English Immigrant Voices

The 1830s immigrants to Upper Canada whose letters are included here wrote – or dictated – to tell loved ones in England that they had survived the voyage across the Atlantic and their travels inland. They told family and friends about their new country – work, food and drink, weather, opportunities, the stuff of their daily lives. The letter-writers were mostly from Sussex, with a few from Surrey and Cambridgeshire. Most were part of family groups; some had emigrated on their own. In England, they had worked for wages as agricultural labourers, in service, or in rural trades, and they emigrated with the assistance of their parishes or landlords. As they explored the work opportunities of 1830s Upper Canada they often sent advice to individuals who might follow. Their compressed accounts of what was most important to them reveal much about the lives they had left as well as demonstrating their resourceful determination to seize the new opportunities immigration offered.

This collection of letters opens new ground in Canadian social history – presenting a first-hand basis for Upper Canada's reputation as "a poor man's country." Editors Wendy Cameron, Sheila Haines, and Mary McDougall Maude confront the questions of authenticity that surround working-class letters of this early date, using their work on assisted emigration under the Petworth Emigration Committee to identify the writers and place their letters in the context of the emigration scheme that enabled them to come to Canada.

In addition to an introductory essay explaining the historical background of the letters, letter-writers and their families receive careful attention. The text has been annotated to sketch the stories of individual writers, link letters by the same author or members of the same family, and explore the connections between writers. Sources of letters are documented and the letters are fully indexed.

WENDY CAMERON is a partner in Wordforce and a visiting scholar at the Northrop Frye Centre, Victoria University at the University of Toronto.

SHEILA HAINES is a partner in Kinship and has recently retired from the Centre for Continuing Education, University of Sussex, England.

MARY McDOUGALL MAUDE is a partner in Wordforce and Shipton, McDougall Maude Associates, a coordinator of the Publishing Program at Ryerson Polytechnic University, and a visiting scholar at the Northrop Frye Centre, Victoria University at the University of Toronto.

ENGLISH IMMIGRANT
Voices

LABOURERS' LETTERS
FROM UPPER CANADA
IN THE 1830S

Edited by
Wendy Cameron,
Sheila Haines,
Mary McDougall Maude

McGill-Queen's University Press
Montreal & Kingston • London • Ithaca

© McGill-Queen's University Press 2000
ISBN 0-7735-2035-X

Legal deposit third quarter 2000
Bibliothèque national du Québec

Printed in Canada on acid-free paper

Publication of this book has been made possible by a grant
from the Jackman Foundation.

McGill-Queen's University Press acknowledges the financial
support of the Government of Canada through the Book
Publishing Industry Development Program (BPIDP) for its
activities. It also acknowledges the support of the Canada
Council for the Arts for its publishing program.

Canadian Cataloguing in Publication Data

Main entry under title:
English immigrant voices : labourers' letters from Upper
Canada in the 1830s

Includes bibliographical references and index.
ISBN 0-7735-2035-X
1. Immigrants—Ontario—Correspondence. 2. Working
class—Ontario—Correspondence. 3. English—Ontario—
Correspondence. 4. Immigrants' writings, Canadian (English)
5. Immigrants—Ontario—History—19th century—Sources.
6. Working class—Ontario—History—19th century—
Sources. I. Cameron, Wendy II. Haines, Sheila. III. Maude,
Mary McD.
FC3071.1.A1E54 2000 971.3'00421 C00-900037-Z
F1056.8.E54 2000

CONTENTS

Maps and Illustrations   vii
Foreword   ix
Preface   xi
Introduction   xv
Abbreviations   lii
Editorial Note   liii

LETTERS
    1832 [1–49]   3
    1833 [50–93]   89
    1834 [94–98]   159
    1835 [99–103]   175
    1836 [104–125]   191
    1837 [126–131]   243
    1838 AND LATER [132–144]   263

ADDITIONAL CORRESPONDENCE AND MEMOIRS
    Wilson Correspondence [145–164]   305
    Chantler Correspondence [165–173]   336
    Frederick Hasted Letters [174–175]   381
    Wells' Letter [176]   391
    Knight Correspondence [177–179]   393
    Charles Adsett Autobiography [180]   398

APPENDICES
    A Transcribed original manuscript letters   405
    B Identification of People, Places, and Terms   409

Notes to Preface and Introduction   414
Sources   419
Acknowledgments   425
Letter-writers by Letter Number   429
Letters by Place of Origin   437
Index   441

MAPS AND ILLUSTRATIONS

MAPS

1   Portsmouth to Toronto: Routes of the Petworth immigrants   xliv
2   Southeast England in the 1830s   xlv
3   Upper Canada in the 1830s   xlvi
4   Locations of Petworth letter-writers – townships and towns   xlvii
5   Location of Petworth letter-writers – Hamilton-Woodstock area   xlviii
6   Location of Petworth letter-writers – Adelaide-Plympton area   xlix
7   Sussex parishes at the time of the Petworth emigrations   l
8   Sussex and Surrey parishes assisting Petworth letter-writers   li
9   Southern Cambridgeshire and surrounding counties   308

ILLUSTRATIONS

Fete in Petworth Park   xii
Statue of George O'Brien Wyndham, 3rd Earl of Egremont   xiv
Thomas Sockett   xvi
Egdean Parish record   xvii
An English family sketched by J.M.W. Turner   xxv
Extract of a letter describing St Lawrence route   xxxvii
List of parishes with proportion of expense to be paid by Egremont   3
Steamboat towing sailing ships from Quebec to Montreal   10
Cedars and the Rapids at Cedars   12
Character reference brought by James Napper   14
Tall trees, Upper Canada   15
Newfoundland dog   22
Entrance to the passage behind Niagara Falls   24
Steamboat *Great Britain*   41
John Racher and his second wife, Ann Burns   49
A cobbler's home in England   72
Houses built by Richard Neal, Dundas, Upper Canada   81
Hamilton, Upper Canada   84
Advertisement for the *England*   89
The Noah's Ark, Lurgashall, West Sussex   93
A Sussex barnyard, Petworth   96

A shanty and log house   99
Harvest celebration, England   113
Mother and children, Sussex, 1832   122
Rapson family Bible   131
Edward and Hannah (Streeter) Bristow   139
Broadsheet for the *British Tar*   159
Rideau Canal   164
Saturday night, England   167
A clearing and cabin, Upper Canada   172
Petworth Emigration Committee announcement for 1835   175
Toronto, 1835   182
An English dairy   186
Announcement for the *Heber*   191
Gingerbread moulds of an Oxfordshire horse and coat of arms of William IV   196
Henry Mann in round-frock coat   197
Guelph, 1840   202
Francis Jackman, Henry William Jackman with their ships   239
Broadsheet for the *Diana*   243
Easebourne Workhouse, Midhurst, West Sussex   253
Five of Ann Mann's sons   254
Letter from James Lannaway   263
A "bush road" in winter, Upper Canada   273
Shooting of Colonel Moodie   275
Four generations of Rapleys   281
A Sussex woman making bread   285
St Mary the Virgin Church, Petworth, interior   291
Envelope   303
Letter from Maria Wilson   304
Obed Wilson and his wife, Betsy Martin   314
William H. Hall and George Muncey   332
Four daughters of Moses Chantler   351
William Nathaniel Chantler with his wife, Margaret Booker   366
Clearing the land, Upper Canada   382
A frontier cabin   383
London, Upper Canada, 1840   385
Church of St Peter ad Vincula, Wisborough Green, West Sussex   394
Mann family, 1891   402

FOREWORD

It gives me great pleasure to write this Foreword to *English Immigrant Voices,* one of two companion volumes on the Petworth immigration scheme. The idea for this volume came not from myself but from its three editors: Wendy Cameron, Sheila Haines, and Mary McDougall Maude. I was more interested in the history of the immigration scheme itself, while others were touched by the human reactions to the working out of the scheme in the lives of the emigrants. Perhaps that is the difference between the masculine and the feminine way of looking at life. Thus, *Assisting Emigration to Upper Canada: The Petworth Project, 1832–1837* deals more with the objective point of view, this volume with the subjective.

I was, however, most happy to sponsor this second volume. These are the stories of the arduous voyage to and into Canada, the hardships of pioneer life in Upper Canada, the feelings of loneliness in being separated from family and friends back in England, the old country. Above all, there is the novelty of the entire process of migration from one country to another. All these experiences and many more are captured in the letters that follow. We all can enjoy and benefit from reading them. May we also particularly thank those who wrote them and especially those who have preserved them over these many years. Happy reading and remembering!

Reverend Edward John Rowell Jackman,
sponsor and patron of these volumes,
and a proud descendant of the Petworth pioneers

Toronto, Ontario
March 2000

PREFACE

Historians collect and edit immigrant letters because it is always interesting to read other people's mail. The letters of Petworth immigrants give first-hand accounts of the immigrant experience; they capture for us impressions of individuals from over a century and a half ago. And they are fun to read. Their stories are of adventure and tragedy. The people writing (or dictating) these letters led lives of hardship and deprivation by the standards of anyone likely to read this book, but they were resourceful and took advantage of opportunities that came their way. Many of them had a good turn of phrase and an eye for vivid detail in describing a scene or situation.

Our first object in preparing this collection is to bring the letters of Petworth immigrants together in one place and to make them better known. As a collection, these letters are noteworthy both because they were written by steerage-class passengers and because they date from early in the nineteenth century. We hope that by tracing the individuals and families who sent the letters, and by placing them and the letters in their contemporary context, others will be encouraged to use a very interesting source.

This edition of letters grew out of a project on the history of the Petworth emigration scheme. At first we thought of these letters only as part of the story of the emigrations sponsored by Lord Egremont and Thomas Sockett's Petworth Emigration Committee. We soon found, however, that the challenges facing the people in charge of assisting Petworth immigrants were different in kind from those facing the immigrants and that they brought different sources into play. Our plans evolved to include a edition of immigrant letters in addition to a book on the history of the Petworth emigrations.

When Charlotte Erickson prepared *Invisible Immigrants: The Adaptation of English and Scottish Immigrants in Nineteenth-Century America*, her classic collection of written by people from England in the United States, published in 1972, she chose to report the results of her work on census manuscripts, county histories, and port records in separate articles now collected into the book *Leaving England*. Robin Haines intends *Emigration and the Labouring Poor: Australian Recruitment in Britain and Ireland, 1831-60* to provide an overarching framework, the separate context needed to interpret the personal experiences described in the letters and diaries written by British immigrants after they settled in Australia.[1] In our companion volume to this one, *Assisting Emigration to Upper Canada: The Petworth Project, 1832-1837*, we write of Canada using sources different from Erickson's and Haines's, but we have made a similar division of our material. *Assisting Emigration* discusses the unfolding of Thomas

A large fete in the grounds of Petworth House: Egremont is on horseback to circulate among his hundreds of guests.

W.F. Witherington, *The Fete in Petworth Park*, National Trust Photographic Library

Sockett's scheme of emigration to Upper Canada. The letters from his immigrants – the subject of this book – can be enjoyed on their own. If they are read with *Assisting Emigration,* each book supplies a further context for the other.

The division between sources in each of these studies of nineteenth-century English emigration is in part a division between the rulers and the ruled, but it is more than that. The worlds of the people with national and local political and economic power who stayed home and made decisions about policies and assistance were far removed from those of the people who actually moved from Britain to a distant colony. Petworth immigrant letters barely hint at the structure of the elaborately organized scheme that brought them to Upper Canada and helped them to settle there. What they do is present the experience of people emigrating from small communities of village and field in England to the colony of Upper Canada.

The first letters sent were written while the writers were travelling under a superintendent; other writers sent word home only after they had secured food and shelter and a way to survive their first winter. As social history these letters document the daily lives and working conditions of labouring people – they reflect a shared heritage at home and they carry precise information back to family members and friends who were thinking of emigrating. As personal records, they reveal hopes, aspirations, fears, loneliness, excitement, and wonder. If these people had ever been the stolid, incoherent countrymen and women pictured by English Victorian commentators, emigration jolted them out of it. Their letters are full of colour and energy.

THIS VOLUME is the result of a transatlantic collaborative effort, and the key person in that effort is the Reverend Edward Jackman, who supported our investigations – intellectually, practically, and financially through the Jackman Foundation – over a number of years. He has acted as a personal link between the two teams, one in Sussex and one in Ontario, and has himself covered the ground in both areas. We are conscious of and grateful for his assistance at every stage of the project.

Leigh Lawson in England and Brenda Dougall Merriman in Ontario have given invaluable help with the genealogical research on which this volume rests. Leigh Lawson assisted in newspaper and manuscript research in addition to her work in parish records. Brenda Merriman investigated genealogical sources in Canada and prepared the family trees for the Chantlers and the Wilsons. They have both assisted in pulling together and analysing the results of their work in family history. Gwen Peroni advised on setting up our computer files, helped in creating them, and translated them from files to final text with patience, accuracy, and good humour. We have been fortunate in having the assistance of Susan Rowland of the Geography Laboratory at the University of Sussex, who prepared the English maps, and of Byron Moldofsky of the Cartography Office of University of Toronto, who prepared the Canadian and the migration maps. As editors we, of course, take responsibility for the final result, but collaboration has made the work an enjoyable task.

A statue of Lord Egremont at Petworth
Photograph: Patrick Burrows

INTRODUCTION

Immigrant letters give us a personal, individual insight into population migrations, while collections of letters provide a context for the individuals involved. The people who wrote the letters in this collection had much in common. They sailed in the six years between 1832 and 1837, part of a group of some 1800 men, women, and children who emigrated from the south of England on ships chartered by the Petworth Emigration Committee. In addition to connections of place and time, almost all had personal ties to others of the group. These were ties of family relationship, of work, of neighbourhood, and of the network of acquaintances in rural communities where the course of daily life brought the same people into frequent contact with each other. Although relationships through women are difficult to trace in conventional sources, these letters show that women's connections and ties, as well as those of men, were important to the emigration decision.

The 144 letters at the heart of this book were written and sent to England by labouring people. They crossed the Atlantic from Portsmouth to Quebec under arrangements made by the Petworth committee, all but a few taking advantage of an assisted passage (see map 1). Most of the Petworth letter-writers, like the majority of Petworth emigrants, came from rural districts of West Sussex, although East Sussex, Surrey, and Cambridgeshire are also represented in this collection (see map 2). Letters were sent from places along the route inland from Quebec City in Lower Canada (Quebec) to Upper Canada (Ontario) and from within the province.

Petworth emigrants were fortunate in sailing as part of a well-organized scheme which was devised and organized by the Reverend Thomas Sockett*, the rector of Petworth, under the patronage of George O'Brien Wyndham, the third Earl of Egremont*, an aristocratic landowner noted for his benevolence towards the poor. Some emigrants had direct assistance from Egremont with their passage, others embarked on ships chartered in Egremont's name but with the assistance of other sponsors who chose to send them with the Petworth committee. In Upper Canada, they were often identified as "Lord Egremont's emigrants," a connection Sockett used to get them more official attention as a group than was accorded to poor immigrants arriving as individuals.

We have been able to identify, with a fair degree of certainty, some 1600 of the 1800 Petworth emigrants whom Sockett recorded as embarking at Portsmouth for Quebec and Montreal (there are no original ships' lists for these emigrations), and the list of emigrants is found in Part Two of *Assisting Emigration*. Our evidence for information provided about the letter-writers among them is generally good. Common names make it difficult to trace some people in parish records and to pick them up in Canadian

Thomas Sockett photographed in old age
Courtesy Barbara Brydone Calder and Peter Jerome

sources, but we know that the people behind these letters existed. We have also included a few letters from the handful of cabin passengers on Petworth ships, two memoirs by emigrants who came as children, and correspondence from others who throw additional light on the experience of the Petworth emigrants (145–180).[†]

In the 1830s, settlement in Upper Canada was rapidly expanding, and the places Petworth letter-writers first settled reflects that pattern. In its broad outline, their set-

---

† Numbers in parentheses refer to letter numbers.

tlement patterns also reflect a tendency among English immigrants to bypass eastern Ontario in favour of Toronto and places farther west (see map 3).[1] The clusters of letter-writers who were the focus of our research settled in the Home, Gore, Niagara, London, and Western Districts. A few settled in towns and in urban occupations, but most of these people sent their letters from places where they could use their rural background to advantage. (Maps 4, 5, and 6 plot the addresses of the letters.)

Egremont's assistance was a gift; other sponsors might get up a subscription or extend their help in the form of a loan to a parish. With or without such help, the parish was the basic unit of organization sending emigrants and was responsible for all or part of the costs. (In sending emigrants, an English parish acted in its civil capacity under poor laws that made each individual parish accountable for social services

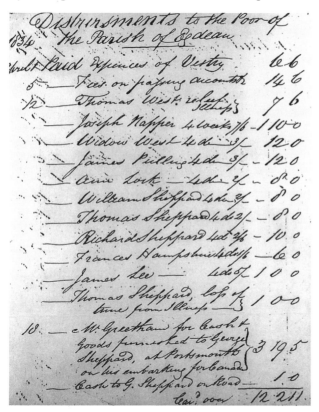

Egdean's record of parish spending on emigration
WSRO, PAR 79/31/1

in that parish.)[2] In parishes where Egremont provided the passage, the parish still had to provide an outfit, transportation to Portsmouth (where all Petworth emigrants embarked), and money to be distributed by the Petworth superintendent at Toronto. Although some Petworth parishes or sponsors gave more than the one or two pounds per adult suggested by government officials, this "landing money" was a small sum for immediate expenses. Advocates and sponsors of assisted emigration from England in the 1830s based their assumptions on the belief that there was a constant demand for labour in the Canadas and that the sober and industrious immigrant was sure of finding work. Sockett stands out among them for testing this belief by going out of his way to collect letters sent home by his immigrants, and his committee was unusual in sending their people all the way through to Toronto where they believed opportunities were greatest.

Individual emigrants gathered as much as they could in the way of supplies and money to take with them. Even poor emigrants took large amounts of luggage in casks and boxes: clothing, bedding, and utensils for the journey, sometimes the tools of their trade, and food, in addition to that supplied by the Petworth committee. An adult passage included a 500-pound luggage allowance. Everyone aged fourteen and up was classified as adult. Children aged thirteen or less travelled as a half passage and infants travelled free. The first Petworth emigrants discovered that steamboats in the Canadas had lower limits for the amount of baggage and food that could be carried free, and that inland transport was expensive. After 1832, the main tenor of advice received at Petworth was that emigrants should select goods for transport carefully and bring more of their resources in money. Sockett responded by encouraging emigrants to assemble as much of their own outfit as they could, rather than relying on purchases by the parish. Where his influence prevailed, the parish allocated a sum for each emigrant or family and put all that was not spent on the outfit in the committee's hands to be given to the people concerned on their arrival in Toronto.

Almost 100 parishes had a part in sending emigrants with the Petworth Emigration Committee (see maps 7 and 8). Potential emigrants applied to their parish of settlement. A settlement in this period was usually acquired by birth or marriage and, no matter where they lived, this was the parish to which people applied for all forms of relief, including assistance to emigrate. We know which parishes sent the letter-writers included in this text (see map 4), and they are noted in the introductions to the letters. Although baptismal records indicate that several families had moved about in search of work, parishes were small, so that a family moving only a short distance could cross a boundary. Most children on Petworth ships had grown up in the district around the parish that sent them.

As an example of British immigrant literature, the published letters of Petworth immigrants belong to a distinct period of enthusiastic "discovery" of Upper Canada at the beginning of the 1830s. From 1829 to 1830, arrivals at Quebec almost doubled to 28,000 and they were over 50,000 in each of the next two years. The total number of emigrants recorded as departing for British North America in 1832 was 66,339 as against 32,827 who gave the United States as their first destination.[3] All this movement was accompanied by an increase in the demand for information, particularly about Upper Canada; which drew the lion's share of emigrants who stayed in the British North American colonies rather than using them as a staging point on the way to the United States.

Government in these years began the publication of official notices giving advice intended to put emigrants, and those who assisted them, on guard against fraud and deception. Private authors elaborated the brief overview of Upper Canada supplied by government agents and recounted their own experience of Upper Canada as travellers or settlers. The publication of letters from labouring immigrants addressed a market with little money to spend on books, but sponsors such as the Petworth committee were willing to subsidize publication in order to encourage parish emigration. For this purpose, letters from Petworth emigrants were published in small pamphlets or on single sheets. Letters also circulated through newspapers. Some Petworth letters were sent by Sockett to the editors of Sussex newspapers, but these also editors had their own sources. For instance, Sockett reprinted William and Sarah Jackman's letter from the *Brighton Guardian* (126).

Published letters extended community and family networks where letters were passed from hand to hand and copied to share with distant family members. Some Petworth letters survive in their original manuscripts. There are also manuscript copies made by family members or descendants of the immigrants, and letters Sockett had copied and sent to the Duke of Richmond at Goodwood House near Chichester. Charles Lennox, the fifth Duke of Richmond, was a member of Lord Grey's Whig cabinet from 1830 to 1834 and the chairman of an Emigration Commission appointed by the colonial secretary in 1831-32. Sockett sent Richmond copies of immigrant letters when he asked for Richmond's help or in order to underline points he hoped Richmond would take up with the government.

BACKGROUND TO THE LETTERS

The Petworth emigrations contributed significantly to the literature of 1830s emigration to Upper Canada. Sockett, using Petworth printer John Phillips, published five collections of emigrant letters, his own accounts of the emigrations of 1832 and 1833, and Superintendent James Marr Brydone's *Narrative of a Journey*, a published version of Brydone's reports to the committee from Upper Canada in 1834.[4]

For the first three years of Sockett's scheme, interest in Upper Canada was at a high point. London co-publishers readily took up the work of regional printers such as Phillips. An evolving list of books on Upper Canada carried for sale by Phillips and approved by Sockett could be drawn almost entirely from very recent publications.[5] These books describe the rapidly expanding settlement that accompanied high immigration at the beginning of the decade. After 1834, the province became a less popular destination among the middle-class, book-buying public, but the same books remained on the market, read by English men and women unaware that much of what was described applied best to a particular moment in time.

Sockett and others continued to publish immigrant letters to encourage the emigration of labourers or small farmers. In every year, Sockett produced single sheets and small pamphlets of one or more letters to distribute for free or for one or two pence. When he had difficulty finding sufficient emigrants to fill the *Diana* in 1837, he again published letters in larger collections, which were still of considerable contemporary interest. When Phillips was unable to find a London co-publisher in 1837, he found at least one London bookseller willing to distribute on his behalf.[6] The directors of the Canada Company, a London-based company selling land in Upper Canada, continued to order 1000 copies of each of Sockett's publications.[7] Production numbers are not available for any of Sockett's published collections, but he must have achieved a quite considerable circulation.

The manner of survival of immigrant letters varies remarkably in different countries and for different groups of emigrants. Some modern collections are based entirely on manuscript letters that remained in family hands or were deposited by families in archives after being kept for several generations. The families of Polish immigrants whose letters are edited and translated by Josephine Wtulich never received them, or the money and tickets sent with them. They are all that remain of a much larger number of letters confiscated by Czarist police in 1890 and 1891 in the Congress Kingdom of Poland, sent to Warsaw, and, with these exceptions, destroyed in the Warsaw uprising during the Second World War.[8] Under less traumatic circumstances, we have found letters from Petworth immigrants in private and public collections, in government records, and in contemporary printed sources such as newspapers, pamphlets, or books.

In collections and studies that have personal letters as a major source, the writers are usually presented as spokespersons for an ethnic group in a particular country.[9] With immigrants who wrote in languages other than English, translated letters tell their stories to people on the other side of barriers of language as well as of time.[10] Charlotte Erickson subtitled her study of "invisible" nineteenth-century English immigrant letter-writers "The Adaptability of English and Scottish Immigrants." Although we have a sense of very different personalities among the people writing in the letters presented here, something like a family resemblance begins to emerge if letters from nineteenth-century English immigrants are compared with those of people from other countries. There are common themes, even if there is always a subtext supplied by the voices of people who had another opinion than the majority. If we had to chose a single determining characteristic for Petworth immigrants, it would be their willingness to turn their hands to whatever opportunity to earn a living came their way – the adaptability Erickson attributes to English immigrants, on a different economic level and in another guise.

Petworth immigrant letters-writers shared working-class origins in England, came mainly from rural areas, and emigrated under similar circumstances within six years of each other. Their letters allow a detailed look at a particular experience – particular enough that we decided to present them chronologically so that the senders in any one section are grouped with people who shared the experiences of that year. The individuality of this experience comes out in the variety of the strategies these immigrants adopted to support themselves and their families through their first winter. Once they arrived in Upper Canada, Petworth immigrants sought out people they had known at home and tried to keep in touch with them, but they settled where they found the best opportunity and worked at the occupation offering the best return. Their letters reflect the formation of clusters of Petworth immigrants around two places – Adelaide Township and Woodstock – where government made land available to some of their number on favourable terms, but they do not show the determination to settle among their own people, even if they did so at the price of economic disadvantage, that Marianne McLean documented among Glengarry Scots.[11]

Most of these letters were written early in the nineteenth century (before most of those in the collections noted above). The people sending them grew up before education was universal in the English countryside – a subject we will return to. The letters in this collection are early in another sense – almost all were sent during the first months or years of the writers' emigrating. At the time of writing, the immigrants who had arrived poor were still poor, although these letter-writers do not represent the very poorest immigrants or the gangs of rootless people who followed work on canals back and forth across the border with the United States during the 1830s and 1840s.[12] We know of a few Petworth immigrants reported to have hired on at public works, but we do not have letters from them. The people writing these letters were working for others or beginning the clearing of a backwoods farm. In cases where we have a sequence of two or more letters from the same person, they can be seen consolidating their position. Where we can, we have added their later stories to the brief biographies that accompany the texts.

The letters given here describe a recent journey and give impressions of Upper Canada seen through the eyes of a newcomer – they reflect a particular stage in emigration rather than the whole story. In this respect the letters from Upper Canada are different from the Wilson letters (145–164), which are an example of a family correspondence that extends over three generations, during which first-hand contact between the immigrant and his people at home becomes ever more remote. These immigrants wrote home to families who lived in rented housing and cramped spaces, unstable conditions for the survival of letters, however valued by the recipients. We have a few letters in manuscript, some manuscript copies, and letters that survive as copies in more than one version. Our largest single source, however, is the letters published by Thomas Sockett between 1832 and 1839 with a view to promoting the next year's emigration under the Petworth committee.

Some editors who work with immigrants' letters have excluded all but those in manuscript form.[13] The small amount of extant correspondence from poor immigrants who went to early nineteenth-century Upper Canada does not offer that luxury. In order to examine the correspondence of labouring people in the first third of the nineteenth century, we have made use of letters in whatever form they survive. We take comfort from Erickson's observation, made after comparing letters sent to newspapers with family letters, that even private correspondents had their own agendas so that "private letters were no more unbiased than published ones."[14] Furthermore, the published letters of Petworth immigrants have the saving graces that Erickson sees in private correspondence: we are able to identify the people writing and to explain their circumstances. The evidence we have does not entirely make up for the absence of manuscripts, but we think it is sufficient to authenticate the experiences described in the surviving texts.

PARISH-AIDED IMMIGRATION TO UPPER CANADA

References to emigration as a safety valve for pressures at home date from the era of English history considered here. The Petworth emigrants were economic migrants, leaving rural areas of the south and east of England where wages were low and seasonal unemployment an annual problem. In the parishes that sent them, the Swing disturbances of 1830-31 were a recent memory: machine breaking, arson, strikes, and mobs of labourers who gathered to give force to their demands for better wages and working conditions. Collectively named for threatening letters signed with the name of the mythical Captain Swing, these disturbances were local in character, without collective leadership, and the men of any one community were easily dispersed by the army. Politicians, however, remained uncertain that harsh sentences against the ring leaders had been enough to undo the example of the power of numbers. In the months after the Swing disturbances, and again when they feared renewed unrest in reaction to the changes in welfare policies introduced to these same parishes in 1835 and 1836, they encouraged landlords and parishes to send their "redundant" labourers as emigrants.

In the parishes, fear of unrest was only one reason to sponsor emigrants. Some sponsors responded to persistent nagging from people set on finding a new life; others tried to use this means to rid themselves of troublemakers and expensive, chronic paupers. Humanitarian motives also came into play, and the Petworth emigrations are an example on a large scale of an assisted emigration in which concern for the people involved played an important part. As a group, Petworth emigrants had an edge over those whose assistance was less and less well thought out. Immigrants who sailed under a Petworth superintendent on a ship chartered by the Petworth Emigration Committee had a good chance of reaching Toronto and of getting there in reasonable health. Once they arrived at the place where they would make their first home, however, agents of the Crown Lands Department had the same expectations of Petworth immigrants that they had of other immigrants of a similar background who managed to make their way inland. The amount of assistance provided by the Petworth Committee was intended to place the people helped on a level with the poorest immigrants arriving at their own cost who might be expected to succeed – success being defined as getting permanently established in Upper Canada.

Before the 1830s, only a few people emigrated from the Petworth area and they went mainly to the United States, which was the destination of choice among English emigrants at the time. In the years from 1831 to 1837, the numbers of immigrants arriving in Quebec from England in general increased, and the proportion of parish-aided immigrants among them also increased substantially. The better-off often chose to come to Upper Canada via New York, a route that promised more comfortable ships and a shorter passage. Immigrants for whom cost was a factor found the cheapest fares on timber ships, which carried passengers on their return trips to Quebec. There is no good information on the total number of parish-aided immigrants among Quebec arrivals during these years. The most reliable records were kept by agents stationed in the port by the British government. They counted just under 10,000 immigrants assisted by parishes and landlords in 1831 and 1832 and another 9131 between 1833 and 1837. In the years 1833-37 they recorded 60,656 coming in from all English ports of departure, a figure that included Irish immigrants coming via Liverpool. If they stayed in the Canadas, most immigrants arriving at Quebec went to the upper province, the destination Sockett chose for the Petworth immigrants.[15]

The increase in parish-aided immigration in 1831 and 1832 coincided with a general increase in immigration to the Canadas. In 1835 parish-aided immigration increased against a general downward trend in immigration as a whole. It was buoyed in 1835 and 1836 by provisions in the Poor Law Amendment Act passed in the summer of 1834. Two clauses in the act allowed parishes meeting certain conditions to apply to the newly appointed poor law commissioners for government backing in raising loans to send emigrants. Many parishes with high unemployment took advantage of assisted emigration to reduce the numbers of the working poor aggrieved by the loss of parish allowances.

Parish emigration slowed in 1837, and in 1838, in common with all immigration from England to the Canadas, it was reduced to a trickle by dramatic news of rebellions in the Canadas. In Upper Canada in 1837, economic problems had contributed to political turmoil. Both Upper and Lower Canada had had a period of poor harvests, and a banking crisis which began in Europe was felt across North America. Active rebellion broke out first and most seriously in Lower Canada, occurring from mid-November until the defeat of the last Patriote forces at Saint-Eustache on 14 December. A second rebellion in Lower Canada in early November of 1838 was quickly put down. In Upper Canada, the forces taking part in William Lyon Mackenzie's abortive attack on Toronto, which began on 5 December 1837, were scattered by the 8th, and Charles Duncombe's smaller rising in townships near Brantford was quickly dispersed by forces under Allan Napier MacNab of Hamilton. Alarms continued through 1838, however, as rebels who had taken refuge in the United States and their American sympathizers mounted raids at several points along the border between the two countries.[16]

The check in emigration to the Canadas caused by the rebellions came at a particularly difficult time for Sockett, whose scheme lost its patron with Egremont's death in November 1837. Only one family came forward for emigration to Upper Canada in 1838, and Sockett missed his best chance of convincing Egremont's son to continue his father's plan of assisting emigration from Sussex. By 1839, Sockett reported a renewed interest in Upper Canada, but by then the new owner of Petworth had turned his attention to emigration from his Irish estates. George Wyndham allowed the Petworth Emigration Committee to continue its work, but on a much reduced scale. He sponsored perhaps one hundred emigrants from Sussex to Canada and a few more to Australia. By contrast, he is recorded to have sent 220 families, 1505 individuals, from his estates in counties Clare and Limerick to Quebec in Canada and Sydney in Australia.[17]

Immigration to the Canadas supported by parish sources other than the Petworth committee resumed after 1838, but it was never again as important. Government agencies in Britain encouraged emigration to Australasian colonies willing to pay the passage of assisted immigrants, and rural agricultural workers of the sort who had sailed with the Petworth committee were diverted to these colonies. Although less likely to be helped by the parish, rural labourers in later years still sought local assistance in raising the money needed for a compulsory outfit and deposit in order to qualify for a government-assisted passage to Australia.[18] The immigrants in this book were probably similar in background and character to many rural English immigrants assisted under schemes financed by Australian colonies in the next two or more decades.

THE LETTER-WRITERS

Sockett described typical economic migrants. He wrote of people who feared that they were losing ground at home and believed that no amount of hard work or frugality could remedy their situation. Whether married or single, most adult males among Petworth immigrants had been wage-earners. Sockett once mentioned sons of farmers as being among his emigrants, and some few, particularly emigrants from the wealden areas north of Petworth, may have worked small plots of land. As a group, however, Petworth immigrants were landless labourers and artisans, and, for the most part, the children, and probably the grandchildren, of people who thought of their wages as their income.

Men were the principal wage-earners in rural Sussex. The average male farm worker's wage in Sussex hovered around ten shillings a week, a wage so low that under the old poor law, though not under the new, families attempting to support more than two or three young children on this wage received an additional "child allowance" from their parish. Day labourers were hired on a casual basis, employed during much of the year but only certain of work during the busy harvest season. Young, single men had difficulty getting a toehold in the labour market. Their wages might be lower than those of married men and they were the last hired and the first laid off. As winter tightened its grip, even married men might find themselves applying to the parish overseer for road work.

Most of the men sent by the Petworth committee had farming or other skills that were useful in finding work in Upper Canada. The broad term "agricultural labourer" has to be clarified for each group of immigrants to whom it was applied. The county of Sussex had very different regions, adapted to quite different kinds of agriculture, but most of the Petworth immigrant agricultural workers seem to have gained their experience on arable farms. Some had worked in woods or coppice, and some had experience in a trade, usually a practical trade such as carpentry, shoe-making, or bricklaying. For many, season and opportunity determined their tasks and some combined farming skills with knowledge of a trade.[19]

A number of the women writers of these letters seem to have been in service in England before marriage, but as married women they had few opportunities to contribute to the family income and were paid miserable amounts for the very few jobs available to them. Few labouring families had ground beyond a small garden rented with their cottage, and cottage industries were a thing of the past. Children taken into service, boys or girls, earned nothing more than their board for years. Families with young children depended largely on the wages of a single breadwinner and these wages were so low that the children lived in poverty, often severe poverty.[20]

After immigrating to Upper Canada, men were still the principal breadwinners, and their occupations receive a corresponding amount of attention in letters sent to England. There is, however, considerable information in these letters about the activities of their wives and children. Attitudes of the English countryside are evident in the satisfied reports of finding useful work for children, an approval the middle-class Sockett echoed. In describing the ease with which his 1832 emigrants had found employment, he noted as "very striking" that "girls and boys, even as young as ten years, seem sure of immediate places."[21] Census takers in 1851 in the area around the Adelaide settlement of Petworth immigrants found "Petworth" young people in the households of other Petworth immigrants, suggesting that some of these children were working and learning with relatives or friends. In the early days of their arrival, however, the immigrants reported their children as in service, sometimes at a considerable distance. Formal apprenticeship for the very young appears to have been reserved for special cases, such as that of Charles Adsett (180), but older boys learned a trade this way if they could not learn by working alongside a father or an uncle.

If girls were still at home and not in service by their mid-teens, their parents sometimes write to explain why they were needed at home, suggesting that it was more usual for them to be working outside the home. Once a young woman married, and particularly once she had children, attitudes seemed to change. Her focus was

J.M.W. Turner had a studio at Petworth House and painted and sketched in the area. This Sussex family is typical of those who might have emigrated.

J.M.W. Turner, "Man with Wife and Children," Courtesy Tate Gallery, Studies near Brighton sketchbook, cat. 66

expected to be on her own home and family. No one, male or female, can have worked harder than Elizabeth Voice who, with the help of her daughter, maintained a large family in a small log house in addition to sewing men's clothes "when they have time to work at it" and making as much as twenty pounds of butter a week (98 and 101). Her earnings from her sewing and anything she may have made from her dairy were from home-based activities. William Upton reported a childless couple as being better off than a single man because "there are so many situations for them in gentlemen's families: the woman as housekeeper; and the man as in doors servant" (26), but most Petworth immigrants sought their own living quarters after marriage, as was the custom in England. Before she had children, Ann Cosens lived in the house of her husband's employer, "a large farmer," but she specified that she did needlework and was paid by the piece. John Gamblen would not hear of his wife working "while I can get a good living without her help" (100). The gentry who tried to persuade married women such as Ann Gamblen to come to work for them as domestic servants seem to have contended with a strong cultural bias against living in as a servant after marriage.[22]

Whose Letters Survived?

The writers of these letters reflect the overall composition of the adult population on Petworth ships. Of a sample of 93 letters (the sample looks at only the first letter sent home by an individual or family), 34 were written by single men, 14 of the men we know travelled with a family. About half the adult male Petworth immigrants were single. The single women on these ships were fewer than the men and, with very few exceptions, they sailed as part of a family group. Our two unmarried female letter-writers travelled with their family. Twenty-seven letters were attributed to a married man and 9 to a married woman. Another 21 letters were sent jointly by couples. Of these, 3 appear to have been written by the man and 3 by the woman.

Although the writers are broadly representative of the rural, labouring immigrants coming to Upper Canada from the south of England in the 1830s, they are not equally representative of them all. Even within the pool of immigrants from Petworth ships, they are better described as a sample than a cross-section. Chance survival played a part, but the letters of some immigrants were more likely to be collected and published by Sockett than those of others. To begin with, Sockett collected only letters from immigrants in Upper Canada or on their way there. Petworth emigrants who settled in the United States may be mentioned in these letters, but they do not appear as primary writers.[23]

In England, Sockett's informal methods of acquiring letters resulted in a certain bias in his collections towards parishes in his neighbourhood. A large number of letters from his own parish of Petworth is only to be expected. In addition, a high proportion of the letters he collected were written by people sent from parishes where Egremont paid all or part of the passage for the emigrants. (Egremont paid the full passage for those from five parishes immediately around Petworth and a portion of the passage for thirteen others.[24]) Sockett had good connections, and therefore reasons to visit, in a number of these parishes. The Reverend John Knight Greetham*, for instance, organized the Kirdford group of emigrants in 1832 and is a likely source of letters from his parish. Closer to home, families brought letters to Sockett. He encouraged them to do this by providing news of other emigrants and by letting it be known that when shown a letter he would give a shilling towards the postage that had to be paid to get it from the post office.

In his published collections, Sockett corrected the imbalance to some degree by obtaining letters through sponsors in more distant parishes, and we have been able to add letters from other published sources, notably the letters from the Dorking area of Surrey, and from private collections such as the letters sent to Obediah Wilson from Cambridgeshire. Still, we have no letters from places such as the Isle of Wight, which according to Sockett's records sent 138 emigrants under the Petworth committee.

All immigrant letters of the nineteenth century, not just those of Petworth immigrants, are questioned as sources of historical evidence on the grounds that there are selective processes at work in determining both who would write and which letters among those written were most likely to be kept.[25] Out of the millions of private letters sent from North America to Britain in the nineteenth century, some had a better chance of survival than others. The survival of a letter depended on both the desire of people to keep it and their ability to preserve it.

Petworth letters are probably, for the most part, the letters Sockett characterized as "good letters," written by people who applied to emigrate to Upper Canada after careful thought. Some of them reported illness and deaths and economic setbacks in Upper Canada, but they were written by solid emigrants who left with a good prospect of being able to improve their standard of living in Upper Canada. If the people who fit Sockett's description of "the scum who rose to the top just at the last"[26] – people the committee took reluctantly at the last minute in order to fill their ships – wrote home, Sockett was less likely to include their letters in his collection. Not all misfits, however, were excluded. Single young writers sometimes took a lighter view of life than their elders and sometimes admitted a less than perfect record. As well, in the small world of the parish, Sockett was able to collect letters from people who had been at odds with the authorities: for example, before he emigrated, David (Cloudesley) Sharp had been jailed for defaming Egremont's estate agent (86, closing comment). These were, however, people with strong connections in a parish community who were sent in the belief that their background did not preclude a fresh start. The fact of a middle-class editor between us and most of these letters increases the probability that the letters which survive are those of motivated people whose letters stood out in some way.[27]

Rural Workers and Letters

Petworth "letter-writers" seem to belong in a category of emigrants "not ... from the letter-writing classes."[28] At the time she compiled *Invisible Immigrants*, Erickson believed that ordinary labourers, "those who may have gone for the most straightforward economic reasons," were out of reach of her collection because they were illiterate.[29] Although Terry Crowley makes some use of Petworth letters in describing rural labour in nineteenth-century Ontario, he suggests that some source other than written records must be found to obtain glimpses of "the lives of illiterates and the largely destitute."[30] These opinions follow the lead of English historians. In *Captain Swing*, the most complete account of the Swing disturbances, Hobsbawm and Rudé set themselves the task of "reconstructing the mental world of an anonymous and undocumented body of people" – people who were for the most part illiterate and who had few occasions to write even if they could.[31]

Books such as *Captain Swing*, however, look at English labourers and their parishes at times of deep stress. Normal times produced occasions when distance required paupers to use the mail and middle-class preoccupations led to their letters being preserved. Thomas Sokoll, investigating the papers of Essex overseers, found a cache of some 1000 letters sent in the years up to 1834 by paupers living and receiving support far away from the parish where they had their settlement.[32] Pauper letters have also been discovered in the context of emigration, although Petworth sponsors seem to have expected emigrants to apply in person as they would for poor relief. Following the large exodus of parish-aided emigrants from Norfolk and Suffolk in 1836, Gary Howells reports that applicants denied assistance in 1837 sent letters to distant London under the impression that they could appeal decisions of their local poor law union to the central commission. The new poor law did not work that way, but their letters remain.[33] When the Petworth immigrants reached Upper Canada, even the illiterate and barely literate among them were well aware of the value of the mails for keeping in touch with England. They either struggled on their own or they found someone to write on their behalf.

Letter-writers and Literacy

In 1830s England there were a good many labouring people in rural districts who were illiterate and a significant number who could read but not write. Others could read and write but only imperfectly.[34] The men who carried on the Chantler correspondence were clearly highly literate; John had been sent to London to school and his cousin Joseph had a clear copy-book hand which allowed him to pack an amazing amount on a single sheet of paper by crossing (writing one way and then turning the page to write across the lines). At the other end of this spectrum, the fact of dictation seems to have been taken for granted in the circles of people who sent, received, and printed Petworth letters.

The parish record of marriages for Petworth letter-writers suggests a low level of literacy, with just under one-third of those whom we can count achieving a signature.[35] Signatures as evidence of literacy are a subject of debate, but, for our purposes, it seems that someone uncomfortable with a simple signature would have had difficulty writing and addressing a letter. There may be exceptions. Ann Mann was one who used a mark (127). Was it she or someone writing for her who added the note to her letter to "please to pick it out as well as you can, for I have made many Baffles?" Nevertheless, the numbers for the thirty-three couples for whom we have good examples of entries in marriage records are suggestive. Both partners signed in only four cases. In total there were signatures for nine men and seven women. All the remaining people used a mark.[36] In addition, Henry Harwood was the only one of five men who wrote as widowers who had signed a marriage register in England: the other four used a mark. The wives of Thomas Adsett and Henry Smart had signed, but both of them died before the letters in this book were written.

The little evidence that we have shows Petworth immigrants turning to people within their own circles to write personal letters. Ann Mann told her sons in England "Aunt Belchamber will write for you" (127). Frederick Hasted stated in 1839, apparently with reference to the Adelaide settlement where he lived among Petworth emigrants, that he had written letters for several of his neighbours. (He probably wrote 133 and 135.) Charles Haines and James Rapson identify themselves in letters they wrote for other Petworth immigrants, but they did so only because they wanted to add a short message of their own (64 and 72). Although slight, this evidence fits the picture of a stage in the spread of literacy described by David Vincent in which members of the working poor regarded literacy as but one of many skills which could be shared within the family or community. When they needed it, those who did not have it knew where to borrow.[37]

Not having manuscripts for most of the letters limits what can be said on the subject of how they were composed, but we have examples of what David Fitzpatrick has described as "collaborative composition" – several people contributing to a letter written in a single hand. There is one example in the Wilson manuscripts, and there are sequences in the printed letters which fit the case. There are of course other reasons than illiteracy to dictate: people who could write a bit may have chosen to dictate to someone with a better hand, with more confidence in a seldom-used skill, or with better eyesight.[38] George Hills sent his love to sister Elizabeth and said to tell her that, "if she thinks she cannot write a whole letter, to write a few lines of it, as it would give me a great deal of satisfaction" (63). Asked about literacy in his neighbourhood, Sockett said there had been constant improvement since he first arrived at Petworth in 1796 and since he became rector in 1816. In a place like the market town of Petworth, as a result of the introduction of national schools, "there are few boys now [1838] of 12 years old who could not write something in the shape of a letter."[39] This had been less often the case with their parents' generation whom he sent as adults to Canada, but he did not mention having seen any letters actually written by children. He also did not give an opinion on the pace of improvement in rural districts around the town.

WRITING FROM UPPER CANADA

This is a family correspondence. Parents figure in the address or salutation of half the letters in this book and other letters carry messages for the writers' parents. The next most frequently mentioned recipients are brothers and sisters. There are also a smaller number of letters sent to members of the middle class who had an interest in particular immigrants or in emigration. The Reverend Robert Risdale received a letter from Thomas Adsett on a sheet of paper that he had supplied and self addressed (49). These letters shade over into a different kind of connection. Elizabeth Wackford's letter to Sarah Green seems to carry a hope that Green would help her parents with correspondence and, perhaps, with postage (72). The Tribes and Jesse Penfold kept in touch with their English acquaintance through the owners of their local pub (54 and 50).

Although Petworth emigrant letters carried news of family and friends, they were a substitute for a conversation around the kitchen table rather than an intimate discussion or private gossiping session between two people. The Cooper brothers, James and William, wrote to their mother that she should not expect letters from them individually as we "are together … and makes one letter do for us all" (133). In England, immigrants expected that their letters would be shared and often asked that they should be. Sockett's collecting and publishing of their letters must have been based to a degree on personal trust. He won this trust more easily because he was extending an existing network of informal circulation rather than starting something new. Sockett believed that his immigrants had improved their prospects by going to Canada. Immigrants who felt the same way were anxious to have their opinions heard and to encourage their family and friends to join them.

Petworth immigrants shared letters, or wrote to several people in one letter, in part because letters were expensive to send across the Atlantic. They relied on the recipient to send on or copy their letters, or to carry them to people living at a distance, and they sometimes chided in the next letter if they did not. Edward Boxall, for example, wrote: "copy this letter, and send it to my sisters" (7). William Chantler (in a letter copied and sent on to Canada by his London cousin) wrote to John describing his tour of relatives and friends around Horsham with John's letter and their tearful joy at news from Canada (168). William Voice asked his sister to send to Horsham "for fear they should not get their letter" (98). The salutation in Ann Mann's letter is "Dear Sons and Friends," but in the body of the letter she asked that the letter be sent to her sons Henry and George and also that it be "copied off" and "stuck up" at the Onslow Arms (127) for all her acquaintance in her former community to see.

One letter often served a number of people. In addition to showing them around the family, those writing asked repeatedly to have their letters shown to friends or to people who had asked them before they left to report on Upper Canada. They sometimes mention workmates or a former employer. Immigrants sent messages to Sockett in these letters and to other sponsors. If immigrants were willing to go out on a limb and recommend emigration – many preferred a neutral stand – they named people who should be urged to come, sometimes suggesting that they be shown the letter. Other writers, such as William Spencer, a widower lonely for contact with home, seemed to enjoy the local fame of a published letter. Spencer was upset when people coming from Petworth told him that his parents had not received two "long and intelligent letters, informing you [of] all the particulars relating to myself and the country that I possibly could" (125). He repeated the exercise, adding a request at the end that, if this letter was printed, it should be printed in full rather than in part like the extract from his first letter to them "which I had the pleasure of seeing."

In addition to concerns about the cost of a letter and difficulties in getting it written, Petworth immigrants and their families worried about whether their letters would arrive saying the same thing as when they were sent. Labouring emigrants had many reasons to feel anxious. The emigrant trade to North America was tainted by tales of sharp dealing and deception. Then there were the colonies themselves. All emigrant destinations had their enthusiastic supporters and their detractors, and public opinion might in a very short time swing radically from the one opinion to the other as had been demonstrated by the 1829 venture to colonize Swan River in Western Australia. A fiasco such as Swan River was much more complicated than a simple case of deception, but the people involved felt betrayed and their feelings were conveyed to communities in England.[40] For many assisted emigrants, the facts and rumours associated with emigration became the more sinister in the light of their own mistrust of the motives of their sponsors. In areas like Petworth, where parish emigration was actively promoted, the letters, which were a prominent part of this promotion, came in for their share of suspicion.

On the simplest level, Sockett reported rumours in this area that the letters published after the parish-aided emigration from Corsley in Wiltshire in 1830 had been faked.[41] The letters in this collection contain a number of references to fears of substitution and of tampering with the text. Sockett addressed this issue in his correspondence with Richmond in 1833 and returned to the subject in his evidence to the 1838 committee on postage. He blamed these fears partly on trouble makers – "there is always a certain class of persons who seem to have pleasure in making mischief, and in setting the lower class against the higher class." Word was spread that Egremont and Sockett supported emigration only to reduce the expense of the poor rate and were therefore circulating false letters. Such rumours gained credence because of "the want of the habit of writing letters among the poor . . . they are hardly acquainted with their own children's handwriting, because they do not often see it."[42]

Phillips kept the originals or "well attested copies" of published immigrant letters at his office, and newspaper editors sometimes added a similar note saying that the letters they published were available at their offices, although we have no evidence that this opportunity to check the printed record was used. In his correspondence and publications Sockett called attention to those strategies taken by the senders to reassure their relatives that there had been no substitution. Petworth emigrants set off prepared. Probably the favourite measure was to tear off a corner of a sheet of paper which could be left behind to be matched up with the first letter received. They also carried with them signed pages, pages with a portion cut off through a signature, and a variety of agreed tokens, seals, and signs to include in a letter from Upper Canada. According to Sockett, Jesse Penfold took a sheet signed by no less than eight inhabitants of Petworth, a sheet which served the double purpose of reminding the recipients of the others who wanted to see the letter.

Not long after arriving in Waterloo Township, Cornelius Cosens wrote that "some people in England think that letters are opened, but there is no such thing" (34), but rumours arose in Canada as well as in England of mail being opened. Although it did not stop her asking that her letter be copied for relatives and friends, Mary Holden wrote from Adelaide Township: "but you may understand that the letters be all opened, before they go out of this Country, to see that there is not any falsehood sent; and if there is any thing in them, against the country, they are kept back." She did not send the letter right away and thus was able to satisfy herself by making enquiries "to know the fact and truth about their being opened by the head gentleman [Roswell Mount, the superintendent of the Adelaide settlement]. So that we are sure now that they are not opened until you receives them" (47).

When they emigrated in 1833, James and Hannah Tilley were concerned about forgery rather than censorship. They took the case a step further by taking a copy of the printed volume of 1832 and showing it to "several that sent letters." These people said "that they are exactly as they sent them" (83). Immigrants wrote at intervals to tell their relatives not to worry about letters being opened, but these concerns seem never to have been put entirely to rest. Lydia Hilton sailed on the *Heber* in 1836 leaving part of a sheet of paper with her family. William Courtnage, who had emigrated in 1832, sent a letter five years later in 1837 on a page signed "Pannell, Haslemere." He told his brother and sisters to let Mrs Pannell see it to identify her handwriting.

Transportation and the Mails

These letters do not record assisted immigrants using water transport in Upper Canada unless their fare was paid for them by someone else. The Petworth committee promised the immigrants transport to Toronto or any port at the head of Lake Ontario as part of their agreement. In 1832 the government of Upper Canada chartered schooners which took some Petworth immigrants through the Welland Canal to Port Stanley and in 1833 carried others up the Detroit and St Clair rivers to Sarnia. The government also paid the passages of a large number of Petworth immigrants sent on steam boats to Hamilton.

On land, assisted immigrants walked unless they travelled with families and luggage. When a group of poor families travelled by road, there must always have been people walking beside the wagons. When Durham boats encountered rapids on the way up the St Lawrence, all or most of their passengers were put on shore to lighten the load while oxen or horses dragged the boats to the next stretch of navigable water. (Sometimes they did not lighten the boats enough. As she walked on the road by the towpath with her husband and parents, Sarah Rapson saw the boat still carrying her children being cut loose from the struggling oxen and flying backwards with the current until the boatmen regained control and brought it to the bank (12).)

Edward Longley described the wagons in 1830s Upper Canada as quite different from those of England: "much lighter and drawn by horses" in the same manner as carriages in England (106). William Phillips Sr described the typical wagon as being like "a great chest, without a lid," with a straight board on each side and at the front and back (74). In 1834, superintendent Brydone hired four wagons to carry the women and children of thirteen families from Hamilton to Woodstock as well as ten more for the luggage of 100 immigrants. By contrast, the party of the wealthy Admiral Vansittart*, also bound for Woodstock, had left Hamilton the day before with 21 wagons.[43]

A long walk undertaken from necessity, for business, or for the purpose of visiting made a good subject for a letter home, but immigrants did not mention the journeys of daily life, such as those that must have been made by children in service. They did recount long trips made under special circumstances: John Stedman's walk from Cobourg to Toronto and Toronto to Port Stanley in 1832; James Rapson's journey with his brother, William, and John Dearling in pursuit of a cask and money brought by Brydone from England in 1836; and, also in 1836, George Hilton's three-week journey from Toronto to the Adelaide settlement and back (18, 115, 119). On a journey to find his brother, Hilton walked almost the full distance to London and then branched off into the townships of Delaware and Adelaide to visit members of his brother's family.

During the course of the Petworth emigrations, the mail service between North America and England relied on sailing ships and pre-dated the introduction of the penny post in England and the many improvements in internal mail delivery introduced in Canada later in the century. Mail in the Canadas in the 1830s was carried by road, by stagecoach, by wagon, by couriers on horseback and on foot, and, during the open season, on steamboats and on some schooner routes. Despite military interest in routing mail through British ports, the best established route for letters between Upper Canada and England was through New York.[44] From the Canadas, the expensive government packet service from Halifax was effectively limited to government correspondence, and merchant ships leaving Quebec were not much of an option for Petworth immigrants once they reached the upper province. They thus recommended sending letters by New York (the route had to be specified) as cheapest and quickest, an opinion Sockett confirmed from the English side of the correspondence. Charles Rapley, in the Adelaide settlement at the western end of the province, said that his letters from England were two shillings cheaper if sent through the United States.

Even via New York, sending letters was a significant expense for poor immigrants and their families in England. A portion of the postage had be paid by the recipient in either direction. Although the Canadian mails were controlled by the British postmaster general through deputies in the various provinces, the British and Canadian systems were not integrated. The recipient in England had to pay the cost from "the water," the port where the letter arrived, and, as their Canadian relatives warned, they also had to pay for this first leg of the journey for their own letters if they were to arrive in Canada. Sockett estimated the usual cost to the English recipient at about a shilling. So that their relatives would know that the letter was worth redeeming, he supplied some Petworth emigrants with a sheet of paper folded to show his own signature on the outside.

Costs associated with sending letters in this period account for their appearance and the habit of cramming in as much as the writer could possibly fit on a page. The basic postage was for a single sheet of one ounce or less and increased for each additional sheet. If a second sheet was used as a "cover," the price doubled.[45] Hence people wrote on a single sheet folded to allow space for an address. Postal regulations also help to explain serial letters addressed to several people and letters from different people on the same page. So long as there was one sheet of paper and one address for delivery, the basic rate applied. Apart from weight and the number of sheets, the other factor in cost was distance. When Edward Longley at Guelph sent a message to his family that a letter directed via New York "will save me three or four postages" (106), he referred to the incremental costs associated with a longer journey for the letter.[46] John Barnes in Toronto could get a letter to England for 2 shillings, but those farther inland paid more.

How long a letter might take to arrive at its destination was hard to guess. A letter from James Rapson dated Waterloo Township, 30 August 1836, arrived in England on 1 October, while one dated 4 September 1836 and sent by John Denman from East Flamborough took nearly a month longer and was received 4 November. In another example, a letter from Thomas Adsett's father dated 10 March 1833 did not reach his son in Canada until 19 June. Yet, a letter sent by George Coleman from Woodstock dated 17 December 1835 reached its destination in England on 10 February 1836 and was printed in the *Brighton Herald* three days later.

Upper Canadians in this era complained that there were not enough post offices to serve new settlements. Politicians blamed this situation on the postmaster general in England, who insisted that each post office pay its way.[47] A number of letters in this collection either mention a post office at some distance from where the immigrant lived or give the post office as their address. Thus Ann Cosens, living on a farm in Blenheim Township in 1839, gave the Preston Post Office in Waterloo as her address (141).

Roswell Mount, who in 1832 was both postmaster in Delaware and superintendent of the government settlement opened that year in Adelaide, used his position as postmaster of the more settled township of Delaware to promote correspondence from his new settlement. During the months that he visited the settlement regularly, Mount picked up and delivered letters. Some Petworth immigrants gave their families Mount's address in Delaware or used the closest of his depots as their address. A post office was opened in the Village of Adelaide in 1833 but it was still some distance from the lots on concessions 4 and 5 where most Petworth emigrants were located. They did not have a convenient post office until one opened in Katesville in 1837.

The postal service was not always to blame when letters were delayed or went astray. Edward Longley began a letter in Guelph on 28 September 1835 but concluded it the following March, "not having an opportunity of sending the above" (106). Immigrants gave vague addresses. Like all new immigrants, they moved frequently. On her travels in Canada, Anna Jameson saw a long list of uncollected letters at Brantford and agonized for emigrants too poor to pay to claim them.[48] However, Sockett, from long experience, claimed that even the very poor would scrimp to claim a letter; the unclaimed letters at Brantford were more likely to be letters addressed to people who had travelled on to western Upper Canada or to Michigan. If Petworth immigrants knew they were going to move, they sometimes waited to write until they thought they were settled.

If immigrants could find someone to carry a letter for them, they did not use the postal service. Brydone, Petworth superintendent from 1834 to 1837, carried a number of letters in both directions. Rather than pay, immigrants were ready to give a letter to almost anybody travelling to England. According to Sockett, these informal postmen were unreliable, and letters might take five or six months to arrive, if they arrived at all. John Worsfold provided a good example of letters carried as a favour. He sent three letters from Quebec, Montreal, and York (Toronto) as he passed through these places in June and July of 1832. At mid-December he still did not know if they had arrived. He had given the one he sent from Toronto to a man who sailed on the same ship as he did. This man planned to return to England to fetch his family and had promised to post it in London. A doctor (perhaps the ship's doctor) also promised to take a letter from Montreal to Dorking. Of the three letters, Worsford expected his family to pay for only one, a letter he had been unable to prepay from Quebec (48).

Sockett described the high cost of postage as an impediment to emigration because it reduced the flow of information from the colonies to England. Promoters of immigration in Canada took the same view, as we saw with Mount going out of his way to collect letters in Adelaide Township. The Canada Company carried mail for settlers in its Huron Tract free of charge, and the few Petworth immigrants settled on company land used this service. Sockett sometimes used the funds at the disposal of his committee to pay for the letters of people who had their passage from Egremont, and he would have liked the government to facilitate all immigrant letters. He lobbied the Duke of Richmond, postmaster general until 1834, and claimed that Richmond had been receptive to his proposal to allow poor immigrants cheap postage similar to that afforded soldiers and sailors from the lower ranks, but nothing came of it.[49] However, despite the costs and difficulties, immigrants continued to send letters as the best way they had of maintaining contact with family and friends in England.

THOMAS SOCKETT'S EDITING OF IMMIGRANT LETTERS

Although we do not have the originals of letters copied by Sockett, we do have other examples of manuscript letters written by Petworth immigrants, and some of the letters he published survive in more than one copied or published version. With this evidence, and the work of other editors of immigrant letters, we can speculate about how complete and accurate the letters he published may be. Stephen Fender examined a wide range of sources while writing *Sea Changes* and remarked on the similarity of the language in immigrants' letters printed in promotional tracts to that of letters preserved in archives without contamination by any third party.[50] The manuscript letters in our collection that can be identified as originals are also reassuringly similar in content and expression to the printed letters, but these similarities do not dispel all concerns.

Sockett's personal reputation, and the fact that migration from and to the same places took place over six years, should have been insurance against major fabrication, even without the extra vigilance of Petworth immigrants and their families. In collections such as this, where people and places are named and the letters can be localized in a community if not in a family, outright forgery is not the main concern. The greater problem in using the texts of printed letters of the first half of the nineteenth century is the editorial standards of Sockett's day.

Editors sometimes left clues to the changes they had made which can be teased out in a careful reading. In a study of the letters of emigrants from Corsley, which Petworth rumours had branded as fakes, and of a second collection from nearby Frome in Somersetshire, Terry McDonald did not find forged letters. He did discover that the experiences and achievements described were not, as implied, those of immigrants just starting out in Upper Canada. The writers of these letters included former soldiers who had served in North America during the War of 1812, some who had had land granted to them in 1820, and one family from Frome who had been in New Brunswick for ten years.[51]

This sort of misrepresentation did not occur with Petworth immigrants, who arrived in Upper Canada at the times stated. Questions arise, however, around material Sockett chose not to use, not to publish, or not to include in an "extract." Contemporary editors of extracts from immigrant letters exercised their own judgement in dropping words or passages without indicating where this occurred, a practice which naturally raised suspicions that were not always quieted by assurances in a preface or introduction that everything important had been retained. In his first collection, Sockett sometimes noted his excisions and even summarized the material omitted, but he seldom bothered as he published more letters.

Sockett set out his editorial principles more than once and proved consistent over time. At the beginning, in 1831, before he had sent any emigrants himself, he published letters from local people who had gone to the United States, explaining that the text was from the originals with no changes other than to correct the spelling. "The parts omitted [from letters given as extracts] are either repetitions of the same or similar statements as those given, or relate solely to the private affairs of the Parties: not a single word has been altered or added."[52] His statement in the introduction to *Emigration: Letters . . . 1832* was similar: "[the letters] are faithfully given in the very <u>words</u> of the writers, and even where, in some instances, the sense might seem to require a little alteration, that liberty has not been taken: the spelling alone (to save extra trouble, in copying and printing) has been corrected." Sockett left out proper names in some letters, perhaps because he was asked to do so, and regard for the feelings of the family may well have prompted him to drop the sentence from John Capling's letters in which Capling described his rough burial of family members who died of cholera near Stratford in Upper Canada (21). With regard to his selection of letters, he wrote that "many others [letters] have been received, but they are either not so explanatory, as those which are given, or merely contain repetition of the same facts."[53] Sockett's practice as explained in this introduction was not very different from that of many modern editors of immigrant letters.

In matters of content, however, Sockett made some additional editorial decisions for less obvious reasons. Why did he not publish James Rapson's admittedly depressing account of his trip up the St Lawrence (12) when he was willing to include the far worse experience of the Capling family? The answer seems to be that he was most cautious where he felt his emigration project was most vulnerable.

In his relationship with would-be emigrants, Sockett was confident that in offering assisted emigration he offered a chance for a better life. He wanted emigrants

Sockett sent this extract to Richmond as evidence of the hardships of the St Lawrence route (see 77)

Goodwood House Archives, MS 1470, f.217

Courtesy of the Trustees of the Goodwood Collections and with acknowledgements to the West Sussex Record Office and the County Archivist

to understand, however, that he offered improved opportunities, not certainties. So far as the future of his scheme were concerned, his insecurities were about his sponsors. He was particularly anxious about Egremont, his elderly and autocratic patron. Egremont gave Sockett a free hand in administering the emigrations on the understanding that he himself would not be bothered. Sockett, for his part, was both protective of Egremont's reputation and wary of his reactions, and he went to great lengths to avoid criticism that might touch his patron.

Sockett's defensive attitude resulted in his dropping passages from letters, omissions that are not discussed in any preface. The first instance deals with the general belief among the ruling classes – a belief Sockett shared – that assisted emigrants should travel on British ships and settle in a British colony. Sockett took to heart account of hardships and suffering on the St Lawrence route in 1832 and 1833, but in published letters he dropped his immigrants' advice to travel via New York and the Erie Canal. The results can be seen in the two versions of William Cooper's letter (8).

Sockett knew that omitting passages like Cooper's advice to travel via the United States was of limited use – "tho I have not printed these recommendations, yet the letters containing them have been much read, & they will have their effect"[54] – but he was buying time, hoping that the Canadian route through Bytown (Ottawa) and the Rideau Canal would provide an acceptable alternative to the St Lawrence route. He was disappointed in 1833, and criticized in England, when his party found the Rideau Canal closed for repairs and could not use it as he had promised. His instructions to Superintendent Brydone in 1834 show him prepared to consider sending emigrants by New York and the Erie Canal, but a successful trip through the Canadian canal that year made Brydone's inquiries unnecessary. Without Sockett's private correspondence, we would know that immigrants had advised the more comfortable American route, but we would have no idea that "most" recommended it or that Sockett thought that they did so with "good reason."[55]

In different circumstances – those surrounding the conduct of the Petworth committee's superintendents – criticism reported by the press led to the publication of material from immigrants' letters that we would not otherwise have seen. In 1833, newspapers across Upper Canada, and then in Brighton, carried charges that Captain Hale, the superintendent of the *England*, had been drinking heavily and stealing stores intended for the immigrants. These charges, originating with Petworth immigrant George Turner, received qualified editorial support in Toronto and Montreal. In distant Sussex, Sockett was in a quandry. His fears of serious ill effects from the negative publicity reaching England forced him to make a public statement on behalf of his committee before he knew if he could find any better superintendent than Hale for the coming season. He issued a pamphlet stating his confidence that Hale was not guilty of "peculation" and his hopes that accounts of his drinking had been exaggerated, but he was uneasy. In the absence of solid evidence, Sockett published all the circumstantial evidence he had collected on both sides of the issue in a pamphlet issued in the name of his committee. The committee's *Statement* included: a letter recommending Hale from the shipping agent Carter and Bonus, James Knight's favourable account of Hale's conduct in 1832 (177), newspaper reports, letters Hale solicited in his support in Canada, and extracts from all immigrant letters shown to the committee which made any reference to Hale. These extracts contained "every word that is said [about Hale], whether favourable or otherwise" (Thair 70 and 78; Rapson 76; Barnes 75; Habbin 80 and 81; Tilley 83; Dearling 85; and Sharp 86).[56]

We have printed the extracts Sockett used in the *Statement* in their chronological sequence, placing them, if possible, in the context of the letter of which they are a part. While Hannah Tilley spoke well of Hale and Henry Habbin dismissed him as "not fit to drive a pig to market," Rhoda Thair summed up the general sense of these extracts best. She praised the food and grog on the *England* (the committee's conduct of the emigration), but she wrote plainly that on the St Lawrence River Hale was "three parts of his time tipsy." Sockett's handling of her letter shows his part as editor. When he first published it he omitted "some remarks about the private character of an individual." When his hand was forced, he made public the missing passage in one of the extracts printed in the *Statement*.

In 1837, a single letter printed in the *Brighton Patriot* made similar charges against James Marr Brydone, the superintendent from 1834 to 1837 and a close friend of Sockett's. In this case, the accusatory letter was anonymous and there was no corroboration. Sockett responded strongly, and the matter dropped from view (see 130 and 131).

As much as we know of the record that Sockett kept private or, in the case of Hale, would like to have kept private does not greatly change the story of the Petworth emigrations, although these incidents add colour. From a historical perspective, letters revealing that the organization did not operate entirely without hitches and problems lend credibility to the Petworth committee's considerable successes in a difficult task.

PETWORTH LETTER-WRITERS AND UPPER CANADA

A collection of letters such as this one challenges the stereotypes of English immigrants in 1830s Upper Canada as officers and gentlewomen. It makes clear that the published travellers' and settlers' narratives of the middle classes represent only a partial survey of "English" reactions to the province. In the writing of contemporary British travellers and settlers, and in official records, people such as those sent under the Petworth committee often lack even the individuality of a proper name.[57] These letters portray a different world, a world in which it is the employer and the government official who are shadowy figures identified vaguely as "the squire" and "the gentleman." In writing to relatives and friends in England, their authors give us a valuable perspective on the immigration experiences of poor and assisted emigrants.

Contemporaries of the Petworth immigrants believed that "after the impulse has once been given towards countries readily adapted to emigration, the letters of the settlers themselves ... serve to maintain and propagate the disposition to resort to the same quarter."[58] Historian Eric Richards puts this point more simply, describing emigrant letters as "the central link in chain migration."[59] The letters of Petworth immigrants show the forging of this link. Sockett wrote in 1833 that labouring people in his neighbourhood would not stir until they received reports from the immigrants of the year before.[60] Looking back in 1838, he touched on the more personal side. He said he knew of "individual instances" when people had come to him saying "I was thinking of going out to so and so this year; and I will go if any letter comes before the ship sails." When the letter did not come, the person did not go. In these cases the issue was not distrust of the scheme, or of the authenticity of the letters they had seen, "but each one preferred having a letter from his own individual relation or near friend."[61] Once assistance had induced the first emigrants to go from a community, chain migration hinged on the reports they sent back. The first Petworth immigrants wrote that they had explored the way: "you will not have the care on your mind as we had, not knowing where to go to, or what we was going to do, for you know that we tried the road for you" (20). Emigrants who followed them would have an easier time getting settled: "you will have a home to come to until you can get one, and some friends to converse with" (138).

The conditions in England that drove these people to emigrate were low wages and competition for employment, which had been intensified by a dramatic increase in population in a largely static rural economy. In letters from Upper Canada, the importance of these factors in the emigration decision is apparent from the emphasis placed on their opposites – on the ease with which immigrants found work and abundant food. Certainly they had fears as well, and many letters reveal the writers' concern about what will happen should their health fail. But letter after letter repeats the sentiment of George Carver: "there is always plenty of employment, for any person who is willing to work" (95). Carver claims he has "got to be quite steady since I came to this country, and have almost given over drinking. Whisky is very cheap here," he goes on. (This last comment is repeated by many, sometimes in warning tones.)

The worries of those at home – about the winter's cold, about wild animals, about what would happen if the immigrants got sick, about the native peoples – are assuaged by the letter-writers. They sent advice about what to bring – advice which took into account the different needs of emigrants planning for a settled district or the backwoods. Some letters reflect the desire to be seen at home as having made the right choice, as having made good. The most common message is that sent by Henry Heasman to his father: "you have no cause to weep for me, for I am better off here, than I can ever be in England" (96). Hard work is stressed by some: "not play as half of it is in England" (100); and plentiful food is emphasized: "I may have beefsteaks or other meats for breakfast," boasts John Worsfold (48). The rudimentary housing is commented on, but in a very matter of fact way; except for the journey, immigrants are clearly not less comfortable than in England. After only a year or two, they can see a future of comparative prosperity, one that our research in Canadian sources demonstrates that was often fulfilled. This kind of confidence attracted others to emigrate.

The picture of Upper Canada provided by these letter-writers is most accurate when it relates to their daily lives. Martin Martin's general description of soil and landscape, for example, suggests that he had been influenced by emigrant guides aimed at newcomers to the province. When he wrote of his immediate prospects as a carpenter, however, he offers the perceptive comment that he was benefiting from a surge in building activity that would last only as long as new immigrants continued to arrive (29).

Immigrants set out the details of agreements that they or their family members and friends made with employers – a few warned that the newcomer had to be wary – and described the price and terms on which they agreed to buy land. The people writing were experienced by labourers, very aware of the seasonality of their work and used to calculating board and other payments in kind in addition to wages. When they turned from work to their domestic economy, their letters gave snapshots from different parts of the province of the costs of basic groceries and other necessities. The evidence they record of prices comes from people poor enough to watch what they paid, and it was sent from places some distance from towns which had chambers of commerce and newspapers to keep such records.

In the circles where these letters were first received, where the success of the harvest, a small change in prices of foods, or a slight shift in wages could mean the difference between getting by and a winter of want, such letters were read very closely. For family members trying anxiously to read between the lines and find out how children, brothers, and sisters were really faring, these familiar markers were reassuring evidence of their welfare and lifestyle. For potential emigrants considering their options, information on prices, wages, and the demand for labour or for their trade could be a deciding factor.

If family news and practical information were important parts of these letters, most writers also tried to convey how they felt about their new home. Though almost all were working people, immigrants varied greatly in education, in social attitudes, in aspirations, in religion, and in temperament. Some common themes and preoccupations, however, can be identified.

Writing home, immigrants described Canadian society in terms of their English background. Much of it seemed strange, too strange for some. When the letters talk of people returning home, they seem to have gone back quickly, perhaps discouraged at not finding work immediately. Richard Neal wrote pragmatically that "there is a great many don't like this country, nor more do I myself: but I can get plenty [of] work here" (47). (He stayed and, after the death of his employer, took over and successfully continued his contracting business.) Apparently contrary advice to stay at home and frequent disclaimers of any attempt to persuade, are a reminder that adjustment was not easy. As the people whose letters we have were those who hoped to sustain family networks through their letters, they were people who missed the emotional support of family. Some of them also missed the physical support of those back home. Offers of generous help and to share land may reflect the needs of those in Upper Canada, especially those in backwoods settlements, as much as the needs of the people invited. At the same time, they found much to praise.

The "independence" letter-writers found in their new homes had more to it than better paid work, cheaper food, and fuel that was often free for the taking. They enjoyed free access to the forest, the right to keep a hunting dog and to hunt and fish at will, and the right to walk where they pleased and to turn out their cows and pigs. They could make their own candles without fear of prosecution for avoiding a tax. They reported these differences with pleasure, but they gave no sign that they compared Canada to a less-industrialized England. Instead, Petworth immigrants seemed rather to be creating a new nostalgia – remembering the society of English villages, the good English beer, more varied gardens, and the flowers, fruits, and vegetables they hoped to discover or to have sent to Upper Canada as reminders.

If Petworth immigrants remembered happy times at home, they also remembered why they had left. When bitterness crops up in these letters it often centres on how they were treated as workers. Many of these people felt a new sense of control over their lives, brought on in part by their new relationships with employers: "no running after masters" here, comments Henry Heasman (96). Charlotte Willard records that this difference was reflected in the language used: "they dine along with the master and mistresses as you call them in England, but they will not be called so here, they are equals-like and if hired to anybody they call them their employers" (20).

The people who wrote the letters in this book had no illusions that they had come to a classless society, but they noted the lack of the extremes of wealth and poverty: "there is no beggars, nor any carriages" wrote George Hills (17). George Coleman's letter was unusually self-conscious, and, by admitting that his tongue had caused him to be "discharged twice in a fortnight" at home, he came closer to "republican" sentiments than most. Yet, his quarrel with England was on a personal level; he wanted to be well treated as a hard-working farm labourer, not to overturn the social order. In Woodstock, he had been ill and had missed five weeks of work in consequence, but "[I]now have not to meet the frowns of the overseer, and be called a poor pauper, but I am looked upon, and receive kindness without grudging" (103). Being looked upon, being noticed and valued by employers, eating a full meal at the farm table rather than snatching at dry bread and cheese under a hedge, these are images of better working conditions that recur.

On first arriving in Upper Canada, Petworth letter-writers adopted a range of strategies for earning a living. A few, such as Thomas Holden, who settled immediately on a government lot in Adelaide Township, came with the single ambition of becoming farmers (47), but most were more flexible in seizing the best opportunity that presented itself. A majority of Petworth letter-writers arrived in Upper Canada with training that made them desirable employees as skilled farmhands, as artisans, or, usually in the case of unmarried women and children, as servants. For most of them, work and farming were complementary activities. They might work, when work was available, for money to improve their farms. Or they might occupy a smaller plot and give their first attention to work – a strategy that received official recognition in the government plan to allow parish immigrants the use of five-acre lots as pioneered by Petworth immigrants in Woodstock (98 and 101). Some of these immigrants worked with a view to buying land of their own in the future, either on a new frontier or in more settled townships where the hardships were less. Others with a profitable trade saw it as a better opportunity than a farm: for Charles Adsett, ownership of a farm seemed to be a form of insurance, a refuge in case of bad times rather than an ultimate goal (180). Although some of the older Petworth immigrants lived all their lives as labourers, there were others, especially among those who came as children or young adults, who prospered in fields as diverse as the land acquisitions and hotel of Obediah Wilson or the shipping enterprises of William Goldring.

Letters written by Petworth immigrants have been used, with those of other immigrants, as a source of knowledge about the opinions and priorities of rural labourers in southern England, and Canadian social historians cite them as examples of opinion among poor immigrants in Upper Canada.[62] Unless the provenance of the letters and how they came to be written are known, however, the use that can be made of them is limited. Bringing the Petworth letters together, explaining how they came to us, and providing as much information as possible about the letter-writers should make them more useful to historians but, more than that, it should make them accessible to a wider audience who, we hope, will find them as fascinating as we have.

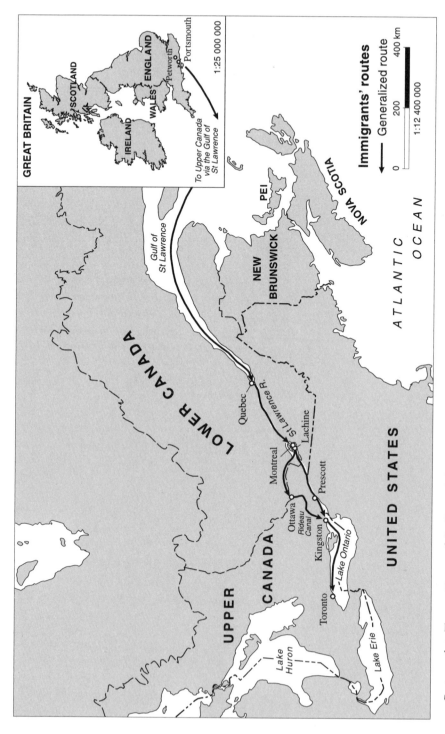

1 Portsmouth to Toronto: Routes of the Petworth immigrants

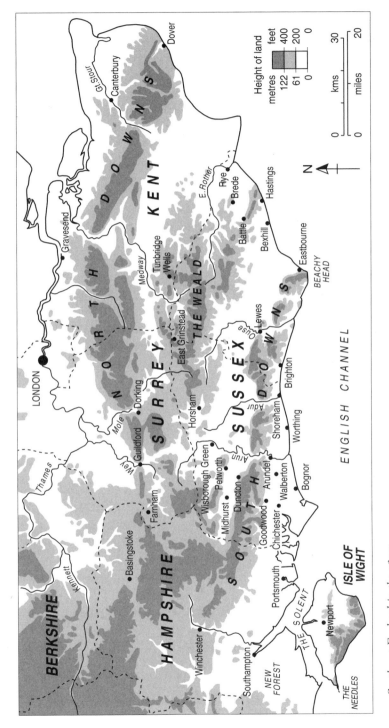

2 Southeast England in the 1830s

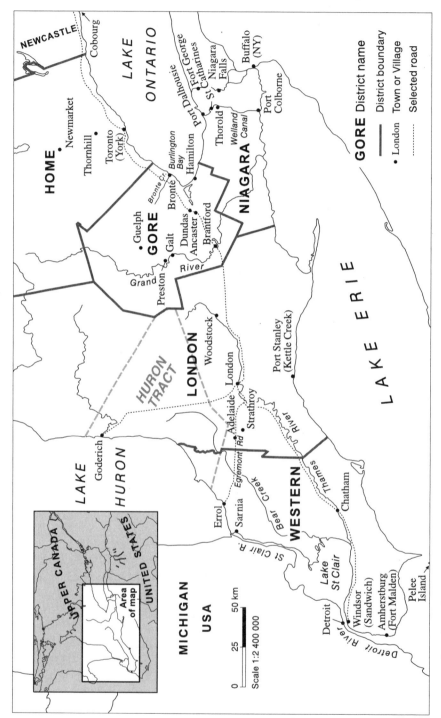

3 *Upper Canada in the 1830s*

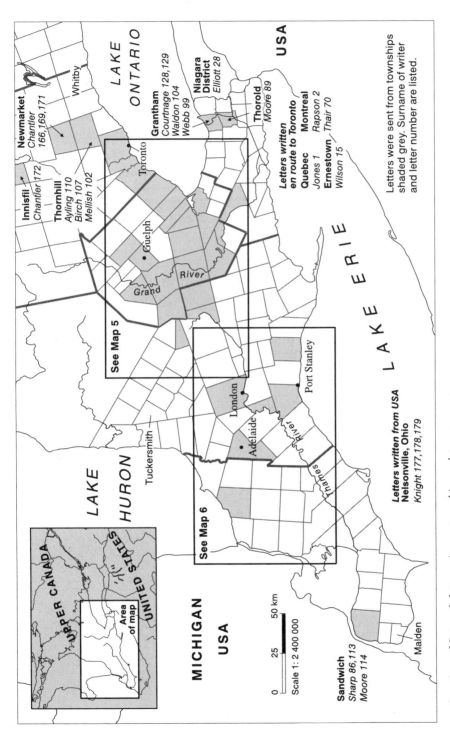

4 *Locations of Petworth letter-writers – townships and towns*

Note: District and township boundaries of the 1830s are used.

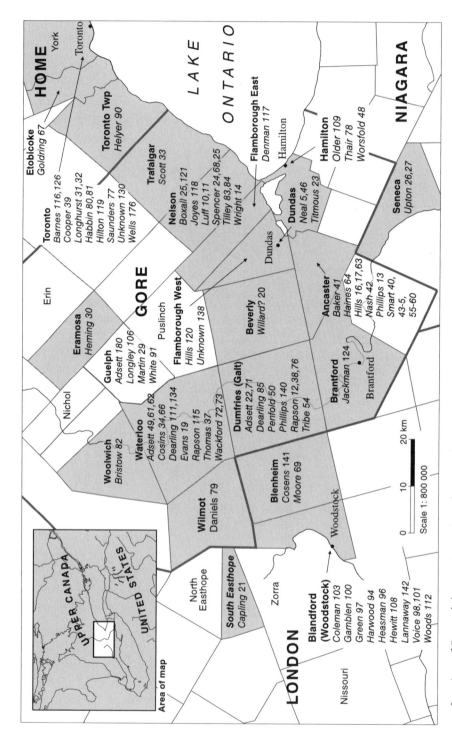

5 *Locations of Petworth letter-writers – Hamilton-Woodstock area*

Note: District and township boundaries of the 1830s are used.

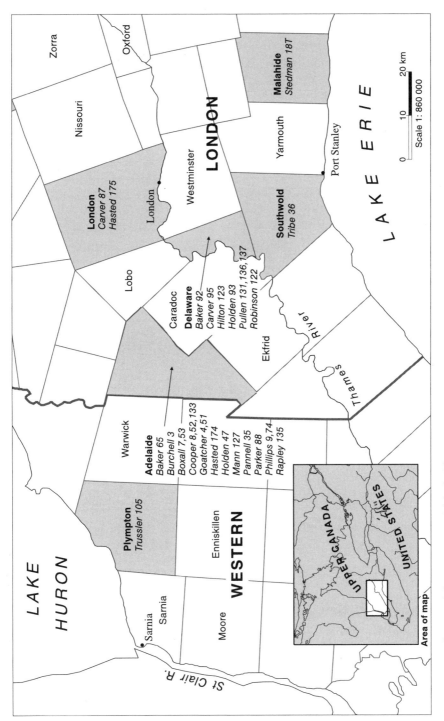

6 *Locations of Petworth letter-writers – Adelaide-Plympton area*

Note: District and township boundaries of the 1830s are used.

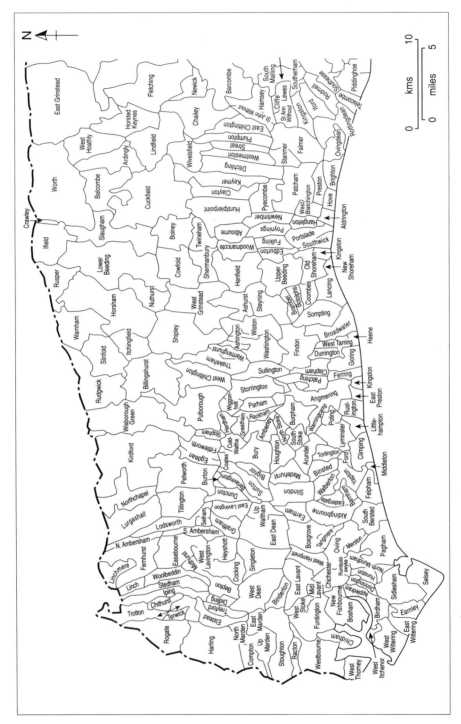

7 *Sussex parishes at the time of the Petworth emigrations*

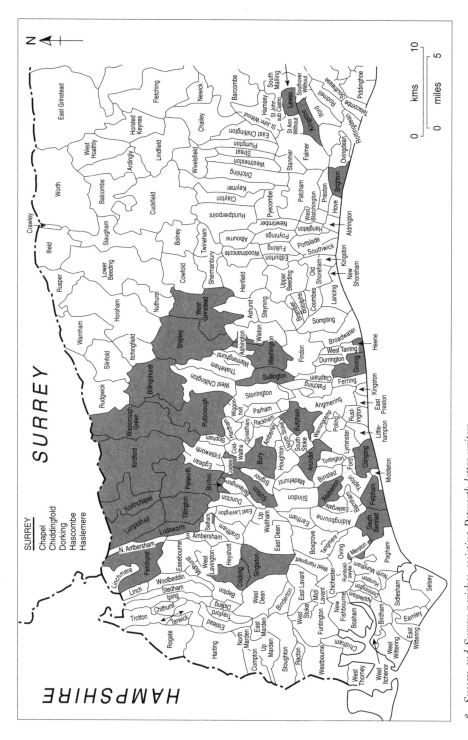

8 *Sussex and Surrey parishes assisting Petworth letter-writers*

Note: Sussex parishes are shown and shaded; Surrey parishes are listed.

ABBREVIATIONS

Add Ms	Additional manuscript
AO	Archives of Ontario
BL	British Library
CIHM	Canadian Institute for Historical Microreproductions
CO	Colonial Office
ESRO	East Sussex Record Office
GMR	Surrey Record Office, Guildford Muniment Room
HO	Home Office
IGI	International Genealogical Index
IOW	Isle of Wight
IOWRO	Isle of Wight Record Office
KPL	Kitchener Public Library
MH	Ministry of Health
MP	Miscellaneous paper
NA	National Archives, Canada
OGS	Ontario Genealogical Society
P	Parish record (Cambridge County Record Office)
PAR	Parish Record (ESRO, WSRO)
PEC	Petworth Emigration Committee
PHA	Petworth House Archives
PRO	Public Records Office, England
SER	South of the Egremont Road
WSRO	West Sussex Record Office

EDITORIAL NOTE

We have tried to let the writers of these letters tell their own stories. The letters are arranged chronologically and we introduce each writer the first time he or she appears in the collection, presenting the basic known facts of that writer's life up to that point. At the end of the letter, as seems appropriate, we indicate where complementary information may be found, provide links between immigrants and letters, and for the final letter, set out the information we have about the writer's subsequent life in Canada. We have added footnotes to identify people or on occasion supplied a name in square brackets, but we have tried to keep our interventions to a minimum. We have tried to explain terminology or references that are obscure to today's reader. Some references, of course, remain obscure. Many of these letters were written for public consumption. The writers knew that everyone in their home parish or town or village would want to know about the first few letters that arrived from Upper Canada so that their letters would almost certainly be read out and reach people beyond the family circle. As time went by, they also knew that they might be published (as many of these were). These people were writing for the most part to loved ones whose lives they knew well. The letters must be read with this in mind. Letter-writers and recipients knew who could read and write and who could not; they knew the rhythms of life at home. Therefore what is not commented on is as interesting as what is.

Presentation of entry

Each letter is numbered and identified, wherever possible, by the name of the letter-writer (according to the letter's signature), address, recipient, recipient's address, date. Letters are preceded and followed by our editorial comments, which introduce writers, identify the parish that sent them, provide explanations and links to other letters, or tell the reader what we know of the letter-writers' subsequent life. These introductions always indicate when people came with family units, and information on the immediate family unit (husband, wife, children) and on the extended family is given when we have it. If we have traced a marriage, a note indicates whether or not a husband and wife signed the marriage register. Readers seeking more information about Petworth immigrants who were not letter-writers should consult the list of Petworth emigrants in Part Two of *Assisting Emigration to Upper Canada*.

Spelling of names

Names of letter-writers are given in the entry listing according to the most accepted spelling of the family name. In our editorial comments we also use what seem to be the most accepted spellings, based on a variety of sources, for the people mentioned. The spellings used in the letters, which were often copied by someone other than the signer, may differ from the entry listing.

Source

The source of each letter is noted before the text of the letter. Any additional copies of the letter found are also recorded here, as well as any special notes about versions of letters. Editorial comment that appeared with a letter when originally published is reproduced after the source line and before the text of the letter.

Editing of published letters

Those letters published by Thomas Sockett or Charles Barclay were edited by them to omit repetitions, to correct some spellings, and to standardize punctuation. Because these changes are helpful to the reader, we have used the published versions even when we have a contemporary copy in manuscript or a version published in a contemporary newspaper. We have compared different published versions carefully and compiled composite texts to include variations of substance; the variations are explained in the notes to the text.

Spellings in original letters, especially those written by the older generation, tend to be phonetic or reflect the local dialect, and we found that Sockett's and Barclay's changes simply brought the letters into standard English. Thus "witch" becomes which, "the" becomes they, "haney" becomes any, and so on. We do not have sufficient original letters to draw any firm conclusions but it would appear – as one might expect – that these spellings are found in letters written by the generation born before 1800; those born a generation later used a more standard English.

Some of the original letters are completely unpunctuated, and it is the punctuation of the published letters that seems most different from late twentieth-century English. Again we can only conjecture based on limited samples, but it would appear, comparing newspaper versions and versions published by Phillips, that Sockett's punctuation was eccentric. Exact transcriptions of examples of original letters are found in Appendix A for those who wish to compare. Some of the originals were (and are) difficult to decipher, and ellipses or repeated asterisks were used by Sockett and other contemporary transcribers to indicate an omission, such as personal details or something illegible. In a few published letters, dashes were used to replace surnames.

We, too, have made similar editorial changes to spelling, punctuation, and capitalization. Our most significant editorial change is to add paragraphing, so that modern readers are able to read and comprehend the letters fairly easily. Significant changes in spelling or other editorial changes are given in square brackets.

Composite letters

Letters were often collaborative efforts. They may be signed by a couple, but written by one or the other. Sometimes it is evident whether the husband or the wife is writing the letter; sometimes one can guess with confidence. We have not attempted to do so. On occasion Sockett indicates that a letter is written by an individual when the letter is signed by a couple, and one or two of his attributions are clearly wrong.

Letters may be addressed to one individual but have sections addressed to different members of the family. We know from the manuscript letters that composite letters sometimes result from one person writing for a number of people, and sometimes from each person in a group composing a part of the letter in turn. We have followed the published versions in numbering and treating letters as separate items. In cases where we had originals, we followed the format of the letters, distinguishing between a composite letter written by several people on one or more pages and, after envelopes began to be used, two letters sent in a single envelope.

Annotation

Letters are footnoted as appropriate. Some notes were included in contemporary published letters and these have been retained but incorporated into the footnote numbering system. All such notes begin: Original annotation.

Other letters

The numbers of any other letters by a letter-writer are noted at the end of each letter and before any editorial comment. In addition, letters by other family members or close connections are noted either here or in the editorial comments.

Asterisk

An asterisk following a name in the text indicates that the person is identified in Appendix B and is used for people who are referred to frequently in the letters. Persons mentioned only occasionally are identified, when possible, in the notes.

Bullet ■

A square bullet is used in the margin to signal each letter number. An open bullet □ is used in the index for letter numbers with the page numbers for that letter following in parentheses.

Identification of people, places, and terminology (Appendix B)

Certain individuals are mentioned in a number of the letters or in our introductions because they sponsored emigrants or assisted them once they arrived in Canada or were otherwise involved in their lives. These people are identified in brief in Appendix B, and their names are noted with an asterisk in the text: for example, the Earl of Egremont*.

During the 1830s many places in Upper Canada were named and renamed. We have included in Appendix B some of the place names that change in this period. We have also listed here a few of the terms that may be unfamiliar to readers on one side of the Atlantic or the other. Our maps show the boundaries of parishes and counties in England, and of townships and districts in Canada, as they were at the time most of these letters were written. We have used some modern place names in Canada to help readers refer to current maps.

Letters

1832

A

Emigration — 1832.

Expenses to be borne by Lord Egremont formed with
reference to the proportion of land he holds in the
different undermentioned parishes.

The total expense for each Adult to York in
upper Canada being estimated at £10.

Parish	Portion of property	Expense to be D.r by Ld Egremont	Expense D.r by other Landowners	Remarks
Petworth		10 . 0. 0		
Tillington		10 . 0. 0		
Duncton		10 . 0. 0		
Egdean		10 . 0. 0		
Northchapel		10 . 0. 0		
Sutton	4/5	8 . 8. 0	1. 12. 0	
Kirdford	1/8	3 . 10. 0	6. 10. 0	
Lurgashall	1/5	3 . 5. 0	6. 15. 0	
Norrington	1/14	3 . 5. 0	6. 15. 0	On the passage
Sullington	1/14	3 . 5. 0	6. 15. 0	to ationtreal
Fittleworth	1/5	3 . 5. 0	6. 15. 0	by Ld. E.
Ambersham South	1/16	3 . 0. 0	7. 0. 0	
Wisboro' Green	1/20	1 . 2. 0	8. 18. 0	or 1 in 3
Pulborough	1/36	0 . 16. 3	9. 3. 9	or 1 in 4

CHRONOLOGY FOR THE YEAR 1832

26 January The first entry was recorded in the minute book of the Petworth Emigration Committee.

11 April The *Lord Melville* and the *Eveline* sailed from Spithead (outside Portsmouth harbour).

2 May At about 4:00 AM the berths on the larboard (port) side of the *Lord Melville* collapsed, an incident mentioned in several letters.

8 May The *England* set sail.

22 May Charlotte Willard saw land for the first time.

28 May The *Lord Melville* and the *Eveline* arrived in Quebec.

31 May The *Eveline* arrived in Montreal.

8 June The *Lord Melville* arrived in Montreal; the emigrants from the *Eveline* arrived in York (Toronto).

9 June First death from cholera reported in Montreal.

14 June The Chantler families left Montreal.

c. 15 June Cholera spread rapidly up the St Lawrence River route to towns in Upper Canada.

19 June Three schooners carrying emigrants from the *Eveline* departed on or about this date: two went to Hamilton, one to Kettle Creek (Port Stanley).

21 June Two cases of cholera were confirmed in York.

19–22 June The emigrants from the *Lord Melville* arrived in York.

24 June Stephen Goatcher reported seeing Niagara Falls.

late June The Adsett family arrived at Preston, having travelled by way of Hamilton, Dundas, and the road through the Beverly swamp.

1 July The emigrants from the *England* arrived in York.

1 July Beginning 1 July through to August Hale conducted a party made up in Wisborough Green and consisting of six families and three single men (some 40 people) to Knight's settlement in Nelsonville, Athens County, Ohio.

6 July Edward Boxall arrived in Adelaide Township.

31 July Albert Cooper was paid for the transport of 8 wagonloads of goods belonging to the settlers sent by the Earl of Egremont from Woodhull's Mills to the "English settlement" in Adelaide (on an earlier trip he took 13 loads from Captain White's in Lobo to Adelaide).

17 September The Petworth committee sent copies of letters from Boxall and Cooper, and extracts from Hill's letter, to the *Portsmouth Herald*.

21 September Sockett wrote to the Canada Company enquiring about the likelihood of travelling via the Rideau Canal in 1833.

20 October Mary Holden and her family moved into the log house built for them in Adelaide Township.

6 November Sockett reported that letters "continue to be received by every mail from our emigrants."

SOURCES: PHA 137; WSRO, Goodwood MS 1461; NA, RG1, E15B; Cameron and Maude, *Assisting Emigration to Upper Canada* (Montreal: McGill-Queen's University Press 2000); Geoffrey Bilson, *A Darkened House: Cholera in Nineteenth-Century Canada* (Toronto: 1980); *Courtauld Family Letters 1782-1900* vol. 6 (Cambridge 1916); contemporary newspapers; letters.

PREVIOUS PAGE: List of parishes with proportion of expense to be paid by Egremont, WSRO, PHA 137

SHIP: *Lord Melville*, A1, 425 tons (registered tonnage)
MASTER: Captain Chancellor
SUPERINTENDENT: William Penfold

SHIP: *Eveline*, A1, 301 tons
MASTER: Captain Royal
SUPERINTENDENT: Stephen Goatcher

SHIP: *England*, A1, 320 tons
MASTER: Captain Lewis
SUPERINTENDENT: J.C. Hale

BACKGROUND

The Petworth emigrant of 1832 rode a wave of enthusiasm for emigration to Upper Canada which had gathered force from the previous year. After the *Lord Melville* and the *Eveline* sailed on 11 April 1832, there was still sufficient interest to fill the *England*. Although Thomas Sockett* made a distinction between the first two ships, which were "under the management of the Committee," and the *England*, which was sent "under similar arrangements," the relationship was close enough that he counted the *England*'s passengers in with the others and reported a total of 767 emigrants for the year.

Lord Egremont's assumption of much of the risk and a large share of the costs of the Petworth emigrations allowed his committee to act with confidence. It chartered ships, purchased supplies, and hired superintendents. Parishes helped emigrants to assemble an outfit, and arranged for transportation to Portsmouth. Parishes or interested sponsors provided "landing money," which the committee arranged to send to Toronto through the Canada Company. Emigrants sold what they could and packed their belongings in chests and boxes, some to go in the hold and others for use on board ship. People who might never have seen a sailing ship had to select what they would need for the six to eight weeks until they arrived at Montreal. Most had rations provided and took only some additional food for their personal use; a few on the first ships took their own supplies.

At Portsmouth, Sockett and his associates did their best to see the emigrants on to their chartered ships on the day they arrived at the docks. In the years of the Petworth emigrations, few other emigrants embarked at Portsmouth, and prompt boarding protected them from the frauds and sharp practices that gave the boarding houses and docks of the principal emigrant ports their bad reputation. By all contemporary standards Petworth emigrants travelled on good ships. The committee used

Carter and Bonus, a reputable firm experienced in the emigrant trade, and they insisted on ships certified as A1 by Lloyds of London. Each ship had a superintendent and a doctor. Despite the confined space and low, crowded berths, the Petworth committee took significantly fewer people than the total numbers allowed under contemporary Passengers' Acts. All their ships were kept clean and free of major outbreaks of disease. However, a row of berths on the *Lord Melville* collapsed during a storm, an event mentioned in several letters.

In 1832, Petworth ships passed through the Quarantine Station established that year at Grosse Isle. After more paperwork at Quebec, the emigrants stayed on their ships while they were towed upriver to Montreal by a wood-fired steamboat. They became part of the main horde of emigrant traffic only upon disembarking at Montreal. Between Montreal and Toronto, Petworth superintendents had a more difficult time keeping their parties together. A few emigrants left the party deliberately and others straggled behind or were delayed by sickness. The emigrants boarded Durham boats at Montreal to go through the Lachine Canal. At Lachine, they transferred to another set of open boats for the trip to Prescott, a journey broken by rapids where the people had to walk or take wagons. In towns such as Lachine or Prescott the merchants who transported the Petworth emigrants allowed them to sleep in empty warehouses. Between Montreal and Prescott, several emigrants mention sleeping outside after an uncomfortable day packed in the boats. Once they reached Prescott, regularly scheduled steamboats took them to Kingston and then to Toronto. All Petworth letter-writers reached Toronto free of cholera. Although the Chantler families can have been only a few days later in leaving Montreal, they were less fortunate and lost two members of their party to cholera on the river between Montreal and Prescott.

FIRST SETTLEMENT IN UPPER CANADA

The cholera epidemic of 1832 created conditions verging on chaos on the overcrowded emigrant routes of Lower and Upper Canada. Officials concentrated all their energies on dealing with the emergency. The numbers of immigrants arriving in York (Toronto) were overwhelming: officials recorded the arrival of over 20,000, about four times the settled population of 5000 to 6000, and there is no doubt that these figures are incomplete. Although the transmission of cholera was not understood, authorities in both Lower and Upper Canada could see the dangers of the crowded and unsanitary conditions in the temporary immigrant quarters that sprang up around the docks each summer. Lieutenant Governor Sir John Colborne met the epidemic with a determined strategy of dispersing immigrants throughout the province as quickly as his agents could manage to send them forward. The Upper Canada government paid to send poor immigrants westward. In consequence most Petworth immigrants went to communities the government had chosen to develop.

Obediah Wilson was a rare exception among Petworth immigrant letter-writers in settling some distance to the east of Toronto. Although even in 1832 a few Petworth immigrants stayed in the Toronto area, most of the 1832 letters were sent by people who went to the Gore and London districts. The letters of these immigrants caused others to follow, and the settlement pattern of 1832 influenced that of later Petworth emigrations.

In 1832, Petworth immigrants were sent to Hamilton and Burlington Bay on Lake Ontario or through the Welland Canal to the Lake Erie port of Kettle Creek (Port Stanley). Hamilton was the main port of entry for the Gore District, but passenger vessels also stopped at other places along Lake Ontario. Immigrants of 1832 wrote from Ancaster and Dundas as well as Hamilton, and from townships such as East Flamborough on Burlington Bay. Letters sent by people who travelled farther inland within the Gore District come mainly from communities in the valley of the Grand River. Immigrants travelling by land to townships behind Lake Erie also left from Hamilton, which was the starting point of the road leading into the Canada Company's Huron Tract. A party of Petworth immigrants from the parishes of Lurgashall and Lodsworth lost almost half their number to cholera on this road at a quarantine camp set up at the Fryfogel Inn near Stratford.

Government agents forwarded fewer poor immigrants through the Welland Canal (opened in 1829) to Lake Erie than they sent to Hamilton, but those they sent represented a bold initiative by Colborne to introduce British settlers to the western end of the province where most previous settlement has been by Americans. British immigrants began to travel directly from Quebec to the London and Western districts in large numbers in 1832. Petworth immigrants who made this journey found themselves in the agency of Crown Lands Agent Roswell Mount*, who was stationed in the interior of the London District. Those who chose to take land with the government's assistance were sent to the townships of Adelaide and Warwick.

Mount claimed to have had some 4000 immigrants under his care in the summer and autumn of 1832. He claimed that roughly half these people had found work or otherwise provided for themselves while he had located just over 2000 in the townships of Adelaide and Warwick. He placed most of the actual settlers in Adelaide, where our letters-writers settled in a cluster of Petworth immigrants on the 4th and 5th concessions. Immigrants who went to this settlement disembarked from lake schooners at Kettle Creek and travelled inland by wagon to camp at one of Mount's depots. For the last stage of their journey, they were conducted by guides over newly opened bush roads to lots where a rough log house had been put up in advance for anyone bringing a family.

In addition to immigrants intending to settle in Upper Canada, in 1832 the *England* carried the only group of Petworth emigrants who had left home with the stated intention of going to the United States. The *England*'s superintendent, J.C. Hale, had been engaged to take this party from Wisborough Green via Quebec to Ohio and a settlement being promoted by letter in Sussex by James Knight, a former maltster and inn keeper in Wisborough Green who was acting as an agent for the Courtauld family. After travelling with Hale all the way to Nelsonville in Athens County, these immigrants were unhappy with what they found and soon left. There is no further mention of them in surviving letters of Petworth immigrants.

■ I

MRS SARAH ELIZA (COOPER) JONES, QUEBEC, LOWER CANADA, TO HER BROTHER, 2 JUNE 1832

In England there was great concern to hear news of the 1832 emigrants. The extract and paraphrase that follows was introduced by Thomas Sockett* and was published in a local newspaper. The final sentence concluded the article.

SOURCE: *Portsmouth, Porsea, and Gosport Herald*, 22 July 1832

A Mrs. Jones, who went out in the Lord Melville, with her children, to join her husband, who is settled in Upper Canada, says in a letter to her brother, dated Quebec, June 2: – "We arrived safe and have passed the examination of the surgeon of the quarantine, but not one is allowed to go on shore …" She expresses a strong sense of the kindness and attention showed by the Captain (Chancelor) and chief mate (Barlow), to herself and family, and to all the passengers. They have had only one death (hooping cough) but considerable illness from rough weather. The Superintendent's wife[1] was safely delivered of a boy, and both were doing well. May 30.–They hailed the ship Carrick in the St. Lawrence, from Dublin. Out of 170 she had lost forty.[2] Many families were left without parents, and there was no medical man on board.[3]

We have great pleasure in adding that a certificate from Mr. Penfold, the superintendent of the Lord Melville, of the safe landing at Montreal, has been received, June 8, of every individual emigrant except the child above named. The Melville party left for York, June 12th.

Mrs Jones and her children were cabin passengers who were going to join her husband Thomas Jones. He was probably Welsh in origin and seems to have sent for his family after acquiring land in Guelph Township. Their daughter, also named Sarah Eliza, married Edward Francis Heming at Guelph on 1 November 1832. Edward Heming (6 and 30) had also travelled as a cabin passenger on the *Lord Melville*. In 1835, Sarah "barred her dower right" (or gave up her future rights as a widow) in the sale for £300 of two lots Heming had purchased in Guelph Township to his relatives in England. She died in 1850, shortly after the birth of her seventh child.

■ 2

JAMES RAPSON, MONTREAL, TO HIS FATHER, PHILIP RAPSON, LODSWORTH, SUSSEX, 4 JUNE 1832

When he emigrated, James Rapson was a 29-year-old sawyer from Lodsworth, a wooded parish north of Petworth. He was sent by the parish of Lurgashall with his wife Sarah Tribe, her daughter Charlotte Tribe, and Sarah and James's six children, Hannah, Mary, Philip, Isaac,

---

1   Sarah Penfold

2   The *Carricks* lost 42 passengers, her carpenter, and one boy. She was traditionally considered to be the first ship to carry cholera to Canada, but this possibility is unproven (Marianna O'Gallagher, *Grosse Isle: Gateway to Canada, 1832-1937* [Quebec: Carraig Books 1984], 24).

3   See Sockett's introduction to letter 2.

Rhoda, and James (a baby born 1 January 1832).[4] Sarah's parents, Henry and Charlotte Tribe, emigrated with seven of their unmarried children at the same time, as did her sister Jane and brother-in-law, Jesse Penfold (see 50 and 54). Pregnancy was one of the elements that increased the journey's hazards and discomforts, and Jane Penfold was one of a number of pregnant women among the emigrants that year.

Despite the introduction to his letter that appeared in the *Herald*, Rapson's letter actually makes clear that he was on the *Lord Melville*.

SOURCE: *Portsmouth, Portsea and Gosport Herald*, 22 July 1832

The following letter has been received by Philip Rapson, of Lodsworth, in this country, from his son, James Rapson, who went out with several other emigrants in April last, we believe in the Eveline. We have given the writer's own words, without alteration. Our readers will here see the effects of the very judicious regulations under which the Sussex emigrants left their native country, for which they are indebted to the liberality and benevolence of Lord Egremont, and the indefatigable exertions of his committee. These effects are the more apparent when we compare the healthy state of those who emigrated from Sussex, with that of the 170 who went from Dublin in the ship Carrick, and out of whom no less than forty died during the passage:–

Montreal, June 4, 1832.

Dear Father,

April 10th, set sail to Spithead, where we stopt until four o'clock the 11th, when I think 275 out of 300 were sick.

13th, all my family, except myself and Isaac, very bad.

14th, all better, except James and Sarah, her mother poorly; all their family quite as well as any.

15th, in the Bay of Biscay, in a calm.

19th, the four last days very bad, with the wind against us.

20th, a calm. Twelve o'clock at night a grievous hurricane blew the vessel on one side so that the water ran over the side of the vessel – the sea so rough that fifteen of our beds or berths fell from one side to the other, people and all; this happened at midnight.

The 21st, twelve miles on, and very rough at night, continues very rough.

28th, very bad myself.

May the 1st, one of our sailors fell and drowned; fell from the mast head. Continued very rough until 6th.

From April 25th until May 6th, very bad, so bad that the Captain said he could compare it to nothing but a wreck all the time, but now, thanks to him that holds the sea in the hollow of his hand, for he hath said to the winds and the waves be still. All well, Sarah's mother poorly, and so is Jane Penfold.

May 10th, met the ship Malborough, bound to London, which was to report us

4   When James and Sarah were married, he signed his name to the register while she signed with a mark. The children in the family Bible begins with Charlotte Tribe, born 9 July 1817 (see p. 131).

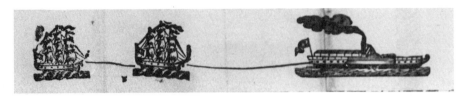

Steamboat towing sailing ships from Quebec to Montreal
Detail from "Montreal Towboat Company. Rates of Towing Vessels," wsro, Petworth House Archives

and the Eveline in the news. Passed two ships before, and spoke to them. Vessels passing almost every day.

12th, very fine, all well, pleasant, as the sea is calm.

13th, a child died[5] – it was sewed up in a piece of canvas and sunk. Thank God it continues fine.

22nd, in the morning, came in sight of an island by the name of Cape Breton, and in the afternoon St. Paul's Island; passed the first on the left, St. Paul's on the right; all the party quite well. James, the child, is very bad. Sarah's mother and Jane Penfold well.

23rd and 24th, in the Gulph; very pleasant.

25th, came in sight of America, on the left, and Anti-Costi on the right.

26th, in sight of the American coast, a very favourable wind.

27th, rode quarantine [at Grosse Isle] for four hours, within thirty miles of Quebec; buildings on each side [of the St Lawrence River], very pleasant, but no gardens. Churches on each side, not more than ten miles apart.

28th, reached Quebec about eight o'clock.

29th, just went to the town which stands on a high rock, old pieces of timber for pitching, going up [from the Lower Town] with steps forty or fifty feet in a place. A young man of the name of John Hilyar, from Haslemere, got tipsy, with many more of our party, and came to the boat, jumped out, and was drowned. Port wine 9d. a bottle, rum 1s. a quart, brandy 1s. and gin the same. I could have had plenty of work at once, James very bad.

At twelve o'clock the 29th, left Quebec, a steamer engaged to tow us up, by the name of John Bull, and she had one of each side of her and four behind, all the six vessels as large as our's, the most beautiful sight I ever saw.[6] Reached Montreal in thirty-six hours; very pleasant passage; James, the child, very bad, has fits.

31st, came into the harbour.

June 2nd, left the ship to go up with part of our things, and a man ran to me,

---

5   Hester Longhurst
6   Nathaniel Gould, *Sketch of the Trade of British North America* (London 1833), confirmed that the *John Bull* could tow six vessels. The engine had 260 horsepower and burned 512 cubic feet of wood per hour.

and said to me, that James, the child is dead, and now I say, from the bottom of my heart, "the Lord gave and the Lord taketh away and blessed be his holy name."

June –, Charles Boxall, brother to William Boxall at White's Green,[7] went to the town and came back tipsy, and sat down in the fore part of the vessel and went to sleep, fell down and drowned.

3rd, went to a Wesleyan chapel and heard an excellent sermon, in the evening heard one of our own Ministers, but they have not yet a chapel.[8] On Monday morning our child was buried, in an English burying ground; another child at the same time; very much pleased with the burial service. Mrs. Barnes[9] remember to Mrs. Steyning; they are well. Let Robert Tribe know. Write as soon as you can, and send to Mr. Goldsmith. The voyage has not so much as made my Isaac nor his grandfather poorly; Sarah's mother is two years younger. Rhoda poorly; Philip, with all the rest, well. Tell George there is plenty of brick making, 4s. 6d. per 1,000 with the earth prepared and put on the bench. My love to all my brothers and sisters, and all enquiring friends, when I arrive at York I will write and I then shall be able to say more, so no more from your affectionate son,

JAMES RAPSON.

June 5th, Jane Penfold put to bed; Sarah takes mother's place; Jane, with child, well; this morning met with a man that would engage with thirty pair of sawyers, at the same per hundred as reported.[10] We are now about to leave for York, we are all well and very thankful for our safe arrival.

OTHER LETTERS: 12, 38, 76, 115

■ 3

MRS J. BURCHELL, ADELAIDE TOWNSHIP, UPPER CANADA, [CIRCA JUNE 1832]

Thomas Sockett* included this description of the emigrants' voyage up the St Lawrence rapids from Montreal in a letter to the Duke of Richmond, prefaced as follows: "Extract of a letter from Mrs J Burchell who emigrated with her husband and some relations,[11] from Arundel, and sailed from Portsmouth in company with a party from Wisborough Green on the Ship England, May 10 1832." The party reached Quebec in mid June and York on 1 July.

7 Whites Green, near Lurgashall, West Sussex

8 Phillip Rapson's house in Lodsworth, Wood Common, was licensed as an Independent Meeting House in 1807. James Rapson was licensed to use his home for dissenting worship in 1824 (Michael Reed, "Social and Economic Relations in a Wealden Community, Lodsworth, 1780-1860," WSRO, MP 2027). Both the Rapsons and Thairs had children baptized in the Petworth Independent or Congregational Chapel.

9 Probably Mary Barnes from Tillington, West Sussex

10 The figures given in the *Portsmouth Herald* were 7s 6d per hundred feet of pine and 8s 9d per hundred feet of oak.

11 Elizabeth Goatcher, wife of the superintendent of the *Eveline*, was born a Burchill.

Cedars and the Rapids at Cedars on the St Lawrence River
William Henry Bartlett, "Village of Cedars" and "Rapids on approach to Village of Cedars,"
NA, C2340, C2338

SOURCE: WSRO, Goodwood MS 1460, f115, in f112, Sockett to Richmond, 14 October 1832

From Montreal we were taken in a Canadian Batteau to Lachine fastened on to a Steamer and crossed Lake St Frances to the Island of Cedars, where we waited 3 days for horses to commence our journey up the rapids of 140 miles, which took us 5 days; at times drawn by horses but at the west parts by oxen, this was a most fatiguing part of our journey as we were obliged to walk a good deal at the dangerous parts of them, the water at some places flowing at such a rapid rate, it was unsafe to pass through in a boat, we travelled by day and encamped in the woods or barns at night, whichever was most convenient.

■ 4

STEPHEN GOATCHER, EN ROUTE TO KETTLE CREEK, UPPER CANADA, TO HIS WIFE, ELIZABETH BURCHILL, PULBOROUGH, WEST SUSSEX, 6 JULY 1832

A Pulborough farmer, Stephen Goatcher had been sworn in as a special constable during the Swing disturbances in 1830. In 1832, he sailed as superintendent of the *Eveline*, leaving his wife behind on the farm at home. Goatcher's own letter suggests that he felt less than competent to deal with the confusion and delays experienced by the immigrants who sailed with him on the schooner bound for Kettle Creek, but the threat of cholera certainly exacerbated the situation (see 18 by John Stedman).

SOURCE: *Emigration: Letters* (1833), 3–4

July 6th. 1832.

DEAR WIFE,

(*The first part is omitted, as it relates entirely to family affairs*) * * * * * * * I never was sick at all, but there were a great number that were very sick. The weather was very cold when we came to Newfoundland; snow lay on the mountains; they had a hard winter at Quebec: they were sowing wheat. It is a very cold place. I saw the waterfall (June 24th) at Niagara (our schooner lay about 2 miles off): it was the most wonderful sight that ever my eyes beheld. It is much the same as Mrs. ...... book relates. James Parker, his wife and family are all well, also Napper, and his wife and family, and hope all their friends are well at home.[12] I cannot give you much account of Canada at present, only most of things dear. The flies are very troublesome; there are great numbers, and are different from those in England. We are now on our way to Kettle Creek, which I expect to be my home. The people seem very bad farmers. Whisky very cheap. I should like to know how you are doing, and how your crop is coming along. I hope you will have a plentiful harvest, and all things going

12 James and Amy Parker and three children and James and Avis Napper and three children all emigrated from Pulborough in 1832. The Parker family went on to Adelaide Township, while the Nappers evidently stopped in York (Toronto).

on well. I hear the reform bill is thrown out. It has been reported the Duke of Wellington is dead.[13]

The people are very much afraid that we had got the cholera; we have often been inspected by surgeons. I would advise any of my friends not to come to this country in so large a party; if they do, they will find it unpleasant. I had a great deal of trouble, 250 people to feed every day. When I arrived at York, I went to the Governor [John Colborne*], a very fine man; it was like a king's palace: the gold laid on his shoulders. He said he would send us to the best land in Canada. I lived with Captain Royal, in the ship Eveline, in the cabin, on fresh meat and fowls.

You will think it long before you receive this letter; I hope it will find you all well with Wm. and his family. I often think of you all. Remember me to my sisters and brother, and Mr. Clements, and Mr. Parry, and my old friend Mr. Comper[14] and all the family, Mr. Challen and his family, and all my old friends wheresoever they may be.

We are now arrived in the woods, but what we are to do, we do not know at present. The musquitoes are very troublesome. I think of having some land, but it is not settled at present; the land is very good. I think of taking James Parker and family with me. When I get settled I will write to you again. We are too late for any crop this year, but I hope we shall find one another year. The land is very full of tim-

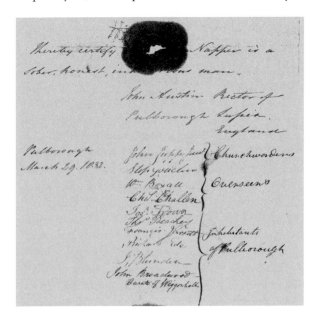

Character reference brought by James Napper
Courtesy Jean Hodges, Elizabeth Hodges, and Jane Thompson

---

13 Wellington did not die until 14 September 1852. Goatcher was writing on 6 June and the Reform Bill had finally been passed on 4 June, after a long and stormy passage since its introduction in March 1831. It was to further the process of redistributing parliamentary seats and extending the franchise, a process that continued through the nineteenth century and into the twentieth.

14 The Compers were long established in Pulborough. This may be Henry Comper, a farmer with several children.

The tall trees of Upper Canada as they looked to an Englishman
James Pattison Cockburn, "Making a road between Kingston and York,"
NA, C12630

ber, very tall, three times as lofty as yours in England. Now, Mr. Comper, you wish
to know something about the country: it looks very well to me at present. You wish
to know the appearance of the country: by what I can see at present, the land is the
best quality, but it is all covered with heavy timber. They say they can clear an acre
for about £4. There are no underwoods nor bushes at all, but the timber is cut and
burnt altogether. The system of farming is this: they burn it off, and harrow the wheat
in, without ploughing. In this place there is not one stone to be found; it's black loam.
Their wheat is very fine; barley they do not sow, but I think it would bear good
barley. They raise a great deal of Indian corn. Where I think of settling, the government are making a new road through; they say that a coach will pass through before
long. There is a mill not far distant, and a saw mill is making.[15] There is plenty of

15 Probably a reference to the mill built by John S. Buchanan* close to the site of Strathroy.

good land for all the people in your country; they would not want to work on the road, as they do in your country. The people are very kind to us: they are very fond of the English. The weather is very hot; more so than in England. Last winter was the hardest that ever they remember.

I cannot tell you where to write to me at present. Remember me to the Rev. J. Austin.[16] I shall write to you before long, and then I shall give you more account. John Burchell I forgot.[17] I hope it will find you all well. So no more from your ever loving and dutiful husband,

STEPHEN GOATCHER.

To MRS. GOATCHER,
   Pulborough, Sussex.

OTHER LETTERS: Goatcher's second letter is 51; the Parkers' is 88.
Sockett reported a fleeting possibility that the Petworth community in Adelaide might be named for Goatcher, but Goatcher did not stay.

▪ 5

RICHARD NEAL, DUNDAS, UPPER CANADA, TO FRIENDS AND RELATIONS, [SUTTON, WEST SUSSEX], 20 JULY 1832

Richard Neal was a bricklayer sent by the parish of Sutton. People in the building trades were suffering from recession in many parts of Sussex, and Neal left a community where the predominant building material was a local sandstone found near Pulborough.

In an introduction to this letter, Sockett explained that "an impression prevails to a considerable extent among the common people, that all the letters said to come from emigrants to the United or the Canadas, are fabrications." He used Neal as an example of one of several Petworth emigrants who took steps to make sure his letter would be recognized as genuine. Neal's method was to tear a strip off the top of a sheet of paper and leave the strip with his friends. "The letter, of which the following is a copy, has been found exactly to fit to the slip left behind, to the great satisfaction of the writer's friends."

SOURCE: *Emigration: Letters* (1833), 5-7. There are three other copies of this letter: one is found in WSRO, Goodwood MS 650, f.110, a second appeared in the *Portsmouth, Portsea, and Gosport Herald*, 16 September 1832, and a third in *Emigration: Extracts*, 23-4.

Dundas, North America.
July 20th.1832.

DEAR FRIENDS AND RELATIONS,

I take this opportunity of these few lines to you, hoping to find you all in good health, as it leaves me at present. Thank God we landed safe at Quebec, after seven weeks sail. We had a very rough passage. I enjoyed good health all the way over; I

16 John Austin, rector of Pulborough
17 Possibly the husband of Mrs Burchell (letter 3), although he would have sailed on a different ship.

never had one hour sickness all the time we were on the sea. They were most all sea sick. Joseph Leggett and Elias [Elliott] were a little sick, but not much. On the first of May we lost one of the sailors,[18] and was one of the roughest days we had, but [we] were tost about very much. We saw a large quantity of porpoises coming over, and whale fishes blow water as high as the mast head. We were about six weeks out of sight of land. The first land we saw was Cape Breton, a large mountain covered with snow the 19th and 21st May we entered the river of St. Lawrence, which was 400 miles long before we came to Quebec, some places 50 miles wide, and some places not so much. We saw snow for about 200 miles up the river, and the trees were coming out in leaf: as fast as we go up the country, the forwarder the land is.

When we landed at Quebec, a great many of the men (spirits being so cheap) drunk so much, it made them crazy: one of them got drowned there, and another at Montreal.[19] We were at Quebec two days then sailed to Montreal.[20] There was six large ships towed up the river by one steam boat: the name of the steam boat was John Bull, 245 horse power. 180 miles from Quebec to Montreal. They were all French people there. You can buy rum 10d. per quart, port wine 1s.3d. per quart,[21] all the other liquors very cheap: cider about 6d. per quart.

I was offered 5s.6d. per day at Montreal, but I did not wish to stop.[22] We went into the woods and found plenty morels, just like them in England, but the people did not know what they was. Then we started for Little York, which is about 500 miles[23] further, all by water. When we landed at York, some went one way and some the other. I stopped there; Elias and Joseph Leggett went on with Hilton,[24] 180 miles further.[25] They promised to write to me, but I have had no letter from them. But I saw two men that went up with them. They both got work[26] for one man, and Sefton Charman's wife's brothers[27] they have got a good place, 12 dollars a month and their board. A man will get more a month here with his board, than in England without. I have not seen any game about here, but there is pheasants and hares, and thou-

18 See James Rapson, 2. Neal is one of the emigrants who can be identified as travelling on the *Lord Melville* by a reference to this sailor or to the berths that collapsed during this storm.

19 John Helyer drowned at Quebec and Charles Boxall at Montreal. See letter 2.

20 The words "then sailed to Montreal" appears in the manuscript copy, WSRO, Goodwood MS 650, f110.

21 The version printed in the *Portsmouth, Portsea, and Gosport Herald* gives 1s. 3d. per pint.

22 The version printed in *Emigration: Extracts* begins with this sentence and its punctuation and spelling varies slightly. Omissions or substantive differences are noted.

23 Original annotation: "355 miles."

24 Hutton in *Emigration: Extracts*.

25 Charles and Mary Ann Hilton emigrated in 1832 with their children. Neal may be referring to Charles, or more probably to their son Alexander. The original annotation noted "To Fort George, Niagara." See letter 46.

26 Version in *Emigration: Extracts* reads "they told me that they both got work."

27 Probably William and James Moore, who emigrated from Petworth in 1832 (see letter 181); their brother Luke emigrated in 1837, and brother Edward may have emigrated in the intervening years.

sands of pigeons, and a few bears, and wolves, but a very few. There is a great many cherries in the woods, and currants,[28] gooseberries and nuts.

I promised to send you the state of the country: I will as well as I can. This is a good country for one thing, the people are all of one sort, pretty much: their servants lives with their masters, and they gets good wages. *But it is very hot in the summer, and very cold in the winter. I do not like this country so well as England, for men are not so strong as they are in England; nor the meat is not so good, but very cheap.*[29] I left York, and went to Dundas, and got a job there for a man of the name of Pope. He has been here five years, and is doing very well. I have 5s. a day, and board and lodging, for which I have to take 2s.6d. per day in store what they call it. You must take clothes, shoes, hats, or any thing that your master works for, and I take 15s. a week, paid in money. Clothes is very dear here. Any man can earn enough in three days to keep a wife and family a week. Dear father and mother [William and Abigail Neal], do not make yourselves uneasy about me, for I am doing very well; *but I do not like it so well as in England, but I can come back when I like, if it pleases God.* Bricklayer is a good trade here, and can earn a great deal of money after you gets known.

Send me all the news you can, and I will send you more next time. Tell James Clarke that I do not persuade him to come over to stay, but here is plenty of work, and good pay.[30] I will send you another letter in the course of a few weeks; then I shall be able to say more about the country.   Direct to

RICHARD NEAL, Bricklayer,
Dundas, Upper Canada,
Near the Lake Ontario.
North America.

Put down *By New York.*

You must pay the letter to the water. So no more at present, from your affectionate brother,

RICHARD NEAL.

Kind love to father and mother, and all my friends, which there is too many to mention. Write to me as soon as you gets this letter.

OTHER LETTERS: 46

■ 6

[JANE PAYNE?, JULY 1832]

This extract of a letter written by the aunt of Edward Francis Heming was included by Thomas Sockett* in his collection of letters written by the 1832 emigrants. Heming was the son of Canon George Heming of Chichester and Anna Maria (Payne). A friend of Heming's wid-

---

28 The Goodwood MS version adds "and currants"; *Emigration: Extracts* reads "there are a great many cherries in the woods, currants, and gooseberries."

29 Italicized words here and below are omitted in the version in *Emigration: Extracts.*

30 Version in *Emigration: Extracts* ends here.

owed mother recommended him to the authorities in Upper Canada as having a "well grounded Farmer's education" and capital to invest. He was living in Bognor when he left England. In Upper Canada, he employed Martin Martin to finish the inside of a log house (see letter 29). A later house on the same site was named "Bognor Lodge."

SOURCE: *Emigration: Letters* (1833), 4–5

The gentleman named in this letter is Mr. Heming (son of a late clergyman at Chichester.)

[23 July 1832]

* * * * * * I am happy to say that my sister[31] received a letter from her son on Sunday last; we did not hear of it until the next evening. He writes from Guelph, on the 19th. of July, but the letter is dated on the outside the 23rd. It is a very satisfactory account. I only hope he has not been too precipitate in settling himself, for he has already bought an estate; but he seems to have made his choice with some discretion, as far as we can judge from our own inferences drawn from his letter. He has bought 230 acres of the company, only 2½ miles from Guelph.[32] The land is *uncleared*; he says that almost all the land that is to be bought cleared, having been first taken by people with little or no capital, is generally exhausted, and must be left fallow for three years to recover itself, and therefore does not answer. He says the land near Guelph is higher in price than he expected, that it sells for 17s.6d. per acre, so I suppose he has given that for it. The chief timber is maple, bass, (a sort of pine I believe)[33] beech, and oak, and these I believe, bespeak a good quality of land. There is a good road, (he is on the *Eramosa* road) a grist mill, and two saw mills. The situation is high; and, he thinks, it must be healthy. And, as the land is selling off fast there, it must be an improving place, and not so far out of the world as Goderich. There are three or four springs of good water on the lot; he thinks he shall be able to procure three acres more, which will give him the command of a river.

York, he says, is in a very unhealthy situation, the land about it not near so good as at Guelph. He was still with Mr. Penfold,[34] from whom, he says, he has experienced great kindness and attention, and I should rather suppose he thinks of settling thereabouts, but Edward does not say so. * * * *

I hope Edward will do well: he seems quite delighted with his prospects. * * * * * * * He says he makes sure of seeing us all out there ere long, he hears such bad accounts of poor old England: we are going to send him out as quickly as we can a collection of seeds, and his saddle, which he has written for.

OTHER LETTERS: 30; see also letter 1, from Mrs Jones, a fellow cabin passenger on the *Lord Melville*.

31 Anna Maria Heming
32 The land and colonization Canada Company, which owned the vast Huron Tract, founded both Guelph, in the interior, and Goderich, on Lake Huron, in 1827.
33 The basswood tree, also known as linden, is a hardwood like the others on her list.
34 Probably William Penfold, superintendent on the *Lord Melville*.

Heming's aunt might have been even more apprehensive if she had known that Heming had purchased a part lot on the 7th concession from the Department of Crown Lands in July in addition to buying the two lots on the 6th and 7th concession from the Canada Company. His purchase from the Canada Company was finalized in September when he built his home on lot 8 concession 6 which was probably the lot that Martin Martin (29) described as having some improvements on it.

■ 7

EDWARD AND CATHARINE BOXALL, ADELAIDE TOWNSHIP, UPPER CANADA, TO MOTHER, 28 JULY 1832

Edward Boxall had been living in Coldwaltham when he and his wife, Catharine, were sent to Canada by the parish of Petworth. At that time, he was working as a gardener, but he had served as a private in the 36th Regiment of Foot long enough to be entitled to land in Upper Canada.

SOURCE: *Emigration: Letters* (1833), 8. This letter is also found in WSRO, Goodwoood MS 1460, f35; and *Letters from Dorking*, 12.

Adelaide, Upper Canada.
July 28th. 1832.

DEAR MOTHER,

I take this opportunity to acquaint you that we arrived here safe, and in good health, on the 6th July. Dear mother, I was very fortunate, in bringing my discharge with me, for I found, when I landed at York on the 23rd June, that all who could shew their discharge was entitled to a hundred acres of land from the crown for their service, which I accordingly got.[35] So if either of my nephews, or both of them, should like to come over here, I will give them some land to work upon. Tell them to bring some tools, and all the money they can get, with them, and some upland seed of all descriptions, and garden seeds too, and barley in particular. Wm. Cooper's land joins mine, but he have got to pay two dollars per acre for his, and 6 years to do it in. Here is a river runs through the corner of my lot,[36] and plenty of fish in it; and here is wild deer, and turkeys, pheasants, partridges, and rabbits: and any body may kill them.

Catharine is very well at present, but she was very sea sick coming over, for some time: she sends her kind love to Ruth, and all their brothers and sisters, and all friends. Copy this letter, and send it to my sisters, and tell them I will build them a house, if they will come over here to live. So no more at present from yours,

EDWARD & CATHARINE BOXALL.

OTHER LETTERS: 53

35 In 1832 Edward Boxall was granted E ½ lot 26 concession 4 SER Adelaide Township for military service.
36 Probably Bear Creek, now the Sydenham River.

■ 8

WILLIAM COOPER, ADELAIDE TOWNSHIP, UPPER CANADA, TO HIS
FATHER AND MOTHER, BROTHERS AND SISTERS, 28 JULY 1832

According to Sockett*, William Cooper, whose settlement was with the parish of Burton,
was living at Graffham when he emigrated.

Two surviving versions of Cooper's letter provide an example of Sockett's policy in 1833
of deleting references to travel via New York before publication. He allowed Cooper's advice
to stand when he sent the letter to the Duke of Richmond, whom he was lobbying for
improvements in the all-British route via Quebec. In his covering letter he noted: "tho I have
not printed their recommendations [to travel through New York and the Erie Canal], yet
the letters containing them have been much read, & they will have their effect."

SOURCE: *Emigration: Letters* (1833), 8-9. Other copies are found in WSRO Goodwood MS 1460, f.35; *Letters from Dorking*, 43-4; and *Emigration: Extracts*, 22-3.

Adelaide, Upper Canada.
July 28th. 1832.

Dear father and mother, brothers and sisters,

I hope this will find you in good health, as it leaves me at present. I have been
very well ever since I left England. We were seven weeks coming to Montreal, and
five weeks more coming up to Kettle Creek.[37] I have got 100 acres of land, at 2 dollars per acre, and one fourth to be paid at the end of 3 years, and the rest in 3 years
more. In English money, it comes to £41.13s.4d. in all. Tell my brother James I saw
Richard Carter and his wife at Little York. They are doing very well, and said this
would be a good opportunity for them to have come out to this country. I should
like for all my brothers to come here, for here is plenty of work, and no doubt but
we shall do very well after next harvest. Edward Boxall, and his wife, and Wm. Phillips
from Merston, and we have built us a Shantee, and lives and works altogether on
our own land. We have got above 2 acres cleared, and shall sow 6 or 7 acres of wheat
this autumn, and more in the spring. [38]

Dear father, I should like to have a malt mill, and a few pounds of thread, and above
all things, a Newfoundland dog for myself. And take this letter to Merston, to Phillips'
father,[39] and tell him to be sure to bring him a dog – to catch the deer – and [tell
him to be sure to] tell you what time of the year they means to come out, so that
you may all come together. Answer this as soon as you receive it. [if you come in the
Spring or fall be sure & come by New York and from thear to Buffalo and then cross
the Niagara river at the ferry and whait for the Chippaway steem boat to bring you
up to Kettle Creek, when you arrive at New York send us a letter and we Will meet

37 Port Stanley
38 The version included in *Emigration: Extracts* begins with the second sentence and ends here; it varies
slightly in punctuation and spelling.
39 See 74.

you at Kettle Creek.][40] I have to tell wheat is now selling, at 1 dollar a bushel; beef at 2½d. per pound; and mutton the same; and pork 4d. per pound in English money. Spirits is very cheap here. Farmers' men gets from 3 to 12 dollars a month, and board and lodgings, and washing and mending. I have no more to say at present, so I must conclude, with my kind love to you all. I remain your dutiful son,

WILLIAM COOPER.

Direct to William Cooper, Township of Adelaide, to be left at Colonel Mount's, Delaware, North America.

Newfoundland dog
Thomas Bewick, *A General History of Quadrupeds* (Newcastle 1790)

OTHER LETTERS: 52

When Cooper wrote to his family again at the beginning of 1833, he still wanted a dog for deer hunting. He knew by now that venison could be bought from the Indians more cheaply than he could bring it in, but he was one of many Englishmen of all classes who were delighted to find that there were no game laws in the Canadas. Deer hunting and a dog (part New-foundland) come up again in James Cooper's letter (133).

■ 9

WILLIAM PHILLIPS, ADELAIDE, UPPER CANADA, TO HIS FATHER AND MOTHER, WILLIAM AND ELLEN PHILLIPS, MERSTON, WEST SUSSEX, 28 JULY 1832

William Phillips Jr was sent by the parish of Merston.

---

40 Sockett, wanting to discourage emigrants from travelling via the United States, left out the brack-eted passage. In his published version Sockett also standardized spellings.

SOURCE: *Emigration: Letters* (1833), 46–7

Adelaide, Upper Canada,
July 28th. 1832.

DEAR FATHER AND MOTHER,

(The first part contains an account of the voyage as far as York.)[41]

Here [York] they put us on board 3 schooners. Two went to Hamilton:[42] they are not got here yet:[43] ours went across the Lake into the Welland canal, only 18 miles long, and only 37 locks in it, to Chippewa, 2 miles above the falls, which I went under to see, down a well stair case, 172 steps. I have heard Eden say, you could turn a waggon there, but it must be a very small one. Here we was towed by oxen, 9 miles up the Niagara river, opposite to Buffalo; there the Yankey doctors came to inspect us, but would not suffer us to cross the river. Here we staid 6 days for a fair wind; then sailed for Kettle Creek, or Port Stanley, 170 miles, where we landed on the 6th of July, but was not allowed to cross the river, on account of Mrs Hilton[44] being sea sick. They brought us boards, to make us shanteys, and victuals to eat. We now went by land, to Delaware, 25 miles, to Colonel Mount*'s. He had orders from York to let us have 100 acres of land each in the township of Adelaide at 2 dollars per acre: one fourth to be paid in 3 years time, and the remainder in 3 years more. This is said to be the best land in Upper Canada; it is well watered and level, not a stone to be seen, they say, for forty miles. I have plenty of timber on my land: some of the trees will square 6 or 7 feet; 89 feet from the roots without a branch.

Dear father, I hope you will come and help me next summer; and bring me all sorts of seeds that grows in England: you had better stay till after harvest, and bring some cuttings of gooseberries, apples and grapes,[45] that I may have some English fruit; you can bring them in a tub. Dear father, I would not advise you to come here, if I did not know it would be to your advantage, even if you spend your last shilling to get here. And bring uncle Carpenter with you, and he, nor you will never repent coming here, for I can get you both a farm, if you want one; and you can earn money enough, in one year, to pay for it yourself.

Dear father, William Cooper, and Edward Boxall, and his wife, and I lives together, and works on our own land: we shall sow 6 acres of wheat this fall, and more in the spring. Their friends live at Graffham; some of them will come here next year, and

---

41 Parentheses in original; the square brackets in the following sentence are also in the original.

42 Original annotation: "Those who went by them, settled at, and near Dundas, Ancaster, Galt, Guelph, etc."

43 William Cooper (letter 8) also referred to the expectation on the part of people on the schooner for Adelaide that those on the two schooners which took emigrants to Hamilton were also to go to for Port Stanley and the Adelaide settlement.

44 Mary Ann Hilton

45 Grapes had been grown in Sussex since Roman times.

Entrance to the passage behind Niagara Falls (see p. 23)
Samuel Oliver Tazewell, "Niagara – View of the Entrance under the British Falls, c. 1833"
Toronto Reference Library, T14667

I hope you will come with them. I must conclude with my kind love to you, and all enquiring friends. So no more at present from your dutiful son,

WILLIAM PHILLIPS.

Direct to William Phillips,
    Township of Adelaide, Upper Canada, to be left at
      Colonel Mount's Delaware, North America.

William Phillips's parents emigrated from Merston in 1833 at their own expense, with at least one other child, to join their son in Upper Canada, but whether they brought the dog William Cooper was asking for in letter 8 we do not know. (Brydone* quotes their account of their journey in his "Narrative," 20-1.) William Jr married Mary Pullen of Adelaide on 13 December 1834. Two years later William and Mary's first child was born in Warwick. In 1838, Phillips sold the right to a half lot on the 4th concession of Adelaide to his father in law Richard Pullen for £75. Mary's father, Richard Pullen (not the Richard Pullen who emigrated to Adelaide with his family as Petworth emigrants in 1837), eventually joined them to live in Warwick.

■ 10

JOHN LUFF, NELSON TOWNSHIP, UPPER CANADA, TO THE OVERSEER OF BURY, WEST SUSSEX, 29 JULY 1832

John Luff of Bury, Sussex, sailed on the *Eveline* in 1832. He was about 16 and "somewhat deaf" (see letter 68). Sockett* noted: "This lad has neither father nor mother living, and made repeated applications to the Overseer of Bury to pay the expence of his conveyance to Canada. – His request was at length complied with, and the above is addressed to the said Overseer."[46] A Mr Bishop sent £3 to be paid to him at Toronto.

This short note to the overseer and the one following to his aunt at Fittleworth were on the same sheet of paper.

SOURCE: *Emigration: Letters* (1833), 9–10

Nelson, July 29th. 1832.

DEAR SIR,

This letter is to inform you of your humble servant, John Luff: we arrived at York on the 23rd day of June. I might have got three places at Montreal but as I was a waiting for Mr. ..... I did not go, so I came to York, and from York about 30 miles up the country; and I went to work on the road, and Mr. ... did not come for me; so I am living with Jacob Triller, and I am living in the Township of Nelson, District of Gore, County of Halton, the Province of Upper Canada, and I like Canada far better than England.

OTHER LETTERS: 11

Luff was employed by the same Jacob Triller who hired William Spencer. Triller's farm bordered Lake Ontario on broken front lot 4 concession 4 of Nelson Township.[47] In May 1833, Spencer wrote in more detail about Triller's farm, see letter (68). Luff was bound to Triller as an apprentice until the age of 21. This relationship gave his master the authority of a parent and the right to put someone else in charge of him so long as he continued to be trained in the same business.[48]

■ 11

JOHN LUFF, NELSON TOWNSHIP, UPPER CANADA, TO AUNT FOSTER, FITTLEWORTH, WEST SUSSEX, 29 JULY 1832

Source: *Emigration: Letters* (1833), 10

DEAR AUNT FOSTER, AT FITTLEWORTH, NEAR PETWORTH;

I hope you will give yourself no more uneasiness about me at present; though the distance is far that we are from each other, I should like to see you once more, though I am resigned to the will of him that devised all things. I think at present

---

46 Charles King was overseer of Bury in 1832.

47 AO, Gore District Census, 1832 Census & Assessment Nelson Township, mfm MS700 r2. According to the 1851 census of Nelson Township, Jacop Triller had been born in the United States, was 57 years of age, married, and an innkeeper.

48 Jeremy Webber, "Labour and the Law," in Craven, *Working Lives*, 129–30, comments that while indenture was used in Upper Canada to provide for orphan children and those whose parents could not look after them, apprenticeship was "above all" an economic relationship. See 180, Charles Adsett, "Autobiography."

that the country above mentioned, that I now live in, is a good, and a wholesome, and a pleasant one, as far as I am judge. The prospects of gaining property are pleasing, and may say the same of my master.[49] Whether we shall have the pleasure of seeing each other in this world again, God only knows; if we should not, I wish you would join with me in writing, it seems to be the only satisfaction we can truly have here. Nothing more at present, but remaining yours truly,

JOHN LUFF.

OTHER LETTERS: 10

■ 12

JAMES RAPSON, GALT, UPPER CANADA, TO HIS FATHER, PHILIP RAPSON, LODSWORTH, SUSSEX, AUGUST 1832

Sockett* sent this manuscript copy of a letter from Rapson to the Duke of Richmond as dramatic evidence of the hardships of emigrants travelling up the St Lawrence River, and most of the underlining was his, intended to draw the Duke's attention to particular passages. Although anxious to emphasize that such reports would turn the tide of emigration to the United States, Sockett was inclined to attribute the tone of this "*least* encouraging" of the letters he had received to the pain Rapson suffered from neuralgia on the journey.[50] In England, the Rapsons had attended an Independent, or Congregationalist, Chapel.

SOURCE: WSRO, Goodwood MS 1460, f.114.

Dear Father

We left Montreal after staying until the 8th of June I think that to be a very nice place, many good people, and blessed with good Ministers of the Wesleyans, our people[51] have not any place, only a dwelling house; they have not had a Minister any time; here are flies in such abundance that if the wind blew, they fall against the houses like snow, and they might shovel them up, they last about six weeks, they are what they call the grass flies. Benjamin[52] and I took Jane Penfold[53] in a chair and carried her into the Durham boat, where we were *stuffed in so thick we were not able to sit down and were obliged to stand*: then we came two miles through a canal [the Lachine Canal] where we were with seven batteaux boats, towed across the lake [Lac Saint-Louis] about 70 miles *all one night* in *this miserable situation*, and the cabin where Jane was is like your barges and that let the water in.

10th came to a canal where we just had *to take out our beds and lay them down on the ground under the bushes and lay down on them*, in the morning at peep of light just

---

49 Jacob Triller

50 WSRO, Goodwood MS 1460, f.112, Sockett to Richmond, 21 October 1832. Sockett annotated the letter: "(The spelling is occasionally corrected, but there is no other alteration, whatsoever) TS."

51 Congregationalists

52 Benjamin Tribe, brother of Sarah Rapson

53 Marginal note in Sockett's handwriting: "lately brought to bed."

squeezed into the boat again; all well, (*and better than any one would expect as we were not able to get any provisions from morning until night*)[54] except Jane. She very bad and my face very bad; here they charged us *two shillings* for a loaf, and we should have starved if we had not bought it ourselves so we bought a little peppermint at 1od. per quart, and a little port wine, some of the party spent all by the time they came to York; from the time we left Montreal until we came to Prescot was 8 days and 8 nights. During the time we was in the Durham boat sometimes very pleasant to see the rafts of timber coming down and passing us nearly as fast as a horse could gallop, and we have *16 horses in the river drawing as hard as possible and sometimes not go a mile an hour* and when we came to a place that is called the rapid of Matilda,[55] we had *2 yoke of oxen and the boat being over burthened began to draw the oxen back the drivers jumped in and chopped the rope and then they were driven back like the wind. Wife and self with her father and mother were a walking – Charlotte with the children with all her brothers and sisters – wife with us saw it and I thought it would have frightened her into fits.*

Took Sir James Kemp, a steamer, and came to Kingston, where we expected to have overtaken the common trader of the lake; but Sir James Kemp had undertaken to convey us under price, so he left us at Kingston two days and two nights *in the wharf* when he came up again they obliged him to convey us to York [Toronto].[56] I think this was the handsomest place in the province but my face was very bad.

15th left at night 180 miles from York, 10th just at daylight a thunder storm which upset the steamer we were only 18 miles from York and drove us back to Coburg 85 miles, 17th at night left, reached York 18th. Every thing now appeared very strange, our things all out exposed to the weather, very heavy rains, stopped all night, a monday night I just went to see Mr. Goldsmith and he would have got me a place in a saw mill, the next morning the Agents, as came down to us as our things were in the wharf, and said that there was three schooners that would take us forward, and they would take us to the place where we should have 50 acres of land, and 15 pounds given to us to help us through the winter, carriage and board free. I went to Mr. Goldsmith, and told him what the agent said, and he said that he thought it was best to go, if they would do as they promised. They gave us a letter to take to the agents at Hambleton [Hamilton].

19th left York, Colonel FitzGibon[57] the Agent said that they were all going to the same place, and we sailed together, and Goacher[58] went straight across the lake Ontario to the falls of Niagara, and we to Hambleton; this was the most distressing sight I ever saw, some of their things in one vessel and they in the other; wives in

54 Marginal note: "underlined thus in the original."

55 Matilda (now Iroquois) is in Matilda Township on the St. Lawrence River between Morrisburg and Prescott.

56 The *Sir James Kempt*, 200 tons, was built at Gananoque in 1831.

57 James FitzGibbon, secretary of the Society for the Relief of Strangers in Distress. FitzGibbon was a colourful Irishman noted for his success in quieting riots and his part in protecting Toronto during the 1837 Rebellion.

58 Stephen Goatcher, superintendent of the *Eveline* (see letters 4 and 32).

one, and husbands in the other, one brother in one vessel, and his brother in the other; so we they placed before the wind for the wind to separate us.

20th at Hambleton, my face very bad; so bad I thought I must have died; here we laid, expecting every day to be forwarded to the Huron tract: here we was obliged to find ourselves in every thing, and bread *2 shillings a loaf.*

2nd July the teams came, and our things all loaded and then they stopped us for the carriage; and my things would have been 6£ besides provisions, so we left them,[59] and came to Waterloo. my face so bad when we left Hambleton, and on the road that I almost lost my senses. The doctor of the ship bathed my face with hot water, and scalded it so that the skin came off, and at Kingston I went to a doctor and he said it was the Ticdoceleureux, he let me have some stuff, done good for once or twice, then at Hambleton Sarah poured cold water, and I held rum in my mouth, and I have not had the pain since.[60]

Waterloo is a nice place, houses about a mile apart. Jesse & Benjamin and James Wack-ford and I went to Guelph but there was nothing to do, 11 miles from Waterloo, so we bought 48 acres of land at 4 dollars an acre, and set to cutting and clearing; have just raised a house 20 feet by 30 and 13 feet high, two stories high. I have got a cow, and are by the mercy of God all well. I am sorry to say we are 20 miles from hearing, here is a Presbyterian charge but no Minister. I think I shall not stop, so I hope you will write as soon as possible. Dear Father I have waited expecting a letter for 8 weeks, and am quite uneasy as I have not heard from you, Sarah's mother [Charlotte Tribe] has been very bad so that she has not been able to sit up for 8 weeks, but is a little better, her father is quite well but very thin, *all our clothes is got a deal too big.* Sarah is poorly, Rhoda is poorly, Mary and Hanah is well, Philip is grown but very thin, Isaac quite well, Self is well. Dear Father I need more than ever your prayers that the Lord would guide me and bring me to that place where I may again hear his Gospel preached. Remember me to all my brothers and sisters, say how mother's face is. I can say no more but that the Lord God bless you all in time and to eternity.

Believe me to be your loving Son

James Rapson.

Direct to Me
James Rapson
Galt, in the township of Dumfries
Upper Canada
North America

---

59 The Canada Company had two "good covered Stage Waggons, with Teams of four horses each" constantly travelling a route between Hamilton, the Wilmot line, and Goderich, and had in addition 12 extra wagons in readiness at Hamilton to convey people to the same place (*Emigration: Letters* [1833], 68-9).

60 Tic douloureux, a form of neuralgia. In July 1838, Caroline Dearling mentioned in 134 that James had recently had severe pain in his face but had recovered.

THER LETTERS: 2, 38, 76, 115

■ 13

WILLIAM PHILLIPS, ANCASTER, UPPER CANADA, TO MRS NEWELL,
5 AUGUST 1832

This William Phillips was a shoemaker from Singleton, near Midhurst, Sussex. Two other men
of the same name, son and father, emigrated with the Petworth Committee from Merston
to the Adelaide settlement.

SOURCE: *Emigration: Letters* (1833), 12–13

Ancaster, August 5th. 1832.

MRS. NEWELL,

At your request, I have now taken the opportunity of sending this Letter hoping to find you, and all friends, in good health, particularly my father, and mother,
and brother.[61] I am in very good health at present, thanks be to God for it, and have
been ever since I left England. Here is a great deal of sickness in the country, the
cholera morbus is raging very much in some places.

I promised I would send the best account of the country that I could: so I intend
to do. It is a fine country, but it is not half like England, every thing being very mean,
when compared to that. Yet a person may get a very good living by working hard:
for there is a great many hardships in coming out here. So I would advise them that
can get a comfortable living at home, to bide there, but they as cannot, why they
cannot change for the worst. Here is plenty of work, but it is very different for what
it is at home. They here all work by the month: so much for a month and their board.
They have not much money; so that you are obliged to take part in money, and part
in goods, here being a great deal of barter amongst them. If you work a month, and
can get all your wages in cash, it is thought much of. You can sometimes, and that
is best for single men. But they that have families, why it is not much difference, as
they must buy for them, if they did not so, as it is almost always in provisions. *(Here
follows a long list of prices, and explanations about the currency, which have been omitted, as
they are more correctly given in Cattermole, Doyle, &c.[62])*

I am working at my trade for a master, and likes it very well at present. I have
been here 3 weeks. Ancaster is 50 miles above York; it is a pleasant village. The land
in this country is, as in England, some very good and some bad; and so are the crops.
Here is fine orchards, but the fruit is not half so good as with you, it being more of
a wild nature. As for their gardens, there is no variety in them, as they plant very little but french beans and potatoes, the winters being too cold and the summers too

61 Thomas, Sarah, and Thomas Phillips Jr

62 Sockett is referring to a a couple of 1831 publications that he had been promoting: William Cattermole, *Emigration: The Advantages of Emigration to Canada* (London); and Martin Doyle, *Hints on Emigration to Upper Canada, Addressed to the Lower Classes in Great Britain and Ireland* (Dublin).

hot for vegetables, so they say. I have a great deal more to tell you all, but I have not room for it in a sheet of paper, so I hope you will be satisfied with this little.

I want to tell you a little about how we got here. I sailed in the ship named The Eveline. There was 450 passengers on board, but they were all strangers to me. We left Portsmouth the 11th April, and arrived at Quebec May 28th. I was very well all the passage, and was not the least sea sick; yet a great many were, nearly all the passage, as it was very stormy and rough. * * I am very much obliged to ..... and Mrs. ..... for their charity to me, as I had £2 to take at York, and the superintendant said they gave it me.

Tell my father to write to me as soon as possible, as I long to hear from them all. My love and respects to all Singleton folks: I have not mentioned any of their names, for it is to them all. So no more at present from your well wisher,

WM. PHILIPS.

Direct to W. Philips,
   Ancaster, Upper Canada,
    North America.

OTHER LETTERS: 140
Phillips evidently returned to England but was able to go back to Canada with the Petworth Committee emigrants in 1837.[63]

■ 14

WILLIAM WRIGHT, NELSON TOWNSHIP, UPPER CANADA, TO JAMES WRIGHT, HIS FATHER, NEAR DORKING, SURREY, [CIRCA AUGUST 1832]
This letter from William Wright was published with others from Dorking emigrants. Although he was not on Charles Barclay*'s list of those sent from the parish of Dorking by the Dorking Emigration Society, Wright was part of the larger group of 1832 emigrants from Surrey which Thomas Sockett* characterized as from "Dorking & Neighbourhood."

Wright mentioned paying his way from Montreal. The Petworth Committee accepted a few emigrants who paid their own passage, and in 1832 it accepted emigrants whose way was paid only as far as Montreal. He could have fallen into either of these categories.

Wright was young, baptized in 1814, and a member of a large family. Three of his younger brothers – James, David, and George – were old enough to have been the one mentioned as being with him in Upper Canada.

SOURCE: *Letters from Dorking,* 22–4

North America,
Upper Canada and Township of Nelson.

DEAR FATHER,

I feel myself happy to have this opportunity of writing these few lines to let you know the situation of things, and how circumstances are with me at present. I am

---

63 *Brighton Guardian,* 1 January 1840

in the enjoyment of good health, and hope that these lines may find you my dear mother [Rebecca], and all my friends in the same enjoyment. I will now let you know what kind of a passage I had; after embarking we had a fair wind for three days, in which we sailed off in high glee, but after that we had a rough passage, all the way being contrary winds. But the hardest time was on the 2nd of May, when the wind was so heavy that they reefed all the sails and let her go with the wind, which lasted four-and-twenty hours, and after a long and tedious passage of eight weeks we landed at Montreal. I was sea-sick three weeks; for fear of wearing your patience with this scrawl I shall be as brief as possible. After landing at Montreal I drew 25s. from the bank, which with the help of some money I drew at York when I came from Montreal, paid my passage to York in Upper Canada.

After coming to York I was only three days idle, when I found work about twenty miles from York, where I worked thirteen days on the road, at the rate of 2s. per day and board,[64] and when I had been there the time above-mentioned, there came a farmer by the name of William Dornorman to me and wished to hire me for a year, which offer I accepted, and am now to work at the rate of £22 a year. Wages are from £22 to £23 a year; a fresh hand coming from Europe cannot get as much at first as an American, not being acquainted with the work of this country. The land is of various prices: wild land or that which is uncultivated is from half-a-pound to £2 per acre, and that which is under cultivation is from £3 to £4 an acre.

PRICES OF THE PRODUCE		EXOTICS.
	£ s. d.	Tea from 3 to 9 shillings a pound.
Wheat	0 5 0	Tobacco 7½d. a pound.
Potatoes	0 2 0	Superfine broad cloth 15s. per yard.

Some cloths are as cheap as they are in England. My brother is bound apprentice to a Blacksmith, and as I expect he has wrote home I will not say any thing more about him. I expect to come home next summer, but no certainty. I hope you will write me an answer as soon as possible, ***** ******* has led his brother in a *snare*, and they are both in prison for stealing.[65] Give my love and respects to all my enquiring friends. I add no more but remain your obedient and affectionate son,

WILLIAM WRIGHT.

N.B. Direct your letter to Nelson Post-Office for me.

■ 15

OBED WILSON, ERNEST TOWN, UPPER CANADA, TO HIS PARENTS, JOHN AND MARIA WILSON, [BASSINGBOURN, CAMBRIDGESHIRE], 5 AUGUST 1832
Obediah Wilson was one of a group who emigrated from Cambridgeshire with the Petworth

---

64 In 1832 work on the roads was being subsidized by government in order to give employment to new immigrants.
65 Possibly Richard and George Broughton from Dorking. See letter 33, note 136

Emigration Committee in 1832.[66] They were sponsored by Charles Beldam, a Royston brewer, who in the spring of 1832 consulted with Thomas Sockett* about sending emigrants from Bassingbourn, Wilson's home parish. Beldam and the committee agreed to pay for 19 passages at £9.10.0 per passage; Sockett recorded a total of 24 people in the group.

SOURCE: *Emigration: Letters* (1833)

Ernest Town, August 5th. 1832.

DEAR PARENTS,

I take this opportunity to inform you, that I am well; hoping that these few lines will find you the same. I was seven weeks coming over: I was three weeks sea sick; but I arrived safe. I have seen Edward Clear, at Montreal. I have got a place, at one Silvester Lambkin's, a new married couple, and I like them very well, at present. I have sixty dollars a year. I live thirteen miles from Kingston. I like the ways of the place very well, at present. My mate and the rest have gone on to York, and I have not heard of him since. I want to know whether Edward[67] is coming over; if he is, put it in your letter. Remember me to my old master and mistress, and all enquiring friends. So no more at present. I remain your dutiful Son, until death.

I want you to write as soon as possible. Direct your letter to R. Hough, at Ernest Town, thirteen miles from Kingston.

OTHER LETTERS: The surviving letters from Wilson's family in England extend from 1840 to 1889 and are thus an unusual correspondence. We have grouped them together in the section on Additional Correspondence and Memoirs; see Wilson Correspondence beginning with 145 sent by his mother, Maria Wilson.

For the group of Bassingbourn emigrants whose names were recorded by the vicar as going from Portsmouth, see 23 from Simeon Titmouse.

■ **16**

GEORGE HILLS,[68] ANCASTER, UPPER CANADA, 5 AUGUST 1832
George Hills, a labourer, and his wife, Ann Charman, emigrated from Sullington, West Sussex, with six children; Jane, George, Caroline, John, Ann, and Henry.[69]

---

66 Why they travelled a considerable distance to sail from Portsmouth with the Petworth Committee we do not know for certain. It was probably because of a personal connection through Charles Beldam, who sponsored and organized their emigration, or Thomas Prime, the Bassingbourn overseer, who may have been related to Richard Prime of Walburton, West Sussex, a staunch promoter of emigration.
67 His brother Edward did not emigrate.
68 Hills seems to be the preferred spelling despite this letter, which was published with the spelling Hill.
69 Both George and Ann signed the marriage register with a mark.

SOURCE: This letter is found in *Emigration: Letters* (1833), 10–11; WSRO Goodwood MS 1460, f.36; and *Letters from Dorking*, 40–1; *Emigration: Extracts*; and *Brighton Herald*, 2 March 1833.

Ancaster, August 5th. 1832.

* * * * *We were six days coming up from Montreal to Prescott, which was a very tedious journey. The boats are drawn up the rapids in some bad places, with 8 or 10 yoke of Oxen. * * * [70]We have been here 5 weeks: I like the country here very much, but my wife don't seem to be quite so well contented yet. I got work the first day I got here, and have had plenty of work ever since. I got 6s. per day (New York currency which is 3s.9d. English money), and be boarded. Farmers and labourers all sit at one table here. We get 5s. per day English money [in harvest],[71] and be boarded. {I don't wish to persuade any one to come over, for they must expect to see a good many hardships; but}[72] I know that a poor man can do a great deal better here than he can at home. He is sure to get plenty of work if he is steady, and can live cheaper. Puddock and me have rented a very good house at £1. per month English money. I have bought a cow for £5, and a young sow for 12s.6d. We work here from sunrise to sunset, but we don't work so hard as we do at home. We rest through the day very often; they are not particular here about losing a little time as they are at home. Jane (she is twelve years old) is out at service for a year at 10s. per month English money. George (aged ten) is with a Mr. Gabriel Gurnett, of Horsham,[73] a saddler.

Dear father and mother, we left you almost broken-hearted, but you may be satisfied that we have bettered our condition by coming here. * * * * *

OTHER LETTERS: 17, 63

■ 17

GEORGE HILLS, ANCASTER, UPPER CANADA, TO HIS BROTHER AND
SISTER ELIZABETH, 6 AUGUST 1832

SOURCE: Like letter 16 this letter was printed in *Emigration: Letters* (1833), 11; and *Letters from Dorking*, and is found in WSRO, Goodwood MS 1460, f.36.

Ancaster, August 6th. 1832.

DEAR BROTHER AND SISTER,

If you think anything about coming you must come by New York.[74] I do not persuade you to come against your will: we can live cheaper here than you can in Eng-

---

70 The version printed in *Emigration: Extracts* begins here and includes some minor variations in punctuation in style. Omissions are noted.

71 As given in the copy in the Goodwood MS and published in *Emigration: Extracts*.

72 Material in French brackets is omitted in *Emigration: Extracts*.

73 Original annotation: " i.e. late of Horsham, Sussex." Gabriel Gurnett was a brother of George Gurnett, the proprietor of the *Courier of Upper Canada*.

74 Sockett left this first sentence out in *Emigration: Letters*.

land. There is a great many difficulties in getting here. If you come you will have me to come to; when I came, I had no one to come to. Dear Brother, if you do come, it will be the happiest hour I ever knew. * * * * * * No beer in this country; plenty of whiskey, 1s. a quart, but that is only 7½d. in our country. We likes the country very well, and it is a pleasant place. * * * * There is no beggars in this country, nor any carriages.[75] Dear Elizabeth, Sister, here is my kind love to you, and all your family. I hope you will be satisfied that this letter comes from me; make yourself contented, for I think I shall do myself some good, better than if I had been in England. * * * I neglected writing to you before, but it was on account of my child being so ill so long: {she never knew a well day after we left Portsmouth};[76] through my having so much trouble, that made me wish I had never left England, but I think I shan't after a while. Almost all my neighbours come from the States, and they likes this country best, &c. &c.

OTHER LETTERS: 16, 63

■ 18

JOHN STEDMAN, MALAHIDE TOWNSHIP, UPPER CANADA, TO JAMES G. STEDMAN, HASCOMB, SURREY, 7 AUGUST 1832

John Stedman was sent by Hascomb in Surrey. He one of a number of 1832 emigrants from the Dorking area who seem to have travelled by a direct arrangement with the Petworth Committee rather than as part of what Charles Barclay* referred to as the Dorking party in *Letters from Dorking*. When Sockett* sent an extract of Stedman's letter to the Duke of Richmond, he explained that, having sent a letter which "seemed to complain of some neglect on the part of the agents for Emigrants [in Upper Canada]," he was now sending one which "speaks most favourably" of their efforts.

See 36, for John Allen Tribe's account of the journey. The parish of Chiddingfold, Surrey, which sent Tribe was not far from Stedman's parish.

SOURCE: *Emigration: Letters* (1833), 13-15. A shortened version is in Goodwood MS 1463, f. 329.

August 7th. 1832.

Dear Father and Mother and little John.

* * Thank God that I am in a state of health at present, and as happy as any person in the world; and I hope you are all the same. * * We landed at Quebec the 28th of May; that made our passage 7 weeks. I went on shore there, about 6 hours, on purpose to see the Town, and I was glad to step my foot on land again. I had 1 lb. of beef steak and 2 quarts of cider; then come on board of the ship, and sailed to Montreal; which was 160 miles farther. We was towed up by the steam boat called the John Bull; then we left the ship. We laid in the store house 3 days before we could get boats to take us to Prescot, which was 160 miles further. When we got to Prescot,

---

75 The original spelling was charrages.
76 Sockett omitted these words also.

we took steam boats to take us to York, (which) was 160 miles further still, but I in good spirits all the time. I thought we should get there some time, if it was please God. But when we left Prescot for York, we crossed a lake; we was overtaken by a dreadful tempest. We was within 30 or 40 miles of York; we then was driven back on the shore, about 80 miles from York again.[77]

Then Matthew[78] and I thought that we would walk to York then, as it was no further than 80 miles. We thought we [should] get there as soon as the boat could. Dear father and mother, and when we got to York, the boat had been there and unloaded all the passengers, which was 250, and all from the same ship as I sailed in, called the ship Eveline from London. We all thought of going by land to any place where they get to when we got [to] York, but all them that was sent out by the parishes, was put into large Canada boats, and sent to Kettle Creek, at St. Talbots settlement,[79] 280 miles further still, and [they] had been gone just two hours [when] we got into York town. We went to the emigrant's office, to know where they was gone to, for they had all our things on board, a long [with] the other luggage, that was all together all the way over. Then we got directions, and steered across the country to Kettle Creek, which is 170 miles by land, but they gave us a letter at the office, to give the tavern keepers along the road, as long as we lost our passage, to get victuals, and a place to lie down in, when night come, and to direct us the best road they could.

But we got to our journey's end before the rest of them got [there, by] a week. As we was waiting for [our] things to come ashore, a man wanted us to go and cut some grass for him. We then thought we might as well go to work, as to wait about after our chests, as [we] should be getting something in pocket. In a week after we went to work, we heard the boat was come in with our things. Then we went [to] get the chests, which was just 8 miles from the place where we was at work. We was mowing 16 days there, and 3 days of harvest; then he give us the chance to go [and] seek for some reaping, as his was not ripe. We went to farmer ..... for reaping; he asked me if I would hire by the year. He said that he would give [me] one hundred dollars, board, lodging, washing [and] mending for the year; so I thought it wise to hire, as long as I had that chance, as I was a stranger in the country. Then, I thought, I should be sure of a home in the winter, as they say it was very cold last winter. I thought that the best [thing] to do. Thank God, I have got a good master and mistress, and we lives upon the best of every thing. I never wish to have a better home than I got at present. Thank God, I am well and hearty, and hope that I shall remain so.

Dear friends, I will give my opinion of this country, which you call it, America, but [if you] knew so much about it as I do in this short time, you would wish you

---

77 Tribe identified the port where they took refuge as Cobourg.
78 Probably Matthew Stedman, baptized in Hascombe, Surrey, but apparently not John's brother.
79 The version of this letter in the Goodwood MS reads Talbot settlement. Thomas Talbot, a former aide-de-camp to Lieutenant Governor John Graves Simcoe, supervised the settlement of an area on the north shore of Lake Erie which included portions of 29 townships. Malahide Township was named after his birth place in Ireland.

had America at home: for I can assure you that this [is a] good country for any person. If [he] do not choose [to] go [to] farming, he may always get work in, if [he] choose. But I myself, please God, I have health and strength, [and] when my year is out, I have 100 dollars to take. Then if [I] have good luck, I think I shall get me 100 acres of land, as I may work for myself at times, and not work for other people any longer than I am forced. For when [I] get a bit of land cleared, and get tired of this country, I (can) sell my land, at any time: for that is [the] best thing that a man can do in this country, is to get land as soon as he can. I can get land, not cleared, at from 1 dollar to 5 dollars. The man that I live with, had nothing when he begun, but 1 dollar, when he (bought) 200 acres for 400 dollars, and 4 years credit for it. Now he has 700 acres where I live, and has just bought 1000 acres more. He gave a man [a] job of chopping of land, and gave him so much land for clearing of some for him every year. He (sowed) 70 acres of wheat, and is going to sow as much this fall. Wheat is very dear this fall: it is 60 pence per bushel; peas is 30 pence; and Indian corn is all cut off by the frost, for it is a very cold place in the winter. But I like the country very well at present, but it is a short time; but I have never wished myself at Hascomb, not as yet, thank God for it.

So my dear father and mother, give my love to uncles and aunts, and all enquiring friends, and tell them if [they] lived as [I] can in this country it [would be a] comfort to them; for [I] can get what clothing I want, in about 3 miles where I live, and as cheap as it is in England. You think there is nothing to [be] had, but I can tell you better: there is any thing you want. Tell little John that he must grow as fast as he can, and come to me, [and] never abide in that country. So no more from (your) loving (son),

JOHN STEDMAN.

You are there, and I am here; I live in hopes (to) meet again where the Angels do also.

Direction for John Stedman, at Mr. Fozer's, the Town[ship] of Malahide, County of Middlesex, in London District, Upper Canada, North America; which I am about 4000 miles from home.

For Mr. JAMES G. STEDMAN,
    At Hascomb,
        Near Godalming,
            in the County of Surrey,
                Old England.

We have not been able to trace Stedman beyond the time of writing this letter.

■ 19

CHARLOTTE (TRIBE) EVANS, WATERLOO TOWNSHIP, UPPER CANADA,
TO HER BROTHER, ROBERT TRIBE, DEAN, NEAR PETWORTH, SUSSEX,
18 AUGUST 1832

Charlotte Evans emigrated with her parents, Henry and Charlotte Tribe, and other members of the family from Dial Green, Lurgashall, West Sussex; she married Joseph Neuroke Evans in Canada. Jesse Penfold wrote of the marriage in letter 50 that "Charlotte Tribe is married to [a] man worth money." This letter to Charlotte's brother seems to have been a joint production but was signed by Charlotte's new husband. Two of Charlotte's married sisters also emigrated with their husbands and families (James and Sarah Rapson and Jane and Jesse Penfold), and they therefore had the comfort of a large family group. See letters 2, 12.

Joseph Evans was granted E ½ lot 8 concession 6 Medonte Township in July 1832, before he married Charlotte. The sickness that prevented them from going to Joseph's land was undoubtedly cholera. John Capling in letter 21 describes the trip inland on the Canada Company road taken by him and other Lurgashall people mentioned in this letter.

SOURCE: *Emigration: Letters* (1833), 17-18

Waterloo, August 18th. 1832.

* * * * Robert Chalwin is dead; he wished to make his home with us, but his Uncle[80] would not let him stay, but took his things with him. 14 that came out of Lurgashall Parish, Mrs. [Sarah] Morley, Joseph Kingshott, Henry Lander and Brother [George Lander], Ned Luff, Henry Gogger is dead. Dear Robert, Benjamin [Tribe] says, if he could have the two Robert's and Neddy, (or Biddy) between them, he never should want to see England again. Give Ben's love to Henry Baker, Robert Kingshott. Our love to Mr. and Mrs. Hill, and all the children. Jesse [Penfold], James [Rapson], and Benjamin [Tribe] are building a house; and you and family shall have a house when you come.

Dear Father and Mother! and we all send our best love to you; and Wife, and her Father, and Mary's love to Mrs. Sanders; and give my best love to Miss Upfold; and let her see the letter: and tell her when she writes to Mrs. Evans, to give my love, and let her know that I shall write when I get settled, as I have altered my name since I came to this country. I have married an Irishman, that has got land from the King,[81] and we should have been on it before, but for the sickness that prevails in the part of the country where the land lies.

When you come bring 2 pair of shoes, high; very strong:[82] Chalwin to make them. Bring your clock; also bring every thing you want (for) housekeeping. In this country, as you pay no duty for any things coming, you will not be examined. If you could, I wish you would bring 12 yards of waistcoat flannel, and I shall refund you the money with thanks. Bring some net for caps, and some for borders. In fact any things in the wearing way, you will get paid for in this part of America. Your trade, working by the day in this country, pay 5s. and the best of boarding, and abundance of employment.

Wishing you and your family, a happy voyage to this country, which shall be the prayer of your affectionate Charlotte and myself.

---

80 Chalwin's uncle, John Capling (or Capelain), describes the journey in letter 21.
81 If Evans had been a soldier, he would have been eligible for a grant of 100 acres of land.
82 Boots extending to the ankle are what she recommends.

(The Letter is signed by Charlotte Tribe's husband.)

JOSEPH NEUROKE EVANS.

Directions,

HENRY TRIBE, *Galt, Upper Canada.*

OTHER LETTERS: *See also* letter 54, written by Charlotte's parents, Henry and Charlotte Tribe. Thomas Adsett, on 25 June 1833 (71), wrote of a recent visit he had made with Jesse Penfold, James Rapson, and Benjamin Tribe to Elizabeth Kinshott (Joseph Kinshott's widow) and Charlotte Evans. He did not give any very precise location, but he did say that Mrs Kinshott was keeping a school in Blenheim, a township just east of Woodstock.

Charlotte and her family apparently remained in Blenheim. Joseph Evans died in Blenheim Township on 2 April 1867, survived by his wife, two sons, and five daughters; he left an estate valued at $5787. The 1871 census for Blenheim records Charlotte Evans, a widow aged 68 and born England, who stated she was a member of the United Brethren Church (an evangelical sect of Germanic origin that came to Canada from Pennsylvania amd were well-established in neighbouring Waterloo County). She was living with Joseph Evans, aged 29 and probably her son, his wife, Elizabeth, and their two children.

■ 20

CHARLOTTE AND WILLIAM WILLARD,[83] DUNDAS, UPPER CANADA, TO MRS MARIA WOLGAR, CHARLOTTE'S SISTER, MILTON STREET,[84] DORKING, SURREY, 26 AUGUST 1832

William and Charlotte (Longhurst) Willard sailed on the *Lord Melville* in 1832 with their nine children, Maria, William, James, John, Charlotte, Henry, George, David, and Charles.[85] The costs incurred in sending this family of eleven with the Dorking Society were £87.14.2. Six of the children travelled at half price making a total of eight passages. At Sockett*'s recommended amount of £10 for each adult passage to Toronto, and £5 to cover the outfit, transport to Portsmouth, and landing money, his parish of Petworth would have paid as much as £120 for eight passages. Thus, emigrants provisioned by the Petworth committee should have had a better diet during the passage than Charlotte's family who depended on the Dorking Society.

William's father and his brother, Henry, also went to Canada in 1832, but they do not appear in the emigration records of the parish of Dorking.

---

83 Original annotation:"William Willard was a Carpenter by trade; a dispute have arisen relative to his settlement, the parishes interested in the solution of the question, viz. Dorking, Shiere [Sheer], and Albury, rather than spend money in litigating so doubtful a case, wisely contributed £30 each towards the expense of conveying himself, his Wife, and seven boys, all young, to Canada. The ages of the respective members of the family were not taken, but the father was about 45."There were also two daughters, but these do not seem to have warranted a mention.

84 Milton Street is about one and a half miles west of Dorking.

85 Both William and Charlotte signed their names to the marriage register.

SOURCE: *Letters from Dorking*, 15-22

August 26, 1832.

MY DEAR SISTER,

No doubt you are very anxious to hear from us, I am thankful to say we all arrived safe in Upper Canada. We are 60 miles from York, 15 from Dundas, though we travelled all the way by water, except 20 miles by land. We are very near the back settlements of America. We are situated in a very pleasant spot, 12 acres cleared land, two houses, outbuilding, beautiful spring of water like your orchard water at Milton. Twelve shillings we give for a sow and 5 pigs, but we expect to have a cow, and there is about half-a-dozen here, and every thing are so much cheaper to what they are at England. The man that built this house lived here five years, he said he had not a penny, he was a shoemaker; he had 4 cows, 2 oxen, pigs, chicken, ducks, geese. There was'nt a tree cut down when he came; now there is a garden and 12 acres clear land and plenty of wood around us they are glad for us to burn. A plenty of maple tree that we make sugar of the sap they get in March. We live under Capt. Roberts who has 200 acres of ground, and this spot he will let us have at 25 dollars a year which is £6.5s. English money.

My dear sister, I can assure you we live in a good friendly Christian country. There is a chapel[86] about a mile from us and 20 houses. My father and Wm. has a dollar a day and their board. James has 1s.3d. a week and his board. John and Charlotte is out. Dear sister I don't repent leaving England. The children are all very happy and well; David is very stout. They were at home a board of ship. I wish we had come years ago. Dear sister please give my kind love to my father, brothers and sisters and their family and all our friends, and wishes you were all here for you could never repent leaving England, for my brother Henry Willard has got a place and they wants to keep him till he is 21 years old, but we are not determined about it. And if Uncle James is in the same mind he was when we left England, I hope my dear sister you will not be backward in coming for we did not fear the water. You will not have half the care as I have had with the children, fearing that they will fall overboard, but you will not have that care on your mind, and I hope you will come next April if it is possible for you to come. Put forward for Sarah Britt, Tommy and Amey to come. We have great reason to thank God that we all got here safe, and there is the same Providence over you as there was over us. It was very hard parting with you thinking never to see you any more, but I hope you will try your best to get here. You will not have the care on your mind as we had, not knowing were to go to, or what we was going to do, for you know that we tried the road for you. And I hope you will follow us, and now shall tell you a few things about what I think you ought to bring. We was very sorry that we did not bring our grate, for it would have been very useful, and many other things would have been very

---

86 The two youngest children were baptized at the West Street Independent [Congregational] Chapel in Dorking; the older children had been baptized in the Church of England. William Willard Sr had been received as a member of the chapel in 1828.

useful. Get a good strong chest. Do not come away without things for your use, such as dishes, pots, embden grits.[87] And now I am going to tell you what will be on board ship, bring a few onions, a little arrow-root, and a little vinegar, and plenty of bread baked hard, and I can tell you that we should have been very glad to had a morsel of bread before we got to Quebec. My dear sister we are very thankful that you did not come with us, for we had a very uncomfortable set to come with. There was not a day went over our heads but what there was a quarrelling or a fighting, with it, made it very uncomfortable, and for that reason I am very thankful that you did not come with us.

On Tuesday the 22nd of May we saw land, on the 24th we came to the gulf [of St Lawrence], on Sunday the 27th of May we saw the snow on the hills. I was so cold, we could not stand upon deck, and there was such mountains as never was seen in England. The Pilot came on board the 28th, the Dorking fair day. It was just 8 weeks when we got to Quebec, on Saturday afternoon. Tell Mrs. Tocker of Albury, there was two gentlemen came on board Sunday morning, I shewed them the letter, and they knowed the gentleman well, and was with him the day before, and told me if I could get to go to shore that they would direct me were to find him, but our Captain [Chancellor] would not suffer one to go ashore, except the Doctor [Lascelles] and himself, and I ask the Doctor to take the letter to the gentleman, and the Doctor left it but never see the gentleman himself, and so I heard no more about that. We have nobody to thank for but the Captain. They had plenty of every thing in the cabin, we had nothing but musty biscuit and salt beef, I mention this because you should not come away without necessaries.

We arrived at Montreal, Wednesday morning, and Saturday morning we went out of ship, and then we went into the stores, and we stop there till Monday, and then we got into the boat. We was a week going up the river to Prescot. We was one night there. We went into a very fine steam boat, Great Britain. The last voyage it carried 700 people. There was 500 when we was in, and we arrived at York Friday morning, and it is a very beautiful place, and if we had stop there we could have got work, but lodging was so dear. Mr. Harper[88] and John Worsfold we understood went to Hambleton [Hamilton] by land. We arrived at Hambleton on Monday morning. We have heard no more about them, and we are very anxious to find them, and [if] they have wrote home to England, I will thank you to give the directions. Give our kind love to John Wolgar and Mary, and tell them that it is the best thing as ever they did to come to America, they will never wish to go back again.[89] They dont put up dinners in this Country, but they dine along with the masters and

87 Embden grits, the seeds of *Avena sativa*, the common oat. "When bruised ready for use, they are denominated Embden grits," *The National Encyclopaedia: A Dictionary of Useful Knowledge* (London: William MacKenzie 1884-88), vol. II.

88 James and Sarah Harper emigrated from Dorking with two sons.

89 Members of the Wolgar family did emigrate in 1833; we do not know if they included John and Mary.

The steamboat Great Britain *carried many Petworth immigrants from Prescott to Toronto. It was described as the largest vessel on the Great Lakes when it was launched at Prescott in 1830.*
Henry Francis Ainslie, "The Steamer Great Britain," NA, C522

mistresses as you call them in England, but they will not be called so here, they are equals-like and if hired to anybody they call them their employers.

John Wolgar is to bring a good long rifle gun, for the Bears comes around us; I expect we shall get some in the fall, and there is pigeons, and pheasants, partridges, quails and rabbits. Dear sister you know that we could hardly get a taste of meat in England, but now we can roast a quarter of meat. Mutton is 2½d. per lb., pork 3½d., veal the same, butter 7½d., sugar is the same as it is in England, and we are in hopes of making some sugar next season. One 100 weight of flour for 12s.6d. They do not reap their wheat in this country, but they cradle it here, and it is worth anybodys while to lease here, for one good leaser could get a bushel of wheat a day, for they rake it in this country.[90] There is no leasers in this country; they let the hogs eat it. I hope we shall be able to get a good grist this harvest.[91] You must not be afraid to come across the water, I have been upon deck when the moon and stars shone beautiful, and have said that we must put our trust in God, for he is our only refuge, for

---

90 To lease, to glean. In England, gleaning was a task for poor women and children, who gathered up the ears of corn left by the reapers. A cradle was an adaptation of a scythe, designed to catch the grain as it fell.
91 Corn to grind.

I have thought of it a great many times, that Providence have been on our sides, and we have great reason to thank God for his kindness that we all got here safe. I should think it a great mercy that near 400 people came over in one ship and only one little infant died of them, and there was four births before we got there.[92]

Give our best respects to all kind friends at Dorking, London, Broadmore, and all that enquires after us. Tell James Willard that we wishes that he would bring a pitsaw with him for there is plenty of timber here,[93] we may have it for cutting. There is two families arrived here this spring from London, one family's name was Heath, brother to Counsellor Heath below Cold-harbour, and Maria have got a situation and gone with them to the gulf, about 20 miles from us. She is to have a pound a month; she would have got plenty of places coming up the country, but would not leave us till we got a little settled. We are very anxious to know where [James] Harper is. We shall not take any land till we find out them.

We conclude, so no more from your affectionate brother,
WILLIAM and CHARLOTTE WILLARD.

Dear sister, I was deprived of my new blankets they was stolen out of my berth and one old one placed in the room, and many more things, James's best hat, Charlotte's bonnet, Maria's shawl and caps besides, I know where they went to, some had them.

When we were at Hambleton there is an old gentleman living there, the man's name Mr. Horezen, 77 years of age, he has been here ever since the American War, wished me when I wrote to give his compliments to Mr. Barclay*'s family, was quite old playmates together when Mr. Barclay was in the States. I am thankful to say we are all well at present, and happy, not wishing to return. If it's possible for you to see the children you would be astonished. The country agrees with us all at present. Maria, I am afraid you will not be able to read this scribble, hope the next will be better. Our best wishes to all. The Lord be with you.

My dear sister, since I wrote this letter Captain R. has sold this 100 acres; we have another house to go to, 2 acres of ground and garden. We are to live there all the winter for nothing, about a mile from this. Sovereign, 24s., half-sovereign, 12s. one shilling is 1s.2d., sixpence is 7d. Tell John to bring as many farthings as he can get, and old halfpennies, they go for as much as a penny-piece, they call them coppers. Clothing is as cheap as in England. I mention this if the kind friends would be so kind as to give in money what they will give you, it will be more to your advantage. Give our love to sister Hannah, tell her I hope she will come when you come. James's family will be no burden to him here. I wish my poor father and friends was here, they would not want bread I can assure you all. It is a friendly and Christian

---

92 Hester Longhurst was the infant who died; see letter 31. The four births were William and Elizabeth Bloes's daughter, Jesse and Jane Penfold's daughter, Henry and Jane Smart's daughter, and Ann and Edmund Thomas's son.

93 On pitsaws, see James Rapson's letter 38.

country. We left David Percival at York well. I hope you will send a letter soon as possible, a long one. Send word how much this letter is [costs] coming.

Directions. – William Willard, Carpenter,
   Beonley, [94]
   to be left at the Post-Office Dundas,
   District of Upper Canada,
   America,
   by way of New York and Liverpool.

The Willards found Mr Harper and John Worsfold some time before Worsfold wrote to his parents in December 1832 (see letter 48)

   In England, gleaning in the wheat fields following the harvest was one of the few ways Charlotte could have made a direct contribution to the family store of food. Thus, she could expect her sister to recognize a measure of abundance when she told her that hogs were turned into these fields in Upper Canada.

■ 21

JOHN CAPLING, SOUTH EASTHOPE TOWNSHIP, UPPER CANADA, TO HIS BROTHER, LURGASHALL, WEST SUSSEX, 28 AUGUST 1832
John Capling (Capelain or Caplin) emigrated with his wife, Jane (Booker),[95] a nephew, Robert Chalwin, and 11 children (George, Thomas, Caroline, John, William, Mary, James, Stephen, Edmund, Jane, and Charlotte, who was baptized in March 1832, just before they sailed for Canada). Capling was a labourer. In November 1830 he was given £1.10s by his parish, perhaps to help with his rent, and he would have received a child allowance for his younger children. A minute of the Petworth Emigration Committee of 27 October 1832 records sending letters to James and John Caplain to the Canada Company to be forwarded to Upper Canada.

SOURCE: *Emigration: Letters* (1833), 16-17. A manuscript copy is in WSRO Goodwood MS 1460, and notes on the letter are found in WSRO, PHA 137, Minutes of the Petworth Emigration Committee, 1832.

Huron Tract, Upper Canada,
August 28th. 1832.

MY DEAR BROTHER,
   I take the opportunity of writing these few lines to you, to inform you of our distress and trouble. After a very rough passage of twelve weeks, by the help of the Almighty God, we arrived safe to land,[96] except the loss of two babes, Ned Luff's

---

94 Probably meant to be Beverly Township
95 Both John and Jane signed the marriage register with a mark.
96 At this point in the Goodwood MS copy, the handwriting changes. The first few lines were probably written by Sockett; the remainder may have been copied by one of Sockett's daughters, who did on occasion copy materials for their father. (See the evidence of T. Sockett to the Select Committee on Postage, 23 May 1838.)

youngest and Wm. Tickner's youngest child. But we then thought ourselves safe, but the Almighty was pleased to send a very great affliction upon us. In a few days after we arrived at our intended place of settlement, I lost my poor little Mary for the first, then my poor dearest wife, then my two youngest, and little Edmund, all in the space of eight days. *And what was more hard for me I was obliged to wrap them up in the rinds of trees and dig holes and put them in myself.*[97] But, dear brother, I am not the only one the Almighty was pleased to send the affliction upon. Poor Joseph Kinshott was the first; and his sister, Nathan Morley's wife [Sarah Kinshott], were next; and, I am very sorry to inform my poor brother in law, poor Bob [Robert Chalwin] is gone: likewise the two young Landers [George and Henry]. There was 32 of us that came up into the woods together, and there is twelve of the 32 dead. The complaint was the cholera morbus; they all died in the space of a fortnight. There (was) none laid ill but a few days. Dear brother, I should like to know what my brother in law should like to be done with poor Bob's things: he had no money. I think his things to (be) worth £6; (it) is now in (the) possession of Nathan Morley.

My dear brother, I am very sorry to send you this unpleasant account, but it is all owing to the affliction the Almighty was pleased to send upon us: for I can see (a) good prospect for a good living to be got. Flour is 7 dollars a barrel, which is 3½ bushels. That is the highest price; after another harvest, it will be lower, no doubt, as we shall all grow our own, and now it is brought a long way up the country. Mutton I kill, and sell out. I can afford to sell it 3*d.* per lb., beef 2½*d.*, butter about 9½*d.*, but I shall keep a cow, and make my own next summer. I have nothing, no keep for a cow, this winter. Dear brother, if my brother William could take the heart to come, there shall be a home for him, as soon as he comes; for I have got a comfortable house up, and 100 acres of land, full of timber, and he shall have part of it. But I will not persuade any one to come, tho' I can see much better prospects here than in England. If he should, let him bring what ready money he can, and not provide a parcel of things, as I did. For things is as cheap *here*[98] as in England and tools cheaper. Let him bring a few onesided oats,[99] a little barley, gooseberry and currant cuttings.

My dear brother, remember me to all relations, and all enquiring friends. I hope, by the blessing of God, you are all well, as I thank God it leaves me, and the remainder of my family, at present. I hope you will write to me, as soon as you can. I remain your affectionate brother,

JOHN CAPELAIN.

97 The words in italics were omitted by Sockett in the published version. Robina and Kathleen Macfarlane Lizers, *In the Days of the Canada Company* (Toronto 1896), 417-18, write: "The manner of burying them out of sight was most primitive. They dug a kind of grave, put a piece of bark at the bottom of it, laid the dead upon it, then placed another piece of bark, and cover all with earth."
98 Original annotation: "i.e. In the Huron Tract."
99 *Collier's Encyclopedia* (1995) defines sided or banner oats as "a class or variety in which the panicles hang from one side only. Climate and soil determine the choice of variety."

Mrs. [Elizabeth] Kinshott's (love) to all her husband's family, and is sorry to say, she has the inexpressible grief, to say she lost her dear and only friend, 29th June, in about 28 hours; and in sixteen days after, her youngest child. She expects every day to go to Oxford, 25 miles distant, to settle with a school. As soon as Mrs. Kinshott gets to Oxford, she will send her friends all the particulars. She, and her two children [Eleanor and John], is very poorly. She wants for nothing; she meets with the greatest of friendship. I have not heard of Wm. Tickner, since we left York. He went in another vessel farther up the lake. We have not heard that any more died than those who came here, except Edward Luff, and he died at Hamilton. We are 100 miles from York.

Direct to me No. 13, 1st. Concession,
    Huron Tract,
        South Easthope, Upper Canada,
            America.

Left with seven surviving children who ranged in age from 6 to 20, John settled on 100 acres of lot 13 concession 1 South Easthope, a lot belonging to the Canada Company. He completed the purchase in 1854 at which time he and his eldest son, George, both paid off mortgages on their lots. George married Mary Morley and settled in North Easthope.

Capling is one of the few Petworth emigrants of 1832 who we know followed through with the intention to buy land belonging to the Canada Company. Because they were on company land, Sockett was able to send the Caplings' mail free of charge to them through the company's office in London.

Mrs (Joseph) Kinshott, the former Elizabeth Child, lost her husband and a baby to cholera. In June 1833, Thomas Adsett (71) reported that he with Jesse Penfold, James Rapson, and Benjamin Tribe had gone to see her in Blenheim where they found her keeping school. Adsett reported that she was making "1½ dollars a per week, and most provisions found" (she likely received part payment in kind).

■ 22

THOMAS ADSETT, GALT, UPPER CANADA, TO HIS FATHER-IN-LAW,
THOMAS SCUTT, BIGNOR, NEAR PETWORTH, WEST SUSSEX,
9 SEPTEMBER 1832

In December 1830, Thomas Adsett had been working as a labourer under Egremont*'s land steward. He and his wife, Sarah Scutt, sailed on the *Lord Melville* with their four children, Emma, Charles, Sarah, and Harriet, sent by the parish of Northchapel.[100]

---

100 At their marriage in Petworth in 1824, Thomas signed the register with a mark and Sarah signed her name.

SOURCE: *Emigration: Letters* (1833), 18–19

September 9th. 1832.

DEAR FATHER,

I am sorry to be the messenger of bad news, but we are in a land of disappointment: if we go to bed at night, well and hearty, we may not rise in the morning alive.

April 11th. Set sail from Portsmouth. Fair wind for some days. Children and Wife quite well, self quite sick, and so I continued for a month.

May 19th. Harriet failed with the hooping cough, and continued getting worse. Wife and the children quite well, all the way over.

June 2, reached Quebec.

7th, to Montreal, after a passage of 8 weeks and 1 day, and almost all the way very rough sea. Here we left the Melville, and took the Durham Boats. Here we was put hard to it, being exposed to the weather until we reached York.

19th, reached York. Harriet kept getting worse: we did not stop at York above 5 or 6 hours. Next came to Hamilton: wife failed in eating. Left and came to Waterloo. Child very bad; wife quite poorly, and kept getting worse.

July 1st, Harriet died. 2nd, wife very bad. 3rd, died.[101] The doctor said that it was the scarlet fever: the other children all well. Sara (2½ years old) a gentleman by the name of Chapman, a Carpenter, came and took her, the 7th.

Charles (6 years old) is at a Weavers; Emma (7 years old) is at Mr. Tottles, in Dumfries; and are well; and like the place quite well. I get plenty of work, at 5s. York, that is 2s.3½ of your money, and board. Here is plenty of whisky, at 1s. per quart; here is no beer; and the water is not so good in many places as in England. They live in quite a different way to what they do in the old country, but they live much better. The produce is wheat, oats, winter barley, rice, indian corn, and potatoes, but this is truly the wooden world. If we find so many houses as at Crouch,[102] we should think that we should be in a city: the houses are about half a mile a part. Here is plenty of pheasants, and pigeons, and deer that will weigh 20 stone, and bears, foxes, wolves, and hares. I can say no more at present. Write to me as soon as possible, and send word how they all are. Direct, Thomas Adsett, Galt, Dumfries, U. Canada, N. America.

OTHER LETTERS: 49, 61–62, 71, and Charles Adsett, 180

■ **23**

SIMEON TITMOUSE, DUNDAS, UPPER CANADA, TO —— JACKSON, 11 SEPTEMBER 1832

Simeon Titmouse, a farm labourer, and his wife, Sarah Jackson, emigrated with their children, Charles, Ann, and George, from Bassingbourn, Cambridgeshire.[103] They were part of a

---

101 Sarah died on the site of the village of Preston (surveyed in 1834) in a drive shed that had been given over to immigrants. See Charles Adsett, 180.

102 Crouch Common, a tiny hamlet two miles north of Bignor, West Sussex.

103 Simeon and Sarah both signed the marriage register with a mark.

party of five families and one single man. The vicar of Bassingbourn supplied a record of baptisms and marriages from his parish register; the group included the families of Titmouse's married sisters, Edith Racher and Mary Shambrook or Shambrink. The single man was probably Obediah Wilson (letter 15).

SOURCE: *Emigration: Letters* (1833), 19–20

Dundas, Upper Canada, North America.
Sept. 11th. 1832.

DEAR SIR,

After we left home for America, we were seven weeks before we reached Quebec, and about a fortnight after, we arrived where we now are. Our passage was very rough, but we landed safe. This country is quite different from home; but there are better things for labouring people here than at home. We can make a better living than we could in England. People are generally engaged by the month, and get about ten dollars for that time. I have been with the principal man of this place a month, and may stay some time. The wife and children are well at present, but this is rather a sickly country, the people being very subject to ague. We hope we shall, in a little time, like America very well. Corn is about 5s. a bushel. Pork, mutton, beef, &c. 3d. or 3½d. per lb.; capital good tea, from 4s. to 5s. per lb.; pretty good sugar, at about 4d. or 5d. per. lb.; potatoes, about 1s. 6d. per bushel; clothing pretty reasonable, but tailors wages are very high. The women generally make mens apparel; but mark! money, or cash, is very bad to catch. People must be very wary when they first come into the country, otherwise they will be very much imposed on. People often hire new comers for a month, and then take occasion to quarrel with them and turn them off, without their wages; but still, if one place does not do, another will.

The appearance of the country is no way enticing, being principally woody. The houses are not so comfortable as at home, as they are all wooden ones, or mostly so. Land may be purchased at 1½ dollars to 4 dollars an acre, uncleared; or, in other words, a perfect wood. Cleared farms will cost much more an acre. Wm. Bloes has not engaged for the month yet, but has ½ a dollar a day for every day he works, and has had work most of the time. But the work we have to do is quite different to what it was at home. John Shambrink, and John Racher live about two miles from us: Racher is engaged for a year, 115 dollars his wages; house rent free; ½ acre of land for a garden; and fire wood found gratis. Shambrink has had the ague; and his daughter[104] is living where I am engaged by the month.

The country is discouraging at first, but the longer one is in it, the better one begins to like it. Any stout, hard labouring man, with a family, may do better in this country for them, than he can do at home. But remember, he will have to work pretty hard and long days. But abundance of trouble and disappointment await those who come at first, and it takes a little time, and patience to get over them; and many a

104 John and Mary Shambrook had three daughters, Lydia, Hannah, and Sophia.

one loses his life in the encounter, either by sickness or misfortune. But I am happy to tell you, we are all safe and well. Simeon Titmouse[105] and Wm. Bloes live in the same village, (viz. Dundas) and [are] engaged in working as above stated. Summers are hotter here; and we are told, winters are colder and longer than in England. A good cow may be purchased from 3 to 4 pounds; apples, in abundance, about 1s. per bushel. But with all these appearances of things being cheap, they are dear enough in proportion to the money we receive, because they often pay wages by shop goods, either eatables, or wearing apparel. Please give our best remembrances and respects to all friends, particularly fathers and mothers, brothers and sisters and remain

> Dear Jackson
> Yours very faithful
> SIMEON TITMOUSE.

Wm. Bloes' wife was confined at Montreal: a little girl, quite well and hearty. This event took place on the 4th June, 1832. She had a very good time, and got very good friends.[106] Please to let us hear from you as soon as convenient after receiving this; and acquaint us with all particulars, and how you all are. Give my love to John Flanders, and tell him, he might buy 5 acres of land for what he might give for a rood at home.

Simeon Titmouse was recorded in census records in Flamborough Township in 1842 and again in 1851 when he was on 50 acres of lot 1 concession 6 Flamborough. He gave his denomination as Baptist in 1851. At that time he had remarried and his wife was listed as a Roman Catholic named Catherine born in Ireland. Five children, Richard, William, Joseph, Elizabeth, and Benjamin, were noted as born in Canada. George Titmouse, who was about one year old when the family emigrated, married in Beverly Township in 1854 and moved to Michigan two years later. His Canadian-born brother, Joseph, also married in Beverly in 1866.

The Bloes family were in Dundas in 1835 and in Ancaster in 1842. John and Edith Racher settled on half of lot 32 concession 6 in Beverly Township. They arrived with two children and had another six before Edith died. John Racher's second marriage, to Ann Burns, produced another eight children.

Also living in Dundas was Richard Neal; see letter 5.

■ **24**

WILLIAM SPENCER, NELSON TOWNSHIP, UPPER CANADA, TO HIS FATHER-IN-LAW, FRANCIS COOPER,[107] PETWORTH, WEST SUSSEX, 16 SEPTEMBER 1832

William Spencer and his wife Sarah Cooper emigrated from Linchmere, Surrey (now West Sussex).[108]

---

105 We do not know why the third person is used here, although we do know that someone other than Titmouse or his wife likely wrote the letter since they both signed the marriage register with a mark.

106 William and Elizabeth Bloes already had a young son, Isaac.

107 Letter 68 gives Francis Cooper's address as Mountpillier, near Petworth.

108 Both William and Sarah signed the marriage register with a mark.

*John Racher and his second
wife, Ann Burns*
Stockton photograph
collection
Courtesy Margaret Stockton
and Glenn W. Racher

Source: *Emigration: Letters* (1833), 24

September 16th. 1832.

Dear Father, and Mother, Brothers, and Sisters,

  * * * *[109] We arrived safe in York, in Upper Canada. We came further up the country, about 30 miles, and there we went to work on the road, for 3s.3d. per day. We were staying with Mr. Jacob Truller [Triller]; and was enjoying a good state of health till the 22nd August: my dear wife was taken ill with typhus fever, and she departed this life on the 7th of September. She was attended with all the neighbours; and we have found them very kind, much kinder here, than ever we did in England. I have hired with Mr. Truller, by the year, and I am getting good wages; and, if you feels any ways inclined to come, I think it would be better for you, for I think you will

109 See William's comments on these omissions at the end of letter 125.

get [a] better living here than you ever will in England. I will find you a home for you, till you can suit yourselves better. I am going to write to my brother in London, and I should wish for you to let all my friends see this letter; and I should be very glad to hear from you, as soon as you could make it convenient to write. So no more at present, from your affectionate son,

WILLIAM SPENCER.
So adieu.

OTHER LETTERS: 68, 125.
Spencer's letter 68 gives detailed information about Jacob Triller's farm.

■ 25
GEORGE AND MARY BOXALL AND WILLIAM TILLEY, NELSON TOWNSHIP, UPPER CANADA, TO JAMES TILLEY, PETWORTH, WEST SUSSEX, [16 SEPTEMBER 1832]
George, a sawyer, and his wife, Mary (Tilley) Boxall, emigrated in 1832, along with their young son, Alfred, and Mary's brother William Tilley.[110] George and Mary were sent with the assistance of W.H. Yaldwyn* and the parish of Fernhurst, West Sussex; William was sent by Petworth, the parish of his parents, James and Hannah Tilley. This letter was written on the same sheet of paper as that of William Spencer, letter 24.

Source: *Emigration: Letters* (1833), 25

Dear Fathers, Mothers, Brothers, and Sisters.
    * *We arrived safe in York, in Upper Canada; and we travelled up the country, and were settled near Wm. Spencer, and my brother; and we have got plenty of work, of sawing of steam boats,[111] and we gets good pay for it. And we like this country much better than old England. My dear Alfred grows, and gets fat, and funny, and hearty: thank God for it. Dear father and mother, Hannah and James Tilley: if you feels any ways inclined to come out, and my brother William Boxall, I think it would be better to get [a] living [here] than in England, but I shall not persuade you against your inclination. But, if you comes, I will find you a home, till you can better yourselves. Boys and girls can have good places here; and I should be glad if you would let all my friends see the letter. Write to me as soon as you can. Remember me to Mr. and Mrs. ..., Mr. ..., and Miss ..., Mr. ..., and to all of my enquiring friends. There is but one thing grieves us: that will be leaving Elizabeth and Crank[112] behind: and, if you comes, pray leave my poor mother, at Henly,[113] a sovereign; and I will pay you

110 When George and Mary were married, he signed his name to the register while she signed with a mark.
111 They were sawing wood to be used as fuel by wood-fired steamboats.
112 Original annotation: "His sister Elizabeth's husband."
113 A hamlet between Midhurst and Fernhurst, West Sussex.

again. Be sure and do not forget the directions. So no more, at present, from your affectionate sons and daughter,

WM. TILLEY, MARY AND GEORGE BOXALL.

So adieu.

This is the prices of this country. Barrel of flour, 196 lbs. price £1.5s. Pork, 3d. per lb. Best green tea, 3s.9d. Best butter, 7½d. Sugar, 6d. Tobacco, 1s. a pound. Best mutton and beef, 2½d. a pound. We makes our own soap, and candles. Price for work: sawyers, 10s. per hundred; single men about £20. at farming. If you comes, be sure and do not come under any superintendent, but mind, and buy plenty of flour, and bacon, and good cheese, tea, sugar, butter, currants, raisins, [and] tobacco. Buy your furnishings at Portsmouth. Get your flour in barrels; pack up all your goods, as you can iron hoop your boxes; and cord them strong; do not trust no locks.

Direct as follows. William Spencer, Mr. Jacob Truller's, Township of Nelson, County of Halton, District of Gore, Upper Canada, North America.

OTHER LETTERS: 121

Mary's parents, Hannah and James Tilley, followed in 1833. Her mother wrote to England in July 1833 with an update on the family; see letter 83.

■ 26

WILLIAM TAYLOR UPTON, ANDROSS [ARDROSS] MILLS,[114] NELLES SETTLEMENT,[115] UPPER CANADA, TO GEORGE WARREN, PETWORTH, WEST SUSSEX, 16 SEPTEMBER 1832

William T. Upton, aged 23, emigrated with his 13-year-old brother, Clifford, from Fittleworth, Sussex, in 1832. William's parents, William and Frances Taylor Upton, had married at Petworth in 1804 when they both were minors. Born in 1806, William Jr was the eldest of ten children. Three of his sisters died in England and Frances Upton Jr emigrated to Tasmania in 1829. William Sr, a timber merchant, had deserted the family by 1831.

SOURCE: *Emigration: Letters* (1833), 23-4. A version was also published in *Emigration: Extracts.*

Andross Mills,
Niagara District, Grand River,
September 16th. 1832.

DEAR FRIEND,
* * * * *[116] I dare say you have heard bad accounts of Canada, from the Petworth

---

114 Ardross belonged to James Hector Mackenzie, a merchant and miller in the village of York, part of the Grand River Tract, later Seneca Township. He named his lands on Mackenzie Creek Ardross in honour of his home in Rossshire, Scotland (W. J. Quinsey, *York, Grand River: Its Early History and Directory 1834-1860* [n.p.: The York, Grand River, Historical Society 1991]).

115 Henry Nelles and his sons, Robert and Warren, were Loyalist settlers from New York State who obtained large land grants on the Grand River. Warner Nelles built a residence at York on the Grand.

116 This and the following indications of omissions are not included in *Emigration: Extracts.*

Party; for I know that they wrote home in the midst of their trouble in travelling, before they knew what it was, or had time to get situations. *I was above a month coming up the country, on account of my waiting at York for my box, which was put into the wrong ship at Portsmouth.*[117] I went from York to Hamilton, and, after a weeks illness, and quite broke down for money, I got a situation at a Mr. Mc'Kensey's[118] saw mills, on the banks of the grand river, at 12s.6d. per week, and board and lodging. I am the lowest, not understanding it: the others [get] from £1. to 32s. per week. I enquired at York and Hamilton, cabinet makers wages, which is 30s. per week, board and lodging, and plenty of trade to be got. I have been in my place now 9 weeks, and what with my wages, and what I have made with them, am now worth £8.10s. There is a man of property in 9 weeks. * * * * If trade is as bad as it was, any one would do better in Canada, for here any one can soon gain an independency. * * * Tell J. Lucas that his brother Ned and C. Edwards are living close to me: they get 11s.3d. per week, and board and lodging, and are quite steady.[119] Write as soon as possible.

I cannot give you a more true account of the price of provisions, *and men's wages,* than *Doyle's Hints to Emigrants.*[120] There were plenty given to people about Petworth.

The following letter, 27, is to Upton's mother

■ **27**

WILLIAM TAYLOR UPTON, ANDROSS [ARDROSS] MILLS, NELLES SETTLEMENT, TO HIS MOTHER, FRANCES TAYLOR UPTON, PETWORTH, WEST SUSSEX, 16 SEPTEMBER 1832

William T. Upton and his brother Clifford seem to have sailed on different ships in 1832: William on the *Eveline* and Clifford with the Penfolds on the *Lord Melville.* The family paid an apprentice fee of £20 or £21 to William Penfold for Clifford on 6 April 1832, just before the ships left Portsmouth.[121]

SOURCE: *Emigration: Letters* (1833), 22–3; an edited extract was printed in the *Brighton Herald* in March 1833.

Andross Mills, Nelless Settlement,
September 16th. 1832.

DEAR MOTHER,

I arrived at Montreal on the 1st of June, where we stopt 1 week. From there we came up the country in Durham boats, and steam boats to York, where I stopt another

---

117 Italicized words here and below were not included in *Emigration: Extracts.*
118 "Kersey's" in *Emigration: Extracts.*
119 This message was significant since Ned Lucas and Charles Edwards, both "loose and runagate fellows," were suspected in July 1831 of setting fire to a barn, part of a stable, and a hayrick at Northlands, part of the premises of the rector of Petworth, Thomas Sockett* (WSRO, PHA 8618).
120 The 1831 edition of *Doyle's Hints* was the first; the second and third appeared in 1832 and 1834. Martin Doyle was a pseudonym for William Hickey.
121 WSRO, PHA 9015.

week, waiting for Clifford [his brother] with my box, as it was put into the wrong ship. When he came to York he had lost it, by its being misplaced in one of the boats. I was in a terrible way about it, but I thought it must be gone either to Hamilton, Kettle Creek, or left in the steam boat. I therefore started to Hamilton to look for it, and there found it in a storehouse. I was ill at Hamilton for a week; after which time, I was hired by the agent of the Canada Company, to go to a Mr. Mc'Kensey's, at Andross Mills, on the banks of the Grand River, Niagara District, where I now am. I get 12s.6d. per week, and board, and lodgings. I have been in my situation 9 weeks, and [with] what I have made by my wages; I am now worth £ . . . .

It is a beautiful country, and all young people may make money fast. If they could bring out £100. with them, they would be sure of making a fortune, if they were steady, in a few years. Young men with a wife, without family, is better off than a single man, as there are so many situations for them in gentlemen's families: the woman as house-keeper, and the man as in doors servant, where they get high wages. We have an Eng-lishman and his wife, living with Mr. Mc'Kensey, who has been in the country only 5 years; and is worth now, above £500, and was not worth 5s. when he first came. The mills I am living at are saw mills: we cut 10,000 feet of board per day. I wish Clifford had not been bound to Penfold, as they give money for boys, instead of taking it. I could have had an agreement drawn up at York for him to have had 300 dollars at the expiration of his 7 year's apprenticeship, to a carpenter. If you think of sending the other boys out, do not apprentice them, but send them to Hamilton to me. When you write, tell me [whether] you intend them to come or not: if you do, write again, and tell me, when they are to leave England, and I will meet them. I believe Penfold has taken some land near Guelph; but where, I do not know; so, if you have heard of Clif-ford, send me his address, when you write, which I hope will be as soon as you receive this; and tell me, how all the family are getting on at home. * * * *

I will send you some assistance in the spring, if nothing happens to me. Remem-ber me to all friends, particularly to Mr. and Mrs. J.***, not forgetting G. Hawkins: tell him he will hear more of me by G. Warren. Direct to me, Wm. Upton, County of Wentworth, Gore District, to be left at the Post Office, Hamilton, till called for. Give my love to all my brothers and sisters. Tell them that can write, to write to me soon: and, if they cannot get a living in England, to come to Canada, where they may soon get an independency.

I remain, my dear mother,
Your affectionate son.
WM. T. UPTON.

N.B. Tell me whether the times are better in England, since the Reform Bill has passed.

OTHER LETTERS: *See also* letter 26.

William Upton's brothers, Frederick, Egbert, and Percival, sailed on the *British Tar* in 1834. Frederick had served in the British navy for six and a half years, on his last ship as a stew-ard. He served Superintendent James Marr Brydone* in this capacity on the *British Tar* and volunteered to go on with him from Hamilton to assist in conducting the convoy of emigrants and wagons bound for Woodstock. Brydone took charge of the first contingent and Upton followed with a second group which travelled more slowly, arriving in Woodstock on the third day after leaving Hamilton. The three Upton brothers from the *British Tar* found work in Hamilton where William was already settled.

In 1835, Frances Upton herself sailed on the *Burrell*, taking her youngest son, Albert, and Frederick's fiancée, Hannah Palmer. They heard on their arrival in Hamilton that William had died a few months earlier, in March. Frederick and Hannah were married in Hamilton on 15 July 1835. By 1851 Frederick was harbourmaster in Toronto Township and there were eight children in the family.

■ 28

ELIAS ELLIOT, NEAR FORT GEORGE,[122] UPPER CANADA, TO HIS
BROTHER RICHARD ELLIOTT, SUTTON, WEST SUSSEX,
24 SEPTEMBER 1832

Elias Elliot was sent by the parish of Sutton in 1832, one of thirteen emigrants: five men, two women, and six children under age fourteen.

SOURCE: *Emigration: Letters* (1833), 26

September 24th 1832.

DEAR BROTHER,

I now take this opportunity of writing a few lines to you, for to let you know that I am well at present, hoping that when these few lines reach you, they will find you all in good health. We had a safe arrival across the ocean, landing at Quebec, thence up the river St. Lawrence, to Fort George,[122] where there were several of us stopt, about twelve miles back in the country, where we expect to tarry for the winter. And the rest have gone on about a hundred miles further, into the country. We have all had the fever ague that stopped here, but we are getting over it. I am getting quite right again, and I feel happy that I ever took the resolution to leave my native home, [for] a country far easier to get an easy, and honest living. I feel happy to think that we are here. Dear brother, we have not landed among thieves, nor robbers, but among christian people, where we can hear the gospel preached. I have nothing to regret, only that my friends were not here and as well suited with the country as I am. I wished to [be] remembered to Mr. Charman, and Hannah Charman. I feel a desire to see you all, and I think, if I have my health a few years, to pay you all a visit. Dear brother, I wished to be remembered to James Francis, and Mary White, and to my brother Daniel: I should feel happy if he were here with me now. Joseph Leggett is well, and wishes to be remembered to all his enquiring friends; and William Moore and his brother[123] is well. Brother, I don't know but I shall come

---

122 Located on the Niagara River, at Niagara-on-the-Lake.
123 Probably Edward Moore

to see you next fall, or the spring following. We left Richard Neal[124] at Little York. Brother, I hope you will improve the first opportunity of writing to me, as I have nothing more to write at present, but I remain, your affectionate brother,

ELIAS ELLIOTT.

To

MR. RICHARD ELLIOTT,
Sutton.

Richard Neal (letter 5), writing in July, reported that Elliot and Joseph Leggett, another man from Sutton, had promised to write to him. He had not heard from them but a third person had told him they were both working for the same man. In this letter, Elliot implied that he would be moving on in the spring. He seems, however, to be the Elias Elliott recorded in nearby Louth Township during the 1870s. The census of 1871 recorded an Englishman of this name, and an appropriate age, as a labourer with an English-born wife and six children. He was probably the owner of 96 acres of lot 18 concession 4 and probably the same Elias Elliott who died in Louth Township in 1878, aged 64, born in Sussex. We have not found any further record of Joseph Leggett in the area.

■ 29

MARTIN MARTIN, GUELPH, UPPER CANADA, TO MR SPARKS, FELPHAM, WEST SUSSEX, 24 SEPTEMBER 1832

Martin Martin was a carpenter who emigrated from Felpham, West Sussex, with his wife, Fanny Hollis, and six children, Frances, Richard, Louisa, William, Marion, and Esther.[125] According to family sources, he had been a pauper boy. One source said that he was born in Brighton. After only three months in the country, he gave a very thorough summary of his findings and impressions.

Fanny's brother, John Hollis, his wife, Jane, and their four children, John, Jane, Mary, and Sarah, also emigrated in 1832. A tailor, he settled in Thornhill.

SOURCE: *Emigration: Letters* (1833), 27–30; a long extract was printed in the *Brighton Herald* on 16 March 1833. The letter was also printed with minor changes in punctuation and style in *Emigration: Extracts* and by J. Phillips as a four-page pamphlet.

SIR,

You have, no doubt, expected to hear from me long before this time, but the reason I did not send sooner was that I had not seen enough of the country. To give you a short description of our voyage, we had a very rough one, continually winds blowing against us, so much that before we arrived to the banks of Newfoundland, we was above 700 miles too far to the south: and on the 2nd May, about half past

124 Original annotation: "He afterwards went to Dundas." See Neal's letter 5.
125 Four of their ten children born between 1811 and 1827 died before they left England.

4 o'clock in the morning, all at a sudden crush, the whole of the births on the lar-board side of the ship fell down; but no one happened to be hurt, but caused a con-fusion in the ship. This brought the captain to his senses; for he never laid the ship to, till this happened. But from this time, till the next morning, she was laid to, under a close reefed main top sail. But I hope what I have said about this will not dishearten any one from crossing the Atlantic, for I assure you, that I had so much confidence in a ship, that I would give the preference to travelling by water.

We was just 8 weeks from Portsmouth harbour, till we arrived at Montreal, which town is a large, flourishing, and very fast improving place; immense quantities of mer-chandise exported and imported, to and from this place. We staid there a few days; and then we started in the boat for York in Upper Canada, which we reached in about a week. This passage is a very difficult one, on account of the different rapids[126] in the river St. Lawrence: and whoever should come this way to America, I should advise them to travel by land from Montreal to Prescot, and wait there for their luggage; and from Prescot to York, there is steam boats, which will take luggage and passen-gers in about a day and a half. But this land travelling will not do for a poor person. The expence from Montreal to York, for one passenger, which is 450 miles, 19s.7d.

I arrived at York, the capital of Upper Canada, and was much surprised to see such a large town. The trade, and the many great shops of all sorts, is quite equal to Chich-ester, but the town I think is larger, some of the streets 2½ miles in length. There I stayed about a week, but did not like to settle there. I again set off in the steam boat for Hamilton, which is quite at the west end of Lake Ontario; and this is also a flour-ishing place, but a small town. Here you will see the farmers come riding in and out of this place, with as good breed of horses as in England. I staid here six weeks, trav-elling by land from Hamilton to Guelph, where I may perhaps settle; and I made it my business, as I went along, to make all enquiries about land, and its price and qual-ity, &c.&c. I went through several different townships, and the farther I got to the west, the better is the land. You may always judge the depth of mould where the trees are blown down. The present price of land in the township of Guelph is 3½ dollars, or 17s.6d. currency; in the township of Nicholl, is 3 dollars, and better land; in Wool-wich township, 4 dollars; in the township of Garrafraxa, is 2 dollars an acre; in the township of Wilmot, is 2½ dollars an acre; and in the Huron Tract is 1½ dollars.

This land is not so difficult to clear as you might suppose; as the trees all grow up very straight, and there is no bushes grow amongst the trees. The way of clear-ing the land is, they chop, with a very superior sort of axe, off the tree, about 3 feet

---

126 Original annotation; "With respect to the Rapids, See Advertisement from Canadian Courant in the Appendix." The appendix to *Letters from Sussex Emigrants* (1833) contains a report from the Mon-treal *Canadian Courant* on 29 September 1832 on the launching of the steamer *Iroquois*, which will "ply between the head of the Long Sault [rapids] and the village of Prescot," a stretch of the St Lawrence previously "considered unnavigable by steam." This note was omitted in *Emigration: Extracts.*

above ground; as soon as 'tis dry, they burn it; leaving the stumps still standing on the land, which will rot in about 6 years; and when they have burnt the brush wood, and the logs they spread the ashes. They sow the land with wheat, and the produce is from 25 to 35 bushels, which now sells for a dollar a bushel; and this first crop generally clears the whole expence of buying, and clearing, and burning. Suppose you say the purchase to be 3 dollars; the price of chopping, burning, and fencing, is, from 12, to 14 dollars; so that your land will not cost you, when chopped, more than four pounds per acre; and when harvest comes, there is your money again. Here is no expence of ploughing the land the first nor the 2nd. year; they harrow the seed in for the first 2 crops. Oxen is mostly used for this, because they are more steady than horses. A yoke of oxen is worth about 50 to 70 dollars; a horse about 100 dollars; a cow about 20 dollars. Mutton and beef is about 3½d. per lb. English money, butter 7½, sugar the same; tea is 4s. per lb. Whisky is mostly the drink. The whole of the taxes for 100 acres is about a dollar a year, but no poor's rates, nor any other taxes to a farmer. Here is all sorts of farming implements suitable to the country, from the spade to thrashing machine, as well as the fanning ditto. And for about 5 gallons of whisky you can get a loghouse built; this is done by, what they call, a "*Logging Bee*." When you have cut your logs, you invite all your neighbours round you, to a certain distance, and they will raise the house in one day, rearing high, but must roof it yourself, which is covered with shingle, and when finished, looks like slate; all this you can get on your own land.

Mr. Heming has bought 365 acres in this township, with some improvements on it, and he is next week a going to have his "*Logging Bee*," and I am just a going to finish the inside of his house, such as sashes and doors.[127] And you would be surprised to see what a quantity of respectable people daily, a coming and settling, some buying 700, some 1000 acres of land. Here is a tailor, that come from Oxfordshire, that brought £600. He has 600 acres of land, 60 cleared, he has a capital framed barn, and a good dwelling house, and out houses; in short, his premises are very complete.

Here is plenty of work for labourers, at about a dollar a day; and will be while there is so many settlers coming out: and no labouring man need to be afraid to come. When he gets to York, Captain Fitzgibbon will forward them to Hamilton. But almost all the labourers get farms, and I have never seen any body in distress since I have been in the country. There is a great many people that goes to the United States, but that is not so well for a farmer, the taxes are so much higher. I believe I may say as much as 8 to 1 more than it is here; but for all that, provisions is much cheaper, there than here. But for a mechanic, the United States is the best, but not so healthy. The climate here in the summer is much the same as in England, but more fine weather. We had about a fortnight's very hot weather, in the beginning of July, but not but what we could work as well as you could, in the old country. But the

127 See letter 30.

winter, from what I can learn from people that has experienced it, is colder, but not at all unpleasant.

I am very much deceived in the idea that I had formed about this country, as you may travel from the east to the west part of the province in tolerable good roads, through towns and villages, and not at all lonesome. Whoever comes to this country, should pack all their luggage, that is not wanting in the voyage, in casks. And it is best for poor people to board themselves, and to bring plenty of flour; it will be better than so many biscuits; and plenty of potatoes. Since I have been writing of this, I have heard about the quality of the land in the Huron Tract, which is exceedingly good at 1½ dollars per acre. I think of going to see it.

Mr. Huntly, the bearer of this, is waiting for it. I shall write to you again before the winter is over, and let you know what it is. I would thank you to make it known, that I intend to fulfil my promise in writing to several friends in Felpham, and its neighbourhood. Here is certainly a good chance for farmers and labourers. The cholera has been very bad in several parts, this summer, but it is a little better now. So no more at present, from your obedient servant,

M. MARTIN.

Guelph, Upper Canada,
    North America.

Sept. 24th. 1832.

P.S. Mr. Huntly, the bearer of this, has bought a good deal of land in this township, and is going to England to take to a wife.[128] I think that this conveyance will do away with the idea of letters being intercepted: I know there is several people silly enough to think, that all letters are broken up; there is no such thing. Tom Sturt gave me a piece of foreign money, to put under his seal, when I wrote to him, for the purpose; please to tell him, I will shortly write to him, and Tate, at Bognor. I forgot to mention a chance for labourers. As soon as they arrive at York, that is the capital, they may have 50 acres of land at Lake Simcoe, 6 years to pay for it; nothing the first 3 years, and sent to the place free of expense, and the price of the land is only a dollar per acre.[129]

Martin Martin was definitely in the village of Elora in 1837 and in 1836 or 1837 built and operated the first tavern there for a few years before selling it to return to farming. (He had at one time been landlord of the Fox at Felpham, West Sussex.) In 1839, he had cleared 10 of his 100 acres on lot 5 concession 2 in Woolwich Township; a year later, he had cleared 10

---

128 In 1834, Mr Huntly returned with his wife on the *British Tar* and settled in Guelph (Brydone, *Narrative of a Voyage*, 14, 42).

129 Another area, in addition to the Adelaide settlement, where the government was placing indigent emigrants. Sockett printed a notice concerning employment for emigrants on a road being opened from Kempenfelt Bay to the Township of Sunnidale under the supervision of crown lands agent Francis Hewson (*Emigration Letters* [1833], 70).

more. Martin also worked for extended periods on farms belonging to others, though whether as a farm hand or a carpenter is not clear.

In August 1850, Martin obtained the patent for the northeast ½ lot 11 concession 3 Pilkington Township, which he sold five years later to William Martin (presumably his son). Fanny had died some time before 1851. When he wrote a will in December 1871, his residence was given as Woolwich. He died in Pilkington Township, 30 March 1872.

■ 30

EDWARD FRANCIS HEMING (HEMMING), NYTON FARM, NEAR GUELPH, UPPER CANADA, TO HIS MOTHER, ANNA MARIA (PAYNE) HEMMING, [BOGNOR, WEST SUSSEX], 25 SEPTEMBER 1832

Edward Francis Heming's home farm was on lot 8 concession 6.

SOURCE: *Emigration: Letters* (1833), 30

September 25th. 1832.
Nyton Farm.

MY DEAR MOTHER,

Since my last letter I have been so engaged, getting in my harvest, &c. &c. that I have hardly known which way to turn myself. I have bought 134 more acres of land, with 30 in crop, and a loghouse to put Chase[130] into. I have now 367 acres in all. The last lot is only 3½ miles from Guelph, on the same road as my first purchase. Emigration has so greatly increased this year that, before this letter reaches you, all the land within 8 miles of Guelph will be sold. It is, in my opinion, a most beautiful country, and excellent land. I am going to build a good loghouse, to get into before the winter sets in. My stock at present consists of 1 yoke of cattle, 10 pigs, 1 cow and calf, 1 pony, Neptune, and another dog, 1 cat, and 30 fowls, including hens and chickens. My land is paid for, excepting the 100 acres bought of the Canada Company. The improved land sells for much more than we conceived in England: quite rough land sells for 17s.6d. per acre, if at all in a desirable situation. I have not been up to Lake Huron; therefore I can only speak from report, but am told, land, of the best quality, sells for 11s.6d. per acre.

OTHER LETTERS: *see also* letter 1 and 6.

According to family tradition, Heming and Eliza Sarah Jones were married upon the completion of his log house. The Hemings had seven children between January 1835 and 1850, but in December 1850, Heming – a widower – returned to England with three of the chil-

---

130 Original annotation: "A labourer who went out with Mr. Heming." William Chase was from Pagham, a short distance along the coast from Bognor, and he brought his wife Lucy (Gregory) and two very young children. His £5 deposit with the Petworth Emigration Committee was paid by a Mr Goddard. Chase stayed with Heming into 1833. He moved to St Catharines some time before 1835 – long enough to be described as "still" living there in January 1835 by Joseph Webb (99).

dren. The three oldest boys and the infant born that September remained with the Jones family in Guelph. His second son, Charles, took over the farm in Canada. Walter, one of the three children who went with him to England, returned to Canada and lived near Owen Sound. Heming himself never returned. He died at no. 2 "Canada Villas," in Bognor on 19 August 1892 at the age of 82.

In 1834, Heming was assessed for about 370 acres in Guelph Township, an assessment probably made before he purchased two additional lots. Edward Longley (104) wrote that he had worked for Heming for six weeks in the summer of 1835 and reported that he had declined Heming's offer to work his farm on shares. In 1835, Heming sold some of his land to the Paynes, relatives in England. In 1836, he arranged to have Southdown and Leicester sheep sent from England. A year later, he was assessed for 467 acres and only one adult male was reported in the census return for his farm.

31
REBECCA LONGHURST, LITTLE YORK, UPPER CANADA, TO MRS WELLER, HER MOTHER, COLD HARBOUR, DORKING, SURREY, 4 OCTOBER 1832

George Longhurst and Rebecca (Weller) Longhurst, from the parish of Capel, Surrey, sailed on the *Eveline* in 1832 with their infant daughter, Christiana.[131] They were part of a larger family group since George's parents, Joseph and Sarah (Hosmer or Osmer) Longhurst, and his brothers and sisters emigrated at the same time. The Longhurst families were sponsored by Thomas Broadwood, a member of the piano-manufacturing family.

SOURCE: *Letters from Dorking*, 25-7

October 4, 1832, Little York.

DEAR MOTHER,

I write these few lines hoping to find you in good health, as thank God it leaves us at present. George has been very ill with the fever and ague, is the reason I did not write to you before, but he is quite well now. Dear mother we arrived at Little York just 12 weeks from the time we left Capel, father and mother and the younger brothers and sisters are living 20 miles from us, but they are quite well. Charles and [his?] Mother is living with us and they are quite well. I saw Mrs. Chantler in July, she and her children was all well then, but her husband died in coming up the river Lawrence.[132]

Dear mother you will want to know a little about our passage. We had but very little wind till the 1st of May, and then it was very awful for a few hours, and we all wished ourselves on land, and the next day the wind was so much against us, that we lashed the helm and let the ship go where the wind might blow her, for they

131 Both George and Rebecca signed the marriage register with a mark.
132 Sophia Chantler, her husband Nathaniel, and their children emigrated in 1832, but not on a Petworth Emigration Committee ship. See Chantler letters 165–173.

could steer her no longer. But we met with no further accident than a few of the berths fell down. Little Hester[133] died on the salt water, and that was all that died in our ship. We were out of all necessary provisions in less than three weeks, but we had beef and biscuit enough to last us all the way.

Dear mother, we like the country very well, and we have all plenty of work. George and Charles has built two houses, and they have got a driving shade [shed] 50 feet square, and a genteel cottage to build this winter. And if George has his health this winter we shall be able to purchase a hundred acres of land in the spring, which we have already looked out. Dear mother, we like Canada too well to come to England to live again, but if God spares us we shall see you as soon as we can work our land so as to pay our passage, but we will send you another letter before then. Dear mother, Mrs. Chantler told me you fretted yourself very much about me, which I was very sorry to hear, for I am much better off than I ever should have been if I had stayed in England. I shall be glad to hear from you all as soon as possible; give my love to all my brothers and sisters, and to all friends.

Dear mother, I shall hope for a long letter as soon as possible, to George Longhurst, at Thomas Montgomary's Tavern in Dundas Street, in the Township of Little York, Upper Canada, North America. Dear mother, I must conclude with my love to you, ever to remain your dutiful daughter Rebecca Longhurst. I had almost forgot to say any thing about my little Christiana, but she is quite well and almost runs alone.

OTHER LETTERS: 32

In England, George was said to be a fellmonger, a dealer in animal skins and hides, but Rebecca's letter suggests that he had also worked as a carpenter. By 1850, George and Rebecca had had eight sons and another daughter and they were leasing W½ lot 5 concession 1 Mulmur Township in Simcoe County. George died there about 1865. Rebecca died years later in 1888 in Watt Township, Muskoka District, where she probably lived with Christiana.

■ 32

REBECCA LONGHURST, TOWNSHIP OF LITTLE YORK, UPPER CANADA, TO ROBERT SWAN, [4 OCTOBER 1832]

SOURCE: *Letters from Dorking*, 27

Mr. ROBERT SWAN.

SIR,

You were kind enough to say you would forward our letters to any part of England, therefore we should be glad if you would send this to Mrs. Weller, at John Edward's, Cold Harbour, Dorking, Surrey. Sir, we can say but little about the country in this letter, as we have been here so short time, but the climate is much the

---

133 George's youngest sister, an infant.

same as England, but vegetables quite as good, but fruit is not so fine, clothing is nearly as cheap as in England, all except flannel, and that is very dear. The Cholera Morbus has been very bad in York, but we are in hopes it is abated. Now I remain your humble servant,

R. LONGHURST.

OTHER LETTERS: 31
Original annotation: "(Written across where there are marks of sealing wax.) 'I have dropped some sealing wax as I promised you.'"

■ 33

GEORGE SCOTT, TRAFALGAR TOWNSHIP, UPPER CANADA, TO JAMES AND MARY SCOTT, HIS FATHER AND MOTHER, [DORKING, SURREY], 6 OCTOBER 1832

George Scott was a single labourer sent by the Dorking Society with his younger brother, John. At the time of writing, Scott was 27 years old and John 21. The ages listed for single men sent by Dorking ranged from 17 to 40.

SOURCE: *Letters from Dorking*, 24–5
Copy of a letter from George Scott, dated Trafalgar, district of Gore Head off Lake Ontario, Upper Canada, 6th Oct. 1832.

DEAR FATHER and MOTHER,

This comes with my kind love to you, hoping to find you in good health, as leaves me at present thank God for it. Me and John[134] my brother is now living about half a mile from each other, and likes the country very well, so far a great deal better than we expected at first, and James Rose[135] is living about a mile from me and likes [it] very well; he sends his love to father and mother, and all friends; and for two ****** they were well when they left me and **** ***** he is with them, I expect they are in New York prison at present for breaking open stores, but the truth I don't know as yet.[136] Please to send me word whether John Sturt is at home or not.[137]

We arrived safe but had a very long and rough passage of eight weeks and three days to Quebec, but instead of my being sorry and sick, I had a great deal of fun on the passage. You must give my love to James Murnick, and Mr. Steadman, wife and

134 Original annotation: "John Scott, aged 20"
135 Rose was also from Dorking and emigrated in 1832.
136 In his "Address to the Inhabitants to Dorking," introducing his *Letters from Dorking*, Charles Barclay writes: "The only case of failure which has come to my knowledge is that of an individual, who narrowly escaped transportation for life at the Assizes for this County, in the Spring of 1832; who, upon his arrival in Upper Canada, broke open a store, and was committed to prison in the town of York, upon his liberation worked his passage home, and is now in confinement in Guildford Goal [sic] for disorderly conduct."
137 Sturt paid for himself to emigrate in 1832 from Dorking.

family, and if he thinks of coming, I think this country would suit him very well, for Bricklayers has from 1 dollar to 2 dollars a day and plenty of work in the season. If Steadman should come out I wish he would be so kind as to fetch me a wife out with him, and if not give my love to my little girl; give my love to my brothers and sisters, and all friends, and you must excuse me for not writing before as I was not settled, and I hope my father and mother is more reconciled than they were. I hope if any emigrants is coming they will be aware of liquor, for it is so very cheap a coming up the country.

So no more if we are never spared to meet again in this world, may we meet again in heaven, for Jesus' sake, so no more at present,

From your affectionate Son,
GEORGE SCOTT.

■ 34

CORNELIUS COSENS, WATERLOO TOWNSHIP, UPPER CANADA, TO JOHN BARTLETT, DORKING, SURREY, 7 OCTOBER 1832

Cornelius Cosens (or Cosins) was single, 20 years old, and identified as the son of Charles Cosens, "the late occupier of Redland Farm," when the family emigrated in 1832. Charles Cosens Sr, aged 59, and his wife, Ann (Goodchild) Cosens, 43, brought eleven children, ranging in age from 5 to 21.[138] In addition, two married children also emigrated, son Charles Cosens Jr and his wife, Ann (Miller), and daughter Jane and her husband William Tilt. John Bartlett, the recipient of this letter, was a blacksmith and may have been Cornelius's former employer.

SOURCE: *Letters from Dorking*, 14–15

SIR,   October 7, 1832.

According to promise I write to you at last. I should have wrote before but I had not any chance. I have had plenty of work since I have been here. I hired with a Dutchman[139] the first month, 12 dollars and my provision. I live in a Dutch settlement in the township of Waterloo, 700 miles up the country. I have not worked at Blacksmithing not yet. I can earn plenty of money here at any work. Sometimes I can earn a dollar a day and my board. I like this country very much; it's a far better place than old England. There is fine land here full of timber, the finest I ever saw. Some of the trees is 250 feet in length. This country is improving very fast. It wants people to come here with money; they will do some good here. You may buy land very cheap here. Pray tell some of the Dorking gentlemen to come out with the next they sends out of Dorking. We was used very bad in coming over the seas. ******* *****[140] got into the cabin along with the captain and the steward and they used us very badly.

138 The oldest was Hester, followed by Cornelius, Thomas, Mary, Elizabeth, Caroline, Nathaniel, Francis William, Ann, John, and Jesse.
139 German
140 Probably Christopher Abel, the superintendent sent by the Dorking Emigration Society.

We did not have the things that was put aboard for us. We had a long passage; we were nine weeks on the seas but we all got safe to land at last.

The Cholera has been very bad here. There is thousands died but it's got better now. There is a great many people come out this year with money. The people that means to come here, they better come as soon as they can, for the land gets higher every year. It's of no use for poor men to come here with young families, for they find a great deal of trouble to get the children up the country; young men and women does best here. It's no use to bring much luggage, you will find it a good deal of trouble to you. You can buy every description here and as cheap as you can in England. Please to tell Mr. Marsh that Mary[141] has got a situation as soon as she got here. She is living with an English gentleman in the town of Guelph, 12 miles from where I live. No more from me at present.

CORNELIUS COSINS.

P.S. Some people in England think that letters are opened, but there is no such thing. If a man land here with two hundred pounds, he can do wonders.

OTHER LETTERS: 66, 141

■ 35

WILLIAM PANNELL, LONDON DISTRICT, UPPER CANADA, TO HIS FATHER AND MOTHER, WILLIAM AND JANE PANNELL, KIRDFORD, WEST SUSSEX, 14 OCTOBER 1832

William Pannell from Kirdford was one of the single men who settled and stayed in Adelaide Township.

SOURCE: *Emigration: Letters* (1833), 31–2

October 14th. 1832.

DEAR FATHER AND MOTHER,

I have wrote these few lines to you, [hoping] to find you in good health, as it leaves [me] at present. I have been very poorly, with fever ague. I had it for 5 weeks, but it has left for 5 weeks. I like the country very well at present, and I get plenty of work; . . . I get about 3s.6d. per day, and my board. And I do not get the highest wages at first; and there is plenty of work for them that comes. But I did not find it as them told us, by a good deal;[142] but I am working at carpenter's work, at present; but I [shall] have a few jobs at wheel making, in about a month's time. And I have got 100 acres of land; and I have 2 dollars an acre to pay for it; and I have six years to pay it in; but half to pay at 3 years hence; and it is very good land; but it is

---

141 Original annotation: "Mary Cosins, aged 18, the sister of the writer, and late in the service of Mr. R. Marsh, Draper."

142 Original annotation: "Meaning that he did not find so much work at his own business, (a wheelwright) as he expected; and this may be accounted for, by his having gone into a part of the country, where wheels are not yet much used."

very full of timber; and it is very large timber; and there is a great deal of white oak; and red oak; and white oak is very tough; and there is white ash; and sugar maple: that is, what they get sugar out of. And we have plenty of game in America; plenty of deer, and turkeys, pheasants, partridges, and black squirrels, and red squirrels. And there is all sorts of wild animals, a great many bears and wolves, but they will not meddle with any body. They will run away from you, as fast as they can: but the bear, if set by a dog after them, they will run up trees. And there is the finest river in America, as I ever saw; and there is [the] finest waterfall at Niagara. It falls for 100 feet down; and is about ¾ mile wide. It is near Chippewa.

And the Cholera has been very bad in America, but it is all done. And old Mr. Rapley is dead.[143] William Haslett is dead too.[144] And if any one comes to this country, they should not bring any axes; for they will not do for cutting down trees; but hand bills[145] are very good.

Desire to remember me to all my acquaintances: and I should like to hear from all; and when you write, I should like to hear from John Baker, and Henry Hellyer, and Benjamin Barns, and remember [me] to James Mitchenor, and James Hellyer. And, when you write to me, direct the letter to me, at Mr. Moulton's, London District, in Upper Canada: I should be near that place. There is a great many fish in the rivers; but we had a long voyage over sea. We were 8 weeks going from Portsmouth, to Montreal. Quebec is about 450 miles nearer England; but we are about 700 miles from Quebec; and from Montreal, 250; York, 150 miles, up the Country.

WM. PANNELL.

Jane Smart died with cholera, at Prescot.[146] William Baker is with me, when I write this letter. Thomas Thomas is very well, and family. James Thomas, they are all very well.[147] Benjamin Bachelor[148] is very well. William Baker desires [to be] remembered to his father and mother, and all the family; but he should like to see his brother Thomas over here next summer. I should like an answer back, as soon as you can write. William Baker should have an answer from his friends. Tell them to direct a letter to the same place. I should like to see some Kirdford people over; but I will not persuade them, but it is a great deal better than England. Every one that comes out has got 100 acres of land, at 2 dollars an acre. It is as good land as any in England; but, if any body comes out, they should bring out some lucern seed, bent seed, tares.[149] There are all sorts of grain, but them. If any body comes out, they should

143 James Rapley, aged 51, of Wisborough Green, West Sussex, died of ague contracted on the voyage (WSRO, MP 1031).
144 William Haslett, from Kirdford, "died of a bilious fever, he laid ill only a fortnight." See letter 60.
145 Bill or billhook, a sickle-shaped tool.
146 Jane Smart was William Baker's sister; see letters 40 and 44 from her husband Henry Smart.
147 Two brothers from Kirdford. See 37.
148 Bachelor also was from Kirdford.
149 Lucern, or alfalfa, a clover-like fodder plant; bent, a stiff-stemmed grass; tare, a vetch used for fodder.

not lay it[150] out in England, for they can get cloathing very near as cheap. We have not any singing birds in this country, but the toads and frogs mount the trees, and sing very delightfully. There is no rubber,[151] to sharpen scythes, in this country. So no more, from your affectionate son,

WM. PANNELL.

In January 1833, William Pannell married Mary Holden, who also had emigrated from Kirdford to Adelaide with her family (see letter 47).[152] Mary Holden died in 1850, and on 6 May the following year he married a second time, to Mary Marshall, who also had children from a first marriage. At the time of the 1851 census they were living with four of his children and two of hers on E ½ lot 22 concession 3 Adelaide. He remained in the Adelaide settlement until his death in 1882.

■ 36

JOHN ALLEN TRIBE, SOUTHWOLD TOWNSHIP, UPPER CANADA, TO GEORGE FIELDER, HAMBLETON HOUSE, GODALMING, SURREY, 14 OCTOBER 1832

John Allen Tribe was sent by the parish of Chiddingfold, Surrey, with his brother, James, and uncle, Thomas Tribe. (Other Tribes who emigrated with the Petworth committee came from Lurgashall, West Sussex, just across the county border.)

SOURCE: *Emigration: Letters* (1833), 32-4

Township of Southwold, London District,
Upper Canada, October 14th. 1832.

DEAR FRIEND,

* * * We lost our passage from Coburg, 250 miles, to where I am now. My brother was in the schooner, and my box, or else I would not gone up so far: so I, and my uncle, and two more, came up by land, walking through the woods; finding all kind of wild animals. We slept in the woods, two nights; we made a large fire, to keep the wild bears from us. The place that the vessel was going was to Kettle Creek, Upper Canada. We are all about the country. I know not where any of them that came with us is, but my brother and uncle: some is one place, and some is another.

But I am in a good place now; I get £20. a year, and every thing found me but clothes. My brother gets £15 a year, and every thing but clothes found him. My uncle gets 60 dollars a year, and every thing found him but clothes. Eatables is very cheap

150 Original annotation: "Meaning money."
151 A shaped stone for sharpening tools: "I left him sharpening his swop-hook with a soft sandstone rubber which had lain in the long grass at the foot of a gate-post carefully cradled in a piece of dry sacking" (Bob Copper in conversation with George Attrill of Stopham, West Sussex, c. 1955, Bob Copper, *Songs and Southern Breezes, Country Folk and Country Ways* [London: Heinemann 1973]).
152 They were married by an Anglican minister, but their children were baptized as Wesleyan Methodists and Pannell was buried in the Mt Zion Old Methodist Cemetery.

in this country, and labour is dear. You have heard the price of it before, so I did not send the price. Give my love to Charles Parkins, and let him see this letter. Charles, I have sent you a few lines, to tell you, that a shoemaker is a good trade in this country. Leather is about as cheap as it is England, but not so good; a shoemaker may earn a dollar and half a day, if he will work. And I wish all the young men that is in Chiddingfold was here in Canada, for there is a good living for every one that comes here; not as I will persuade any one to come here, but if any of them comes, I should like to see them. For the most trouble is coming over here, and up the country, for there is great trouble and fatigue. A carpenter, and a blacksmith, and a shoemaker are three good trades in this country. Clothes is very dear; cotton and calico is the dearest. The living is very good in this country: there is plenty of whisky, brandy, rum, and gin, and all very cheap. I can get a pint of brandy for two shillings, York;[153] a pint of whisky for one shilling, York. York money is not like yours; one shilling, English; is two shillings, York, all but one penny.

This is a fine country, and a free country; you can go where you like here, and no one to hinder you; shoot anything as you see, of wild fowl. And there is plenty [of] deer, there is a great many of them. James is very sick at present, with the ague. Every one that come into this country have it, but I have not had it yet. There is no church within ten miles of us, now; but we have got a place of worship to go to. It is a log house, and there they keep school for boys, and girls. Where I live is about a mile from the Lake Erie, past Talbot [Talbot Mills (Selborne)].

Give my love to my aunt and uncle, give my love to Mr. Elliot, and to Mr. White and Mrs. White. Give my love to Harriet Jones, and to Mary Ann White. Give my love to Mr. Sadler, and tell him that it was the best thing he could do for me, when he sent me here to Canada, North America.[154] Give my love to all that is in the house, both young and old; and give my love to William Fielder, and all your children. Thomas Tribe is very well; and he sends his love to his sister, and he will send her a letter in a short time. I should send more, but had not time; so no more at present, from your humble servant,

JOHN ALLEN TRIBE.

If you sends, please to direct for me, John Tribe, Township of Southwold, London District, Upper Canada.

To be left at the Post Office, Port Stanley, till called for.

For Mr. George Fielder,
Hambleton House,
Hambleton, Godalming, Surrey,
England.

---

153 Eight shillings New York currency equals one dollar. By the 1830s it was not much used in Upper Canada.

154 James Sadler, of Hambleton House, Chiddingfold, Surrey, was a local landowner.

John and his uncle must have walked from Cobourg to York (Toronto) and on to Kettle Creek with John Stedman (see letter 18). In 1839, Tribe married Unis Ward at Malahide in the Talbot settlement. In the 1851 census, John and Eunice were still in Malahide, and were listed as Baptists with four children, living on ten acres of lot 8 concession 6; his occupation was given as teacher. We do not know the fate of James, whom he followed to the western end of the province, but the Tribe name occurs occasionally in parts of Elgin County and London/North Dorchester.

■ 37
ANN THOMAS, WATERLOO TOWNSHIP, UPPER CANADA, TO HER FATHER, THOMAS PUTTOCK, STROUD GREEN, KIRDFORD, WEST SUSSEX, 15 OCTOBER 1832

Ann (Puttock) Thomas[155] and her husband, Edmund Thomas, a farm labourer, emigrated from Strood Green, Kirdford, sailing on the *Lord Melville* with their four children. Another son was born on board ship. Ann's sister, Sarah Puttock, went with them.

Edmund's brothers, Thomas and James, were also sent by Kirdford. With Thomas Thomas was his wife, Elizabeth (Durrant or Deront), and two children, Rhoda and David. Baptized in 1795, Thomas was the oldest of the three and had served as a private soldier in the 5th Regiment of Foot from 5 April 1814 until 2 March 1817. He was described in his army discharge papers as "under size, 5'2¼", dark brown hair and brown eyes" (UCLP T21/5). James, who was two years younger than Edmund, emigrated with his wife Mary (Bell) and two children, Henry and William. Both James and Thomas went to the Adelaide settlement.

SOURCE: *Emigration: Letters* (1833), 34–5

October 15th. 1832.

MY DEAR FATHER,

I write these few lines to you, hoping to find you in good health, as, thank God, it leaves us at present. We had a very long voyage over. We were 9 weeks on the seas. We landed the 7th of June. We were tossed about very much indeed. The 3rd of May we all thought of being lost; the births all fell down, from one end of the ship to the other. And I was not well after that till I was confined, and that was the 3rd of June. I got about again quite as soon as I could expect. It is a fine boy, and goes on well.

I am happy to tell you, that America is quite as good as we expected to find it. Edmund has had plenty of work, ever since we have been here. We have no reason to repent leaving England at present, and I hope we never shall. He has earned 3s.9d. a day, and his board, and sometimes not so much. Give my love and Sarah's [her sister] to my brothers and sisters. Sarah is about 30 miles from me, in service, and is doing very well. Give Edmund's love to his father and mother, and all. Thomas [Thomas]

---

155 Both Ann and Edmund signed the marriage register with a mark.

and James [Thomas] are about 100 miles [off] they are all well, and send their love to all. If Thomas and William [her brothers] should come out next spring, it is Sarah's and my wish for you to come with them, as I think we should [be able] to help support you here. The worst of it will be getting over. Edmund's brothers has got 100 acres of land each. We might have 100 acres, if we liked to go where it is; but we don't like to leave the place where we are, at present. The cholera has been very bad indeed in this country, but thank God, not one of us has had it. Henry Smart's wife is dead; and both his children. She was confined the same night that I was. Please to thank Mr. Greetham* for his kindness to us, and I hope he will do the same for you, if you should come.

We have had a very fine summer, but hotter than in England, and they say the winter is much colder. But there is one great comfort here: we have as much wood as we like to burn. If you should come, you had better send us a letter on, when you get to York, for us to meet you. Please to answer this, on the first opportunity, as I should very much like to hear from you. I have no more to say, at present. I remain your affectionate daughter,

ANN THOMAS.

Addressed.

 Thomas Puttock,

  Stroud Green, Kirdford, near Petworth, Sussex.

   England.

Direct to me, Waterloo Township, Gore District, Upper Canada.

———————

Ann and Sarah's father, Thomas Puttock, emigrated in 1833: "64 years old, and held his journey as well as any of the young people" (see letter 82 from Edward Bristow). In 1834, Ann and Edmund were in Woolwich Township, west of the Grand River, with oxen and cattle on their farm, and evidently only one daughter at home. Three years later they had two acres under cultivation on the south part of lot 86 German Company Tract and a much larger family: two males and one female over 16 and five males and two females under 16. They still had seven children living with them in 1851, of whom at least two seem to have been born in Canada.

Thomas and James were still in the Adelaide settlement in 1837. Roswell Mount* had located Thomas Thomas on E ½ lot 18 concession 4 SER in 1832. He received this lot as a military grant in 1837 when William M. Johnston sent a certificate to Toronto attesting to his military service and stating that he had performed his settlement duties: clearing and chopping five acres and chopping the full width of the concession road. Children of Thomas Thomas married in the Adelaide area.

■ 38

JAMES RAPSON, GALT, UPPER CANADA, TO PHILIP RAPSON, LODSWORTH, SUSSEX, 16 OCTOBER 1832

By the time James wrote this letter to his father in October 1832, the Rapsons were sharing a house with Sarah's sister Jane Penfold and her family and were about 300 yards away from the house occupied by Henry Tribe (either Sarah's father or her brother Henry). See letter 50, written by Jesse Penfold, and 54, written by Henry and Charlotte Tribe.

SOURCE: *Emigration: Letters* (1833), 35–7

Galt, Dumfries, Gore.
October 16th. 1832.

DEAR FATHER,

(The first part relates only to the voyage and progress up the country; which is described in other letters.) * * * * * And now I shall tell you all that I know about the country. The place where we are, is most like Lodsworth,[156] of any in the province, as I have been in. We had, in the middle of August, a very severe frost; the ice at Guelph, was ½ an inch thick: and killed the produce of the country. That is 14 miles from us; and, in the Huron Tract, the frost have been far more severe, than in any other part of the province. Until the middle of August, very dry; and more hot than in England; it dried up the Oats: very good crop of wheat; it killed the Indian corn, potatoes, and pumpkins, and cucumbers; and the vines. The produce is wheat, oats, Indian corn, rye, winter barley, peas, very fine. Potatoes, and pumpkins grow in the fields, 4 feet 8 in. round, and cucumbers with them, and melons; good cabbage, but very backward; no beans; plenty of dwarf, and french beans; fine crop of apples at Hamilton, and Dundas, at 7½d. per bushel. We are 20 miles from Dundas; 25 miles from Hamilton. I must say, that I think that we should have half died, if it had not been for the pigeons; we shot 30 of a day: one man shot 55 at 5 times; and he pitched a net, and caught 599 at one draw; here is plenty of pheasants; of rabbits; and ducks; and geese; deer; foxes; wolves; and bears; which come into our ground: they have killed a hog, and got it over a fence, 7ft. high, and 5 pigs. Here is squirrels, from the size of a mouse, to a rabbit, numbers of them. I will now tell you, who is dead. Henry Gogger, E. Luff, J. Kingshott, 1 child of his, Mrs. Morley, their youngest child, Mrs. Capelain, and 5 of her children, B. Chalwin, George, and Henry Lander, Mrs. Adsett, and 1 child, and many more:[157] so the Lord hath thinned us out. The cholera have raged very much, in Quebec, and Montreal, and York, and swept off thousands; and it followed us all along up the river, about a day behind us; and it have been all around us, but not within 2 or 3 miles of where we live: so we have cause for gratitude.

I must say, that little James Penfold have been to work a month, and earned enough, to find us all in flour, a month, and his own board; 16 of us. I have been to lime burning, and we took 2 houses to finish: had 24 dollars. I have ½ a dollar a day, and board; but Jesse Penfold, a dollar. Plenty of work; but the people live in a different way to what we have been used to; but, they live well; the people have never seen a pitsaw[158]; and, when I talk about sawing, they laugh at me; and I can buy inch boards, at the mill, for 1s.7¼d. per hundred; better boards than ever I saw in England. I wish you would see what the merchants would give me if I get 6000 feet of

---

156 Original annotation: "A village near Petworth."

157 Henry Groggin (Gogger), Joseph Kingshott, Sarah Morley and her son Thomas, Edward Luff, Jane Capelain, Robert Chalwin, and George and Henry Lander were all from Lurgashall. Sarah Adsett and her daughter Harriett were from Northchapel, an adjoining parish.

158 A large, two-handled saw: the lower of the two men working a pit-saw stood in a pit.

our pine, hewed, and towed in a raft, to Montreal. Our ground is within 300 yards of [the] grand river: we have 47 acres, and timber, 200 feet long, 4 feet through. We have a good house up, and I have 2 good cows: and seems, if [it] please God, as if we should do well. Tell Robert Tribe that his mother says she would go a thousand miles to meet him. We are all well, except Henry, he is poorly: tell him, all is well. I shall expect some, or all, of my brothers, next spring; I wish they were all as well off as I am. I wish you to go to Mr. Chrippes*, and the Rev. Mr. Sockett*, and tell them, that I return them many thanks, and Lord Egremont*, for his kind benevolence, with Esq. Yaldwyn*. Tell them, that I hope and pray; not that the Lord would give Canada, but make them meet for the heavenly Canaan.
Believe [me] to [be] your loving son,

JAMES RAPSON.

* * * * Here is a Scotch presbyterian minister, who preaches in a grist mill, which is crowded very much; but it is not what I have been used to. Charlotte [their eldest daughter, aged 15] is with us, and will be until Sarah gets up stairs. She might have a dollar a week. The children are all well; and are grown very much; and are often running out, to see if they can see any of you coming: sometimes they say, Here comes grandfather! or, Here comes grandmother! Indeed we want you, [in] many ways: we want you to make cider; as there is nothing to drink, but whisky. We want a malt mill, very much, as here is no such thing in the province. Remember me to all my brothers, and sisters. Sarah's love to all, and tell Rhoda that she will look for her, next spring. God bless you all.

OTHER LETTERS: 2, 12, 76, 115. See also John Capling's and Thomas Adsett's letters, 21, 22, 49, 71.
James's sister, Rhoda, did come the next spring with her husband, George Thair; both James and Rhoda wrote describing their reunion (letters 76 and 78).

■ 39
HUMPHREY AND CHARLOTTE COOPER, YORK, UPPER CANADA, TO MR J. TURNER, FITTLEWORTH, WEST SUSSEX, 25 OCTOBER 1832
Humphrey and Charlotte (Boswell) Cooper and three children were sent to Upper Canada by the parish of Tillington. Humphrey was cited as the father of an illegitimate son born in the Pulborough Poor House a couple of months after his marriage to Charlotte, who was herself illegitimate.[159]

SOURCE: *Emigration: Letters* (1833), 47–8

York, October 25th. 1832.
SIR,
[*In the beginning of the letter he states, that altho' he might have had land near Lake Simcoe, he found that he could not settle there comfortably, without more capital than he at present possesses.*]

159 Charlotte signed her name to the marriage register; Humphrey signed with a mark.

J.M.W.Turner, "The Cobbler's Home"
Courtesy Tate Gallery (cat. 258) c. 1825

＊ ＊ ＊ ＊ ＊ So I thought I had better give up all thoughts of land, and go on with shoemaking, which I think it is the most profitable trade here. The journeyman's wages are very high; if you put out the best top boots to make, they are £1.5s. making; wellington boots 14s;[160] and common boots that people wear, instead of high shoes, are 7s.6d. making; women's low shoes 8s. I have got more work than I can do myself. I am happy to tell you, I never had a better chance in my life to do well. We have got a nice house, built up on purpose for us; it belongs to an English gentleman. The rent is high; we pay £20. a year, and a favor to get it; as if you go for a single room, you will not get one under 7s.6d. per week. We have had every thing to buy for our use, which have been a great expence. We now have got a stove to

---

160 Top boots had a high top, often of a different colour to give the appearance of being turned down. Unlike modern Wellingtons, Wellington boots, named after the Duke, covered the knee.

get, for the winter; as the cold is so great, every body haves them in their houses. The cold weather lasted 7 months last winter, and snow laid on the ground 13 weeks.[161] The people say it is nice dry weather, though cold: flannel must not be spared. * * *

In respect to trades, journeyman's wages are very high, from 5 to 7s. per day, and the meanest laborers have 3s.9d. per day. Meat is reasonable, beef 3½ per lb., good stakes 5d., hog-meat 3½ per lb., bullocks heart 7½d. Spirits and wines are as dear here, at the inns, as in England; but if you go to a store house, you can get a quart of port wine for 15d., a quart of whiskey for 9d., brandy 1s.6d. and 2s. per quart. I have a great wish for William [his son] to come over, as soon as an opportunity serves, as I know that here is a good chance for him to do well, if he have a mind to it, or any other person that is industrious, that comes over. My wife, and myself and family, wishing you health and happiness, and to all enquiring friends. I hope, some time, I shall have an opportunity of coming to England, to see my friends.

I am &c.

HUMPHREY & C. COOPER.

P.S. I am sorry there is so many people that comes out of England, gives the country a bad name; it is that sort of people that wont work, and give their mind up to drink and idleness.

————————

The Coopers' son William evidently emigrated in 1833, since the Tillington vestry records noted on 28 March 1833 that he was to get £3 and be taken to Portsmouth (WSRO, PAR 197/12/1). An H. Cooper, boot and shoe maker, appears in the Toronto directory for 1833-34 at 8 Market Lane. In 1836, Lydia Hilton wrote that Humphrey Cooper was keeping a tavern in Toronto (*see* letter 119).

■ **40**

HENRY SMART, ANCASTER, UPPER CANADA, TO JOHN AND SARAH BAKER, HIS FATHER- AND MOTHER-IN-LAW, KIRDFORD, WEST SUSSEX, 5 NOVEMBER 1832

Henry Smart, a labourer, and his wife, Jane (Baker), emigrated with their son, Frederick, a toddler. The parish records of Kirdford show that Smart had married Jane in December 1829[162] and received some parish aid the following year. Frederick was baptized in Wisborough Green in January 1831, but it was Kirdford that sent the family to Upper Canada.

Henry's letters to three different people, and the notes he sent from William Baker (his brother-in-law) and Frank Nash (a cousin), were described as all on the same sheet of paper (40–42, 44–45), and they were sent to James Napper of Kirdford.

————————

161 Original annotation: "The snow does not lie so long by 3 weeks or a month at Adelaide, Niagara, or Guelph."

162 Henry signed the marriage register with a mark; Jane signed her name.

SOURCE: *Emigration: Letters* (1833), 37–9

Ancaster, (5th November,
and I hope you will remember,[163] *1832.)*

DEAR FATHER AND MOTHER[164]

I hope this will find you all well, as it leaves me at present. I am sorry I had to send you such bad news, the last time I wrote to you, or the last time you heard from me, by the way of Penfold. We had a very long passage; and a very rough one. My wife was sea sick three weeks, but she was no worse, after that, than she was before she left home. But she was unwell, at times, the same as she was at home. Frederick was but very little sea sick, but was taken with a very bad fever, and, for three days, I did not expect he would live, from one hour to another, but he recovered, a little. We had a bad squall, one morning, which threw us, and our berths out, altogether; but we received no damage, any more than a fright.

When we crossed the banks of Newfoundland, Jane was taken very ill, and we expected she would be confined; but she passed on, for about a week, much the same as she was when she was confined before. We sailed into Quebec harbour, the 10th of June, about 8 o'clock, and she was confined, about 12 o'clock, while the ship was at anchor, thank God for it! the ship being still. She was confined with a girl, but it did not live, but four and twenty hours, and we left it in the harbour where it was born. Jane was better than we could expect; we was in the ship four days after she was confined, before we landed in Montreal. There she was taken out, and put into a large house, and she got her strength, very fast, for I got her every thing she could wish for. We staid there four days. When she wanted to go out for a walk, I took her out, and she was very much pleased with the country, and said, she was not sorry that she had left England.

Then we started up the river, in a Durham boat; the weather was very fine; we was in the boat, 7 days, when we landed at Prescot. The weather was fine till the last day. We stopped at Prescot, three days, and she was very pert,[165] and getting on very well; but the third, I was very sick; but she was as pert, as ever. I saw her till about noon. She was very cheerful that day, and laughed, and said, that I should die first. But, about four o'clock, she was taken very ill; and said, if there was not an alteration soon, she should soon be gone; and I went and got a doctor to her, but he

---

163 Please to remember the fifth of November
Gunpowder, treason and plot.
I see no reason why gunpowder treason,
Should ever be forgot.

Guy Fawkes day, 5 November, commemorates the plot by Fawkes and others to blow up the Houses of Parliament in 1605. It is remembered in parts of England with torchlight processions, bonfires, fireworks, and the burning of an effigy of Guy Fawkes.

164 Sockett noted in the original published version: "[i.e. his late wife's father and mother.]"

165 Original annotation: "In Sussex this word means lively, cheerful."

gave a very poor account of her. As soon as he see her, the doctor said, he would do all he could for her, and I believe he did. All the rest went out in the steam boat, the next morning at 6 o'clock; and left me, all alone. I applied to 3 doctors, but two of them said it was no use. They would not pay any attention at all to her. But the other did, and done all he could for her. He told me, it was no use; she had the cholera; and she could not live, but a few hours. She was insensible at that time; but, at 10 o'clock, she came to her senses, and talked to me for an hour. She told me she was going; she told me not to fret for her; she should be better off than I was. But all she wanted of me was to promise her, to take as good care of her child, as I had done of her; which I promised her I would. So she died that day, at 12 o'clock, the 25th June. She died; and never mentioned father, mother, sister, nor brother, any more than her sister, Martha, who was dead and gone, and who said, on her death bed, that she would soon be after her; and she was going. She wanted to be buried in the way her sister was, but I could not bury her so well as I could wish. About an hour before she died, Frederick was taken very ill, with the bowel complaint, and died 8 days after. I was obliged to go on to Hamilton, on account of the cholera, and I was still very ill then; but still, I kept about. I buried my wife at Prescot; and my child, at Hamilton. I am as much as two hundred miles from where I buried my wife; but my child, I can look upon every week. I kept about all this time, but after, I was confined to my bed for a week, which the doctors said was brought on me by trouble.

Remember me to Charles and Ann Street. Tell Ann, I am very sorry her words are come so true, as she told me before I was married. Jane told me not to reflect upon her dying out of England; she did not think she died any the sooner for that. Tell Ann Street that I am very sorry, I have heard the worst account of her brother, of any, that is come out. I shall see him, next week; and I shall give it him.[166] He is as much as a hundred miles from me, but I am a going up next week, and I shall see him. So no more from me at present,

HENRY SMART.

OTHER LETTERS: 43, 45, 55–58, 60.
Ann Thomas, who was on the *Lord Melville* with the Smarts, knew that the Smart's baby had died but believed that it had been on 3 June, the same date as her own (37).

■ 41
WILLIAM BAKER, [ANCASTER, UPPER CANADA], TO HIS MOTHER, SARAH BAKER, KIRDFORD, WEST SUSSEX, [5 NOVEMBER 1832]
William Baker was a brother of Jane (Baker) Smart, who died of cholera soon after arriving in Upper Canada (see letters 40, 44–45, 55–60 from Henry Smart).

---

166 That is, he will be angry with Ann Street's brother, Charles Newman. There is better news in letter 60.

SOURCE: *Emigration: Letters* (1833), 41

On the same sheet, from William Baker, late of Kirdford.

DEAR MOTHER,

    * * * I am very sorry to do as I have done. When I left Montreal, I left my sister [Jane Smart] very ill; little thought but I should see her again. Not but what I am satisfied, she was done as well by, as if I was there; for Henry attended to her, both night and day, while we was aboard the ship, and so he did afterwards to all account. I never saw my brother,[167] till three weeks ago; and then I had cut off one of my fingers, and very near another. I could not work, and I got out of money; and my sister troubled me: so I was determined to find him out, if I could. I travelled down to Ancaster, a hundred miles, and I begged my way, (though I never wanted any thing) for three days, and there I heard of him. He was very angry with me at first, but I owned myself in fault. I staid with him four days, and he relieved me with seven dollars. Then I started back up the country, and I will never leave him for so long a time any more. My fingers are got nearly well, and I shall soon be able to go to work; and I can do a great deal better here, than I can at home; and I should be very glad to have my brother Tom come out. So no more from me, at present.

Wm. BAKER.

Baker is unusual among Petworth emigrants for admitting to a rocky start in Upper Canada; his letters 65 and 92, written in 1833, showed that he was making up for lost time.

42

FRANK NASH, ANCASTER, UPPER CANADA, TO HIS MOTHER AND FATHER, [KIRDFORD, WEST SUSSEX], [5 NOVEMBER 1832]

Frank Nash was 17 years of age, a sawyer, and single, when he came to Upper Canada at the same time as his cousin Henry Smart. The Petworth Emigration Committee recorded receiving a down payment for William Nash and his wife at the same time as Frank.[168] William was 21 and also a sawyer.

SOURCE: *Emigration: Letters* (1833), 41

    Frank Nash, to his mother and father. He is well, and doing well; and, never means to come to England, any more; unless his cousin, Henry, does. He takes me as his friend, and tells me, he will do as I wants him to do, and he will do very well.

Direct to Henry Smart, Ancaster, Upper Canada, (and say) by the first packet ship, for New York.

---

167 He is referring to Henry Smart, his brother-in-law.
168 The down payment was for £8 for 4 passages; presumably another adult or two children under 14 were also in the party: WSRO, PHA 137.

■ **43**

HENRY SMART, ANCASTER, UPPER CANADA, TO JAMES AND CHARLES
RAPLEY, GOWNFIELD,[169] WEST SUSSEX, [5 NOVEMBER 1832]

SOURCE: *Emigration: Letters* (1833), 40

James and Charles Rapley, Gownfield, there, or elsewhere.

I have heard from your brother, William, but your father is no more.[170] He has
been dead about five weeks; but you need not fret about your younger brothers, and
sisters, for they will do better than you will, if you bides there. William is very steady;
and takes a father's part well, by what I have heard. I have not seen them, since they
have been in this country, yet; but I shall see them all, next week.

OTHER LETTERS: 40, 44–45, 55–60.

The recipients of this letter were two sons of James Rapley Sr who did not emigrate with
their widower father. (Their mother, Mary (Collins), had died at Wisborough Green in 1831.)
William was the oldest of James Rapley's sons in Canada.

See 135 for the letter of a different Charles Rapley who also reported on the children of
James Rapley in the Adelaide settlement.

■ **44**

HENRY SMART, ANCASTER, UPPER CANADA, TO JAMES NAPPER,
KIRDFORD, WEST SUSSEX, [5 NOVEMBER 1832]
Smart wrote this to the son of the man to whom all these letters were directed.

SOURCE: *Emigration: Letters* (1833), 39-40

JAMES NAPPER,[171]

This comes, with my kind love to you, and all the family. I hope this will find
you all in good health, as it leaves me at present. Remember me to all my brothers
and sisters, if you please, and to Charles Brockburn, and Mary Court, Gunshot;[172]
and to all enquiring friends at home; and tell them of my downfall; as they have heard
before. I don't repent of leaving England at all, because my wife did not; no more
would not you, if you was once to get here. I should be happy to see you here, and
Tom Baker, and sister Rhoda,[173] and her family. I don't persuade you to come, but
I should be glad to see them, for I know they would do much better here than there.

169 About a mile south of Kirdford.
170 James Rapley Sr, a widower, emigrated from Wisborough Green in 1832. He was under a doctor's
     care while the Petworth immigrants were camped in Lobo Township waiting to be assigned their
     lots, and he died in October of ague (a malarial type of fever) contracted on the voyage.
171 A James Napper also emigrated with the Petworth Committee from Pulborough in 1832, but he
     belonged to a different family of Nappers.
172 A farm at Wisborough Green, West Sussex.
173 William Baker's brother. Rhoda Smart was married to Thomas Whitington.

Ask my sister, Rhoda, if she will accept this little present, and tell her she must keep it till I see her again. If she don't come here, I intend to come to England, after a few years, if life lasts; but never more, not to stay. You need not dread the water; I don't at all. I should take a deal of pleasure on the water, had it not been for my ill luck. Look to that book, that you got of me, about the country,[174] for I fully agree with it. Tell Matthew Puttick, that he can keep three such families as he has got in this country, better than he can keep one there.[175] Tell David Smart, I saw Tom Mitchell, about a week ago. They are all well, and doing well; and Tom says; he never wants to come to England any more. If any of you comes out, don't buy a parcel of clothes to bring here. If you do, you will lose money by it. You can get them fully as cheap here. I would not advise you to bring out any thing, excepting blankets, and flannel. Why you think things are so dear, here, is: because, on account of the money; thirteen pence, of your money, is two shillings, here.

Write me an answer, as soon as you can, if you please, and let me know all the news you can, and how the cholera is there, for it has been very bad here. And let me know who talks of coming out, as well as you can. If you, or any of my relations, come out, I will do all I can for them, at first coming. They shall not want for a bed, nor for something to eat, when they once get to me. You need not be afraid of coming out here, on account of not getting a wife. You can get one, of any country, and any colour you like. You can come here, and go back again in a few years, a better man than ever your father was. If you are not here by the 5 July, I shall be gone from here, but my directions will be, at Mr Gurnett's, which you will see as you go up the town. At present Matthew Crooks Esq. Ancaster, Upper Canada.

OTHER LETTERS: 40, 43, 45, 55–58, 60.
The Crooks family were merchants and entrepreneurs. They owned a large amount of land in West Flamborough and their enterprises in Burlington Bay included milling and manufacturing complexes on Spencer Creek and the Speed River. Matthew Crooks might have employed Henry Smart in a number of ways, although Henry's letter written in March 1833 (55) suggests that he was working on a farm.

■ 45

HENRY SMART, ANCASTER, UPPER CANADA, TO THE REVEREND J.K. GREETHAM*, KIRDFORD, WEST SUSSEX, [5 NOVEMBER 1832]
J.K. Greetham, the vicar of Kirdford and an active proponent of emigration, may have had a part in copying and sending on letters sent by Henry Smart. He very probably gave copies to Sockett.

SOURCE: *Emigration: Letters* (1833), 41

---

174 Original annotation: "*Doyle's Hints to Emigrants.*"
175 Matthew Puttick, a labourer, had six children by November 1832; his wife was Mary Smart.

Mr. Greetham,

I am much obliged to you, for what you have done for me. I wanted to beg one more favor, if you please; that is, I shall be much obliged to you to take my register out and send it to me, if possibly you can.[176] You will find it in the church at Kirdford; but you want to look back, as much as nine and twenty years. I forgot to say before, as Wm. Haslett is dead; but he has been dead as much as three weeks. No more from your humble servant, at present,

HENRY SMART.

OTHER LETTERS: 40, 43–44, 55–60.

William Haslett was a young single man born in September 1808. His life seems to have been one of poverty. His parents had been sent with five-week-old William and his two young sisters from the parish of Whitley in Surrey back to Kirdford under a removal order. If they could prove that applicants for relief had a "settlement" in a different parish than their own, parish officers were entitled to send them back. Smart reported in 60 that Haslett died of a billious fever, possibly cholera.

■ 46

RICHARD NEAL, DUNDAS, UPPER CANADA, TO HIS FATHER AND MOTHER, WILLIAM AND ABIGAIL NEAL, [SUTTON, WEST SUSSEX], 18 NOVEMBER 1832

SOURCE: *Emigration: Letters* (1833), 42

Dundas, November 18th. 1832.

DEAR FATHER AND MOTHER,

* * * * * I have sent you a letter, in July; but I have not had any answer, yet; but I hope you will send me one, soon. Dear Friends, I hope, if any body is coming to America, you will give them my directions, and let them come to Dundas. I sent Edmund Harwood a letter, last sunday, by a man that is coming to England, and I hope, if you receive the letter you will go to Littlehampton, and so, his name is Reeves. I have not seen Joseph Leggatt, or Elias Elliott, since I left York, but I heard from them last week. They are getting on very well. I hear they have hired for twelve months, but I shall go and see them in the winter, when I cannot work. Charles Hilton is about 100 miles further up than I. He took 100 acres of land.

The 5th of November, my Master was buried, which I worked for ever since I have been in Canada. His name was Thomas Pope, from Northhamptonshire, England. He has been here 5 years: he left three children in England, when he came to America. He have, a fifty acres of land, and a house; it is all to be sold, and debts

176 Smart wants the Reverend Greetham to write out a copy of the entry of his baptism from the Kirdford parish register. These parish registers were the official register of baptisms, marriages, and burials in England before the introduction of the national General Register in July 1837.

paid, and the rest of the money sent to England, for the children. He owes me, about £15, but I expect to be paid, in two weeks. I have took his work. I have four men, to work for me, and I have work enough for two more, if I could get them. Brick-layers gets, 7s.6d. per day. I never seems contented here, as I was in England. I do not like Canada, so well as England, but in England, there is too many men; and here, there is not enough. There is more work than we can do here. There is a long winter here, and very cold, they tell me; but, if I live to next spring, I shall be able to tell you more about it. Here have been snow and frost, here, but it is mild now. I expect we shall not be able to work, more than 3 weeks longer. We have plenty of plastering to do.

Tell my brother William; if he feels inclined to come, here is plenty of work, and good wages: but I will not persuade any body, to come, without they like: but here is plenty to eat, and drink; and cheap. But there is a great many don't like this country, nor more do I, myself. But I can get plenty [of] work here, and I cannot in England, with it [is] altered since I was there. I can earn £2.5s. a week, English money, if I have my health. * *

I am your dutiful son,

RICHARD NEAL.

OTHER LETTERS: 5.

If 5 is the letter Neal says he wrote in July, it did arrive at its destination. This letter also arrived, although – to Sockett's great frustration – many letters miscarried when they were given to people on their way to England to deliver as best they could.

In June 1835, Richard Neal evidently started building "a series of one storey, solid brick, houses that are peculiar to Dundas, and are easily recognizable because he used the 'Flemish Bond' type of brick layering in the front walls of these houses."[177] This method of bonding alternates a regular horizontal brick with a tie brick, placed end first, to give a checkerboard effect.

■ 47

MARY HOLDEN, ADELAIDE TOWNSHIP, UPPER CANADA, TO SERGEANT HOLDEN, 2ND REGIMENT, TOWER HAMLETS MILITIA, LIGHT INFANTRY, LONDON, ENGLAND, [POSTMARK 21 NOVEMBER 1832]

Mary Holden was apparently the eldest child of Thomas Holden, a widower, who emigrated from Kirdford, West Sussex, with three other daughters and three sons between 16 and 5 years of age (Ann, Ruth, Harriet, James, Thomas, and Moses). The Holdens were part of the large group of emigrants who came to Adelaide Township from Kirdford. As the eldest girl, Mary was keeping house for her widowed father and three young boys. The youngest of the three girls who were out working was 12.

SOURCE: *Emigration: Letters* (1833), 43-4

177 T.R. Woodhouse, *The History of the Town of Dundas*, pt 2 of A series (Dundas, Ont.: Dundas Historical Society 1967), 16

A number of the houses built by Richard Neal, some using the typical Flemish-bond brickwork, were still standing in Dundas, Ontario, in the 1990s

DEAR BROTHER, – *When you are in Canada, fill this up, and send it to me; send all the news you can; say the truth, and nothing but the truth. Sarah Holden, Slinfold near Horsham, Sussex, England.*[178]

DEAR FRIENDS,

This comes with our kind love to you all, hoping to find you all in good health, as, thank God, it leaves us alive, and well at present. We were all very sea sick, and had a very long and rough voyage. On the 2nd of May, about half past 4 in the morning, the sea was very rough, and the ship was tossed, so that the berths, on our side, fell from one end of the ship to the other, but no one was hurt a great deal.[179] We were driven so much towards the north, we had very hard frosts and snow, and it was very cold, and we often thought that we should go to the bottom; but our heavenly father, that awful Protector of persons, brought us safe to land at last. We were six weeks getting to Quebec. We did not go a shore there; we landed at Montreal, and we were then towed up the river by [in] Durham boats to Prescot, and then in steam packets to York, and from York, 350 miles, in schooner vessels to Kettle Creek. And we were then carried in waggons up the country, 66 miles.

It was the 22nd of July, when we got to where we are settled.[180] Father has got 100 acres of land, and has to pay for it two dollars per acre, in six years time. Father thinks of getting in two acres of wheat this year. We have got a cow. Father gave 30 dollars for her. We expect to find very hard times this winter. We have ten miles to go for flour, and all our provisions, but I hope, please God will help us through it this winter. The Gentleman is going to have a log house put up for us. Ann, and Harriet, and Ruth, have got places 40 miles from us. Father says, he can see a good prospect of doing well after a few years. It is good land.

Father sends his kind love to all of you, and hopes that you will make up your minds, and take a good resolution and come here, for here is a good prospect of doing well, and getting a good living. Father says he would not come back to England again for no respects. Dear friends, if you should come, this is where I'll direct you to come to, Kettle Creek, the township of Adelaide. To Kettle Creek, and then to the township of Adelaide, in Upper Canada, as that is where we are. But you may understand that all the letters be all opened, before they go out of this Country, to see that there is not any falsehood sent; and if there is any thing in them, against the country, they are kept back. I hope you will be so kind as to send this letter, or write another and send to all our friends, and pray do send to poor mother's friends at Chiltington *William's letter*, and tell them in their letter, to write to poor aunt at Goring.[181] Please to write again as soon as you can. We have heard that the old ship that we came in, is drowned, and 5 were saved, and 10 drowned. We are 500 miles from Montreal.

So no more at present, God bless you all.

---

178 Sockett noted that "The heading was written on the paper, before it left England."
179 This reference to the berths' falling indicates the Holdens travelled on the *Lord Melville*.
180 July 22 was probably the date on which Thomas Holden took possession of his lot.
181 West Chiltington and Goring, West Sussex

[182]Dear friend,

we have enquired about the letters, to know the fact and truth about their being opened by the head gentlemen. So that we are sure now that they are not opened, until you receives them. Father have sowed 2 acres of wheat, and thinks of getting in one acre of potatoes, and one acre of Indian corn, in the spring, if please God. We have got a warm house now, thank God. We have been exposed to all weathers ever since we came out of the old ship, until the 20th of October: so I will leave you to guess, dear friends, what we have gone through. We did not enjoy our tea what you gave us, dear aunt, for the wet got through the chest, and wet it; and when we came to open it, behold it was all spoiled, the *strength* was gone, and stained some of our things. I hope you will excuse my bad writing. If any comes, which I hope you will, please to bring some dried yeast, for there is none here. We wet our flour, and bake it on the ashes. Poor father has been very ill: had the ague. I thought he would have died, but the Lord raised him up again, and is as well now as ever he was, thank God. So God bless you all.

I was obliged to open the letter again, to put in the right direction, that you should direct to us: To *Colonel Mount, Carradoc,* in Upper Canada: by so doing, it will be sure to come to us.

To Serjt. Holden,

Second Regt. Tower Hamlet Militia, Light Infantry,

London, England.

Postmark, Delaware, 21st. November.

A Mary Holden married William Pannell, both of Adelaide Township, just a couple of months after this letter was written, on 29 January 1833. See William's letter 35. Her father, Thomas Holden, married widow Ann Mann (née Downer), on 20 February 1837 in Adelaide, thereby marrying into a large Adelaide connection. Ann's letter 127 describes her experiences after emigrating in 1836 with her husband Samuel and nine of eleven surviving children. In May 1837 Thomas's daughter Ruth married Ann's son Thomas Mann. Although Thomas Holden died in Michigan in 1854, he was buried in the Mt Zion 4th Line cemetery in Adelaide. The Holden and Mann families were typical of many families in the area in the ease with which individuals moved back and forth across the border between Ontario and Michigan, whether to settle, to work for a period of time, or simply to visit.

■ 48

JOHN WORSFOLD, HAMILTON, UPPER CANADA, TO HIS FATHER AND MOTHER, DORKING, SURREY, 15 DECEMBER 1832

John Worsfold, a painter and decorator, emigrated from Dorking in 1832. He was one of only a few immigrant letter-writers with such skills.

---

182 Original annotation: "The latter part seems to have been added at a much later period."

A view of Hamilton, Upper Canada, from the Mountain
Attributed to Owen Staples, 1845?, Toronto Reference Library, T15382

SOURCE: *Letters from Dorking*, 35-8

Hamilton, North America,
December 15, 1832.

MY DEAR FATHER AND MOTHER,

I take pen in hand to write to you after so long an absense, but I hope this will find you in good health as this leaves me at present. With pleasure I have to inform you that I like this country better than I did at first, and I make not the least doubt but that I shall do much better than at home; we had many difficulties to undergo before we arrived in this place, but we all have prospects of doing well. Mr. [James] Harpur and J. Knight, and me have taken a farm and have got six acres of it cleared and sowed with wheat, and hopes to have 10 acres of other grain in the Spring, it is at Flambro East about 12 miles from Hamilton and 13 from the Gulphs, 8 from Dundas and 40 from York, and all the places have good markets. I am at present at work at the town of Hamilton and there I am treated as a gentleman for the art of graining and flatting[183] is not much known there, I get one pound a week English

183 Graining, painting to imitate the grain of wood or marble; flatting, a uniform undercoat of paint

money and board and lodging, I have every thing that I want; I may have beef steaks or other meat for breakfast and what I like to drink. But I think I shall start for myself next Summer and if I do I shall have 7s.6d. per day, which is the regular price that masters have for journeymen.

Tell John Fuller this is a fine country for him and his family, and if he chooses to come next year I will be bound that he will get on saving money fast, and if he comes tell him I should like him to go in partnership with me, and tell him to bring a badger's hair softner as I cannot get one, and diamonds are worth in this country 6 or 7 pounds.[184] It is much easier to start in business than at home, and every prospect for him as he is so good a workman; tell him that I am the head man and best work-man in the Upper Province, tell him if he comes he will do well.

I hope that you received the letters I sent you before; I have sent 3, one from Quebec, one from Montreal, and one from York, and I hope they cost you nothing as the Doctor promised to put them in the Dorking post or call and deliver them to Mr. Patching. The one sent from York I gave to a person who came out in the vessel with us and was going back again to fetch his family, after getting home for them; he promised to put it in the London post for me, and the one from Quebec I expect will cost you; I could not pay the post to England for you. I have not yet seen the *wild* Indians you told me of, but I have seen the Indians, but they are a dif-ferent kind of people to what you expect they are, a very good sort of people and bears a much better name than the wild men and are a very honest people. As for wild animals I have seen but few, there are some bears in the wild parts of it, and a few wolves, but they are very shy; there is plenty of deer, rabbits, pheasants, and pigeons to shoot at. It is a fine country to live in, for there is little danger of starv-ing, and the country appears generally pretty well settled. The Upper Province is a good deal like England; there is plenty of towns as good as at home, the town of Hamilton is as good as Dorking, and will be in a few years much better. And as it regards money I get money for labour and likewise for grain of all descriptions. Wheat is about 5s. per bushel, beer is the dearest article and 6d. per quart wine measure, but there is plenty to be bought. Mr. and Mrs. Williard[185] have been to see Mr. and Mrs. Harpur, and they are very comfortably situated, and I understand are doing pretty well, but I suppose you have seen the letter that they have sent. They are quite well and desires their kind regard to you and their love to Mrs. Wolgar, and hopes she is in good health. Edward Hunt has been with us, but went away to Prescot for a box that he left there, and we have not heard of him since, neither can trace any thing of him, which is now nearly six weeks since, and I am afraid something has

184 A paint brush and presumably a diamond for glass cutting.

185 William and Charlotte Willard, see letter 20. When the ship's captain refused to allow emigrants to land at Quebec, Charlotte Willard also gave a letter to the ship's doctor, although hers had a local destination. Charlotte wrote that Worsfold and Mr. Harper/Harpur had travelled to Hamilton by land, but she made no mention of a family with either man.

happened to him; if that is the case and I can obtain any information, I shall write to his mother, but not till then, I hope that nothing has happened to him; Prescot is 300 miles from Hamilton.

You know you used to talk of the rattle-snakes, but I do not fear them now, for I have killed two this summer; they are not so bad as is represented. You can get plenty of Hyson tea[186] at 3s.9d. per lb. English money, sugar 6d., butter 6d., and things generally much cheaper than in England. We have got a house built on our farm with two rooms up and two down and nearly all paid for; farming men gets 3s.4d. per day and in harvest 4s.10d. per day English money, good beef 2d. and 3d. per lb., and mutton 2d., pork 2½d., and flour 14s. and 15s. per hundred weight. Tell Mrs. Marden she had better come here and bring her wash tub with her, for it is a fine country for washing, it is as good as a trade. I wish you to give my Christian regard to Mr. and Mrs. Patching, and tell them I am comfortably settled in Hamilton, Upper Canada; I should like to see them but I must wait a few years first; give also my Christian regards to Mrs. Botting and family, and Charles Grinstead, and enquiring friends. Please to write to me soon and send me a long letter, and tell me all the news you can. Good bye, for I must write no further, but leave room for the direction.

So no more from your dutiful Son,

JOHN WORSFOLD.

Direct to me, Hamilton, Gore District, Upper Canada, North America. Hamilton Post-office.

Worsfold had been received into the Independent (Congregational) West Street Chapel in Dorking, in 1829. James and Sarah Harper, with whom he was farming in East Flamborough, had also been received into the Independent Chapel, where their two oldest children were baptized. James Harper acquired title to the 100-acre farm, located at lot 13 concession 8 of East Flamborough Township, from the Canada Company in 1838, and 50 acres were still in the Harper family until the mid 1980s. He gave his name to Harper's Corners, which was on his property on the road that divides East and West Flamborough.[187] Neither Harper nor J. Knight, the third person sharing the farm was on the list of emigrants sent by the parish of Dorking. Worsfield was living in Beverly Township in 1842 and evidently working as a painter. We have not traced him after that date.

---

186 Chinese green tea

187 Now lot 13 on the road between concessions 7 and 8 of East Flamborough and the junction of highway 6.

■ 49

THOMAS ADSETT, WATERLOO TOWNSHIP, GALT POST OFFICE, UPPER
CANADA, TO THE REVEREND ROBERT RIDSDALE, RECTOR,
NORTHCHAPEL, WEST SUSSEX, 21 DECEMBER 1832

SOURCE: *Emigration: Letters* (1833), 45–6

[Written on a sheet of paper, which Mr. Ridsdale had directed to himself, and given to the man when he went away.]

December 21st. 1832.

(In the early part he speaks of the voyage &c. and mentions the death of his wife and youngest child.)

* * * * My son Charles is with [me], and I am going to bind him to be a tanner, with the man I am now living with.[188] And my oldest daughter is in a very good place, and my other little girl is in another place, near the other, and will remain there, till they be able to do for themselves;[189] they are people that has no children of their own, and was very glad they could get them, from me: so that I shall have no more trouble, but go and see them, when I please; and if it had not been that I had lost my wife, I could have [been] more comfortable. I thank God, that my children has got two such good homes as they have, and I am a great deal contenter, than in England, and can make a good living. I can live better with working one day, than in England in seven, and there is a great many people living near me, that comes from the same place that I did.[190] And it is a very healthful place, and the climate good. The land is in middling way, for being good; and some raises very good crops. [*Here comes an account of produce and prices, much the same as in many others.*]

The people where we are, they are most Dutch,[191] and a great many English and Scotch. All people in this country that will work, may gain property very fast, with care, and industry. The country is increasing with ministers, and hearers very fast, and I think, the people in this country is seeking after religion more than in England, but they have more time, and enjoys more pleasure, than in England. There is little or no tax in Canada; but we can have the goodness of it, ourselves. We do not have to take a piece of dry bread, in our pockets, and go to our 6d. a day work here; but we go to eat with our master and mistress; and have the best that the world can afford of all kinds, and spirits, and ale on the table, every time we sit down to eat.[192] All the farmers that I see, is independent, and has plenty. And I wish that the poor people in England had the leavings of their tables, that goes to the dogs, and hogs;

---

188 Charles, aged six, was first apprenticed to a weaver "but the weaver started tavern keeping . . . and as I and my father were tea-totalers I could not stop with him." In November 1832, he started work for Mr Betchel, master tanner. He was apprenticed for 14 years, until he was 21; see 180.

189 Emma, aged seven, and Sarah, aged two and a half.

190 In letter 71 he mentions Jesse Penfold, James Rapson, and Benjamin Tribe.

191 German

192 Thomas was perhaps not always a teetotaller, despite his son's memories.

they live better than most of the farmers in England; that is, our dogs. I do not see any body going from door to door, like in England, that would be a disgrace to the country, and the people that is in it.

I must conclude, for I have not room on my sheet to write. I hope that you will be so kind as to send for my father [Thomas Adsett], or let him see it, if he is spared in the world; and tell my poor old father to send me a letter back, and direct for Thomas Adsett, Waterloo, Galt, Post Office, Halton.

Direct your letter to, province of Upper Canada, Halton County, Gore district, Galt post office.
    To the Rev. Robert Ridsdale,
        Northchapel, near Godalming, Surrey,
            England.

OTHER LETTERS: 22, 61–62, 72

1833

The Petworth Emigration Committee
have engaged CAPT. HALE, the author of "*Instructions
to Emigrants,*"to go out with their Party, in the Ship
ENGLAND, to sail from PORTSMOUTH, on *Wednesday the 24th. instant.*

On the arrival of the Emigrants at MONTREAL,
CAPT. HALE will proceed with them through the
Rideau Canal (avoiding entirely the Rapids of the
St. Lawrence,) into *Lake Ontario,* and land the
different Parties at YORK, or *any other Port* at the
head of that Lake, as may be wished.

CAPT. HALE sailed in the same Ship, *England,*
last Year, with Emigrants from *Wisborough Green,*
and conducted them from QUEBEC, up the *Canadian Lakes,* and a long journey over land to
NELSONVILLE, in the *United States,* where they
all arrived in good health.

*Capt. Hale's success on the occasion above mentioned,
and his long experience, and compleat acquaintance
with Canada, have induced the Committee to avail
themselves of his services, on the present occasion.*

The Committee have also the satisfaction to state, that the
SURGEON engaged, is a most respectable Person, a Member
of the College of Surgeons, London, and also of the Apothe-
cary's Company,

The space allowed to each individual, being much greater than before, the number of Passengers is necessarily limited; applications
should therefore be made to Mr. PHILLIPS, PRINTER, PETWORTH,
as soon as possible.

Five hundred weight of Luggage is allowed on *board Ship,* for each Person above 14 Years of Age,
and in proportion for those under that Age; but in proceeding up the Country, all above 1 cwt. must
be paid for.

The Passengers to be on board on MONDAY, *the* 22nd, *before 6 in the Evening, or not later
than NOON on* TUESDAY, *the* 23rd.

Petworth, April 8th. 1833.

PHILLIPS, PRINTER, PETWORTH.

Chronology for the Year 1833

12 April	Sockett was in Portsmouth seeing to the "fitting out" of the *England*.
25 April	The *England* sailed from Spithead
30 April	The *England* in Portland Roads (off the coast of Dorset)
1 May	The *England* put to sea and on 5 May passed the Lizard, the southern tip of Cornwall.
24-5 May	Hale reported having problems with turbulent emigrants.
4 June	Caroline Dearling reported sighting land.
16 June	The emigrants landed at Grosse Isle; they re-embarked the same day.
17 June	The *England* arrived at Quebec, departing the next day under tow.
20 June	The emigrants arrived at Montreal, where they stayed on the ship until the 22nd.
22-23 June	The emigrants were at Lachine, camped in McPherson's warehouse.
24 June	The emigrants embarked on Durham boats at 4:00 AM and were towed to Cascades.
24-26 June	Cascades to Cornwall in the rain, by Durham boat and by road.
28 June	The emigrants arrived at Prescott.
29 June	The emigrants left Prescott for Kingston on the steamer *United Kingdom*.
1 July	Arrived at Toronto from Kingston on the steamer *Great Britain*.
1-2 July	The schooner *Trafalgar* was chartered by the UC government to take emigrants to Plympton Township. The following men embarked with their families: J. Trusler, George Turner, J. Phillips, J. Randall, T. Elliot, and the Georges of Chichester.
3 July	A party made up of the families of William Rapson, George Thair, John Dearling, John White, and George Trussler embarked in a schooner for Dundas (Hale)/Hamilton (Thair).
5 July	James Rapson's family greeted the Rapsons, Thairs, and Dearlings at their home near Galt.
4-6 July	The party going to Plympton passed through the Welland Canal.
14 July	The *Trafalger* put the emigrants on shore at the Rapids, the landing place for the Indian Reserve on the St Clair River; Hale returned to Toronto with the schooner.
17 August	The *Canadian Emigrant*, a newspaper in Sandwich, Upper Canada, printed George Turner's accusations against Hale.
29 August	George Sockett, Sockett's eldest son, sailed from Gravesend for Canada on the *Ottawa* (he settled outside Guelph in Eramosa Township, near Edward Heming).
17 September	The Montreal *Gazette* published a long article bringing together evidence against Hale. (Sockett's response did not appear in this paper until 2 January 1834.)
17 October	The *Brighton Gazette* printed a story repeating allegations against Hale from Canadian papers.

Sources: WSRO, PHA 138, 140; WSRO, Goodwood MS 1469, 1470; AO Fonds 129, Canada Company, series A-6-2, vol. 2; Cameron and Maude, *Assisting Emigration to Upper Canada* (Montreal: McGill-Queen's University Press 2000); contemporary newspapers, letters.

PREVIOUS PAGE: Advertisement for the *England,* WSRO, Goodwood MS 1465, f.19

SHIP: *England*, A1, 320 tons
MASTER: Captain Lewis
SUPERINTENDENT: J.C. Hale

BACKGROUND

The officially recorded immigration to Quebec in 1833 was less than half that of 1832. In 1831 government had held out promise of legislation in support of parish emigration, and in 1832 sponsors still had hope of financial support; these hopes had died by 1833. Although Egremont* increased the number of parishes to which he gave support, the Petworth committee sent only one ship in 1833 and in each year thereafter. A majority of the passengers on the *England* were from West Sussex, but they were accompanied by emigrants from Wiltshire, the Isle of Wight, and Surrey.

The Petworth committee dispensed with the services of a broker, and instead supplied the ship themselves, hiring J.C. Hale, a former master of a merchant ship and a professional superintendent. It assigned berths in advance, and supplied emigrants with Hale's "Instructions," a useful booklet of practical information on what to bring, how to fit up a berth, and how to stow possessions so as to be as comfortable as possible. The committee also modified the rations to bring the emigrants' diet closer to the tastes of country people.

The wind was against the *England,* and the ship was obliged to stop and anchor twice before getting clear of the Isle of Wight, a rough beginning to the voyage during which the swell made almost every passenger seasick. On the ocean voyage, Hale admitted to some difficulty controlling a group of young men. In a quieter moment, Caroline Dearling told her parents that on 1 June "we all" went down to have tea with the sailors, "very civil men." Her letter is one of few accounts of contact with the crew who were usually kept as separate from the emigrants as possible.

FIRST SETTLEMENT

The first letters in this section were written by immigrants of 1832 and represent
the letters being received up to the time of departure of the *England*. Many of the
immigrants of 1833 left England hoping for land near their friends in the Adelaide
settlement and the same assistance. Their hopes were disappointed, despite the good
will of Lieutenant Governor Sir John Colborne*, a strong supporter of assisted immigration. Colborne's instructions from the Colonial Office were to cut back aid to
new immigrants. His own discretionary spending was curtailed as the entire surplus
in the Crown Lands Department had been swallowed up in coping with the cholera
epidemic of a year earlier. The best he could offer Petworth immigrants in 1833 was
land in Plympton Township with assistance for travelling and easy terms of purchase.
The government would not give rations or more than minimal help to get settled.
Although Plympton was not far west of Adelaide on the map, the newly named Egremont Road that led to it was virtually impassible and the emigrants faced another
long journey by water.

Many Petworth immigrants stopped in Toronto and a number found jobs there.
Our letters, however, are mainly from people who made their first settlement in towns
at the head of Lake Ontario or in the hinterland of Hamilton in the Gore District.
Before he left for Plympton, Hale made good the Petworth committee's promise to
pay the way of immigrants who chose to go to the Head of the Lake. The families
of William Rapson, George Thair, and John Dearling (who went to join James Rapson) and those of George Trussler and John White took advantage of this offer.

Relatively few immigrants remained with Hale to set out from Toronto for
Plympton on a schooner chartered by government. They sailed through the Welland
Canal (where a few of their number found work), and travelled the length of Lake
Erie to the Detroit River, Lake St Clair, and the St Clair River. Hale put no more
than forty immigrants, and perhaps fewer, ashore on the dock at the Indian Reserve
on the site of Sarnia.

A few of the Petworth immigrants sent to Plympton Township actually settled
there, but they were too few to form the nucleus of a community. Edmund Sharp's
letter (74) reflects the resentment of Hale and dissatisfaction with Plympton that motivated George Turner to take his complaints about Hale to the newspaper at Sandwich (Windsor). These were copied from paper to paper and carried through the
Canadas and across the ocean to Sussex and Egremont's Brighton house. Although
Turner's complaint against Hale received a great deal of newspaper attention (attracted
in large part by Egremont's name), it reflected the temporary hardship of the people involved, very real for them but not affecting the other immigrants.

The Noah's Ark, Lurgashall, West Sussex
Photograph: Patrick Burrows

■ 50

JESSE PENFOLD, GALT, UPPER CANADA, TO MR AND MRS NOAH HILL,[1]
NOAH'S ARK, LURGASHALL, SUSSEX, 1 JANUARY 1833

Jesse Penfold, a carpenter, went from Lurgashall with his wife, Jane Tribe, and their children,
including Matilda, Jesse, Caroline, and Harriett.[2] Jane was pregnant and gave birth to a girl
named Esther on board ship. James Rapson in letter 38 describes Jane's journey up the St
Lawrence soon after the birth of her baby; the "little James Penfold" mentioned in this letter was probably a child of this family.

SOURCE: *Emigration: Letters* (1833), Supplement, 1–2.

Galt, January 1st. 1833.

MR. AND MRS. HILL,

I have wrote this few lines to you, to inform you, that we are all in good health,
and we hopes to find you all the [same]. Now I am going to state [in] this letter,
about this country. We are settled in Galt township[3] at present, and we likes it; we
get plenty of work, and very well paid. We tradespeople get from 5s. to 7s.6d. per

---

1 Noah Hill was landlord of the public house, The Noah's Ark. Parish meetings, at which decisions
   were made to emigrate, were held at The Noah's Ark.
2 Jesse signed the marriage register when he and Jane were married, but she did not.
3 They were in fact in the village of Galt in Dumfries Township.

day; board, and lodging, and washing, if [we] wish it; and now I have 3 houses in hand, and expects 5 or 6 in the spring. I have a house in hand now, 42ft. by 26ft., besides the outbuildings. We square all the main timber, and find, at 10s. per hundred run. We can square 150 and from that, to 200; 2 of us: and we do not want to work every day. We oftentimes have a day's hunting, and sporting: we kills hares, rabbits, pheasants, turkies: and have killed 14 in a week. There is plenty of deer here; but we cannot get them with our shot guns; any person who comes to this country, tell them, to bring a good rifle. We gets plenty of ducks in the river; we lives about 16 rods from the river,[4] and close to the main road to Goderich.[5]

We have got 48 acres of land, very good, fine land, with scants of timber in it. We have cleared 1½ acre, sowed of wheat; and we have a very good house to live in, 30ft. by 20ft. loghouse: and we have got 2 cows; but out a keeping: but we can keep them in the woods, in the summer: if we had 10, we could keep them: we do not expect that we shall remain [in] this place, long, for here is not land enough for us all. So we think that we shall get some of the land cleared, and then sell it. It is a very good place for one family; for I myself are going to have 100 acres given to me from government, for my servitude. All soldiers, that have served 5 or 6 years in regular service, is entitled to 100 acres of land. He will have to pay £1.5s. for their trouble; then, he will have it free.

I will advise any person to come in this country that have been in the army; for it is better to have land give to them, than to pay for it. But if any person comes in this country, [they] will get a good living; but the more money they bring with them, the easier it will be for them. Land is very high in some townships. We gave £1. acre for our land; now, it is selling at £1.10s.; but we can buy land, 12s. per acre; but we lives betwixt two townships. There is 2 corn mills on each side of us, 1 mile to one and 2 miles to the other, and plenty of shops; and public houses; plenty of whisky, 2s.6d. gallon. Rum and brandy is a little dear. Beer and cider, 7½d. pot. Buy good beef for 2½d. lb; mutton, the same; venison, for 1d.; flour, 5s. per bushel. So we can live well if we work half our time, but I do not dare keep any holidays, for I have 3 or 4 people after me in a day for to go to work.

Now Mr. Hill. I hope that you will let my father [Jesse Penfold Sr] see this letter; and I will send another, before it is long. The names at the bottom must see this letter; [they] lives at Petworth.[6] I hope that I shall see some more of our country people here next spring, for it is a good country for any person to get a living, whether they are a trade or not. Tell Robert Tribe[7] to come; plenty of work, as soon

---

4 Grand River
5 The line to Goderich on Lake Huron was laid out in 1827 to give access to the Canada Company's lands known as the Huron Tract.
6 At the end of the letter Sockett noted: "The sheet of paper on which this letter was written had been prepared before Penfold went away, by having the signatures of 8 inhabitants of Petworth, at the bottom of it."
7 Robert was one of Jane's brothers who did not emigrate in 1832.

as he gets here, at 5s. a day, bed, and board; and send some carpenters, and some wheelers, and some blacksmiths. Tell Thomas Lickfold, here is a very good place for him if he like to come. Tell John White, here is plenty of work for him. Tell Mr. Ralph Chalwin, we wants he here very bad, but give my best respects to him; and I hope [he] is well. Now to include one and all; give my best respects to them, and tell them that we are all in good health, thanks be to God for it.

We returns many thanks to all gentlemen that assisted we here. Thank Mr. Yaldwyn*. Caroline gives her best respects to Biddy. Tell Robert to bring Bumper. William Barnes is dead: he died at York.[8] Charlotte Tribe[9] is married to [a] man worth money. Let father see this letter, as soon as you can, I hope he is well. Any person might see it after; be sure and carry it to Petworth. So we all joins in our love to Mrs. and Mr. Hill; and tell Noah Hill, if he likes to come, I will find him plenty work.

JESSE PENFOLD.

Answer this letter, and give us all the news you can.

(Received at Petworth 8 February [1833])

SEE LETTER 54, from Jane's parents, Henry and Charlotte Tribe.
While he still lived in Dumfries in 1833, Jesse was granted 100 acres for his service of 8 years, 156 days, as a private in the 57th Regiment. This grant was not located; perhaps he chose to stay in a settled area so that he could continue to work mainly as a carpenter. Census records for 1837 and 1840 show the family in Waterloo Township. In each of these years they had only one cow, and they did not have any land under cultivation at the time of the 1840 census. In 1837, Penfold was hiring out three breeding stallions to local farmers; in 1840 he no longer had the horses but he kept a yoke of oxen. On 21 December 1844, Jesse and James Penfold received the deed to the E½ lot 6, Beasley's New Survey, Waterloo Township, which Jesse had occupied at least since 1840 and probably before. James died in 1847 and this property was sold a year later. On 1 June 1849, Jesse bought 116 acres of lot 64 in the German Company tract in Woolwich Township. Jesse still lived in Woolwich at the age of 90 in 1871.

■ 51

STEPHEN GOATCHER, ADELAIDE TOWNSHIP, UPPER CANADA, TO HIS
WIFE, ELIZABETH BURCHILL, NASH, PULBOROUGH, WEST SUSSEX,
17 JANUARY 1833
These extracts from Stephen Goatcher's letter to his wife were printed by Sockett* as a pamphlet, which the latter sent to the Duke of Richmond.

SOURCE: Along with letter 54, this letter was part of a 4-page pamphlet printed by J. Phillips at Petworth; copy found at WSRO, Goodwood MS 1465, f.18, in Sockett to Richmond, 9 April 1833.

---

8   Letter 75 is an extract of one from Mary Barnes, widow of William.
9   See letter 19 from Charlotte (Tribe) Evans.

A Sussex barnyard
W. Backshell, eng., WSRO

Dear Wife,

* * * * *

If any of my old friends like to come out and live with me, I shall be glad of their Company to live with me to manage my dairy. J. Parker is going on his own land. If any person likes to live with me, I have plenty of land, I have 14 acres clear now, enough to keep me as long as I shall live.

* * * * *

If any person will come, send me word as soon as you can. I can tell you what things will be useful. Bring out as much clothing as you can of all sorts; and some for me, 2 pair of shoes from C. Greenfield, one pair high shoes; but put no iron on them. Bring plenty of clothes, it is 3 times dearer than in England:[10] bring a malt mill, that will be very handy: we can grow our own barley and make our malt. Bring out as many hops as you can, whatever you bring will be useful.

* * * * *

There are about 1500 souls come into this township this year. It is accounted as good land as any in Canada. I want to know how you are getting on. I am fearful the times are bad for farming in England. I do not have the overseers call on me for poor taxes[11] as you have; that is the beauty of the country. After we can get in our harvest we shall get things as we want. I should like to see all my old friends. I hope they are all well, I think if they were here they could do better than in England. Earthenware is very dear here, cups and saucers are, very. * * * * * J. Parker and his

---

10 Original annotation: "That is in Adelaide – In the Huron Tract clothes are not dear."
11 A tax levied on property owners in a parish for the relief of the poor.

wife and family are all well, and desired to be remembered to Father and Mother, and all friends: Charles Rapley and the children are all well, and desired to be remembered to his friends.[12]

    * * * * *

I shall leave it to you to look out some family to come to me. Labour is very high, a man will get ½ dollar a day and board. I hope if any person intends coming out, he will send me word as soon as he can. Bring some crop seed, there is no such thing here. Direct to me, the Township of Adelaide, Upper Canada, to be left at Col. Mount*'s, Delaware, that is the post office. I live about 10 miles from that place. Remember me to Mr. Challen, Comper, Jupp, Clement, Parry, brothers, and sisters, tell them I should be glad to smoke a pipe with them. Remember me to all my old friends wherever they be. I hope William, and wife and family are all well. T. Burchell, I should be happy to see you all again, but that I do not expect, except I should return after a few years. So now my dear wife, I will bid you and all my friends farewell. God bless you all.

    Upper Canada, N.A.

    January 17th. 1833.

OTHER LETTERS: 4

Although Goatcher was the original nominee for lot 20 concession 5 SER in Adelaide Township, he seems to have moved away from the Adelaide cluster of Petworth emigrants in search of a more suitable site for his dairy. His plans did not work out as envisioned here, and he returned to England. He may have been back in England by November 1833 (see letter 93 from John Holden). He certainly was by 1839 when he was said to occupy Upper Nash House, Pulborough.[13]

The family working for Goatcher, James Parker and his wife, Amy (Steer), stayed on in Adelaide; see letter 88.

■ **52**

WILLIAM COOPER, ADELAIDE TOWNSHIP, UPPER CANADA, TO HIS BROTHER, CHRISTOPHER COOPER, GRAFFHAM, NEAR PETWORTH, WEST SUSSEX, 5 FEBRUARY 1833

William Cooper wrote this enthusiastic letter early in 1833 urging his family to emigrate and refining the wish list of things to bring (see letter 8).

SOURCE: *No. 1 Continuation, 5-6*

DEAR BROTHER,

I received your kind and welcome letter, February the 2nd. If father and mother will come over, and keep house for me, I will keep them without work. £50. will

---

12 Charles Rapley, a widower from Wisborough Green West Sussex, sailed on the *Lord Melville* in 1832 with two young daughters.

13 WSRO, TDW/99, Pulborough Tithe Apportionment Book.

be of great service to buy stock, as there is plenty of keep in the woods; and I hope that you will all come, for I think you will do better here than in England, as you may all draw land. The men are employed on Government roads, at 12 [dollars] a month, and board; and boys half pay. One dollar [is] 4s.2d. England, 5s. our money, 8s. the States.[14]

Here is foxes, wolves and bears, but you need not be afraid of them, they will shy off. We shoot them, or catch them in steel traps. We have plenty of deer, rabbits, black squirrels, racoons, porcupines, ground hogs, that are all good for food; birds of prey, eagles, two kinds of hawks, ravens, owls, turkeys, ducks, large partridges, wood pigeons, plenty; some kind of birds leaves us in the winter. Wheat is one dollar a bushel with us, Indian corn the same, barley the same, pease the same. Our winter begins about Christmas; shortest days about 9 hours sun: we have somewhat more snow than in England, the night is colder, the days are clear and pleasant. We do not mind it; we have plenty of wood. I shall buy 100 loads of wood and faggots, and much more timber, this spring.

I have got in 2 acres of wheat, I shall [have] about 4 acres more for spring crop. We cut the small trees close, the big timber we cut about 2 feet high, and cut them in lengths, and draw them with oxen, to burn them; and sow our corn, and harrow it in with oxen. Our land is a sandy soil: we grow melons, cucumbers, [and] pumpkins, on our land. There is a river runs through Boxall's land, called Bear Creek. If any of you are coming out in the autumn, bring some apple pips, and pears, plum stones of all kinds, cherry stones, nectarines, peaches,[15] gooseberry and white currant seed: I am fearful the trees will perish on the road.

The Government have built houses for the married people, but not the single. I have built mine, a log-house, 16 feet by 22. I shall build a barn in the summer, 20 feet by 30. I hope that some of you will come and help build it. Bring me a hay cutter, a large steel trap, with a chain, and padlock; a rabbit trap or two, a saw, gimblets, 2 inch chisels, 1 pair of high shoes from Graffham; bring a load of sacks if you can, 12 pairs tan leather gloves, 4 lbs. rabbit net thread; bring a dog that will catch a deer; bring out bedding, as much as you can; blankets, and woollen, worsted stockings, and thread, needles and pins; buy some salt water soap, or pipe clay, to wash aboard ship. Tell Francis Smart if he comes, he will get from 1 dollar to 1½ dollar per day and board. Bring all your fire irons, and cooking utensils, knives, forks, metal plates, and panekins for your voyage; Bring my bottle; bring out 2 lbs. powder, 1 bag of shot, 1 bag No. 5. Guns are cheaper than in England.

I hope you will send me word who is a coming, as soon as you can. Bring garden seed of all sorts. Direct to me in the Township of Adelaide, Upper Canada, to

---

14 "Our money" is Halifax currency; the eight shillings refers to the conversion rate of New York currency.

15 Nectarines and peaches are unlikely to have been grown in a cottager's garden. It would seem that one of William's correspondents had access to the walled garden or hothouses of a large house.

Titus Ware Hibbert, "Log House in Orillia Township," (left) and "Shanty on the Coldwater Road, Orillia Township," 1844, Toronto Reference Library, T14376, T14396

be left at Colonel Mount⁺'s, in 4 Concession South, No. 21.[16] I now must conclude. I hope this will find father and mother in good health: my love to brothers and sisters, and all friends at Burton. Bring as many farthings and old halfpence as you can; no penny pieces, they [do] not go [for] more than 1 farthing. The Indians are very civil, but [do] not love work: they more love hunting. They will bring venison cheaper than we can kill it. Beef 4 dollars a hundred, pork 7 dollars. So no more from your dutiful son,

February 5th. 1833.   Wm. COOPER

For Mr. Christopher Cooper,
    Graffham, near Petworth, Sussex,
        England.

———————

OTHER LETTERS: 8, 133
William Cooper's letters led to an interesting example of extensive chain migration that began with one single man. William's brother, James, mentioned by name in his first letter, brought

———————

16 Colonel Mount's, lot 21 concession 4, seems to have been the temporary depot Mount established at or near the future site of Strathroy to supply these settlers.

his wife Harriet and family to the Adelaide settlement in 1836 (see 133). Harriet's sister Mary, married to James Budd, also emigrated with a large family on the *Heber* in 1836. The Budd family went to Woodstock. A third Cooper brother, John, did not emigrate until 1844 when he came to Upper Canada with four children of his first wife (who had died in childbirth), his second wife, Harriet (Challen), and their daughter (born in 1841). The parish vestry of Graffham/Woolavington assisted him with £30, believing that it was "highly advantageous" for John to join his two brothers who were doing well in Canada. John was described as "an honest, ambitious labourer ... [who] has behaved well & shewn a great willingness to assist himself in [emigrating]." The 1851 census found John and Harriet Cooper and a family of eight children on the 2nd concession of Adelaide.

When James Cooper wrote in 1838 on behalf of himself, his wife Harriet, and William (133), he made no mention of a family for William. This letter, which recounts William's service with the militia in 1837 and 1838 and a visit to the Budds and other Petworth emigrants in Woodstock, is our latest certain reference to William.

■ 53

EDWARD AND CATHARINE BOXALL, ADELAIDE, UPPER CANADA, TO HIS MOTHER, WIDOW BOXALL, GRAFFHAM, NEAR PETWORTH, WEST SUSSEX, 9 FEBRUARY 1833

SOURCE: *No. 1 Continuation*, 7-8

Adelaide, Upper Canada,
February 9th. 1833.

DEAR MOTHER

I take this opportunity to acquaint you, that I received your letter on the 4th. instant. and rejoice to hear you are in good health, as it leaves us at present, thank God. Now if any of you comes out this season, bring me a little crop grass seed, swede turnip, and stone turnip seed,[17] mangel wurzel seed,[18] carrot and onion seed, and all kinds of working tools, and bedding, and clothing. Now if David or William would come out here, it would be much better for them, than to bide starving in England.

Dear mother, we have got a log house, 16 feet by 22, covered over with boards, but the house is not finished, the floor is not laid, nor the chimney built yet; but we make shift to live in it. We can make our own sugar and soap, and starch, and I buy the deer's fat of the Indians, to make my own candles, which is generally one shilling a pound; and I bake my bread in the iron pot, with a leaven which I keep from one time to another. Dear mother, Charles Boxall was drowned at Montreal, through getting drunk: he fell overboard, down between the ships, and was never seen more,

---

17 The Swedish turnip is "cultivated in a field for the use of cattle ... The garden-turnip is called the stone-turnip by some" (W. Cobbett, *The English Gardener* [1829]).

18 A large variety of beet used for cattle food

although two men jumped overboard to save him.[19] We have heard that William Barnes died at York, and left a wife and four children; and Rapley died here, and left eight orphan children; but Government finds them in provisions. I intended to have taken one of the little girls, but it have not been convenient; but I shall take her in the summer.

Dear mother, there is plenty wolves here, they makes a terrible noise in the night time. But we can never see any of them; all the bears are laid up now. Here is plenty of black squirrels here, they make a very nice pudding; and turkeys, and deer, and foxes, and partridges, and racoons, and porcupines, and ground hogs, and eagles, and owls, which makes a dismal noise in the night, and humming birds, the most beautiful in [the] world; and 5 or 6 sorts of woodpeckers, very handsome; and the night hawk, which sings, Whip poor Will, as plain as you can speak.

Give my kind love to Mrs. Henly, and tell her I should have wrote to her, but letters are very expensive: we pay 3 shillings and six pence each for them. Dear mother, when you write, let us know what you pay for a letter: and how Mrs. Henly and family is. The next time I write it will be to my sisters; I shall desire them to send to you immediately. Give our kind love to my brothers, and sisters, and nephews, and accept the same yourself. We remain your dutiful children,

EDWARD and CATHARINE BOXALL.
To Widow Boxall, Graffham, near Petworth, Sussex.

OTHER LETTERS: 7

Many Petworth emigrants left their mothers anxiously watching for a letter from Canada. In the spring of 1834, after "an unusually long interval of time ... elapsed since his last letter," Edward Boxall's widowed mother persuaded the Reverend Henry Manning to write to the Colonial Office on her behalf. A year later, a reply signed by Sir John Colborne*, the lieutenant governor of Upper Canada, and copied by the Colonial Office to send to Manning, relayed the message that a letter would reach her son in Adelaide Township if directed to Mr Thomas Radcliff*, the postmaster at Adelaide Village.[20] At mid-century, the Boxalls were still in the Adelaide settlement, living on E ½ lot 21 concession 4 SER. Catharine died 26 October 1857, aged 67, and was buried at Mount Zion 4th line cemetery, Adelaide Township.

■ 54

HENRY AND CHARLOTTE TRIBE, GALT, UPPER CANADA, TO NOAH HILL, NOAH'S ARK, LURGASHALL, SUSSEX, 12 FEBRUARY 1833

Henry Tribe was a bricklayer in his mid 50s when he emigrated from Dial Green, Lurgashall, with his wife, Charlotte, and children Charlotte, Henry, Benjamin, Mary, Richard, Ann, and Jonathan.[21] We do not know if their son Robert followed later as they expected, but their

---

19 See also letter 2.
20 PRO, CO 42/425, 348, Colborne to R.W. Hay, 15 May 1835, replying to a letter of 26 May 1834.
21 Both Henry Tribe and Charlotte signed the marriage register.

married daughters Jane and husband Jesse Penfold and Sarah and husband James Rapson also emigrated in 1832. Daughter Charlotte married Joseph Evans in Canada.

SOURCE: Along with letter 51 part of a four-page pamphlet printed by J. Phillips at Petworth; copy found at WSRO, Goodwood MS 1465, f.18, in Sockett to Richmond, 9 April 1833.

To Noah Hill, at the Noah's Ark, Lurgashall, near Petworth, Sussex, Old England.[22]

Galt, February 12th. 1833.

I have wrote this few lines to you, hoping to find you all in good health, as it leaves all of us at present, we thank [God] for it. We have sent 4 letters, and we have had no answer. We do not know whether the letters passes from England, or not; we think that the letters are stopped, as we cannot get no answer, but I hope that you will answer this few lines by return of post, for we long to hear from you.

We are all very happy and comfortable; we lives in two houses, Jesse and James Rapson lives together, and Henry Tribe lives in a house about 3 hundred yards from them. So we all assists one another, as well as we can; we [get] pretty good living. When we work, we gets 5s. a day, and our board, and plenty of whisky. And tell Richard, that he must come, for he will [get] a very good living here; without going to the gentlemen farmers, as they call themselves, he will earn enough in the summer to keep him in the winter. If he bring a good gun, he will get plenty in the winter; a good rifle is a very good thing to kill the deer, and tell him to bring Bumper.

Mrs. Tribe gives her best respects to Mrs. Hill, Biddy, Fanny, Esther, and Jane, and to all her old friends. She gives her best respects to them. Henry Tribe junior wishes to know how John Trigg is, and to know whether he have built his new house; but he says he do not wish to come back again, for he likes this place very well. He wishes to be remembered to his old master. I saw George Kinshott last Sunday, and he and James [Kinshott] is very well;[23] and have good places. And tell Robert [Tribe], when he comes, he must stop at the first tavern in Waterloo; we lives 1 mile this side. Now we be in hopes that you will send us as many as you can: it signifies [not] whether they are married, or single, they will get a good living, and any that have been in the army will get 100 acres of land. Remember me to Wm. Saunders, and to brothers and sisters, and all enquiring friends. Benjamin wishes Robert Kinshott to come, here is a good place for him. Mr. Hill, you tell Robert Richards at Little Park, that Edmund Thomas and his family are well, and they lives near us.[24] Jesse Penfold wishes to be remembered to his father, and to all enquiring friends. Tell Charles Enticknap to send my knife by Robert T. We give our best respects to you all. So no more at present from

HENRY and CHARLOTTE TRIBE.

Direct to me Dumfries, Galt.

---

22 Original annotation: "This address was written on the paper by Noah Hill himself, before the man went out."

23 George and James Kinshott also emigrated from Lurgashall in 1832.

24 Edmund and Ann Thomas emigrated from Kirdford in 1832.

OTHER LETTERS: 50

Henry Tribe died during this first winter in Canada.

At the end of the Tribes' letter Sockett printed the following:

A letter from Thomas Mitchell, (who also went out with the Petworth Party) dated February 21st. 1833, speaks of the mildness of the winter, and confirms the statements of former letters, as to the demand for labor, and the ease with which an industrious man may earn a livelihood.

■ 55

HENRY SMART, ANCASTER, UPPER CANADA, TO JAMES NAPPER, KIRDFORD, WEST SUSSEX, 1 MARCH 1833

Smart addressed this letter to James Napper, but he again wrote letters and notes to several people on the same sheet of paper; see 56–60 to other friends and family. The letter appears to pick up from his first account of the country given in 44. See also letters 40, 43, 45.

SOURCE: *No. 2 Continuation*, 9

Ancaster, 1st March, 1833.

To JAMES NAPPER.

This comes with my kind love to you, hoping it will find you well, as it leaves me at present. I received your letter on the 12th February. I received it a month sooner than I expected. I received it as I was riding up the town with the esquire. I was sorry I could not write more to your satisfaction before, but I mean to do it now. As I describes the country to you, I describes it to one and all.

This is a very fine country, and plenty of room. I don't persuade any one to come out, but if all the labouring folks in Kirdford was here, they would not want to go back again. For my part, I don't mean to come back again to bide. Labouring people's wages here is six shillings per day, this money, or three shillings and six pence your money. In hay and harvest time, they get five or six shillings per day your money. We don't do as you do in your country; wherever we work, we live. If they hire by the month first coming in, they will get from 8 to 10 dollars; and after they have been here some time, they will get more. Single men that hire by the year, will get from one hundred dollars to one hundred and twenty. I have been up the country 120 miles, where all our old parishioners are settled, nearly altogether.[25] They have all draw'd their land, and all settled upon it; but they are pretty much in the bush, at present. They have all got 100 acres of land, apiece, at 2 dollars an acre. There is no money wanting for the first 3 years, and after that, they must pay interest for it. I have been up and draw'd mine, but I am not gone to it, nor am not sure as ever I shall. I draw'd mine in the township of Warwick.[26] There is so many people gone up there, that things are very dear, but they have

25 By "up the country," Smart meant the Adelaide settlement which included the neighbouring Township of Warwick.

26 Smart's late application for land and his lack of resolve to settle on his land seem to explain why he was assigned a relatively remote lot at a distance from his friends.

not wanted for any thing, as Government helped them to provisions. Wheat up there fetches one dollar per bushel, but down here 'tis only 3s.6d, your money. Meat here is 2½ d. your money, per lb. There is not a great deal of cheese in this country, and not so good as it is at home: it is too new; but plenty of every thing else. There are bears and wolves in this country, but not so many as you have been told; there is no danger of them; they are very seldom seen; and they never trouble any person. I saw one bear, one morning about 2 o'clock before me, but I did not know what it was; but about a week ago, I saw one tied up at a gentleman's house, and then I knew what it was.

This is generally a very level country, and very good land, but we want some of the English farmers to shew them how to make the most of it. They let their manure lay in the barn yards, till they are obliged to hoist their fences. The fences in this country are made of rails: there is no hedges, ditches or posts.

OTHER LETTERS: 40, 43–45, 56–60

■ 56

HENRY SMART, ANCASTER, UPPER CANADA, TO SARAH BAKER,[27] [KIRDFORD, WEST SUSSEX], 1 MARCH 1833

SOURCE: *No. 2 Continuation*, 10

To SARAH BAKER.

I have not seen William [Baker],[28] but I have heard from him by Tom Thomas: he is very well, and doing very well, and working on his land. And Tom Thomas desires to be remembered to all his friends; he is very well, and his family is very well, and likewise his brother's family.[29] There is neither of them that desires to come to England again; and Tom desired me to tell you, that he would not come back, if they was to lay him down a hundred pounds. I fully agree with him; for if any body had a hundred pounds there, they might soon spend it; and here they may soon find a way to get it.

OTHER LETTERS: 40, 43–45, 55, 57–60

27 Presumably his mother-in-law, to whom he wrote letter 40.
28 Henry's brother-in-law, who wrote on his own behalf from Adelaide a couple of weeks later (65).
29 Thomas Thomas, his wife and two children, emigrated from Kirdford in 1832 and settled in Adelaide. Two other families named Thomas emigrated that year: James, his wife and two children, and Edmund, his wife, and four children. See letter 37.

■ 57

HENRY SMART, ANCASTER, UPPER CANADA, TO CHARLES RAPLEY,
[KIRDFORD, WEST SUSSEX,] 1 MARCH 1833

SOURCE: *No. 2 Continuation*, 10

To CHARLES RAPLEY.[30]

Your brother and sisters are all well; there is three of them at service, and the others are doing very well on their land, and not in want of any thing at present. By your orders, I sent word up to them, if they got really in distress they should send to me; but if they get through this winter I think they will be better able to help you, than you will to help them, if you live there.

OTHER LETTERS: 40–45, 56, 58–60

■ 58

HENRY SMART, ANCASTER, UPPER CANADA, TO HIS BROTHERS AND
SISTERS, [KIRDFORD, WEST SUSSEX], 1 MARCH 1833

SOURCE: *No. 2 Continuation*, 10–11

DEAR BROTHERS AND SISTERS,

This comes with my kind love to them, hoping it finds them in good health, as it leaves me at present. I was very glad to see their letter, but I should have been more so to have seen them. I shall live in hopes of seeing Thomas Whitington[31] and his family, in the spring, and likewise Elizabeth Puttock, or any the rest of them that likes to come; but I don't expect any of them has heart enough to come. But if any of them do come, I will do the best for them I can, upon their first coming in; or for Charles Street, James Napper, Thomas Baker. I don't advise any of them to go into the bush at first starting. I would rather they would come to me, if they feel inclined. They will be just as well for a year; and they won't see so many hardships. You need not bring much of any thing here, nor lay your money out for much new clothing to bring here; but if they go up in the bush, you can't take too much. If you intend to come here, when you get to York, you must come up to Hamilton, and not go to Lake Huron. And if you will write to me from Montreal, you shall be took to at Hamilton wharf, by the time you get there, any of they that I have mentioned.

The winter is colder here, and a little longer; the summer is a little warmer. The summer don't begin here so soon as it does there. The days, in summer, are as much as an hour and a half shorter here, than they are in England; but, in winter, the days

---

30 Original annotation: "The father, James Rapley, a widower, who went out in 1832, with 7 children, died soon after his arrival, and the relations at home fearing the family would be in distress, had written to offer assistance. T.S." See letter 37.

31 Thomas Whitington was married to Rhoda Smart, Henry's sister.

are much longer here than they are there. There's not difference enough neither in heat or cold, to make any difference to any body. So no more at present, from your absent friend,

HENRY SMART.

OTHER LETTERS: 40, 43–45, 55–58, 60

■ 59

HENRY SMART, ANCASTER, UPPER CANADA, TO THE REVEREND J.K. GREETHAM*, KIRDFORD, WEST SUSSEX, I MARCH 1833

SOURCE: *No. 2 Continuation*, II

To MR. GREATHAM.

I am very much obliged to you, for what you sent to me;[32] I received it all safe; and likewise for what you had done for me before; and so are a great many others that I have seen. I think it was the best thing you could have done for the poor people of Kirdford, to send them out here; and so it will be if you send any more. If you send any more as you did us, give every one account of what they are to receive on board ship. A better lot of sailors than we had aboard, never need go on board a vessel; particularly the chief mate. No more at present, from your humble servant,

HENRY SMART.

OTHER LETTERS: 40, 43–45, 55–60

■ 60

HENRY SMART, ANCASTER, UPPER CANADA, TO CHARLES STREET, [KIRDFORD, WEST SUSSEX], I MARCH 1833

SOURCE: *No. 2 Continuation*, II

To CHARLES STREET.

I am happy to give a better account of Charles Newman, than I did before.[33] I see him about a week after I wrote before, and what I said was all right: he left that place immediately, and he is now living in a very good place, in Hamilton, about 7 miles from me.

William Hastlett died of a billious fever: he laid ill only a fortnight.

OTHER LETTERS: 40, 43–45, 55–59

This sequence of letters is the last reference we have to Henry Smart.

---

32 See letter 43.
33 See letter 40; Newman was Street's brother-in-law.

■ 61

THOMAS ADSETT, WATERLOO TOWNSHIP, UPPER CANADA, TO FRIENDS,
4 MARCH 1833

Thomas Adsett wrote three months after his son Charles was indentured to the tanner John
Betchel. Charles gave his perspective on the relationship in his "Autobiography" (180).

SOURCE: *No. 2 Continuation*, 12–13

March 4th. 1833.

Respected Friends,

I now take my pen in hand to write to you, hoping these few lines will find you
in health, as it leaves me and my children, at present, thank God, for the same which
is, and which I hope will come. You were in earnest to hear of my wife's decease,
and how she was buried; and how me and my children is situated, in a strange country like this. That is true which you said about your daughter, we was in a strange
country; but it is a country that me and her was likely to live happy, and enjoy our
pleasant situation, where there is many of our country people, and all is likely to do
well, if all keep their health. And about my wife being buried: she was respectfully
buried, in a graveyard of a class of people called methodists, and was held by a great
number of stranger friends to the place of her residence. And now I must speak of
(a word here is unintelligible) my wife. I am to say, that she wanted for nothing, me nor
my children wanted for nothing; and I hope that we shall never, by all appearance,
want for any thing in this world, but that one thing before mentioned, my dear wife.
But the Lord says we must go the way of all flesh.

My children is in good places: my two girls is in [as] good places as the world
can afford; and they are bringing them up like two young ladies. The people that
they reside with, is people of great respect, and will keep them till they are 21; or
till they have a mind to go away, to find a place for themselves. And my boy is at
another place, about three miles from my girls; and he is going to learn to be a tanner and currier; and I think that it is one of the best places in the country; the people is so agreeable here. The people I am now among is Dutch, and English, in
general. The place is called Waterloo, where I live, and my children. I am with the
man that has my boy Charles, and expect to remain for some time. It will be likely
that I shall remain there the remainder of my days.

OTHER LETTERS: 22, 52, 62, 71

■ 62

THOMAS ADSETT, WATERLOO TOWNSHIP, UPPER CANADA, TO FATHER
AND MOTHER, 4 MARCH 1833

Letters 61 and 62 were written on the same sheet.

SOURCE: *No. 2 Continuation*, 12–13

Dear father and mother,

I want you to write to me; and I want to send you some money in my letters that I send to you: the next, if I can get about it without having the money lost. I want you to send me a few lines back in the letter, to let me know whether Lord Egremont franks these letters;[34] or how the money is paid when they come to me; for it costs me very little or nothing, when I get them; and I want to know who pays the amount. So no more from me.

Give my best respects to all enquiring friends, and in particular them that enquire after my welfare.

THOMAS ADSETT.

OTHER LETTERS: 22, 49, 61, 71

■ 63

GEORGE AND ANN HILLS, ANCASTER, UPPER CANADA, TO FATHER, MOTHER, BROTHERS AND SISTERS, [SULLINGTON, WEST SUSSEX], 8 MARCH 1833

In this letter, the Hills are thanking their sponsors, John Hampton and George Gibson and his wife. If their daughter Jane had found a place in England at 13 (she was baptized in September 1819), she would typically have worked for her keep and relied on her parents for clothes.

SOURCE: *No. 2 Continuation*, 12-13

Ancaster, March 8th. 1833.

DEAR FATHER, & MOTHER, BROTHERS, & SISTERS,

I take this opportunity of writing, hoping to find you all well, as it leaves us at present. George has been very ill, with the scarlet fever, but is better now. Dear father and mother, I wish I had you here, I could keep you from my labor, better than you can live at home. I expect to leave my situation about next Michaelmas, after getting the wheat in the ground: then I shall have one crop off, and another in the ground. Jane has left her first situation, and has got another, where she gets 3s. per week. Jane sends her kind love to grandfather, and grandmother, uncles and aunts; so does George, John, and Ann, and Henry. The children often speak of their grandfather, and grandmother.

Please to remember me to Mr. Hampton,[35] and tell him I am a great deal better off than I was at home, and plainly see I shall do better in time, please God to

---

34 The Earl of Egremont*, as a member of the House of Lords, was allowed to send ten letters and receive fifteen letters daily with a frank for free postage. This right was abolished in 1840.

35 John Hampton, of Sullington Farmhouse, a farmer and landowner. In 1835, Petworth emigrants took to Upper Canada with them two rams and four ewes from Hampton's flock for "Mr Riddle and Mr G. Sockett" (*Hampshire Telegraph*, 27 April 1835) (see 106, Edward Longley). Brydone stayed with a Mr Riddel in Zorra Township in 1834 (*Narrative*, 42).

spare my health. Please tell him he might not take any notice of what people might say, that he persuaded me to come to America; for he never did persuade me. For he and Mr. Gibson[36] were the best friends I could find. I never took so much pleasure before, as I have done this winter, since I have known what it has been to work.

We received your letter on the 15th of February, and I hope they will write again as soon as convenient. I hope, my dear father and mother, they will send all the news they can, and let us know whether they know what is become of Hugh's wife. I hope my brother Hugh will take care, and do all he can for his children; and if any of them should think of coming to America, they will do better here than ever they will be able to at home.[37] But tell them, never to leave England to come to America, saying I persuaded them. Dear father and mother, please send me word where my brother Charles is quartered now, and if he enjoys a good state of health. We should be very glad to know, whether William Charman, my wife's brother, ever received our letter, as we have wrote two, and think it strange we never received any answer. Give our love to brothers and sisters, and am very sorry to hear Eliza is going to get married again; but hope she will do well. We wish to know, whether you know where James and Edward Charman is, and how they are. Remember me to James Terry, and all enquiring friends about Sullington. Respecting Penfold, he is settled at Guelph, about 40 miles from this, and is doing very well: his wife died shortly after they got up there: he has since married his wife's sister, Eliza Brooks, only 7 days after the death of his late wife.[38] I see Standen in Hamilton wharf, where we first came up, but have not heard of them since.

Respecting the prices of things in America, wheat will bring a dollar in the summer, when the river is navigable, so that they can carry it down to Montreal; but in the winter it will fetch no more than 3s.9d. or 4s. English money: barley ½ dollar; Indian corn ½ dollar; buck wheat ½ dollar; rye ½ dollar, per bushel. If any of you should come to this country, bring a few tares, as the people do not know what they are.[39] A turkey will fetch ½ dollar; geese from 8d. to 1s.; fowls 7½d, English money; butter 7½d. in summer, 1s. in winter; tea 3s.9d. or a dollar; cheese is very dear, 7½d. per lb. is the lowest price; whisky from 1s.10½d. to ½ dollar.

Give my love to my sister Elizabeth, and tell her if she thinks she cannot write a whole letter to write a few lines of it, as it would give me a great deal of satisfaction. I should be glad to know whether father and mother lives with you, and I hope you will ever be kind to them, and do all in your power to comfort them.

GEORGE & ANN HILLS.

---

36 George John Gibson, Esq. of Sandgate Lodge, Sullington. The Gibson's lent the parish a further £40 in 1835 to send another family on the *Burrell*. This loan was repaid in four annual instalments at 3 per cent interest.

37 A Hugh Hills and family emigrated from Climping, West Sussex, in 1835; we have no evidence that he was George Hills's brother.

38 In 1835 Parliament passed an Act making it illegal in England for a man to marry his deceased wife's sister; the Act was not repealed until 1907.

39 Vetch, used for fodder

OTHER LETTERS: 16, 17
The Hills remained in Ancaster at least through 1833. Their son William, born 15 July, was baptized there on 26 December 1833.

■ 64

CHARLES HAINES, [ANCASTER, UPPER CANADA], 8 MARCH 1833

Charles Haines, who apparently wrote 63 for George and Ann Hills, was the son of Charles Haines, a gamekeeper. He was from Ashington, West Sussex, and was assisted to emigrate by John Hampton, who also helped send the Hills. He added this brief note to their letter.

SOURCE: *No. 2 Continuation*, 14

This letter is wrote 8th day March, 1833, by Charles Haines, of French Land, Ashington; and if you should see his father or mother, give his love to them, and brothers and sisters: tell them to send word where they are now, that he might write to them.

CHARLES HAINES.

P.S. Let Mr. Hampton see this letter.

Here is not a great deal to shoot about here: I have only had one good shot, then I killed 17 pigeons at one shot. I have drawed 100 acres of land, at 2 dollars an acre, but think I will not go on it, as it is 100 miles from here: think of getting some nearer here.

■ 65

WILLIAM BAKER, ADELAIDE, UPPER CANADA, TO HIS FATHER AND MOTHER, JOHN AND SARAH BAKER, AND TO HIS BROTHERS AND SISTERS, [KIRDFORD, WEST SUSSEX], 13 MARCH 1833

SOURCE: *No 2 Continuation*, 15-16

Adelaide, Upper Canada,
March 13th. 1833.

DEAR FATHER, & MOTHER, BROTHERS & SISTERS,

I take this opportunity to acquaint you that I am in good health, and the country agrees with me very well; and that I have heard from you all on the first of March, by Henry Smart's letter, and rejoice to hear that you are all in good health. Dear father, I have got 100 acres of [as] good land, as any in England, with a very good stream of clear water running through it. Now, my dear friends, if any of you will come here, and live with me, you shall have part of my land; or, if you choose, you may draw another 100 acres, and you will get 6 years to pay the money in; one third at the end of 3 years, and the rest in 3 years more; at 10s. per acre, as I have got mine. I have got about 2 acres for a spring crop. And William Rapley[40] and I have got one

---

40 Son of James Rapley of Wisborough Green. James, a widower, emigrated with seven people in his party in 1832 and died before settling on his land.

yoke of oxen between us, to do our work, which shall be at your service also. We give about £10, in English money, for them; and I have got two good hogs, about nine months old, to fat after harvest, when I have got corn of my own. And I hope some of you will be here to help me eat them; for I am well sure that you can do better here, than any of you can in England. For, although every kind of provision is almost twice as dear as when we first came, even now we can buy beef at 2d. per lb.; pork at 4d.; butter 7½d.; sugar from 2d. to 9d. according to the time of the year; tea 4s.; tobacco 1s.; flour 8d. per gallon; venison about 1s.6d. per quarter. I have stated the price in English money, that you may understand it; but whiskey, rum, and brandy, is very cheap; and beer is very dear.

Farmers men get about £2.10s. per month, and board, and lodging, and wash-ing, and mending; and Government work[41] is £3. per month, and board, all above sixteen years old; and under that half price. Cows from £2. to £6. each; oxen from £9. to £14. per pair, they are very small; [horses] from £15. to £30. each; hogs from 1s. to 20 shillings each; sheep from 5s. to 7s. each; fowls 6d. each, ducks the same, geese and turkies 1s. each, guinea fowls the same.

Dear father, be sure to bring me a hay cutting knife, but no other tools; for you can get them cheaper here. Bring me some tares, about half a gallon of each sort, and a little lucern seed; swedish turnip seed, but no white rounds; and all kind of garden seed; and one gallon of bents grass seed, and a little good barley, and a little nonsuch seed;[42] and a clock; and all the money you can get. A farthing, or old plain halfpenny, and a penny piece are all the same value here; they are all called cents, and 100 of them makes a dollar; 4½ dollars makes one sovereign; and 4 English shillings and 2d. makes one dollar.

Dear father and mother, I am sorry to say that my sister Jane died at Prescot, with the Cholera; and I had it myself, but recovered; and little Frederick died at Hamil-ton, about a week after his mother. I was sorry I was not with her when she died; she seemed pleased with the country when I left her, at Montreal. I did not hear of her death for above two months, then I went above 100 miles, to a place called Ancaster, to find them, and saw Henry Smart.

Dear friends, you will find the living very different on board of ship, from what you have been used to. You ought to get some good hams of bacon, and pickles, to eat after being sea sick, and good white biscuit, and a little spirits; and tell the farm-ers at Kirdford, that if it please God I have my health, in three year's time, I shall be as well off as John Downer, at Marshall's;[43] though he used to cut such a swell over us at the meetings. James Joiner wishes to see his brother in law, William Covey, here.[44]

---

41 Immigrants were hired to work on the roads. William Rapley was listed as one of those labouring on the Caradoc- Adelaide-Warwick road in August-October 1832.

42 Lucerne with black pods, medicago lupulina. Lucerne is also known as alfalfa.

43 A farm on the road between Petworth and Kirdford

44 James Joiner emigrated with his wife and three children in 1832. James's sister, Hannah, was mar-ried to William Covey.

I conclude, with my kind love to you all, and remember me to all friends and acquaintances, and I remain [your] dutiful son,

WILLIAM BAKER.

Dear father,

It is very hot here in the summer, but the winter is no colder here than in England, as I can find; but there is a good deal more snow. We expects the winter to break up in a week or fortnight, at most. Answer this as soon as you can.

Direct to William Baker,

Township of Adelaide, 5th. Concession, Lot 18, South, District of London, County of Middlesex, Upper Canada, North America.

OTHER LETTERS: 41, 92

Mount* did not record a location to Baker on lot 18 concession 5 SER of Adelaide Township, but the Rapleys were on the adjoining lot 19.

■ 66

ANN AND CHARLES COSENS, WATERLOO TOWNSHIP, UPPER CANADA, TO HER FATHER, MOTHER, AND SISTER, [DORKING, SURREY], 31 MARCH 1833

Ann Miller and Charles Cosens married in Dorking, Surrey, in February 1832.[45] They emigrated a few months later, aged 20 and 19, respectively, at the same time as Charles's parents and brothers and sisters. See letter 34, by Charles's brother Cornelius.

Although William Upton in letter 27 had identified an opportunity (such as the Cosens had) to hire out as a couple without children as an excellent way to make money, Ann seemed less than comfortable with the arrangement.

SOURCE: Cosens family papers, Gowanstown, Ontario

Waterloo, America
March 31, 1833

My Dear Father, Mother, and Sister:

After a long delay I now improve the opportunity of writing to you, hoping that it will find you all well as, thank God, it leaves us at present. We have both been laid up with the fever and ague. Charles froze three of his toes. They were very bad but, thank God, they are almost well.

He has hired with a large farmer for 12 months. His wages is 10 shillings English money a week ($2.50) and his board. I live in the house with the family and do needlework and I am paid by the piece. We are both very comfortable. I have no incumberence now and no signs of any at present.[46] We were very glad to hear that you were well when Bushby sent his letter. Again glad to hear that my sister Jane is doing well

---

45 Both signed their names to the marriage register.
46 But see letter 141.

A labourer and his master at a harvest celebration, an annual feast hosted by an English farmer.

Jefferys Taylor, *The Farm: A New Account of Rural Toils and Produce* (London 1832), University of Sussex Collection

and that she has got a little girl, I long to know and to name. And so pleased to hear from my dear sister that has got so comfortable. We often wish that we could see you all again. I will not persuade you to come to Canada unless you could bring some money with you. It is a very poor country for a person without some money, but if a person had some money thay can do well, much better than they can do in England. We do not like the country as well as we did England but I think that we shall like it better after a time. The winter is colder and the summer is hotter here than what it is at home. The days are shorter in the summer and longer in the winter. There is plenty of very fine wood here without any expense. We can get it any where by cutting it. We need not get cold. I often think of poor Jane, she told me that I would freeze to death in Canada. There is no danger of that. We do not suffer either with cold or hunger.

There was nothing said about Jane's husband in that letter that Cornelious had. Charles' friends [parents] live about 8 miles from us. His father has a house for one year. They are getting along as well as can be expected but they have a lot of serious trouble. They lost two of their daughters, Jane and Mary Ann. Jane (Mrs. Tilt) died in childbirth[47] and Mary Ann from the effects of scarlet fever. Some of the rest

47 Jane Tilt died 17 October 1832 and was buried in the Turner Cemetery in Tuckersmith Township where she, her husband William Tilt, and her parents had gone to settle. William subsequently moved to Waterloo Township.

of them are quite poorly. Have not recovered from their trouble yet. I should have wrote you before but Cornelious' letter laid 2 months in the post office. I wrote to you in the summer as soon as we landed but we never had any answer so we thought that you had not received my letter.

Please write to us as soon as you receive this letter and let us have all the news you can. We long to hear from you.

When you write you must pay the post through England or it will not reach us. Charles saw Cornelious a little before we wrote and he said that he was going to write to Mr. Bushby and Charles desired to be remembered to Thomas Skildon and Wm. Mason and tell them that there is no cricketing in Canada. They don't know what the game is. You may tell Mason that he might have done well if he had come. The working man is thought just as much of as his master. We are not obliged to set down to a piece of bread and hard cheese. The table is set all the time, loaded like as though there was feasting.

Charles heard from young Jos. Taylor and he is quite well, and he had a suit of nice blue cloth. Please tell his father that he is quite well. Dear Father, there is plenty of good potter's clay and the pottery is a very good business here if a man had a little money. There is no duty to pay and the pottery sells here as dear as in England.

Give our love to all our friends and [accept] the same yourselves. From your affectionate son and daughter,

Ann and Charles Cosens

Direct your letter to Charles Cosens c/o Breugremen Snider[48]

Township of Waterloo. Upper Block, Holton Co., Gore District of Upper Canada, North America.

OTHER LETTERS: 34, 141

■ **67**

JAMES S. AND WILLIAM GOLDRING, YORK, UPPER CANADA, TO THEIR UNCLE, THOMAS GOLDRING, SOUTH BERSTED, WEST SUSSEX, 9 APRIL 1833

James S. Goldring was 23 and his brother, William, was 19 when they emigrated in 1832 from South Bersted, a coastal parish, with their parents, James and Sarah (Pratt) Goldring, and their sister and brothers, Frances, Eleanor, Michael, George, and Edward. James Sr's brother, Henry, also emigrated at the same time with his wife, Mary Ann (Rayner), and four children, Eleanor, Samuel, Emma, and Caroline. A James Goldring – either the father or the son – had in the past been fined for smuggling.[49] The Goldrings settled on Lake Ontario near York (Toronto). Their first employment came from government: in October 1832, John Gamble reported James Sr, Henry, and James Jr on his "List of Emigrants employed on the Lake Road."[50]

---

48 Possibly Bürgersmann
49 WSRO, Add. MS 1476
50 NA, RG 5, A1, Upper Canada Sundries, p.67508, mfm C-6876.

SOURCE: *No. 3 Continuation*, 17–18

April 9th. 1833.

DEAR UNCLE,

I take the opportunity of writing to you, hoping to find you all in good health, as it leaves us all at present. But father has been very near of losing his life: he was ill for 6 months. It was in the autumn, and the doctor gave him over; but he is quite well now, and just begun sowing.

We have taken a house, and bought 2 cows; and some hogs, but we have killed them. We have got 1 acre for a garden, and the garden runs down to Lake Ontario, where we can get fish, and ducks, if we have any time to spare. The pigeons go away in the winter, the same as the swallows; so when they first come, I can get a plenty of them: they are blue with a long tail. We have not got any land that will suit us yet; we find the country just as that book was that Mr. Phillips* had; so we all like the country very well. We need not want to come back again at any rate.

We have a very pleasant house, with a very large ball room at the top: we have had one ball since we have been here. Now I will tempt laundress women a little: they get from 2s.6d. to 3s. per dozen, for washing. It would have been a good job, if my aunt Fanny had come with us.

We live about 8 miles above York, Upper Canada.[51] It is pleasant here now. We had not a very cold winter this winter; but it was colder than it is there; but we can get firing for nothing here, that is a fine thing. My brother James is hired out for one year, for £20.; but that is very low wages. I have a plenty of work at my trade, more than I can do very well. I can earn as much in one day, as I did there in a week; so we can afford to enjoy ourselves. There is no good beer in [this] country; but there is some very good grog; and we can sit down and drink it, as well as Mr. R.A. Esq. We have nobody to run over us here, and to order us out of their fields. We can take our gun, and go a deer hunting, when we likes; so we hope all that can come, will have heart enough.

We have not seen [Thomas] Joice, nor heard from him; for he had 50 acres of land gave him on account of his being an old soldier.[52] Any old soldier can get land if he seek for it. We saw Mr. R. Wonham last summer, but he is come back to England to fetch his family; but he left his eldest boy here, at the college,[53] until he return. [John] Hollis, the tailor, is in York, doing very well.[54] My uncle Harry has took a house and 3 acres of land. C. Raynor is hired in a saw mill; I think he will get on after a bit. I should be glad if you could find out Stowe's directions, or any one else that we know. I have sent two letters before, but I don't think that you ever had them.

51 They were probably in Etobicoke. In 1837 a Henry Gouldring was on lot 12 broken front concession Etobicoke Township (*Directory of Toronto & Home District*).
52 Thomas and Rachel Joice (Joyes) and their five children emigrated from South Bested in 1832.
53 Possibly Upper Canada College, founded in 1829 by Lieutenant Governor Colborne*.
54 John Hollis emigrated with his wife and their four children from Felpham, West Sussex, in 1832.

If you come, board yourselves if you can; bring cheese, red herrings,[55] a little brandy, and bacon. But you will wish yourselves back again, when you are sea sick; but keep up your spirits. So no more at present from your well wishing friends,

J.S. and W. GOLDRING.

Direct your letter, J. Goldring, York, Upper Canada.

Remember us to all enquiring friends; and tell grandmother to expect a letter in about a week.

For Thomas Goldring,

Southbersted [South Bersted], near Chichester, Sussex.

Henry and James both evidently continued to live west of Toronto in Etobicoke. James was still there in 1851. In the 1851 census for Etobicoke, James Sr and Sarah gave their ages as 69 and 65. A James Goldring, probably James Jr, is reported as a sailor or mariner in Toronto directories in the decade from 1846 to 1857; there is also a James Goldring who was a labourer recorded in the 1851 census.

William Goldring is described in the 1851 census as a widower, aged 40, working as a shoemaker and living on 2–3 acres on lot D concession 1 Etobicoke. By 1888, he had a brick house at 75 Duke Street, Toronto. William died in 1891 leaving an estate valued at $56,000.

In 1943, C.H.J. Snider interviewed 84-year-old Captain Richard Goldring, "one of six sailor sons" (five sons and a stepson) of William Goldring, and published his reminiscences in the Toronto *Evening Telegram* on 4 and 18 December. As we have found to be the case more than once, this article identified William, who came to Toronto at the age of 20, as the pioneer and "captain of his family's fortune" and does not mention his parents or other members of the large family group who emigrated at the same time.

Richard's memories give a specific shape to the impression of great versatility left by many Petworth emigrants. His earliest memory was from the time his father had a fisherman's licence and a fish lot at the mouth of the Etobicoke river (now a small creek). He recalled all the family being put to work as his father built a scow out of materials salvaged from a wrecked schooner in between setting and hauling nets, marketing fish, working a garden, gathering coal, and making shoes (probably the "trade" mentioned in this letter). Richard grew up living all or much of the time either in the old-fashioned poop cabin of this scow or in its two increasingly larger successors. Like his brothers, he worked on the "Goldring fleet" of coasting vessels: "small neat schooners" and some "butt ended scows," which supplied Toronto with such cargoes as crude oil and the fill for construction sites. As his enterprise grew, William moved to Toronto and rented a wharf at the foot of Frederick Street where he directed a "family enterprise, employing all his sons and a dozen more men."

---

55 smoked herring

■ 68

WILLIAM SPENCER, NELSON TOWNSHIP, UPPER CANADA, TO FRIENDS
(ADDRESSED TO HIS FATHER-IN-LAW FRANCIS COOPER),
MONTPELLIER, NEAR PETWORTH, WEST SUSSEX, 6 MAY 1833

SOURCE: *No. 3 Continuation*, 18–20

Nelson, May 6th. 1833.

Dear and affectionate friends,

I received your letter, dated November 5th, which gave me great satisfaction, to hear that you was all in good health, and yet in the land of the living; for which cause we have reason to thank God. I therefore once more submit to the duty incumbent as children doth in obedience to their parents, which through the mercies and indulgence of God, I improve these passing moments in return, to write to you in sincerity; trusting in an all-wise God, to convey these home once more to distant friends.

About 3 weeks after I wrote to you before, I was taken sick with a fever, and lay for the space of 3 weeks, during which time I suffered much pain; though revived again, and have had reasonable good health since, and am in good health at present, and hoping that this intelligence may find you in the same state, which God grant they may. I am still living at Jacob Triller's, whose farm I have taken to work on shares, for which I am to have one-fourth of all that I can raise on the cleared land, and am found in all except clothing; and have John Luff, a lad about 16 years old, to work with me. He came out with us, and is bound to Jacob Triller, till he is 21 years of age. He is in good health excepting somewhat deaf. He has an aunt living at Fittleworth, near the sign of the Swan [Inn]; her name is Henley. He wishes to hear from her, if you could see her, and if so, should you have the opportunity of writing to me again, enclose the particulars from her in my letter. The distance is far that we are from one another, though intelligence is near. I frequently see people from England, and converse with them, though it is not so gratifying as to have a letter.

Speaking of cleared land above in my letter, that is land of which the timber has been cleared off, or mostly off. The land in its nature through these parts is very heavy timbered, generally speaking. The timber through these parts are oak, pine, ash, maple, elm, beech, hickory, and bass wood, some hemlock, and cedar. Soil and productions: the soil is fertile, fitted for all the purposes of agriculture. The air is generally clear and healthy. The snow laid about six weeks, and went off quite sudden, with some rain. The time of harvest comes here with us, about the same time it comes with you. The heat in summer exceeds the heat with you; though I have seen some as hot days there, as ever I have seen here, though not in general. Wheat is the staple article, though there are various other kinds of grain, raised in the country. Wheat yields from 16 to 25 bushels to the acre; and [I] have heard of its raising more.

Now to let you know, you perhaps will be deceived in the country, for the forest is quite different from what I thought it was. I found no such great landholders here, like as there is in England. I live along the banks of Lake Ontario, and I believe it is inhabited for 60 or 70 miles back: the land is surveyed into townships, then into 200 acre lots; and I believe the greater part has been drawn from the Crown; and almost every one that wants land, can get it by industry, if he likes. The forest is something like the North Woods. You wanted to know something about the natives of our land. Of what I have seen, I believe [they] are all naturalized, and become subject to the law of the land; how they are back in the interior parts I cannot tell; for what I know, they are almost as far off perhaps as you are. The wild beasts of the forest are such as generally do no harm; the bear and the wolf are the worst, and they scarcely ever do any harm. Fowls of various kinds, geese, ducks, and fowl, of all kinds, not so many as was represented; though we have the opportunity of fowling where we choose. Fruit of various kinds, though none but what is raised in the same way they are with you. The fruit is plentiful here in places; I believe apples have been sold for 1s.½d. per bushel, in places through the country, though not all over so plentiful. There is a great deal of cider made from apples in this country, for which we can get 16s. per barrel. The barrel that you spoke of in your letter, I left at Kinshott's, and Kinshott's son brought it out with him to this country; and I believe he is about the head of the Lake, in the township of Ancaster.

Clothing, in this country, is quite cheap. Other persons coming from England, had better bring their money, and what other things they need, they can get almost every thing they need here, quite as cheap as they can get [it] there. You spoke in your letter something about liquor: we have spirituous liquors of all descriptions of prices; brandy, 10s.; spirits, 5s.; wine, from 6s. 3d. to 10s.; whisky, which is made mostly in our own country, is 1s. 6d. per gallon.

Now my dear friends, I am a far distance from you, and, in sincerity, I do not regret my coming yet; for things looks more prosperous in my estimation here, than they do there, for a poor man. Now if you think fit to come to this country, I think you would better your situation. I know of a man that has a farm, that wants to get a man on for two years. It is not far distant from me: I think it would suit you very well. Will you please tell my brother James to come; for I think it would be a great advantage to him if he was only here. A bricklayer is worth 5s. at the least, per day, and found. I know of a job of work, where I am, that he could get if he was here. Now if you come out this season, come out soon.

Now I wish that you, after reading this letter, would send it to all enquiring friends, that they may see and hear for themselves. And I have one other request, please if you know where my brother Samuel is, you would confer a favour on a friend, by sending a letter to him, to let him know where I am, that he could write to me; and I will answer him as soon as I get a letter from him. William Reeves, from Littlehampton, left this country, and said that he would go back to England, in the latter part of the season: he had a number of letters for different ones: you would know by sending to James Bays or Solomon Matthews. Nothing more at present, but remain your most affectionate son, until death do us part. Write to me as soon as possible. When you write, direct your letter by the way of New York: direct your letter, Upper Canada, District of Gore, County of Halton, Township of Nelson, Post Office.

WILLIAM SPENCER.

To Mr. Francis Cooper, Montpillier, near Petworth, Sussex, England, by the way of New York.

OTHER LETTERS: 24, 125

As Spencer noted, Triller's farm was very close to Lake Ontario, about midway between Bronte and Wellington Square (Burlington), on broken front lot 4 concession 4 Nelson Township. Spencer bought a half-acre town lot in Bronte some time before November 1836, the date of his next letter, 125.

■ 69

CHARLES MOORE, BLENHEIM, WATERLOO TOWNSHIP, UPPER CANADA, TO HIS FATHER, WILLIAM MOORE, [PETWORTH, WEST SUSSEX], [CIRCA JUNE 1833]

Charles Moore married Rhoda Willett on 29 March 1832 in Petworth, just before they were sent to Upper Canada by his parish of Tillington.[56] He was a minor (under twenty-one) and married with his parents' consent. Rhoda's young daughter, Eliza Willett, accompanied them.

SOURCE: *No. 3 Continuation*, 23–4

Blenheim, America, in
Upper Canada.

Dear father,

I write these few lines, in hopes to find you well, as it leaves me at present. I am very sorry to think, that I did not send you a letter before, but I was never settled before. Me and my wife do send our best respects to you, and mother [Frances], and James, and the baby. We are a doing very well, and we are in hopes to do better in a little while. I have bought me a cow. And I hope you are doing the same. You might tell William Sageman, that Eliza is doing the same.[57]

I do not wish to see you come to this country, if you can live at home, for it is not fit for old people. Father! it is a country that a man can live if he will work; but you must work hard. I can earn 5 shillings a day for working about farming work. I am about[58] buying one hundred acres of ground for myself, shortly. The country is all trees, so when you buy ground you goes right in amongst the trees, and chop them down, and burn them up, and so we make a clearing. The climate is about the same here as what it is there in the summer; but the winter here is much colder. We

56 Charles signed the register and Rhoda made a mark.
57 Eliza was probably the illegitimate child of William Sageman and Rhoda Willett, born in Easeborne Poorhouse and baptized July 1830.
58 close to

had snow about 4 feet deep last winter. We found a large mistake in having one hundred acres of ground, as they promised us in England; but we had the money that was coming to us at England.[59] We will leave that, so turn over the other side of the letter.

Well, father! we have got one child, a boy, and his name it is George. Now, father! I would wish you to give my and my wife's best respects to her father and mother [Thomas and Mary Willet], sisters and brothers, and to all my uncles and aunts, and to Mrs. Steer, and to Mr. Steer, George Steer and William Steer. And to satisfy you that I did send this letter, I will put in about that razor that you gave me. But send me word whether uncle Charles' little baby is alive or dead. So no more at present,

CHARLES MOORE.

Father, send me [a] letter back as soon as you can: direct it to Upper Canada, America, in the Township of Waterloo, Upper Block, C. MOORE.

To Frank Moore, England, in the County of Sussex, in the township of Petworth.

■ 70

EXTRACT FROM A LETTER BY RHODA THAIR, MONTREAL, 22 JUNE [1833]

Rhoda (Rapson) and her husband George Thair, a brickmaker, emigrated in 1832 from the parish of Lodsworth, with three children, John, Tom, and Fanny, and an extended family group. The Thairs and Rapsons were one of relatively few family groups whom we were able to identify as non-conformist while they lived in England. Rhoda's son John was baptized in 1832 in the Independent and Congregational Chapel at Petworth.

Rhoda's brother, William, was married to George's sister, Maria. Both these families, in addition to the Dearlings (letters 85 and 111) emigrated as a group with the intention of joining James Rapson. Hale made good Sockett*'s promise to send emigrants to any destination at the Head of Lake Ontario by paying their passage to Dundas, the nearest port to James's land.

———

SOURCE: Petworth Emigration Committee, "Statement," [October 1833]. When the statement appeared in the *Brighton Guardian*, 16 April 1833, this passage had some minor changes of punctuation, style, and spelling. The most significant changes are noted in square brackets below. The statement with the extracts was also published in the *Montreal Gazette*, 2 January 1834.

15th. (June) staid [stayed] quarantine at Grosse Island. 16th. all went ashore: staid all day, but we did not take but one box, with changes, which was taken [shaken]

———

59 The source of his information in England (incorrect if he expected the land for free) is not clear. In 1832, he could have had land if he had been among the Petworth emigrants sent to the Adelaide settlement; there were no crown lands set aside for indigent emigrants in Waterloo or surrounding townships.

out to see if it was clean. We was [were] obliged to wash all our things the week before, and clean our places before the doctor came on board. There was 8 ship loads on the island; some had to stay six weeks. One ship had 36 [thirty] died; our ship have not lost any, but those two babies.[60]

17th. came to Quebec. 22nd. we are all well now, and very busy getting ready to start for York. We have not been ashore at Montreal; the boats came to the side of the vessel and takes us. We had [have] grog every other day, and plenty of provisions, and very good. Give our love to them all; tell them we have not had the trouble we expected to have yet.

OTHER LETTERS: 76, 80, 78

■ 71

THOMAS ADSETT, GALT, DUMFRIES TOWNSHIP, UPPER CANADA, TO HIS
FATHER, THOMAS ADSETT, NORTHCHAPEL, WEST SUSSEX,
25 JUNE 1833

SOURCE: *No. 4 Continuation*, 25-6

June 25th. 1833.

Dear and honoured Father,

I have just received your letter, and am very glad to hear that you are well and hearty. Your letter was dated 10th March, and I had it 19th June. I have the pleasure to say, that I am quite well and hearty, never better in my life. Emma is quite well, and grown very much, so that you would not know her. She have an excellent place: the people are quite genteel folks; they have no child, and they takes her as their own child; and they could not be fonder of her if she was their own; and they are bringing her up to learning. Charles is well, and grown very fat, and can talk Dutch as well as any of them. I have put him apprentice to a tanner [John Betchel], but he goes to school, and his master will, I have no doubt but he will, make him a good scholar: they are Dutch family: he is bound for 14 years. I have lived with them 8 months, and they seem very good people. They are to board, lodge, wash, mend, and find him in clothes and every thing; and when his time is out, he is to have £17.10s. currency; that is, 70 dollars, and a new suit of clothes from top to bottom. He has a bad foot, something come of itself, but [I] am in hopes it will soon get better. Sarah is with a master builder, and cabinet maker: they are quite genteel folks: they have no child, so they are very fond of her. They sends her to school, and she is drest like

60 The babies were the two-day-old daughter of William and Maria Rapson and Harriet, the daughter of George and Elizabeth Trusler who was baptized 1 July 1832.

Mother and children, Sussex, 1832
Daniel Fowler, sketch, NA, C45184

some gentleman's daughter: she is quite well, and looks well. Sarah and Emma are at Galt, and Charles is only 4 miles west of Galt; and I have worked ever since I have been [here] just around them.[61]

Now I will answer your request concerning my poor wife and child, and how she was buried. My child was taken to a Wesleyan meeting house or chapel, where there is a man appointed to perform the office of the burial service, when he delivered an excellent address; after this it was taken to the burying ground, and interred in its grave, and concluded with prayer. In the same manner, my wife was taken in a waggon to the same chapel, where the man gave a most affectionate address on the uncertainty of life: then conveyed to the church yard, this being the way of all living, to remain until the great rising day: the service being ended with a most solemn and appropriate prayer concluded. I think enough hath been said to satisfy you on this subject.

I would just say that William Davis was very sick, so he could not come with us any further than Montreal; but Penfold took him to Prescot, there left him in the hospital. Since that he got better and came to Hambleton, and is now married to an Indian woman, a black; she has two hundred acres of land, and a grist mill. I wish

---

61 Original annotation: "On comparing this letter with those given in … the Sussex letters of 1832 [letters 22, 49], it will be seen that the kindness shewn to these children, on the death of their mother, was not a mere feeling of the moment, but has been steadily persevered in. T.S[ockett]" This letter is the last reference we have to Thomas's children, Emma and Sarah. Sockett's note perhaps misses the spirit of a relationship which appears to have been that of adoption by childless couples. Adsett's memoir (180) made no mention of his sisters.

you would send me word where James Johnson is, and what they did to him, because he did not come out with us to Canada; say whether uncle John ever had my letter. I do think it very hard that he have not wrote to me: I should think that they all (I mean all my uncles and aunts and cousins) would join and pay for the letters for you, when by doing this they will shew their love to me by so doing. I should be glad to hear from you all as often as you can.

I will now give you all the account I can of the country and weather: the country is very little different from England, only colder, and hotter, and the winter longer, and sharper; and the summer very short, only 3 months at the most: the snow came November the 1st and the last April 5th. Frost in August ½ an inch thick, and on the 22nd June, very frosty nights and hot days. Jesse Penfold, James Rapson, Benjamin Tribe, and I, went and seen Joseph Kinshott's widow, and Charlotte Tribe[62] as was. They are all well; and Mrs. Kinshott keeps a school in Blenheim [Township]: she have 1½ dollar per week, and most provisions found.

We heard that there were many more coming out this spring, should be glad if you would send word who is coming, and when they set sail, and whether they are coming by Quebec. My best respects to old Mr. Mills, and James Etherington and his wife, may God bless them all; but I should be glad to see them. And tell my old work mates, that we do not do here as they do in England. I am a mowing grass, but we do not sit under the hedge to eat a bit of bread and cheese, but go in doors, and have the best that the country affords. Tell old Jesse Penfold, that his son Jesse, with his family, are all well. Old Mrs. Tribe and her family are all well. Jesse Penfold desires that you would tell John Mann that he is a fool that he did not come. So no more from your affectionate son,

THOMAS ADSETT.

Direct to me Galt, Dumfries, Gore, U.C.

The prices of provisions are as follows: flour 4 dollars per barrel, pork 4d. lb., butter 6½d. lb., beef 3½d. lb. mutton 1¼ dollar for a sheep, whisky 2s. per gallon, spirits 5s.6d. per gallon brandy and wine, beer 7½. per quart, and cider the same.

Of work: labourers 3s.3d. per day, and board and whisky; tradesmen front 5s. to 7s. per day, with board and whisky. Write as soon as possible, and fill it up as full as possible.

Wrote by James Rapson: his wife and family are all well.

To THOMAS ADSETT,
    Northchapel, near Petworth, Sussex, England.

—————————

OTHER LETTERS: 22, 49, 61, 62

Thomas married Petworth emigrant Matilda Penfold, daughter of Jesse, probably before 1837 when he was recorded as living on part of lot 11, Beasley's Tract, Waterloo Township. By 1840, he was on the west part of lot 6 in the same Tract and two years later, he was on a lot in

—————————

62 Charlotte Evans (see letter 19)

Dumfries Township. The 1851 census-taker found Thomas Adsett on lot 3 concession 1 Woolwich Township. By the 1840s, the Adsett family were all Wesleyan Methodist, and Thomas
became a trustee of the Woolwich congregation. He died in 1870.

See 180.

■ 72
ELIZABETH (NASH) WACKFORD, WATERLOO TOWNSHIP, UPPER
CANADA, TO MRS SARAH GREEN,[63] PETWORTH, WEST SUSSEX,
25 JUNE 1833

Elizabeth and James Wackford emigrated from Petworth with the assistance of the Earl of Egremont* and Mrs Sarah Green in 1832.[64] Elizabeth had previously worked for Mrs Green and
was a hatmaker. There were six children in the family: Sarah, James, Emma, Thomas, William,
and Abraham. We do not know the ages of the oldest two, but Emma was 14 at the time they
emigrated, and the three younger boys (all baptized in Lurgashall) were under 6.

SOURCE: *No. 3 Continuation*, 21–2

June 25th. 1833.

Dear and honored Friend,

I suppose you have been looking for a letter for a long time, but I have been
detained in writing, because we have been in an unsettled state, and I thought I would
stay until we was settled: but I have now the pleasure and happiness to say, that we
are all quite well and hearty, hoping this will find you all the same. I find myself in
duty bound, to thank you for the many favors I have had to enjoy at your hands. I
will now give you some of the outlines as to the passage. We had a very tedious passage of 8 weeks, but I soon overcame my sea sickness; but I could not stand the rock-
ing of the ship, and it was a very rough sea almost all the way over; but I may say that
I was as well as any of the party. The children was as well as any of the children, but
my husband was very ill all the way; so bad, that he could not go up on deck above
once or twice all the way, and for the first nine months there were, that he could not
earn any thing; but I have been quite well, and have had plenty of work hat making.
I have had to maintain the family myself; but we have not wanted any thing.

Labouring men earn 3s. per day, and board; here is plenty of work for every body,
and provisions are very cheap; but here is but very little money. The price of provisions are as follows, as nigh as I can tell. Flour is 4 dollars per barrel of 196 lbs.
weight; 4d. lb. pork; 3d. lb. beef; 3d. lb. mutton; and a fat sheep for 7s.6d.; butter from
7½d, to 9d. lb.; cheese here is none in this country; sugar, 6d. lb.; tea, 5s.3d. lb.: candles, 9d. lb.; and other things much the same as in England; clothing very little dearer;
shoes are very dear in this country, and very bad leather; cows are from 4£. to 5£.

---

63 Sarah Green to whom both this letter and 73 were directed was the sister of John Hampton of Sullington, also a sponsor of Petworth emigrants. Her husband, Thomas, was a grocer.
64 Both Elizabeth and James signed the marriage register with a mark.

per head; oxen are from 15£. to 18£. per yoke; horses from 10£. to 20£.; no good barley in this country; it is winter barley.

The produce of Canada: very fine wheat very plentiful, oats, peas, no beans, potatoes, carrots, cabbage, onions, peas, french beans; pumpkins, cucumbers, melons, all grow wild in the fields with turnips. The weather is colder in the winter, and hotter in the summer, here is only 3 months of summer, and then very hot days and sometimes frosty nights; these months are June, July, and August. Then September, October, and November, are the fall; these months are something like your winter. Then December, January, and February, are very sharp frost and snow: March, April, and May, are like your winter. I had 3 bushels of wheat for 2 hats, and I have flour enough to last until harvest.

Please to send me word how all your family is, and what additions to your family. Remember me to Miss Ann [Green], and Miss Mary [Green], and my kind love to all.

Please to let mother [Massey Nash] see this as soon as you can: should be very thankful to have the letters franked. Can say no more at present, from your affectionate servant,

ELIZABETH WACKFORD.

Wrote by James Rapson: his love to all. Please to let him [his father] know that his son and family are all well.

OTHER LETTERS: 73

■ 73

ELIZABETH (NASH) WACKFORD, WATERLOO TOWNSHIP, UPPER CANADA, TO HER FATHER AND MOTHER, RICHARD AND MASSEY NASH, AND FRIENDS, [PETWORTH, WEST SUSSEX, 25 JUNE 1833]

SOURCE: *No. 3 Continuation*, 21–3

I must write now to my dear friends. My dear father and mother, as I have said so much about the country, I shall say nothing, because as you will see this. I have the pleasure to say, that I am quite well and hearty, and can keep myself quite well, and I have kept my family, owing to my husband's being so ill, and we have not wanted any thing. The people are very kind to us: they are Dutch mostly, but very good to us. Emma is quite well, and never wishes to return to England; but sends her love to all. James is out at service for 8 months, for 31 dollars: he is quite well and sends his love to you. Sarah is at home with us: she have been out at service a week, she is quite well, and wishes to be remembered to you all. Thomas is out, and will be until he is 18 years old. He is not bound yet; he have a good place, and the people are very kind to him. He is quite well, sends his love to you. William is very lusty. Abraham is grown very tall, so that you would not know them.

My husband sends his kind love to you all, hoping this will find you all in good health: he is better now than he have been since he have been in this province; he says he would not return to England for £200. He would like to see you all here; here would be a living for them. I thought to have heard from all my brothers and sisters by Mr. Gibbs, and did not; so I hope you will write and send all the news you can. Frank [Nash] is at Hambledon: he have had 3 dollars a month, ever since he have been here. [Thomas] Adsett saw him last week; he is quite well, but I have not seen him since we have been here; he have promised to come and see us next week.

My love to aunt Spooner, and uncle William and his wife, and Mary [and] Ann Green. My love to Charles Adsett and all my dear brothers and sisters; here would be a good living for them all. I hope Charles Woods will come, as a blacksmith is a good business. I can say no more, your loving daughter,

E.W.

I wish mother to go to Lavant Hill, and tell Mr. Noel and Mrs. how we are; and remember us to all friends; and send how they are all; with all the news you can. Write as soon as possible, and direct, William Wackford, Waterloo, near Galt, Dumfries, Gore, Upper Canada.

To MRS. SARAH GREEN, PETWORTH.

OTHER LETTERS: 72

In 1834 and 1837, the family was recorded in Woolwich Township, probably on part of lot 22 on the town line with Peel. In February 1849, James purchased the rear of lot 21 concession 2 Peel Township, and he had a one-storey log house when the 1851 census was taken. He still owned this lot in 1861. Despite Elizabeth's concerns for his health when they first arrived, James lived to the age of 77, dying on 21 December 1870, two days after his birthday. Elizabeth was 75 when she died the following month. James Jr and Thomas seem to have married and settled in Woolwich.

■ 74

EXTRACT FROM A LETTER OF WILLIAM PHILLIPS SR, ADELAIDE TOWNSHIP, UPPER CANADA, [SUMMER] 1833

William Phillips of Merston, West Sussex, paid his own way and that of his wife Ellen and one child in order to join his son in the Adelaide settlement. Phillips, like James Rapson, Rhoda Thair, and Caroline Dearling, wrote a letter that was in part journal entries of his travels. James Brydone* used this extract in his *Narrative* to contrast the hardships encountered by the Phillips family on the St Lawrence route with the comparatively easy journey his 1834 emigrants made using the Rideau Canal.

SOURCE: Brydone, *Narrative of a Voyage*, 62

In the morning, we with our luggage, went on board two large Durham boats, and was carried through the locks in the Lachine canal, there we were forced to unload the boats, to have everything weighed; it was six in the evening, before we left this place, and got to Lachine at eleven at night; could go no farther, for the lock.

We expected some place to go to, but no place was provided for us; so we sat in the boat all night; in the morning the men went, and stole wood, and made a great fire. The next day, being Sunday, we stay all day and night, we made tents, and slept on the ground.

Monday morning, at break of day, sailed the remainder of the canal, and crossed a small lake, into another canal, called the cascades; with a great many locks, every one taking us several feet higher up a hill. This canal is cut through a rock, to miss the rapids in this place. We were now drawn by oxen, up the rapids; they walked at the edge of the water, taking us as near the outside of the water, as the boats could go. Our travelling this way is very tiresome, and took us eight days, to get to Prescot; the first night we reached a village, and after begging hard, we prevailed with them to let us lay on their floor: we carried our beds, and slept there, at the charge of 6d. each. At break of day, we went on board, and stopped at night, where there was no houses: we borrowed the sail, and as many as could get under did. The others made a large fire, and sat, or slept by it; the next day, it rained all day, and at night we stopped at a village, and prevailed with some poor people, to lodge us, a house full, on their floor; they let us make tea, and dryed our clothes. In the night, I was taken ill, with the spasms, and a fever followed; I did not eat one mouthful, of food, for eight days; only drinked a little port wine often. I could not hardly get in, or out of the boat, nor did I think I should ever see Adelaide. We at last came to Prescot; *sleeping on the ground every night, but two*. The boatmen were all Frenchmen, and no way obliging; we could not make the kettle boil, by the fire. When we came to Prescot, we were all very wet with rain, so we was forced to remain, as we was. At five o'clock, we went on board the steamer, to Cornwall, in a close room; should have been comfortable, if we had been dry.

We got to Cornwall, about five in the morning; the boatmen said, we must walk nine miles, the rapids run so strong. A great many walked; but myself, so ill, I could not; so myself, and Ellen, and three more women, with small children, hired a waggon, and two horses, to carry us twelve miles, for two dollars. These waggons are not like yours, they have one straight board, on each side, one at the head, and one behind, just like a great chest, without a lid; they are like this all the country through; but we had spring seats, and a man to drive. The boats did not get here until the afternoon. The roads are very dirty, and rough; but this is one of the best, being where the coaches run. The men walked on, but the women and children got in the boats, for we were as much in the rapids, as before; the middle of the stream is worse, by far, than the edge of the water, where we were drawn by oxen; when we got at last to Prescot, we took the steamer for York, across Lake Ontario.

– I have told you wrong; we came to Cornwall, before we came to Prescot; the other place's name, I have forgot: Prescot is where we took the steamer, for York.

SEE LETTERS of William Phillips Jr (9) and William Cooper (8).

William lived to the age of 88 and was buried in the cemetery of St Paul's church in Warwick.

■ 75

EXTRACT OF A LETTER FROM MARY BARNES, YORK, UPPER CANADA,
JULY 1833

William and Mary Barnes emigrated from the parish of Tillington, West Sussex, with their
six children in 1832. This extract was chosen by Sockett* for use in his pamphlet defending
his committee from the newspaper accusations made against Captain Hale, and it includes
no personal information. We know, however, from Edward Boxall (letter 53) that William died
some time before February 1833.

SOURCE: Petworth Emigration Committee, "Statement," [October 1833]. This extract was was printed
in the *Brighton Guardian*, 16 October 1833, and the *Montreal Gazette*, 2 January 1834.

Lord Egremont*'s Emigrants are just arrived at York, Monday the 1st of July, after
10 weeks voyage: they are all over the place at present, not knowing what to be doing.
They had a better voyage over than what we had, and we felt glad to see them, as
coming from Petworth; therefore, instead of any complaint being made, every one
ought to feel highly indebted to The Earl of Egremont, and Mr. Sockett*, for the
great favors conferred on them; as the inconvenience they feel, is nothing equal to
the expence that we are sure must have been to him.

Mary Barnes family was a source of concern to Sockett both before and after emigration. His
fears as well as his hopes for this family came out in a letter he wrote in September 1832 to
the Duke of Richmond in the hope that Richmond might use his influence on their behalf.[65]

A man named William Barns, a Parishioner of Petworth, with his wife and six children,
emigrated with our party. He was so weak as to suffer himself to be decoyed up the country by a stranger who robbed him of all his money – between £60 & £70 leaving him
pennyless. He has left some money behind him in this country, and has written home to
have a supply sent out, and I sent out £20 last night, to the Secy of the Canada Company, to be forwarded to York, for his use, but in the meantime the man & his family are
living at an Inn at York U.C. (Cooper's Black Horse Tavern Church Street) and before
the £20 can get to him he will have run up a heavy bill, and I much fear will be overtaken by the winter, & perhaps reduced to great extremities. Barns has been Bailiff to different people, & had got together a little money, by industry & frugality – finding that
an experiment at farming on his own account, did not succeed, he determined on emigrating; but before he went, his mind seemed depressed, & not quite in a sound state –
his conduct since he arrived in U.C. (remaining back at York instead of going on with
the party, & suffering himself to be thus imposed upon & robbed) seem to shew that he
is not competent to manage his own affairs – but his wife is a clever managing woman,
& the family a fine rising one, just fitted for Canada; and some more money could be
sent if it would be made good use of. If therefore any thing could be done to retrieve

65 WSRO, Goodwood MS 1460, f. 34, Sockett to Richmond, 18 September 1832

the false step the poor man has made & to get them thro' the coming winter they might yet do well. I am not aware whether any representation made by your Grace to the Governor or any other leading person could be of use, but I have ventured to state the case in a faint hope that something might be done in behalf of the unfortunate people. The man who robbed Barns is in prison at Port Hope, & is to be tried in Octr but I fear very little if any money will be recovered.

Sockett sent at least one, and perhaps more, credit notes to this family through the Canada Company. By 1833 William had died at York (letter 53) and by 1836 two of the boys were apprenticed to a butcher (letter 133).

■ 76

JAMES RAPSON, GALT, UPPER CANADA, TO HIS FATHER PHILIP RAPSON, LODSWORTH, SUSSEX, 9 JULY 1833

James Rapson was joined by his brother William and sister Rhoda Thair and their families. William Rapson and his wife, Maria (Thair) had been married for nearly four years when they were sent to Upper Canada from Lodsworth. They had one young daughter in addition to the baby girl who died at sea.

SOURCE: *No. 4 Continuation*, 28

Galt, July 9th. 1833.

DEAR FATHER,

I have the pleasure to say, that my dear brothers, and sisters, arrived here the 5th. July, all well and hearty; with John White, and wife, and child; John Dearling, his wife, and all his children; George Trussler, his wife, and all his children; but G. Trussler have had great accidents with two of his children.[66] William's wife [Maria] was put to bed on the 12th. of May, (they are all with us) very good time, and was quite well; but the child lived only two days; but as they will write within a week, I shall say nothing more, only that they came all unexpectedly, as I have not had a letter for a long time; nor knew any thing of it, till I saw William coming, near a quarter of a mile before he came to our house; and he held up his hat. I knew him, but I could not believe my eyes for some time; but I was highly pleased to see them, and especially as they are all so well. I think that William, Rhoda, and Thomas, look better than ever I saw them. George and Maria[67] are both well, and have enjoyed themselves well; their love to all, and will write to them in 5 or 6 days; but they wish you to let them see this. They have had quite a comfortable passage, and are all enjoying themselves much better than any one could expect.

I must now tell you that we are all quite hearty; and I may say that I am, and have been, better for the last 9 months, than ever I have been for many years. You must excuse this short letter, as I am so busy; it is now one o'clock. They was hurried

66 See letter 78 from Rhoda and George Thair.
67 George and Maria, Rhoda's husband and William's wife, were brother and sister.

through Montreal, so that they could not go to the post office. The weather is not so hot as it was last summer, and much healthier than with you. Sarah is not strong yet, but quite well, thank God.[68] Hannah is out still, quite hearty: she came here to day, and saw them all, quite pleased. Mary is with us. Philip, Isaac, and Rhoda, with the little one, are all well. I do not know how to express my thanks to the gentlemen that have sent them out so honorably; and that they provided for them; for I think they came out like gentlefolks.[69] I have received a letter from the Rev. Mr. Sockett, and as soon as I can get time, I will write to him. I am very thankful to him for his kindness. Remember me to Mr. Chrippes, and to all friends: may the blessing of God rest on them all, through life, and for ever, is the sincere prayer of J.R.

Dear Father, I should not have wrote you such a letter as this, only I was forced: you would not have their letters, as they could not have time to go to the post themselves: they wrote a letter to you, and to George's mother [Sarah Thair], and sent them to the post as they came; and I was afraid that they did not put them in; and as they will write by next Tuesday, I shall say no more. We sends our united love to you all. Your affectionate son,

JAMES RAPSON.

To PHILIP RAPSON,
    Lodsworth, near Petworth, Sussex,
    England.

Described as an extract, the passages from this letter that Sockett used as part of his evidence of Hale's conduct in Petworth Emigration Committee, "Statement," [October 1833], are taken from different parts of Rapson's letter and are more accurately a compilation. The wording is very slightly adjusted.

I have the pleasure to say, that my dear brothers, and sisters, arrived here the 5th. July, all well and hearty; they came all unexpectedly, as I have not had a letter for a long time; nor knew any thing of it, till I saw William coming, near a quarter of a mile before he came to our house; and he held up his hat. I knew him, but I could not believe my eyes for some time; but I was highly pleased to see them, and especially, as they are all so well. I think that William, Rhoda, and Thomas, look better than ever I saw them. George and Maria are both well, and have enjoyed themselves well; their love to all, and will write to them in 5 or 6 days; but they wish you to let them see this. They have had a comfortable passage. I do not know how to express my thanks to the gentlemen that have sent them out so honorably; and that they provided for them; for I think they came out like gentlefolks.

OTHER LETTERS: 2, 12, 38, 115. Other members of the party greeted by James have letters in

---

68 Sarah's daughter, Jane, was born in 1833.
69 These families were assisted by Egremont, W.H. Yaldwyn, and the Parish of Lodsworth.

this collection; see Rhoda (Rapson) and George Thair 70, and John and Caroline Dearling 85; and Timothy Trusler, brother of George Trusler, 105.

James and Sarah Rapson had several more children in Upper Canada, fourteen in all. The family was still living in Waterloo Township in 1840, but by 1854 James Rapson was leasing land in Goderich Township. The 1871 census of Huron County describes Rapson as a Baptist, and according to his obituary he was one of the founders of the Base Line Church. He and Sarah are buried in Balls Cemetary, not far from the family farm in Goderich Township.

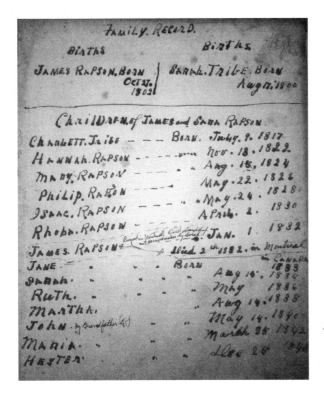

A page from the Rapson family Bible
See letter 2

77

EXTRACT OF A LETTER FROM JOHN SAUNDERS, YORK, UPPER CANADA, 11 JULY 1833

We think that the John Sanders of this letter was a bricklayer sent from Lurgashall in 1833, possibly accompanied by his wife and children. Sockett* sent a manuscript copy of this extract in which Sanders complained of the hardships he experienced on the St Lawrence between Montreal and Prescott to the Duke of Richmond. It seems to have been enclosed in a letter Sockett wrote to Richmond on 5 November 1833, along with another extract taken from Captain Hale's report for 1833. Hale reported that delays in repairing winter damage to one of the locks on the Rideau Canal had forced his party, and several others, to use "the old tedious & comfortless Batteaux by the Rapids of the St. Lawrence." As a result, Sockett and his committee, who had promoted the 1833 emigration on the assumption that the Rideau Canal would be open, were being "charged with having given the people false information."

SOURCE: WSRO, Goodwood MS 1470, f217
Extract of a Letter from J°. (John) Saunders, dated York Upper Canada July 11th 1833.

"We arrived at York July 1st after 10 weeks voyage, and glad enough we all were to reach that place. [It was stated to us that we should *not come up the rapids*, but <u>we did</u> and I think no poor creatures ever could suffer more than *we all* did, lying out at nights, and getting into any outhouses to lie down for an hour or two. Therefore I expect that it was being thus exposed that caused me to get the cold I have in my arm and, hand, what with wet clothes, and other inconveniences."][70]

■ 78

RHODA AND GEORGE THAIR TO PHILIP RAPSON, LODSWORTH, SUSSEX, 13 JULY 1833

SOURCE: *No. 4 Continuation*, 28-9.

July 13th 1833.

DEAR FATHER AND MOTHER,

June 23rd. 9 miles from Montreal, staid there all day Sunday, very hot.

24th. started on at 4 o'clock in the morning.

25th, very wet in an open boat; wet through all day; men all obliged to walk; the sailors and captain very cross, threatened us very much.

26th. told Captain Hale of it, so he let all the women and children go in the steamer, and the men in the boat.

27th. in the boat, had 4 oxen to draw us, sometimes had 2 horses.

28th. came to Prescot, staid in the storehouse all night.

29th. went on board a steamer, by the name of the *United Kingdom*, a most beautiful thing it was.

30th. all well, came to Kingston: it is as large a town as Chichester: houses are mostly built of stone: all goods are as cheap as in England.

31st. a thunder storm about 12 o'clock in the night, our beds were spread on deck, and we were all in bed: we got wet through, and our beds soaked with rain. In the morning, George Trusler's little James was getting some water, and the board gave way, and he fell over; he was about 11 years old. They stopped the steamer and let down the boat, but they could not get him. It was the most distressing sight I ever saw; they said they could see him for 200 yards: he had his caul in his pocket.[71] His

---

70 The square brackets show the passage marked by Sockett.

71 Children are occasionally born with a caul, a portion of the inner membrane enclosing an infant before birth which remains on their head. The caul was (and is) thought to be lucky and to protect its owner from drowning.

mother has not been well since.[72] Blessed be the Lord he brought us safe and well to land.

July 1st came to York, our things all out exposed to the rain.

. . .[73]

3rd. went in a schooner: 4th. came to Hamilton, slept in a stable. 5th. hired 3 waggons, gave 8 dollars a waggon for families. Wm. and George went on, and James came to meet us, we got here just as it was dark, all unexpected, we were glad to see them all looking so well: met the children about a mile from home, without any shoes or stockings, they all go so here. Old Mrs. Tribe looks better, I think, than ever I saw her. The next day, poor Hannah came in, did not know that we were here, she looked very hard, and at last begun crying before she could speak. Mrs. [Charlotte Tribe] Evans came to day, she looks very thin, but she expects to be confined very soon.

15th. James has been to Hamilton, and agreed for 200 acres of land for us, so will part it in 4 lots, they are all gone this morning to work on it, to put up houses and clear. Nothing to be paid for three years. It seems dismal at first, but I think we shall like it after a bit. Tell aunt Madgwick that Isaac Berry is somewhere near York, little George died when they got to York.[74] Harriet White, the young woman that came out with us, staid at York. Tom is with James, he seems to like it very much; he has been to work with Richard Tribe, a chopping; he will write as soon as he can, but he will be busy now with James and the rest. I had the letter from Jane, at Portsmouth, with the half sovereign for Tom. We are all well, except John, who has been bad ever since we have been here. I have been to a doctor; he gave me some powders for him to take every night and morning, and to keep his head wet with whisky; he said it was the sun fever in his head. Fanny has been poorly, but she is got better. George has been poorly, but he is quite well now. He was not the least sea sick all the way over, nor Tom but very little. Old Mrs. Tribe was very much hurt because Robert was not come with us, but she hopes he will come next year. I shall write to George's mother within a week, so you will hear how John is, I think he is rather better; I hope, if it please God, he will be well when I write. George Trusler has took a house and land, and is gone to it; brother John went to Adelaide.[75] Sarah sends her love to all, and is very glad with what mother and Ruth sent her. Tell Jane she should write to me soon, and tell me her direction, and I will write to her. John Dearling

---

72 George and Elizabeth Trussler emigrated from Fernhurst, West Sussex, with seven children. Their baby Harriet died on the *England*. Hale, the superintendant, countered Trussler's complaints by writing that he was the "most helpless on the voyage and received the most attention." The family settled in Plympton Township.

73 Original annotation: "*(The passage omitted contains some remarks affecting the private character of an individual.) T.S.*"

74 Isaac and Emma (Curtis) Berry with their five children emigrated from Fernhurst, West Sussex, in 1832.

75 John and Jane (Childs) Trusler emigrated in 1833 from Fernhurst with 11 children and took them to Plympton Township.

went out one day, and met with a bear, but as soon as the bear saw him, he turned and run away. He, John, is going to have part of ground: his wife is very poorly, he, and the children, is quite well. I am quite well, and have been ever since I left home, except sea sick, and so has Tom. They have seen several deer, and shot at them with their shot guns, but they have not killed any one yet. We have not had many pigeons yet. There is a fish pond on the ground we are going to, that covers 4 acres of ground, and full of fish. I think little John is a little better, but he is very much altered. As Wm. has wrote to George's friends I shall not write so soon, but Tom will write next time. We miss the beer and meat very much, as there is no getting any without we kill, ourselves. Here is strawberries and hurts[76] by the bushel, that grow in the woods.

Dear father, I hope I shall have a letter from you soon. I wish I could get at some of our home doctors; there is none so good doctors here as Mr. Hicks. I have been to two doctors with little John, but he is not much better yet; he was quite well all the way over. I shall write to the Rev. T. Sockett soon. Give our love to all my brothers and sisters and all friends. Tell me, when you write, how mother's face is: James' face was bad the night we came, but is quite well now, thank God for it. So no more at present, from your affectionate son and daugher,

God bless you all.

RHODA & GEORGE THAIR.

To PHILIP RAPSON, Lodsworth, Sussex.

OTHER LETTERS: 70, 76

Sockett selected a passage from Rhoda's journal for publication in Petworth Emigration Committee, "Statement," [October 1833], including material he had suppressed when he first published the letter.

24th. (June) started at 4 o'clock in the morning.

25th. very wet all day: men all obliged to walk: the sailors and Captain very cross, threatened us very much.

26th. told Capt. Hale of it, so he let all the women and children go in the steamer, and the men in the boat.

July 1st. came to York. Capt. Hale would not pay our way any further: kept us there two days; then, afterwards, he paid our way to Hamilton: we were obliged to buy all our provisions, all the way up: he was three parts of his time tipsy.

From Hale's journal sent to the Petworth Committee, we know that his party was circumventing the Long Sault Rapids at Cornwall on the 26th. His version of her report that he was "three parts of his time tipsy" was that his supply of spirits was "plundered" on this date.

---

76 Whortleberry or bilberry

He described sending Rhoda's party to Dundas at an extra charge as "the steamer did not go that way." He may have been referring to the schooner that sailed with the Plympton party.

We have been told of a family memory that James Trussler was throwing garbage overboard when he drowned. The circumstances are the same; the rail or gate gave way and he fell.

■ 79

WILLIAM AND ELIZABETH DANIELS, WILMOT TOWNSHIP, UPPER CANADA, TO BROTHERS AND SISTERS, ADDRESSED TO MR GEORGE SHARP, PETWORTH, WEST SUSSEX, 14 JULY 1833

William Daniels, a labourer, and Elizabeth (Horton) Daniels emigrated in 1832 with the assistance of the parish of Tillington; William had been drawing poor relief at the time. They had been married at Petworth in 1814[77] and at the time they emigrated had four girls and one boy between the ages of 15 and one.

SOURCE: *No. 5 Continuation*, 34–5

Wilmot, 14th July, 1833.

DEAR BROTHERS & SISTERS,

I write these few lines to let you know that we are all well, and hope this will find you all in the same. We had a great deal of sickness when we first arrived in this country. I did not [do] any work worth speaking of, for twelve months, but I am quite well now. I have got 100 acres of land, and intend to go on it this fall. I have got 8 acres of wheat growing. Dear Brothers, I wish you was here to help cut it; and expect to have as much more next year, and some in grass.

The prices of land in this country is various; in Wilmot it is 12s. 6d. currency, per acre; in the Huron Tract, it is 7s. 6d.; in some places it sells at £2. 10s. per acre; wild land according to its situation and goodness. The prices of provisions is as follows: flour 22s.6d. per barrel of 200 lb.; pork generally sells about 14 dollars per barrel of 200 lb., but is now 18 dollars; butter 7½d. per lb.; beef 6 dollars per 100 lbs.; tea 5s. per lb.; sugar 6d. to 8d. per lb.; a yoke of oxen from 60 to 80 dollars; a cow from 16 to 24 dollars. The prices depend on the season of the year you want to buy them. I have told you all I can. I hope that some of you will come out, for it is a much better country than England: here is peace and plenty. Labourers have from 2s. 6d. to 3s. per day, and found. A man, to hire by the year, has from £24. to £32. per year. Sovereigns passes here generally from 23s. 4d. to 24s. currency. When we came to York, our money amounted to 14£. 12s. currency. We left Frances Hall[78] 70 miles from York, with an English Family. We are 38 miles from Mr. Standing: they go on the same way they did when they were at home. They lost all their clothes.[79]

---

77 Both signed the marriage register with a mark.

78 Frances Hall or Hale was a single woman from Tillington, who apparently emigrated in 1832.

79 The Standings must have been somewhat notorious in Petworth; the Tilleys (83) use almost the same words to describe the family.

Dear Brothers and Sisters,

If any of you think fit to come, I will be very happy: it will be much better for you, than it was for us; for you will have a place to come to, as we only had the woods to shelter us. Dear George, please to write to London, and let them know our situation. We send our love to James Hooker, and his wife, Thomas Horton,[80] and wife, and to all my nephews and nieces. Give my duty to Mr. Sargent, tell him I am much obliged to him for the book; and also to Mr. Wiggens; to Mr. and Miss Ayling; to Mr. Burgess; and tell them we are doing well.

Dear Father and mother,

This comes with our kind love to you, hoping it will find you alive and well, as we are all at present, thank God for it. Dear Father, I will be glad to hear from you as soon as you can; you might write with my brothers. I should have come and seen you, but did not like to it; but I have [been] sorry many a time since, that I did not see you before I left England. Give our respects to my sister, and tell her I would have come and seen her, but she often came near, and never came nigh [us]. So God bless you all.

Dear Sisters,

Charles Boxall was drowned at Montreal, the last of May 1832,[81] or else he would have been back to England before now. His sister's daughter took what belonged to him, and returned to England in the same ship we came out in. She went back with the Captain's mate. I have told you all I can, So no more at present. Your affectionate brother and sister,

WILLIAM & ELIZABETH DANIELS.

Direct to us, Wilmot, Gore District, Upper Canada, North America, by way of New York.

Mr. George Sharp, Petworth, Sussex, England.

Daniels does not explain where or how his family had lived in the year since emigrating, but it sounds as though they had spent some time in a shanty. Wilmot Township, settled by a largely German population, was on the road to Goderich just before it entered the Canada Company's Huron Tract. The family had three more children in North America, one of them recorded in the 1851 census of Wilmot as born in the United States.

William, described as a joiner in 1851, received a deed from the Canada Company for the whole of lot 25 concession 1 in Wilmot in 1850 and in 1858 bought another 100 acres on the N ½ lot 23 concession 1. At different times, three of his sons occupied land on these lots, apparently as farmers. Two of them were still there in 1871. William was by then 84 years of age, his occupation was given as labourer, and he and Elizabeth rented one quarter acre

---

80 Thomas Horton was Elizabeth Daniels' brother.

81 Charles Boxall, a single man from Tillington, drowned after drinking. His sister could be Sarah Boxall who was married to William Tickner; their eldest daughter was Jane.

of lot 26 concession 2 Wilmot. William died in 1876; Elizabeth lived to be 90, and at her death in 1883 she was described as a "labourer's wife."

■ 80

HENRY HABBIN, YORK, UPPER CANADA, 17 JULY 1833

Before emigrating from the parish of Petworth in 1832 aged 19, Henry Habbin had applied to the Duke of Richmond (in his capacity as postmaster general) for a job in the post office. The reply he received in March informed him that there were so many applicants that he did not stand a chance.

SOURCE: This extract, printed in Petworth Emigration Committee, "Statement," [October 1833], was the first of two taken from letters sent by Habbin.

Extract of a Letter from Henry Habbin, lately of Petworth, (one of the Passengers of the England, 1833,) dated York, July 17th. 1833, to a Gentleman at Petworth.

On the 16th June, we landed at Grosse Island, just this side of Quebec, where we were obliged to land on purpose to see if our clothes was clean, or to see that there was no sickness on board. We landed, and our boxes were over-hauled, but we were so clean and free from sickness, that we came on board the same evening very safe: but some vessels were obliged to stay on the Island some time, through filth.

OTHER LETTERS: 81

■ 81

HENRY HABBIN, YORK, UPPER CANADA, TO HIS MOTHER, PETWORTH, WEST SUSSEX, 17 JULY 1833

The second extract, from a letter Habbin sent to his mother, a widow living in Petworth, was blunt and to the point on the subject of Hale.

SOURCE: Extracts printed in Petworth Emigration Committee, "Statement," [October 1833]; copied in *Brighton Guardian*, 16 October 1833

As for Captain Hale, he was not fit to drive a pig to market to be sold: and not only me have sent word in their letters about it, for others have sent word, and many more will.

OTHER LETTERS: 80

In a note following this extract, Sockett warned: "The Committee think it right to state; that Sharp [86], Turner, and Habbin, are all persons to whose testimony very little credit is attached by those who knew them."

In a letter written from Sandwich on 21 August 1836 (113), David Sharp sent "our love" to Mr and Mrs Habbin, suggesting that this group of people from Petworth may have still been in touch with Henry.

■ 82

EDWARD AND HANNAH BRISTOW, WOOLWICH TOWNSHIP,
UPPER CANADA, TO HIS BROTHER, SHIPLEY, WEST SUSSEX,
20 JULY 1833

Edward Bristow, a labourer from the parish of Shipley, sailed on the *Lord Melville* in 1832 with his wife, Hannah Streeter, and their three young children.[82] Emigrants from Shipley were under the sponsorship of Egremont*'s son- in-law, Sir Charles Burrell*.

SOURCE: *No. 6 Continuation*, 41-2

Woolwich, July 20th. 1833.

DEAR BROTHER,

This comes with my kind love to you all, in hopes it will find you in good health, as it leaves us at present. I wrote to you to inform you, that we was greatly disappointed that you did not come out this spring, as you promised the last time you spoke to me. This is the 4th letter I have wrote to England, and have never received any answer; please to answer this letter as quick as possible, and let me know whether you have a mind to come or not, to join me in partnership on my land, as it would be a great pleasure to us. I have got one yoke of oxen, and 3 cows. Stock is dear at present. – George Streeter[83] is an apprentice to a blacksmith, for 3 years, and has nothing to pay; but is to receive £35. for 3 years, and be boarded, and washing and mending done, and nothing but his clothes to find himself. So * * * may see which is best, and if he had been a man, instead of a coward, he might have got as much for half the time; so he had better make up his mind to come next spring.

I wrote 2 letters to England last fall; whether you had them or not I cannot tell, for I never received any answer. There is an excellent account of this country, and it was [illegible in letter] as I promised; it is truly a very prosperous country for labouring people, and neither heat nor cold is not anywise disagreeable, but we have a great deal of snow. I am very sorry that you are all so hard to believe the good news of this country, for surely all the good news that ever you heard of by letters, are the truth. The children have been very healthy since they recovered of the hooping cough; they enjoy the country very much, but they are sadly disappointed that their little cousins did not come to play with them.

May 6th 1833, Hannah was confined of another son, which we have named John. We are in a very obliging neighbourhood, and as friendly people in such a case as any in the world – it was as cheap a time as ever I had in England, and for [far?] more necessaries for the woman than ever she had in England. This is the correct direction, so I hope your letter will come safe this time. – Edward Bristow, at David

---

82 Edward signed the marriage register and Hannah used a mark when they were married on 31 July 1827.

83 Hannah's brother, who also emigrated in 1832. He was apprenticed to Michael Eisenhauer and settled on the 50 acres above Bristow after he married Eisenhauer's daughter, Susan.

Edward and Hannah
(Streeter) Bristow
Woolwich Historical
Foundation

Musselman's,[84] Woolwich Township, near Waterloo Post Office, Gore District, Halton County, Upper Canada, North America.

– Give our love to all enquiring friends, especially to Fathers, Mother, Sisters and Brothers. I should be very glad to see all, or any of you in Woolwich, to join friends. If Fathers and Mother could make up their minds to come, we can make them a very good home, without being in any care about a living; and your age is nothing if you can only make up your minds, for there is people come out this spring from England 80 years of age, and held their journey quite well. Our nearest neighbour is Edmund Thomas;[85] he came from Strood Green[86] with us in the Lord Melville – his Wife's Father came out this spring to them, 64 years old, and held his journey as

---

84 David Musselman was located on lot 88 German Company Tract (GCT), having bought the full 350 acres from Martin Wenger in 1828. Family information is that Edward and his brother John worked at one of Musselman's mills in Conestogo, walking daily from their lots.

85 Original annotation: "See letter from Ann Thomas" [letter 37].

86 South of Kirdford, West Sussex.

well as any of the young people, and if you cannot believe, if any of you go to Strood Green, and enquire for Thomas Puttock, you will find the same story. If any of you mean to come, write me an answer with speed, get it franked if you can; then I will send you word what to bring, and what is best for you to bring, so that you may come out next spring. For if any of you mean to come, the sooner you come the better, for the Township is good land, and settles so fast, that the joining Lots will soon be taken up. So I will not say any more to entice you, nor I will not persuade you; but the best thing any industrious people, and there will never be too many come, if only they come far enough, they may do well. Publish this letter to all that wish to hear. Remember us to James Newman, tell him I should be very glad to see him, or hear from him, for I wrote him a letter, as I promised him, but have never received any answer – but I wish to hear from some one very shortly, for the time seems very long, without hearing from you.

This is to tell you what chance there is for fatherless children; there is plenty willing to take them, and bring them up till they are 16 years of age, and give them plenty; but for common, they stay till they are 18 or 19 years of age. Then if it be a boy, he will receive 100 acres of land, 1 yoke of oxen, 1 plough, and harrows and chains. If it be a girl, she will receive 1 cow, 1 bucket, 2 beds and steads, a sufficient quantity of earthenware for housekeeping, and plenty of clothes. So no more at present, from your affectionate brother and sister,

EDWARD & HANNAH BRISTOW.

Edward and his younger brother John Bristow married sisters Hannah and Sarah Streeter. John Bristow (who may have been the recipient of this letter) and Sarah came on the *Burrell* in 1835 at the same time as another John Bristow.

Edward Bristow was one of the leading pioneers of the Elmira area. About 1843, he opened a tavern, the Troy hotel, and started a small general store and an ashery. He was first postmaster of the West Woolwich Post Office, known locally as Bristow's until 1856 when he moved away to start another community, Shipley, in Wallace Township.

Edward and Hannah had seven children in Upper Canada; John and Sarah, who also settled in the Elmira area, had six more children in addition to the three who came with them from England.

■ 83

JAMES AND HANNAH TILLEY, NELSON TOWNSHIP, UPPER CANADA, TO
FRIENDS AND NEIGHBOURS, [ADDRESSED TO THOMAS LUCAS, RED
LION YARD,] PETWORTH, WEST SUSSEX, 29 JULY 1833
James Tilley, a labourer, and his wife, Hannah Chesman, emigrated from Petworth in 1833.[87]
They mention three children who accompanied them, Maria, Henry, and Frederick, and two

87 When they married at Petworth in 1801, both James and Hannah signed the marriage register with a mark.

grown children – William Tilley and Mary (Tilley) Boxall (with her husband George) – had emigrated the year before. Others of their children may have remained in England.

SOURCE: *No. 4 Continuation*, 30–2. A short extract from this letter – noted in italics below – was published with minor punctuation changes by Sockett* in the Petworth Emigration Committee's, "Statement." Sockett attributed the letter to Hannah Tilley.

Nelson, July 29th. 1833.

Dear Friends and Neighbours all,

This comes with our kind love to you all, hoping it will find you all in good health, as thank God it leaves us at present. Thank God we have arrived safe, after a long and tedious voyage of 10 weeks, where I found my children enjoying good health, and plenty of work. We had a comfortable voyage, except a little sea-sickness. *Captain Hale behaved very well to us, and did every thing in his power to make us comfortable;*[88] *and we had plenty of every thing we could wish for. Mr. Sockett's words I found very true, for I believe every thing was done that laid in their power, to make us comfortable*; and tell him, that the letter he wrote to Mary, she never received, which makes me think there must be some mistake at the Post Office; for if you send by New York, which is the best and quickest way, the letters should be paid to the water. If you enquire at the Post Office, you will know the rights of it; and when you answer this, let me know whether Mr. Sockett received the letter Mary sent to George's friends, after we had left England. You need not think the letters are forged which have been sent home; for I have shewed the book[89] to several that sent letters, and they say, that they are exactly as they sent them.

Tell Mrs. Tanner I have heard of her daughters, and son-in-law, and they are all living in service, at Dundas, and doing well.[90] Tell Mrs. Heather her son [George] has got a situation with a gentleman, and is doing well. Tell Mrs. Burgess that I heard of her son, he was in York about a fortnight before we arrived there, and he was in good health; but I cannot say where he is now, for he left York to go and work at some other part of the country, but I did not hear where. Tell Mrs. Smith, that her brother was at York, to receive his pension, the day we arrived at York; but I did not see him: I heard he was living a little way below York, and I will send her letter to the Office, and put a line inside to let him know where I am. Thomas Lucas is not living with his wife, but she is doing very well.[91] William Standing goes on about the same [as] he did in England. Tell Mrs. Peacock I have not heard of Mrs. [Elizabeth] Daniells yet,[92] but I intend going to Dundas as soon as I get a little settled, as

88 Captain Hale noted in his log of the voyage on 27 April 1833: "Many of the people distressed with sea-sickness, Brandy administered in pretty plentiful doses, sometimes mixed with laudanum as a booster."
89 Original annotation: *"Collection of Letters from Sussex Emigrants, 1832."*
90 Eliza Tanner and Mary (Tanner) Stemp, married to Arthur Stemp.
91 Ann (Mitchell) Lucas; she and Thomas Lucas emigrated with two young sons.
92 William and Elizabeth Daniels emigrated from Tillington, West Sussex, in 1832 with five children; see letter 79. The Daniels had in fact settled further west in Wilmot Township.

I hear there is a great many of them there; and when I write again, I will send the whole particulars.

I am living about nine miles from Dundas, and Tilly is at work for Government: him and George have taken a job of ditching, for 100 dollars, which is £25, and they make very good wages at it. I had two gentlemen offer to take Frederick, till he is twenty one, and give him 100 dollars, but Tilly would not let him go. Henry is at work with his father. Maria attended on the cabin passengers all the way over, and has been very lucky; she has got a good place, for 12 guineas a year, at Brockville, about 200 miles below where we are. Tell Mrs. Matthews, at Bunker's Hill, if she had let her daughter come with me, I could have got her a place next door, for the same wages. Tell Mrs. Herrington, I took Mary Rice[93] in the mess with me, and would have taken care of her all the way up the country, but she turned out so very bad; and I had to leave her at Montreal, with the Captain [John Lewis, of the *England*]. William Edwards, from Sutton, came up the country with us, and has got a place a little way from us, for 10 dollars a month.

With regard to the country, I will tell you as far as I am able. The country certainly is a very good one, and there is plenty of work for all England, if they were to come out here; but it is nothing like England. A man may get a good living by working hard, and enduring a great many hardships for the first year or two, till he can get his land cleared, and raise his own provisions. Then they can go on a little more comfortable, and I think it would be folly, for persons who are doing comfortably at home, to come to Canada; but they that cannot do comfortably at home, they cannot change for the worse. There is one great evil, I am sorry to say, in this country. A great many write about the cheapness of whisky, but they say nothing about the evil of it; so I would not advise any, who are given to drink, to come to this country, for they will do worse here than at home. For a man has to live here by the work of his hands, and not the assistance of the parish, which they can do comfortably, if they are steady; but if they spend half their earnings in drink, and lose half their time in getting drunk, where is their living to come from? Besides injuring their health, and shortening their days: as I have heard most of them that died of the cholera last year, were persons given to drink; but I do not mean to say all. But, thank God, I have nothing of that in my family to trouble me.

George has been very sickly since he has been here, and William has been very unfortunate in sawing for the steamboats: he is afraid he will not be paid his money. I had a misfortune and scalded my foot, on board of the ship, and have been lame ever since, but I am much better now. I do not mean to say but the country is a very good one, and a man may get a good living in it, but it does not altogether suit my feelings, for it is nothing like home; for there is no place near me where the gospel is preached, which makes me feel uncomfortable.

To be continued in No. 5.

---

93 Mary was the illegitimate daughter of Mary Rice. Her sister Frances, also illegitimate, was to emigrate in 1845. Whether Mary was "very bad" physically or morally we cannot say.

■ 84

Continued.

From James and Hannah Tilley: continued from No. 4.

SOURCE: *No. 5 Continuation*, 33–4

and wish I was with you again, and I shall never think myself at home in Canada. There is a friend at home that I shall write to very shortly. Please ask Mrs. Andrews to copy a few lines of this, and send to Hambleton to my brother Henry; and get a few lines from him, to know how my mother and all are; and likewise Tilley's father and mother, at Lodsworth.[94]

Please to remember us to Mr. and Mrs. King; Mr. and Mrs. Sockett*, and family;[95] and Miss Herington; also to the Messrs. Stovelds, and thank them for the many favours I have received of them; and to Mrs. Ball, and family, and tell her I will write to her before long; and also Mr. and Mrs. Price; and Mrs. Clement Burgess, and let me know how her health is; also remember us to Granny Boxall, and indeed all Petworth if I could mention them. I have heard of John Nevett, the Tailor: he is living at Westminster,[96] and works at his trade, and is doing pretty well. I have heard of Thomas Nevett, but I do not recollect where he was living, but he was in good health, but not doing as well as I could wish.[97] Please remember me to Miss Daintrey, and all her family, and let me know how she is, as she was very unwell when I saw her last; likewise remember me to Mrs. Nevett, the Tailor,[98] and Mrs. Bridger at the shop, and Mrs. Dawtrey, and all her family, and I could remember fifty more names, if time and paper would allow me. So I must conclude with my respects to you all, and I wish I was with you. So no more at present, from your well wishers, and old neighbours.

JAMES AND HANNAH TILLEY.

Please to answer this as soon as possible and let me know all particulars. Mary joins in love to Mrs. Andrews, and all of you, and our children, to all the children in the yard.

Direct to us,

To the care of Mr. George Chisholm, in the Township of Nelson, County of Halton, District of Gore, Upper Canada, North America.

There is one thing more I should like to mention, that is, we are always so fortunate as to fall in with a good Landlord and good Neighbours. There is people of all countries around me, and they behave very kindly to me; and if a person is sick,

---

94 Hannah's mother was Sarah Chesman, and James Tilley's father was John.

95 Thomas and Sarah Sockett, Frances, Caroline, and Henry. Frances and Caroline were Thomas's daughters by his first wife.

96 Presumably he was in Westminster Township, south of London.

97 John Nevett and Thomas Nevett may have been related but they were not brothers. They emigrated in 1832.

98 Rebecca Nevett, not the mother of either John or Thomas.

there is no fear of their starving in this country; for every body will assist them if they behave well, but drunkards they cannot bear, though I am sorry to say there is a great many in this country. One great blessing, there is no beggars in this country; and if a person is travelling, if he calls at a house for something to eat, he is treated as an old friend, and has the best they have in the house.

To Mr. Thomas Lucas, Red Lion Yard, Petworth, Sussex, Old England.

SEE ALSO letters from Mary and George Boxall: 25, 121
In November 1836, William Spencer wrote from Nelson Township (125) that the Tilleys were living about five miles from him and that he visited them often "as they are the only people that I am acquainted with from the old country."

■ 85
JOHN AND CAROLINE DEARLING, GALT, UPPER CANADA, TO HER
FATHER, JOHN FRANCIS, LICKFOLD, LODSWORTH, WEST SUSSEX,
30 JULY 1833
John Dearling and his wife, Caroline (Francis) Dearling, emigrated from Lodsworth, West Sussex, in 1833 with three young daughters, Phoebe, Jane, and Caroline.[99] Unlike the other three heads of family in the Lodsworth group, who were in the building trades in England, John Dearling had been a labourer.

SOURCE: *No. 5 Continuation*, 35-6

July 30th. 1833.

DEAR FATHER & MOTHER,
I now take the opportunity of writing to you, hoping it will find you in good health, as it leaves us all at present, thank God.
April 24th, sailed to Spithead, where we stopt [at] Thursday night 8 o'clock.
27th. wind against us, I very [sick], John and the children all well: cast anchor at Portland [Bay], could not get along.
May 1st. sailed again, the wind against us, cast anchor at Torbay, Brexham.[100]
4th. sailed again, *I was very sick, the children never sick to hurt them, they eat hearty, and got quite lusty. We had very good living, all the way over. John was never sick, but one day.*[101]
17th. very rough, the water flung over the vessel.
18th. continued very rough untl sunday night, it never was so rough as to shut us down under. We always had the hatchways open.

<hr/>

99 Caroline signed her name to the register when they married in Selham parish in 1824; John signed with a mark.
100 Brixham, Devon
101 The italicized sentences were among the extracts published by Sockett* in the Petworth Emigration Committee's *Statement*, issued in response to published complaints about the behaviour of Captain Hale on the voyage in 1833.

23rd. very cold. 29th. very cold: pieces of ice passing us as big as the vessel.

30th. all well except myself; when it was calm I was not quite so sick, but I was sick every day. 50 pieces of ice in sight, one piece came close to us, as big as Lickfold Green; one piece further off, which they said was 4 miles round it.

June the 1st. we all went down with the sailors to tea: they were very civil men. Caroline was afraid of one, because he had so much hair on his face.

4th. came in sight of land, Cape Breton, which is most part of it covered with snow.

6th. in a calm, pleasant to see the Whales, 60 feet long, and the thrashing fish.[102]

8th. very cold snow for two days. 15th. laid quarantine, at Grosse Island.

16th. all went ashore for to show that we were all clean: carried a box with us, every one a clean change: we were obliged to wash everything we had dirty: we went ashore in the morning, back in the evening.

June 22nd. we landed at Montreal, after a long voyage, but safe one, thank God. I cannot tell you any more of the passage, my paper is small. We got to James Rapson's, July 5th. we are staying there now.[103] We have got 50 acres of land, at 3 dollars per acre: we have nothing to pay for 3 years. Our house will be done before long, then we are going to it. John can get work, he is a harvesting. I hope you will let John's father see this letter, and I will write to him as soon as harvest is over, then I will tell you about the country.

July 14th. I was taken ill with the bowel complaint: 15th. no better: 16th. no better: 17th. 1 o'clock, I was taken worse; about 3 o'clock, I called them up; in about half an hour I was confined, with a 6 months child, it was a boy. The doctor was not with me at the time: he only charged me 5s. Dear Mother, I am now enjoying a good state of health, [so are] John and the children thank God. So no more at present from us, your loving son and daughter,

JOHN & CAROLINE DEARLING.

Direct, John Dearling, Galt, Dumfries, Gore, Upper Canada, North America.

To John Francis, Lickfold, Lodsworth near Midhurst, Sussex, England.

OTHER LETTERS: 111, 134

■ 86

EDMUND SHARP, SANDWICH, UPPER CANADA, 11 AUGUST 1833

Edmund and Sarah Sharp emigrated from the parish of Petworth in 1833. Sarah Clowser (née West) was a widow when she married Edward Sharp in 1806.[104] Their daughter, Elizabeth, also emigrated in 1833, along with her husband, George Turner, and their five children, the youngest of whom was baptized just before they left.

---

102 Perhaps flying fish.
103 Rapson described the arrival of the 1833 party in letter 76.
104 They both used a mark in the marriage register.

SOURCE: Petworth Emigration Committee, "Statement," [October 1833]. Another version, substantially the same, was published in the *Brighton Guardian* which copied the "Statement" into the issue of 16 October 1833.

Extracts of a Letter from Edmund Sharp, late of Petworth (whose daughter is married to George Turner, an Army Pensioner, also from Petworth, and supposed to be the "Mr. Turner" spoken of by the Sandwich Editor.)[105]

Dated Sandwich, August 11th. 1833.

We was 8 weeks a coming from England to Montreal. We was boarded to Montreal, no further. Capt. Hale, our Superintendent, at Montreal, gave some a little bacon, and some none; and then we sailed for 4 weeks in great want of victuals and drink; which Capt. Hale keep a tub of Petworth pork; and some of the hams of bacon.[106] Some days we got our grog and sometimes nothing, for he was the greatest part of his time drunk. We sailed with some of the emigrants up Lake Huron, and then put into a storehouse, where we could get nothing for money, for some had none. He come away and left us the next day after we got to Lake Huron; the next day, we men all went up 16 miles further, to a gentleman by the name of [Henry] Jones,[107] at Plympton, as that was the place they told us the Government work was for us, making roads; but when we got there, there was not a day's work to be got; but George [Turner] and Thomas [Sharp] got their pension, and their paper, at Little York, for to have their 100 acres of land, at Plympton.[108] and Edmund and I, could have had 50 acres of ground apiece, at Plympton, where Thomas and George was to receive theirs. We might have had it, and had 9 years to pay for it, at three instalments, for 2 dollars per acre; but it is all in the woods, and bigger timber, than the Earl of Egremont*'s pleasure ground, for there is timber bigger than ever I saw in England. We was forced to leave that part, and come about 100 miles back down the river again, to a little village opposite a town called the Detroit, is in the United

105 On 17 August 1833, the *Canadian Emigrant* (published in Sandwich, Upper Canada), contained a statement attributed to Turner attacking Captain Hale, the superintendent of the *England*, for peculation, habitual drunkenness, and unfeeling conduct towards those in his care.

106 The "some who had none" might well have been some of the young boys in the party sent from the House of Industry on the Isle of Wight. Hale had charge of a guinea for each boy, which was to be given to them on their arrival in Canada. However, investigation revealed that Hale had gone ashore at Torbay, as the *England* went down the Channel, and had bought herrings, cakes, eggs, and cider, which he sold to the passengers, deducting the cost in the case of the Isle of Wight boys from their guinea. Some had apparently spent their guinea on food before their arrival.

107 Henry John Jones, the crown lands agent charged with looking after the Petworth emigrants sent to Plympton.

108 George Turner and Thomas Sharp (who emigrated in 1832) had both been soldiers. Thomas's army record described him as 5'7" in height with brown hair, grey eyes, and a fair complexion. He had served in the East and West Indies and was discharged as "worn out" after serving for 20 years. Thomas returned to England in the autumn of 1832 and then came back to Canada in 1836 with his nephew David Clowser Sharp.

States of America, and we are in the British side.[109] We get work now this harvest time, but there is not but very little in this part, where we are now; for we cannot tell where George and Thomas will have their ground; for they will try to get it somewhere else near to a town. We gets a half dollar a day, and board. Bread is cheap, and meat: whisky we have for 7½d. per quart, rum 9d. per quart, but no beer.

If you think of coming to this part of the country, I hope that this letter will not shy any one in coming; for if we had been boarded all the way to our journey's end, we should have had a little money, what we received at York. Now Mary, you see Mr. Sockett*, and tell him we sends our best respects to him, Mrs. Sockett, and all the family, hoping they are all well. We thank the Earl of Egremont, Mr. Sockett, Mr. Knight*, and Mr. Chrippes*, for they done the best they could for emigrants, at Portsmouth, for to make them all comfortable.

Mr. Colebrook, Sir, I told you that I would send you the state of this country, it is a beautiful level country as any in the world, plenty of good water; its all wood like the Earl of Egremont's pleasure ground full as big timber, you may buy what quantity of acres you like, for 2 dollars per acre, and have 9 years to pay it in; good black soil, not a stone to be seen. I hope that you will make yourselves happy about us: and we like the country, but we are not settled, so do not write till you hear of us again, for we are in view of some ground. I hope that we shall see you all in America, next spring with us; as there is a plentiful country for every thing; but do not come without I send for you, then I will find a place for you all to come to, for it is a great deal of trouble to come here, in getting about, for here is no road waggons nor carriages here. I hope that this letter will not put out of heart, in coming to America next spring, for it is a good country, much better than England. We shall do after a while; but I hope that the gentlemen of the [Petworth Emigration] Committee will never let Captain Hale come out with no more emigrants from England.

The Committee think it right to state; that [Edmund] Sharp, [George] Turner, and [Henry] Habbin, are all persons to whose testimony very little credit is attached by those who knew them.

Sockett used Sharp's letter as evidence against Captain Hale, although he hesitated to give it full weight. In a private letter to the Duke of Richmond, Sockett went much further than his public reference to little credit being attached to the testimony of these men. He described Sharp as a "man of very bad character." His son-in-law, George Turner, an army pensioner, had some time earlier been condemned to hang for housebreaking. He was "reprieved, and finally pardoned, on the ground of having, at the time of the Robbery interfered to prevent murder."

The Sharps' private opinions of Sockett were never recorded, but we do have a record pertaining to Egremont's land steward, William Tyler. In August 1834, Sarah's son David Clowser Sharp, who had remained behind in Petworth, was jailed for a month for "wicked & malicious libel." He had been found guilty as a confederate of a man who had paraded

---

109 They travelled via the St Clair River and Lake St Clair to Sandwich (Windsor, Ont.).

with accusatory placards and an effigy of Tyler on market day at Petworth and at the Egdean fair. David, his wife, and children emigrated to Upper Canada in 1836.

SEE LETTER 113 from David Clowser Sharp.

■ 87
GEORGE CARVER, LONDON, UPPER CANADA, TO HIS FATHER AND MOTHER, JAMES AND SARAH CARVER, BIGNOR, WEST SUSSEX, 18 AUGUST 1833
George Carver, Joseph Leggett, Richard Neal (5 and 46), and Elias Elliot (28) were all from Sutton, West Sussex. Carver also included Charles Hilton in his group of Sutton acquaintances (Hilton's parents lived in Sutton).

SOURCE: *No. 5 Continuation*, 37–8

London, [Upper Canada] August 18th. 1833.

DEAR FATHER & MOTHER,

I take this opportunity of writing to you, to let you know that I am well at present, hoping that this will find you in the same state. I should be very glad to see some of my brothers come to this country, as I think it is much better than England. I am at present in the Township of London, working by the month, and there is always plenty of employment, for any person that is willing to work. If any of my brothers have any notion of coming to America, I will give any one of them a cow, as soon as they arrive here, to start them. All sorts of clothing is reasonable in this country, and provisions are quite low, so that I think it is an excellent country for poor people.

I have drawn 100 acres of land, but I have not done any thing upon it yet, as I think I can make more by working out. Wheat in this country sells at about 3s. 9d. per bushel, Barley 3s., Rye 3s., Corn 2s. 6d., Oats 1s. 3d., Potatoes 1s. 3d., the Winchester bushel. Pork sells at about £1. per cwt. Butter about 5d. per lb., Beef and Mutton in proportion. Land sells in this country at about from 12s. 6d. to 15s. per acre, with no improvement upon it. You must remember that I have board, washing and lodging along with my wages, as every person hired by the month, get their board. Charles Wilson is well, and he lives in the Township of Westminster. I should like to see all the young chaps in our country come off to America, and not stop lingering about home. I have got to be quite steady since I came to this country, and have almost given over drinking. Whisky is very cheap here, it sells at 2s. 6d. per gallon; Rum 5s.; Brandy 6s. per gallon. People can make their own candles, and soap, without paying any duty; and we can make our own malt, and brew our own beer, without paying any duty upon it.

It is of no use of high spirited farmers wishing to come out to this country; for they will not get their servants to wait upon them as at home, and to sit down at a second table to eat their crumbs. The servant is made equal with his master, in all respects of that kind, and not treated as a great many of the light headed farmers at home treat them, as dogs.

You will please to give my respects to all enquiring friends, and acquaintances; and let them know, that I like this country much better than Old England.

I should like to see any of my acquaintances out in this country, if they would but think fit.

I should be glad to have a letter from you, as soon as you receive this, to know how all are, and how times are in England.

Direct to George Carver,

To the care of Mr. George Robson, Township of London, Upper Canada, N. America.

I am your ever dutiful son

GEORGE CARVER.

To Mr. JAMES CARVER,

Bignor, near Petworth, Sussex, England.

––––––––––

OTHER LETTERS: 95

■ **88**

JAMES PARKER, ADELAIDE TOWNSHIP, UPPER CANADA, TO [HARVEY WHITINGTON, PULBOROUGH, WEST SUSSEX,] 1 SEPTEMBER 1833

James Parker and his wife, Amy (Steer),[110] emigrated with three children, Amy, George, and James, from Pulborough, West Sussex, in 1832. Parker was to receive £8 on arrival at York, paid by Mr Challen of Pulborough.

––––––––––

SOURCE: *No. 5 Continuation*, 38–40

The contents of the letter under written are contained in a sheet of paper sent from Pulborough, with a bit torn off at the bottom by Harvey Whitington, and the following written upon it.

Pulborough, April 8th. 1832.

'Please to fill this up, and sent it with the best information you can. Harvey Whitington.'[111]

Adelaide, September 1st. 1833.

I now take the opportunity of writing to you to give you the best information I can of this country. I can keep my family here, better by working three days, than I could by working all the week in England; for here I can earn a dollar a day, and my board and lodgings, and I have plenty of work. I could have a dozen masters, but I am obliged to work for myself as much as I can, at present, as I want to get sown 4 or 5 acres of wheat this fall, to keep my family next year. This year I have got about 3 acres of Indian corn, and potatoes, which look very promising at pre-

––––––––––

110 Both James and Amy signed the marriage register with a mark.

111 Harvey and William were the sons of Henry and Mary Whittington of Pulborough.

sent. I being with Mr. Goatcher,[112] was a great hindrance to me; it not only prevented my getting wheat sown last fall, but hindered my earning 15 or £20, besides. I have one hundred acres of as good land as any in the country, at two dollars per acre, one-fourth to be paid in two year's time, and the rest in three years more

Now I will not persuade you to come here, but I would not go back to England again on any account. Now, if you should come out here, I am certain you would do better here than in England. If you should come, I wish you to send me word as soon as you receive this letter, that I may get you some land as near mine as possible, and if I cannot, you shall have half mine 'till you can suit yourself.

I wish you to bring me all kinds garden seeds, and tell father to send me some of his crookhorn peas,[113] and you bring a little barley, and a few sacks, and rubbers to sharpen scythes, for they cannot be got here, grafting tools, and hay cutting knife. Now I want some sprig and plain muslin for caps, and cotton and thread of all sorts, about six pounds; and some lace at about 5 pence and 8 pence per yard, and stay and shoe laces, and 3 or 4 shillings worth of tape, and worsted, and some silk for bonnets, and wire for the bows, and stiff cambrick, and bring butter and cheese ware cloths. Now I wish you to bring all the bedding, and clothing you possibly can, and pack every thing in casks, and do not bring any more than you find absolutely necessary, because of the expence of getting up the country. Bring your clock, but not the case; nor the bedsteads; you may bring a set or two of bed screws, and nuts; you may get them at Chichester or Portsmouth. You may bring me 4 pair of cotton stockings of the largest size.

Do not be afraid to cross the ocean: the boys, nor I was not sea sick at all, but Amy and her mother was a little at first. You had better find your own provisions for your passage, and be sure not to chuse your berth in the ship opposite the main hatchway, as the water is apt to come in there when the ship rolls; get as near the stern of the ship as you can, you will not find so much motion of the ship.

Here I make my own sugar and soap and candles. We have but a small house at present, but I shall build a larger next summer. We have one cow and calf; I hope to get another in the spring. Now, if your brother William and his family would come here, they would do well. I wish you to bring me a malt mill. When we first came here, we had to go 7 or 8 miles for provisions, but now we get it within 2 miles. Here is a saw mill building here, and there will be a grist mill built next summer, by Mr. [James] Buchanan*.

Charles Hawkins left York, and called here yesterday: he is gone to live in Warwick, about 12 miles from here. Tell Mr. Goatcher, Captain Hale keeps charge of his chest of clothes, and said he would carry it to England again. To conclude, give our best respects to all friends, and accept the same yourself. We remain yours,

JAMES & AMY PARKER.

Tell James Pollard if he would come here, and bring his discharge with him, he would get 100 acres of land for his servitude, from the government.

---

112 Stephen Goatcher, superintendent of the *Evelyn*; see letter 51.
113 Crookhorn peas were field peas, grown for seed and possibly animal food and known as "grey" peas.

Direct to Mr. James Parker, Lot 15, fourth concession South of the Road, Township of Adelaide, District of London, Upper Canada, North America.

After leaving Goatcher's employ, Parker was located as an indigent emigrant on W ½ lot 15 concession 4 SER. Later land records indicate that he bought the east half of this lot in 1844. About this time he had also agreed to pay Frederick Hasted $500 for the W ½ lot 19 concession 4, a sum that included improvements made by Hasted. There were difficulties with the sale and he did not receive the deed until 1850 (see 174, 175). At his death in 1863, Parker left an estate valued at $250. Both James and Amy are buried in the Mt Zion Old Methodist 4th line cemetery, Adelaide Township.

Their son George married Sarah Ann Hilton and their daughter Amy married Charles Napper, both in Canada. Charles Napper was eleven when he emigrated in 1832 with his family, also from Pulborough. James Napper Sr was lent £47.10.0. "For to emigrate with his wife [Avice Downer] and 3 children to America."[114] Charles Napper died in 1907 and his wife Amy died the following year; they are buried in Mt Zion Old Methodist 4th line cemetery.

■ 89

WILLIAM MOORE AND JAMES MOORE, THOROLD TOWNSHIP, UPPER
CANADA, TO WILLIAM MOORE, PETWORTH, WEST SUSSEX,
5 SEPTEMBER 1833

Brothers William and James Moore were the sons of William and Hannah Moore of Petworth. They were single when they emigrated in 1832.

SOURCE: *No. 5 Continuation*, 40

Township of Thorold, District of Niagara, Province of Upper Canada.

September 5th. 1833.

Dear Father,

I embrace the opportunity of writing to you, to inform you that me and my brother James, are in good health at present, thanks be to Almighty God; and we are doing well, and are very comfortable. We received word from you by Thomas Sharp, and rejoiced to hear that you were all well. We intend to return home in twelve months from this time if we are well. I wish that my brother in law and sister would not come over here until I return, or send them some other word from here.[115] I would have wrote to you before, but was so little acquainted with the country that I could not tell you how it was. We like the country much, as labouring people are much more comfortable, and are more looked upon here. We are sorry that we gave you so much trouble and uneasiness by coming away as we did, but we think it is much to our advantage. We were both sick of the fever the first summer some time, but have been

---

114 WSRO, PAR 153/12/3
115 Sefton Charman and Mary Ann Moore of Sutton. They did not emigrate.

healthy this summer. We send our affectionate love to all our brothers and sisters, and to my brothers wife, and her family, and remain your affectionate sons,

William Moore, James Moore.

P.S. We wish you to give our love, and affection, to all our kindred, and acquaintance you may see.

To Mr. William Moore, Petworth, county of Sussex, England.

OTHER LETTERS: 114

By 1836 James Moore seems to have moved west to Sandwich (Windsor); see letter 114. A third brother, Edward, indicated in 1832 to Petworth parish officials that he wished to emigrate but this letter and Elias Elliot's reference to William Moore and his brother suggest he may have come to Upper Canada at a later date.

■ 90

JAMES HELYER, TORONTO TOWNSHIP, UPPER CANADA, TO PETER
SCOVELL*, HASLEMERE, SURREY, 29 SEPTEMBER 1833

Sockett* recorded that Haslemere, which is in the southeast corner of Surrey on the boundary with Sussex, sent nine emigrants with the Petworth committee in 1832, and 13 in 1833, the year James Helyer and Charlotte (Goble) Helyer emigrated. Charlotte was baptized in Heyshott and married in Easebourne, both places close to Midhurst and a short distance into Sussex from Haslemere.[116] The Helyers took seven children on the *England*. Their eldest son, James, whom they were seeking in New York State, was probably 16 in 1832 when he sailed on one of the Petworth committee's ships of that year. A John Helyer, who emigrated at the same time as James, had drowned at Quebec.

SOURCE: *No. 6 Continuation*, 43-4

Sept. 29th. 1833.
Toronto, near York, Upper Canada.

DEAR SIR.

I embrace the present opportunity, according to promise, to write you a few lines, hoping they may find you and family in good health. I have the pleasure to inform you, that I arrived with my family, safe and well, by the providence of God, in this country, after a roughish passage of 10 weeks, and arrived by the steamer Great Britain, at York, the capital of Upper Canada, the 1st July. Many of our passengers proceeded to the London District, to settle on the Canada Company's lands;[117] but for my part, I have rented a farm in shares, as it is called here, from a Mr. Maquire, an Irish gentleman, for 3 years. I have put in 16 acres of wheat this fall, and have a tolerably comfortable log-house, and plenty of provisions. My daughters, Eliza and

---

116 James and Charlotte signed the marriage register with a mark when they married on 24 December 1808.
117 These would be people planning to go to Plympton.

Jane, are at service, one in York, and the other near where I live, which is within 15 miles of York.

I bought a cow and calf for £5.7s, and 4 hogs for about £4, and 100 bushels of potatoes, at 1s.3s. per [bushel]. I went into the State of New York, about 500 miles, to enquire after my son James, but could get no intelligence of him, but have advertised him in the newspapers. I saw John Saunders[118] in York, 2 weeks ago, he was in good health. Wm. Hetzel is well, lives in my neighbourhood. You will expect me to mention something concerning this country, and as far as I can judge from my short residence in it, I have every reason to be satisfied. It is a fine healthy climate, and a fertile soil, after it is brought into a state of cultivation, but requires a good deal of labour to clear, and bring it into that state. Those who emigrated to this country a few years ago, though poor, and having to undergo many privations, are now in a state of comfort and independence, having fine farms cleared, plenty of stock, and all the necessaries of life in abundance; but earn it by the sweat of their brow. But there is one comfort enjoyed there, that taxes are a mere trifle: and as to the hateful tithe system, and poor rates, they are unknown this side of the Atlantic. There has been a very abundant harvest this season; good wheat rates at 4s.6d. a bushel, oats 1s, peas 2s.6d. There has been a great many emigrants arrived in this country this season, many of them persons of capital, who are purchasing cleared farms, and lands are rapidly increasing in value. A neighbour of mine sold a farm of 100 acres, partly improved, which he purchased 4 years ago for 500 dollars, for what he got 2000 dollars. York promises to be a flourishing town, and affords one of the best markets in Upper Canada. Goods are in general, as far as I can judge, very reasonable, except flannel, which is 2s.6d. a yard. I received my money at York, £60. Province currency, as £1.4s. a sovereign. I hope you will send an account of how my property was disposed, and who it was that purchased it. Richard Tanner is well, and lives with me, and requests to be remembered to Edward and Henry Helyer. Mr. Chase, from Epsom, wishes to be remembered to Mr. George, Mr. Fielding's butler. In the course of a week I shall write to Henry Court. My wife and family send their love to my brothers and sisters and remain your much obliged humble servant,

JAMES HELYER.

P.S. – Direct to me in care of Mr. John Maquire, Toronto, Upper Canada.
For MR. SCOVELL, King's Arms, Haslemere, Surrey, Old England.

■ 91
JOHN AND ELIZABETH WHITE, GUELPH, UPPER CANADA, TO HIS
FATHER, EDWARD WHITE, AND MOTHER, LURGASHALL, WEST SUSSEX,
27 OCTOBER 1833
John White and Elizabeth (West) White were living in Lurgashall when William, their first child, was baptized in January 1832.[119] White was probably the 27-year-old shoemaker on

118 See letter 77.
119 Both signed with a mark when they married at Fernhurst in August 1831.

whose behalf Sockett* wrote to the Duke of Richmond in March 1833. Sockett explained that White lived in Lurgashall but that his settlement was in the parish of Boxgrove, near the Duke's Goodwood House. The walk to Boxgrove would be a long one for White who had a club foot, and he could ill afford to take the time away from his work. Sockett asked the Duke to refer the case to the proper authorities. Richmond referred the letter to his agent, John Rusbridger, for an opinion.

Sockett offered to take the White family to Toronto, or any other Canadian port along the lake as far as Hamilton, for £20 "provisions & medical attendance, [emigrant] tax paid & everything found."

SOURCE: *No. 6 Continuation*, 44–5

October 27th. 1833.

DEAR FATHER AND MOTHER,

This comes with kind love to you, hoping to find you all in good health, as, thank God, it leaves me, and my husband, and children. I was confined with a young sailor on the ocean, on 8th May, and we call him young England.[120] We stayed with Mrs. Tribe[121] a month, but we did not see any prospect of getting a living there, so John went to Guelph, and there he got a seat of work; and he let himself for 3 months, for 7 dollars for the first month, and 8 for the next two, and his board, and for me and the children[122] to be found with every thing we want, except clothes, and for me to have 1 dollar a dozen for binding of shoes for myself; and a dollar is 5s. and we have no reason to repent for leaving of England, at present.

Give my kind love to my dear sister Sally and her child, and to little Charlotte. But I am very sorry to let you know that John lost the sheet of paper which he brought over with us, out of his pocket, which we promised to send you back again: and we live 14 miles from Jesse Penfold, and Benjamin Tribe. My best respects to Mr. and Mrs. Curtis, and all the family. So I conclude with my kind love to fathers and mothers, sisters and brothers, and all enquiring friends. Direct to John Horning, boot and shoe maker, Guelph, Gore District, Upper Canada, North America.

Tell Mr. Stenning we see Mrs. [Mary] Barns at York, and she is doing well and all her family.

Dear father and mother, brother and sisters, this comes with my duty to you, hoping to meet you all in good health, as thank God it leaves me at this present; and I am very happy to inform you, that I never repent for leaving the old country at present, for I have plenty of good eating and drinking, some times beef, and sometimes a young roaster, and I know that any industrious man can do a great deal better here,

---

120 Hale noted the arrival of Mrs White's son in his log. He was invited by a deputation of married women to "birth" his "pretty little grandson" by broaching his brandy cask. This request was repeated on 12 May when Maria Rapson gave birth to a little girl.

121 Charlotte Tribe was in Galt; see letter 54 from Henry and Charlotte Tribe.

122 Original annotation: "One of them was born on the voyage out, as stated above."

than ever he can in England; for a young man that have a mind to let himself out by the month, he can get from 10 to 14 dollars a month, and his meat. And a shoe maker's wages is by the piece, making jockey boots £1 5 in English money, welling-tons fine 14s., coarse fine 12s.6d., coarse pegged 7s.6d.,[123] mens fine shoes 4s.4½d., coarse fine 3s.9d., womens boots 4s.4½d., coarse 3s.9d., womens shoes 8s.3d. If a pair of shoes come to a dollar, a journeyman gets half, and so in proportion for all mend-ing, and I shall be very glad to see my brother Edward in this country, for he can get a better living here, than he ever will in the old country.[124] We live along side of Mr. William Penfold, of Easebourne work-house.[125] I met with a friend that was a coming to England, and so I sent this letter free of expence, and I wish you to send me word what the letter cost you.

There was no signature, but this is evidently meant as the joint letter of husband and wife.

To EDWARD WHITE, Lodsworth, near Petworth, Sussex, Old England.

In August 1836 James Rapson mentioned that the Whites had their house framed but not yet completed; see letter 115.

■ 92

WILLIAM BAKER, DELAWARE TOWNSHIP, UPPER CANADA, TO HIS MOTHER AND FATHER, JOHN AND SARAH BAKER, KIRDFORD, WEST SUSSEX, 3 NOVEMBER 1833

SOURCE: *No. 6 Continuation*, 46-7

November 3rd. 1833.

MY DEAR FATHER AND MOTHER,

I take the opportunity of writing to you, I hope it will find you all well, I am quite well at present. I received your letter, I heard you were all well, I should like to hear from my brothers and sisters, father and mother. I am doing well. I am liv-ing with Mr. Charles Ford, that married Amelia Cooper, from Frightfold.[126] I shall have 3 acres of wheat of my own to reap next year, off my own farm. I have 1 horse and waggon harness. They are all doing well that come with me on their own land. Benjamin Batchelor is along with me, doing well on his farm, he is hoping to get

---

123 Wellingtons (named for the Duke of Wellington), high leather boots covering the knee in front and cut away at the back; jockey boots, top boots of a type formerly worn by jockeys; pegged boots, wide at the top and narrow at the bottom.

124 Edward White and his wife, Louisa Lotton, emigrated in 1835.

125 The superintendent of the *Lord Melville*. See page 253 for a photograph of the Easebourne Work-house.

126 Frightfold or Frithfold, located between Northchapel and Kirdford, West Sussex. Both names seem to have been in use in the early part of the nineteenth century before Frithfold became the more usual spelling.

in 3 acres of wheat this michaelmas: he don't want to come to England no more, he is very sorry to hear his brother Matthew is gone for a soldier, he [had] better come to Canada, he would be better off. I was glad to hear from my mother, and brother Charles. William Pannell is doing very well on his land, he was glad to hear all his friends were well.

Your son, William Baker, and Mr. Ford, have been butchering this summer, and do well at it, and sells at two pence a pound, good fat beef and mutton; pork, three pence pound. You be not forced to go down to Spooner, and give nine pence a pound for pork. Come to Upper Canada, then you won't go to bed without your suppers; there is plenty to eat in Upper Canada: any man work three [days] in a week will get a good living. Young girls that wants to get married, must come to Upper Canada, they will soon get a husband: girls are wanted for wives. I should like to hear from W. Rapley. There is no black man, there is plenty of Indians in this country; bears and wolves in this country; they be very civil, they don't hurt no one. There is plenty of deer; pheasants; poultry; rabbits; squirrels, are black; ducks. Winter is very cold, but not over three months. You can get plenty of whiskey, and rum, brandy six pence a quart, beer sixpence, cider, two pence a quart, tobacco six pence a pound. Price of work, 5 shillings a day, in your mint. Bring no tools, in this country; tools are better in this country, and cheaper. Any one that come in this [country] come by New York, come much cheaper and quicker to Upper Canada. Cows and oxen are cheap. There is no small birds; bull frogs, plenty, up the trees singing in the spring; first one I saw I took my gun to shoot him, thought it had been a duck, but when I shot, it was a bull frog.

London District, County Middlesex, in Upper Canada, North America, Delaware. That is where you must write to me, I sent a letter in March, I had no answer, I should like to have an answer from this one, as quick as you can. So no more from me at present.

Dear Father give this to Thomas Heather, Wheelwright, at Lord Egremont's, Petworth, from his son,[127] he is very well; and write the same directions as my letter is, do not forget it.

To MRS. JOHN BAKER, Kirdford, near Petworth, Sussex, Ebernow Common.

OTHER LETTERS: 41, 65

Benjamin Bachelor and William Pannell (letter 35) were also from the parish of Kirdford. The address in Delaware that Baker gives in this letter may be the post office kept by Roswell Mount*.

By the time of the 1851 census there were several William Bakers in the London District. The one most likely to have been the Petworth emigrant married in 1846 and was living with his wife, Amanda, and two young children on a farm on E ½ lot 4 concession 3 SER Adelaide Township.

---

127 George Heather emigrated from Petworth in 1832.

■ 93

JOHN HOLDEN, DELAWARE TOWNSHIP, UPPER CANADA, TO THOMAS
AND SOPHIA HOLDEN, HIS FATHER AND MOTHER, 6 NOVEMBER 1833
John Holden was 19 when he emigrated from the small parish of Washington, West Sussex,
in 1832, one of two young bricklayers sponsored by a Mrs Goring. The other was William
Lelliot, probably the William Elliott mentioned in this letter.

SOURCE: *No. 6 Continuation*, 47–8

Delaware, November 6th. 1833.

DEAR FATHER AND MOTHER,

I hope these lines will find you in good health as it leaves me at present. I now
take the opportunity of informing you of my present situation in life. I am very happy
to tell you I have had a very good summer's work; I am the only one of the trade
in this village. When I first came to Canada, there was only 6 houses in Delaware,
but now here is about 20. Here is but one tavern with licence yet, but 2 more are
about to be finished: here is 4 large stores containing hard ware and linen drapery.
Here will be a grist mill built next summer. I am boarding with George Robinson
and his wife at present, from Angmering, but I shall get my house, so as I can live
in it, in about 2 weeks. It is but a very small one, 16 ft. by 22, I shall build a larger
next summer, if the Lord Almighty only restores my health and success, as it is the
only thing I have to depend on. I intend this building for a grocery and bakery, if
ever I should have the means to go on with it.

Dear Brothers, this comes with my kind love to you all, I should be very happy
to see you come to Delaware next summer, as I think it would be much the best
for you, if you can but think so; I will by no means persuade you, but come if you
please, you will find a home. If you come I shall have plenty of work next summer.
William and Joseph, you would both be of great service to me, and yourselves as
well. I expect you can find a friend to assist you, if you only want to come, and you
had better come by way of New York, if you can make it convenient, if not do not
set out before May. Dear Henry, I hope you are in good health, and your wife and
children, Eliza and Charles more or less. I have not heard from Wm. Elliott, since
last Christmas, when I went to see him. I desire my kind love to Uncle Charles and
Aunt and your family. I should be very glad to see you in Canada, but I shall not
expect to see you until I return to Chiltington, which I expect will be within a few
years.

As for the country, it is quite to my expectations, preferable to the States, by the
account I have heard. Please to write as soon as you receive this letter, for I have
not had no answer since last February. I hope you will let me know how Mr.
Goatcher is getting on, and if he do not want to come to Canada again. Please to
send me word how uncle is getting on at Worthing, and my cousins. Dear sister, I
sends my kind love to you, I should be very glad if you would come and keep my
house, as housekeepers are so very scarce in this country. I sends my kind love to

you all, my grandfather, uncles, and aunts, and cousins, one and all. I hope you will send word of any thing as happens to any of you, whether it is for the best or the worst. I sends my kind love to all Washington young people, and old: in particular to my old acquaintance. I see Charles in April just before I left. I particularly wish to hear from William Bowley.

So no more at present from kind and dutiful son,

JOHN HOLDEN.

Direct to me John Holden, Delaware, Township of London, Upper Canada. By New York.

Holden moved to Woodstock some time before 1839 when he was mentioned by William Phillips in letter 140. John Holden and his wife, Sarah, had a son, Henry Edward, baptized at Old St Pauls, Woodstock in 1842.

1834

THE SHIP
BRITISH TAR,

A 1. coppered and copper fastened,

Burthen 383 Tons per Resister,

is engaged by the PETWORTH EMIGRATION COMMITTEE,

to sail from

PORTSMOUTH

FOR

MONTREAL, DIRECT,

On THURSDAY, the 17th. of APRIL next,

(Passengers must be on board before 6 in the Evening of Tuesday, the 15th, or at latest by Noon on Wednesday, the 16th.)

with Emigrants from different parts of the County of SUSSEX.

The Committee have much pleasure in stating, that they have prevailed on a Gentleman of high respectability, a SURGEON of nearly 30 years standing in the Navy, and whose practice has been considerable, both on shore and afloat, to take the entire charge of the Emigrants who go out in the BRITISH TAR. He will have the controul of all the arrangements to YORK, Upper Canada, (or to any other Port at the head of *Lake Ontario*); and though he will not be authorized on the part of the Committee, to incur any expences for Conveyance, &c. beyond the head of the Lake, yet he will, with the assistance of the Government Agents, use his best endeavours towards forwarding the different Parties to those places where they have Friends already settled, or to which they may wish to proceed; and also in finding Employment for those who have no particular engagements.

A large number of Passages being already engaged on board this Ship, applications must be made as early as possible to **Mr. J. PHILLIPS, Petworth**; of whom, or of **Mr. KENNARD, 20, Penny Street, Portsmouth,** further Information may be obtained.

A few Cabin Passengers could be accommodated, and Berths may be secured in the Intermediate Cabin, at a small advance on the Steerage price.

J. Phillips, Printer. Petworth.

Petworth, March 22nd. 1834.

CHRONOLOGY FOR THE YEAR 1834

17 April The *England* Sailed from Spithead.

28 April The Ditton's child born at sea.

14 May Newfoundland is sighted..

15 May The emigrants, including Mrs Ditton, danced on the deck of the *England*.

23 May The *England* arrived at Grosse Isle – delayed in quarantine because of measles among the children.

27 May Emigrants landed at Grosse Isle for inspection.

28 May Emigrant re-embarked; William Dighton was rescued after falling overboard.

31 May Cleared quarantine.

1 June The *England* anchored at Quebec.

3-4 June Towed to Montreal by the steamboat *St George*.

5 June The emigrants spent the night in Cushing's warehouse.

6 June To Lachine.

7 June On the Ottawa River. As there were no horses available, the emigrants dragged their barge through the Carillon Canal. They were detained overnight at Grenville.

9-13 June Bytown to Kingston. Taken in tow by the steamboat *Toronto*. In the Rideau Canal system, they stopped at night between Long Island and Burrett's Rapids, at the mouth of the Tay or Perth River on Rideau Lake, at the Isthmus (4½ miles from the Narrows), and at Kingston Mills.

13 June Boarded the steamboat *Cobourg* for Toronto.

14 June At Toronto, emigrants scattered to find their own accommodation in preference to the house and sheds offered by the government agent.

18 June "Some" boys bound as apprentices at Toronto; the government agreed to pay for the passage on the schooner *Superior* of the young men going to the work on the canals.

19 June Twelve families and the remaining single men left Toronto with Brydone on the *Queenston*.

20 June Brydone's party started from Hamilton for Blandford Township (Woodstock) with 14 wagons: 4 for women and children and 10 for baggage.

21 June Mary West's baby was born at the tavern where the emigrants stopped for the night.

21-22 June The emigrants arrived at Woodstock, where the families camped in John Hatch's barn.

8-17 July Brydone's tour of inspection of lands belonging to the Canada Company.

19 July The Petworth families moved into log cabins built for them on five-acre lots on the government reserve at Woodstock.

21 July The Rapsons had a visit from Brydone at their home about 5½ miles from Waterloo.

1-7 August Brydone travelled from Niagara to Lockport and through the Erie Canal to New York.

14 August The Poor Law Amendment Act, 4&5 William IV, c.76, received royal assent.

8-28 August Brydone sailed from New York to Liverpool on the American Packet *Independence*.

Sources: WSRO, PHA 139; WSRO, Goodwood MS 1476; J.M. Brydone, *Narrative of a Voyage* (Petworth, England: 1834); Cameron and Maude, *Assisting Emigration to Upper Canada* (Montreal: McGill-Queen's University Press 2000); contemporary newspapers; letters.

PREVIOUS PAGE: Broadsheet for the *British Tar*, WSRO, Goodwood MS 1474, f.330

SHIP: *British Tar*, A1, 402 tons
MASTER: Robert Crawford
SUPERINTENDENT: James Marr Brydone

BACKGROUND

In 1834 Sockett claimed to have no lack of willing candidates for emigration, but he had a problem with sponsorship in the Petworth area, his district of first choice. Sponsors who had not been repaid for past loans refused to advance more money to the same parishes, and new sponsors were harder to find. This was the only year in which a minority of Petworth emigrants were from West Sussex. Sockett was able to fill the *British Tar*, but only because plans initiated by the Earl of Chichester to send an emigrant ship from East Sussex also ran into difficulties and the Brighton and Lewes emigration committees sent their emigrants with the Petworth committee. These emigrants and emigrants from the Isle of Wight made up Sockett's numbers. Brighton sent mostly families, while the Isle of Wight and Lewes sent mainly single men. The *British Tar* carried more single men and a smaller proportion of children than other Petworth ships.

While he worked to secure emigrants in 1834, Sockett was able to consolidate his administration. His search for a satisfactory superintendent ended when the navy put his friend James Marr Brydone on half pay without a job. Brydone was a career naval surgeon whose background included some years of farming experience and a voyage to Australia in 1819 as surgeon-superintendent on a convict ship. Hiring Brydone meant that the committee did not have to find a doctor for the ship, but, above all, he was a person Sockett trusted, and trusted to negotiate on behalf of his committee and of Lord Egremont with merchants and government officials in Upper Canada.

As superintendent of the *British Tar*, Brydone imposed order on shipboard life. He appointed Frederick Upton as steward, and had all the adult male emigrants busy performing or supervising duties such as cleaning the living quarters, issuing rations, and doing the communal cooking. In 1834, he reported ready cooperation from the emigrants. Letters from emigrants who sailed under Brydone have little to say about his organization, but several emigrants reported with pride the compliments they received at Grosse Isle on the cleanliness of the ship.

The 1834 emigrants were the first sent by the Petworth committee to go from Montreal to Kingston by way of the Ottawa River and the Rideau Canal. Although longer in miles, this route was somewhat shorter in time than the trip up the St Lawrence River to Lake Ontario. The real gain, however, was in comfort and increased security for people and luggage. On the Rideau route, Petworth emigrants travelled in a larger vessel all the way from Montreal to Kingston. There was a full deck and a cabin, and Brydone was able to assign space so as to keep emigrants together who had grown used to travelling together on the *British Tar*. In his *Narrative of a Journey*, Brydone contrasted this trip with William Phillips Sr's account of his harrowing journey up the St Lawrence River in Durham boats in 1833 (74).

FIRST SETTLEMENT

Although Canada had another cholera epidemic in 1834, it struck later in the immigrant season and Petworth letter-writers were not directly affected. Authorities at Toronto, however, sent them on quickly, paying for almost all of them to travel inland. Two groups disappeared from our records: the boys whom Brydone apprenticed in the Toronto area and the twenty or so single men sent at the governor's suggestion to find work canal building on the Grand River or improving the harbour at Port Stanley. The main party of twelve families and a few single men went to Hamilton and Woodstock.

At Woodstock, families sent by the Petworth committee pioneered a government experiment in settling parish-aided immigrants. The idea was to bring labourers and artisans needing work together with settlers who had some capital and who needed workers. So that these poor families did not spend all they earned supporting themselves over the winter, each family was allowed temporary possession of a five-acre lot – the size of a standard park lot – laid out on a government reserve near the fast-growing townsite. The Petworth immigrants were housed in a barn until log huts built by the government on their lots were ready for them to occupy. When they were not employed by their neighbours, they were expected to clear and work a subsistence farm. This plan of assistance can be seen at its best in the letters of William and Cornelius Voice (98 and 101).

Despite his difficulties in filling the *British Tar*, Sockett won Egremont's support for a project to buy land in Upper Canada on the Earl's behalf. By the time Brydone sailed, Sockett had realized that this purchase would take time, and he had scaled back plans for an immediate start. The Woodstock immigrants found work quickly, and Brydone set off on the inspection tour that was the second part of his mission in 1834. However, in a search concentrated on lands owned by the Canada Company around Guelph and between Guelph and Goderich, he failed to find a tract suitable for Sockett's proposed settlement.

■ 94

EXTRACT OF A LETTER FROM HENRY HARWOOD, BLANDFORD
(WOODSTOCK), UPPER CANADA, [1834]

Henry Harwood, a shoemaker from Lewes, was one of the East Sussex emigrants sent under
the patronage of the Earl of Chichester in 1834. He was a widower when he emigrated with
three of the four sons of his first marriage (Henry, Alfred, and Richard), which is why he
and his sons were all working for board despite having possession of a lot on the government reserve at Woodstock.[1]

SOURCE: *Sussex Advertiser*, 8 September 1834

*Extract of a letter received from Henry Harwood, one of the Emigrants who went from Lewes in April
last to Canada.*

We sailed from Spithead 17th April, with 135 passengers, and left the Land's End
the 19th. The first land we saw was Cape Ray, in Newfoundland, on the 14th May,
after a passage of only 25 days from leaving the Land's End. We arrived at Gross [sic]
Island the 21st which is 30 miles below Quebec and came to Quebec June 1st. We were
then towed to Montreal by a steam boat [*The St George*], 160 miles, in two days. We
left Charles Townsend[2] and several more passengers here that got work. I saw Charles
Page, the saddler from Lewes, at Montreal; he was very well, and got plenty of work;
we stayed here three days; this is a fine large town, and shops as large as any in Lewes.

We here left the "British Tar" and were put in a packet-boat, and sailed to
Kingston, about 200 miles in seven days, and then went on board a steam-boat
[*Coburg*] and sailed up Lake Ontario to York, 160 miles. We stayed here five days,
then started again for Blandford, about 90 miles further, where we are now.

I saw M. Kemp and Gates the shoemaker at Ancaster, 45 miles from where I live,
Kemp has got a very fine shop of business, keeping on two or three men. We arrived
at Blandford 20th June. This is a very fine country as ever a man set his foot on, and
the people are very friendly, kind and obliging; here a man can find plenty of employment, and well paid for it and a man that has got a family may do well here. Each
family of us are allowed five acres of land, with very high trees, that my gun will
not kill birds off the tops of them. This is a very fine level country, and the best of
land; here are as fine wheat and corn as ever I saw in England, pease in particular;
the grass is very good, and mowers are in great request. Land is selling here at 3, 4,
and 5 dollars per acre, allowing 4 or 5 years to pay it in. Henry and I intend to buy
100 acres very shortly. I have the pleasure to inform you we are all in good employment. I have plenty of work at shoe-making, and can earn three shillings and my

1 Henry Harwood signed his name to the marriage register when he married his first wife, Sarah Wise,
in 1810.
2 Also from Lewes. Brydone in his *Narrative*, 14, wrote: "Mr. and Mrs. Huntley, and Mr. and Mrs. Bassam, and child, who had paid for their passage, only to Montreal, quitted our party. George Townsend,
Charles Crossing, William Rackett, and George Walden; left here, but without permission."

The Rideau Canal: the Petworth immigrants of 1834 were the first to use this easier route

John Burrows, Hartwell Locks, Rideau Canal, c. 1835, NA, C92922

board per day; Henry is working in a brick-yard at three pounds per month, board and lodging, washing and mending; Alfred is at service with Mr Birch, for six dollars per month, board and lodging, washing and mending, which is twenty-five shillings English; Richard I put apprentice to a blacksmith for five years, his wages will average twelve pounds per year, with board and lodging etc.

My Dear Friend, words cannot express the satisfaction I feel when I look around me and see my family so comfortably siutated, and all in good health, and I sincerely thank Mr Hurly and Mr Rogers for their kindness in sending us here;[3] we have neither of us had a day's illness since we have been here.

Henry's first wife had died in 1818, at about the time of Richard's birth. He married again in Canada (to a second Sarah) and had six more children. In 1844, Henry received the patent for lot 1 of range 1 (north side of Barwick Street), Woodstock, a lot he and his wife sold in 1855. In 1871, at the age of 80, Henry Sr still gave his occupation as shoemaker. He died in Ingersoll in 1879.

Although the two Henry Harwoods are not always easy to distinguish, his son Henry appears to have been the farmer who was assigned a lot on concession 11 of East Zorra Township. Henry Jr also married twice and had children with both his wives. His first wife was Petworth emigrant Lucy Coleman, the daughter of George Coleman (George had been a witness at Henry Sr's first marriage in England in 1810; see letter 103.) In 1846, Henry owned his first lot in East Zorra and part of another. The census-taker for the 1851 census reported

3 Henry Hurley, a Lewes banker, owned Iford Manor House. Henry Harwood married his first wife, Sarah Wise, at Iford. Mr Rogers was a "gentleman" of Southover, Lewes.

that Henry, Lucy, and their children were living in a one-storey log house. A generation later, Henry Jr's farmer son left an estate valued at $3000.

▪ 95
GEORGE CARVER, DELAWARE TOWNSHIP, UPPER CANADA, TO HIS FATHER AND MOTHER, JAMES AND SARAH CARVER, BIGNOR, WEST SUSSEX, 30 JUNE 1834

A single man, George Carver emigrated from the parish of Sutton, West Sussex, in 1832.

SOURCE: WSRO, Goodwood MS 1476, f278, in f276, Sockett to Duke of Richmond, 26 August 1834

The following is a correct copy of a letter from George Carver who emigrated in 1832 without the addition or omission of a single word. [T. Sockett]

Delaware June 30th 1834

Dear father & mother,

I now take this opportunity of writing these few lines to you hoping to find you in good health as this leaves me at present thank God for it. I received your letter in March requesting an answer which I now send to inform you. I left working by the month, and have taken a farm for 3 years on shares, now *I earnestly request that some of you will come over if possible, my brother, and brother in law, and sister at least, and not stay starving in England* any longer, for here you may live on the fat of the land, on the best of every thing you can wish for; you can get 4 bushels of wheat, and your board for a weeks work, if you like to work for other people. If not I will get you a farm for yourself either or both of you, and then in a few years you will be independent of the world, and all that is in it.

And I should like to see any of my poor old neighbours, and their families, for I say this is the country for poor labouring people to come to, and the larger their families the better they are off when they gets once settled, but there is a great many hardships, and difficulties to be met with in coming over the sea, and more in coming up the country, which you will find to be between eleven and twelve hundred miles. But this country will not do for your high spirited farmers & their wives for they would not like *to sit down at table after their servants have done* meals & eat what they have left, for here they would be obliged to beg, and pray to get a man for a few days to help them instead of blustering, and swearing as they do over you in England. Here if a man wants any common labour done he must do it himself or let it go undone, but if he wants to raise a house or a barn or any such thing as that all his neighbours readily come & assist him, and he does the same in return.

As for Joseph Leggatt I have not seen or heard of him. I left him above 100 miles back, and Richard Neal, and Elias Elliott stopped back,[4] Charles Hilton and family are all well, and send their best respects to their father, and mother, and all enquiring friends, they live about 2 miles from me. Please to remember me to Mr & Mrs Puttick,

---

4 See letter 28.

and *Mary*, and tell her to come over here for *I want a wife very bad, and women are very scarce here, we wants about ten thousand sent over here*, and then we should stand *a better chance to get a wife amongst them.* Tell James if he comes *to bring a wife for himself, and one for me.* I have nothing more in particular to say at present only *if my father & mother will come over I will keep them as long as they live without working.*

Please to give my best, and kindest respects to all my old neighbours and all enquiring friends & accept the same yourself. I remain your dutiful Son George Carver.

 Please to direct to George Carver
   Township of Delaware
   County of Middlesex
   District of London
   U.C. N.A.
To Mr. James Carver
  Bignor near Petworth, Sussex
  England

OTHER LETTERS: 87

Carver did not manage to find a wife until March 1842 when he married Isabell Marrell of London, Upper Canada. He was also living in London at that time. One of his witnesses was Benjamin Woodhull; Woodhull's Mill had been a staging point for the Petworth emigrants of 1832 on their way into the Adelaide settlement.

■ 96

HENRY HEASMAN, BLANDFORD (WOODSTOCK), UPPER CANADA, TO HIS FATHER, HENRY HEASMAN SR, SISTERS, AND BROTHERS, WEST GRINSTEAD, WEST SUSSEX, 19 OCTOBER 1834

SOURCE: Printed, 2 pages (Petworth: J. Phillips [1835]), page 2 has an advertisement for Brydone's *Narrative*, "just published"; copy in PRO, CO 284/39, ff.316-16v, with Sockett to Hay, 14 February 1835, f.312

From Henry Heasman, late of West Grinstead, Sussex, who went out with the Party sent by the Petworth Emigration Committee, to Upper Canada, in 1834.

Blandford, London District,
Upper Canada, 19th. October, 1834.

Dear Father, Sisters, and Brothers,

No doubt, you have long expected a letter from me. We arrived at Quebec, on the 1st of June, after a tolerable good passage, very pleasant, I never for a moment sick, plenty to eat and drink, and an excellent captain [Robert Crawford] over us. We of course, were landed at Montreal, and then had steam accommodations provided for us, up to Toronto. To tell you of what I only saw in the going up to Toronto, by the steam boat, of timber, stock, and such like, would only surprise you. I delay my tale.

When we got to Toronto, we found, all the married folk had a grant of land, and a shanty (that is a house) given them here. I expressed to Mr. Brydone*, our super-

Saturday night. The weekly pay of a West Sussex agricultural labourer was
around 10 shillings without board.
Jefferys Taylor, *The Farm: A New Account of Rural Toils and Produce* (London 1832),
University of Sussex Collection

intendent, that I should like to move with them, and he immediately acceded to my
wish, and here I am well settled, and never for a moment sick. I have apprenticed
myself to a blacksmith, a Mr. Jones, (a very worthy man) for 4 years: the first year, I
have nine pounds, the second year, eleven pounds, and the third year, thirteen pounds,
and the fourth year, fifteen pounds. My master provides me my board, lodging,
clothes, and washing, and I hope, dear father, that you have no cause to weep for
me, for I am better off here, than I can ever be in England. I desire that you will
remember me to Mary, Harriet, Anne, George, and Sarah, and they must all come
out: plenty of work, and well paid: labouring men get 3s.6d. and 4s. the day, and board
provided them, plenty. And if father will come out, in two years time, I can give him
twenty acres of land of his own: beautiful land it is. Jack is as good as his master here.
Masters are glad to get servants, and come to hire them: no running after masters.
    George Morgan apprenticed himself at Toronto, to a carpenter, about 100 miles
below us, and I have no doubt that he will do well.[5] I desire to be kindly remem-

5 Brydone, *Narrative,* stated that George Morgan went as far as Hamilton where he found employment "and left us."

bered to Jane Jupp, and tell her that I have that little bottle that she gave me. I hope that Jane has not lost that shoe brass, which was given her by me, and she must come out in two years hence: she must remember this very seriously. I desire to be remembered to Mr. and Mrs. Coates, and beg to say, that I have the little comb which Mrs. Coates gave me. Give my respects to Mr. Jupp, and thank him, for the good usage which we received from him, on our road to Portsmouth. Arthur Greenfield must now eat his hat, for I am now in America.

We have had the cholera here, in Canada, but it has never reached us here in this part. Blandford is considered the most healthy, no diseases; but very hot in summer, and cold in winter. We have now thunder and lightening, with a white frost on the ground. I desire to present my respects to Mr. Woodward,[6] and thank him for the truly christian-like kindness which I experienced from him and Mrs. Woodward, and live in the hope, that a day will arrive, when I shall have it in my power to return their benevolence.

I am, dear father,
Your affectionate son,
HENRY HEASMAN.

Henry Heasman was one of the young single men who chose to accompany Brydone to Woodstock in 1834. It is interesting to compare Heasman's careful account of the terms of his apprenticeship with Brydone's statement in the *Narrative* (page 55) that Heasman had been hired at £20 per annum with room and board. Despite being well placed to get information on his people's wages, Brydone's information was far from accurate. Wages in Upper Canada were already high by English standards, and inflated reports raised the expectations of new immigrants who were sometimes disappointed as a result.

■ **97**

EXTRACT OF A LETTER FROM WILLIAM GREEN, BLANDFORD
(WOODSTOCK), UPPER CANADA, RECIPIENT UNKNOWN,
20 OCTOBER 1834

William Green had served in the 36th Regiment of Foot for just short of 19 years, half of that time with the rank of colour sergeant. His service had taken him to the Iberian Peninsula during the Napoleonic Wars, to the Mediterranean, and to the West Indies. As an ex-soldier trying to find work as a labourer, Green, with a wife,[7] and three children, was proving costly to the parish of Pulborough. When the family was sent to Canada on the *British Tar* in the spring of 1834, they had had £42.5s.6d. from the parish over the previous two years.

---

6 Original annotation: "The Rector of West Grinstead."

7 A William Green married Mary Hawkins at Pulborough on 9 September 1812; Mary signed her name to the register, William made a mark.

SOURCE: Brydone, *Narrative*, 62

Extract of a letter from William Green, late of Pulborough, Sussex, who emigrated to Canada, in 1834, in the British Tar.

Town Plot, Blandford,
20th. October, 1834.

* * * * *

Relating to myself and family we are all well; and doing very well just now; have got my order for 200 acres of land, which I intend to go to, in Spring. People may say what they will concerning America, it is one of the finest countries for a poor man that is industrious, for he has to want for nothing. Please to give my thanks to Mr. Sockett* for his kindness to me.

The Greens were one of the families settled on lots on the government reserve in Woodstock. Green was entitled to 200 acres for his military service. As he explained in a petition of 3 September 1834, Green was too nearsighted to work at his trade as a whitesmith (or tinsmith). He therefore wanted to take up his grant and hoped for a location close to one of the areas settled by Petworth emigrants. His request in 1834 for a lot in Zorra Township near Woodstock was denied, and on 24 September 1834 he was granted lot 14 concession 2 in Enniskillen, a sparsely settled township south of Plympton. He was still in Woodstock in September 1837 when his request to exchange the Enniskillen lot for one he had chosen in the Adelaide settlement was also denied.

Apparently resigned to becoming a frontier farmer, Green was visiting Adelaide on his way to Enniskillen in 1837 when the Rebellion offered him a chance to return to the profession he knew best. He enrolled in the Adelaide militia under Colonel Thomas Radcliff*. When it was discharged in February 1838, Green joined Radcliff's Western Rangers until they too were disbanded that July. After one more year in the militia based at Sandwich (Windsor), Green took out the patent for the Enniskillen lot in 1839 and apparently lived there until he sold it in 1846.

■ 98
WILLIAM VOICE, BLANDFORD (WOODSTOCK), UPPER CANADA, TO HIS SISTER, MARY ELLIOT, ASHINGTON, WEST SUSSEX, 27 OCTOBER 1834

William Voice was the eldest son of Cornelius and Elizabeth (Smallwood) Voice and travelled with them, his brothers and sisters, and a cousin John from Billingshurst, West Sussex, to Woodstock. At 23 years of age, he was one of the younger Petworth letter-writers. Sockett* noted that William's account of the voyage on the *British Tar* and the journey upriver – written from an emigrant's perspective – nicely parallelled that of superintendent James Brydone* in his *Narrative*.

SOURCE: Printed, 4 pages (Petworth: J. Phillips [1835]), page 4 has an advertisement for Brydone's *Narrative*, "just published"; a copy is found in PRO, CO 284/39, ff.317-18v, with Sockett to Hay, 14 February 1835, f.312. The italic words in parentheses represent Sockett's editing.

From William Voice, late of Billingshurst, Sussex, who went out to Upper Canada in the British Tar, in the spring of 1834.

October 27th. 1834.

DEAR SISTER,

I write these few lines to you, hoping to find you all well, as it leaves us at present. I am going to tell a little about our voyage, a coming over: we had a very pleasant week first, when we sailed from Portsmouth, and then the weather begun very rough, the wind was against us for two weeks, and very rough, and cold; there was 135 of us, and one born,[8] coming on a very rough night, then there were 136. The third Sunday, just as we were going to take up our dinners, our coppers turned over and our dinners were rolling to and fro on the deck,[9] for the sea was very rough, the water dashing over on us, but we were not much afraid for we all trusted to the Lord to protect us. Mother was very sea sick, but all the rest of us was not sea sick, all the voyage of any account. When we came to the banks of Newfoundland, we met with lumps of ice, as large as your farm, floating on the water on the 8th of May, and it was so cold, that we could not get on deck. George and Joseph[10] laid by mother, to keep them warm, as she was so sick, and we were about a month without seeing any land, and sometimes we were like to be thrown out of our beds. When we came to the mouth of the gulf, mother soon got better, and never enjoyed her health so well as she has since.[11]

About 25 miles before we came to Quebec, at an island [Grosse Isle], we were stopped for the doctors to come on board, as no ships were allowed to pass, on the account of the cholera being brought into the country in that way; then 43 ships laid there that morning, (*torn out* **) in the river was of them. We had the measles on board; we were detained nine days, two children were sent to the hospital,[12] but we had no more failed. We all were sent on shore, and all our luggage, to be examined to see if we were clean and we staid there one night. There was 1767 people staid in a shed that night, that was built for that purpose, and most of them Irish. The next day were examined, and was the cleanest ship load that ever came to that

---

8 Ann, daughter of Thomas and Tabitha Ditton, born 28 April 1834.

9 "The ship rolling much, the cooking coppers were upset before dinner, without other injury, than that of dirtying the beef and frightening John Barton the cook," J.M. Brydone, *Narrative of a Voyage*, 5.

10 The two youngest brothers, George and Joseph, were both baptized at Billingshurst parish church on 9 January 1831; the older children were baptized in Hayes Independent Chapel in Slinfold, but in 1831 there was no longer a registered Congregational minister in Slinfold.

11 Brydone had pea soup made for all the emigrants when it was so cold off Newfoundland. When the *British Tar* came to the mouth of the St Lawrence, it seems that everyone felt better for they danced on deck to the violin.

12 One of the inspecting physicians was Dr Fortier.

island; and then we sailed for Quebec, but did not go ashore, only our captain, to get a steam boat for to draw us up to Montreal, 180 miles.

We were two nights and one day, and at Montreal went ashore and staid there two days, then we went on for York (*now Toronto*) in a barge;[13] sometimes we were drawn by horses, and sometimes by steam boats, which was 480 miles, we were two weeks a going, and when we came to York, we took a house and we remained there 4 days. We had a doctor [James M. Brydone*] on board, that came up with us, to get us all work, and he went to the Governor [Colborne*] of York, to say what he could for us, and they gave every family five acres of land, to go to Blandford [Woodstock], and built us a house on every one's land: this house was some round trees put on one another.

From York to Blandford is 110 miles; we went to Hamilton in a steam boat, that was 50 miles; from Hamilton to Blandford, we travelled in waggons, that was 60 miles; the road was very rough, I [did] not much mind it, for whisky is only 6d. per quart [to those] that carry a bottle. When we came to Blandford, we were put into a 'squires barn,[14] 11 families, that we had plenty of company; and we remained there 4 weeks, till our houses were built. Our houses had no door way, nor window, nor chimney, they always cut out the door ways and windows, and build the chimney afterwards.

We arrived at Blandford the 17th June. William Voice, John [a cousin], and me went to seek for work, and got work for father, Trap, and all of us, thank God for it. Father, and we, are earning 6s.3d. per day, John 5s., and plenty of work, that we hardly get time to do any thing to our own house. I forgot to tell you, that Government paid our passage from York to Blandford, which was very expensive. But now we have got our house very comfortable; we have got a front door, and a back door, two great sash windows, a brick chimney, and oven at the side of the chimney, a good roof on our houses, shingled, for there are no tiles nor slate in Canada.

Dear sister and brother, that is all I shall tell you about our voyage at present, now I am going to tell you a little about this country. The land in general is very good, the land that we were on is very good, but was very full of timber, and very large trees. We chop them all down with an axe, and burn them, and plant or sow it three times without plowing. We have got a cow, and the calf we fatted and killed, four young sows, six hens, and a cock, and a large fat hog, thank God, it is all paid for, and if we had stopped in England we should not had so much. There is land to sell for 12s. per acre, full of timber, it is very expensive, labour is so dear, labouring men get 2s.6d. a day, and their board, but no taxes, or tithes to pay. This is a fine flourishing country, a great many gentlemen settle round here. Provisions are as handy here, as you have at home. We live

13 "This vessel ... was entirely decked over, had a good commodious cabin ... the access to the cabin was by a good stair, or what is called, a companion ladder. The vessel had a main hatchway ... and a fore-hatchway [which gave access to the berths below the deck]." Brydone, *Narrative*, 13. This 1834 party was the first Petworth group to use the newly constructed Rideau canal.

14 John Hatch's barn. Hatch was one of two magistrates at Woodstock.

A clearing and cabin, Upper Canada
Philip John Bainbrigge, "Bush farm near Chatham" NA, C11811

about half a mile from the village; a new church is as near to us as you have to you. We can grow good Indian corn, good wheat, and good oats, and good peas.

John and me are going about 100 miles further up the country, to get 100 acres of land, they are giving out land to get inhabitants, and when I write again, if we have got it, I will tell you. I should like for you to be here to go with us, for you could get it as well as us, for we expect it will become very valuable in a few years. Wheat is 3s. per bushel, here; oats are 1s. per bushel; peas are 2s. 6d. per bushel; Indian corn 2s. per bushel; beef is 2½d. per pound; mutton 2½d. per pound; venison 1d. per pound. Clothing is rather dearer here than in England; boots and shoes are rather dearer, but not much. Mother and Elizabeth can earn 2s.6d. per day, making of men's clothes, when they have time to work at it. Martha is at service, has been ever since we have been here, and likes her place very well; she is 10 miles further up the country.

We all like the country very well. We have seen a good many people in this country that [we] knew in England; they all like this country very well. Father is working at the 'squire's, and John and Trap, and they have their dinner every day along with the 'squire and daughter, sits down after they have done to the same. We all live well in this country: we have roast meat twice in one day; and whisky is so cheap, that we can take our grog after supper, so that we enjoy ourselves at home: that is the ways of this country. Beer is about the same price as whisky, but very scarce, but there is two breweries a building; father has not tasted any since we have been here. This place is very much improved since we have been here: there is about forty houses built this summer, some gentlemen's and trades-people's houses. The cholera has been very bad this summer, in Montreal, and York, and Hamilton, but has not reached us, and we want to know if it have been bad in England.

When you writes, mother wishes to know how they all are at Horsham, but we have wrote there. Father and mother send their kind love to John and Sarah, and all the family, and wishes they were here, then aunt would not work so hard as going to market; but we would not persuade any one to come. Dear brother and sister, if you think of coming to America, I think of coming to England, please to send me word. * * will come to England at the same time. But father nor mother will not persuade any of you to come, although they would like to see you here; it would be better for me to come with you, as I should know better how to come again. Please to send to Horsham, for fear they should not get their letter.

Dear sister, please to give my love to Sarah * and I am very sorry that I did [not] go to see her before I came away, but I was afraid it would hurt more than it did before, but tell her I wish she was here with me, I would make her very comfortable. Please to show her the letter, tell her I wish she would make up her mind to come out with me, when I come home. Please to give my respects to Joseph Wood, tell him it would make a man of him, for it is all new work here; to William Phillips, the old man. Remember me to Mr. Bridger, and Rhoda, to all of them, to Mary * to Mr. * to William Botting's family, tell them I am saving 5s. a day. Father has saved £45. in 18 weeks in property and money; and I have saved £20. I have no more room, so good bye, God bless you all, until we hear from you again. Dear brother and sister, the reason why we did not write before, we did not know the ways of the country, and now we can tell you better, a little better about it. Give my respects to John Harwood, and Mrs. Harwood, and Mary Harwood, till I shall see them again.

Direct to us, Blandford Townplot, London District, Upper Canada, North America. By New York.

Please to shew Joseph Wood this letter, for we have plenty of game here, and deer plenty, your gun has killed three deer, we have all liberty to carry a gun; and we are going to make some sugar this spring, out of maple trees, they are very large trees here.

To JAMES ELLIOTT, Ashington,
Near Horsham, Sussex, Old England.   By way of New York.

OTHER LETTERS: *See* letter 101 by Cornelius Voice.
At the height of the building season in July 1834, William's father, Cornelius Voice, told Brydone that he, his two sons, and his nephew John were making a total of six pounds a week, a figure close to that given by William in this letter.

Although William said they had little time for their own house, the two doors and two sash windows must have set it apart from many of the log houses in which immigrants began life in Upper Canada. Brydone wrote of competition between this family and the Colemans, Dittons, Gamblens, and Martins in finishing their houses. As not all were carpenters and joiners like the Voices, some families paid the contractor for a "regular" shingled roof in place of the sloping roof of the shanty. Ditton, according to Brydone, had thatched his with straw, "quite a novelty in this part of the country."

Beginning in 1835, Sockett made special arrangements to offer reduced fares to "a few single women, not belonging to families now emigrating, but who may wish to go to friends already settled in Canada." We do not know if Sarah did take advantage of this opportunity, or even if William married.

1835

The Petworth Emigration Committee

will engage a **SHIP**, to sail from *Portsmouth* to *Montreal* early in April next.

————————

Mr. BRYDONE, Surgeon, R. N. who conducted the Party that went out in the Ship **"BRITISH TAR"** last year, has engaged to take charge of those who may go out, under the management of the Committee this season.

Mr. Brydone will be commissioned to purchase Land for the **EARL OF EGREMONT**, in **UPPER CANADA**, it is therefore necessary that he should get to that Country, as early as possible, in order that the operations of clearing and building, may be forwarded before the season is too far advanced.

Persons disposed to take advantage of this opportunity, must apply to *Mr. Phillips*, Library, Petworth; or to *Mr. Kennard*, No. 20, Penny Street, Portsmouth, without delay.

Petworth,
Feb. 24th. 1835.

————————

J. Phillips, Printer, Petworth.

3 February   The Petworth committee published a notice that the Poor Law Amendment Act, ss. 62 and 63, enabled parishes to borrow money for five years to assist emigration.

20-21 April   Egremont and his son-in-law, Sir Charles Burrell, authorized Brydone to negotiate the purchase and improvement of land in Upper Canada.

23 April   The *Burrell* sailed from Spithead.

1 May   Eight days into the Atlantic crossing, Brydone sent a letter with a ship on its way to England reporting everyone well after some rough weather.

c. 7-8 June   The emigrants were landed at Grosse Isle for inspection.

9 June   The *Burrell* arrived at Quebec. Edward Longley reported that they travelled to Montreal under sail without a tow and took almost a week to get there.

18 June   The emigrants arrived at Montreal; they travelled to Toronto through the Rideau Canal.

25 June   Emigrants from the *Burrell* landed at Toronto.

26 June   The Petworth families left Toronto for Hamilton on the steamboat *Britannia* in Brydone's charge.

27 June   Emigrants departed Hamilton for Brantford with 13 wagons.

21 July   With a view to purchase, Brydone and a survey party explored crown lands situated north of Goderich on Lake Huron between the Huron Tract and Indian lands.

3 August   The survey party returned to Goderich.

15 August   Brydone left Toronto on a tour of inspection of lands west and east of Balsam Lake.

12 September   Brydone submitted a proposal to Colborne to purchase in the tract north of Goderich: 60,000 acres to be bought immediately and 40,000 more reserved.

20 September   Cornelius Voice reported that his sons William and John had gone from Woodstock to see Brydone's tract north of Goderich; "they said it was a lake, but rather unsettled."

10 October   Brydone left Nicolet, where he had been inspecting lands of the British American Land Company, on his way via Lake Champlain to New York and Liverpool.

Sources: WSRO, PHA 140, PHA 1068; PRO, CO42/427; Brydone Family Papers; Cameron and Maude, *Assisting Emigration to Upper Canada* (Montreal: McGill-Queen's University Press 2000); contemporary newspapers; letters.

PREVIOUS PAGE: Petworth Emigration Committee announcement for 1835, PRO, CO384/39, f.374

SHIP: *Burrell*, A1, 402 tons
MASTER: J. Metcalfe
SUPERINTENDENT: James Marr Brydone

BACKGROUND

In 1835, the *Burrell*, a larger ship than the *England* or the *British Tar*, was easily filled, mainly from West Sussex parishes. Sponsors and parish officers had responded to the Poor Law Amendment Act. Some took advantage of the loan guarantee available on application to the poor law commissioners, and others used money from the sale of parish poorhouses and cottages no longer needed because Poor Law Unions had taken over the task of housing the destitute poor. Sockett's numbers increased as part of a general renewal of interest in parish-aided emigration, and he proceeded confidently with his plans to buy land in Upper Canada. Brydone sailed with authority to make a purchase in Egremont's name and to make the preparations necessary to begin a settlement in the spring of 1836.

Sockett's plans for Egremont to buy land in Upper Canada were a logical extension of his scheme to use Egremont's private patronage to provide assistance not given by government. When government in Upper Canada pulled back from assisting poor emigrants to settle, as had been done in Adelaide Township, Sockett wanted Egremont to buy an "estate" where he could offer Petworth immigrants the same security. He did not expect that they would all go to this estate, but they would sail knowing that there was a place where they could be certain of land to purchase or work when they first arrived. Sockett had become an enthusiastic colonizer, and his plans in 1835 were on a grander scale than those of the year before.

The *Burrell* seems to have had an uneventful passage and cleared Grosse Isle without mishap, but, apparently at Brydone's insistence, she refused the services of a steamboat and spent the better part of a week making her own way between Quebec and Montreal. Some of this lost time was made up by a relatively quick trip through the Rideau Canal, and the emigrants reached Toronto by mid June.

FIRST SETTLEMENT

In 1835 Upper Canada experienced an exodus of new and recent immigrants who travelled west in search of cheaper land in Michigan. Some Petworth immigrants may have joined this migration, but a number of the immigrants on the *Burrell* had people to join in Upper Canada or a destination in mind. As their letters indicate, Frank Mellish (102), who had contacts from his parish of Walberton, and Edward Longley (106), who was an experienced farm worker, found work without difficulty.

The chief emigration agent for Upper Canada continued the policy of assigning parish immigrants temporary occupancy of five-acre lots and expanded the program from Woodstock to Brantford and Paris, other areas where settlers of means clamoured for labourers and artisans. Petworth families set out under Brydone's supervision to go to Brantford. As was always the case, some, such as John Walden (104), dropped off along the way to go to other destinations on their own.

These letters hint that the newer townships offered fewer opportunities than in more prosperous years. William Cooper had warned Walden that he might best stay in St Catharines rather than looking for work in the Adelaide settlement. Although Brydone was aware of signs of a recession in the provincial economy, he negotiated for a purchase according to his instructions, choosing a large triangular tract the size of a township between the Canada Company's Huron Tract and Indian lands to the north. Lieutenant Governor Colborne recommended the sale to the Colonial Office, but officials there chose to insist on standard procedures whereby a sale could not be made until after a formal survey. Thus matters stood still awaiting the survey.

■ 99

JOSEPH AND ANN WEBB, ST CATHARINES, UPPER CANADA, TO HIS FATHER, WILLIAM WEBB, BROTHERS, AND SISTER, FELPHAM, WEST SUSSEX, 11 JANUARY 1835

Joseph Webb and Ann(e) Richards married in South Bersted in 1821[1] and they had five children by the time they emigrated (Sarah, Joseph, Ann, William, and James), though only Joseph and Ann are mentioned in this letter. They were sent with the Petworth committee in 1832 by the parish of Felpham where Joseph had grown up with the label of pauper boy. Their lame son, Joseph, was about ten at the time of writing.

Felpham was a parish in which £150 of the sum raised to send emigrants in 1832 and 1833 remained to be paid in 1835. It was also one of the Sussex parishes in which the authorities feared serious disturbances once parish paupers felt the full effect of the new poor law. Egremont*'s decision to assist emigrants from this parish on the strength of a tenuous personal connection as one of six governors of a charity no doubt reflected his concern for law and order as well as his benevolence. This extract of a letter from a Felpham emigrant was printed in the *Sussex Advertiser* in February, the month of decision for assisted emigrants.

---

1 They both signed the marriage register with a mark.

SOURCE: *Sussex Advertiser*, 22 February 1836

Extract from a letter from Joseph Webb, who emigrated with the Petworth Party, in 1832.

St Catherine's, January 11th 1835

Dear Father, Brothers & Sister,

We now take the opportunity of writing to you, sincerely hoping the same will find you in good health, as it leaves us at present, thanks be to God for it. We received your letter from brother Charles, and I am happy to hear that you are all well, and that Charles is happy in his new situation; he told us that it was the woman that kept his house, but we do not know who that was, we should like to know when you write to us again. Joseph is got the better of his lameness, and can get about without a stick. I am working on a farm for a Scotch gentleman, and I have my house rent, and firing, and board for all my family and [£3] a month clear; my wife washes for the gentleman and his wife, for three dollars a month, besides my wages, so that I am doing well, and not at all sorry that I left Old England for America. Carpenters' and bricklayers' wages is 5s a day, and board, which is 30s a week; a labouring man is from [£3] to 4.10s a month and board. Provision is cheap: beef and pork is about the same as when we wrote before.

Dear friends, we shall be happy to see any of you that may make up your minds to come, but I will not persuade any of you; but I have told you how I am doing, and you may think with yourself, and see who has got the best chance. Your wages is ten shillings a week, and every thing to buy, and mine is fifteen shillings a week, and nothing scarce to buy, but my clothing: only see the difference ... Give our love to all enquiring friends, and tell them they would do better in America than in the old country. Wheat is very cheap, it is only 3s per bushel now; it is cheaper than since we have been here: the regular price is about 4s 6d. Joseph and Ann are grown very much, they both goes to school, we have not any more in family, nor an appearance of any. If you should come, bring all the clothes you can, for clothing is cheaper there than here. William Chase is still living near us.[2] Write to us an answer, as soon as you receive this, and direct to Joseph Webb, St Catherine's Upper Canada, North America.

We have heard from Martin, and he is living fourteen miles from Guelph, which is about 80 from us.[3] Hollis[4] is living at Little York [Toronto].

So no more at present, from your loving daughter and son, brother and sister

Ann & Joseph Webb

To William Webb, Felpham, Sussex

2 See letter 30.

3 Martin and Fanny (Hollis) Martin and their family were among those who emigrated from Felpham in 1832; see letter 29.

4 John and Jane Hollis and their four children emigrated from Felpham in 1832.

We cannot identify Joseph and Ann Webb in later records with any certainty. William and Lucy Chase prospered; in 1871 they were living with two adult children in St Catharines and William worked as a locktender, presumably on the Welland Canal. They moved to Grantham Township to the "farm lot," lot 21 concession 6, before William died on 17 April 1874. Lucy and the youngest son, Edwin, were the executors of an estate valued at $2000 which included a lot in St Catharines.

■ 100

JOHN AND ANN GAMBLEN, BLANDFORD (WOODSTOCK), UPPER CANADA, TO DANIEL KING, BRIGHTON, EAST SUSSEX, 18 FEBRUARY 1835

John and Ann Gamblen brought one son with them when they emigrated in 1834 from Brighton to Woodstock. Gamblen's reference to his 12 years at sea explains why James Brydone* chose him, with William Green and William Martin, for a position of responsibility on the *British Tar*. On a daily basis, these three men saw to the issuing of provisions and water, checked the berths, and made sure the emigrants' quarters were ready for Brydone's inspection.

SOURCE: *Brighton Gazette*, 23 April 1835

The following letter has been received from one of the party of emigrants who went out from Brighton last spring. It will no doubt be interesting to many of our readers. A few passages only, relating to private matters, are omitted:

—

18 Feb 1835

Sir, – With the greatest pleasure I now address you, hoping this will find you and all your family well and hearty, as it leaves us at present, thanks be to the Lord. We set sail from Spithead in the brig British Tar, on the 17th April, and after a very good passage we arrived at Toronto, late York, on the 14th June, all in good health; and from thence all us married people proceeded on to the township of Blandford, where we are still remaining, and doing very comfortable, upon five acres of land each, granted to us by his excellency Sir John Colburne,* for three years, and at the expiration of three years we may purchase the said five acres at 80 dollars per acre. The cause of its being so valuable is it is the town plot [of Blandford (Woodstock)]; the money [is] to be paid in four instalments, four years to come, so we have a great advantage by living on it three years to do as we please with it, and live rent free, with plenty of good firing and good water, and can grow the finest of vegetables and corn. Also we have plenty of gooseberry and currant trees growing wild in the woods and millions of beautiful raspberries – so all we have to do is to remove them from the woods into our gardens, then we have plenty of fruit for gathering ...

We can also accommodate ourselves with a fine pheasant or quail, hare, woodcock, plenty of pigeons, wild ducks, and many others. At times, I have seen fine deer pass close by my house, but they took great care not to wait until I had got my gun out for them; not but we get a great plenty of venison at 1d. and 1½d. per pound; beef, 3d. per pound, very fine and very young, two and three years old; mutton, veal, pork, the same price. Sir, I hope you will be pleased to understand these are English prices, what we call currency,[5] goose, 1s.3d., turkey, 20 to 30 pounds weight, 3s.6d., a fowl, 7½d., eggs per dozen, 7½d., flour, 3s. to 3s.6d. per bushel, oats, 1s.3d. bushel, peas, 3s.6d. bushel, potatoes, 1s. bushel, turnips, 1s.3d. bushel, Indian corn, 2s.6d. bushel. Tea, sugar, and candles much the same as in England. Tobacco, 1s. pound; boots, shoes, and clothing rather dearer than in England. Such things you all know cannot be obtained at those reduced prices in England, excepting a very great alteration has taken place since we left; and if people cannot live in this country it is a wonder, when tradesmen's wages are 6s.3d. per day, and labourer's 3s. and 3s.6d.

Sir, I will also give you an account of the prices of spirits, as well as eatables, not that I make very free with it, nor ever intend to it. Buy whiskey, 3s.6d. gallon; rum, 6s., brandy, 12s.6d., gallon; port and white wine same price as brandy. All these luxuries are to be obtained by *hard work only* – not painting alone, far from it; plenty of other hard work in addition to painting, such as tree cutting and farming, and work downright hard too, not play as half of it is in England. It is true we lay a good foundation before we go to work, and when the days work is over.

I am sorry to add that my wife was very ill the whole of the passage, but thank God she enjoys her health far better in this country than in England. My little boy is particularly hearty, and fat as a pig; and I am also sorry to add that I have been laid up ten weeks with a fistula, shortly after my arrival at Blandford. I underwent an operation for it, most dreadful sharp time of it, I assure you Sir, but I thank the blessed Lord, I am quite recovered and hearty. Sir, pray do you remember Martin, the carpenter, that came with us from Brighton, his wife and family?[6] If you do, I am sorry to say his poor wife is now in a truly dying state, with an abscess in her side. We expect to hear of her death every moment; it is impossible she can live. I hope the blessed Lord will be pleased to receive her poor soul.

Sir, I hope and trust you will be pleased to excuse the liberty which I now beg of you, that is, Sir, if you will be so kind as to give our respects, both myself and wife, to –. Be pleased to say we are happy and comfortable, that my wife enjoys her health a deal better than in England, for she is not obliged to work so hard, – thank God that lot falls upon me, – who is much the fittest to do it. Here is a great plenty for her to do, but I will not suffer her to do it while I can get a good living without her help. We have plenty of gentry here at Blandford – they strive their utmost to get her to work but their labour is all in vain.

* * *

Toronto is certainly a very smart place; I may say truly handsome; it is so much like an English town I canot tell the difference. Can purchase anything and everything the same as in Brighton; and again, Montreal is a splendid place – a place of great

---

5 Probably Halifax currency.
6 William and Jane Martin and four children.

Toronto: King Street looking east from Toronto Street, 1835. On the left can be seen the jail, courthouse, and St James Anglican Church

Thomas Young, "Toronto, King Street East," Toronto Reference Library, T10248

trade, full as large as Brighton – to see the carts, waggons, etc. driving as bad as at Whitechapel in London – and coaches with six horses, most beautiful greys.

* * *

Sir, amongst the residents at Blandford, we have Admiral [Henry] Vansittart and family; he has lately lost his wife, while on a visit to the Falls of Niagra;[7] also Colonel [Alexander Whalley] Light and family, and many other officers, both of navy and army. Great quantity of the settlers at Blandford think it is a very healthy situation. Blandford at present is but small, but bids fair to become a place of great importance. Sir, I have said all that I can think of, and I hope my letter will give you every satisfaction, and all that may see or hear its contents; and, Sir, I should be happy to receive an answer to this letter to satisfy me that you did receive it, and in the course of twelve months more I should wish to send you another with a still more flourishing account, I hope

7 Vansittart's party travelled to Upper Canada through the port of New York. As his wife was ill, she stopped at Saratoga and died about two weeks after her husband reached Woodstock (Mary Byers and Margaret McBurney, *The Governor's Road: Early Buildings and Families from Mississauga to London* [Toronto 1982]).

and trust particularly of my own concerns, as I have good promises in view; and if you should be pleased to write, Sir, which I trust you will be so kind as to pay the postage of the letter you send to the water edge, or otherwise I shall not receive it. I now conclude, with my wife, returning our most sincere thanks to you for all the kindness we experienced of you, and may the Lord bless you and your good lady and family.

We remain your very humble Servants
JOHN AND ANN GAMBLEN

When you should be pleased to write to me, please to direct as follows: – John Gamblen, painter, township of Blandford, district of London, North America; by the way of New York.

P.S. – I trust, Sir, you will be pleased to give my respects to – Puget Esq.,[8] and all that so kindly assisted me; tell them I am perfectly satisfied with the exchange that I have made, and so is every body that I see, and well they may be, many that I know having arrived here with not a shoe on their feet, and after three or four years to possess beautiful farms, with cows, oxen, pigs, poultry, of all sorts; finer my eyes never seen in any part of the known world; and of course you will grant that I must know something of the world after having sailed twelve years on the salt water, east to west, north to south. Sir, I have also sent a letter to his Lordship the Earl of Chichester*. From my beginning this letter until I closed it, some days had elapsed, sufficiently to acquaint you with the death of Mrs. Martin; she departed this life Friday, 6th February, 1835 after a long illness, five years come the next August.

Sir, we are 900 miles up the great river St. Lawrence. An emigrant is just gone to England, named Carter, gone to reside down in the borders of Hampshire, labourer, turned to farming, in a very few years made [£]1,300, and took it with him, and gone to enjoy a handsome fortune left him in England also.

To Mr. Daniel King, Provident and District Society,
High-street, Brighton, Sussex, Old England.

Set against Brydone's opinion that he was "a decided radical," Gamblen's deferential letter offers a glimpse of the complexities of Sussex society and of the long reach of the influence exercised by a patron such as the Earl of Chichester.

The Gamblens disappeared from the records of Woodstock, and we have not been able to trace them in the area.

101

CORNELIUS AND ELIZABETH VOICE, BLANDFORD (WOODSTOCK), UPPER CANADA, TO BROTHER AND SISTER, 20 SEPTEMBER 1835

Cornelius Voice signed his name to the marriage register when he and Elizabeth Smallwood were married in Horsham in 1807; she signed with a mark.

8 John Hey Puget, from a Huguenot family, supported several charitable institutions in Brighton and was vice-president of the Provident and District Society.

SOURCE: *Continuation of Letters from Sussex Emigrants, 9–11*

*From CORNELIUS VOICE, who emigrated from Billingshurst, Sussex, in a ship sent by the Pet-
worth Committee, with his wife, 5 sons, and 2 daughters, and a nephew, in the Year 1834. He was a
Carpenter and Joiner,[9] and his two eldest sons and his nephew who were grown up, followed the same
trade.*

BLANDFORD, UPPER CANADA,
September 20th. 1835.

Dear Brother and Sister,

This comes with our love to you, hoping it will find you all well, as thank God,
it leaves us all. Cornelius has still a wound in his leg, but he is a great deal better.
Brother, I should [have] wrote to you before; I wanted to get settled, to see how I
like the country. We all like America very much, it is a pleasant country, particularly
Blandford: there is a many settled round here, most English.

We had a good passage over; we landed at Quebec the first of June, but our vessel came as far as Montreal: there we left, and went on shore, and staid two days,
before our doctor [Brydone*] could get a boat, as he was to see the whole party up
to Toronto, Upper Canada, and that was where we paid our passage to. From Montreal to Toronto is 600 miles.[10] We travelled in a large boat like a barge, up a new
cut, and it being so much up hill, that we past through a great many locks. Sometimes we were drawn by horses, sometimes tied to a steam boat. We travelled this
way 400[11] miles, to Kingston, there we left the boat, and all got in a steam boat. We
had 200[12] miles up to Toronto, 12th June. As soon as they stopt the steamer, we saw
a gentleman on the wharf, we thought we knew. As soon as we got out, he came to
us: he ask us if we did not come from Horsham. I said no, my name is Voice, from
Billingshurst. He said his name was Gurnett, from Horsham.[13] He is living at Toronto,
carrying on the printing business. He told me to come to him, he would help me
to work: he got work for me and William.

Before we begun, our Doctor come to our lodging; he said he had been to the
Governor [Colborne*], to speak for the party, and the Governor said the married
men were to come to him, he [would] give 13 families each 5 acres of land, and build
us a shanty as they call it, at Blandford, and take us there free of expence.[14] Our doc-

9 As carpenters, they constructed houses; the joiner did the lighter and more ornamental work of finishing a house and built furniture.

10 Original annotation: "The writer appears to be under some mistake with respect to this distance, it
being only about 410 miles." Since the 1834 party travelled from Montreal to Toronto via the newly
constructed and longer Rideau canal route, the distance estimate is not as far out as Thomas Sockett*, who annotated the original, suggested.

11 Original annotation: "240."

12 Original annotation: "170."

13 Presumably this was George Gurnett.*

14 Brydone took twelve families sent by the Petworth committee and the Rivers family was put under
his protection by the emigration agent at Toronto.

tor was sent with us: it is a 100 miles further up the country. We come 50 miles in
the steamer to Hamilton, that was as far as we could come by water. Our doctor
hired 20 waggons to carry us and our luggage the 50 [miles] to Blandford. We reached
there the 21st June: we were all put in the 'squire's barn, while our houses were building. Our houses were built with round trees laid one on the other, with a few boards
for the roof, without any door, or window, or fire place, we had to do the rest as we
could. Our land was full of large high trees. We were in the barn just one month,
and some were there longer.

William and John went out the next day to get work, and got work for all. We
get 6s.3d. a day, English money. We were glad to begin work, for we had but 3 sovereigns. We soon earned some money, and then we all went to work at our house
and land. We had a new brick chimney and oven, we have 2 pair of sashes, a front
door, and a back door, and a good roof, and shingled: we have no tiles nor slates; we
have got this done before the cold weather comes. We have cleared our 5 acres of
land. The way we clear is, chop the trees down with an axe, then chop them in
lengths, and draw them together with oxen, and burn them; this is a hard job to clear
land, but thank God, we have done. Brother, now I will tell you what I have got,
and what I have grown. I have got 4 cows, and 4 calves, them I am raising up. I have
4 sows, and 20 young hogs. There is plenty of beech-nuts, we are in hopes they will
be good pork, without any more fatting: we have about 100 fowls, little and big,
besides geese and turkeys: we sell none, but eat them all, for they are very cheap here.
Your sister is making 20 pounds of butter a week. We have a good garden; plenty of
potatoes, and we have all sorts of vegetables, cucumbers and melons grow on the
ground, the same as cabbages; the other part of our ground with Indian Corn and
Oats, for cows and other things in the winter. Our cows and hogs cost nothing in
the summer, they run in the woods and keep themselves. I only wish you had been
here last month, to see your sister and the girls making sugar in the woods, sometimes up to their knees in snow, but they made 150 lbs. of sugar, and 60 lbs. of treacle.[15] The Yankees called it a good bunch, being a bad sugar year. Your sister has learnt
to make her own soap and candles.

Our house is about half a mile from the village. We have a new church, and [an]
English preacher came up the day before we did.[16] There was but two shops when
we came here, but there is five more shops now built since we have been here, and
about 50 framed houses. We can get any thing for money, the same as in England.
Brother and sister, if you can get here, I think it would be a good thing for your
family, as there is plenty of work for your boys, and girls, and good pay. The same
doctor came out with Lord Egremont's vessel last April, as came out with us; he came
to see us and told us he brought out 250 from Sussex. He settled all the families at

---

15 Elizabeth and her daughters, Elizabeth and Martha
16 Cornelius and Elizabeth had been members of the Hayes Independent Chapel, Slinfold, West Sus-
    sex. The Church of England "preacher" was William Craddock Bettridge, a missionary sent by the
    Society for the Propogation of the Gospel who travelled in Admiral Vansittart's party.

Brandtford, on a five acre lot each, the same as us. We came through Brandtford, about 25 miles back; he told us that he was coming out with another vessel load next April: he said that he was going to take them that liked to go, to farm a new tract at the side of Goderich, about 60 miles further up the country than we are. William and John has been up there: they said it was a lake, but rather unsettled. If you think of coming, I can get you a five acre lot near ours, as I am acquainted with the 'squire. You can change your money here, but you must get that settled at home. You had better go to Mr. Sockett, at Petworth, and you may shew him this letter, and he will tell you the best way to get out. Go soon, as the vessel will start the beginning of April.

We wrote home, but we have not received any letter from them, but we have had a letter from Mary.[17] I staid at home to write to you. All four boys are gone to play a game of cricket: they play 11 on a side, 10s. to 5s., the trade against the gen-

An English dairy, perhaps like the one where Elizabeth Voice learned to make butter
"The Dairy," Jefferys Taylor, *The Farm: A New Account of Rural Toils and Produce* (London 1832), University of Sussex Collection

17 Their daughter Mary married James Elliot of Ashington, West Sussex, in 1827 and remained in England when the family emigrated.

tlemen. I cannot tell you which beat, they are not come home. So I must conclude with all our loves to you, and all your family.

CORNELIUS & ELIZABETH VOICE.

I forgot to say that Elizabeth was married 18th July, to a young man, the name of [George] Coleman: he came from England with us, they live on a 5 acre lot, joining ours.[18] Brother, I hope you will write as soon you receive this. This letter is by the favor of a young lady that is coming home, she has been out on a visit to her sister.

Direct to me, Cornelius Voice, Blandford Town Plot, London District, Upper Canada, North America.

OTHER LETTERS: *See* letter 98 from William Voice.

The letters of William and Cornelius Voice give a full account of a successful family emigration in which the presence of several adult children contributed to rapid progress. Although they say nothing of the daily round of looking after a large family in a small log house, these letters also give more recognition than most to the work done by the women of the family.

Although Cornelius sounded quite settled in Woodstock in 1835, and William and his cousin John seemed to be of two minds about leaving the familiar people and amusements of a settled community to pioneer in the bush, we were unable to determine what happened to this family. Lot 3 range 1 (on the north side of Barwick or St Mary Street), the three-acre Woodstock lot first occupied by the Voices, was patented in 1844 by Ham Voice, a Petworth emigrant of 1836, also from Billingshurst, and perhaps a relative. By 1844, Ham Voice had built a new house to replace the one described by William and Cornelius.

■ 102

FRANK MELLISH, THORNHILL, UPPER CANADA, TO HIS FATHER, WILLIAM MELLISH, AND HIS MOTHER, WALBERTON, WEST SUSSEX, 8 NOVEMBER 1835

Frank Mellish emigrated as a single man from the parish of Walberton. Walberton emigrants on Petworth ships were sponsored by Richard Prime*, the principal landowner. This letter adds to the story begun in 1831 by George and Emily Wells (176) of the community of Walberton emigrants settled in Thornhill, on Yonge Street, north of Toronto.

SOURCE: *Letters from Sussex Emigrants*, 6–7

Thornhill, Young Street, Nov. 8, 1835.

DEAR FATHER AND MOTHER,

This comes with my kind love to you, hoping that these few lines will find you in good health, as it leaves me at present, thanks be to God. We landed in York on the 25th of June, after a nine weeks passage. The 29th of May we saw the first land

---

18 George Coleman emigrated from Kingston, near Lewes, East Sussex, with his parents and brothers and sisters (see George Coleman Sr's letter 103). Young George and Elizabeth had one son in Canada and then emigrated to the United States; five sons were born in Illinois and one in Kansas.

after we left England, covered with snow. When we arrived Thomas Messenger came on board the steamer and gave directions where to find George Wells and the two Birchs, and I have been at work for George Wells ever since. [William] Cole is working just bye, and Charles Leggatt is working about three miles from here.[19] Now we have had £2 10s. a month ever since we have been here and *our board*, so we have nothing to get but clothes.

Dear Father and Mother we have a Church and every thing as comfortable as we can wish, and I like the country very well at present; it is far better than being beholden to the Parish. But in my next letter I shall be able to tell you more about it, after I have been here a winter. Mr. Birch, Mrs. Norris, G. Wells and all the Walburton people live close together.[20] James Birch is married to Frances Viney, from Climping.[21] Remember me to J. Ayling, R. Suter, and Master and Mrs. Millyard. I have not seen George Suter yet, but I have heard that he was 50 miles from here.[22] I can assure you that any one can get a good living here if he will work. So to conclude I send my kind love to you all, so no more at present from your affectionate son,

FRANK MELLISH.

Remember G. Wells and Family to his father and mother. Direct to me at G. Wells' Thornhill, Young Street, Toronto.

To William Mellish – Walberton.

OTHER LETTERS: *See also* letter 107 from Mary and Edmund Birch (Burch), and 110 from John Ayling.

Mellish married Eliza Savage in 1839 at Thornhill. In 1851 he was occupying one acre on lot 37 concession 1 Vaughan Township and gave his occupation as labourer.

■ **103**

GEORGE COLEMAN, WOODSTOCK, UPPER CANADA, TO
MR J. MARTEN, RODMELL, EAST SUSSEX, 17 DECEMBER 1835

Like most of the letters printed in newspapers, this one lacks the personal information that Sockett* often included in his publications. George Coleman and his wife, Sarah (Pollard), were sent by the parish of Kingston by Lewes. We know that they had at least ten children, and that two died before they emigrated. Some of the other children may have stayed in England.

SOURCE: *Brighton Herald*, 13 February 1836

---

19 All the people mentioned emigrated from Walberton, the Messenger family at an unknown date, James and Edmund Birch (Burch) in 1832, and William Cole and Charles Leggett in 1835.
20 Mr Birch is probably a reference to Edmund Birch; Charlotte and Henry Norris probably also emigrated in 1835.
21 Sisters Frances and Emily Viney emigrated in 1835.
22 George Suter probably emigrated in 1835 and settled in Woodstock where his son George was born about 1837. He evidently moved to Thorah Township by 1851 where he occupied N ½ lot 11 concession 6. He died in Thorah in March 1887.

Extract from a letter, received last Wednesday (Feb. 10th), by Mr. J. Marten, of Rodmill, from George Coleman, who emigrated from Kingstone, near Lewes, in April, 1834:

Woodstock, Dec. 17th. 1835.

I have passed one winter, and so far on my second, which you will see by the date of my letter. This winter began sooner than the last, and we had snow from 12 to 18 inches thick as early as the beginning of November, with sharp frost. This day the cold is 16 degrees below Zero, and, in the lower province, at Quebec, as much as 30. Here, then, you must keep moving; but, to make amends, plenty of firing, plenty of good beef, pork, venison, mutton, bread, brandy, rum, whiskey – yes, all this, for the poor, honest, working man; but mark, he must be what he ought to be, or he will find want here as in England.

The land varies very much in difference of soil in the space of half a mile. In some places, nothing but sand – then light, rich mould – and then fine, deep, black mould; and, all of a sudden, you come to stiff, hard clay; the higher ground, in general, is light, with sand hills; but there is some good land where the ground is level: stiff soil, where the oak, walnut, beech, and maple wood grows, in the best land – keep away from the pine-wood, the cedar, and the swampy ground. The farmer sows 1½ bushel of wheat per acre, and on new ground gets from 20 to 30 bushels per acre. Oats and barley about in proportion. Most excellent crops of peas grow here; we eat green peas in abundance; if you have none growing of your own, which was the case with us the first summer, you can get plenty of your neighbours; my wife had leave of 4 or 5 farmers to take what she pleased, and we ate of green peas until we were tired. Turnips are very good here, and potatoes excellent – much better flavoured than any I have eaten in England; but perhaps you will say there is reason for this, when I tell you that we never eat them but with good beef, mutton, pork – yes, and plenty of butter.

Oh, my brother labourers in England, how much do I feel for you; may Providence send you here; but not without you mean to acquit yourselves like men, and then, and only then, may you expect to find these things. Oh, England, I weep for you, being my native land. I am still at work for the same master that I began to work for the second day after I arrived, and not one angry word has passed between us as yet – something different from being discharged twice in a fortnight. I speak my mind, here, the same as I did in England, but the masters in this country love to hear the truth.

I am now in my own log-house; a good cow of my own; a good pig put in the tub to-day. I have not been able, through illness, to work for five weeks; but, thanks to Providence, I am fast recovering, and now have not to meet the frowns of the overseer, and be called a poor pauper,[23] but I am looked upon, and receive kindness without grudging. Dear Sir, I am happy. We make our candles, soap, and sugar. If I

---

23 The overseer was the parish officer in charge of poor relief.

had room, I would tell you the process; but I have room to say, that we have no excise-man[24] to interrupt us.

 To all my old acquaintances, I desire my best respects, and, those that can, let them follow me.

G. Coleman.

OTHER LETTERS: *See also* letter 101 from Cornelius and Elizabeth Voice, and letter 94 from Henry Harwood Sr.

Within a year or two of arriving in Canada and settling in Woodstock, Coleman's daughter Lucy Susannah married Henry Harwood Jr and his son George Jr married Elizabeth Voice; both the Harwood and Voice families had travelled to Canada with them on the *British Tar*. (Indeed the Harwoods were very old friends since George Sr had witnessed the marriage of Henry and Sarah Harwood in England in 1810.) George's health cannot have improved as he died seven months after writing this letter, on 26 July 1836 at the age of 57.

---

24 The exciseman collected duty payable on goods manufactured inside the country, such as candles. It was illegal to make your own candles in England as they were taxable. William Cobbett in *Cottage Economy* (1821-22; 17th ed., Oxford: Oxford University Press 1979) gives precise instructions for making rush-lights to avoid buying expensive candles.

1836

THE
HEBER,
Of 441 Tons Register, A. 1.

Built at Whitby, and only One Year old,

ENGAGED BY

The Petworth

Emigration Committee,

ACTING FOR

The Earl of Egremont,

Will be ready to take her Passengers on Board in PORTSMOUTH HARBOUR, on FRIDAY, the 15th. and will positively sail from thence (wind and weather permitting) on MONDAY, the 18th. of APRIL under the superintendence of Mr. JAMES MARR BRYDONE, R. N., who will conduct the Party through the RIDEAU CANAL (thereby avoiding the dangerous Rapids of the St. Lawrence) to

TORONTO.

The COMMITTEE having been highly gratified, by the system of management adopted by Mr. Brydone, on two former occasions, and the success that attended it, (not one casualty having occurred) have the greatest pleasure, and confidence, in placing the Party this Year, under his charge.

Passengers to be on Board before SIX in the Evening, of FRIDAY, the 15th. or at latest by NOON of SATURDAY, the 16th. of April.

No Passengers can be taken on Board on the Sunday.

The CABIN BERTHS in the HEBER are of a superior description, and two are still disengaged.

For Particulars, enquire of the PRINTER, or of Mr. KENNARD, 20, Penny Street, Portsmouth.

Petworth.
April 2nd. 1836.

J. PHILLIPS, PRINTER, PETWORTH.

Chronology for the Year 1836

January	Sir Francis Bond Head replaced Sir John Colborne as lieutenant governor of Upper Canada.
20 March	Edward Longley at Guelph reported the snow beginning to melt after covering the ground since 11 November.
27 April	The *Heber* sailed from Spithead.
24 May	First sight of land.
25 May	William Ayling and John Barnes reported heavy snow and a lively snowball fight on deck.
26 May	The twentieth anniversary of Sockett's induction at Petworth was celebrated by a dinner at the Half Moon Inn.
5 June	The *Heber* arrived at Quebec.
9 June	The emigrants reached Montreal.
16 June	Abraham Randall drowned, an apparent suicide.
23 June	The emigrants arrived in Toronto after travelling in Durham boats from Montreal up the St Lawrence to Prescott.
7 July	Brydone arrived at Preston bringing casks and money sent from England for the Rapsons, Penfolds, and Dearlings
8 September	Brydone renewed his offer to purchase crown lands north of Goderich but reduced the size of the tract and his price.
18 September	Mary Hills, who was living near Dundas, wrote a letter for Brydone to take to England to deliver to her sponsor, John Drewitt.
12 September	David (Cloudesley) Sharp reported that several of his friends from the *Heber* had joined him in Sandwich.

Sources: WSRO. PHA 140; Cameron and Maude, *Assisting Emigration to Upper Canada* (Montreal: McGill-Queen's University Press 2000); contemporary newspapers; letters.

PREVIOUS PAGE: Announcement for the *Heber,* PRO, CO 384/41, f.338

SHIP: *Heber*, A1, 441 tons
MASTER: Captain Rue
SUPERINTENDANT: James Marr Brydone

BACKGROUND

After 1831 and 1832, 1836 was the year of the largest parish-aided immigration to Upper Canada. The Petworth committee took slightly more emigrants than in 1835, and apparently turned others away. The majority of these emigrants, as Sockett preferred, were sent by West Sussex parishes. Sockett's relations with the new assistant poor law commissioner for Sussex were not good, but parishes continued to get the poor law commissioners' approval for loans to send their emigrants on the Petworth ship. Possibly because of all the turmoil over the introduction of the new poor law in England, more than one immigrant to Canada wrote answering questions about relief in that country. Their very positive reports outlined a spontaneous charity that was not, however, always forthcoming, especially in cities where heavy immigration had given a whole new dimension to poverty; Toronto in fact was introducing its first workhouse.

We know nothing much about the *Heber*'s Atlantic crossing or the voyage from Quebec to Montreal, but available dates suggest that the journey went as planned until the emigrants reached Montreal. There, a closure on the Rideau Canal forced them back into Durham boats for the trip through and around the rapids on the St Lawrence. They complained about exposure and discomfort; the trip to Prescott had not improved since 1832 and 1833. From Prescott to Toronto, they travelled on the regular steamboats.

FIRST SETTLEMENT

Economic difficulties persisted, getting worse in Upper Canada in 1836. Although vigorous campaigning by Colborne's successor, the eccentric Sir Francis Bond Head, helped conservative candidates to win a sweeping victory in elections to the House of Assembly that summer, the campaign polarized opinion and contributed to political discontent. Brydone continued negotiations to buy the tract of land north of Goderich, but he was apprehensive in view of "the present state of the province," and in particular of the stagnation, if not decline, of Goderich itself. He reduced the acreage requested and sought a better price, citing the widely held opinion (shared in private by many government officials) that government must reduce the price of crown lands in Upper Canada to a level competitive with the United States.

Letters from Petworth immigrants of past year who wrote in the early months of 1836 suggested that they were doing all right, with subsistence farms or wages to support themselves. Few of the new immigrants on the *Heber* stayed in Toronto – Lydia Hills wrote that her family and the family of John Barnes were the only two who remained. As in 1835, Petworth families again travelled to Brantford for five-acre lots. Head allowed this plan of providing for parish-aided immigrants to continue, but he reduced funding as part of cut-backs on assistance to able-bodied immigrants. Petworth immigrants seem to have had to pay for their own food on the way to Brantford. There were some log huts built by the government that year, but the Jackman family reported living in rented quarters and made no mention of having a home supplied.

■ 104

JOHN AND RUTH WALDON, ST CATHARINES, UPPER CANADA, TO
FRIENDS, [JAMES COOPER], TILLINGTON, WEST SUSSEX,
9 JANUARY 1836

John Walden, a husbandman, and his wife Ruth (Rewell or Rule), a cook, emigrated in 1835 with their five children, Elizabeth, Mary, Ann, Charles, and Jane. Ruth wrote this letter.[1]

SOURCE: *Sussex Advertiser*, 14 March 1836

Letter from John Walden who emigrated from Climping Sussex, and went out in the Burrell in 1835.

Dear Friends, according to my promise, I now take up my pen to write to you, which I hope it will find you in good health, as I am happy to say it leaves us all at present, I thank God for it. Dear friend we did not go to your brothers as you wished us to do, for when we got to St Catherines, William Sturt[2] and we got into work. And I wrote up to your brother,[3] and he wrote back to us again, and he said money was scarcer with them than it was with us; so we thought we had better stay where we were, for I have got a good place. I am working for an English Esquire, I gets 20 dollars a month, which is about 4 pounds in English money, and provisions is cheap.

---

1 Both John and Ruth signed their names to the marriage register.

2 William and Elizabeth (Fowler) Sturt of Felpham, a parish just west of Climping, emigrated in 1835 with their six children.

3 The brother would be William Cooper, who emigrated in 1832 and settled in Adelaide Township (see letters 8, 52).

Beef and pork is now selling at two-pence half-penny a pound, and that is counted very dear for this country; wheat is about 4 shillings a bushel, but I have not wanted to buy any since harvest, for we picked up 25½ bushels of wheat,[4] and Walden was cutting of wheat and rye.

[sic] Here is no women do not go out into the fields here to work; they are too independent for that, but I went on about the same as I did [at] home. Dear friends, I hope you will not fail in coming, for I wish I had come ten years before I did; for here we can get a good living and be independent of any one. We have about a hundred stone[5] of pork to carry us through the year, and that is what we could not do at home, but it is no trouble to do it here. As for your children, you can get places for them that are big enough: they take them out very young, they board them and clothe them, and put them to school; and that is a good thing for the children.

Dear Friends, I hope you will not doubt my letter, for what I say is true; and the letters are never opened, nor interrupted; for as this letter leaves me so it will come to you; and I hope you will come, for I would sooner see you come here than any one I know. Please to give our love to Mr & Mrs Goatcher,[6] and tell Mrs Goatcher I wish they was here; they would make money as fast as they could tell it, in their business; for I have never seen any goods as they can make, since I have been in Canada.

As to what Mr Barnet had to say, about going barefooted, it is true enough, for they do, but it is because it is so hot; it is not for want, it is for their pleasure. My children wanted to go without, but being just come out, I would not let them; and people is not so proud here, as they are at home, in their dress; if you were here, you would see they had plenty of clothes now it is cold. I wish Harriet and King[7] had come with us, it would have been the best thing they ever had done in their lives; for I have every reason to bless the day that I left Old England. I wish I could see you, I could tell you more; but you may believe this, as well as if I come home, as it is almost too soon to come home this year, but I think I shall come home in the course of a year or two, but do not wait for that; come as soon as you can; and I shall not get into any business for myself, until I see whether you comes or no, and if you do, I will go anywhere with you; and we can get a good living anywhere, or anyhow, and no trouble to us, dear friends, if you make up your minds to come, which I hope you will, for the sake of your family, and do not live there in that distressed place, for I can assure you, that we do not flatter you at all. We can have anything that heart can wish for; we can have a fat goose for 1 shilling and a penny of your money, and a good fowl for 6 pence halfpenny; so we can have a treat cheap when we like; they are never more than that.

If you come out with the Petworth party, as I expect you will, do not board yourselves, for we had everything as we could expect in such a place, we had plenty. You

---

4 This is another reference to gleaning.
5 A unit of weight equal to 14 pounds or 6.35 kilograms.
6 Robert Goatcher, of Petworth, was a baker and confectioner.
7 Harriet King and her husband.

Examples of wooden gingerbread moulds, the horse from Burford Museum, Oxfordshire; the coat of arms of William IV, which belonged to a Horsham baker, now at Preston Manor Museum, Brighton.

Drawn by Leigh Lawson.

might get oatmeal for gruel, as that is not on board the ship; bring vinegar, and lemons, and pickles, and oranges, and a ham of bacon will be very good, if you are sick. Walden and the children were very well, but I was sick, at times, all the way, until we got into fresh water, and then I was very well; but do not mind that, but think what a fine thing plenty is, for what it is where you are now. I hope and trust you will come. Please to answer this as soon as you receive this, whether you come or no. Your brother sent us word he had let his farm, and had some people in his house, so he had no room for us, but he offered us some bush land, if we liked to go, but it is said by many, that this is as good place as any we can get in, for money; for in many places when they work for a farmer, they are forced to take corn, and hogs, or anything they have but we get all our money, and go where we like.

Dear friends, bring your gingerbread blocks with you, and prints, for I have never seen any seed, gingerbread, or gingerbread nuts, since I have been in Canada.[8] It will be a good trade here. I can sell sugar goods as fast as I can make it. And bring all the

8 Henry Mayhew, in *London Labour and the London Poor ...* (London: Frank Cass & Co 1967), gives a detailed description of the making and selling of cakes and gingerbread. Seed cakes were flavoured with caraway seed. Writing in 1861–2 of the use of gingerbread prints and moulds, he observed that "the sale of gingerbread ... was much more extensive in the streets than it is at present. Indeed what was formerly known in the trade as 'toy' gingerbread is now unseen in the streets, except occasionally,

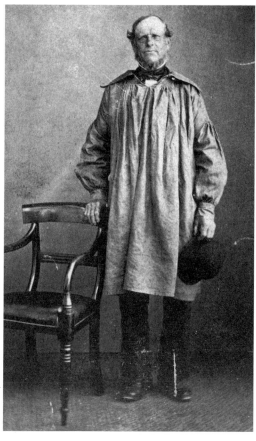

A round-frock worn by
Henry Mann
Courtesy Margaret Parsons

clothes you can. Clothes is rather dearer here, than it is at home. Do not bring any heavy nailed shoes, for they are not wanted here, as here is no stones to wear them. I have not seen a flint stone since I have been in Canada.⁹ You can bring some stones to strike a light with. Here is no round frocks,¹⁰ nor breeches worn here.

Dear friends, you will come to Toronto with the party, and you can leave them, and you come on in the steam boat to Niagara, they charged us 7 shillings and 6

and that only when the whole has not been sold at the neighbouring fairs . . . twenty or thirty years ago 'King George on horseback' was popular in gingerbread. His Majesty, wearing a gilt crown, gilt spurs, and a gilt sword, bestrode the gilt saddle of his steed, and was eaten with great relish by his juvenile subjects. There were also sheep, and dogs, and other animals all adorned in a similar manner." Gingerbread nuts were nut-sized, hard knobs of gingerbread sold already packed in paper bags. Mayhew's informant said they sold at 40 for a penny.

9 West Sussex has an abundance of flintstones in its chalky soil; they were used extensively as building material.

10 The round-frock was a loose, over garment of coarse material, usually black when worn as a working garment. For Sundays and special occasions, the frock would be white and, when ornamented with intricate smocking, it became a smock-frock.

pence each, Sturt and we. That is about 12 miles from us. You can hire a waggon and 2 horses, and they will bring you to St Catherines. You enquire at Mr Murray's or at Doctor Cross's shop, or at Mr Bole's shop, and they will tell you where I live – So no more at present, from your very well wisher.

Ruth & John Walden

St. Catherines, January 9th 1836

Direct: John Walden, St. Catherines in the District of Niagara, Upper Canada, North America.

To James Cooper,[11] Tillington, near Petworth, Sussex, England –

By New York & Liverpool

The town of St Catharines was flourishing as a result of the opening of the Welland Canal. We have not traced the later history of this family.

■ 105

TIMOTHY TRUSLER, PLYMPTON TOWNSHIP, UPPER CANADA, TO WILLIAM LUFF, FARNHURST CROSS, SUSSEX, 8 FEBRUARY 1836

Timothy Trusler, a sawyer, was the eldest son of John and Jane (Childs) Trusler. Assisted by the parish of Fernherst and W.H.Yaldwin*, the Truslers emigrated as a large family group made up of two families: Timothy's parents and nine of Timothy's brothers and sisters and his uncle and aunt, George and Elizabeth (Gilbert) Trussler, and their seven children.

The misfortunes of these families during their travels vividly illustrate the risks of emigration for young children. In John Trusler's family, Timothy's two youngest brothers travelled all the way to the site of present-day Sarnia. They died there, camped in a storage shed on the wharf while their mother waited for John and the older boys to prepare their lot to receive the family. In George Trussler's family, Timothy's infant cousin died during the ocean voyage. Another of his cousins, 11-year-old James, drowned in Lake Ontario, having fallen while fetching water over the side of the steamboat as they approached the harbour at York (see 78 by Rhoda Thair).

SOURCE: *Letters from Sussex Emigrants*, 9–10

Plympton, half-past 7 o'clock, Monday Night, Feb. 8, 1836.

Dear Sir –

I received your letter in Sept. ... I am sorry to hear the sad state that England is in, I think you had better come to this country if you wish to be independent of any other man – a man in this country have no business, to ..... for any body but his self after he have been in this country three years if he is industrious. We are now living on our own produce, pork is scarce in this township – we have just killed a Sow that weighed about 250 lbs. ... we have 3 young sows, about 5 months old, so we shall have plenty

11 James Cooper and family emigrated from Tillington in 1836 and settled in Adelaide Township (see letter 133).

another year, and every thing that we wish for – we have a yoke of Steers to break in the spring, 2 good cows and 2 calves a year old – we have no mill in the township as yet, we are sawing the timber for one to be built in the summer, it is a long road to one – we have plenty of sawing handy home about half-a-mile, and from that to 5 miles more than we can do, but thank God we shall not want to do any much longer.

Tell Thomas West he should not fail in coming, for it will be the best thing he ever done for himself – when first I came I thought I would go back to England, but I got acquainted after a little and thought no more about it – if Thomas West comes out and thinks of getting land, he had better come up pretty handy to us, for it is good land, but if he do not mean to farm, labour, I think, is better further down the country; but if a man wishes to do good for himself he had better farm – but tell him not to take cleared farms at halves, for there is plenty would let farms at halves, or so much a year; it is a bad plan, for when you leave it you are no better than when you first came to this country, but when you clear a farm yourself it is your own. – here is trouble you will find when you come to this country for 2 or 3 years and then you will begin to be comfortable. We have 9 acres of land to clear off in the spring, we have 6 acres of wheat sewed – we have built a barn 32ft long, 22 wide – we had good crops of every thing last year that we could wish for –

Father's family is small now, only 4 at home besides myself and Absolom – we have 240 acres of land amongst us – Eliza lives at her old place still – tell Grandmother, Reuben is a good thrasher – Mother and Eleanor have many a battle about the barn, she is so fond of thrashing she cannot keep her out of the barn; here is not hardly a man in the township that can thrash as much as them two.[12] Apples about 40 miles from us have been selling at 2d per bushel all this last year – you take 2 barrels they will fill one with cider for you for the empty one, and as many as you like on the same terms. Provisions are not so cheap as when we came, but cheaper than in England – they have been bringing fresh pork from Upper Canada and selling 4d per lb, and it is getting lower – flour 6½ dollars for 196 lbs – tell Thomas West if he comes to bring some seeds such as clover and grass – plum stones and apple pips.

Yours &c. &c.
TIMOTHY TRUSLER.

P.S. If Thomas West comes I wish he would bring me ½ doz sacks, ½ doz Birmingham reap hooks, a prong[13] that will answer for a pitch prong or barn & a hog killing knife & I will pay him.

To Mr. William Luff, Sawyer,
Farnhurst Cross, Sussex,
Near Haslemere, Surrey, Old England.

OTHER LETTERS: 143, 144

12 Eleanor was probably 11 years of age (she was baptized in October 1824) and Reuben 9.
13 A hay fork. He is asking for one suitable to clean the barn as well.

John Trusler settled in Plympton Township and in 1843 purchased E ½ lot 9 concession 9 SER with Timothy. Several members of the family were living in Plympton at the time of the 1861 census. At some point after emigrating, this branch adopted a spelling of their name with one "s."

Timothy's uncle George seems to be a case of an apparently undesirable emigrant who did well for himself in North America. He was suspected of poaching at home, his family had problems on the journey, and both Captain Hale and Jones characterized him as dissatisfied and a complainer. He moved his family from Plympton to Waterloo Township where he settled successfully on the German Tract.

■ 106

EDWARD LONGLEY, GUELPH, UPPER CANADA, TO WILLIAM MITCHELL, HEENE, WEST SUSSEX, 28 SEPTEMBER 1835 AND 20 MARCH 1836

Edward Longley and his wife emigrated from Heene, Worthing, West Sussex, in 1835. Although this letter was started on 28 September 1835, Edward did not finish it until 20 March 1836. Longley's first wife, Lucy, had died in 1817. Four of her five children survived, but apparently none of them accompanied their father and his second wife in 1835.

SOURCE: *Brighton Guardian*, 11 May 1836

Excerpt from a letter received by Mr William Mitchell,[14] of Heene Sussex, from Edward Longley, labourer, who emigrated to America last April on the Ship Burrell under the management of the Petworth Committee

> Guelph, Upper Canada,
> 28th Sept. 1835

RESPECTED SIR –

Agreeable to your request, I take the earliest opportunity of acquainting you with my proceedings since I left England.' In the first place, I will commence with our voyage, which was a very tedious one, being obliged to lay to for five days in crossing the wide Atlantic. I am happy to say the Captain behaved to us like a Briton. We fell in with a considerable number of ice-bergs, as big, I should suppose as the whole of the buildings on your farm; also shoals of porpoises from two to three hundred in number and from ten to twelve feet long. We also met with a few small whales or grampuses. As we approached the banks of Newfoundland, the weather became very cold and foggy; but as we approached America, the atmosphere became much warmer.

On our arrival at the river St. Lawrence, we were obliged to perform quarantine, to our great annoyance, a day and night, at the Quarantine Islands [Grosse Isle], and then take all our traps[15] ashore to be inspected; after which we proceeded to

---

14 The Mitchell family were farmers in Heene. William was chapel warden and he and Thomas Hill were the overseers for Heene.

15 Personal effects.

Quebec, where we arrived exactly seven weeks after our leaving Portsmouth. We stopped at Quebec two days, but did not go on shore. We then started for Montreal, which took us nearly a week to get up, owing to Mr Brydon*, "under whose care we were," refusing to [bear] his part of the expences of a steam boat, which would have towed us up in little short of a day and night." The Captain [J. Metcalf] was very willing to pay his part.

We stopped at Montreal one day. It is a pretty town about – miles long and broad. At this time it was very dirty. We were here put on board a Durham boat, which is a vessel like the barges that travel the canals in England, only not quite so large, which took us up the river St. Lawrence to a town called Prescott, about twelve miles from Montreal. Sometimes we were drawn by horses or oxen, sometimes were pushed along by long poles, and when the wind was favorable we sailed. Prescott is situated on the Canada side, it is a pretty town and a great deal of business done there. Here we took a boat and proceeded up to Hamilton at the mouth of the lake Ontario. On our way thither we stopped at Kingston, and at York, the capital of Upper Canada, but now called Toronto, where we received our money. We then proceeded for Hamilton, which is about forty miles further, which finished our water carriage, a distance of upwards of seven hundred miles from the gulf of St. Lawrence to the lake Ontario. We could not see much of the country up the river and lake sufficient to form an opinion of it. The mouth of the St. Lawrence is 90 miles wide and is navigable for ships of war as far as Quebec, a distance of 360 miles.

At Hamilton I left George Poland[16] and the rest of the emigrants who went up to a place called Blandford [Woodstock],[17] since which I have not heard of him. I took a waggon and went on to Guelph, about 30 miles, which cost me five dollars. Waggons here are somewhat different to yours; they are much lighter and drawn by horses similar to the carriages in England. Guelph is a delightful little town; it has only become a settlement within these last seven years. At that time there was not a single tree cut, and now it contains three or four hundred houses, three churches, seven or eight stores or shops and as many taverns, and a great deal of business is done there; it has also a fair twice a year and a market every Saturday.

On my arrival at Guelph, I immediately set out to find Mr Sockett,[18] who, I ascertained upon enquiry, lived about eight miles in the country. I informed him I had left the hogs and cattle which had been placed under my care by his father at Hamilton. I told him the conversation that passed between his father and myself previous to my leaving England; but he said he did not want us, as his house was not large

16 George Poland, 40, was also sent by Heene. He was a widower when he married Mary (Grimwood) in 1822, and they sailed for Upper Canada in 1835 with six children. A farmer's labourer, he had received £3.8.6 in parish assistance in the year before he emigrated. Brydone recommended Poland as "an industrious hard-working man, handy with carpenter's tools and well-behaved on the voyage."

17 He probably meant to write Brantford, rather than Blandford.

18 George Sockett, the eldest son of the Reverend Thomas Sockett* of Petworth; George emigrated in 1833 and settled in Eramosa Township.

Guelph, 1840
Water colour from a drawing by Miss Neeve, Toronto Reference Library, T16579

enough to accommodate us. I immediately got work at a Mr Hemmings, a neighbour of Mr Sockett's for six weeks.[19] He, Mr H., wanted me to take his farm by paying him half the produce for rent, he finding seeds and cattle for the first year; but
I declined it. I am now in the employment of one Mr John McCrea, an Irishman.
I have a house to live and 150 dollars per year; but there are higher wages given by
some in the country. As I only agree by the month, I am at liberty to better my condition should an opportunity occur. I can keep a cow and pigs, which will get their
own living in the woods all the summer and only cost me a trifle for food in the
winter. The poorest persons here keep a cow and make their own butter. The woods
here being free for all cattle to run in, they would pick up a good living from the
green weeds which grow in great abundance. We put a bell round their necks similar to your sheep bells, so that we may know where to find them when they do
not regularly return home. It is an invariable rule here to give all your cattle salt once
a week at least and they are so fond of it that when they have been salted (as it is
called here) they will regularly return home.

We can live much cheaper and better here than in England; we make all our own
sugar, soap, and candles, the fat costing us 4d. a lb. Whiskey we get for 7½d per quart,

19 Edward Francis Heming; see letter 30.

good beef 3d per lb. Mutton the same. Good fat pork 6d per lb, tea 3s9d per lb, a barrel of best flour (196 lbs) for 3½ dollars, at which price it was selling last summer, but is now selling at between 5 and 6 dollars, owing to the very wet harvest and most of the crops being spoiled by a very hard frost which came early in August.

The land in this township is selling at five dollars per acre, wild land; but in the townships that are not so much settled it is less, some as low as 1½ dollar. But there are plenty of farms for sale already cleared with buildings upon them which may be bought very reasonably, owing to the proprietors being very short of money. They will sell out and take wild land [far back] in bush which they get so much cheaper and the overplus allowing them to buy a stock of cattle. A yoke of cattle here will plough as much as three yokes on your farm. Here the wild land is entirely covered with trees from the huge spreading oak whose diameter is from 4 to 5 feet, the lofty pine whose top seems to pierce the clouds, to the smallest sapling, all planted by the hand of nature and so thick that a squirrel may traverse thousands of acres without ever touching the ground. Still you may get the heaviest of it cleared and fenced fit to dig in your seed, – we never plough for the first crop, – for 15 dollars per acre, and if a good crop [it] will pay the first year for clearing.

The climate here is very salubrious. The summer is generally warm, but not more so than the warmest weather in England; the winters, they tell me, are very cold, but the old settlers say they like the winter best. Then it is that all the travelling is done on the snow with sledges. You may travel 50 miles a day and take very heavy loads. What I have seen of the country, I like it very much and would recommend all poor people that are able to work immediately to come out and not be afraid of crossing the water; and those that can muster large families will do much better than those without; and "though last not least," I would recommend all young single women to come out as quickly as they can, and I will warrant they will soon meet with an object to fix their affections, for many young men are at this time keeping bachelors' hall in the bush for want of a wife. Should they not feel inclined to tie the conjugal knot, they can get good wages and are very much wanted.

Not having an opportunity of sending the above, it has enabled me to give you an account of our winter. A tremendous fall of snow came on the 11th of November; although this being the 20th of March, we have not as yet seen the ground for more than four months. It is now, I am happy to say, just upon leaving; it has been a very severe winter. Even now the snow is more than three feet deep, and at times the cold has been so intense we could scarcely endure it and were obliged to keep up good fires day and night to keep us from being frozen.

Tell Mills he could get plenty of good tobacco at 1s. a lb. and a glass of stiff toddy to wrap him up for the night. I intend to purchase a cow at the next fair which will be held on the 2nd of May. Please give my wife's respects to Mrs Haylor and family and would strongly recommend her and her husband and all her squad to come out here, and in a year or two they would be in very comfortable circumstances. I can assure him it would be much better than staying at home; he should make direct for Guelph and enquire for me at Mr McCrea's and he will find me out. I should feel greatly obliged to you if you could ascertain from my brother or father where my son William is. Would you write to him and tell him I would very much wish him to come out to me. As I think of taking a farm of my own in a short time, he would be a very great assistance to me, and I could make him much more comfortable here than he ever will be at sea. He can easily work his way out, either to Montreal or New York, and £3 would take him up to Guelph.

I now conclude with my best wishes for your future welfare and many thanks for your past kindness. Give my love to my father, mother, and friends, and let them know how we are getting on. Should either of them write, tell them to direct via New York, as it will save me three or four postages.

Your obedient servant,
ED LONGLEY.

Brydone described Longley as having employment "in view," and internal evidence in Longley's letter suggests that Sockett expected him to be hired by his son, George. In the very different conditions of Upper Canada, George was as likely to have been unable to afford to hire Longley as to find space for his family.

In 1851 Edward and his wife, Jane, were recorded in the census of Puslinch Township.

■ 107
MARY AND EDMUND (EDWARD) BIRCH (BURCH), GEORGE ST, THORNHILL, UPPER CANADA, TO HIS UNCLE, GEORGE BURCH, AND HIS AUNT, 13 APRIL 1836

Edmund or Edward Birch, an agricultural labourer, and Mary (Caiger) Birch, with five of their children, Charles, Mary Ann, William, George, and Emma, emigrated from Walberton in 1835 with the intention of joining their sons Edmund Jr and James.[20] The latter had emigrated as single men with the Petworth committee in 1832 and settled at Thornhill, a few miles north of York (Toronto). At the end of the 1835 voyage, superintendent James Brydone* described Edmund Sr as "a very discontented and impudent man."

SOURCE: *Letters from Sussex Emigrants*, 7–8

Thornhill, April 13, 1836.

DEAR UNCLE AND AUNT,

I take opportunity of writing these few lines, hoping they will find you as well as when we left, I am happy to tell you we are all well, and doing well at present; I like this country surprisingly. We were nine weeks on our passage, and had a very rough one. Give my love to brother Ben and sister Jane, I do not persuade them to come out, but if they should come, they would do a great deal better here than at home. I had to go thirteen miles after I had left the ship to my sons' and there I

---

20 Both Edmund and Mary Birch signed the marriage register with a mark. Although this letter was signed Edward in the printed version, the parish register gives him as Edmund.

found a good home; they came to meet me when I landed. I have got a good place, farming for an English gentleman, my wages are £4 2s 6d per month.

Give my love to Thomas Burch and his wife, and I hope they are as well as when we left. I hope you will write as soon as possible, and if any of you like to come out, you would do better than at home – but I will not persuade you. Little George bids me tell you, some one cut his pockets and took his six-pence. Ask Ben if he has seen anything of George, I should like to hear of him – when you write I should like to hear of my old master; tell him this is a good place for farmers, but they must not think to do here as they do at home, telling men if they do not like it they may go, for the masters here must humble more to the men, than the men to the master.

I should like to hear from all my aunts and uncles, how they are, and how they are doing, for we are all well and doing well, and likely to do well. You may ask my sister, [Winn?], if she recollects what she said on Yapton Bridge, when I said I hoped to do better here; she said, she wished I might find it so; tell her I do find so; all I am sorry for is, that I did not come sooner.

Frank Mellish is well, and doing well; Charles Leggatt is well and doing well, he makes my house or my son's house his home. William Cole is with George Wells, he is very well.[21] Tell Mr. Jay I have not heard anything of Henry Jay, nor my son that came out before me. Edmund & James send their love to uncle, he must tell George Blackman not to think we sent for father and mother to eat one another. Remember Edward to George Ostand. Instead of eating one another as *George Blackman said*, I can buy a whole Hog at a time. Direct to me Thornhill, George Street, Upper Canada. Tell Thomas Falkner we have better windows here than he has in his church. I must conclude with best wishes for your welfare – your affectionate nephew and niece,

MARY & EDWARD BURCH.

To Mr. George Burch, thatcher.

On 20 September 1835, James Birch married 19-year-old Petworth emigrant Frances Viney at Thornhill. She had been assisted by the parish of Climping and travelled on the same ship as his parents. George and Emily Wells were witnesses at the marriage. James and his father and brother stayed in the Thornhill area. Edmund Sr was buried at Thornhill, 11 October 1843, aged 53. Edmund Jr married and was on lot 9 concession 4 Vaughan Township in 1850-51.

■ 108

WILLIAM HEWITT, WOODSTOCK, UPPER CANADA, TO HIS FATHER AND MOTHER, WILLIAM AND ELIZABETH HEWITT, COCKING, WEST SUSSEX, 6 JULY 1836

William Hewitt was a 21-year-old agricultural labourer when he decided to try his fortunes in Upper Canada and travelled to Woodstock to join the Petworth emigrants there in 1836.

---

21 Frank Mellish, Charles Leggett, and William Cole all emigrated in 1835; George and Emily Wells were already in York in August 1831.

His emigration, and that of others from the parish of Cocking, was financed in part by a loan made by Charles Caplen, a linen retailer from the town of Midhurst.[22]

SOURCE: *Continuation of Letters from Sussex Emigrants* (1837), 11–12

WOODSTOCK, UPPER CANADA,
July 6th. 1836.

Dear Father and Mother,

I take this opportunity of writing these few lines to you, hoping to find you in good health, as they leave me at present, thanks be to God for it. I am very glad to say, that I am got here quite safe, and I tell you, that I do not repent my journey, for I find it as good as it was said it was, and I am very well satisfied with it. And I am happy to tell you that we had a very short, and good pleasant voyage of 7 weeks to Quebec, and three afterwards to Blandford [Woodstock]; and I was used very well all the way over, and we had every thing for our use, and a very good living; and was not sick only 4 days, and that was not very bad, but there was some very bad for a great while.

I tell you, that I have got a very good place. I have hired for 5 months, at 10 dollars per month, board and lodging; and I am about 4 miles from Blandford, where I go every Sunday in the waggon to my own church. James Budd[23] lives at Blandford, and have got a very good place, under a captain, a very great gentleman. Master Budd works on the farm, and Mrs. Budd works in the laundry, and the boys are all in places. They all live in the houses in this country, and so do I, and lodge in the houses. They are all English and Scotch, and they are very good people.

(Here follows an account of the country, the same as given in several other letters before published.)

Here is plenty of work for men, and women; and boys you may apprentice; they will take them, keep them, and clothe them, and wash for them. George Budd is gone to a tailor, and John is gone to a blacksmith, and Henry is gone to live with *** and they are all at work, Joseph and all. They are all very well in health, and desire to be kindly remembered to you all. And I pray you to remember me to all my brothers and sisters, and all my friends and relations, and all friends. I am very sorry I have not any more time to write now. Tell Mrs. Wingham that her brother stopped at Prescott, because his children was not well, and so he got work there, and stopped there. * * * * I will write again in a very short time, and will write to Mr. Challen, and will tell you all about, and pray forgive all my mistakes and blots, for I have no time at all. And so God bless you all, from your affectionate son,

WILLIAM HEWITT.

22 Cocking was in the Midhurst Poor Law Union and the £100 loan from Caplen was negotiated by the Union with a guarantee from the central government arranged through the poor law commissioners.

23 James and Mary (Carter) Budd, also of Cocking, emigrated with Hewitt, "sent in great distress" with their six children, John, James, George, Joseph, Mary, Barbara Ann, and their nephew Henry. Joseph was eight years old. See also letter 133.

The following is my direction,

William Hewitt, Woodstock, Oxford, London District, Upper Canada, North America.

Please to answer this as soon as you can, and tell me all the news you can.

To MRS. WILLIAM HEWITT,

Cocking, Midhurst.

———

Single men did typically hire out to obtain their board, though most Petworth immigrants thought further ahead than Hewitt, whose six-month contract could have left him unemployed in mid winter. Woodstock, four miles away, was apparently his closest post office.

William Cooper reported that his brother James had seen Hewitt at Woodstock in 1838 (133). Hewitt married and lived on in Blandford Township. He and his wife, Sarah, had five young children at the time of the 1851 census.

■ 109

GEORGE OLDER, HAMILTON, UPPER CANADA, TO JOHN DREWITT*, LITTLE PEPPERING, BURPHAM, WEST SUSSEX, 7 JULY 1836

George Older, an agricultural labourer, his wife, and two children were sent by the parish of Wisborough Green, His wife's name may have been Sarah Gilbert. Drewitt gave Older " a very good character" to take to Upper Canada (see letter 122). Sockett* included this brief extract from a letter written as the family passed through Hamilton on their way west.

———

SOURCE: *Continuation of Letters from Sussex Emigrants . . . Written in 1836* [1837], 8

Extract of a Letter from George Older, who emigrated to Canada, in the ship Heber, which sailed from Portsmouth, April 23rd. 1836, to Mr. Drewitt,[24] of Peppering, Sussex.

Sir,

There has been a great deal of fault found, about the living on board ship; but I say, we had a plenty of every thing to eat, and to drink, and that was very good.

Hamilton, July 7th.

———

All we know of the later history of this family is what William Robinson wrote of them in letter 122 in October 1836, when they were in Delaware Township working for him.

■ 110

JOHN AYLING, YONGE STREET, THORNHILL, UPPER CANADA, TO WILLIAM AND MARY AYLING, HIS FATHER AND MOTHER, WALBERTON, WEST SUSSEX, 24 JULY 1836

———

24 Drewitt had probably helped fund the Olders' emigration. The *Brighton Gazette* on 10 November 1836 noted that "Mr Drewitt" of the "Arundel Banking Firm" had sent out tare, turnip, and beet seeds to another emigrant, Mr Holmwood, formerly of Angmering and now living near Dundas, Upper Canada; the seeds had produced "fine crops."

Eighteen-year-old John Ayling was one of a group of young men sent by the parish of Walberton in 1836. He went immediately to join the "little Walberton" based on Thornhill. *See* letter 102 from Frank Mellish, 107 from Mary and Edmund Birch, and 176 from George and Emily Wells..

———————

SOURCE: *Letters from Sussex Emigrants*, 8–9

Thornhill, Young Street, July 24, 1836.

DEAR FATHER AND MOTHER,

I take the pleasure of writing a few lines to you hoping by the blessing of God it will find you all well, as I am happy to say it leaves me at present, thank God for it. Dear Father and Mother, we had a very fine voyage indeed, we were six weeks coming to Quebec; we had no rough weather except two or three days, the 2nd and 3rd of May, when the sea was very rough. I was sea sick three days and so we were all, but poor Jemmy Millyard was sick for three weeks; he was very bad indeed. But I should not care no more of coming over the water than I should of going over the sheep-wash. On the 10th of May we saw icebergs and we saw nearly fifty, and on the 25th of May we had snow four inches thick on the deck, and we snow balled one another till we got wet through.

Dear brother Henry, I wish you was here my boy, but stop till next spring and come out with Bob, and don't hire till you get up to me, for you don't know who you may hire with. Dear friend, when we landed at Toronto, we were walking up the Town, and we went to where Mark Messenger[25] lived, and we went up to his house and slept there that night, and we came up to Thornhill the next day with Edmund Birch, he goes down to Toronto every day, so we got up to George Lintot with Edmund and we stopt with George that week, and we have all got work.

George Leggatt is at work about one mile from Thornhill, he have 8 dollars a month and his meat.

John Norris and George Booker is about ten miles from George Lintot; George has ten dollars, and John eight dollars a month.

George Cole is with George Wells.

Charles Richards is about four miles from George.

James Millyard is eleven miles from here, he is gone prenticed to a Carpenter.

Thomas Norris has got a place, and has hired for a month.

Richard Cooper is at work for Mark Messenger and Cornelius Cook is at work at Toronto, he hired the second day we landed; and John Ewens he hired at Toronto as a Butcher's boy, he has not been up to Thornhill at all.

Ruth Leggatt is with Edmund Birch, and I have hired up at Newmarket for eleven dollars. I have got a very good place about eighteen miles from George Lintot. I got

———————

25 Mark Messenger is listed as a brickmaker living on Duchess Street in George Walton's *City of Toronto & the Home District Commercial Directory and Register* (Toronto 1837).

a horse and came down to write this letter home, but I must get back to night. I have been at farming work, and been a mowing a day or two and a shoveling about; I don't work hard, but I lives very well, that is £2 15s, a month and my board and lodgings, that is better than working in England. There is Charles Leggat and William Cole and all the Birch's, Henry Norris and wife [Charlotte] and two children, George Wells, B[enjamin] Lintot, George Lintot and wife is quite well, they have one child. Frank Mellish and all is quite well, and all close together; makes quite a little Walberton all together. Never be afraid to come to America, don't be afraid to come, you will do better here. Give my love to Robert and all enquiring friends. When you write, direct to me at George Lintot's, Thornhill, Upper Canada. I will write soon and tell Bob all about it. Give my love to all, and write again soon.

JOHN AYLING.

Mr. William Ayling,
Walburton, Sussex, near Arundel, England,
by way of New York.

A member of a Congregational Church, Ayling married and raised his family in the area. In 1851 he was farming 10 acres on lot 7 concession 8 Vaughan Township.

■ III

JOHN AND CAROLINE (FRANCIS) DEARLING, WATERLOO TOWNSHIP, UPPER CANADA, TO THOMAS FRANCIS, LODSWORTH, SUSSEX, 24 JULY 1836

This letter, written jointly by Caroline and John, updates the experience of the four families who settled together on the lot chosen by James Rapson. On 11 July 1836, James Rapson received a deed from Hamilton land speculator Richard Beasley for 206 acres on lot 8 "Beasley's old survey" (also identified as Beasley's lower block).[26] This lot was shared by the families of James and William Rapson, John Dearling, and George Thair. By the time this letter was written, Caroline and John have had two more children born in Canada, John and Hannah. Caroline's family must have been relatively well off to send her £20 in addition to the gifts she reported receiving.

SOURCE: *Continuation of Letters from Sussex Emigrants ... Written in 1836* [1837], 1-3.

Waterloo, July 24th. 1836.

Dear Father and Mother,[27]

This comes with our kind love and best respects to you both, hoping you are well and happy, as it leaves us at present, thank God for it. I was sorrowful when I heard of your calamity, but comfortable to hear that you was so patient with it. I

---

26 A tract of land west of the Grand River at the south end of Waterloo Township.
27 Thomas and "Phebey" Francis

hope, dear father, that you will set your mind stedfastly on the Lord: he is our maker, and redeemer: without the Lord we can do nothing.

Dear father and mother, we received a letter on the 7th. of July from you, out of James Rapson's cask, and a parcel, which contained a piece of nankeen,[28] 4 pair of socks, a small piece of print, 3 balls of worsted,[29] a reel of cotton, two pieces, a shilling; I was well pleased with it. We received the money safe, that you had the goodness to send us. Mr. Brydone* was in Preston, on the evening, the 6th. of July, but was gone before we knew of it, when we had to go to Eramosa, to Mr. Sockett's house, to Mr. Brydone. We received £20. the 11th. of July. He went to Hamilton, paid part on our land; we have only 50 dollars more to pay. Mr. Besley give him time to pay, one year from next September. They have got a deed for the land; will have a deed taken off for the other, as soon as they get it from the recording office, at Dundas. We have 51 acres and a half, and we are much obliged to you, very thankful for your kindness, dear father and mother. May 12th. received a letter from you, the first thing I heard in him, was of my brother James. We heard of brother John's misfortune two or three days before the letter came, expecting every day we should hear he was dead. I am happy he is well again, about his business. Give my love to sister Phoebe, John and all the family. Sister Jane, my love to you, to tell you, that I received the note that you sent me. Give my love to Mr. Tribe, if you please.

Dear sister, Jane is much pleased with her nankeen, and Phoebe with her shilling: she is going to buy a string of beads to keep for your sake. Now I must tell you we had a little school all the winter's evenings at George Thair's house. James Hall teached them.[30] Jane have learnt a good deal, she reads middling well. They learned a good many hymns. Give John's love to Dame Till, and tell her that we laughed heartily at her old jokes. Dear brother John, I am sorry to hear such a bad account of your country, I hope it will be better: it must be hard for you and Sarah to bring up your little children. Sarah, when you writes again, write me a few lines of your own hand, tell me all how you are in health.

Dear mother, little Caroline was pleased with her socks. Now I will tell you, our little Canadian,[31] she ran alone a few days over ten months: at 11 months she could run well. I called her little, but she is as big as Phoebe was, she got about as well as Phoebe did at two years old; she is not like the other three, I think she is very much like sister Phoebe.

Now I will say about the winter; it was very cold, and long; and backward spring. We did not begin boiling sugar until about the 9th. of April; we did not make so much as we did the year before, but much better sugar; we made forty pounds of sugar, and some molasses. I take about two tea cups full of molasses, boil it in a gal-

---

28 A strong brownish-yellow cotton fabric originally handwoven in China. It was often used to make trousers.

29 A smooth compact yarn made from long wool fibres

30 James Hall was a shinglemaker. According to William Phillips (see letter 140), he had returned to Singleton, West Sussex, by 1839.

31 Hannah Dearling

lon of water, set it with a little yeast, then put it out in the sun, I have as good vinegar as ever you need of.

August 1st. We have a fine bed of cucumbers, just begun pulling of them. Pease in the garden, are not looking so well as they did last year. My cabbage, beets, and beans, and onions, look well. One acre of pease look well. Half an acre of potatoes looking well. I planted four Englandish Barley corns, I have one hundred ears. Them flower seeds you sent me, the prince's feather,[32] grew; and that beautiful flower that bears a large burr, here is hundreds growing by the sides of the road.[33] I am hobbing[34] my calf, it is a heifer calf, I give her new milk, and make about three pounds of butter a week, we never let her suck at all. We have 5 hogs. I have 21 Chickens. Apples are not so plentiful as they was last year. Raspberries, and gooseberries, very plentiful. Currants also.

Dear mother, I have often heard you say you did not know what mandrakes was, but here is a great many in the woods: they grow on a green, much like the pine flower green; they grow on a stalk, some as large as a hens egg. They are very sweet tasted, most beautiful smelling. We read of them in the 30th. chapter of Genesis, also in the song of Solomon.[35]

August 7th. All busy, harvesting: in a few days we shall cut our own. Sister Jane, I hope you will do the best you can for my dear father and mother, and tell me how they are, and if they be comfortable, or not. I cannot say any more at present. We remain your loving son and daughter,

JOHN & CAROLINE DEARLING.

Dear father Dearling, brothers and sisters, we send these few lines to you, hoping you are well, and all the family. We think it very strange that you do not send us a letter. We wish to know how sister Charlotte and her family is getting along; say if you heard of Mary. How is Hannah, and her husband doing? Give our love to William and Dinah, hoping they are well, and all the family. Daniel, I hope you are well, and your family. Dear sister Jane, we give our kind love to you, I hope you are well, and dutiful to your father: tell us if you are comfortable or not, for we should like to know. I cannot say any thing more to you now, but I hope you will send us a letter. Phoebe sends Jane Hamman a piece of her frock for a present. So no more at present, from us, your loving son and daughter,

JOHN & CAROLINE DEARLING.

Dear father and mother, I wish you would send me both of your ages, for I should like to know how old you are. Remember us to Kitty, and I hope she is well. To

---

32 Amaranthus hypochondriacus, a showy plant 4–5 feet tall with erect crimson flower spikes. A member of the Love-lies-bleeding family.

33 She is probably referring to teasles.

34 Hand-rearing a young animal.

35 The may-apple or podophyllum pelattum; a North American plant of the barberry family, also called wild mandrake, with a white flower and yellow egg-shaped fruit. Rachel and Leah bargained for Jacob's attention with the mandrakes that Reuben had found in the harvest fields, *Genesis* 30:13. "The mandrakes give a smell, and at our gates are all manner of pleasant fruits . . . ," *Song of Solomon* 7:13.

John and Elizabeth Spooner, give our best respects to them, tell them we do not want to come to England for a home, for this place begins to look homely to us. Tell Hannah Enticknap, Thomas was up to see us, three weeks ago, he was well; and George was well; them are four miles from us.[36]

To Mr. THOMAS FRANCIS,
    Lodsworth, near Petworth, Sussex, England.

OTHER LETTERS: 85, 134. For more about the casks, see 115.

Six months after this letter was written, in February 1837, James and Sarah Rapson officially sold 51 acres of lot 8 to James's brother William and another 51 acres to the Dearlings.

■ 112

JAMES AND ANN WOODS, WOODSTOCK, UPPER CANADA, TO MOTHER AND FATHER, 10 AUGUST 1836

James and Ann Woods emigrated from the parish of Tillington with their son George.

SOURCE: A copy of this letter printed on one page is found in WSRO, PAR 5/37/4, a loose page inserted at the back of a copy of *Continuation of Letters from Sussex Emigrants ... Written in 1836* [1837]; an unpaged copy is also found at PRO, CO 384/44, 261.

From JAMES & ANN WOODS, who emigrated in 1836, in the Ship HEBER.
BLANDFORD, UPPER CANADA,
August 10th. 1836.

Dear Mother, and Father,

This comes with my kind love to you, hoping to find you in good health, as it leaves me at present, and my wife, and child, bless God for it. We had a very good passage, but were very sick. Little George is always talking about little ——. Dear mother, we are as well as can be expected after our journey, and I like this country very well at present; and have got into good work, and am getting 3 shillings and nine pence per day. I can see here a good chance for every man to get a good living here, if he is steady; and any man can be independent if he likes in the course of three or four years, if he is steady. He can get a hundred acres of land. And if any of you intend coming to America, be sure and send us word, and whether you come or not, by the return of post.

Dear Sisters, and Brothers, this comes with my kind love, hoping to find you in good health, as it leaves me at present, bless God for it. I like the country much better than I thought I should, and I should like it much better if you were nearer to me. Please to give my love to Charles Edwards, and love to Wm. Long. Please to give Mr. James Tilley's love to Mrs. Long, and likewise William Heather; and they

---

36 Thomas and George were Hannah Enticknap's sons from Fernhurst, West Sussex.

are all doing well, and like the country very well. Tea is from 3 shillings and 9d. to 5 shillings; tobacco is from 1 shilling to 1s. and 3d. per lb.; pork, per lb., 3½d. to 4d.; by the hundred, it is from one pound to one pound four or five. Beef is the same; mutton is from 3½d. to 4d. per lb.; venison 1½d. to 2d. Flour is from 1 pound to 1 pound 5 shillings per barrel. Sugar is from 6d. to 8d. per lb. Every thing is very reasonable here, except clothing, and that is very dear. Be sure and send us the particulars of every thing, when you write to us, and we will send you some back. I have nothing more to say at present. From your ever loving son and daughter,

JAMES & ANN WOODS.

Direct to me, Blandford, Woodstock, London District, Upper Canada.

■ 113

DAVID CLOWSER SHARP, SANDWICH (WINDSOR), UPPER CANADA, TO HIS SISTER, MARY WARD, 21 AUGUST 1836

David Clowser (Cloudsley) Sharp, a labourer, and his wife, Clara Ware,[37] emigrated in 1836 from the parish of Petworth with their five children. David was baptized as the son of widow Sarah Clowser in February 1806. His mother married Edmund Sharp in March 1806. His mother and stepfather had emigrated to Upper Canada in 1833 with their other children. Thomas Sharp accompanied his nephew David and family on the *Heber*. See letter 86. Because Thomas had his army pension of one shilling a day, he received only his passage and a few small items towards his outfit.

In August 1834 David had been in jail for a "wicked and malicious libel"; that is, he was one of a small group parading with defamatory placards and an effigy representing William Tyler, Egremont*'s land steward, at Petworth market and Egdean fair (*Brighton Herald*, 2 August 1834).

SOURCE: *Continuation of Letters from Sussex Emigrants . . . Written in 1836* [1837], 9–10

Copy of a letter from David (Cloudesley) Sharp, to his sister, Ward.[38]

Sandwich, August 21st. 1836.

Dear Brother and Sister,

I dare to say you have by this time heard from us, by the letter I sent to uncle William. I sent you very bad news in that, but I am obligated to tell you a great deal worse in this; for on the next week after I wrote to you, my brother Edmund's child died, on the second of August; and on the fifteenth, my brother Edmund died,[39] and my sister Elizabeth's child, on the seventeenth.[40] We buried them both in one grave.

37 David signed his name to the marriage register; Clara signed with a mark.
38 Mary Sharp married John Ward in 1827.
39 We cannot find a record of a marriage or children for Edmund in England. Perhaps his marriage and the birth of a child had taken place since his emigration in 1833.
40 Elizabeth Sharp was the wife of George Turner.

My dear sister, I hope that you have enjoyed your health the whole of you, since we left you, we are all enjoying good health at present.

William Sageman and his family are with us, and John Moore, and James Moore,[41] and uncle Thomas.[42] I tell you again, for fear you did not have the letter I wrote before, I found my friends all on the twelfth of July, all well, except Edmund, who had been ill five or six weeks at that time. We have been all in one house together, since that time, except George Turner and his family, who are but a very little way from us, so that we can attend to one another at a few minutes notice, if required. George very much wishes you if you can at any time see or hear any thing of his mother, or James Whittington, or his wife, that you would tell them the misfortune they have had, but they are all in good health at present. Give our kind love to all our friends, to John Hollist, and Catharine, and I am in hopes we shall hear when you write, that they are perfectly recovered of their sickness, and in good health now.

Give our love to my wife's friends, and tell them that we are all well, and that we find things very reasonable, such as victuals and drink. We get a bottle of brandy for 1 shilling and 6 pence, English money; gin the same; beer is about 7 pence per quart; whisky 7 pence per quart; beef and mutton from 3½d. to 5d. per pound; pork 7d.; bread at about the same as it was when we left England. Give our love to Mr. and Mrs. Habbin, to Mrs. Palmer and family, Mr. Knight at the White Hart,[43] Mr. Jackson's. Tell my uncle William that I wrote to him 4 weeks ago, if he did receive it. If any time, he or you should think of coming to America, to bring with you some of the largest gooseberry, not the berry, but young trees or slips of the largest sort, for my father wants them: it is a thing that cannot be got here. Put them into some damp earth in a half anker;[44] and some Windsor beans,[45] if you please. I hope you will not think too much trouble to write as soon as possible, and direct to

George Turner, Amherstburgh, Upper Canada, North America.

William Sageman, and his family send their kindest love to his daughter Bertha.[46] Please to remember me to Mrs. Greenfield and Daniel, James Ward, and W. Oakshott, M. Matthews, T. Biggs, Chas. Henley, Josh. Streets, T. Peacock. From your loving brother,

DAVID SHARP.

In 1838, William Cooper reported on a considerable community of Petworth immigrants he had seen while stationed at Amherstburg. He mentioned David Sharp, his uncle Thomas, and two other families of former soldiers who had gravitated to this military town (133).

---

41 William and Mary Sageman and their children had emigrated in 1836, as had John and James Moore.

42 Thomas Sharp had first emigrated in 1832. *See* letter 86.

43 George Knight was landlord of the White Hart Inn, Petworth.

44 Anker, a cask containing a measure of wine and spirits, about 8 gallons or 36 litres.

45 William Cobbett, in *The English Gardener* (1829), specifies two categories of bean, the French and the English, "The English bean . . . has several varieties, the favourite among which is the broad bean or windsor bean."

46 Bertha Sageman was to emigrate in 1844 as a single woman with a young son, James Boxall Sageman.

■ 114

JOHN AND JAMES MOORE, SANDWICH (WINDSOR), UPPER CANADA, TO
FRIENDS AND RELATIONS, [21 AUGUST 1836]

John and James Moore were not brothers. John was the son of John and Sarah Moore. In
1832, he had been employed as a labourer, working under Egremont*'s steward. James Moore
(son of William and Hannah Moore) was a brother of William and emigrated with him in
1832. Another brother of James and William, Edward, may have emigrated in 1835 or 1836;
a fourth brother, Luke, emigrated on the *Diana* in 1837 where he was described by Brydone*
as a "naughty youth." All were single when they emigrated.

SOURCE: *Continuation of Letters from Sussex Emigrants . . . Written in 1836* [1837], 10

From John and James Moore, to their Friends.

Our Dearest Friends and Relations,

We have the opportunity of writing to you all, to inform you we are both well,
and living and working together, in hopes that this will find you all in a good state
of health, and make you comfortable about us, as we are comfortable ourselves. Give
our love to all our brothers and sisters, and all our friends. Give our love to William
Steer, and all the family, and if you send to us, please to tell us if young William is
any better or not. Give my love to Jane Peacock.   JOHN MOORE.

When you write to us, send in a letter with John Ward, the same as this is. Tell
Mrs. Knight,[47] and the servant, Charlotte Nye, that I am well.   JOHN MOORE.

From your loving sons,

JOHN & JAMES MOORE.

OTHER LETTERS: 89

James and John probably sent their letter with David Sharp's (113) to David's brother-in-law
John Ward. In the original, it may well have been a postscript on the same sheet of paper.

■ 115

EXTRACT OF A LETTER FROM JAMES RAPSON, WATERLOO TOWNSHIP,
UPPER CANADA, 30 AUGUST 1836

SOURCE: *Continuation of Letters from Sussex Emigrants ... Written in 1836* [1837], 10–11

Extract of a Letter from James Rapson, dated 30th. August, and received October 1st. 1836.

On the 7th of July, Mr. Brydone* arrived at Preston in the afternoon late. William[48]
was working at Preston, and lodged at the tavern where Mr. Brydone was. When
he went in from work he saw him; he told William he had the money and casks

---

47 Probably of the White Hart Inn, Petworth. *See* letter 113.
48 William Rapson, brother of James

with him. William sent word by Jesse Penfold to me, to be at Preston the next morning at 8 o'clock, and Jesse did not come to me until half-past seven. I started immediately, and met Mr. Brydone about half a mile before I came to Preston, but did
not know him. When I got to William, I found he had been gone about 25 minutes. I tried to get a horse, but I could not; so William and I took the two casks and
came home. We sent for John Dearling, who came about 2 o'clock.

After opening the casks, William, self, and Dearling[49] started after Mr. Brydone at
6 o'clock that evening, as we thought he would have stayed at Guelph all night; but
we were 10 hours after him. It was 10 o'clock when we arrived, and found he had gone
to Mr. George Sockett's, at Eramosa. We stayed there till daylight, and then went to him,
who paid us our money. He charged us nothing for the carriage of casks, only from
Hamilton to Preston. We were all well pleased, as we had no trouble about the casks.
We left Mr. Sockett's (after taking each a good drink of milk) at 10 o'clock, and reached
Guelph at 3 o'clock in the afternoon. Went to John White's, who has a frame up, but
not finished. I gave Mrs. [Elizabeth] White the letter; they have 4 fine boys: they are all
well.[50] We left Guelph and came on as far as we could, but John and self tired out, and
could not reach home until the next morning. William stood the journey far the best.

23rd August. Just done wheat harvest: have a good crop. Not cut oats yet. The
barley you sent looks well. William have nearly the same wheat as I, and in good
order; he have a very fine piece of peas: he is well, but Maria is in family way. Fanny
is well, as are John and Philip, who are two fine boys.[51] Thomas and Charlotte Rapson
are well, and have a little Anthony, 3 weeks old. Sarah [Rapson][52] is well: has a fine
girl, 3 months old. Hannah, Mary, Philip, Isaac, Rhoda, and Sarah,[53] are all well, grows
slowly, but I think learns faster. Old Mrs. [Charlotte] Tribe is as usual, but I think
looks older. Jesse Penfold's family are well. Matilda is married to Thomas Adsett.[54]
Charlotte [Tribe] Evans is well with her three children: they are doing well. Mary
Tribe is married to a Scotchman. Benjamin is well, and have 10 acres chopped and
logged, ready to sow in the fall. Richard, Henry, and Jonathan are well, and all work
together. Ann is well.[55] You see the young women are gone off very much. Saw Isaac
Berry:[56] he is well, and desires to be remembered to all friends.

He told me Michael Foard[57] was living near him; and doing well. John Heather,
from Petworth, wishes you to call at Botting's, to know how his sister is at Redhill:

49 For the contents of Dearling's parcel, see letter 111.
50 *See* letter 91 from John White.
51 Maria, wife of William Rapson, and their children.
52 Wife of James Rapson.
53 All are children of James and Sarah Rapson.
54 Thomas Adsett's second wife was Matilda Penfold.
55 Richard, Henry, Jonathan, and Ann are all children of Henry and Charlotte Tribe.
56 Isaac and Emma Berry emigrtated from Fernhurst, West Sussex, in 1832 with their two children and
   three children by Isaac's former marriage.
57 Michael Ford emigrated from Dunsfold, Surrey, in 1835.

he is well. James Hall still lives in George Thair's house; works shingle-making; has 10 large trees to work up this winter. We have not many apples this year. I wish to return my sincere thanks to the Rev. Mr. Sockett.* Sorry to hear Mr. Yaldwin* has left.

_____

OTHER LETTERS: 2, 12, 38, 76

James and Sarah Rapson had several more children in Upper Canada for a total of 14. The family was still living in Waterloo Township in 1840, but by 1854 James Rapson was leasing land in Goderich Township. The 1871 census of Huron County describes Rapson as a Baptist and his obituary mentions him as one of the founders of the Base Line Church. He and Sarah are buried in Balls Cemetery, not far from the family farm in Goderich Township.

William and Maria Rapson seem to have returned to England where the 1851 census of Lodsworth found them and three children living on Lodsworth common. There are also rumours that William went to Australia (the colonial destination chosen by W.H. Yaldwyn who had arranged the Petworth emigration from Lodsworth in 1832).

■ 116

JOHN BARNES, TORONTO, UPPER CANADA, TO HIS FATHER, BROTHERS, AND SISTERS (ADDRESSED TO ROBERT HASLETT), PETWORTH, WEST SUSSEX, 4 SEPTEMBER 1836

John Barnes, a bricklayer, and his wife, Charlotte Woodford, emigrated from Petworth, West Sussex, in 1836 with four children, Henry, Emma, John, and an infant daughter, Ellen, who was baptized just before they left England. The eldest, Henry, was 14 years of age when they emigrated.

At about the age of 11, Charlotte had received a gift of clothes from the parish of Wisborough Green. (Such a gift from the parish might mark a girl's first time going out to service, if her family could not afford the expense.) John's parish, Petworth, paid £25.10 to outfit the family for Upper Canada. The Barnes family seems to have sailed with the intention of joining John's brother at Pittsburgh in the United States.

_____

SOURCE: *Continuation of Letters from Sussex Emigrants ... Written in 1836* [1837], 12–15

Dear Father, Brothers, and Sisters,

It is now with pleasure I take my pen in hand, to write these few lines to you, in hopes it will find you in good health, as thank God, it leaves us all at present. In the first place, I must tell you about my arrival at the city of Toronto, which I think it a mercy, good one to me, thanks be to God for it. When we landed on the wharf, there was a man, the name of Edward White,[58] late of Lodsworth Common: he went

_____

58 Edward and Louisa (Lotton) White also emigrated under the auspices of the Petworth Emigration Committee.

out to Canada in 1835: his father and mother is living at Lodsworth Common. Now my dear brother Benjamin, perhaps you would call, as you go to Lickfold sometimes, and tell them that they are quite well, and doing well, and he was a very fortunate friend of mine: for as John Pratt and I was standing on the wharf, (I said John Pratt, which I mean from Barnet's Mill, he went out with us) Edward White came up to us, and asked if there was any bricklayers come out with us; and John Pratt said, Here stands one; which I think is all. Then he asked me if I was a going to stop there. I said not for long. He said, that the gentleman he was living with, wanted a bricklayer for a little time; so he told me that he would give me 3 pounds for a fortnight, and board and lodging. I told him I must have somewhere for my family to be: then he said that he would give Henry 2 dollars and his board, for a fortnight; which a dollar is 5s.: so he said that he would go home, and see what could be done with my family, and that he would come to me again.

The next morning, according to his promise, he came with his horse and cart, for to take my things, which was to go to his master's great house, which was at the college,[59] and there I should live rent free. Then I told him, I would stop, and do the work for him, as I thought it good wages altogether; for you cannot get a house here, not under one dollar a week: so that was the luck I had at my arrival at Toronto, which was on the 23rd of June, my dear friends, which made us almost 10 weeks, my dear father, since we had left your house.

I went to work on Saturday, the 25th of June, so I had but one clear day before I went to work; for I thought it best to get on as soon as I could; but my fortnight held for some time. I have been 10 weeks now, and I think I shall be there as much longer, so that will be a good job for me; so you will find that it will amount to a good bit of money; for mine and Henry's money amounts to 35 shillings a week, and board and house-rent free. I have not wanted to take any money, not yet, nor I do not think I shall for as much longer; so you may find that it will amount to a good sum; so I think I shall go to Pittsburgh, to my brother's, with a good bit of money, if please God, all is well.

The gentleman I am working for, built himself a cottage last year, but after he had built it, he found it was not large enough for him; so now I have made it something larger: it is about two miles out of the city, so Henry and me stops out there, all the week. This is an English gentleman, that I am working for, the name of the Rev. Mr. Matthews.[60] He is one of the rectors at the college; he says that I had better stop at Toronto; he says, that if I will stop there, that he will ask all the gentlemen, that he is acquainted with, for work for me, and I might live in his great house,

---

59 Upper Canada College, located at the corner of King and Simcoe Streets

60 The Reverend Charles Stephens Matthews was a graduate of Cambridge University and an original staff member of Upper Canada College, which had opened in 1830. He was for a time the rector of St John's, York Mills, which may be where Barnes and his son were building the cottage. He returned to England in 1843 and lived on the Island of Guernsey.

where I am living now, as he does not want to live in it himself, rent free, so as my wife keeps his house a little clean, which that we should expect to do.

I must tell you my dear friends, I think him a great friend to me, first going into a strange country; but I think it is an old saying, and a true one, the farther you get from home, the better you are looked upon. He told me this last week, that he hoped I would not leave that country, so between both of these places, I know not which to do. If I had got but one chance, I should know what to do; so I will write to you again, in the course of a few months, then I will tell you, my dear friends, where I am settled. So you may tell all my old work-mates that enquire after me, that if I had known what America had been, I would have been there some years ago. I can get paid for my work now. I can earn more money in about 5 or 6 months, than at home in a whole year. So I hope, my friends and acquaintance, I hope all you that reads this letter, may be as happy as I am, and my wife, and children. My wife says, that she never was happier in her life, than she is now, thanks be to God for it.

Dear brother Henry, if you had a come out with me, it would have been the best thing that ever you had done; I could have got a good place for you, with the same gentleman that I am working for: he has got a farm about ten miles from Toronto, which is about 200 acres, and about 50 of it cleared; you might have had 15 dollars a month, house-rent and fueling free. But never mind that, there is plenty of places to be had, for them that be industrious. You may expect, that the next letter I send, will be for you, my dear brother and sister: so you may begin to make up your minds.

Brother Benjamin, I am informed that your trade is very good, but I will tell you more about it in the next letter, as I have not had much time to look into it at present.

Dear brother Robert [Haslett], and sister, I think you have found a small piece of money under the seal of my letter, which is a fivepenny piece of the United States coin: please to give it to your little boy, Robert, and tell him, who sent it; and that he should keep it, till I come to see him, as he may shew it to me again, if we should meet. Like to know how your dear little girl is, dear brother and sister, and all of you, my dear friends, but we must wait a little bit, for I cannot wish you to write to me, not till I send you another letter; for I cannot tell you, my dear friends, where I may be.

Now I must tell you my dear friends, that we had a very good voyage over the seas. Thanks be to God for it, our sea sickness was but little; I kept about every day myself; I was a little swimming at times. Henry and Emma was sea sick, and then mother for a few days. John and Ellen was well, it did not hurt them the least. John was one of the best of boys; was not the least trouble at all; but it is a large undertaking to undergo; but never mind that, thank God, all is well.

Now a few words to our mother at Wisborough Green. Dear mother, brothers, and sisters, I am happy to say that we are all well at present, and I hope you are all well, and as happy as we are. I am not got to our brother's not yet, nor I do not know when we shall; but I have wrote a letter to them, and have received one from them. They are all well: they had been looking for me a long time: they said that they thought I should have been there to a helped them harvest. I hope some of you, my dear friends, will be so kind as to take this letter to [Wisborough] Green, so as they may hear from us, or send for Charlotte's mother to come to you. Give our love to Henry Hunt and his wife, and likewise to John Quelch, and his family, and to all enquiring friends.

Henry Hunt, I must tell you, that if you and your wife was here as I am, you might soon make your fortune, for there is the best chance for them that have no family. Man and wife goes into a gentleman's family, gets 15 or 16 dollars a month, and nothing to buy, but a little clothes, every thing else found them. I can buy a pound of tobacco for one shilling, and some tenpence per pound. I can buy a quart of good brandy here, for one of your shillings, that is 15 pence with us; your sixpence, 7½d.: a half crown, 3s.: a sovereign, 24s.: that is how your money goes with us. I can buy a bushel of malt here, for 3s.9d.; can buy good beef here for 3¾d.; mutton, veal, and lamb, for 4d. per pound; bacon, 7d. per pound; new butter, from 6d. to 7d. per pound; cheese is dear, you cannot get good, not under 10d. per pound. I think it likely, that some that hears this letter, will say that I have wrote fibs to you; but I will assure you, my dear friends, I have not told you any thing but what you would find true, if it was possible for any of you to be along with me, in ever so little a time: you would find as I have told you.

Henry often talks of his grandfather, and his uncle Benjamin, and tells me what he should do, if he was along with you; but I am to tell you, that he will come to old England again, after a little bit; for he says, that he do not mind going to sea, and then he will tell something about it.

Dear brother Benjamin, please to give my best respects to Richard Potter, and tell him that I am happy, and I hope that he is, and shew him the stamp mark[61] that he give me. Now to you, my dear father, brothers, and sisters, all friends and acquaintance, I must inclose my letter with bidding you all farewell. Me, and my wife and children sends our kind love to you all.

I am your affectionate son,
JOHN BARNES.

September 4th. 1836.
To Mr. ROBERT HASLETT, [his brother-in-law].
Petworth, Sussex County, England.
By the way of New York.

OTHER LETTERS: 126
Lydia Hilton, on 10 September, reported simply that John Barnes was earning 7 dollars a week and his board (see letter 119).

---

61 Original annotation: "The Original may be seen at the Printer's. Two Impressions of a Seal within the Letter."

■ 117

JOHN DENMAN, EAST FLAMBOROUGH TOWNSHIP, UPPER CANADA,
TO WILLIAM BOOKER, BILLINGSHURST, WEST SUSSEX,
4 SEPTEMBER 1836

John, an agricultural labourer, and Hannah (Ede) Denman[62] emigrated from Billingshurst, West Sussex, in 1836 with their eight children, William, Henry, Charlotte, James, Sarah, Job, George, and Harriette. William, the eldest, was baptized in 1816; the two youngest for whom the straw hats were requested were three-year-old George and baby Harriette. They also took with them Ann Fair's little girl.

SOURCE: *Continuation of Letters from Sussex Emigrants ... Written in 1836* [1837], 15-16

From John Denman, to his Brother-in-law, William Booker, of Billingshurst. —— Received 4th. November, 1836.

I desire to be remembered to father and mother, brothers, and sisters. I should like to see here John Bridgwater and his wife. All my children are well. Joe has got a dog. Tell Mr. Farhall[63] from me, if he would give me one hundred pounds, and pay my passage back, I would not go; for I like Canada well. Tell brother Sampson, that he should not let his heart fail him, for it is true enough, that we always buy a quarter, or a half of meat, instead of a pound or two. Tell brother Harry, that Ham Foice[64] died the day after we made land, and was buried the same day. Harry [Henry][65] has got a place, and don't want any jobs now. Mrs. Denman wishes to be remembered to her father, brother, and sister, and wishes to know the name of the little stranger; and also that she likes this country well, if only her sister was here too. William desires to be remembered to his grandfather: he has saved money enough since he has been here, to buy a cow: he paid 15 dollars for it. Tell Susan,[66] if she comes, to bring two straw hats for the youngest children. We were 5 weeks on the salt water, and another 5 weeks coming up the river before we got work. Tell John Bridgwater to bring William out a gun, if he comes. Tell Mrs. Denman's father, if he comes out here, she would like him to bring his clock: need not bring any kind of provision with you in the ship, for we had plenty, and to spare. Charlotte is at service. Sarah has had a

---

62 When John and Hannah married in October 1815, they both signed the marriage register with a mark.

63 Charles Farhall, a yeoman farmer, of Clarksland, Billingshurst, owned several farms, cottages, and many acres of land. He was a churchwarden and a guardian of the Petworth Union Workhouse. He was said "to advance money" for Billingshurst emigrants (PRO, MH 12/13060).

64 Ham Voice emigrated with his father, also named Ham Voice, and stepmother, Sarah, from Billingshurst in 1836.

65 The second born, he was 18 when they emigrated.

66 Probably the wife of Sampson Denman.

place ever since she has been here, only she has been ill; but is now well again, and going back.[67] Remember me to Ann Fair: her little girl is very well, and grown very much since she left England. Tell her I hope she will come here with Susan. I hope father [Samuel Denman] will come here, if possible: if he should sell all his things to come, and get the parish to help him.

I hope you are all well, as we are, and write as soon as possible. We should have written before, but the children were not well, and we waited till they were quite recovered. We were in steam boats and open barges while coming up the river. When you come out here and get to Hamilton, enquire at Burley's Inn,[68] for Capt. Shaw, and he will inform you where to find me. Tell John Bridgwater, or Sampson Denman, to bring me out a butter print.

JOHN DENMAN.
Gore District.

East Flamboro', U.C. Sept. 4th. 1836.

The Denmans had two more children in Canada, David and Mary. John Denman appears in the account book of Henry Harwood for 1838 as "logging, ditching, scoring and ploughing" in East Zorra Township. By the 1851 census he was living in Woodstock, where he died in December 1852.

■ 118

LUKE JOYES (JOICE), NELSON TOWNSHIP, UPPER CANADA, TO HIS FATHER AND MOTHER, [BILLINGSHURST, WEST SUSSEX], 4 SEPTEMBER 1836

Luke Joyes, an agricultural labourer, and his wife, Hannah (Dennett),[69] emigrated with a toddler, Daniel (aged 14 months), and an infant, Frederick (aged three months). Joyes's employer, Charles Chitty, resented his going since it meant he was losing a hard-working man. Although neither Joyes's letter nor Denman's (117) mentions the other, both were written on 4 September and received on 4 November, which strongly suggests that they were sent at the same time, if not on the same sheet. Both families were sent by Billingshurst.

SOURCE: *Continuation of Letters from Sussex Emigrants ... Written in 1836* [1837], 16

---

67 Charlotte and Sarah were aged about 14 and 9. Charlotte was married to Petworth emigrant John Budd on 7 October 1841 by a Wesleyan Methodist minister.

68 Plumer Burley operated the Promenade Hotel in Hamilton, "the chief one in town in 1835" (*Inn-Roads to Ancestry: Pioneer Inns of Ontario, Vol. I: Head of the Lake and Niagara* [Toronto: Ontario Genealogical Society 1996], 12).

69 Both Luke and Hannah signed the marriage register with a mark when they were married in Itchingfield on 19 May 1834.

From Luke Joice. Received November 4th. 1836.

Upper Canada, Sept. 4th. 1836.

Dear Father and Mother,

I desire to be remembered to all, father, and mother, brothers, and sisters. We are all well, except Daniel: he has not been well since we come to this country. I wont send for any of my brothers and sisters to come here, but if they like to come, they will find it a deal better country to live in than England. If any of you do come out, come to Hamilton, and enquire for Chatfield's Farm, for Joseph Lyons, and he will direct you where to find me. I have engaged with Joseph Lyons for 100 dollars a year, free house, and fuel, and board for myself, and an acre of ground to keep a cow in summer.

My wife desires to be remembered to her mother, sister, and brothers. I hope I shall see my eldest brother out here next spring, for it is a deal better country for young chaps than England. If my brother comes out next spring, I hope he will bring my sister with him. If she was to come here, it would be the making of her. Remember me to Mrs. P. Miss Pole, &c. &c.

LUKE JOICE.
Nelson P.O. Gore District.

Luke worked in different places, including Hamilton and Brantford, before settling in Westminster Township and raising eight more children, Solomon, Richard, William Henry, Robert, Anna, Cyrus, Edward, and Albert Emanuel.

■ 119

GEORGE AND LYDIA HILTON, TORONTO, UPPER CANADA, TO BROTHER, HENRY HILTON, AND MOTHER AND SISTERS, BIGNOR, WEST SUSSEX, 10 SEPTEMBER 1836

George Hilton and Lydia (Booker) Hilton emigrated from Arundel, West Sussex, where George had been a labourer. Lydia had signed the marriage register at their wedding in 1812, while George had made a mark. In this case, the register probably was an accurate reflection of literacy as Sockett* stated by way of introduction that the letter was written by Lydia.

The Hiltons were accompanied by their children, George, Martha, Henry, Friend, Charles, Charlotte, and Emily. Their son James had emigrated a year earlier in 1835, also sent by Arundel. He and Barbara Bridger were married just before they left on 20 April 1835; James making a mark and Barbara signing the register. Brydone's* description of James as: "For employment. Steady man. Very respectable" seemed born out by his employer's high opinion of him.

George's younger brother, Charles, had emigrated with his family in 1832. This family of Hiltons had started out in Delaware Village (where their eldest son, Alexander, was apprenticed to a carpenter) and spent some time in Westminster Township before settling in Adelaide. George and Charles's mother followed them to Upper Canada in 1837, along with the youngest brother, Henry, and his wife.

SOURCE: *Continuation of Letters from Sussex Emigrants ... Written in 1836* [1837], 3–7

[April 12th. —— Henry Hilton.][70]

Toronto, September 10th.

Dear Brother, and Mother, and Sisters,

I have returned this sheet of paper, which you have *got part of.* We arrived 23rd June at Toronto. Martha and myself was very sick, all the way; father, George, Friend, nor baby, was not sick at all; but poor baby was taken ill with her teeth at Grosse Isle, that is quarantine, that was the 1st of June: she lingered on till the 12th of July, when it pleased God Almighty to take her to himself.[71] We took lodgings in the city, and tried all we could to save my poor child's life, but all in vain. Little George was very ill about 10 days, he got better, and got a place. Martha and Henry got a place directly. George hired with a gentleman for 16 dollars a month, to work on his farm: he let us a house, with 3 acres of land, about 2 miles from the city, which we intend to sow with corn in the spring.[72] We like this country very well. James's master came down on the wharf to us, when we landed; went home, and sent James and his wife to us, with a pair of horses, and four-wheel chaise, jumping for joy; plenty of money; took us to an inn, gave us a supper of the best; staid with us all night, and next day, for he would spend a pound on us. They are the happiest couple I ever saw, and have got the best of characters; no family, nor likely to have any: they are going to housekeeping this Michaelmas.

Dear mother, we did not forget our promise; we had found our son, but we had not found yours; so George worked a month for his master, settled me in our new habitation, and then asked leave to go and find his brother.[73] He was gone three weeks; he had 200 miles to walk; he steered his course for London: he got within 7 miles of London, on a Saturday night; went into a tavern to sleep; asked them if they knew such a man. One man said he saw Charles Hilton two hours ago, at work, about 3 miles from there, digging a well; if he went down in the morning, he would be sure to find him, as his wife[74] and family was 30 miles further. Got up on the Sunday morning, passed his brother, did not know one another: came to the place where he was at work, asked for Charles Hilton: the man said he is just gone for a walk before breakfast: looked up and said, here he comes! George beckoned to him to come on; came to him; George catched hold of his hand; looked George hard in the face; turned pale as death, but could not speak for some minutes; spent the day

70 Original annotation:"This was written by Henry Hilton, and the name afterwards cut through length-wise as a Check, and the upper half kept in England by himself, for the purpose of fitting it to the lower when returned from Canada, in order to be certain that no deception had been practised."

71 Baby Emily was just 13 months old when she died. Charlotte, the only child not accounted for in Lydia's letter, would have been about 6 if she was still alive in 1836.

72 George Taylor Denison who employed George and Lydia was one of Toronto's first aldermen and a member of a prominent Toronto family.

73 Original annotation:"Charles Hilton and Family, who emigrated to Canada with the Petworth Party, in the Ship Eveline, in 1832."

74 Original annotation:"Charles Hilton's Wife" [Mary Ann].

together very happy; went to a meeting house in a wood, where there is hundreds go, for there is no churches built yet. Monday, helped Charles finish his job. Tuesday, went to Delaware, to Alexander;[75] he is apprenticed to a carpenter. Harriet and Charles in service. They went to Carradoc, two miles further, to Ann Evans and her husband [David];[76] found them very comfortable; staid there all night.

Wednesday, went to Adelaide, to see sister Ann,[77] and their little ones, James, William, Sarah, and a baby 2 months old, the first since they have been in Canada. Charles has got 100 acres of land here, about 4 acres cleared, have not been on it two years yet. This is the second crop. He has got wheat, barley, peas, turnips, and pumpkins, a good garden; the pumpkins is for the cow in the winter. He has got a fine cow and calf, pigs, and poultry. Is going to build a new house before you comes. Next morning went to Jane, at Bear's Creek, 7 miles further: she is in service, a very fine young woman grown. David Evans has got a 100 acres of land; have got a good place: saving money to go on their land with: they have got a cow; and a sweet little girl 9 months old. They kept expecting uncle Henry every year, but never did expect uncle George to come. There is land for sale up there. George has applied for a hundred acres, 50 for us, and 50 for brother Henry: we have got no answer yet, as we intend going up there next year. They say they will come down and fetch us, but what we shall come and live near them.

Charles, his wife, and family is well, as ourselves. All wish mother [Sarah Hilton] to come with you, they will do any thing to make you happy, and there can be no fear of a living, when the land is their own. Alexander will be out of his time next April, and then he will come down, and see us; get work in Toronto, and meet you, when you come. They have had many difficulties to encounter, since they have been here, but not so many as they had at home, and that is all over now. George thinks his mother will not be sea sick, because he nor Charles was not: if mother or Ann should be sick, they had better be still, in their berth; that is all there is to dread, as you have a home to come to.

Dear Henry, bring a good ham of bacon; some pickled onions; bake some seed cakes hard, they will keep better; pack them in one of your strong boxes, and keep it in your berth. When you get out to sea, you will want a box to put your provisions in. Be sure you draw your allowance of every thing except biscuit, and take care of it. We did not draw ours half our time, and when we came to Quebec, our provisions were left behind; if we had drawed it, and kept it till we was in the [St Lawrence] Rapids, we should have been right. Bring your wooden bottles full of cider. Bring your home-made wine; a few apples; paper of ginger, nutmegs, oatmeal;

---

75 Original annotation: "The writer of ... letter [123]." Alexander, Harriet, and Charles are the children of Charles and Mary Ann Hilton; the family, including another five children, emigrated from South Bersted in 1832.

76 Original annotation: "David Evans emigrated from Angmering, in the Eveline, in 1832, and subsequently married the Daughter of Charles Hilton."

77 Original annotation: "Ann Hilton, the wife of Charles Hilton."

a 3-quart saucepan, with a hook in front, then you can cook yourselves a bit of victuals in fresh water, when you please. Keep all close till you have been out to sea 2
or 3 days, then you will know the good of it. I would bake some oven cakes hard,
pack them up close, I think they will keep. Bring your feather beds, blankets, and
all your bed healing.[78] Do not bring working tools, they are no use here; sell it all,
and bring the money in your pocket; you will want money. Bring all the old halfpence which you can get; old buttons, or any thing goes at Grosse Island; but they
will not take farthings or penny pieces. You must not change silver nor gold, for they
will cheat you. Bring a warm great coat, and cloacks, stockings, and flannels. Boots
and shoes and women's clothing is quite as cheap as it is at home. James and George
give 11s.8d. for their half boots. Bring your tea kettle. No iron pots, Bring your brand
irons[79] and flat irons. You can put all that in mother's great chest. Do not over weight
yourself, it is very expensive getting up the country. George would be glad if you
could get a peck of Talavera wheat.

Dear mother when you go through Arundel, call on my father, and see if he got
his letter, as I write to him at the same time I do to you. Perhaps he will come out
with you next spring; if he do, he had better take [second] cabin passage, that is only
2 pounds more: you can be together on days, and you can have your meals together;
he will have a place to himself on nights, that will be better than going down among
a lot of young men.

Call on my old neighbours in Poor-house-hill, and Mrs. Piper. If Henry, or if you
should go that way, call on Mrs. Carver, and shew her this letter, she will be very
glad to see you. Tell farmer Boxall, at Barlton,[80] we have not seen his grand daughter, but I saw a person that lives by her: she is married, and got two children; her
father died in Toronto Hospital, 2 years ago. Humphrey Cooper keeps a tavern at
the same place. George saw George Carver, when he went to see his brother, he is
still in partnership with a farmer. John Barns has been very lucky, he got into work
the next day after he came; 7 dollars a week and his board; have never had the least
sickness, none of them: he is the only family stopt here with us.

Charles, and wife, and family, sends their kind love to mother, sisters, and brothers. Please to write back soon, as I shall think you have not got my letter. My children joins with their father and me in love to all. So no more at present from your
dutiful son and daughter,

GEORGE & LYDIA HILTON.

I think my father and you can write both in one letter.

Direct to George Hilton, George Denyson, Alderman, Lot Street, Toronto.
To Mr. Henry Hilton,
 Bignor, near Petworth, Sussex.

---

78 Coverlets or counterpanes (bedspreads).
79 Irons used to support the wood for burning in an open grate.
80 Probably Barlavington, near Sutton, West Sussex.

OTHER LETTERS: 123

With assistance from her parish of Sutton and Lord Egremont, George and Charles Hilton's mother, Sarah [Overington], sailed on the *Diana* in 1837, along with her son Henry and his wife. Reporting on the safe arrival of the *Diana*, the *Brighton Herald* commented on 12 August 1837,

> A female, named Hilton, aged 74, went out with the above party, being induced to do so by the circumstance of several of her children and grandchildren being settled in Upper Canada ... She made application for a passage as long ago as Christmas last, and expressed a great dread of being disappointed ... she bore the sea-voyage remarkably well, and on arriving in the western world, declared herself to be "worth any two of the young ones."

As far as we know, Lydia's father did not make the trip.

We have no evidence that George was successful in his application for 50 acres each for himself and his brother in the Adelaide settlement. The family was probably settled in Delaware by the time Martha Hilton married there in 1841. On 28 March 1845, George and his son Henry Hilton purchased SE part lot 9 concession 1 Delaware Township, a lot where they could have been living for some time. The census taker in 1851 recorded Henry Hilton as the head of a farm household on lot 8 concession 3 Delaware. Lydia Hilton, now a widow, was living with him as was Friend Hilton, his younger brother, who was described as a shoemaker. Henry was 30 and Friend 27. A James Hilton on lots 4 and 9 of concession 1 Delaware could have been their older brother, James.

Letter 123, from Alexander Hilton, is dated a month later than Lydia's letter. Aunt and nephew reflect their very different perspectives on the same family situations.

■ 120

GEORGE AND MARY HILLS, WEST FLAMBOROUGH TOWNSHIP, UPPER CANADA, TO JOHN DREWITT, PEPPERING, WEST SUSSEX, 18 SEPTEMBER 1836

George Hills, a farm labourer, and his wife Mary Ann (Ewens) emigrated from Peppering, Burpham, West Sussex, with their six children, Lucy, Eleanor, Esther, Emma, Charles, and Mary Ann (all baptized at Warminghurst, Heath Common, between 1818 and 1833). Internal evidence suggests that this letter was written by Mary Ann.[81]

The recipients of this letter were John and Frances Ann Drewitt, tenant farmers of the Duke of Norfolk on Great Peppering Farm in Burpham. John Drewitt may have employed George Hills as a farm labourer, or he may have assisted his emigration in his capacity as churchwarden and a member of the vestry. He was also concerned in the emigration of George Older and his family (see letter 109). Mary, however, thanks Frances Drewitt for the trouble she took in sending them to Upper Canada.

81 At their marriage in Arundel, Mary Ann signed her name to the marriage register and George made a mark.

SOURCE: *Continuation of Letters from Sussex Emigrants …Written in 1836* [1837], 17–18

September 18th. 1836.

DEAR FRIEND,

I have taken the liberty of writing to you, and I hope it will find you all in good health, as it leaves me as well as I can expect, at present. I am very happy to say, George and all the children are quite well, excepting Lucy, and she is about the same as she was last year at this time; but thanks be to God, we have not lost a day's work since we came to Mr. * * *. When we came to Hamilton, Mr. Brydone* was very kind to us; he gave us three dollars to pay our expences here. How many times do I thank God for leading us so many miles across the water, to such a kind friend., Mr. * * * took us in the same night we came to the house; and gave us plenty to eat and drink, and found a place to put all our things; and took Ellen for a servant, and agreed to give her two dollars a month; and Hester is going to live with his daughter, Mrs. * * *, and Amy is going to live with his son John, for their board and lodging, washing and mending; and Lucy has had plenty of work to do at Mr. * * * before she took ill.[82] Ellen has been in a great way about her aunt, and she hopes you will be so kind to let her know how well she is; and she is very pleased that her mistress is learning her to write. And Mr. * * * and his sons has been so kind as to put us up a nice little house, close by a beautiful stream of water; and George has got twelve dollars a month and his board, and house-rent, and fuelling, and we have plenty of milk twice a day.

I have so many good things from the house, that we have been able to save twelve dollars since we have been here; and we have bought ten bushels of potatoes, and two pigs; and my children have picked up a nice parcel of wheat; and we have as much wood as we like to use; and we hope God will bless him for taking such a poor family as us; for we were all very poorly when we came here, but Miss * * * was very kind; she gave us all some medicine, so we soon got better, thanks be to God for his goodness. But at the same time, Mrs. Drewitt, I have to thank you for taking so much trouble in sending us out, for we was never so well off since we have been married; for Mr. * * * is going to fence a large piece of ground in, for a garden and orchard for us to use, so long as we are with him; and he said we should have poultry to keep, and I have half for looking after them; and he said he would get us a cow in the spring. They told me at home, I should get no money in this country, but we have our money any when if we only ask for it.

If you please sir, George would be very glad if you would ask his uncle James if he would answer his mother's letter, and let them know where we are. If you please, to remember us to all our friends, and I wish they was as well off as I am, but altho'

---

82 The form of the children's names varies from the baptismal register to this letter, but, if one assumes that the children were baptized within a few months of their birth, Ellen would have been about 15 years old at the time her mother was writing, Hester (Esther) 11, Amy (Emma) 8, and Lucy would have been 18.

I am a poor sinful creature, I find my dear Lord's blessing. I would say more, but I am in haste for Mr. Brydone to take it.

So no more at present, from your servants,

GEORGE & MARY HILLS.

When you please to write to us, direct it, Findon Place, West Flamborough, near Dundas, Upper Canada, North America.

TO JOHN DREWITT, Esq.

Peppering, Sussex.

■ I2I

MARY AND GEORGE BOXALL, NELSON TOWNSHIP, UPPER CANADA, TO HIS FATHER, WILLIAM BOXALL, MOTHER, BROTHERS AND SISTERS, FARNHURST NEAR HASLEMERE, WEST SUSSEX, 25 SEPTEMBER 1836
The letter was written by George Boxall.

SOURCE: *Continuation of Letters from Sussex Emigrants ... Written in 1836* [1837], 18-19

September 25th. 1836.

Dear Father and Mother, Brothers and Sisters,

I have wrote a few lines to you, hoping this will find you all in good health, as it leaves us all at present, excepting our youngest baby, and he is cutting of teeth. I received your letter on the 24th September, and I am sorry to hear that my poor mother is so very ill. I do wish that she was in America with me, for I could get a good living for she, and father too. Dear brother, I am sorry that England is in such a poor state as it is. I do wonder that you stay there, I would sail the ocean over first. I will persuade you all to come here, and then you would be sure of a good comfortable living. I can get two or three of you work, as soon as you comes, for fifteen shillings a week, English money, and they will find you a house and fire-wood free for nothing: for thank the Lord, me and my wife and family do not know the want of food nor children, and I have three children to keep; and I can keep three better than I could one in the old country, and a great deal too; for I can get plenty of work, and good pay too; and if you wants to better yourself, you had better come to me to America, and then you will find friends. You will find more friends in this country in three months, than you would in England in 7 Years.

Dear brother William [Boxall], I would be very glad if you would understand this following, if you please. My mother have the beating at the heart still, I suppose, and if she has, please to tell her that she should take a tea spoonful of hartshorn[83] in half of a tea cup full of tea, and drink your tea as usual, close after it, as you would, as though you never had any thing to take; and your food as usual: for, dear mother, I know one woman that was very ill with the same complaint, and a man too, and they are getting quite hearty now, and I hope she would too.

---

83 an ammonious substance made from the antlers of a deer

Now my dear friends, do not make no delay, but the first chance as you can get to come to America, be sure and come, because it is a good country: and now in three weeks from the date hereof, I am a going to rent about 10 acres of land, and an excellent house; and I shall sell my own house, and I shall look out for you for houses as well as myself, if you will but come. My father[84] and mother-in-law and family is well, and is doing well; they keeps a tavern. And now, my father and mother, brothers and sisters, at home, all that will come out, and can come out, bring all the goods, and clothes as you can, such as crockeryware, you will find it handy; but if you have not got any thing, do not mind about that, for you will have the chance here, so do not neglect coming. So no more from your son and daughter,

MARY & GEORGE BOXALL.

And when you send to me, direct your letter as usual
George Boxall, at Mr. George Chisholm's,[85] Township of Nelson, County of Alton [Halton], District of Gore, Upper Canada, North America.

So God bless you all.
To William Boxall,
Van Common, Farnhurst, near Haslemere.

OTHER LETTERS: 25.

122

WILLIAM ROBINSON, DELAWARE TOWNSHIP, UPPER CANADA, TO THE REVEREND THOMAS SOCKETT*, PETWORTH, WEST SUSSEX, 14 OCTOBER 1836

While in Lower Canada at Quebec, Robinson had purchased lot 2 concession 5 in Ekfrid Township. Sockett published his letter with its offer of employment on the inside and back covers of a volume of letters printed in advance of the departure of the *Diana in* 1837.

SOURCE: *Continuation of Letters from Sussex Emigrants ...Written in 1836* [1837], inside front cover, back cover

Ekfrid Park, near Delaware,
London District, Upper Canada,
14th. October, 1836.

The Rev. T. Sockett,
    Chairman,
Emigration Society, Petworth, Sussex.
Sir,

Understanding that you preside as the chairman of the Petworth Emigration Committee, I take the liberty of addressing you, presuming that the same good, which

84 Original Annotation: "James Tilley, formerly of Petworth, sent out by the Committee in 1833." See letter 83.
85 A George Chisolm, a gentleman aged 37, is listed as living in Trafalgar Township in the 1851 census.

has hitherto been experienced by the many individuals which you have been the means of placing in a comfortable situation in this country, will be followed up during the ensuing spring, by your society sending out more settlers; and being myself in want of labourers on my farm, I beg leave to make the following proposals to those families who may feel inclined to embrace the offer.

First – I will give employment to two men who have wives and children, who are of good reputation for sobriety, honesty, and diligence. The wages that I offer to these men are £30 per annum, with a house rent-free, as much fuel as they wish, and the keep of a cow winter and summer, together with as much land for a garden, or other purposes, as their families may require.

Secondly – I can offer a place to a young woman of steady age and disposition, who has been in service, and can produce testimonials for activity, industry, and capability, as a house servant of all work. And should the families not have a boy of 12 or 15 years of age who has been brought up to farm work, I will also give employment to a youth of the above description, with his board and lodging, and washing; his wages commencing with fifteen shillings per month, and yearly a proportionate increase, with his capability and worth.

My object is, to have people about me whose services I can rely on, at all seasons; and I am persuaded, that the only means of obtaining that end, is to get out families direct from England, who, by being kept together, are less liable to contract wandering habits; and when comfortably housed round their domestic fire-side, with every comfort that reason can dictate, will be more induced to conform to stationary habits, than embrace the roving propensities that too many of the emigrants in this country are addicted to. I have also other reasons for offering employment to families previous to embarkation, and who, on their arrival here, have employment, and a home, ready to their hand; for the more intercourse they have with the older inhabitants, the sooner they lose their native character, imbibe loose habits, become Yankeefied (if I may be allowed the expression), insolent, and independent; for which reason, I would avoid giving employment to any person who came to this country by way of the United States. I am, myself an Englishman, and although not long a settler, have been in the country some years, in the service of the British Government; but as yet, have not lost sight of the good old English manners and habits; and those about me, acting with and for me, I wish to observe the same. I have employed, at different times, men from Sussex, who have been sent out here, under the care and protection of your Committee; and in justice to them, I must say, that I invariably found them well behaved and civil, and I believe, generally doing well.[86] This, I am sure, cannot fail of being pleasing to yourself, and those gentlemen with whom you act.

I have now living with me, a man from the same county, who has a wife and two children, they came out this season. I have engaged with them upon the terms before mentioned; they are at present in my house, waiting the completion of a cot-

---

86 We do not know who these people were.

tage I am putting up for them. His name is George Older,[87] and had with him a very good character from John Drewitt*, Esq.; and although they have been with me but a short time, I have every reason to believe, that they are deserving the praise that gentleman has bestowed on them. They are contented and happy; and according to their deserts, so shall I consider it my duty to contribute to their welfare. He informs me that he is personally known to you.

Emigrants on their arrival here have much misery to contend with, and for a length of time after, that is, when establishing themselves on wild lands; and happy are those who have the good fortune to meet with an employer, who is disposed to place them in a comfortable situation, and aid them in procuring of those comforts without which, life is only a misery; and when they find those blessings bestowed on them, the only means they have of shewing their gratitude is, by faithful servitude. The District of Country from which I now write, is much wanting of able labourers, and particularly mechanics, such as carpenters, a blacksmith, a wheelwright, and in fact, almost any tradesman would find employment, as public works are now commencing, which will for years afford constant work. Having a tolerable large tract of land here, by way of encouraging mechanics, I would engage to settle them, by giving each, at a nominal rent for 3 or 5 years, village lots of about 5 acres, upon which to erect a house, and to cultivate, at periods when their mechanical exertions were not required. By this means, they would at once find a home and employment; during which term they might, if industrious, amass a sufficiency whereby to better their condition, if possible, or to remain with their families, friends, or connections, forming a social society amongst themselves. An able tradesman will earn his dollar per day, besides his board.

I wish it to be perfectly understood, that I in no way am disposed to be at any expence, in bringing out the individuals in question: on their arrival here, I will immediately provide for them in the manner stated, and use every means in my power to render them as comfortable as time and situation will permit: and should your Committee approve of my offer, and make a selection out of those who are fortunate enough to obtain your protection and patronage, I shall expect that they come well recommended for sobriety, honesty, and industry; for without these requisites, no one will do well here; in fact, they must starve, for there is no parish to run to for relief.

I shall be happy to hear from you on this subject, and if your Committee think proper to entertain a favorable opinion of my proposition, I will thank you for timely notice, so that I may make suitable arrangements previous to their arrival. In conclusion, I beg to say, that I consider this portion of the London District worthy of the attention of your Committee, as a part of Upper Canada well calculated to the settlement of the majority of the Emigrants, that you may think proper to send out next year; and I shall feel pleasure in assisting Mr. Brydone*, or any other person

87 Sockett published a brief extract from a letter by George Older; see letter 109.

you may select as superintendent, if such services are deemed of any utility, and this part of the Province eligible. It is healthy, well watered, and excellent soil.

    I remain,
      Sir,
    With much respect,
      Your very humble Servant,
        W. Robinson.

The Pullen family address a letter care of Robinson at Ekfrid Park in May 1838. By 1855, when he sold 350 acres in Ekfrid to Charles Robinson of Toronto, he was living in Wales.

■ 123

ALEXANDER HILTON, DELAWARE TOWNSHIP, UPPER CANADA, TO HIS UNCLE, HENRY HILTON, AND HIS AUNT, BIGNOR, WEST SUSSEX, 16 OCTOBER 1836

Alexander was the eldest in the family of Charles and Mary Ann Hilton, who emigrated in 1832. In addition to Alexander, the family included Ann, Jane, Harriet, Charles, James, William, Sarah Ann, and, by the time of this letter, a baby born in Canada. Hiltons related to him were on Petworth ships in 1835, 1836, and 1837 (see letter 119 from his aunt, Lydia Hilton).

SOURCE: *Continuation of Letters from Sussex Emigrants … Written in 1836* [1837], 7–8

From Alexander Hilton, the Son of Charles Hilton, who emigrated to Canada, in 1832, from Sutton, in Sussex, in the ship Eveline, sent by the Petworth Committee.

                        Delaware, October 16th. 1836.

Dear Uncle and Aunt,

    I take this opportunity of writing to you, hoping to find you in good health, as it leaves me at present, thank God for it. I am doing very well; working at the carpenter and joiner's trade, this two years, and am now getting ten dollars a month; and by next summer, shall be able to get from 16 to 18 dollars a month, as a good workman can get from 20 to 25 dollars a month. Father is living in the township of Adelaide, on land, and doing very well; but he did not go on it till last fall; he raised enough to keep his family through the year. He works about at digging wells and cellars, when he works out; and can earn a dollar, or a dollar and a half a day; but a farmer's man gets from 10 to 12 dollars a month.

    Uncle George is living at Toronto, or York; but he has been up to see us, and to look for land. He found a lot to suit him; he was going to see the Governor [Sir Francis Bond Head*] to see if he could get it; that was about two months ago. He promised to write to me, in three weeks, but he has not wrote yet, and I thinks it very strange he has not: but I have not seen James,[88] since he has been in the coun-

---

88 His cousin, George's son, James Hilton, who emigrated in 1835.

try, but I understand, that he gets a very good living. If you come to Canada, as you had better, for I am certain, that you can do better, than you can in England. Do not stay there to be humbugged about, by those big bugs. In Canada you can have your liberty, and need not be afraid to speak for your rights.

Wheat is in general from 3 shillings and 9d. to 5 shillings per bushel. Peas, oats, and barley, about 2s.6d. Pork and beef, 4d. Butter and cheese, 7½. Potatoes, 1s.3d. If you come to this country, do not bring a mess of old truck, or load yourself with tools, as you can get them as cheap in this country. Bring nothing but good serviceable clothing, and not a great deal of that, for money will be more service than any thing else. Bring no round frocks, for they are not worn in this country. Tell grandmother [Sarah (Overington) Hilton], that she need not be afraid to come to Canada, for her children and grandchildren are able to support her well; and that they will do it. If uncle Clemonds, or any of my uncles and aunts come to Canada, give them what advice you can, from the account I give you; and come by the way of New York, if possible, for it is much the quickest and safest passage.

Ann is married to a young man from Angmering, by the name of David Evans; they have a pretty little girl, about ten months old. Mother enjoys her health a little better than she did in England, and is very happy; but she wants to see her poor mother, and brothers, and sisters, in Canada.[89] Father has got two cows, and a yoke of steers, and some younger stock. I think they will do very well, after this. Jane and Harriet[90] are grown fine girls; and I expect the family will be grown out of knowledge, except me, and I am the same little runt as ever. I forgot to tell you, that mother had a young baby, about four months old. Father and mother sends their kind love to their dear mother, brothers and sisters, and so we do all. Give my love, and respects to all my relations, and enquiring friends. So no more at present, from your ever affectionate nephew, and grandson,

ALEXANDER HILTON.

Direct your letters Delaware, London District, County Middlesex, Upper Canada, either to me, or father.

To Mr. Henry Hilton, Bignor, near Petworth, Sussex.

After learning his trade from John Northwood, Alexander spent about four years in Michigan where he married Martha Humphries in 1841. He returned to Canada and to Delaware Village before settling in Adelaide, first as a farmer on the fourth concession, and later in the Village of Strathroy. His first child was born in Delaware in 1842 and his second in Adelaide in 1844. In the 1851 census of Adelaide, his children were listed as Charlotte, Maria, Martha Jane, Rachel, and Charles. Alexander's occupation was recorded as carpenter and farmer in 1851, leading contractor in 1889, and builder in 1892, the year he died at Strathroy. He had

---

89 Mary Ann Hilton died in 1837; we do not know whether this was before or after the Hiltons had arrived on the *Diana*.
90 Alexander's sisters.

a part in building churches in the villages of Adelaide, Strathroy, and Delaware, and the Presbyterian Church at St Thomas.

Alexander's brothers and sisters married into the Rapley, Parker, and Evans families of Petworth emigrants.

■ 124

WILLIAM AND SARAH JACKMAN, BRANTFORD, UPPER CANADA, TO
THEIR SON, STEPHEN, [GORING, WEST SUSSEX,] 29 OCTOBER 1836
William and Sarah (Lillywhite) Jackman[91] and their family emigrated in a party of 27 people sent from Goring with the assistance of a loan from Levi Bushby, the proprietor of Field Place in Goring. Three of the Jackman's nine children died before they left England and Stephen, their eldest son, remained behind. Ann, Mary, and Frank were about 15, 13, and 12, respectively, when the letter was sent. The other two children, Henry William and Ellen, were under 5. Three Lillywhites emigrated from Findon on the *Heber* in 1836, the brothers Reuben and George Lillywhite and Daniel Lillywhite, but Sarah Jackman apparently was not their close relative.

SOURCE: *Continuation of Letters from Sussex Emigrants ...Written in 1836* [1837], 22-4; it was also published in the *Brighton Guardian*, December 1836, with the following introduction.

A letter was last week received, by Stephen Jackman, of Goring, from his parents who were amongst the last party that emigrated to America from Goring and the neighbourhood: and as two of their companions returned to Goring about a month ago giving a most deplorable account of the parties they had left behind (and more particularly of Jackman's parents) causing considerable uneasiness and grief to their friends in this neighbourhood, the promoters of emigration in the district have thought it desirable to have the letter published, in order to refute the misrepresentations of James Gates and Thomas Grinyer, the parties alluded to. With that view they have sent us a copy, of the letter which we gladly insert. The original may be seen by any one who will take the trouble to call on Jackman at Goring.

Brantford, October 29th. 1836.

DEAR SON

We have taken this opportunity of writing to inform you of our safe arrival in America. We had a very fine passage out, considering the time of the year, but it was very cold. We were just six weeks from the time we left Portsmouth till we arrived at Quebec. We had then to embark on board of a steam boat for Montreal, where we had to take large boats to go up the dangerous rapids at the River St. Lawrence, in consequence of the Rideau Canal being broke. We suffered great hardships and cold going up the rapids. We were all in open boats, exposed to the heat of the sun by day, and to the rain, cold, and fogs by night. We were better than a week going up the rapids, as far as Prescott. We had then to take another steam boat to go to Toronto, where we received our money; but instead of being sent right up to Brant-

91 Both William and Sarah signed the marriage register with a mark.

ford, as we expected, we had to pay part of the expences. We were just ten weeks from the time we left England till we got to our journey's end. I thank God! we were all pretty well coming out, excepting a little sea sickness, which soon wore off again when we got ashore.

As soon as we got here your father got into good employment, and he gets a great deal better paid for it, and need not work so hard. Ann has got a very good place with an English family, and is getting £10 a year. Mary and Frank are both living at one place, and are doing very well. Frank gets as much as Ann; but Mary does not get above half as much in money, but it is more than made up in clothes, for she gets some very good presents from her mistress —— and of the two she is better off. Please to give my kind love to my dear mother [Elizabeth Lillywhite], and likewise to all my brothers and sisters, and to all old friends and acquaintances, especially to Mrs. Martin, for her kindness before we left home. Your father wishes to be remembered to his mother [Ann Jackman], his brothers and sisters, and all his old acquaintances. William Gates[92] is apprenticed to a carpenter; but he does not seem to alter his conduct much since he left home. George Hide is living about 25 miles from us. I have not seen him now for several weeks; but the last time I saw him he was very well, and had a very good place. I have seen George Whitington[93] several times since I have been here, and he appears to be respectable, and seems to be doing as well as the rest. Mr and Mrs Miles[94] and family are all well; and Mr Miles is quite steady to what he was at home.

I thank God this letter leaves us all in good health, and we hope it will find you and Mary the same. Please to give our kind love to Mary's father and mother.[95] As soon as you receive this letter, write an answer, and let us know the full particulars of every thing, and let us know if you have had plenty of work. Tell Mary, if you both intend to come out, that she can get things to suit her here as well as she can at home; and I have no doubt if you come out, but that you will do very well. Little Henry and Ellen look as well as ever they did; but Henry very often talks about his brother Buddy, and says he is sure you are dead, because he has not seen you so long.

We were living with Master Miles till within this month —— now we and Master Ford are living in one house; we down stairs, Master Ford up stairs.[96] The rent is three shillings a week between us, and we are all pretty comfortable. We have not known what it is to want for any thing since we have been here, and we have now a quarter of beef in the house, and cost us only twopence a pound. Ann sends her

92 William Gates emigrated from Goring in 1836. He was a relative, but not a brother, of James.

93 Whittington also emigrated from Goring in 1836.

94 George, "a farming man," and Ann Miles emigrated from Goring in 1835 with their five children.

95 Stephen had recently married Mary Greenfield, probably the daughter of James and Sarah Greenfield.

96 The John Ford who emigrated on the *Burrell* from Goring in 1835 with his wife and two children, Fanny and Ann, gave his occupation as farming man and gardener.

kind love, and wishes to be remembered to Harriet Standen, Martha Martin, and Jane Goulds; and she hopes she will come out next year with you and Mary. Your father wishes to see you out here, as he thinks you will do very well, for here is plenty to do for every one that is industrious.

You can tell Mr. Bushby[97] the land here is very good, as good as it is in England. In some places the plain land here is covered with oak, and small brush underwood. The good ground runs about three inches, and the rest is a red loam, and in some places sand. The flat ground is of a dark, sandy strong nature; it grows oats six feet high, and as thick as any he ever grew on his farm; but it does not bear good wheat. The heavy timbered land is strong moulded ground, and fit to bear any grain. The land in this country, take one place with another, is equally as good as it is at home; and much leveller. When first I arrived here, I took about six day's walk on purpose to look at the country, and this is the best description I can give of it at present; but I shall let you know a little more about it in a short time.

You can tell Mr. Street that I don't find Goring in Canada, nor I don't wish to it; and if but 50 or 100 [acres] in the course of two or three years, I should make a man of myself. Me, and Master Ford, and George Wells[98] are at present clearing land, and some of the trees are four foot through, which we have to cut down with an axe. Brantford is a snug little place, but winter is fast approaching and it is getting cold. So no more at present from your affectionate father and mother,

W. & S. JACKMAN.

P.S. —— You must not believe every letter that comes home from Canada; but what I have said is truth —— it is a great deal better for young men than at home. James Gates and Thomas Grinyer, as soon as they got here, because they could not get employment, started off, and we have not heard of them since; and if they should come home don't believe what they say.[99]

The later history of the Jackman family is told by Brenda Dougall Merriman in *The Emigrant Ancestors of a Lieutenant Governor of Ontario* (Toronto 1993).

Sarah died sometime before 1839 when William married Barbara Smith in Oxford Township. By 1842, the family was on lot 13 concession 1 of Wawanosh Township (just to the north of the Canada Company's Huron Tract). They had five acres of their farm cleared and five chopped and ready to plant in the spring. In 1847, Jackman obtained patents for the southwest quarter of this lot and the east half of lot 28 in the same concession. He died in 1869 in a grisly accident when he fell against the revolving circular saw at a mill near the village of Nile.

Stephen Jackman, the recipient of this letter, was married in Sussex in 1836. He, his wife, Mary, and five of six surviving children, emigrated in 1852 to Toronto, where he worked at

---

97 Levi Bushby of Field Place, Goring, who made a loan for emigration to the parish of Goring in 1836.
98 Wells was another of the 1836 Goring emigrants.
99 James Gates married in Goring in December 1837. Thomas Gringyer was lodging with James Gates and his family at Jupp's Farm, Goring, in the 1861 census.

first as a night watchman and labourer and later established his own business as a grocer and wholesale produce merchant.

Two of William's sons who were emigrants on the *Heber*, Francis (Frank) and Henry William (Harry), made names for themselves in Toronto as captains of sailing vessels on the Great Lakes. In Toronto, they acted as shippers for the successful distillery operation of Gooderham and Worts, founded by English immigrants who arrived from Norfolk in 1831 and 1832. In 1865-6, Captain Frank Jackman achieved local fame by taking the lake vessel *Seagull* on a charter to Natal in South Africa.

■ 125

WILLIAM SPENCER, BRONTE, UPPER CANADA, TO HIS FATHER AND MOTHER, 10 NOVEMBER 1836

SOURCE: *Continuation of Letters from Sussex Emigrants ... Written in 1836* [1837], 19-22

From William Spencer, who emigrated in 1832.

Nelson, 10th. November, 1836.

My dear and ever affectionate Father and Mother,

I have once more, by the sparing hand of the Almighty, taken another opportunity to take my pen in hand, for to address you, my parents; which I hope and trust these few lines will find you comfortable in your persons and in your circumstances, according as I heard in your last letter. As it respects myself, I thank the Lord I am still spared in the land of living, and in good health at present. Dear parents, I have wrote to you two long and intelligent letters, informing you all the particulars relating to myself and the country that I possibly could, which I am informed that they did not come to hand, by several persons that came out of Petworth this spring; which they informed me that you were all in good health when they left, which gave me great satisfaction. I am going to inform you in some particulars relating to myself, viz. Thanks be to Almighty God I am enjoying a merciful portion of health, and I have had no sickness since I received your last letter, except one accident that happened to me: I cut my leg with the axe, which I was unabled to work for three months; but thanks be to God, it is quite whole again.

I have bought half an acre of land in the town of Bronti, which cost me £9. It is a new town, and appears to be in a flourishing state: there has been 25 dwelling-houses and two large warehouses put up this season. I am intended, if the Lord spares me health and days, to put up a house next spring. The town is situated on the bank of Lake Ontario, which is 28 miles from Toronto; and is 14 miles from Hamilton; which is on the main road [Dundas St] betwixt both, and has a large river [Twelve Mile Creek] running through the centre of the town, which would make a beautiful harbour for vessels, and is hoped soon will be accomplished. On the same river, betwixt Dundas Street and Lake Ontario, which is four miles, there is five saw mills, one flour mill. There is another new saw mill a putting up, and there is plenty of work for them all. Each saw mill can saw three thousand feet of boards in 24 hours.

Henry William Jackman (above), Francis Jackman with their ships

Courtesy Jackman family for the photographs of Francis and Henry William; Archives of Ontario, F1194, ACC9379, for "The Jessie Drummond" and "The Sea Gull"

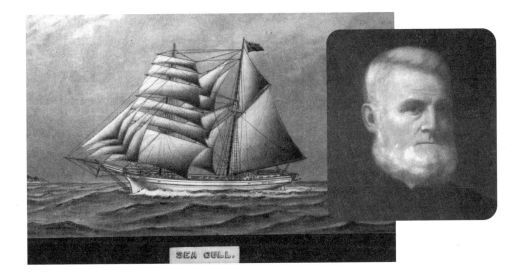

We have a beautiful view of Lake Ontario: we see two steam packets passing and repassing each day. There is four others comes regular past once a week. Forty other vessels. And we hope, that in a short space of time that they will call with us regularly. Any one of the largest vessels can come now within 30 yards of the town.

You requested me, when I would write, to let you know how poor emigrants would get along, when they reached this side the Atlantic, if they had no money and destitute of employ. I never knew such a case but one family, the name of Ladd, which came from Dorking, in Surrey. There was seven of a family, five children and their parents; they came and settled within three miles of me. They had not one farthing to help themselves: there was employ found for as many of them as could work, immediately; it was but a few days till the oldest son, by an accident, broke his leg; their only daughter, which had been sick all the voyage died, and the rest was sick with the fever and ague, except the old woman, and all was unabled to work. You may judge their state, by what I have informed you, whether they were in distress or not. As soon as their case was known, they were immediately relieved with plenty of provision, that was brought to them by the inhabitants of the place, without their own application. There was another case of a family that was burned out: their house was burned, and all their provisions, and all that was in the house; and one child, of two years old, was burned to death. Two of the place went out and made them a restoration of more than they had before, except the child; and the inhabitants of the place put them up a house all within four days time. Also the next request was, how should a man make out for a piece of bread, that has got 100 acres of land allotted to him, if they had no money? The way that they do when they get 100 acres of land, and has no money, they go and work out one half of the time, and the other on their own place. They can earn as much in the half of the time, as is sufficient to maintain them.

We have had a very severe cold winter; as for the summer, it has been very wet and cold for the climate. Also, you requested to know what sort of crops, and what kind of grain we have here. The crops has been very good in general: as for the grain or seeds, we use the same here, as you do there, except India corn, viz. Wheat is 6s.3d. per bushel; potatoes, 2s.6d. per bushel; pork is £1.10s. per hundred; beef is £1.5s. per hundred; as for other things, they are in proportion. And as respects America or Upper Canada, you told me in your last letter, you were hearing various accounts by different people, which came from Petworth and settled here; but it is no wonder, for I am hearing so myself. I am going to give you as near account as I possibly can.

As for the country, it is in some respects not so pleasant as the old country; but there is more privileges here, than is with you: we can fish and fowl as much as we please, and none to make us afraid. There is no gamekeepers, or water keepers here. And as respects labouring, there is plenty of work for every one that will work, and good pay. A labouring man has 2s.6d. per day, and boarded; or by the month, £3. and boarded; in haying, 3s.9d. per day, and do.; and in harvest, 5s. per day, and do.; and mechanics, they have from 5s. to 7s.6d. per day, and do. You told me you were doing well for poor people, in your last letter, which gave me great satisfaction to hear; but I have great reason to believe, that if you were in Canada you would be doing better; but I would not advise you to come, for fear you might reflect on me; but I would be glad to meet with you all in Canada; and I would rejoice; but you must speculate for yourselves.

James Tilley and family is well, and doing well.[100] They are living within five miles of me; I am going often to see them, as they are the only people that I am acquainted with from the old country. I seen Frederick Upton two weeks past: he told me that they were all in good health;[101] that is all the information that I can give you concerning Petworth people.

Dear father and mother, I have one favour to beg of you, that is, to let my own friends see this letter, if you possibly can. If brother Samuel has not the opportunity of seeing this letter, if you would be so kind as to write to him, and give him the directions to write to me, I would be glad to receive a letter from him. And I would be very glad to receive a letter from my own people, if they thought it worth their while to write to me; if not, I would be glad if you would be so kind as give me all the information that you possibly can concerning them.

For want of room, I must draw to a close. I send my kind love to my step-father and mother, and brothers and sisters, and uncles and aunts; and nephews and cousins, and likewise to all enquiring friends. Write to me as soon as you possibly can, giving me all the information concerning yourselves, my own friends, relations, and the country, that you possibly can. I send you my very kind love, dear parents, sisters, brothers, friends, and acquaintances. If we never meet in this side of time, my prayer to God is, that we may all meet in the land of eternal bliss, where there shall be no sorrow, where God shall wipe away all tears from their eyes. I add not. Yours truly. I still remain your affectionate son till death,

WILLIAM SPENCER.

Direct as follows. To William Spencer, Wellington Square Post Office, Nelson, County of Halton, Gore District, Upper Canada, N.A. By the way of New York. I had the pleasure of seeing part of the first letter that I wrote to you in print, I wish if you put this letter in print, that you put it all in.

OTHER LETTERS: 24, 68
Bronte was in Trafalgar Township. Spencer probably dated his letter "Nelson" because his nearest post office was some seven miles away, at Wellington Square in Nelson Township.

---

100 James Tilley emigrated in 1833, following his brother William and the Boxalls who emigrated in 1832 along with Spencer; see letters 25 and 83.
101 Frederik was one of three Upton brothers who emigrated from Petworth in 1833, following two elder brothers (see letters 26, 27). Their mother joined them in 1835.

1837

THE DIANA,

ENGAGED BY

The Petworth Emigration Committee,

ACTING FOR

The Earl of Egremont,

will be ready to take her Passengers on Board on TUESDAY next, the 25th. instant, at TEN o'Clock in the FORENOON.

A few Berths may still be secured on early application either to the COMMITTEE, at PETWORTH, or Mr. PIERCE, HIGH STREET, PORTSMOUTH.

Petworth, April 19th. 1837.

PHILLIPS, PRINTER, PETWORTH.

CHRONOLOGY FOR THE YEAR 1837

25 April Passengers embarked on the *Diana*.

27 April The *Diana* left Portsmouth.

28 April The governor of the House of Industry at Newport, Isle of Wight, submitted a report to the Board of Governors requesting approval for payment of £1068.0.2 spent sending emigrants with the Petworth committee. The sum included £10.16.4½ for taking clothing and other items out of pawn.

3 May The *Diana* resumed her voyage after riding out a heavy gale.

15 June The *Diana* reached Quebec.

20 June The emigrants disembarked at Montreal to travel through the Rideau Canal.

4 July Eight or nine Petworth families were expected in Woodstock.

1 August The Upper Canadian government accepted a bust of Lord Egremont sent with Brydone* to serve as a reminder of their benefactor for Petworth settlers and their descendants.

14 September Brydone gave formal notice that he would not renew the offer to purchase any part of the tract of land north of Goderich.

Egremont caught a cold while at Brighton where he had gone to pay his respects to Victoria, the new Queen of England.

11 November Egremont died at Petworth House "of his old complaint, an inflammation in the trachea." He had succeeded to the earldom in 1763 and would have been 86 on 18 December.

16 November Rebellion broke out in Lower Canada

5 December William Lyon Mackenzie's rebels started their march down Yonge Street

10 December The Coopers in Adelaide Township had still not heard news of the Rebellion in Upper Canada.

14 December William Cooper was called out with his militia unit, the Middlesex Light Infantry.

Sources: WSRO, PHA 140; IOW Record Office, Z/HO/B1, Z/HO/44; Columbia University, Butler Library, X325, T63, vol. 1; Lytton Strachey and Roger Fulford, eds., *The Greville Memoirs, 1814-1860* (London: Macmillan 1938), III: 397-400; *Gentleman's Magazine,* January 1838; Cameron and Maude, *Assisting Emigration to Upper Canada* (Montreal: McGill-Queen's University Press 2000); contemporary newspapers; letters.

PREVIOUS PAGE: Broadsheet for the *Diana*, PRO, CO 384/44, f.263

SHIP: *Diana*, A1, 321 tons
MASTER: Edward Lane
SUPERINTENDENT: James Marr Brydone

BACKGROUND

By 1837, the Petworth Poor Law Union, with Egremont*'s silent approval, was at odds with both the assistant commissioner for Sussex and the poor law commissioners in London. Sockett* had declined election as a guardian of the Petworth Poor Law Union and remained outside the system, but he was drawn into public controversy when the assistant poor law commissioner for Sussex labeled his emigrants as "vicious characters ... steeped in vice and habitual pauperism." Sockett rose to their defence in a letter published in the London *Standard* of 22 February which was sharply critical of the poor law commissioners' handling of parish-assisted emigration. In March, he and officials from the Petworth Union appeared before a parliamentary select committee as witnesses critical of the hasty and uncaring way the new law had been introduced to their area. Although this committee had no particular interest in emigration, the poor law commissioners and the assistant commissioner for Sussex relieved some of their annoyance by making life difficult for parishes that applied for loans to send emigrants with the Petworth committee. Specifically, they made an issue of cost and successfully insisted that at least one parish use a cheaper ship.

As a consequence of these local problems, as well as of bad news from the Canadas, the Petworth committee had such difficulty filling their ship in 1837 that Sockett made enquiries about hiring the use of part of a ship rather than a full charter. The committee did fill the *Diana*, but they did so by taking a large number of emigrants from the Isle of Wight. The two groups on the *Diana* were not an easy mix. Sockett sent mainly families in the West Sussex party with a high proportion of children. The Pullens were probably typical of the large families he believed would be better off in Upper Canada than trying to live on their English wages without benefit of the child allowance taken away under the new poor law. The Isle of Wight sent a few families and a sizable group of single men.

Brydone* named four young men and a boy from the Isle of Wight as well behaved on the voyage. He dismissed 20 other single men and 3 single women as "not recommendable." The captain took Brydone's part, and we do not have any letters speaking for the young men who disregarded Brydone's authority (the writer of 130 printed in the *Brighton Patriot* had his own agenda and only scorn for pauper emigrants). We also do not know what form their defiance took, but they seem to have been disruptive of the other emigrants rather than a threat to them.

At the beginning of 1837, the Courtnages, the Barnes, and the Manns, emigrants of 1832 and 1836, all wrote that they were doing well in three quite different parts of the province. The emigrants who arrived in 1837 are not well represented by letters. Single immigrants whom Brydone had to leave "unprotected" on arrival disappeared from our view. Arrangements were made for several families to go to government plots in Woodstock, but we have no letters from any that did. We do know that a number of the immigrants from West Sussex had family in Upper Canada, and that the Pullens, by going a distance inland, had a choice of employers.

In the later months of 1837, the events of the rebellion overtook all thought of immigration in government circles in Upper Canada. Officials here were silent on the subject of Petworth immigrants. In England, Sockett assessed the situation and made the decision not to buy land in Upper Canada. Brydone reported this decision to the lieutenant governor's secretary in September. Egremont died in November. Once news of the Canadian rebellions reached Sussex, emigrants were too fearful to go to Canada. James Lannaway's was the only family to emigrate with assistance from the Petworth committee in 1838.

■ 126

JOHN BARNES, TORONTO, UPPER CANADA, TO HIS FATHER, BROTHER AND SISTERS, [PETWORTH, WEST SUSSEX,] 1 JANUARY 1837

With four children, John and Charlotte Barnes did not fit the usual pattern of live-in servants. Perhaps because they did not fit the mould, he spells out their relationship with their employer in some detail. They were still working for the Reverend Charles Stephens Matthews, who hired them on the day they arrived in 1836 (see letter 116).

SOURCE: *Continuation of Letters from Sussex Emigrants* (1837), 1–5; the letter was also published in the *Brighton Herald* on 8 April 1837 – three weeks before the *Diana* sailed – with minor editorial changes and the following introduction.

The Earl of Egremont*'s Emigration Committee are busily engaged in making preparations for dispatching their next ship which will sail from Portsmouth in about three weeks. Letters written in high spirits from parties who have gone out under the auspices of Lord Egremont continue almost daily to be received. Among those lately received is the following letter from John Barnes, who emigrated with his wife and family, under the management of the Committee, in 1836:

January 1st, 1837.

Dear Father, Brother, and Sisters,

It is with pleasure I now take my pen in hand to write a few more lines to you, in hopes they will find you all in good health, as thank God it leaves all of us at present. I was quite unwell soon after I wrote to you before for three or four weeks, but I did not leave my work but one week. I kept on till I was obliged to give it up, but the surgeons soon picked me up again. I hope you received my first letter. I am still at the city of Toronto, Upper Canada, and there I shall remain for the present; for I have been doing well since I have been here, and I don't like to leave when I am doing well. I have received another letter from our brothers in States, and they wish me to come on to them as soon as I could, but I cannot go at present; they said they would come to Erie to meet me, which would be 130 miles, all land carriage. I have as much as 300 miles to go to them from where I am, which would cost me £10; but that don't stop me from going, for I have got the money to go with, thanks be to God for it.

I have been working for the same gentleman, as I told you before. I have done working at my own trade about a month, as the frost was too sharp for us; but I have got some more work to do for him in the spring. When I left off work, I had the amount of 147 dollars to take of him; so I drew 40 dollars, which was £10, and the rest I left in his hands, as I do not want it at present; and I am in hopes I shall not want it this winter. I am living in his great house, and the gentleman is living there himself; so we are his servants; so I hope, dear Father, brothers, and sisters, that you will feel happy about me and my family; for we are all very happy. I hope you are all as happy as we are. Henry is at school for this winter, but he did not much like going; he wished to go to service, as he could get 4 dollars a month: that made him very eager to go to service, but I thought that going to school would be the best service for him this winter; as he wants to go apprentice to a carpenter and joiner in the spring, if I can get a place for him. Emma might be at service if we could have let her gone, but we want her at home, for a waiting maid for the gentleman. It is a good place for children, for they may have plenty of places when they get the age of Henry and Emma; they may have a place almost any day.[1]

Henry. – Dear grandfather, I often thinks how I should like to see you, but you see my father is a going to tie me up in the spring if he can get a place for me, and then I must * * *. If please God I shall live to serve my time, and you are all living, I mean to come and see you all once more, which I hope you will.

Dear brother Benjamin, I must tell you that your trade is very good here, of all that I can hear of it; but I am in hopes that you are like to do well in the situation that you was a going in when I left home, and if you are like to do well you will remain where you are for the present, and stop at home with your father. I shall see what turns up here after a bit. I am in hopes I shall see all of you again after a little bit, if it please God all is well with [us]. My dear brother Robert, I think that your

---

1 About 14 and 11, respectively, at the time they emigrated; the other two were much younger.

trade is good here, for I have seen in the windows, as I have walked down the streets, papers for want of hands; not as I think that you will come, only I just mention this to you.

Dear brother Henry and sister, I am now going to tell you what chance I think I have got for you, if you like to come out next spring. A few weeks ago the gentleman I am with asked me if I had any of my friends that was likely to come out to me. I told him that I had a brother and sister I thought would likely come to me if they could get a good living for their family. I told him that I had not wrote to tell you much about it at present, but I must write to you soon. Then he asked me what account I should give you of the country. I told him that I must say that there was a great deal better chance here than at home, for them that was industrious and kept themselves sober. Then he said that I was correct; but it was the case of nine out of ten that gave up to drinking. But I told him that I was not afraid of you about that.

I told him that you was not of any trade, that you was always brought up to farming work. Then he said, I have a farm up the country you know, and if I could light with an industrious man I should let him go on my farm in part with me for a certain number of years. Then I said, that was very good. So my dear brother and sister, I think here is a good chance for you if you think that you should like to come to me. I hope you will please yourself about coming, I do not wish you to come, none the more for the sake of me: but if you do come, I should be very glad to meet you, and will do the best I can for you, in regard of helping you, if you should want any. If you should come, and go on the farm, you might want a little help first going on it.

And if you should come, mind you do not buy so much clothes as I did. If I was coming again I would not buy half so much as I did this time, for clothes is not so much dearer as you might expect, but mind and bring your beds as I did. Let any one say what they will about it, you will come to me free of expence: for the city of Toronto is the place where the superintendant, that goes out of Portsmouth with you, will take you to; and I should be sure to know when you come into harbour, and I will be at the wharf as soon as you are landed, so you may not be afraid that I should not meet you, and if you should come, look up all the old halfpence you can, for they will be as much to you as a new penny is, before you gets up to me: and with us an old halfpenny is as much as a new one, but a penny piece goes with us as with you, for two halfpence. I would be much obliged to you to bring John two blue caps, such as we bought for him at Mr. Halliday's shop; we paid 1s. 6d. for his cap, and with me they are as much as a dollar or more, as I am informed; not as we have bought them. I hope you will make up your mind as quickly as possible, for I longs to hear from all of you, and the sooner the better, for then I shall know what to do. As soon as I know whether you will come or not, and if you should come, I shall have some more talk with the gentleman, as soon as I knows whether you will or not.

I hope, my dear friends, that some of you will be so kind as to take this letter to

[Wisborough] Green, or send for our dear mother to come to your house, so as she might hear from us. Dear mother, I am happy to tell you, that we have been doing so well since we have been in America; and we hope that these few lines will find you all in good health, as thanks be to God it leaves all of us at present. We have had a good bit of snow here, and some frost, it has been very sharp for some time, more so than ever I knew at home. But when frost and snow comes, we wish for it to lay, because it makes good sleighing, that is, the carriages and carts goes without wheels: they slide along: they are drawn by horses, and goes very swift.

We have a large market here every day, except Sundays, when any kind of pro-visioning is brought in. Hogs are brought in by the waggons, and all ready drest. I bought one. They sell now at about seven dollars a hundred weight. Flour is selling at seven dollars a barrel: I thinks they hold as much as four bushels, for I find that it last my family as much as six or seven weeks. Potatoes have been selling at 4s. a bushel, all the winter; so I do not buy many of them. Hay is selling at seven and eight dollars a ton: I bought a load last week for seven dollars: and oats for 1s. 8d. per bushel. I bought some of both, for the gentleman that I am now living with. I do not justly know what peas and barley is selling at, for I did not think to inquire when I was in the market last.

Dear brother Henry, I am going to ask you, or brother Benjamin, if one or both of you will be so kind as to walk over as far as Bury Common, to Samuel Gurr, and to Mrs. Green, so as they might hear from us: they wished me to write to them, but I think this will be as well, for any letter I put in the post costs me 2s. James Green, I am going to tell you that I wish you had been able to come out with me, and if I had known so much then, as I have known since, you should have come when I did: but try and come out this next spring, if you can any how raise the money to pay your passage. If you cannot raise the money yourself, if you know any one that is a coming, and that will help you a little in paying your passage, I will pay them again as soon as you gets to me; you and I could make it right again after a little while, for it is expected that trade will be very brisk in the spring; and if it should, wages will be very good. A dollar and a half have been the regular wages a day, since I have been here. And if Henry Long and you should come, I hope you will assist one another as well as you can. You will find things more convenient aboard ship, than what you might expect. We said that time would seem so long, but I think that it was the shortest that ever I knew, for I scarce know how the time past away, whilst I was aboard the ship Heber.

James, we give our best respects to your mother, your brothers, and sisters, and to George Smith, and to Mr. and Mrs. Gurr, and their family; and tell them that we are very happy in the new country, but we often say we should like to see them. Ellen is quite well, and we are in hopes that Mary Ann is the same. Emma sends her kind love to your sister Ann. James, you may tell Mr. Hills, at Bury Mill, that I have not repented of coming to America yet, he will know what you mean. And give my best respects to Thomas Bridger, and his wife; and to James Shepherd, and his wife; and to Thomas Smith, farmer, as you call him; and all enquiring friends. James, you will send me word, when my brother writes to me, whether you think of coming or not.

Dear brothers, you will be so kind as to take both of my letters with you, so as they might hear them both read. There is not ever a round frock worn in the city: but you may wear what you please in the country. If they see any one with a long frock, they says, there goes an Englishman, with his shirt over his clothes. Shoes and hats are a good bit dearer here than they are with you. Give our best respects to Henry Hunt, and to John Quelch, and his family, and to all enquiring friends. If any of you comes, you must expect that there will be a little trouble through your voyage, wherever there is a family of children; but if you means coming, you must not mind that, it do not last for ever. I do not mean to say that every one have the luck as I had.

I was very fortunate, first coming into a strange country. There was no more of my trade that went out with us, which there was 266 of us aboard. We had two children born in our voyage. We had a good voyage over the seas: we were from the 27th of April to the 24th of May out of sight of land. We had a good bit of snow on the 25th May, had snow-balling on deck. It was in the evening when we came to Montreal. It was to our sorrow, there was a large slip happened in the new river [Rideau Canal], which caused us to go up the river of St. Lawrence, which you would be surprised to see how strong the water run; in some places we were drawn by three or four horses, some places by three or four pair of oxen; if we had not, we should not have got up at all. We had a man of the name of Randall, from Dunsfold,[2] I think that he was got tired of the river of St. Lawrence, for he fell, or jumped overboard, and was lost. It was thought by many that it was his intent to do it; it happened on the 16th June, one night, as we laid to. I could tell you a good bit more about our voyage, but I have not room, so I must let it pass.

I hope you will not delay in writing to me as quick as possible. Direct to me, John Barnes, City of Toronto, Upper Canada, North America, to be left at the Rev. Mr. Mathews' house at the College.[3] By the way of New York.

Now to you, dear father, brothers and sisters, I must conclude my letter with bidding you all farewell. Me, my wife, and children, send our kind love to you all, and to all enquiring friends.

I am your obedient son,
John Barnes.

OTHER LETTERS: 116
We do not know if Barnes ever did go to the United States or if he succeeded in persuading family members to join him in Upper Canada.

2 Abraham Randall emigrated from Dunsfold, Surrey, with his wife, Sarah, and three children Shadrack, Abraham, and Sarah. Three sons, Isaac, Jacob, and Mesheck, emigrated in 1833.
3 Upper Canada College

■ 127

ANN MANN, ADELAIDE TOWNSHIP, UPPER CANADA, TO HER SONS,
HENRY AND GEORGE MANN, AND FRIENDS, [WISBOROUGH GREEN,
WEST SUSSEX,] 2 JANUARY 1837

Ann (Downer) Mann and her husband, Samuel Mann,[4] emigrated in 1836 from Wisborough
Green with their four youngest sons, Mark, Eli, Moses, and Edwin; Noah, their eldest son,
accompanied them, along with his wife, Elizabeth, and their six children. Ann and Samuel's
son Charles had emigrated with the Petworth Committee in 1832, followed by Samuel Jr,
Thomas, and John in 1835. The application from the Parish of Wisborough Green to the poor
law commissioners described John as an agricultural labourer who had been in service: "no
relief until now."

Samuel and Ann were both in their mid 50s when they sailed on the *Heber*, and Samuel,
who must have passed his prime as a labourer, had been depending on the parish to employ
him. Noah Mann, with his six children, must also have been well known to the parish officers of Wisborough Green. He and Elizabeth (Sherwin) were married in Rudgwick in July
1826, removed to Wisborough Green as paupers a month later, and their first child, Noah,
was baptized there in November. Still in 1826, the parish was after Noah about child main-
tenance. In 1835, the year before he emigrated, Noah had been given relief and had been
employed by the parish "occasionally" on the highways.[5]

Ann wrote this letter to two of her adult sons who had remained in England. After Samuel
Sr died at Montreal, the family travelled on with the Petworth superintendent to Toronto
and took advantage of the willingness of the Upper Canadian government to transport them
as far as Brantford. From Brantford, they must have paid their own way to the Adelaide settlement. Edwin, who was still with his mother at the time of writing, was 10 in 1837; Moses
was out at work at 13 years of age.

SOURCE: Copy of letter which came to light through the good offices of Mrs Kemp and Constance
Bayley of Loxwood, June Moffatt of Broadbridge Heath, and the Misses Mann of Billingshurst, West
Sussex; copy in WSRO, MP 4137.

Dear Sons and Friends,
I am ashamed that I have not wrote before but I write with my kind love to you
all and I hope it will find you all in good health; as it leaves me at present, and all
your brethren are in good health and I thank god for it. Dear friends I beg to be
excused for not writing to you before; I could not for I have had a great deal of
trouble since I left England, my dear friend; I lost my dear husband at Montreall,
with a bad complaint in his bowels, and my dear children it made a very hard case
for me; but thank god I am in better health than I have been for these last two years,
dear children. Be not grieved about me, for Thomas [her son] makes me and Edwin

4 Both Ann and Samuel signed the marriage register with a mark.
5 Noah and Elizabeth's children were Noah Jr, Ambrose, Meshec, Shadrac, Hannah, and Ellen, ranging in age in 1836 from ten to the infant Ellen.

a good home; he have bought fifty acres of land in Adelaide belonging to Thomas Holden, Mrs Hawkins brother; we are living with Mr Holden till Thomas can build a house.

Dear children I don't want for nothing; my children are all out at service; I could get them places if I had twenty more. Moses lives in Oxford & is bound till he is twenty years old; Eli lives in North street; Noah and Samuel in North street, John and Mark in London, Charles in London, twenty miles to Charles, twenty three to John, twenty one miles to Mark, sixty miles to Moses, thirty three miles to North street; now my dear sons I wish you and your little children was here; they would be better off here than you are in old England. Here is a good living to be got with working for; but they don't work harder here than you do; they don't mind being still a week. I am two miles from sister Napper;[6] they are all well and gives their kind love to all of you; to James [illegible] brother Napper is getting a good living, he has got a yoke of oxen, three cows, two calves and one horse.

If any of you should come in the spring I should be very happy to see you again; but I shall not persuade you to come for you must expect to find trouble in coming over; don't take a great many things with you for it is a great expence to get up the country with it, bring your pothooks and all your fire irons & cooking vessell. Don't bring any axes, don't bring many tools for you will not want them; bring some rubbers to sharp sythes with; bring all your bedding and plenty of clothes; clothes is very dear in Adelaide because it so far in the country.

I wish you was here and all my sisters and brothers; sister Belchamber,[7] if any of your children should wish to come to America, do not hinder them; for I will say this is a good country to come to; I wish I had come when my first son came; but thank god I am here. What would have become of my children if they had been in England and I had been put into some poorhouse; but now if I go out at the door I do see great comfort; I can say I am as happy and as comfortable as ever I was in all my life; my love to all my friends and relations in Wisborough Green, Loxwood and to all in different places; to Mrs Foster and Mrs Bonsey I wish I could see them here; I would make them as good a cup of tea as ever they drank in their life; I drink as much tea in one week as I drank in a month when I was England; my duty to Mr and Mrs Jenkins, I wish I could see them both here; and tell them to send Mr Taylor here for we want preachers in Adelaide; we have some good friendly neighbours near us; my duty to Mr Parsons, Mr Puttock, Mrs Feilder, Wm Fielder, Mr Knight and to all the rest.

Let my letter be copied off and be stuck up at the Onslows Arms[8] to let every one see that I lives in Adelaide; don't leave no one thing out that I say. Please to send this

6 Avis, Ann's sister, and James Napper emigrated from Pulborough in 1832 with their sons Charles, George, William, and their oldest son, John Downer. John was sponsored by the parish of Kirdford, where he had been born as the illegitimate son of Avis, with James Napper named as his father.
7 Jane Downer married James Belchamber in Kirdford on 24 May 1804.
8 The Onslow Arms, an inn by the Wey and Arun canal at Loxwood.

The "poorhouse" feared by Ann Mann: the Easebourne Workhouse at Midhurst
Photograph: Patrick Burrows

letter to George and Henry. I left you in a great deal of trouble, I often think of that little boy;[9] please to answer this letter as soon as you can for I long to hear from you; dear friends if I send you all I have seen and experienced I should want [another] large sheet of paper as [this.] Noah lost his youngest child [Ellen] at Brandford [Brantford]; we staid there five weeks; it was very expensive going up the country; if we did know when any of you was coming some one [could go] to meet you. Mr [Holden] gives his kind love to Mr Hawkins at Roundstreet Common;[10] they are all well and getting good living; Ruth [Holden] keeps his house at present;[11] send me all the news you can for I long to hear from you; your Aunt Belchamber will write for you; when you get here your trouble will be over; getting over is the most trouble. I wrote to Mr [Botting];I hope he will send it to you, so I must conclude; so no more at present; from your dear loving Mother Ann Mann, also your brother Thomas conclude with me.

Direct to Thomas Mann at Mr Holdens
Adelaide 4th Concession Lot 19 North side Road
Please to send by New York
Please to pick it out as well as you can, for I have made many Baffles. January 2nd 1837.

I should like to know whether you receive the wine that I have left behind.

9 Henry Mann's wife, Lucy, had died in 1835 aged 28, leaving four children, the eldest of whom, George, died in August 1836, aged 9.
10 Half way between Wisborough Green and Loxwood.
11 Thomas Holden's third daughter, aged about 18. Mary, the eldest, wrote 47.

Five of Ann Mann's sons in Canada: from left to right, Mark, Thomas, John, Charles, Eli
Courtesy Margaret Parsons

Ann married Thomas Holden on 20 February 1837 and her son Thomas married Ruth Holden in May 1837. Ann died 9 November 1845, leaving an extensive family of children and grandchildren. Thomas Mann, his wife, Ruth, and their children were still in this part of the Adelaide settlement at mid-century, as were Mark and Sophia (Rapley) Mann and their children. The census-taker for 1851 reported Thomas Mann, James Holden, and Moses Holden all farming portions of the E ½ lot 19 concession 4 SER Adelaide Township.

Charles Mann, who had married Sarah Janes in London, Upper Canada, in 1833, was in Delaware Township in 1837. In November he sold his interest in the lot located to him on concession 4 Adelaide to Frederick Hasted (see letters 174 and 175) for $4 cash and a musket valued at $6. This was the lot Hasted later sold to James Parker Sr (see also letter 51 from Stephen Goatcher)

Ann's two sons to whom this letter was addressed emigrated through New York some time after 1836. Henry settled in New York State and George in Michigan.

■ 128

WILLIAM COURTNAGE, NIAGARA DISTRICT, UPPER CANADA, TO HIS
BROTHER AND SISTERS, 10 JANUARY 1837
William and Ann (Madgwick) Courtnage,[12] both of whom were weavers, emigrated from
the parish of Fernhurst, West Sussex, in 1832 with two young children, Hannah and James.

SOURCE: *Continuation of Letters from Sussex Emigrants* (1837), 6–7

January 10th. 1837.

Dear Brother and Sisters,

This comes with our kind love to you, hoping it will find you in good health, as it leaves us at present. We received your kind letter the 22nd December last, and was very glad to hear from you, but I was sorry to hear of the death of my mother. I thought it very strange that I did not hear from you before. We are very glad to hear that you talk of coming to our country, for I think you cannot do a better thing, for I think you can do a great deal better here, than you can at home, by your talk. You can get land for about 10s. of your money an acre, in a pretty good settlement, and as good land as ever need to be, but you can get it cheaper by going back further in the woods. They will give you, some five years, some ten years to pay the money in, by paying down one part out of ten, as you can get land almost on any terms. As for myself, I am living and Edward Berry, on each of us 50 acres at present. We rent it. We have been talking a good many times of going further up the country to buy us some land, but if you are coming, we will wait till you comes, if you comes in the spring, and go altogether.

I have got along pretty well since I have been here. I have got two cows, and a waggon. I have not got my team at present, I sold them, but I shall get a team in the spring, if I have luck. I have bought a loom, for we follow weaving flannel, for most people have their own cloth wove here. We make our own soap, and candles, and sugar, some springs; but we have not many sugar trees here, but there is plenty further up

---

12 Both William and Ann signed the marriage register with a mark.

the country. Some people makes a large quantity of sugar; some makes a thousand pounds in a spring; them that a good many trees, some more and some less.

This is Mrs. Pannell's hand of writing at the bottom, you might let her see it.

(Pannell, Haslemere.)[13]

You wanted to know the prices of things here, I will tell you the truth as near as I can. Flour is higher now than it has been for 20 years, for the spring was so wet, that it drowned our crops a good deal. Flour is 8 shillings of your money a bushel, but our common price has been 3s.6d. to 4s. a bushel, and fine fat hogs about £1.12s. a hundred weight this season; but other seasons about 1 pound a hundred. Beef, about 1½d, to 3d. lb.; butter in the winter, 9d.; sugar, 6d. or 7d.; tea for 2s.6d.; good green tea for 3s.; tobacco, 6d.; clothing, about the same as it was when we left England: good boots, 14s. per pair; shoes, 7s.; women's boots, 10s. per pair. Strong beer, about 10d. per gallon; strong cider, 8½d.; whisky, 6d. per quart. You can get a good cow for £3. or £3.10s. of your money. A yoke of oxen you can get from £12. to £16. We get 2s. per day for farmer's work, and our board; grass mowing, 3s. and board; harvesting, 4s. and board.

James Enticknap wanted to know how blacksmithing trade was here. Work is different here of what it was in England; but we soon get into the way of it. I think he would do well here, for blacksmiths earn great wages here; it is as good a trade as any here, you may depend; we would be happy to see him here, and his wife, and family, for I know he would do well here. Dear sisters, and brothers, I hope I shall have the happiness of seeing you all here next summer. If my father will come with you, I will take care of him as long as he lives, and I live, and my brother George.

Dear sisters, and brothers, if you comes, bring as little as you can do with, for you can get any thing here, as cheap as you can there for money, you had better bring the money. Dear brother Randall, you say your family is all girls: here is plenty of work for girls. I think you had better come, for I think your girls might get married to the young farmers: for they have plenty of property here. If you come, you had better bring a little brandy, and a few dried herrings, and a piece of cheese, and bake a little bread very hard, and some plumcakes, for fear you should be sea sick, if you are found. I and my wife were not sea sick but a very little, but my children were not sea sick at all. You had better put your things into strong boxes, well bound up. You had better bring a good gun, a flint lock gun or a rifle, if you can get one; for here is plenty of game here. Deer and pheasants, turkeys, rabbits in some places. If you come, bring me a horn lanthorn,[14] for I have not seen any in this country; bring two hay cutting knives, one for me and one for Edward Berry. If you come, you had better come to St. Catharine's, in the township of Grantham, and enquire

13 Original annotation: "This was written at the bottom of the sheet of letter paper which had been taken out by the emigrant."
14 Lantern

for the Griggey's, and they will tell you where I lives, in the district of Niagara, U.C. I hope you will take good courage and come.

Give my love to all enquiring friends. All I forget to tell you now, I will tell you when you comes. So no more at present from WILLIAM COURTNAGE.

OTHER LETTERS: 129

■ **129**

ANN COURTNAGE, NIAGARA DISTRICT, UPPER CANADA, TO JOHN RANDALL, FARNHURST, WEST SUSSEX, [10 JANUARY 1837]

SOURCE: Continuation of Letters from Sussex Emigrants (1837), 8

Dear Brother and Sisters,

I have the opportunity of writing to you, hoping it will find you all in good health, as it leaves us at present. I hope you will not think it too much trouble to take this to my father,[15] to let them know how we are getting on. I think it very unkind that they have not sent no letter, I wish them to send a letter by you, to let us know how him and his wife, and sisters, and brothers are. I am sorry to hear that they has so much sickness, I am feared that they have a great deal of trouble to get a shilling, as we hear the times are so bad. I wish you to send word who my sister Hannah is married to, and where she lives. I want to know all the particulars about them, and whether they thinks of coming to this country.

I have four children. Hannah is grown a great girl; James grows much like his grandfather; they sends their love to you all. John and Mary Ann are young yet. Give my love to my grandfather Deadman, and to all. I was very glad to hear you was all well. If any of you should come, I wish you to bring 2 or 3 pair of black stockings, and a fur cap for William, they are very dear here. The climate is a little colder in the winter, and hotter in the summer, but healthy. I should be glad to see you all in this country. I send my love to all enquiring friends. I must conclude for want of paper. So no more from your loving daughter and son,

ANN & WILLIAM COURTNAGE.

So good bye. If you comes, you had better wear the worst clothes you have got, on board ship. We have plenty of fire wood in this country for cutting. I hope you remember me and Edward Berry to my old friend William Enticknap. So we wish you a happy new year,

WILLIAM COURTNAGE.

MR. JESSE MORLEY,
    Farnhurst, Sussex.

OTHER LETTERS: 128

15 James Madgwick

Three more children, Thomas, Susan, and Maria, were born to Ann and William in Upper Canada, in addition to the John and Mary Ann who were mentioned in the letter. They had a farm in Louth Township, near Rockway Centre, but Ann, at least, continued as a weaver. William died in 1851 and Ann in 1891.

■ **130**

AUTHOR UNKNOWN, TORONTO, UPPER CANADA, 25 OCTOBER 1837

Unlike other letters in this collection, this letter was published to warn against emigration. The editor of the *Brighton Patriot* was influenced by William Cobbett*, the radical politician and poor man's advocate, and reflected Cobbett's dislike of assisted emigration. The editor did not, however, have any obvious personal stake in this particular controversy, and he readily published the material Sockett* sent to refute these anonymous allegations against James Marr Brydone*, the superintendent of the *Diana*. We have been unable to discover anything about the writer of this letter, which was introduced in the *Patriot* of 28 November 1837 as given below.

SOURCE: *Brighton Patriot*, 28 November 1837

We have been favoured with the sight of a letter dated Toronto, October 25 1837, which speaks of some abuses, – and very gross ones too – which are perpetrated by parties connected with the Petworth Emigration Committee; and we take this opportunity of calling the attention of the parties concerned to the facts. It is due also to the public that they should be put upon their guard against any delusive prospects which may be held out as inducements to emigrate – prospects which it is almost certain will never be realised, but in their place come disappointment and misery. The letter before us, which we have read attentively, is written in a frank, feeling, and towards the writer's parents and friends, affectionate style, and we place the more implicit reliance on the emigrant's narrative and assertions notwithstanding his petulant and disrespectful mention of a reverend gentleman resident in Petworth,[16] caused, doubtless, by the total absence of all those comforts on board the vessel, – and that in a time of sickness, – which he was told would be provided by the Committee. We now give the extract:–

I will now tell you a little about the country. No one would come here if they knew how things are; here the labourer has to work a great deal harder than in England, and after all cannot get his money. This has happened with several poor fellows who came out in the same ship with me. Under this infernal Committee the labourer gets 3s9d a day when employed, which is [3s] of our money; and even then he cannot get half employment. If the people knew what poor emigrants have to go through, there would not be many come to Canada. Though, thank God, I have known none, yet I have seen plenty of their miseries. I should have been a middling good sailor, but I was laid up nearly three weeks with a fever, and all the nourishment I could get was the salt pork and beef, and half a pint of porter every other day; and the rascal (of a superintendent[17]) would make game of the people that were

16 Thomas Sockett*
17 James Brydone

ill and say it was idleness. He stopped my porter, as well as that of several poor women that were suckling, and there was nothing served out for the poor little babes, because he said the porter would not last out; and at the same time, when we got to Quebec the steward bottled off several dozen for the use of the cabin passengers.

The book that old S—— gave me was full of lies. There were no preserved meats on board; if there were, he (the superintendent) eat them himself, for I never saw any. When I was so bad that I could not taste anything for three days, I asked the steward to sell me a bottle of port wine, but he told me that he did not dare, and was obliged to go without any, though there was plenty for him (the superintendent) on board. In fact, instead of being treated like respectable passengers we were treated like convicts.[18] His (the superintendent) conduct enraged the men that were sent out by the parish to such a degree – and some of them were the greatest blackguards on earth – that they kept the ship in a state of mutiny all the way over; and we that paid higher than we should have paid had we taken our passage on board a London or Liverpool line ship for superior comforts, as S—— told me we were to have, were insulted and robbed by this villain of a superintendent. The first day we had meat served out, he requested me to assist him which I did, in weighing it up, and instead of a pound each, as their book stated, there was only 5 lbs. between eight of us, two of which was bone.[19] We had soft bread on board, but he (the superintendent) kept it till it got mouldy before he served it out. The scoundrel got drunk on board of the steamer and got fighting with a Paddy, who blacked his eye for him. When he went on shore he got drunk, and kicked a poor friendless boy, who came out with us for which he was taken up and fined £2 and costs, very much to our satisfaction. But I must leave him ...

Sockett was quick to come to the defence of his friend and the integrity of his emigration scheme. The editor of the *Brighton Patriot* returned to the subject on 12 December 1837, referring to the letter published on 28 November and describing the writer as a native of Brighton:

In that letter the writer made charges against the superintendent (Mr Brydone) of so serious a nature, that if true, prove the latter to be a very improper person to be entrusted with the care & well being of any human creature; but if false no consideration of distance should be allowed to stand between the former and justice. With regard to the refusal of a bottle of port wine, during illness, in a place where so many persons of various habits & dispositions are accumulated, discipline, and that of a severe nature, must be observed; but when the writer charges the superintendent with getting drunk & fighting with an Irishman, and asserts that when on shore kicked a poor friendless boy & was fined 2*l.* [£2] by the authorities for his brutality why here are charges about which there can be

---

18 Brydone did take a party of convicts to Australia in 1819 as superintendent of the *Eliza*.
19 The writer's quarrel with Brydone may have begun with a decision by Brydone not to continue him in the privileged position of steward.

no mistake, and either the writer has asserted a foul calumny or he has told the truth. If he has done the first, we hope he will meet his reward.

Gentlemen of the Petworth Emigration Committee have communicated with us, who say that there is no truth whatever in his statements, and we have received the following letters, as contradictory of the allegations put forth. The first is from a young woman [Frances Pullen, 131] who went out in the same vessel as the writer of the letter from which we made the extract, and who lost a child during the voyage, and who, it is concluded might on that account be excused had she uttered complaints, but who on the other hand, expressed herself satisfied with the assistance and comforts she met with on board the vessel; the second (which was addressed to the Rev. Mr Sockett) is from the Master of the vessel (the Diana) and which speaks of Mr Brydone in high terms."

Edward Lane, the master of the *Diana*, had written to Sockett on 9 September 1837 announcing a safe arrival back in England. He described "a very pleasant passage out, barring the misbehaviour of some young men from the Isle of Wight."[20] He perhaps expected that Sockett might hear complaints as he praised Brydone for his assistance in maintaining discipline and singled out "his [Brydone's] impartial behaviour to the passengers throughout in the issue of provisions." In Lane's opinion Brydone "gained the respect of the elder and more sensible part of the passengers."

In 1837, tensions between the people from Sussex and the large group from the Isle of Wight seem to have added to the usual problems arising in the confined quarters of an emigrant ship. Despite Lane's testimony, Brydone's remarks on the passengers indicate at least a private preference for those from Sussex.

■ 131

RICHARD AND FRANCES PULLEN TO SISTER AND BROTHER [ANN AND JOHN SUMMERSELL, PETWORTH, WEST SUSSEX], 9 SEPTEMBER 1837

Richard Pullen, a farm labourer, and Frances (Holden) Pullen[21] emigrated from Colehook Common, Northchapel, in 1837, with their seven children, Ann, Sarah, William, Hannah, Henry, Richard, and Elizabeth. Brydone* described this family from Northchapel as "very respectable." Pullen had had occasional assistance from the parish, such as 2s.6d. in 1830 when he was "going to seek for mowing." In 1836, the year before he emigrated, he had had 11s.5d. in parish relief.

As noted by the editor of the *Brighton Patriot*, Sockett* sent this letter to the paper as a rebuttal of the allegations made by the anonymous writer of 130.

---

20 There were 37 men and 17 boys among a party of 78 emigrants from the Isle of Wight; most of these were sent by the House of Industry. Lane's letter appeared in the *Brighton Patriot*, 12 December 1837.

21 Both Richard and Frances signed the marriage register with a mark.

SOURCE: *Brighton Patriot*, 12 December 1837. See letter 130 for the introduction given by the editors of the *Patriot*.

Dear sister & brother – this comes with my kind love to you all in hopes that it will find you all well, as thank God, it leaves me at present – all that are spared; but I am sorry to inform you of the death of my dear Ann,[22] who departed this life on the 20th of May after one week's illness. We had two doctors on board, and they both told me that the complaint was an inflammation on the brain, which I think it was, for she was never very sensible after she was taken ill; but, poor dear, she never wanted for attendance. We all know my dear friends, that the Lord's will must be done, she was the first that the Lord gave me, and she was the first that he took from me.

My dear friends we arrived at Toronto on the 1st of July and we reached our journey's end the 5th of July after a great deal of trouble and misery. For myself, I never knew one well day from the time I left home till I got here, and we were all very sea-sick for some time. Poor Ann was very sick, but she got well and went upon deck to play, til she was taken all at once with a pain in her head. We had a terrible fright on the sea one evening by a craft of timber running against the ship; but the Lord was merciful and no-one was hurt.

This is a very inconvenient place, for we are fifteen miles from a store. I thought myself bad off when I was at home, but we have been worse since a great deal; but it was not for want of money. But we could not get anything, and the provisions were very dear, flour was fifteen dollars a barrel, and a barrel is three bushels and a half. But we received our money, as we were promised, when we got to Toronto, and, thank God, we have had a very fine harvest, and the flour is fell to eight dollars a barrel; and I think now that we shall do pretty well, if it pleases God to send us our health. Richard did not do any work till the 7th of August, he now comes home to every meal, for we live close to where the gentleman lives, and have a nice house to live in. We have sixteen dollars a month and no rent to pay, and with plenty of wood to burn. [no signature, n.d.]

OTHER LETTERS: 136, 137

Although family history has it that three of Richard's sisters emigrated with him, we do not think that they came at the same time. They may have emigrated at a later date.

Frances's next letter, 136, found her upset by the Rebellion and missing her family, but beginning to sound more settled in her new home. Two letters from the Summersell and Holden families in England to Richard and Frances are 132, and 139.

---

22 Their eldest child, she was baptized in November 1825 and so was probably 11½ when she died.

1838

AND LATER

Emigration to Canada.

From James Lanaway, who emigrated with his wife and family from Petworth, Sussex, in the year 1838.

Woodstock, September 24th. 1840.

I have taken the liberty of writing you these few lines, to let you know that I am in good health at present, hoping this will find you, and all my acquaintances, the same. I have wrote two letters, one to Mrs. Thorp, and another to Mrs. Luff, to both of which I have not received any answer, of which I hope you will not forget to write me an answer to this, and let me know the state of the country, and how are all my old acquaintance, since I left England. I must now tell you, that we are doing well : there is plenty of work in this country, the wages for a labourer is 3s. sterling per day. Provisions are cheap, flour is 10s. per cwt., pork is 3d. per pound, tea is 3s. 6d. per pound. I have also to tell you, that we have five acres of land, and two cows, with a good comfortable house : we have 50 bushels of oats, and a sufficient quantity of potatoes, with other vegetables. I have to mention to you, that vegetables grow here the same as they do in England. I have also to tell you, that the children are all well, Joseph, Rachel, Leah, Sarah, and Lucy we have had in this country. The oldest of the children is often talking about you, Mrs. Hill, Mrs. Baxter, Mrs. Luff, Mrs. Smith, and Mrs. Thorp, and William. We send all of us our love to you all. You will be so good to let me know how James's brothers and sisters ; and James wants to know how is Joseph Richardson, and Mr. Edwards the coachmaker.

This is a good country for a poor man : he can get a good living, if he is industrious. I have also to mention to you, that the winter is a little colder, and the summer is a little warmer than in England. The winter commences in December, and ends in April. We commence making sugar in the month of March, and generally continues for about 5 weeks. I make my own yeast, and bake my own bread. I also make my own soap, which, if I should go back to England, I should be a little more used to, than when I came away. The children never had any sickness since we came to this country. I have also to mention to you, that you will remember us to Mr. and Mrs. King. I have also to mention to you, that all the emigrants that came here two years ago is doing very well. This is a good country, I like it very much, I would not go back to England on no account. I can earn with the needle from 10s. to 15s. per week. I have nothing more particular to mention to you at present, but our blessing to you all, and all enquiring friends.

JAMES and SARAH LANAWAY.

When you write, you will address James Lanaway, Woodstock, Brock District, Upper Canada.

To Mr. WILLIAM THORP, Pound Street, Petworth.

BACKGROUND

While people in Sussex absorbed the news of the rebellions in Lower and Upper Canada in late 1837, there was nothing much that Sockett* could do about emigration from Petworth. He remained as interested as ever in his people in Upper Canada. As news arrived in letters, he recorded vital statistics in a ledger, much as he did for his own parish, and a letter from Frances Pullen became the subject of a sermon at Petworth and of a collection for her church at Delaware.

George Wyndham,* the new owner of Petworth House, was always less committed to assisted emigration than his father Lord Egremont,* and more cost conscious, but he was at first very much influenced by Sockett, his former tutor. When government discussions of supporting assisted emigration from Ireland appeared to be going nowhere, in 1839 Wyndham agreed to sending a ship from Shannon for his tenants in counties Clare and Limerick. The experiment was a success from the point of view of the 181 people on the *Waterloo,* but their costs were very high as many emigrants had dropped out at the last minute. Wyndham did not charter another ship and his estate agent sent future emigrants from Ireland in the same manner as other landlords.

In a separate initiative, Wyndham bought land in South Australia with Sockett's help. This venture turned sour when Wyndham added up his outlay on an investment that showed no foreseeable return. In 1840, Brydone and Sockett were negotiating to buy land on his behalf in Upper Canada – 15,000 acres in Pilkington Township on the Grand River, not far from Guelph – land Sockett thought perfect for a revival of his plans for a "Sussex" settlement. Just when General Robert Pilkington's estate seemed ready to sell, Wyndham made a firm decision not to buy land in Canada.

The Petworth Emigration Committee continued in existence until about 1845, the year that committee member William Knight* died. However, in 1838 they sent only the family of James Lannaway. Their recruiting thereafter was limited to the Petworth area and the Sutton Gilbert Union (which continued in existence until 1869). According to Sockett, they sent mainly emigrants who asked to join family and friends already in Upper Canada, approximately 100 in all, with the largest number going in 1844, a hard year in Sussex. The emigrants sailed from London as individuals on Carter and Bonus ships. We know that some, such as the Lannaways, went to Woodstock to join other Petworth emigrants, and we suspect that others did the same, but these later emigrants were not part of our genealogical research and we have few letters from them.

UPPER CANADA

In the Canadas, the central political events of these years were the rebellions of late 1837 and the raids across the border from the United States in 1838. Although there were Petworth emigrants settled in all the areas where ferment was greatest in Upper Canada in 1837, our letters concerning the rebellions were written by settlers who lived in or near the Adelaide settlement and deal mainly with incursions across the border during the winter of 1837–8 by Canadians who had taken refuge in the United States and their American supporters. William Lyon Mackenzie led the first of these border raids. After a few weeks of stalemate, his small force was dislodged from Navy Island in the Niagara River in late December 1837 by the controversial burning of their supply ship, the *Caroline*, in American waters. This incident was followed by incursions at Windsor in January 1838, at Pelee Island in Lake Erie in late February–early March, at the Short Hills in the Niagara District in mid to late June, at Prescott in mid November (the Battle of the Windmill), and at Windsor again in early December 1838. These raids alarmed authorities for their potential to stir up trouble in the province. They occurred at widely different points on a very long border, always accompanied by the fear – or hope – that a temporary success might bring the local American-born population out in support of the rebels.

English papers gave the Canadian rebellions full play: Obediah Wilson's mother Maria probably spoke for many in England when she wrote of her heightened fears that she was waiting in vain for a letter because her son was dead (145). In Upper Canada, the Cooper family in the Adelaide settlement was probably quite typical of most of their Petworth emigrant neighbours in not knowing or caring much about the course of politics in Toronto before December 1837. In these letters, more than the briefest comment on the political situation of either Canada or England can be a sign of the social aspirations of people who saw themselves as something more than ordinary labourers. (Hasted [175] is an example, and, as a scribe for some of his neighbours, he may be responsible for urging them to write of these events in more detail.) The Coopers waited to send a letter until the end of May 1838 when they were satisfied they could write without giving undue alarm. When they did write, they detailed all their crops and every cat and chicken before getting around to William Cooper's two months' service with the militia. William got in touch with Petworth emigrants settled at Amherstberg, but he made no mention that any of them had seen active service, not even the ex-soldiers (133).

The man most responsible for the militia activity mentioned in these letters was Colonel Thomas Radcliff* of Adelaide, who raised his local unit very promptly. Nonetheless, James Cooper, who "happened to be out of the township at work at the time," and Richard Pullen of Delaware, who was not "forced" to go (136 written by his wife, Frances), stayed at home. William Cooper and Charles Rapley served until the Adelaide militia was discharged in February 1838. William Green, an ex-soldier for whom the Rebellion seems to an opportunity as welcome as it was to Radcliff, managed to extend his service until the summer of 1839, unfortunately without leaving an extant letter from this period.

In addition to describing events of the rebellion and its aftermath, letters such as those of John and Caroline Dearling and Charles Rapley show families who had been settled in Upper Canada for five or six years. As her parents had died, Caroline was having to establish a new connection with England through her brother and seemed anxious to do so.

This group of letters also includes letters in manuscript, and in the Pullen letters we can read both sides of a family correspondence – attempts to persuade family members to cross the ocean did not all originate in Canada. There is no way of knowing how many letters printed as extracts might originally have been as long as these letters in manuscript. As examples, however, manuscript letters give an idea of the kind of detail and the sort of comment that might be lost when a letter was reduced to an "extract" by an editor or newspaper columnist interested only in the facts of settlement.

■ 132

ELIZABETH (PULLEN) HOOKER AND ANN AND JOHN SUMMERSELL, PETWORTH, SUSSEX, TO RICHARD AND FRANCES PULLEN, DELAWARE, UPPER CANADA, 22 APRIL 1838

Elizabeth (Pullen) Hooker was the mother of Richard Pullen. On the same paper as her letter is one from Ann (Holden) Summersell and her husband, John Summersell; Ann was a sister of Richard's wife, Frances.

SOURCE: Thompson Family Papers[1]

Petworth, April 22, 1838.

My Dear Children,

I now write these few lines to you hopeing it will find you all in good health as it leaves me at present I thank the Lord. I am a great deal better than I was in the win-

---

[1] This letter, which we have seen in its original form or an early copy, had no punctuation and about half the words capitalized. It has been edited to add punctuation, to standardize the capitalization somewhat, and to correct the spelling in the interests of readability. The original is transcribed in Appendix A at page 405.

ter, for we had a very severe winter, more so than ever was known since the memory of man for it kild all the furs bushes[2] on the Commons and in the farmers' fields except on the south side of the hills, which I never remember seeing, the furs all dead. I hope that you have not had it colder in Canada. We was in hopes of having a letter from you before this time but as we have an opportunity of sending it by James Lanaway that was Lord Egremont*'s Cotchman [coachman]; he is coming to Blandford.[3]

His Lordship is dead and Colonel George[4] has got the estate. And your sister Martha [Pullen] is come down to the lodge in the Tilington Road to live where the poultry is kept. She has got a good house but Sarah's husband[5] have nothing to do. They have been in view of a place several times but it is all a blank and she have been very poorly, and the children have all had the hoping coff [whooping cough]. And poor little Charles died with it.[6] And the youngest has been very ill but she is a little better. And your brother William [Pullen] is very ill and has been for this 18 weeks with his old complaint, and I'm very much afraid he will never be no better. But we hope he will if it is the Lord's will. But he is a little better again now. And so he have been several times and then he gets worse, he just crawls out to the gate. Now but we must . . . the Lord's will be done . . . I hope and pray and believe that he is very serious. I bless the Lord he have a good hope beyond the grave. His wife and children are very well and I bless the Lord they do pretty well for a living; they have their club money and they have five loaves of bread and a half a crown from the youn[gest] . . . a week.

Your brothers Peter's wife have got another little one[7] and she is pretty well and all of them. Elizabeth will soon have another and they are all well. But Thomas's wife is not like to have any family at present; they was along here the 17th from Billingshurst. The[y] have got a piece of ground now at Midhurst had plenty of work[8]; they are both well but poor James has lost his Master and Mistress. They died both in one week with the Titus [typhoid] fever, but I bless the Lord he has escaped as yet and I hope he will. They have been busy these weeks But he have been in a great deal of trouble there was no one belonging to them Anear[9] that [so that almost] every thing layes on him. I had 5 letters from Sunday to the next Monday morning I have been up to him once and am going again. He is upon taking the business for he says he is quite master of the business and have done it for a great while and so people says about Guildford. I bless the Lord he have an excellent character and I hope and pray he will do well. It will be a good thing for him if he keeps himself steady

---

2 Furze or gorse, a prickly green evergreen shrub, gathered by the poor for fuel.

3 *See* letter 142 from Lannaway.

4 Colonel George Wyndham, the illegitimate eldest son of the 3rd Earl of Egremont

5 Charles Dilloway, alias Bridger, a gamekeeper

6 Buried 11 March 1838, aged five.

7 Peter's wife was Maria Budd. The little one, Harriet Pullen, was baptised 22 April 1838, the day the letter was written. The family lived at Lurgashall, West Sussex.

8 Thomas and Eliza Pullen ran a seed warehouse.

9 nearly, well-nigh, almost, to a nearness (*Oxford English Dictionary*)

and be paruent [prudent?] in business Serving God I hope he will not forget his duty to King and be thankful. He has got a little money of his own and I have found him a friend to lend him a little. Master Hooker is very well. He sends his well wishes to you, and Mrs Winter and her husband, and James Hooker and his family. I see old Jane Baker about a week since, poor old creature she was a planting of potatoes hop[p]ing about as usual.

All Colehook people are all well except William. I forgot to tell you young sister Sarah was got out in Colehook to live to that house where Master May died.[10]

I hope my dear children you received our letter as we sent to you and I hope it found you well and I hope we shall soon hear from you again. And I hope my dear grandchildren goes to school or learns to read and not only learns to read but to serve their Creator in the days of their youth. I long to know whether you have the Gospel preached there or not. But blessed be God you have the Bible, so my dear Children there is trouble and vexation of Spirit for us all. No doubt but you finds it in Canada for that is not our rest because it is perluted but we must look beyond the Grave unto that happy shore where I hope to meet to part no more. All your brothers and sisters join and all friends in love to you. We often talks of you when we meet. So now my dear children and grandchildren I commend you to God and to the [. . .]rde of His Grace. So no more from your loving Mother Elizabeth Hooker.

My dear sister and brother,

This comes with our kind love to you all in hopes it will find you all well and thank God it leaves us all at present, all that is spared. My dear sister I am sorry to inform you of the death of my dear baby who departed this life the 6 of March after six weeks illness. The poor little dear died with the hopping coff. She had several fits with it poor little dear but you know my dear sister and brother that the lord's will must be done, poor little dear; we hope she is at rest but we have had a great deal of trouble but I hope you all that is now liveing will try your best and get back to old England again for we do hear every week in the news paper from Canaday that there is bad going on with some[11] and I your brother John Summersell hope and wish that them that wish for you to go from Old England will be force to pay your passage back again for it have gave me a great deal of trouble to see your sister in so much trouble about you all. And I am sorry my self and it hurt us to hear our daughters Harriett and Ann talk about you all so much and I wish you all well, so no more from your brother John Summersell.

My dear sister, I now take my pen to write about all our dear relations and my dear children Harriett and Ann, both sends their aunt and uncle and all their cousins their kind love and the hopes and we all hopes we shall all meet in this world again. Our aunt Meriah and all her family sends their kind love to you all, and the[y] are

---

10 James Mah of Colhook Common, Northchapel, was buried 1837, aged 49. In 1834 he was paying a standard rent of £1.5s for a cottage and garden (WSRO, PAR 142/30/3).

11 The news of rebellion in Upper and Lower Canada in late 1837 had reached England.

all very well. Our cousins [missing][12] wife is near her confinement if she is [missing] with the second child. My dear sister [missing] not heard from Guildford since I wrote [missing] last I wrote to them but I have not recei[ved] [missing] answer from them. My husband's friend sends their kind respects to you all I saw [missing] danger [daughter?] two or three days ago; Master di[missing] been very ill all the winter but he is [missing] now; they both sends their respecks to [missing] I saw Misses [Holden] yesterday and she s[aid] all the people was all very well in the family except your poor brother William. Old Jane Baker is about the same she goes to [missing] d as she use to do when you lived there. Lord Egremont is dead and your brother John have drawn him to church; we had a very grand funeral; there was hundreds of people; your brother had a sut of close [a suit of clothes].[13] My dear sister, I have not been down in the commonds [Commons] since I wrote to you before. We have had a great deal of trouble all the winter. My dear children have had the hopping coff all the winter but thank God my dear little Ann is a great deal better. It pleased God to take my dear baby to himself, I hope and trust to a better world where I hope we shall all meet to part no more, I hope God will be with you all.

So now to conclude, we remain your loving sister and brother, Ann and John Summersell.

ADDRESS   Mr Robinson, Ekfrid
Delaware, London District[14]
Upper Canada
for Richard Pullen at Mr. Seabrook
Delaware U C

OTHER LETTERS: 131, 136, 137, 139

■ 133

JAMES COOPER, ADELAIDE TOWNSHIP, UPPER CANADA, TO FAMILY AND FRIENDS, c/o JAMES COOPER, GRAFFHAM, WEST SUSSEX, 26 MAY 1838

James Cooper and his wife, Harriet (Carter),[15] were gingerbread makers from Tillington when they emigrated in 1835 with Mary (James's 18-year-old daughter from a previous marriage),

12 A piece of the letter measuring 1 inch by 3 ½ inches, which probably contained a stamp, is missing.
13 It was indeed a grand funeral. Sixteen men drew the funeral car, which was "entirely covered with black velvet, and surmounted by two tiers of black plumes." The coffin was covered with purple velvet, "the handles etc with silver gilt." In addition to local dignitaries and the many members of Egremont's household in deepest mourning, there were 400 labourers in "white [smock] frocks, with black gloves, crape hatbands, and crape round their left arms" (*The Gentleman's Magazine*, January 1838).
14 The Ekfrid Post Office was established in 1837 (Morley Thomas, "Early Mail Service and Post Offices in Middlesex County, Ontario," *Families* 27, no.1 [1988]).
15 James and Harriet signed the marriage register with a mark.

a 14-year-old daughter, Harriett, and seven other children under the age of 12, James King, Emma, Henry, Caroline, Sarah, William, and George. In 1817 James had been removed as a pauper from Graffham to Tillington, his parish of settlement, but he must have returned as all but his two youngest of his children were baptized at Graffham. William Cooper, James's brother, had emigrated in 1832 (see letters 8, 52).

SOURCE: *Brighton Herald*, 25 August 1838; a copy of this letter, printed by J. Phillips, Petworth, is found in PRO, CO 384/S50, minus the *Herald's* heading "Emigration."

The following interesting letter has just been received from James Cooper, who emigrated to Upper Canada, in 1836, in the Heber, *having been sent out by the Petworth Emigration Committee.*

> Woodcut Farm, Lot 21, 4 Concession
> South, Adelaide, May 36th. [sic] 1838.

Dear Father and Mother, Brothers and Sisters, Friends, and Relations all.

We received your kind letter of the 10th of April, 1837, in answer to ours, and we have likewise since received the parcel with the seeds, for which we are obliged; but we did not find your letter sent with the seed, until we were going to sow the seed this spring.

[Dear Mother, you seemed to feel a little hurt that you did not receive a letter from me individually, I thought there was no occasion for that, as we were altogether, and are together now, and makes one letter do for us all. W[illiam] Cooper.[16]]

We now come to state, that we are all well, thank the Lord, and hope this will also find you all in good health and spirits, enjoying prosperity.

We found it pretty hard to get through the last summer, having had much of our provisions to buy, especially flour, which was very scarce and dear, from six to eight dollars per 100 lbs.; but thank the Lord we are better provided this year, having had plenty of grain for seed, for flour, and to fat our hogs, besides which we growed last year 200 bushels of potatoes, and 400 bushels of turnips and Swedes.

We have got in this year 4 acres of fall wheat, and one acre of spring wheat, four acres of rye, five acres of barley, one acre of peas, four acres of oats, and three acres of land ready to sow buckwheat, one acre for Indian corn, and are now burning off three acres more for turnips and potatoes, and we have six acres of grass land. We have now 19 head of horned cattle, one yoke of oxen, one yoke of steers three years old, one yoke of bulls two years old; we work them all to plough, harrow &c. four milch cows, and four calves, one barren cow turned off to fat, one three year old heifer we expect to calve in June, one two year old heifer, one yearling heifer, and one yearling bull, 17 hogs and pigs, 11 hens and 1 cock, 4 cats, and 2 dogs, one is part Newfoundland, a very good dog for cattle, hogs, or deer, the other is a bitch, a little touched of the terrier, very good for cattle or deer, but not very good for hogs.

---

16 Original annotation: "A brother of the writer, who emigrated to Upper Canada in 1832, in the Eveline, sent out by the Petworth Committee."

Our taxes for 1837 amounted to 4s. 3d. English, which is 8s. 6d. York, or 5s. 3¾d. currency of this country.

We think we did not tell you in our last, that we can make sugar, treacle or molasses, beer, cider, vinegar, and ink, from the sap of the maple tree. We made more than 200 lbs. of good sugar, twelve gallons of molasses, and about ten gallons of vinegar, last year. This year we made 374 lbs. of sugar, 30 gallons of molasses, and 30 gallons of vinegar. This season was not so good as the last, or we should have made more, having had more kettles.

We wrote a letter to send you on the 10th. day of December, last, at which time we were all quiet here; but before we put the letter in the post, the rebellion broke out, of which we suppose you have heard, so we would not send it until we saw how things went. All is quiet again now, and have been for some time. Our regiment of militia, the Middlesex light infantry, were called out to go to London, to suppress the rebellion, on the fourteenth day of December, and William went with them; but I happened to be out of the township at work at the time, so I escaped;[17] as every man is a militia-man in this country, from the age of 16 to 60. He was out about two months. London is about 25 miles from us, and after being at London some time, the regiment was next called to the western frontier, to do duty at Amherstburgh, where a schooner was taken from the rebels, with three pieces of cannon, 4 or 500 stands of arms, money, &c. besides 21 men killed, wounded, and prisoners. Amherstburgh is about 150 miles from London; and being rainy, and thawing at the time, it was dreadful travelling, and while he was there, he saw George Goble,[18] his wife and family, who are all well; they have the same family as when they left England; she has had one since, which died with the small-pox. They talked of coming here, if they can get any land to suit them, as they have none there, although they seem to be doing pretty well. He saw also Thomas Sharp,[19] and David Sharp.[20] Daniel Smith and his family[21] are there, and Charles Sageman; his father is about 20 miles off from him;[22] they were then all well. They all left us at Toronto to go there, when we came up here.

We received Christopher's letter about the Langleys, after we had wrote to you. The ship they sailed in arrived safe at Quebec four or five days before us, but we

---

17 Frederick Hasted offered a different version. He wrote that the two Coopers were both drafted but that one of them (James) had had to hire a substitute for $30 because he had a large family of ten children and numerous animals to look after (AO, RG1, C-IV, Township Papers, Adelaide, Frederick Hasted, 3 March 1839).

18 Original annotation: "Went out with James Cooper." Goble was a Chelsea pensioner.

19 Original annotation: "An army pensioner. He went out in 1832, in a ship sent by the Petworth Committee. This man returned to England, in the autumn of the same year, where he remained till 1836. In that year his nephew, David Sharp, here mentioned, being about to emigrate with his wife and family, to join his father and some other relatives who had been sent in a former ship, by the Committee, Thomas Sharp, on his earnest petition, was permitted to accompany them."

20 Original annotation: "These people went out in 1836."

21 Daniel Smith, a former soldier, emigrated with his wife Maria (Lucas) Smith in 1836 from the Lodsworth – Tillington area with six children, Mary, Jemima, Lucy, John, Daniel, and Emma.

22 Charles Sageman emigrated with his parents, William and Mary Sageman, a brother, and some sisters.

A "bush road" in winter,
when snow smoothed the
way for sleighing

Philip John Bainbrigge,
"A Bush Road," Upper
Canada 1842, NA, C11818

have not seen them or heard anything of them since. You wished to know about the widow Barns;[23] we saw her at Toronto when we came here, she was then living in the city, she and her family were well; two of her boys were apprenticed to a butcher. Budd, his wife[24] and his family, John Pratt, William Boxall, his wife and family George Varndell, daughter and son, Thomas Woods and his wife[25] are all settled at Townplat [the townplot of Blandford Township, Woodstock], in the county of Oxford. William Hewitt, Matthew Chalcraft, his wife and family are there also.[26]

---

23 Original annotation: "She went out with her husband and family, in 1832, in a ship sent by the Committee. Her husband died soon after their arrival at Toronto, but she has been able to obtain a comfortable livelihood, and to place out her children." See letter 75.

24 Original annotation: "Budd's wife is sister to James Cooper's wife: they went out with the Coopers."

25 Original annotation: "All these went out with the Coopers."

26 James and Mary Budd emigrated from Cocking with six children. John Pratt was from Petworth. William and Harriet Boxall emigrated from Tillington with seven children. George Varndell, an ex-soldier and widdower, came from Tillington; his two children's passage was assisted by the parish of Petworth. Thomas and Ann Woods were from Petworth. William Hewitt came from Cocking. Matthew and Charlotte Chalcraft emigrated from Tillington with six children. All of them emigrated in 1836.

Mrs. Budd and John Pratt came up here to see us last Christmas twelvemonth, and a neighbour of ours, Mr. Hasted,[27] called on them when on his way to Toronto, in the beginning of March last, and also on Mr. and Mrs. Carter, at Toronto, and William Boxall, and they were all well. Budd has got a town lot of five acres, most of which is cleared, with two houses on it. Henry Budd[28] is apprenticed to a cabinet maker; he is a steady lad, and getting very handy; he has about 3½ years to serve; he was bound for 5 years; he has 50 dollars the first year, to board himself, and increase 20 dollars every year. John Budd is bound to a blacksmith, for 5 years, and got 50 or 60 dollars the first year, besides his board, having learned some before, and to increase every year; but he forgets how much. James Budd and George Budd are both bound to a tailor, but he forgets on what terms; the other three children are at home. Budd had three of his fingers frost-bitten, while thrashing this winter, which made them very bad, taking the nails and skin off; but they were getting better fast. Mrs. Budd made some excellent elder wine last year, and upwards of 200 lbs. weight of sugar; we know not how much she made this year. Mr. and Mrs. Carter were well. The weather has been much more favourable this winter, than any winter since 1832; the present crops look well, and the last season was much more productive than 1836. The present price of wheat is a dollar per bushel, Indian corn a dollar per bushel, peas a dollar, buckwheat and rye about ¾ dollar, barley half a dollar, oats a quarter of a dollar, potatoes quarter of a dollar per bushel.

You wished to know whether William came to meet us with his waggon: he had no waggon, neither did he know we were coming, until we got within about half a mile of his house. We had to pay our own expences from Hamilton here, a distance of about 110 miles from here by land, and the carriage alone cost us near 27 dollars, besides eating and drinking. The line, or street as you would call it, that we live on, is getting pretty well settled. Mr. Hasted is coming to live on it this summer, having lately purchased 100 acres of land within a mile of us. He and his daughter are well, should any of his acquaintance at Cocking, Fittleworth, or elsewhere enquire after them.

Give our love to Mr. and Mrs. Goatcher, and tell them we have not forgot the teapot, but it is wore out, and we hope she will not forget her promise to send us another good one when she can. We do not go to fair-keeping now, but we have horse racing on Caradoc plains, about a mile and a half off from us, once a year, and a stock fair at Amiens, about 7 miles off twice a year.

We had pretty good luck last year with the deer, we killed 7, but have killed none this winter. You wished to know who the father of Mary's child is: it is Henry

---

27 Original annotation: "Many of the readers of this letter, will recollect a respectable man, who used to travel about Sussex, with a dog cart, laden with a variety of articles for sale: he went out to Canada, with his daughter, at his own expense, in 1833, but not in either of the ships sent by the Committee and purchased a farm in Adelaide; from whence he wrote a very descriptive letter, to a friend, which was published, in 1834." See letters 174 and 175.

28 James's nephew, the son of his twin brother.

Colonel Robert Moodie was shot by rebels on the night of Monday, 4 December 1837. Others got through to raise the alarm in the city.

C.W. Jeffreys, after an engraving in Charles Lindsay, *Life and Times of William Lyon McKenzie* (Toronto 1862, vol 2), "Shooting of Colonel Robert Moodie in Front of John Montgomery's Tavern," Toronto Reference Library, T13350

Stephens of Lodsworth;[29] she is still living with the same people as she first hired with, and her child with her, only they are gone to live in another township about 40 miles from us. We have not heard from her since Christmas; she and her child was then well, she gets half a dollar per week. The children all send their kind love to their grandfathers, grandmothers, uncles, aunts, cousins, and all enquiring friends. Caroline's and Sarah's love to Mrs. and the Misses Burgess, and wants to know if the little china dogs have learnt to bark yet. We hope you will excuse our not mentioning our friends by name, as that would unnecessarily fill the letter and lessen your information, for you may be assured we mean well to all of you, would wish you all to see it, and we all join in love and best respects to all of our relations and friends, and remain your ever dutiful and affectionate sons and daughters,

James, William & Harriet Cooper.

Direct in future to us, Lot 21, 4th. Concession, south of the Egremont Road, to be left at the Post Office, Katesville, Adelaide, London District, U.C.

P.S. We hope you will send this letter, or a copy of it, to Harriet's friends: don't forget them, or we shall be obliged to send the next letter to them instead of you.

---

29 Henry Stephens, the father of Mary Cooper's child, was probably Henry Stevens Jr, who emigrated with his parents and four younger sisters and brothers from the parish of Easebourne. He was 17 and she was 18 when they travelled to Upper Canada on the *Heber*.

Harriet has just got another daughter, her name is Charlotte, born May 9th 1838: she is getting pretty well, and the child is well. We have not said much to you yet about the war: it first broke out in Lower Canada, and the Governor of Upper Canada[30] sent every soldier out of this province, to assist against the French Canadians; trusting Upper Canada entirely to its gallant militia; and they drove the rebels into the United States, before the regular troops returned from their successful exploits in Lower Canada. The soldiers reported their losses in Lower Canada, to be about two men in a hundred, of the 24th and 32nd regiments, so that the loss was trifling: they burned down 3 villages and killed a great many people. Since we have been home, except those who volunteered for 6 months, the regulars and some of the volunteers went to attack the rebels at Pele Island:[31] the men went on the ice, advancing in three small columns, the smallest of which, about 90 in number, was fired on by the rebels, and 28 or 30 killed and wounded the first fire, the remainder charged and routed them, to the amount of 3 or 400, and they took to their sleighs, and made off as fast as they could, across the ice, to the States, before the main body of our troops came up. Four were killed, and about 15 made prisoners, of the rebels. Among the slain was their commander: the others fled quick. The killed on our side, were 5 regulars, and 1 volunteer horseman who led on the troops as a guide, and one died of his wounds afterwards: they took 3 cannons, small arms, provisions, &c.

To Mr. James Cooper, Graffham, Sussex.

OTHER LETTERS: 8, 133

Charlotte, the new daughter mentioned in this letter, was their last child. Harriet died of typhoid at Strathroy in 1857. James lived on as a farmer on concession 4 Adelaide Township. He died there at the age of 90 in 1883, survived by his third wife and ten children.

■ **134**

JOHN AND CAROLINE DEARLING, WATERLOO TOWNSHIP, UPPER CANADA, TO BROTHERS AND SISTERS (ADDRESSED TO JOHN FRANCIS), LODSWORTH, WEST SUSSEX, 15 JULY 1838

This letter was written by Caroline Dearling.

SOURCE: *Letters from Emigrants . . . in 1832, 1833 and 1837, 1–2*

From John and Caroline Dearling, who emigrated to Upper Canada, in 1833, in the Ship England, sent out by the Petworth Committee.

Waterloo, July 15th. 1838.

Dear Brothers and Sisters,

I now take the opportunity to write to you again, but am almost ashamed, as I

---

30 Sir Francis Bond Head*
31 The island in Lake Erie was occupied by a force crossing from Ohio on 26 February; the engagement took place on 2 March.

neglected it so long; but I hope this will find you all in good health, as it leaves us at present, thank God for it. Now, my dear brother I must say, as our aged parents are no more, I must tell you, all the potatoes you sent us, we had two gallons and ½ grow. I am in hopes we shall have a good many this year; they look well now. I must tell you what happened on the 9th. September, I was comfortably confined with a son, by a Dutch midwife, and a nice woman she is. We call our little Canadians, Hannah, and John, as you said you did not understand what her name was. Now I will tell you of the wheat sown last fall, 9 acres, and all looking very prosperous. We received a letter from John's dear father, January 8th. We also received a letter on the 15th April. On the 17th. I was taken bad with my eye, it was very bad for 5 weeks. You say in your letter you will come and be bailey[32] for us, but I think you had better come, and help do the hard work, for if the hard work was done, we could bailey for ourselves. We have 3 acres rye, 3½ of oats, 2 of peas, 1 acre of spring wheat, 1 acre of potatoes. It was a backward spring, but every thing grows fast. We have six hogs, and I am hobbing[33] a heifer calf. I have 34 chickens. I think the farmer will be . . . to find fault before harvest. John have been very busy for to do the spring work; now he have finished his chopping for this year; he has 7 acres chopped, but not any burnt off, for it is very showery weather at present, and very hot indeed, hotter than ever it has been since we have been here.

Dear brother, we have heard in William Rapson's letter, that our aged parents was no more. I have been waiting for a letter from you, day after day, and have no letter yet, as you said you would send as soon as there was a change. Pray tell me how my dear father felt before he departed this life, and my dear mother also. I hope we shall all meet again at the right hand of God. Tell me all you can; go to John's friends; ask them to send the particulars of his father's death, and how they all are.

Give our love to brother James, and Jane, and family, tell him I often wish I had him here, that we might have a cup of tea together, but we live very comfortable; we are no ways homesick yet. Remember us to all our friends and relations, I hope they are all well. I hope, dear brothers, when this letter reaches your hand, you will set down and write immediately, if you have not, and I will do the same. Dear sister Jane, I hope you will join with my brother in writing, and tell me all you can.

Give our love to Mr. Tribe, tell him Phoebe grows tall and thin, she is sitting making her a new frock, as I am writing by candle light, so you must excuse my bad writing. Phoebe has been living in Galt, now she is going to be at home until after harvest. James is living in Preston, with Scotch people. Jane looks very pale, but enjoys a good state of health. Caroline grows very much like her poor grandfather. Give our respects to Mr. and Mrs. Rapson, tell them I saw James just before I set down to write; his face has been very bad, [but] it is now better; the family is in good health. William [Rapson] and Thomas, their family is all well. Give our love to all our old neighbours.

32 A manager or steward.
33 Hand rearing

Tell us if you have ever heard of Daniel Smith, and where he is, if you know. You have heard of the death of poor George Thair. We have had a meeting ever since his funeral, some times every two weeks, and three weeks; they are Englishmen that preach and good men they appear to be; they preach in the house that we lived in; they are Methodists but it makes no difference, what religion we are: I think, it is very proper we should have some one to read the word of God. I must now conclude with the blessing of God. We remain your ever loving brother and sister,

JOHN & CAROLINE DEARLING.

TO JOHN FRANCIS,
    Lodsworth.

OTHER LETTERS: 85, 111

John Dearling purchased William Rapson's 51 acres in 1840 in addition to his own. The census and assessment of Waterloo Township of that year listed John Dearling, one female over 16, and 5 females under 16 (we know of 4 daughters and a son) living on the west part of lot 8, Beasley's Lower Block. They had 30 acres cleared, 70 acres of wild land, two oxen, and three cows. In addition to the Rapsons, other Petworth emigrants living nearby in 1840 were Jesse Penfold and his family from Lurgashall and Thomas Adsett and family from Northchapel. John died between March 1842 and August 1843, leaving an estate valued at £263.18.9. His executors, his wife Caroline and Petworth emigrant William Tilt, sold the Dearlings' farm in 1845. We lose track of Caroline after this date, but her brother sent an enquiry about her in a letter from England written by George Trussler in 1863 (see letter 143). This was also the year in which the mortgage from the sale of the farm in 1845 was paid off.

■ 135

CHARLES RAPLEY, ADELAIDE TOWNSHIP, UPPER CANADA, TO HIS FAMILY, [KIRDFORD, WEST SUSSEX,] 14 OCTOBER 1838

Charles Rapley was a widower when he emigrated from Wisborough Green with two young daughters, Sophia (Sophy) and Elizabeth, in 1832. His wife had died in 1826, four years after they were married,[34] probably in childbirth; the child died six months later. James Rapley, who also emigrated from Wisborough Green in 1832 and was also a widower, may have been an uncle or a cousin; certainly the families were close.

James Rapley was ill during the time the Petworth emigrants were camped in Lobo Township waiting to go to their land in the Adelaide settlement. He died in October 1832, but not before he was assigned lot 19 concession 5 SER by Roswell Mount.* This was probably the lot occupied in 1838 by his son David, who petitioned the government on the subject in 1842. In this letter Charles mentions each of the children who came to Canada with James by name: William (who in 1838 was married to Jane, the daughter of Petworth emigrant Charles Hilton), David (who married Harriet Hilton, daughter of Charles in 1840), Lucy (who later married Petworth emigrant John Downer), Ann, Charlotte, Thomas, and Jesse.

---

34 Both Charles and his wife (Frances Adams) had signed the marriage register with a mark.

SOURCE: *Letters from Emigrants . . . in 1832, 1833 and 1837*, 2–5

From Charles Rapley, who emigrated from Kirdford, Sussex, and was sent by the Petworth Commit-tee, in 1832, by the Ship Lord Melville.

Springs Farm, No. 19. 5 Con. South of the
Egremont Road, Adelaide, U.C.
October 14th. 1838.

Dear Father, and Mother, Brothers, and Sisters, Friends, and Relations all,

I hope this will find you all in good health, as it leaves us at present, thank the Lord. Elizabeth is living out about 3 miles from me, and is doing very well. Sophy is living with me, keeping my house. As you are now fast advancing in years, if you are not doing well, and have no better prospect than the parish, I should be very glad for you to come here, and live with me. I have 100 acres of land, and have enough of it cleared, and things enough around me, to maintain myself without going out to work at all; and I continue clearing more; and I will keep you as long as I live, if I live. If my brother Thomas wishes to do himself any good, I should advise him by all means to come here, he would be sure to do well here, either as a brickmaker, a farmer's laborer, or, if he likes, I will give him the choice either of going in part-nership with me on my farm, or let him have half the land, whether he is married or single makes no difference, for children are no burden here; if people cannot keep them themselves, there are plenty of the old settlers, glad to keep them, if you will let them have them for a certain term of years, according to their age. If my brother Thomas will not come, tell Luke Slaughter I will give him the same chance if he will come, and I have no doubt but he will be well satisfied with it; if not, there are plenty other chances that he cannot get in England. Tell any of my brothers in law, or old acquaintance, that I have no doubt but they will do better than when I left. Give my best respects to Mr. and Mrs. Hooker, and I hope they are well, and doing well, and be sure to shew them this letter, and I hope all my old fellow brickmak-ers are well, and doing well; if not, tell them to come to Canada, and never mind about the revolution, for that is over at present, unless it breaks out again.[35]

I was out between two and three months last winter, and was head drummer for our regiment of militia. We had 2 lbs. of the best white bread, and 2 lbs. of beef a day, and 1s.1d. English money. Every man in this country, rich and poor, from the age of sixteen to sixty are militia men, and liable to be called out in case of need, but this being a revolutionary concern, they would not take any that they thought were dis-affected, only the loyal part of our population; nearly all Adelaide were out. In peaceable times they cannot make us train more than four times a year; we sel-dom train more than twice or three times a year, and some townships only train one day in the year, on the 4th of June; this is called the general muster day; all must be

---

35 The most complete account of the 1837 Rebellion and the events in the area of Adelaide was writ-ten by Frederick Hasted, 175; Frances Pullen gave a woman's perspective in 137.

present then, or give a good account of their absence; but any man over forty five, is not obliged to attend on any other day. When we were out our regiment searched houses, and disarmed several persons, but not a shot was fired by any of our regiment at any person, or at any of us by them; there was a schooner with some rebels, and cannon, arms, ammunition, &c. taken after considerable firing by the Chatham and Kent people, at Amherstburgh, about two days before we got there;[36] we went from London to it, a distance of about 140 miles, and the travelling very bad at the time; it had froze, then thawed, attended with heavy rain, then froze again. The marshes at the mouth of the river Thames were overflowed for about 14 miles; sometimes we waded through, and sometimes we walked on the ice.

Sophy sends her kind love to both her grandfathers, her grandmothers, uncles, aunts, relations, and friends all, and would like very well to see you all if she could. Be sure to give her best respects to Caroline Hooker, and Caroline Standen, and Mrs. Dayman. If any of her acquaintance, or any young women should feel inclined to come to Canada, they are almost certain to get good situations, and good wages, from two dollars to five dollars a month.

We have a clergyman of the church of England, and a methodist preacher, in our township, not far from us, the methodist almost close. I have an opportunity of sending this by a neighbour, going to the west of England to see his friends, and have not time to see William and David. William is married, but has no family; he married one of Charles Hilton's daughters, a native of Sutton; he lives about 1¾ mile from me, on the same line of road; and David, and Lucy, are living with him, at present; but David's land joins mine, and he has lately built him a new house on it, the old one having been burnt down, with every thing in it, about 18 months ago; when they were out the logs at the back of the fire place having taken fire behind the clay. They are all well. Ann is married, and lives at Mount Pleasant, in Michigan. Charlotte, and Thomas, are also in the United States. Jesse lives about 20 miles from here, living at the same place he did five years ago, and doing well. Tell my aunt Hannah, that I cannot give any account about Eliza, except that she was living at Woolwich, some time ago, and married to a man by the name of Kingett. Mrs. Mann is married to Thomas Holden, and they are well, he lives opposite David's land, and sends their best respects to you. James Thomas, Thomas Thomas, their wives and families are all well; James lives near me, and his brother is coming to live here soon.

Write to me the first opportunity, pay the postage to the water, and put on it, *via New York*, if you send it by the post, else it will cost me double the postage. Let me know how you all are, or whether any of you intend coming or not. Let me know how my uncle gets on fiddling now, I should like to have a tune with him now. I brought my violin out safe, and we sometimes have a tune, when we raise a new house. Send us all the news you can. It has been too hot this season for some things here, but generally speaking it is the best and finest season we have had since

36 Probably a reference to the schooner *Anne* which ran aground near Amherstburg and was captured with some 30 patriot prisoners in an action in early January 1838.

Four generations of David Rapley's family: to David's right, Thomas, Fred, and Fred (?) Jr. David was a nephew of Charles Rapley.
Courtesy Blake Rapley

we have been here, and every thing pretty plenty. Mr. Hasted, that used to travel with the dog van, is well, and soon coming to live opposite me, having 150 acres of land opposite of the 1st quality; and 300 acres about 3½ miles off me: he sends his best respects to all his old customers, and friends, and would be glad to do any of them a kindness should they come here; he wonders some of his old friends do not come, he would let them have land, or any thing he can, as he wants but little for himself. I must conclude with my kind love to you all, and remain your dutiful son,

CHARLES RAPLEY.

Sophia Rapley later married Mark Mann, a son of Ann Mann. The Manns, like the Rapleys, intermarried with other Petworth emigrant families (see Ann Mann, 127). Members of these families who stayed in the district became farmers and merchants. Charles Rapley died in 1862.

■ **136**

RICHARD AND FRANCES PULLEN, DELAWARE TOWNSHIP, UPPER CANADA, TO ANN AND JOHN SUMMERSELL, AND ELIZABETH HOOKER, PETWORTH, WEST SUSSEX, 31 DECEMBER 1838

SOURCE: *Letters from Emigrants . . . in 1832, 1833 and 1837,* 5-7

From Richard and Frances Pullen, who emigrated to Upper Canada, in 1837, in the Ship Diana, sent out by the Petworth Committee.

December the 31st. 1838.

My dear Sister and Brother,

This comes with our kind love to you all, in hopes to find you all well, as thank God it leaves us all at present; but Richard enjoyed health very bad all the summer; it was a very hot summer, more so than it has been for this ten years, but thank God he is well now. My dear sister, I hope you will not give yourself so much trouble about me, for I know, my dear sister, that we get a better living than we should in England, if it is so bad as it was when we left; but my dear sister and brother, if I had as good convenience to come home, as I had to come here, I would soon be with you, for I think it would be the happiest hour that ever I spent, if I could once more be with you all. But I should make myself more happy if it was not for war, for we have had a great deal of trouble about war since we have been here; and I have been afraid that Richard would be forced away from us, but thank God we have been armed with the Almighty's defence thus far, for there have been a great many forced to go from this place, for the Yankees from the United States, want to gain the Canadas, for now this fall there came over about two hundred and began to fight, but thank God they only killed four of our side before our British soldiers began to fight, and they killed thirty all in one place, and dug a pit, and threw them in like logs, and they took between twenty and thirty prisoners, and the rest fled into the woods and made their escape, and we saw all the prisoners come by our houses all tied together. It was about a hundred miles from us where they were taken, and they were going to London, which is about fifteen miles from us, and they were all obliged to walk, it was an awful sight.[37]

My dear sister and brother, I am now going to tell you, we have left the place that we first went to, and am come back fifteen miles nearer Delaware, and live under a gentlemen by the name of Mr. Seabrook. We are living in his cottage, near his house; and Richard works for him constant; and we are about a mile from Delaware [Village]; and there is a church in Delaware, and we have a very good minister,[38] I thank the Lord, he lives about a hundred yards from us. Here is a great many English people about here, but there is but one that I ever knew before I left England, that is Mrs. Peacock, Amelia Cowper, at Frightfold,[39] as was; I often see her, she lives in Delaware. And I hope, my dear sister, that you will be happy about us. And we send

37 The uneasy situation in the western part of the province was a rich culture for rumour at this time, but the Pullens here are reporting the raid that took place on 4 December when a force crossed the Detroit River near Windsor. According to Colin Read, *The Rising in Western Upper Canada* (Toronto: University of Toronto Press 1982), twenty-five of the invaders were killed (and four of those taken prisoner were shot). Those captured were imprisoned, and later tried, in London.

38 The Reverend Richard Flood

39 Charles and Amelia Peacock emigrated from Kirdford, West Sussex. Amelia was the daughter of John Cooper, who was given as occupier of Frithfold or Frightfold farm in the Northchapel Poor Rate Book, April 1826 to February 1834 (WSRO, PAR 142/30/3).

all our kind love to aunt Maria, and uncle Keen, and all the family, and all our dear relations and friends. And now, my dear sister, I am going to tell you that I was confined the 23rd June, with a little son, and his name is George, he is now six months old. My dear sister, we have fowls and pigs; and I hope, if we live till the spring, we shall be able to get us a cow, if it please God we have our health. And I hope we shall soon hear from you. And Sarah, and William, and Hannah, and Henry, and Richard, and Elizabeth, and George, and myself, and Richard, all send our best respects and kind love to you all, my dear sister and brother, and dear little Harriet and Ann. So we remain your loving sister and brother,

FRANCES & RICHARD PULLING [sic].

■ **137**
(To her mother) This letter continued on the same sheet as letter 136.

And now my dear mother,[40] I take with pleasure my pen in hand to write to you, and I hope it will find you all well, as thank God it leaves us all at present. And we received both your letters, and we were very sorry to hear that our poor brother William was so ill, but I hope he is spared, for the sake of his family, if it is the Lord's will; and we all send our kind love to all brothers and sisters, and I should have wrote to you before, dear friends, had it not been for the confusion in the country, for we did not know how it would be, but it is now a little more peaceable, I thank God. I forgot to tell you the reasons why we left the other place, but he was a commissary in the army, and when there was a confusion, he was obliged to leave his place, and go on duty in London; but we might have stayed a year if we would in his house, but, dear mother, we wanted to get nearer Delaware, on account of the church, for us and our children to attend. Dear mother, we both went to church on Christmas day, and received the sacrament, which was a great comfort to us.

Dear mother, you wish to know more about our voyage, but what I can say it was a very troublesome one, but I bless the Lord he enabled us to go through it. And now, my dear friends, we are too far from home ever to return, we must make ourselves happy, if we can, for you know, my dear mother, we should be happy in whatever situation the Lord is pleased to place us. So now to conclude, Richard and me, and all your dear grandchildren, all sends our kind love to you all, and I hope we shall all meet in the next world, to part no more, and that will be joyful. So we remain your loving son and daughter,

RICHARD & FRANCES PULLEN.

Dear sister, when you direct our letter, direct it to be left at the post office, Delaware. We all send our love to poor old dame Baker, if she is living, and master Keen, and mistress, and all the neighbours on the Commons. So I wish you all well. Our children are all grown very much. Dear mother, one day, when Richard was going to

---

40 Mrs Elizabeth Hooker

London, he met with a man that came from Petworth, his name was Nevett,[41] from the north street, he is a tailor, he talks of coming to Petworth next fall.

For JOHN SUMMERSELL,
    Petworth, Sussex, England.

OTHER LETTERS: 131, 132, 139

■ 138

AUTHOR UNKNOWN, WEST FLAMBOROUGH TOWNSHIP, UPPER CANADA, TO HER UNCLE AND AUNT, 17 JANUARY 1839
The anonymous author of this letter appears to have come from Chichester, West Sussex.

SOURCE: *Letters from Emigrants in 1832, 1833 and 1837*, 8-12

From . . . who emigrated to Upper Canada, in 1837, in the Ship Diana, sent out by the Petworth Committee.

West Flamborough, January 17th. 1839.

Dear Uncle and Aunt,

We received your kind letter on the 12th of this month, and am happy to hear you have made up your minds to come to America. We are all enjoying good health I am happy to say, and pleased to hear you are the same. I can assure you it will be much better here for you than at home. I sent you a very bad account of the country in my first letter, as every thing was very dear; since then provisions are much cheaper. We felt it more, having no home to come to, and no means; but this will not be the case with you, you will have a home to come to, until you can get one, and some friends to converse with. I must tell you we are removed 20 miles nearer home, and we like the country much better; it has more the appearance of home. Now, my dear friends, as regards what you say about grandfather and mother coming out, father and mother says it will be by no means advisable for them to come, as we think the voyage far too much for grandmother; and also, as the Americans are particular in hiring young able men, we fear grandfather would not do well by coming out; we should all be happy to see them, it would to me be a pleasure above any. I hope Billy and Mary Ann will help them as far as they can. Give my kind love to Billy and Mary Ann, and am sorry they should be angry at my not writing to them. I thought if I wrote to one, it would be the same. Believe me, my feeling is towards him the same as ever. We are only four thousand miles from each other.

Now, my dear friends, as regards your coming out, I think from your letter you mean what you say; as regards the wages I named, is not in the harvest, but all the year on. Uncle will find himself at liberty, and will be able to smoke his pipe every

---

41 John Nevett emigrated from Petworth in 1832 and evidently settled in Westminster Township; see letter 83.

night, with a glass of whiskey. Tobacco is one shilling per pound, and you, my dear Aunt, can have two shillings per day and board. The women here will not work, they are so lazy. You need not be afraid of employment, they are making new roads all through the country, and a few miles from us is a canal digging, which will last seven years; they get four shillings per day.[42] Little George will nearly get as much as uncle. Do not leave Harriet and him behind, as they can earn so much more here. I am very sorry to hear Harriet is such a trouble to you, if she is a good girl she can do well for herself. I hope she will think better of it, and come with you. We do not wish to persuade you, my dear friends, but what I tell you is the perfect truth. We all hope you will come; if we were certain you would, here is such a nice house close to us, we would take it for you; but I fear it will be let before we hear from you; but if so, we will get another near. You will find yourself quite independent here: do not remain there, but come here and be at liberty. As regards brother Frank going home, he have quite declined it, as you think of coming: he could not be home until June, and you will I suppose leave in April, and he will have no other friend to go to. Our friends indeed are very few, when you come you might bid them all good bye for me: if they cannot spare one half hour in writing to me, I shall never attempt to write again. I have written to many, and have never received one line.

As regards your furniture, sell all your tables, chairs, and bedsteads; bring your beds, and bed clothes; bring your copper, tea things, and plates, and children's stools: you

A Sussex woman making bread
Daniel Fowler, "Woman Kneading Bread," Rye, Sussex, 1832, NA C45129

42 She is probably referring to the Grand River Navigation.

will find your copper very useful; sew a coarse cloth over it. Bring your tea kettles and cooking pot, with many other little things. Bring your fire irons and bellows: you can get all these here, but it is very high. I would advise you to sell all your large pieces of furniture, as you will find it very awkward in moving it about. We got all our furniture and clothes quite safe. I long to see ———. You will be in time ——— to make the short clothes, if you leave the first of April. Emily and ——— desires you will come without delay, as they are wanting many little concerns done. Emily has made all her own dresses since we have been here; as dress-makers are very scarce here, you will do well. ——— I will seek myself a husband before you get here, and then I will seek for you: here is some very handsome young Negroes in this country, would you fancy one? they are very attentive.

You asked me if we baked our own bread, we do; and have much better than when at home; we get very good yeast at Dundas, there is a very large brewery, it is two miles from us, it is kept by one Mr. Holt, from the Pallant, Chichester. It is those people that go so far up the country, and in the bush, that cannot get yeast; they then use salt rising, but it is not so good as yeast. We can get every thing here, as well as at home. I would not advise any one to go so far up the country, in the bush. I think you frame the country worse than it is. You will need no extra clothing, we wear no more than when at home.

Now my dear friends, you ask me what route you should come by, and what the expence will be after you leave the ship; if you take the same route as we did, or I should say by the Petworth Emigration, they will convey you to Toronto at your first expence, and perhaps to Hamilton, a distance of 47 miles; but the certainty of that you can ascertain of the Committee; you will then be only 7 miles from us, should this be the case. You must buy tin plates and mugs, or you will break your china, and also a spare box to put your provisions in, such as sugar and butter, and meat you will not consume on the sea: you will find it useful coming up the country, as you will leave the ship at Montreal, and then provisions are not so abundant. From Montreal to Toronto is a distance of four hundred miles; you ——— will be delighted with the steam boats on the lake: she will just go fast. If you come by way of New York, your expences will be about 8 pounds, it being a distance of about five hundred miles. If you can get a cheap passage to New York, I should advise you to come by that route, as I think it is a much quicker passage: it cost us eighty pounds to our destination.[43] I think you can get here much cheaper. Bring some brandy, you will find it useful on the sea; some onions and vinegar, and a nice ham would be very nice on the sea. You seem to have a dread of the water, but you will not mind that after you get on board. I felt more going through Portsmouth, than I did all the voyage beside. You will be sea sick I have no doubt, but you must not mind that, it will be soon over: you must lay in bed, and eat as much as you can.

New clothes is not much dearer than at home. ——— will do well, as there are few

---

43 See table at the end of the letter.

dress-makers in this country. Stays are not worn. Bonnet makers and milliners might do well. When I say stays are not worn, they are not used so much as at home, I fear a stay-maker would not do well. We cannot persuade grandfather and mother to come, as they are too far advanced in years; we had one old lady on board, and she suffered so much from the voyage, she was not expected to live when we left the ship; we should not be doing right to advise them to come, we know the difficulty of so long a voyage. Give our kind love to them and we truly hope they will do well. If you have a small trifle to give them, pray do it, and we will pay you as soon as you get here. Now, my dear friends, if you do come, which we sincerely hope you will, will you bring these few articles I am about to name, if you have the means, and I will pay you as soon as you get here. The first for me, a full size cottage tuscan bonnet,[44] about 16s.; next, a neat muslin dress, at 12 or 14 shillings; next, 8 yards of brown irish, for father's round frock; 3 pair of clogs at 1s.; here is no pattens[45] in this country. Will you also bring 3 pounds of small shot, as it is very large here, and a few ballads for the boys, as they wish to learn to sing, and a few rabbit wires, as here is a great many rabbits here. Will you go to Mrs. —— in the North Street, for my bonnet, and say it is for me. Bring no axe, buy no tools, you can buy them much cheaper here. Should any gentleman call on you by the name of —— of —— near —— respecting your coming out, as he have a daughter coming out to her sister; they live near us and are very respectable. I often take tea with them. I named your coming out, and she wished her sister to come with you. I am not certain of his calling; if he should, you can answer him the ship you intend to come by. You must be careful with the children, and not undress them at night, it will be very cold on board. Mother desires you will keep your circumstances private in the ship, as there are people always enquiring what means you have, and what you intend doing when you get here. N.B. you will get 25s. to the pound here. Now my dear friends these are the directions as we are removed, — —— West Flamborough, near Dundas, Upper Canada, North America.

Now a few words to ——. My dear Miss ——, I see from my aunt's letter, my poor dear aunt Kate is still uncomfortably situated. Father and mother say, if she can make up her mind to come out to us, she will do much better, and depend upon a home until she can get one: the boys, with Emily and myself, particularly desire she will come out with Aunt ——; if she cannot make up her mind to come, I hope she will write to us. My dear Miss ——, we often speak of you. Mother often wishes you were here, to take a cup of tea with her. Emily, with Ann and myself, send our kind love to you. We hope you will send a few lines in Aunt's next letter: so now, dear friend, adieu.

We are much pleased to hear Miss —— has been so kind as to interest herself for you so much. Should any part of the family wish to write to us, I shall always be happy to answer it. Bring a few Epsom salts with you, you will find them useful

---

44 A fine straw bonnet.

45 A kind of overshoe, usually with a wooden sole set on an iron ring to raise the foot out of the mud. Sussex was renowned for its mud in winter.

in the ship.[46] We desire to be most kindly remembered to all Mr. —— family; tell —— and —— how much I should like to see them. Give our kind love to —— and John, and hope they are doing well: we will always be happy to hear from them.

Now, my dear friends, you must make up your minds; you will have difficulties to contend with, but never mind, it will soon be over: you, my dear aunt, will not mind the water, after you have been a few hours in the ship. Now, dear friends, note what I say: if you come, please to answer this directly, as we will seek a house for you. Will you go to uncle Henry, and ask him if he has any parcel for us, if so, will you bring it for us? Give our kind love to Mr. and Mrs. ——. Now with a hope we shall soon meet again, is the sincere wish of your affectionate niece,

I forgot to say, wear all your old clothes on board.

Expences from London or Portsmouth to New York by the packets for one adult.

Expences, &c. mls.*	£	s.	d.	Expences, &c. mls.*	£	s.	d.
				Brought forward . 160*	7	19	6
Passage	5	0	0	Albany to Oswego by			
Provisions about	2	0	0	track boat, 50 lbs.			
Cook	0	10	0	luggage free 209	0	15	7½
Hospital Tax at New				62 lbs. luggage extra			
York	0	4	6	to Oswego			
New York to Albany				Oswego to Toronto,			
by steamer, 100 lbs.				1 cwt. luggage			
of luggage allowed				included 170*	0	7	6
free, 12½ cents for				Provisions at New			
every cwt. extra 160*	0	5	0	York, and on the			
				route to Toronto . .	0	8	0
Carried forward ..160*	7	19	6	539*	9	13	7½

[* indicates miles]

■ 139

ELIZABETH (PULLEN) HOOKER AND ANN AND JOHN SUMMERSELL, PETWORTH, WEST SUSSEX, TO RICHARD AND FRANCES PULLEN, DELAWARE, UPPER CANADA, 4 APRIL 1839

This is the second of two letters written to the Richard Pullen family from his mother, sister, and brother-in-law in Petworth, England.

SOURCE: Thompson Family Papers. Parts of this letter are damaged and indecipherable.

Petworth, 1839

My dear children

I now take up my pen to write to you happy to hear you were all well and I hope remain so, as it leaves some of us. But your sister Martha is in a poor state of

---

46 The surgeon's chest was usually very well stocked with pounds of Epsom Salts!

health and has been for some time. She is not able to do anything but we are in hopes she is a little better. Now if it do but last. But I fear it will not for the doctor gives poor account of her. But it is what I ever expected for she always was of a declining constitution and I hope we shall all say the Lord's will be done. But we will hope for the best and pray that the Lord will spare her for the sake of the family. While there is life there is hope.

And poor William is still in a poor way, Not able to work nor do I see any likelyhood of it. But I bless the Lord that he can walk about and comes to Petworth and seems very comfortable and can sit down and read his Bible and is quite resigned to the Almighty's will and he says he hopes he can trust wholly on the Lord for he knows he must go to the strong for strength. He keeps going to that man at Wonish[47] still and he is very kind to him and he tells him he will get better in time, But it is a long time he has been ill, above 19 months. The rest are all middling I thank the Lord, and I am much as usual I never expect to be well. I bless the Lord I can get about and do my work middling. I shall not be right till I get home where I hope to meet you all for this is a dreary wilderness, there is something always to annoy us, some trouble somewhere. This is not our rest because it is perluted and I hope my dear children we shall all be able to look beyond this [perishable world] unto a house not made with hands eternal in the heavens.

Your poor sister Sarah is but poorly off for she have no place nor like to have but she works about a little but no constant thing. But I thank the Lord she is [heartier] then ever she was and gets about to work so you see the Lord fits the back to the burden though she cannot get a living; it is a great thing Peter is where he was. And all well I believe. Elizabeth has got another daughter since I wrote to you last. And they are all well and I have got Emily living with me now and a good girl she is and James is living in Guildford and has got his Master's business and is doing very well. He is married[48] and Thomas is at Midhurst still and has got plenty of work. His wife was confined the Sunday before Christmas with a dead child but they are both well.[49]

Poor old Dame Baker and Mrs Keen and Master and all the people in the Commons sends their best respect to you. All the [same] so rejoiced to hear from you and we were all greatly rejoiced for we thought forever before we did. But I hope you will not stay so long again before you write as I hope to send this not to cost so much as a gentleman is agoing to take it as far as York for me. When you send again I hope some of my dear grandchildren will be able to write part of the letter. But I don't know whether there is any school or not. I hope there is a Sabbath

---

47 Wonersh, Surrey

48 A James Pullen married Avis Smithers at Kirdford on 18 May 1839, the day before this letter was written.

49 Thomas and Eliza Pullen had two sons, John, born 1840, and Frederick, born 1841. Thomas died in December 1846, aged 33. Eliza continued to run the florist and seed business (1851 Census, Midhurst).

School for I think that is the best thing th[at] ever was done for children and for parents; it makes them kind and obedient to their parents and instructs them in the way to heaven for after they have been scholars perhaps they may become teachers in a Sabbath School and what a blessed employment that is for a young person. It keeps them out of bad company. And while they are instructing others they get instruction themselves. I forgot to tell you your sister Sarah has got another daughter to and poor Mrs Spooner at Shop [Farm][50] is dead, died by the sting of a bee. At [least] a bee stung her and she dropt down and died immediately. So you see my dear children in the midst of life we are in death then how ought we to be on our watch tower for we know not the day nor the hour when the Son of Man cometh.

Now my dear children I must conclude with my blessing to you and the dear children; tell them I hope they read their Bibles. Poor dears, how I should like to see them and the dear little Stranger.[51] But I hope we shall meet in that Blessed abode where sin and sorrow never comes, where the Lamb shall wipe all tears from our eyes. Now my dear children and grandchildren, your brothers and sisters and aunts and uncles and cousins one and all send their kind love to you and not forgetting myself and Master Hooker. Mr Lord sends his kind respects to [Mr and Mrs?] Charles Peacock and tell him all the family are well; and he have wrote 3 letters and have had no answer He wonders how it is. He should be very happy to have a letter from him likewise her friends. So no more from your loving Mother, E. Hooker x

My Dear Sister and Brother and to all your Dear Children

This comes with our kind love to you all; we hope it will find you all well, as thank God it leaves us at present. We received your letter the 7th of February and we was all glad to hear from you all, my dear sister, but more happy to see you all in England. My dear sister, that morning I received your letter I was taken very ill and the next day was confined with a little son and his name is Henry and thank God he is doing well. My dear sister and brother, Aunt Meriah and Uncle William Keen and cousins send their kind love to you all. Aunt Fanny at Guildford is about the same and Eliza Jones is confined with two children and no husband and we are very sorry for it.

Now my dear sister and brother, I am your brother John Summersell. I am agoing to tell you the goings on in Sussex; there is at the present time plenty of work but provion [provision?] is dear but the labourers wages is rose. Those men that have got a family gets 13 shilling and six pence per week and all the tradesmen do get more money; for my [work][52] give me 17 shilling per week when I work at day work but now very often we are put to task work and can make a few more shilling per week, thank God; I wish I had your son William with me this summer for there is plenty of work at our trade and I went down to Lurgashall for my cousin and I have got him to work along with me now and he gets 15 shilling per week and will have

50 Shop Farm is about a mile and a half southwest of the village of Northchapel.
51 George Pullen, born 23 June 1838 in Canada.
52 John Summersell was a carpenter.

St Mary the Virgin Church, Petworth, interior. Sockett's church where he preached his sermon on the Pullen's letter.

Photograph: Patrick Burrows

more even he gets a little handier. I hope you will look over my blunders, Fanny, for your sister Ann kept talking and I lay it upon her.

My dear sister and brother. I now take up my pen in hand to write to you all and my dear children all joins their kind love to you all, Harriott, Ann and little Henry. My dear sister I should be most happy to see you all at Petworth. It would be the most happiest day that [illegible] though my dear sister we was very glad to hear such good news from you; I hope you will all do well. I have not been down on the Commons not for more than twelve months. Harriott Holden called on me since I received your letter, my dear sister. She wishes to be remembered to you all and all in the Commons the same, and old Dame Baker says that [little Henry have] not brought that bundle of wood to her that he promised her, but we, please God, we shall have the pleasure of seeing you all again. And when you write again home will send us word if you all should like to come to Petworth again; we will try to help you home for I think we have some friends to help all have you home, for there is another paper post[ed] at Petworth if anybody wishes to go to [Canada to] their friends Col Wingham [George Wyndham*] will send them free, but I hope you will make up your minds [to] Come to England again and [illegible] to get money to you all and I your brother John Summersell will try my best endeavour if you will make up your mind to come to Old England again [illegible] think it be better for you all [and your sister and myself for] all with plenty of friends to help work for you [illegible] tried for a better living than you have at [home but I think][53] if you come back again you would get a better living in England than you will in America, so make up your minds and send back as soon as you can. I am glad to hear you are all back a little nearer and I hope you will get nearer still. Now, my dear sister and brother, that letter that you sent M^r. Socket* was much [illegible] and one Sunday he had a sermon preached in Petworth Church all about your letter, and there was a great deal of money gathered for to send to help your church, and I put some money in the silver plate myself and so did my daughter Harriott and she said she hope Aunt Fanny and all her family will have some of the money. Send us word what their letter caust you for the Rv. Herington at North Chaple was very much pleased with your letter.

So no more at present from your brother John and sister Ann Summersell.
April 4th
Address   For the Richard Pullen
         To be left at the Post Office
         Delaware Canada   May 19, 1839.

OTHER LETTERS: 131, 132, 136, 137.

Frances and Richard Pullen did not return to Petworth. Six more children were born to them in Canada (George, James, Mara Ann, Emily, Frances, and John), and all but the oldest surviving daughter, Sarah, were apparently living at the family farm in Caradoc Township at the

---

53 Parts of several lines are difficult to read.

time of the 1851 census. Frances died in May 1848, aged 43, and was buried in the cemetery in the village of Delaware; Richard died in 1872 and was also buried there.

■ 140

WILLIAM PHILLIPS, GALT, UPPER CANADA, TO HIS BROTHER, THOMAS PHILLIPS JR, OF SINGLETON, WEST SUSSEX, 14 JULY 1839

William Phillips, the Singleton shoemaker, was one of at least two people allowed a second chance to emigrate by the Petworth committee. He returned to England sometime after 1832 and was permitted "at his own earnest request" to work his passage out on the *Diana* in 1837. On that voyage, Brydone* described him as "most respectable." We do not know why Phillips left Canada the first time, but perhaps he was lonely. In 1839 he knew where to go to find a community of Sussex people.

SOURCE: WSRO, PHA 1068; extracts were published in the *Brighton Guardian*, 1 January 1840, and in the *Sussex Weekly Advertiser*, 6 January 1840.

Galt, Upper Canada
July 14th. 1839.

Dear brother

I received your kind letter of the 14th April on the 30th June, and am glad to hear you are all well, as it leaves me at present, thanks be to God for it. This is the first time I have heard from you since I left Drove by letter. I have heard from you twice by William Hewitt,[54] once in February, and then he said you had not heard from me since I left Drove, so I suspected you did not get the letter that I sent by Mr. Brydone, but it appears you did. I received a letter from William Hewitt on the 1st May, and he informed me that you had received my letter of James Hall,[55] so I have been waiting for an answer to it. I knew he had got safe home as here have been some letters received in answer to those he carried home, and as he promised me he would go, and see you. I made myself contented that you had heard from me. I have received your letter that you wrote in October, since I received the one of the 14th April, and it had been taken out of the Post Office, by a man of the same name, and opened, and kept a long time, and then returned, but to prevent any mistake for the future; direct to me, William Phillips, to the care of Mr Thos Gillisby, Hamilton, Upper Canada, North America.

Dear brother[56] I saw in the newspaper that the Colonel [George Wyndham*] had sent a commission to Canada to purchase ten thousand acres of land, and that he

---

54 Twenty-one-year old William Hewitt emigrated in 1836 from Cocking (some 10 miles north of Singleton, West Sussex), to Blandford Township, Upper Canada; see letter 108.
55 James Hall was mentioned in a letter from James Rapson as still living at George Thair's in 1836; see letter 115.
56 The extracts in the *Brighton Guardian* and the *Sussex Weekly Advertiser* begin at this point and end with the words "and I am very sorry for them."

was going to give the same encouragement to emigration, as that given by his father the Earl of Egremont*, and that between three and four hundred of Sussex emigrants were to sail from Portsmouth on the 1st May and that they were to be under the superintendance of Lieutenant Rubidge of the royal navy; but if that had been the case you must have known some thing about it, at the time you wrote your letter. It appears by that that the Colonel is willing, but the people are not.[57] I think they are much to blame as there never was a better time to come to Canada than the present for the late disturbance has kept back emigration for the last 2 years,[58] and hundreds have left the province and gone to the United States, so that there is a good chance for emigrants of all classes. Dr. [Thomas] Rolph[59] of Ancaster is gone to England and I am informed he is going to try to raise emigrants for the next spring, and I think it is not unlikely but he will come and see the Colonel as he always spoke highly of the Earl of Egremont, and the encouragement he gave to emigration. The Doctor is a fine man and is to be depended on for he will not flatter the people, but tell the truth, for he is not a land agent to any party, nor yet a land jobber, as he has no interest in it no more than I but he has the welfare of both countries at heart. I shall say no more on that subject now. I know many would better their condition by coming here.

I saw John Holden and family, James Budd and family a short time ago, and they are all well, they live in Woodstock.[60] James [Philips] is in Hamilton yet, but I have not seen him since March his wife has got another child which makes them four.[61] I have been living in Galt since the 1st April. It is 25 miles from Hamilton up the country. I think I shall go to Woodstock in the fall, for I like the country up there, and there is a great many Sussex people settled about there. They are all Scotch in this part, and I do not much like it for they are very clannish. John Smith is living in Toronto;[62] and when I saw him last he was in the city guards; and that is a very good place for since the disturbance has been we have all been soldiers at times. I am more than fifty dollars out of pocket by it, what with loss of time, and money that I spent; but I hope it is all over now; and thank God I am spared; and I shall do well if I have my health, and strength. I do not want to come to England to live

57 In 1839, Lieutenant Charles Rubidge superintended the emigrants from George Wyndham's estates in the west of Ireland on the *Waterloo*. Rubidge assisted a number of these emigrants to find work in the Newcastle district where he himself lived. He was not involved at any time in the Petworth emigrations from Sussex.

58 The rebellions of 1837-8.

59 Rolph (1801-58) may not have been quite a land jobber, but he did represent the interests of several people with land to sell in Upper Canada. Thomas Rolph, *Emigration and Colonization, Embodying the Results of a Mission to Great Britain and Ireland during the Years 1839, 1840, 1841, and 1842* ... (London 1844).

60 John Holden was 19 when he emigrated from Washington, West Sussex, in 1832; see letter 93. James Budd, wife Mary (Carter), six children, and a nephew emigrated from Cocking in 1836.

61 James Philips and his family emigrated in 1833.

62 This may be the John Smith who emigrated with his wife, Rebecca (Turrell), and six children from Woolbeding, West Sussex, in 1837.

again, for with all the trouble we have had here we are in a much better condition than the poor of old England; and I am very sorry for them.

Dear brother, I should be much obliged to you, if you will send me a newspaper as often as you can; not but we get plenty of news from England, but it is all extracts, and each paper makes such extracts as suit his own politics. I should like to see 'Heringtons Dispatch' some times, and some times the Champion;[63] and as you used to get them, there will be no trouble nor yet expense attend sending them. The post master can give you the instruction about when they ought to be posted. I have sent you some; I do not know if you have had them. I will send you some more now that I am stopping where I can get them, and then you can read for yourself.

[No Signature]

To Thomas Phillips Junior
    Singleton near Midhurst
        County of Sussex
            England

OTHER LETTERS: 13
Phillips may have heard Thomas Rolph speak in Canada. Rolph did speak at Sockett*'s audit dinner in Petworth in the autumn of 1839 while he was in England promoting emigration.[64] Sockett did not pursue the connection, and Wyndham made a firm decision in 1840 that he would not buy land in Canada.

■ 141
CHARLES COSENS AND ANN (MILLER) COSENS, BLENHEIM TOWNSHIP, UPPER CANADA, TO HER FATHER AND MOTHER, [DORKING, SURREY], 28 SEPTEMBER 1839

SOURCE: Cosens Family Papers, Gowanstown, Ontario

Blenheim Township, Sept. 28, 1839.

Dear Father and Mother,

After a long time we will now address a few lines to you, hoping you will forgive and forget our negligence in not writing to you before this. We received a letter from our dear sister on the 26th of this present month and were happy to hear

63 He was probably referring to the *Hetherington's Twopenny Dispatch & People's Police Register* and the *Champion and Weekly Herald*, both radical newspapers published in London.

64 In his address to the dinner on 8 November, Rolph began by stressing how pleased he was to be back in his native land, adding: "Of the Sussex labourers who had made Upper Canada their home, all had done well ... they were to be met with, happy, prosperous and advancing. Respectful in their manner, indefatigable in their exertions, contented in their stations, they proved a natural and impregnable barrier to the ravages which American habits and institutions would fatally entail on us" (*Sussex Advertiser*, 18 November 1839).

that you were all enjoying a tolerable degree of health. As I am happy to inform you it leaves us and our dear children and our other friends in America. We must now inform you what family we have got. We have three boys and our girl and the expectation of another in a few months. The boys we have named Henry, George, and Charles and our little girl we have named after our sister Mary. We thank God that they are all fine healthy children which is a great blessing indeed.

We have to inform you that we are removed from the farm we were on when we wrote to you last, which was in the Township of Waterloo to a farm in the township of Blenheim, which is about 5 miles from where we used to live. We were unfortunate in our crops on the other farm and we did not get on as well as we expected, but for all that we must not complain as we have made out to get a good living and some little property besides. And I trust by the blessing of our Heavenly Father we shall do well on the farm we are now living on. Our crops this year are pretty good. We are happy to hear that our sister was enjoying better health than she used to have and that she was so comfortable in her situation. But how happy we would be to see her and all of you. But I fear that will never come to pass, but we must submit to the will of Divine Providence for He knowth what things we stand in need of, and what is most conducive to our everlasting and eternal happiness. So we must not repine but leave it all in the hands of our gracious Master.

Our sister wished to know if Charles played cricket now but we wish to inform her that he has given up all kinds of games, and the time he used to take up in those transitory trifles he now devotes to his God in meditation and on searching that blessed book the Bible. For in this is found the way to everlasting happiness hereafter. To be brief he has taken to a religious course of life and the satisfaction he has experienced in religion in the last year he would not part with for all the amusements in this world, for his religion can give the sweetest comforts while we live and after death its joys will be lasting as eternity.[65]

She also wished to know where Mr. Uphold, Richard McKean, or James Rowland are but we do not know. She also wished to know how Mr. Cosens family were getting on. Mr. and Mrs. [Charles] Cosens [Sr] and all the family are quite well with the exception of Betsy who is very poorly and at times out of her mind. Mr. and Mrs. Cosens and Betsy and the two youngest boys are moved out of Waterloo to the Huron Tract which is about 50 or 60 miles from where we live [Tuckersmith Township]. They are on a farm of their own up there and we are in hopes will do pretty well. Cornelious [Cosens] and his wife [Emily] are living up there too and they have two children. Thomas is living in Waterloo and he has two children. Esther is living in Guelph and she has got two children. William Tilt is living in Waterloo and is carrying on a very large tannery and currying business in partnership with another man and Nathaniel is living with him. Francis is a cabinet maker [66] and lives

---

65 He had become a Primitive Methodist.
66 Francis Cosens died in 1867 from the effects of inhaling lead paint fumes.

about a mile from Wm. Tilt. Annie Cosens, the youngest girl, lives in Guelph but we think she is coming to live with Caroline before long.[67]

Our sister said in her letter that she lived near Wm. Tilt's sister Ellen, and he wished for her to [tell?] Ellen that his wife and family were all well and desires their love for her, and that he has sent a letter to his father by the same conveyance that I send this, which is by a man who is going home to England into Surrey near Hampshire so you must excuse a long letter this time as we expect the man to call for this letter immediately.

I dare say our little brother has grown a fine boy. Kiss him for us with our kind love to you and our sister and brothers and all our friends and relations.

Hoping you will write soon to us as it is a great pleasure to hear from you and you may depend we will not neglect writing an answer immediately. So no more at present. From your loving son and daughter

Charles and Ann Cosens.

Direct to me Charles Cosens, Jr., Preston P.O., Township of Waterloo, District of Gore, Holton County, Upper Canada America.

OTHER LETTERS: 66; see also 34 from Cornelius Cosens.

Ann's family in England had evidently asked about cricket before (see letter 66). Ann and Charles's previous lot in Waterloo Township appears in the Gore District Census and Assessment for 1833 and 1834. Charles Sr and Jr are both recorded on the west part of lot 20 on the broken front concession of Waterloo although, as we know, Charles Sr took his family to the Huron Tract in 1832.

Charles Cosens Sr and Ann Goodchild stayed in Tuckersmith where they were both buried in the Turner Cemetery. Of the family still at home in 1839, Betsy (Elizabeth) was about 23, and John and Jesse, the youngest boys, were 13 and 12 years of age.

Charles Jr appears to have been in Blenheim Township in 1839, but by 1865 he was settled in Wallace Township, and he purchased village lots in nearby Trowbridge in 1870. Charles and Ann had at least four more children in Canada. Ann had died by the time of the 1871 census. Cornelius Cosens, Charles Jr's brother, had children born in Tuckersmith between 1850 and 1859. By 1860 he was near his brother, settled in Elma Township.

■ 142

JAMES AND SARAH LANNAWAY (LANAWAY), WOODSTOCK, UPPER
CANADA, TO WILLIAM THORP, PETWORTH, WEST SUSSEX,
24 SEPTEMBER 1840

James Lannaway and his wife, Sarah (Coleman) Lannaway, emigrated to Upper Canada in 1838.[68] Lannaway had been a groom and night coachman at Petworth House under the Earl of Egre-

---

67 Letter 34 told of the death of Jane Cosens, William Tilt's first wife, in childbirth in October 1832; Tilt married Caroline Cosens, a much younger sister of his first wife, in 1834.

68 Both James and Sarah signed the register when they married in October 1828.

mont*. After Egremont's death in November 1837 Colonel Wyndham* reduced his staff, and Lannaway was given three months' notice in December. Sarah had worked as a needlewoman in England. Wyndham's offer to aid redundant house servants in emigrating came just before news of the rebellions in the Canadas, and the Lannaways seem to have been the only family sent to Upper Canada by the Petworth committee in 1838. They sailed from London on the Carter and Bonus ship the *Hibernia*, carrying with them letter 132 for Richard and Frances Pullen.

Egremont had paid £10 for the full passage of an adult emigrant from the parish of Petworth and expected the parish to contribute £5 for travel to Portsmouth and an outfit. Wyndham still expected the parish to provide clothing, travel within England, and landing money in Canada, but he paid only half the passage money from London to Toronto for the Lannaway family.

SOURCE: A letter of two folios printed at Petworth by J. Phillips; page 4 includes an advertisement for Brydone's *Narrative*, "just published" [a new edition] (copy in WSRO, PHA 141).

From James Lanaway,[69] who emigrated with his wife and family from Petworth, Sussex, in the year 1838.

Woodstock, September 24th, 1840.

I have taken the liberty of writing you these few lines, to let you know that I am in good health at present, hoping this will find you, and all my acquaintances, the same. I have wrote two letters, one to Mrs. Thorp, and another to Mrs. Luff, to both of which I have not received any answer, of which I hope you will not forget to write me an answer to this, and let me know the state of the country, and how are all my old acquaintance, since I left England.

I must now tell you, that we are doing well: there is plenty of work in this country, the wages for a labourer is 3s. sterling per day. Provisions are cheap, flour is 10s. per cwt., pork is 3d. per pound, tea is 3s.6d. per pound. I have also to tell you, that we have five acres of land, and two cows, with a good comfortable house: we have 50 bushels of oats, and a sufficient quantity of potatoes, with other vegetables. I have to mention to you, that vegetables grow here the same as they do in England. I have also to tell you, that the children are all well, Joseph, Rachel, Leah, Sarah, and Lucy we have had in this country. The oldest of the children is often talking about you, Mrs. Hill, Mrs. Baxter, Mrs. Luff, Mrs. Smith, and Mrs. Thorp, and William. We send all of us our love to you all. You will be so good to let me know how James's brothers and sisters; and James wants to know how is Joseph Richardson, and Mr. Edwards the coachmaker.

This is a good country for a poor man: he can get a good living, if he is industrious. I have also to mention to you, that the winter is a little colder, and the summer is a little warmer than in England. The winter commences in December, and ends in April. We commence making sugar in the month of March, and generally continues for about 5 weeks. I make my own yeast, and bake my own bread. I also

---

69 The letter was written by Sarah.

make my own soap, which, if I should go back to England, I should be a little more used to, than when I came away. The children never had any sickness since we came to this country. I have also to mention to you, that you will remember us to Mr. and Mrs. King. I have also to mention to you, that all the emigrants that came here two years ago is doing very well. This is a good country, I like it very much, I would not go back to England on no account. I can earn with the needle from 10s. to 15s. per week. I have nothing more particular to mention to you at present, but our blessing to you all, and all enquiring friends.

JAMES and SARAH LANAWAY.

When you write, you will address James Lanaway, Woodstock, Brock District, Upper Canada.
To Mr. William Thorp, Pound Street, Petworth.

The Lannaways' five acres in the government reserve at Woodstock was a lot originally given to Ann Kemp in 1834 and was reassigned to the Lannaways by 1838. They mortgaged their interest in this lot to a local merchant who took out a patent for it in 1844. They probably continued to live there, since in 1846 James purchased one acre of the original five on the north side of Henry Street. Although this lot was sold in 1850, the 1851 census found them still in Woodstock, living with three children born in England and three more born in Canada. Their son Joseph died of typhoid fever at or near Woodstock in 1869. The census of 1871 recorded James as a labourer, aged 67 and living in Woodstock.

■ **143**

THOMAS TRUSSLER, BEXLEYHILL, WEST SUSSEX, TO GEORGE TRUSSLER, WATERLOO TOWNSHIP, UPPER CANADA, 10 AUGUST 1863

Thomas Trussler is writing to his brother George, who was 36 when he emigrated to Upper Canada in 1833 with his family and that of their older brother John. See letter 105 from John's son Timothy.

SOURCE: Helen Stover, "Letters to George Trussler in Canada," *Sussex Family History* 8 (1988-89): 326-7

Bexleyhill,[70] August 10, 1863

Dear Brother

I am requested by brother James to write a few lines to you respecting the post office order that you sent to brother James last spring, this being the third letter that I have sent in answer to it. The first I sent by return of post as soon as we received the order and in that I enclosed Robert Eade directions wrote with blue ink which I got from his mother. The second one I wrote on the 21st of June while brother James and John Greavatt[71] stayed at my house. In that I told you William Gilbert's

---

70 A hamlet between Lodsworth and Fernhurst, West Sussex.
71 Their sister Ann Trussler married John Greavatt in 1812.

wife's life was not expected and she died on the Friday following. I must inform you that James Greavatt is about the same as when you were here in this country, like an old man wore out with age. Little John has been dead some time before Ann died, and my son Eli is still lingering in a state of consumption, he has not done any work for 5 years last Christmas, but he do not keep his bed yet.

Dear brother, I am happy to tell you that's a fine crop of corn in this country. Such a one have not been for many years and butiful fine weather to harvest it. Potatoes are very fine, better than have been since the disease came. There is plenty of work in this country in general for all that will work.

My son William and I are plank sawing in Verdley Wood just beyond the old castle[72] for Marshall at Godalming. When you write, John Francis would like to know anything of his sister Caroline Dearling.[73]

Well dear brother, I must conclude by sending all our kind love to all, trusting your family are all well and yourself better, and I remain your affectionate brother

Thomas Trussler

We have heard that George Trussler's last wife have got 1000 pounds left her by old Mr Neal's daughter that Upperfold Farm belonged to. Her mother was a Trimmer from Stanley near Linchmere. Mr Grevatt, Benvill Gate, Easebourne.

OTHER LETTERS: 105, 144

■ **144**

THOMAS TRUSSLER, BEXLEYHILL, WEST SUSSEX, TO GEORGE
TRUSSLER, WATERLOO TOWNSHIP, ONTARIO, 22 NOVEMBER 1879
Although we know of only two letters from Thomas Trussler to his brother George, this one
and 143 from 1863, they suggest a regular correspondence. Thomas by now was 83 and George
82 years of age.

SOURCE: Helen Stover, "Letters to George Trussler in Canada," *Sussex Family History* 8 (1988–89): 326–7

Nov 22 1879, Bexleyhill, Sussex

Dear Brother

I read your kind letter with the postal order for one pound and I gave it to John Greavatt, gave him your directions for him to write to you to thank you for your goodness to send it. Dear brother I trust this will find you well as I thank God I am better again now. I have had another attack of the asthma for this 3 weeks but I am a deal better. We have had 5 weeks of butefull weather the wheat is sown in good

---

72 Probably the remains of an old hunting tower near Bexley Hill.

73 John and Caroline (Francis) Dearling also emigrated in 1833 from the parish of Lodsworth and settled in Waterloo Township. We have no information about Caroline (Francis) Dearling after the death of her husband, John, in August 1843 (see her letters 85, 111, 134).

order. But it began to snow on the morning of the 20th and then all day yesterday. So today we have it nearly up to the knees. I have not seen so much snow for many, many years, and the wind being so still all the time it was falling, the trees are loaded to breaking down. Since I have been writing it is beginning to melt a little. Flour is now 10 shillings a bushell, butter [illegible] cheese from 6 pence to 10 the Brk & D (?) men are taken down to 13 cp per week.

Well, dear brother, trusting this will find you and your family well as, thank God, it leaves all of us well. I remain your ever loving brother T Trussler.

———————————

OTHER LETTERS: 105, 143

George Trussler died 1 September 1882 and is buried in Rosebank Cemetery, Wilmot Township. John Trusler had died at Camlachie, Plympton Township, in January 1878.[74]

———————————

74 Sarnia *Observer*, 8 February 1878.

Additional Correspondence
and Memoirs

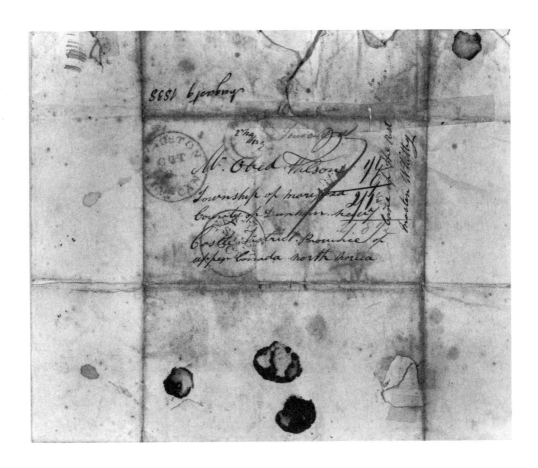

Letter 145 from Maria Wilson (transcribed on page 407)
Courtesy W.H. Wilson

PREVIOUS PAGE: Courtesy W.H. Wilson

WILSON CORRESPONDENCE

Obediah Wilson was the youngest child in a family of seven. In 1832, on his eighteenth birthday, he set sail from Portsmouth for Upper Canada – one of a group sent from Bassingbourn, Cambridgeshire, to travel with the Petworth Emigration Committee. An early letter home (15), sent that August, reassured his family that he was alive and well and was one of those published in the first of Thomas Sockett*'s collections. We have no further letters from Obed but we have a fascinating collection of letters sent to him by his family in England, and his personality reaches us through these letters that he received and kept. The letters were discovered by a family member, years after his death, in a secret compartment in his desk.

The first letter in this correspondence is from his mother, Maria, in 1838. It is the second letter she has written, she tells us, since she has had no answer to her first – and we have letters or parts of letters from her in 1839, 1841, 1848, 1855, and 1859. Maria Wilson had most of her family around her throughout her life, but Obed was the baby of the family and for her his absence was a gap the others could not fill. She was literate but her spelling is phonetic and she does not seem to write easily. (Although several of the letters seem to have been written by her personally and one of the later letters refers to her perhaps having written 149 with her own hand, some of these letters appear to have been dictated to someone else.)

The correspondence also includes letters from his sisters Mary Ann, Elizabeth (Betsy), and Frances Ann (Fanny). It is the women of the family who continue this correspondence and it is only with the next generation that any of the men put pen to paper. Mary Ann's daughter Emma wrote several letters; Emma married her first cousin, Henry Hall, Fanny's eldest son. William Hall, another of Fanny's sons, emigrated to Canada in about 1874 and a letter of his to his uncle survives. And William H. Hall, a son of Emma and Henry Hall, becomes the third generation of the family to continue the correspondence. Elizabeth Crabtree, a daughter of Obed's sister Elizabeth probably wrote letter 160. Some of the letters are combination efforts, with one writer picking up where another left off, and these we have numbered and treated as one letter. In cases where two individuals sent letters at one time (and probably in the same envelope) but each was written on separate sheets of paper, we have numbered and treated them as separate letters.

Because this correspondence was sporadic, because it extended over a long period of time, and because the letter-writers did not know which letters had been received, family information is repeated. Obed's niece Emma introduces herself to an uncle who left home before her birth. Her son, in turn, presents himself and sends a pic-

FIGURE I: OBEDIAH WILSON'S BIRTH FAMILY

Father John WILSON d by June 1841, married 23 Dec 1802 Bassingbourn:

Mother Maria STAMFORD; she wrote letters 145 in 1838, 146 in 1839, 147 in 1841, 148 in 1848, 149 (joint) in 1855, 150 in May 1859, 151 (joint) in Nov 1859

Children:

1 John WILSON, bap 27 Dec 1803 Bassingbourn

2 Mary Ann WILSON, bap 13 July 1806 Bassingbourn, married 6 Dec 1832 William MUNCEY (who d 23 Jan 1855); living in a public house in Kneesworth March 1855); wrote letters 149 (joint) in 1855, 154 (joint) in 1876, 158 in Aug 1881, 159 in Feb 1883, 161 in Aug 1887

    i Frances MUNCEY bap 6 Oct 1833 Bassingbourn (living with Maria WILSON in 1841)

    ii Emma MUNCEY bap 22 Oct 1838 Bassingbourn (living in Royston in 1855); married 12 Sep 1863 cousin Henry HALL; wrote letters 151 (joint) from Hoops, Kneesworth, Nov 1859, 154 (joint) from Bassingbourn Jun 1876, 157 from Bassingbourn Jun 1881, 162, 164 from Bassingbourn 1889

        a Annie HALL b c1865

        b John HALL b 1869, tailor

        c William H HALL b 1871, apprentice joiner, wrote letter 163 Jan 1889, sent his photo to Canada

        d unnamed sister HALL b 1875

    iii John MUNCEY bap 31 May 1835 Bassingbourn

    iv Henry MUNCEY bap 11 Jun 1837 Bassingbourn, d 1 Jul 1854

    v Obed MUNCEY b 22 Feb 1842, bap 7 Aug 1842 Bassingbourn

        a George MUNCEY b c1870, painter, decorator; see letter 163 Jan 1889, sent his photo to Canada

3 Henry WILSON bap 6 Mar 1808 Bassingbourn, d unmarried 1886; lived with Maria WILSON in Bassingbourn; details of illness, death, in letter 161

4 Edward WILSON bap 19 Aug 1810 Bassingbourn, married 20 Nov 1837 Charlotte COURSE; lived with sister Fanny HALL at Broadwater, where he worked with her at the Roebuck Inn.

i – vii at least 7 children born by 1855, youngest son was Obed WILSON

---

ture of himself and his cousin George Muncey. We have used the information from the letters, combined with research in parish records, to prepare Figure 1 on Obed Wilson's parents and his siblings' families. It should enable readers to follow the lives of the various members of the family referred to in the letters.

As far as we know, Obed (in 1832) and his nephew William Hall (about 1874) were the only members of the family to travel so far. Most seem to have lived within a few miles of each other; Kneesworth is less than 2 miles from Bassingbourn, and Broadwater is perhaps 15 miles away. Emma lived in Ireland for a few years but then returned and apparently took work in Royston, perhaps 5 miles from Kneesworth. The family seems to have combined pub keeping with some farming, with Fanny at the Roebuck Inn, at Broadwater, assisted by her brother Edward, Mary Ann at Hoops in Kneesworth, and Maria Wilson at the Fox and Hounds in North End, Bassingbourn. The younger generation of men seem to have taken up trades; Emma's

5 Elizabeth (Betsy) WILSON bap 6 Dec 1812 Bassingbourn, married (1) 23 Jul 1838 Simeon SELL, veterinary surgeon, married (2) c1850 _____ CRABTREE; she wrote letter 149 (joint) in 1855

    i Simeon Leete SELL b 18 Sep 1843, living with grandmother Maria WILSON at ages 5 and 11

    ii Maria Frances CRABTREE b 14 Aug 1850

        a–b had two children in 188[4?]

    iii Elizabeth CRABTREE b 30 Oct 1851, probably wrote letter 160 in 188[4?]

    iv Henry CRABTREE b 6 Dec 1852

    v James CRABTREE b 6 Dec 1852

6 Frances Ann (Fanny) WILSON b Aug 1817 Bassingbourn, married (1) Jul 1838 John HALL, stud groom, (2) by 1855 John HALL, (3) _____ SHORE; she worked at the Roebuck Inn at Broadwater, Hertfordshire, from about 1833 to 1880, managing it for 36 years; wrote letters 149 (joint) 1855, 156 Jun 1881

Children by first husband?

    i Henry HALL b c1839, married by 1863 cousin Emma MUNCEY

    ii Ellen HALL b c1840

    iii James HALL b c1842

    iv Mary Ann HALL b c1844

    v William HALL b c1845; emigrated to Canada c. 1874?, had moved to Buffalo when he wrote letter 155 Nov 1880

        a son HALL mentioned in father's letter

    vi Hannah Maria HALL b c1847

Children by second husband?

    vii Fanny HALL b 1855, wrote letter 153 in 1875

    viii John HALL b Mar 1856, in June 1881 had been in "Lunatick Asylum" 9 months

Probably child by third husband?

    viii Emily SHORE, m by 1883 – FAIREE, referred to in letter 162 of 188[4?]

7 Obediah WILSON, b 11 Apr 1814 bap 10 Jul 1814 Bassingbourn, see Figure 2; wrote letter 15

husband Henry worked for a tea merchant in London, although she seems to have stayed in Cambridgeshire. (See map 9, page 308, for the various locations.)

■ 145

MARIA WILSON, BASSINGBOURN, CAMBRIDGESHIRE, TO OBED WILSON, MARIPOSA TOWNSHIP, UPPER CANADA, 9 AUGUST 1838[1]

The correspondence from Obediah Wilson's family covers the period 1838–89. Obed was the youngest of a close-knit family of seven, and he seems to have been the only one to move more than a few miles from his mother Maria (Stamford) Wilson.

---

1 See Appendix A for a transcription of the original manuscript.

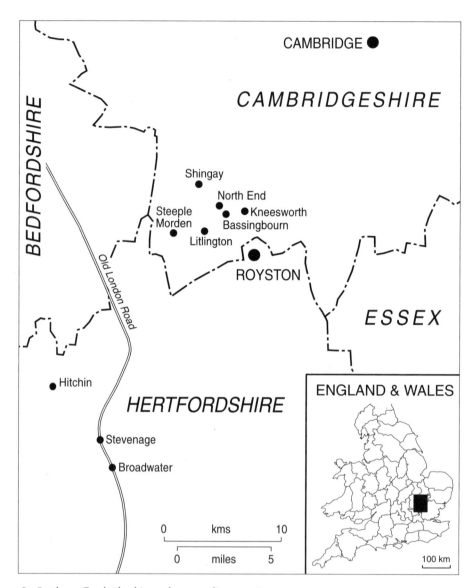

9 Southern Cambridgeshire and surrounding counties

SOURCE: Wilson Family Papers, Obed Wilson correspondence

Bassingbourn August 9, 1838

My Dear Son

This is the second time I have taken up my pen to right [write] to you and have
not reseived haney [any] Answer; if this should reach your hands I hope you will

right as soon as possabel or I shall think you are know [no] more; we hope you still
live and once again will come to old England to see your Affectionate mother as
you are in my thoughts Day And night. This leaves me well. And All your brothers
& sisters as they are more numerous then when you left, as Edward was married 20th
November 1837 to Charlotte Corse, And Faney on the 30 of January 1838 to marie
[marry] Jhon Hall[2] near Broadwater, Elizabeth on 23th July 1838 to Simeon Sell of
Bassingbourn. Your uncal [uncle] Henery is living with me and your brother Henery. Your cousins Willsons are well & send their kind love to you, now my Dear Boy
I must conclude with my kind love, and all your Brothers and Sisters join with me;
I hope the Lord is with you, from your own Loving Mother, Maria Wilson

Bassingbourn
Cambridge Shire
North of England

P.S. If this is not Answered some one of the Family will Come Over
Cover: Mr Obed Wilson

> Township of Mariposa
> County of Durham. New
> Castle District. Province of
> Upper Canada North America

OTHER LETTERS: 15, 146–64. See letter 23 from Simeon Titmouse for the names of the party
emigrating from Bassingbourn.
See Figure 1, which sets out the relationships of this family, retold in the letters.

■ **146**

MARIA WILSON, BASSINGBOURN, CAMBRIDGESHIRE, TO OBED WILSON,
MARIPOSA TOWNSHIP, UPPER CANADA, 22 AUGUST 1839

SOURCE: Wilson Family Papers, Obed Wilson correspondence

August 22, 1839

Dear Obed

I received your letter August the 5th and was glad to hear from you for I never
expected to hear from you again for I quite thought you were dead. We saw by the
news papers the Commotion you were in.[3] We are in a very unsettled state here and
but little work for men; we have very fine Crops of Corn every where.

I have been very fair with the Rumatick; your brother Henery is quite [well] and
sends his love to you; Betsy is married to Simeon Sell the [voster?].[4] Fanny is mar-

---

2 Fanny Wilson and John Hall
3 She is referring to the rebellions of 1837-8, which along with the economic conditions that in part
   lay behind them, meant a virtual stop to immigration from England in 1838.
4 Sell was a veterinary surgeon.

ried to a young man in the name of Hall, stud groom to a gentleman. She has got one young one; she is now very poorly with a bad leg. Mary has four children and they're all well; she sends her kind love to you. Your uncle Henery has left his place and come home and lives with us; Edward is married to Charlotte Course and has got one child; they're living at Broadwater. Your sister Fanny intends writing to you.

Bassingbourn has very much improved; we have a knew [new] house[5] here and a doctor. As you think of changing your conditions in life, I wish you may meet with some comfortable person for I wish you well with all my heart. Your grand father and mother are Both living; father is 79 and mother 82 last June; they send their kind loves to you. Betsey and Judey and Richard[6] send their loves to you and should much like to see you once more. Old Mrs Munsey is living;[7] Isaac Racher is married and got two children; [he] sends his Respects to you, likewise William Haws he is miller at Shingay Mill. Mr & Mrs Chambers send their respects. I think you must have endured many hardships but you not let me know. Be more Explicit in your next for I shall feel more satisfied. Let me know if you meet with any of our people there as we have never heard from William Stamford.[8] Your Aunt is still living at Lilington [Litlington]. Your uncle and aunt are still living at Broadwater; they send their loves to you. Pray answer this as soon as you can for it is a comfort to me to hear from you. Your old friends most of them desired to be remembered to you. John Flanders[?] has made a farm next to us and sends his ... Respects and he is married. Old master Manning is living. They have Built a wind mill in the fen on father's lotment for Conder farm mill[9] has been sold and the people that have bought it have pulled the [old own] down and Built a new one [missing][10] is much improved. My love [missing] and God bless you is the [wish] of your loving Mother
Maria Wilson
Bassingbourn

Bassingbourn
For Obed Wilson
    Newcastle District Upper
    North America[11]

OTHER LETTERS: 15, 145, 147–64

---

5 She is probably referring to a workhouse; in 1835 Bassingbourn was included in the Royston Union and the union workhouse was built within the Bassingbourn boundary (*Victoria History of the Counties of England*, ed. A.P.M. Wright, vol. 8 [1982]).

6 Wilson cousins of Obed.

7 Probably Mary Muncey; she died aged 82 in April 1845.

8 William Stamford emigrated from Bassingbourn in 1832.

9 We found a reference to the sale of "a windmill at Bassingbourn for Mr Wm Condor (£567)" in 1842, but nothing for 1839 (Cambridge Record Office, SR 296.BO791).

10 At some point the stamp marks were removed from the cover, and therefore a section measuring 1½ by 6 inches is missing.

11 Noted on the outside is: "Received this Letter November the 25 1839."

■ 147

MARIA WILSON, BASSINGBOURN, CAMBRIDGESHIRE, TO OBED WILSON, UPPER CANADA, 21 JUNE 1841[12]

SOURCE: Wilson Family Papers, Obed Wilson correspondence

June 21 1841 Bassingbourn

My Dear and Ever Blessed son

I received your kind letter June 11 1841 and was so glad to hear from you I cannot express my feelings towards you my Dear Child, as [I] have no husband, my Children are all my Comforts. I am glad to hear you are well as Bless the lord at this time it leaves us all well. Your grand mother and grand father Stamford are living. She is 80 four this June. Your sister Fanny has been to see me and her Little girl name Ellien, the son Henery & the prettiest Children your ever did see and such a kind husband. She has married into such a respectable family and she wishes so much to see you. I post the letter to her and sent word; she flud into tears for joy to hear from her dear Brother whom she thought was dead. My dear son, pray write often. Your sister Betsy has had 3 stillborn; your sister Mary Muncey has got 4 children, 2 boys, 2 gals; the oldest girl named Frances lives with me as I now do without a servant; she is very handy for me; I have had the rheumatism in my leg so bad but it is better now. I have a nice pony and I drive myself out. Edward has got a little gal and a son; he and his wife sends their kind love to you. He lives near to Fanny; they all say pray mother tell my brother Obed to sell his farm and Come home to England and live happy together with us all, as we are all Comfortable one with another. My dear son, there is a living here for you as well as the rest. They all dined with me on Whitsunday last but the thoughts of your absence was a grief to us all. Oh my son if I could Come over the water I could soon be with you.

Old Mrs Muncey is alive and sends her kind love to you and says how she should Like to see you and many more as well. Your uncle Henry is at home with us 3 years and better. My dear son I thought you was married according to your letter. My dear, if you have got a young woman, bring her to England and we shall love her and use her well. Your sister Fanny will write to you soon. We hear a poor[?] account of the United States for the Banks [are Borok (broke?) and there (are) Bad doing There] there is several gone from here but glad to come back again for they cannot find a better place. Bassingbourn is wonderful improved; our Crops are in some places very good. Isack Racher sends his love to you and says you must Come home as he will spend a happy hour with you; he has got 4 Children. William Hose [Haws?]is so glad to hear of you; he is a fine young man; he is a miller [with] Henry Cullep.[13] Cousin Judy has been very bad, thought she would of died, but she is better. Richard and Betsy are well and they feel very much concerned about your separation from

---

12 Please see Appendix A for a transcription of the original manuscript.
13 The Culleps (Collops) were millers in Bassingbourn.

the rest of the family. Mr and Mrs Chambling and family sends their kind Love to you and many more; I Cannot mention all that wish me to send to you. Asher Racher & his wife send their kind love to you and hope you will find their son John Racher as he [is] at Dundas, Upper Canada;[14] they are a canvassing here and we expect to have a reform.[15] Please to give my kind love to the gentleman that wrote to me. Pray write to me as soon as possible & we all shall [be] glad to hear from you. I remain your loving and affectionate Mother Maria Wilson

OTHER LETTERS: 15, 145–64

▪ 148

MARIA WILSON, BASSINGBOURN, CAMBRIDGESHIRE, TO OBED WILSON, EAST WHITBY TOWNSHIP, CANADA WEST, 21 SEPTEMBER 1848

SOURCE: Wilson Family Papers, Obed Wilson correspondence

Bassingborne
Sep 21/48

My Dear Son

If this letter reaches you I hope and trust that you will not fail answering it as I am very unhappy concerning you as I have been inform^d that there has been war near ware [where] you live and not hearing from you for three years I am fearfull that you must have got killed.[16] I hope my Dear Boy if you are living you will let me here from you as it is the greatest trial I have that I cannot see nor hear from you, my Dear Boy. I am getting in to years verry fast and should verry much Like to see you before I depart this Life. I have all my children round me but you. I do hope my Dear Boy you will try and come home that I may see you be fore I leave this world. Your Brothers and Sisters are all quite well.

I hope my Dear Boy that this will reach you and find you in good health and prospus [prosperous?]. As to my self I am well in health but verry lame and as I get older I find I get worse. Your sister Bettsy [Sell] is still a widow and is living with her sister Fanny [Hall] at Broadwater and her little boy [Simeon Sell] is with me. He is now five years old, the verry image of poor Sim Sell. We have had a verry prospros harvest and there is a home for you if you will but come home.

If you should ever live to come home you will not know Bassingborn as they

---

14 Among the party that emigrated from Bassingbourn in 1832 was John Racher and his wife Edith (Titmouse), and two children. Edith's sister Mary Shambrook and brother Simeon Titmouse also emigrated.

15 Parliament had been dissolved at the end of May 1841, and in the election Melbourne's government was defeated by the Conservatives led by Sir Robert Peel.

16 We are unsure what she might have been referring to here. The Oregon Boundary Dispute in 1846 created tension between Great Britain and the United States and in 1846-8 the U.S.A. was at war with Mexico, but neither of these were "near" Obed.

are building About your cousins Judy and Bettsy [Wilson] are both living and desires there [their] best love to you and feel very anchus [anxious] about you. Your Brothers and sisters and friends join with me in kind love to you. This comes from your verry Affectionet and loving

Mother [Maria] Wilson
Fox & Hound North End

P.S. I hope you will not fail writing.
Good by and god bless you.

OTHER LETTERS: 15, 145–64
We do not know when Maria Wilson began keeping the Fox and Hound at North End, Bassingbourn, but she was still there in 1855; see letter 149.

■ 149

FRANCES ANN HALL, BROADWATER, ELIZABETH CRABTREE, MARY ANN MUNCEY, KNEESWORTH, AND MARIA WILSON, NORTH END, BASSINGBOURN, CAMBRIDGESHIRE, TO OBED WILSON AND HIS WIFE BETSY MARIA, EAST WHITBY TOWNSHIP, UPPER CANADA, WRITTEN BETWEEN 19 AND 26 MARCH 1855

Obed's sister Fanny Hall begins this joint letter; she is now 37 years old and married to her second husband. It is continued by his sister Elizabeth Crabtree, also now married for a second time, by his sister Mary Ann Muncey, and finally by his mother.

SOURCE: Wilson Family Papers, Obed Wilson correspondence

Broadwater March 19th 1855

Dear Brother and Sister

    I can assure you it was with very great pleasure, I perused the content of your letter and was most happy to hear that you, your wife, and family were all well and that you had been so prosperous in all your undertakings. We have often talked about you and thought it very strange we did not hear from you for such a length of time. I sent out a letter by a young woman who went out to Quebec more than 1½ years ago, but you did not state in your letter if it reached you or not. It probably did not. There are great complaints of letters never reaching their destination through some mismanagement of the post Office I suppose.[17]

    I am happy to inform you that my health is tolerably good. I had a bad leg of long standing through a fall from a cart. I have 7 children, 3 boys and 4 girls – viz) Henry 16 years of age, Ellen 15, James 13, Mary Ann 11, William 10, Hannah Maria 8. I must

---

17 Some envelopes survive from the letters sent by Obed Wilson's relatives; they seem to have been addressed to Mr Obed Wilson, 9th concession of Whitby, and post office personnel have annotated them "try Ashburn," "Try Raglan." An envelope from 1881 is addressed to Raglan Post Office, Whitby East, but Canada West rather than Ontario.

Obed Wilson and his wife, Betsy Martin
Courtesy W.H. Wilson

tell you I was a widow nearly 4 years. I am now married again to a person of the same name as my first husband which is somewhat singular to have two of the same name, both named John Hall. I have a baby named Fanny 11 weeks old. John Muncey the son of sister Mary brought your letter to me, he came up to see us on Saturday. He is a you[ng] man grown, nearly 20 years of age, and I hear a very steady industrious young man he is a comfort to his mother who is now left a widow.

We had a very severe winter in England; it has been colder than has been known for some years. There has been a great deal of snow; it was very mild up to Xmas. It has been very hard times for the poor, provisions of all kinds have been so very dear. Potatoes were very good last year; there had been none that you could call good for 8 years previous to the last. Providence has it appears kindly favoured your industry with plentiful crops and in abundance. The Potato failure caused great distress here in England and much worse in Ireland; the crops were very good of all kinds last year and have fetched great prices. Wheat has been 8s. per bushel upon an average. Barley about 3s2d.

Your aunt Stamford has been dead rather more than 3 years. She was a very great sufferer. Louisa Stamford died on the 1st of March she was a poor afflicted creature the last few years. Uncle Stamford continues very hearty for a man at 70 years of age, he desires to be remembered to you. Dear mother will write a few lines to you I hope with her own hand. She has been very ill indeed, but thank God I hear she is getting better. Betsy & Mary will also write. Edward is still with me; he has a family of 7 children living and has buried two; he had his last son named Obed.

I know dear brother there would be a great difficulty for you to leave your home for the time a journey to England would require, but still we hope you will be able to get some trusty person to manage for you during your absence as it is so many years since we saw you. At all events we shall live in hopes of seeing you before long if it pleases God to spare and prosper you. I hope you will write whenever convenient as a letter is always acceptable from you.

Believe me dear Brother to remain your Affectionate
Sister Francess Ann Hall

My Dear Brother & Sister
With pleasure I take up my pen to address a few lines to you which I hope will find you all well as I am happy to tell you this leaves me & my husband & family. I suppose mother stated in her Last Letter to you that I was married again which took place 5 years ago. I have 5 children: Simeon Leete Sell born Sept 18 1843, Maria Frances August 14 1850, Elizabeth Octr 30th 1851, Henry & James Decr 6 1852; you see we have children (lost)? too at birth. I have living close by my brother Edward. I remain your affectionate sister Elizabeth Crabtree

Kneesworth March 25

Dear Brother & Sister
With much pleasure I take up my pen to address these few lines to you as I was glad to hear of you again my dear Brother. I have but poor news to tell you. My son Henry died in [18]54 the 1 of July. Then my dear husband died in 55 Jan 23 so you see I am left a widow. I have a good son which is a comfort to me. My daughter Emma is living at Royston so I have only the two sons at home with me John & Obed. I am now living in a public house in Kneesworth so I think I shall get a living with industry as I have some land, hens, turkeys & ducks. I remain your affectionate sister Mary Ann Muncey

My dear and Beloved Son and daughter
I received your kind and welcome letter on March 13. I so rejoiced to hear from you that I could not do anything all day. My servant took it up town to Cousin Judey Wilson and they was so glad to hear from you and yours and Betsy & Judey sends their kind love to you and hope that the lord will spare their lives to once more to see you and wife. They say they will make you so welcome and my dear According to your wife's statement in her letter that we may expect to see you both in England and your dear children and give them a kiss for me. I knew it is bad for you to leave home for so long a time. I Hope you will try and get someone to take care of your property and come as my time cannot be long. I am seventy-four this last month and I have a bad leg.

Isaac Racher sends his kind love and shed tears for joy for he has got nine children alive. Your old sweetheart Sally Bird as was sends her kind love to you and she is a widow of seven children. Mrs and Mr Chambling sends their kind respects to you and was pleased to read your letter and many more friends which is too tedious to mention. Mr and Mrs Cleaments sends his kind love to you and glad to hear of your doing well. So you see my dear boy I am perfectly satisfied that you have a good wife and I send my kind love to all her friends, thou known the times are very hard here. We are sapress [oppressed?] with rates and taxes. I keep Betsey's oldest son [Simeon Sell] by her first husband. He is eleven years old and we find him very useful. Your brother Henry sends his kind love to you and he so wants to see you all he would come over and see you all if it was not for your mother for she not fit to be left a minute for if she falls down she cannot get up. We still keep the Public house but farming pays the best, and so you see all the family wrote a part of this letter and I hope you will make it out. Please to write as soon as you can and let me know when you are acoming. This from your everloving Mother, goodby and God bless you.

This from
Mrs Maria Wilson
Bassingbourn north end
Cambridgeshire
near Royston
leave me March 26th

OTHER LETTERS: 15, 145–64

■ 150

MARIA WILSON, BASSINGBOURN, CAMBRIDGESHIRE, TO OBED WILSON, EAST WHITBY TOWNSHIP, CANADA WEST, 4 MAY 1859

SOURCE: Wilson Family Papers, Obed Wilson correspondence

Bassingbourne May 4th 1859

Dear Obed

I received your kind and welcome letter on Tuesday the 26th day of April last. Am very glad to hear that you and all your family are quite well, as it leaves me as well as can be expected for my years.[18] We don't know any thing respecting the five families that went out the same time as you did but Wm Stamford and he is dead. His widow has married again. Your sister Betsy's son Simeon Sell[19] is come into some property by the death of Mr. Simeon Sell deceased. He died March the 28th. He left his property in the name of the Sells, and has left them all well. Your uncle Stamford is still living and pretty well. Mrs Hall and family are well and getting a comfortable living.[20] We all feel very anxious to see you and are happy to hear that you have such a good and industrious wife.

We have had a very mild winter, but a cold spring. Mrs Muncey is but middling – her daughter [Emma] is at Belfast in Ireland 600 miles off – she is quite well.

---

18 This is the first letter not written in her own hand.
19 Simeon Sell was living with his grandmother, Maria Wilson, at age 5 after his mother was left a widow and at age 11 after her remarriage to a man named Crabtree. She had four children (including twins) within about three years of marriage. Further details of young Sell's inheritance are in letter 151.
20 Obed's sister Fanny kept the Roebuck Inn at Broadwater.

Cousin Betsy and Judith send their love, and they are pretty well according to their age. I received the newspaper, and shall be happy to have one whenever you think proper to send one. We have had a great many fires this last winter. The man has got transported; times are rather bad here at present, a great many are out of work. Old Master Woods is still living and desires his respects. Uncle has counted up the marbles for the Boys 144 in all. Uncle Henry would so like to see you; he thinks if any thing happens to me, he will come over and live with you. Accept of my love from your ever and Affectionate Mother

Maria Wilson

Your Brother Edward and family are quite [well] and desire their kind love to you. All friends and acquaintances send their respects. Isaac Racher sends his respects. He has a family of eleven children.

Mrs Wilson
Bassingbourne
Near Royston
Cambridgeshire

OTHER LETTERS: 15, 145–64

■ 151
MARIA WILSON, BASSINGBOURN, CAMBRIDGESHIRE, EMMA MUNCEY, HOOPS, KNEESWORTH, AND HENRY HALL, LONDON, TO OBED WILSON, EAST WHITBY TOWNSHIP, CANADA WEST, 7 NOVEMBER 1859 AND 12 JANUARY 1860

SOURCE: Wilson Family Papers, Obed Wilson correspondence

Bassingbourne
November 7th 1859

My Dear Son
    With great pleasure I now take the opportunity of addressing a few lines to you which I hope will find you and your family in good health. I am glad to tell you I am as well as you can expect at my age. Also your dear brother Henry is pretty well at this time. My dear, I have received three newspapers from you But I would much rather see you and your family. I am affraid that I shall never live to see you now. I must now tell you Mr Simeon Leat Sell died the twenty-eighth of March 1859. He left Grandson Simeon Leat Sell four hundred pounds, also his Aunt Edith Sell died June the nineth 1859.[21] She left Simeon five hundred pounds. Mr Sell has left Simeon Grandfather Hemp[?] Sell ten thousand pounds and at his death it will be divided into five parts and Simeon will come in for his part. Also those cottages at the Cross

---

21 Edith Fossey Sell died a spinster at Bassingbourn and left under £12,000 in her will.

will belong to Simeon at his Grandfather's death. Simeon was sixteen years of age the eighteenth of September 1859. He cannot take the money untill he is twenty-one years of age. He will be quite a gentleman if he lives. My dear boy, I think of nothing more to tell you this tim; I must now send with our best love to you and your dear family.

From your loving mother
Maria Wilson

Hoops[22] Kneesworth
November 7th /59

My Dear Uncle Obed,

I dare say you will be quite surprised to receive a few lines from your niece Emma Muncey. But I was at Grandmothers the other day. We were talking about you, so I said I would write to you. Dear Uncle, I must tell you I have not been at home much this last 5 years. I have been living in Belfast, Ireland, more than two years. I have been home from there 2 months I liked that Country very much indeed. I am going to live at Royston now.

Since I have been home I have been to Broadwater a fortnight. I enjoyed myself very much there I have also had a very good holiday at home. Dear Uncle I hope you and will come home to see us all. If you come home, my brother Obed says he will go back with you. You could come home in a very short time now. I am sure you need not to mind the journey on the water. In fact I am very fond of travelling by the water.

Dear Uncle my time is rather short just now so I beg you will excuse my short note. My Dear Mother wishes to be remembered to you, also my two brothers John and Obed. I must now conclude with my kindest love to you dear Uncle & leave me to remain your ever affectionate niece Emma Muncey

18 Rood Lane
London January 12th 1860

My Dear Uncle

I now take the opportunity of addressing a few lines to you which I ought to have done before But being so very busy I hope you will excuse me.

Dear Uncle being the first time that I have written to you I dare say you would like to know who I am. I am the oldest son of your Sister Fanny And I am most happy to say She is quite well. Your Brother Edward is still living at Broadwater and works at your Sister Fanny's place. Dear Uncle I was down at Bassingbourn a few months ago and I am most happy to say I found your dear Mother and Uncle Henry and also your sister Mary in the enjoyment of good health. Bassingbourn looks about the same although a great many old friends are dead. And now Dear Uncle I must tell you a little about your Sister Fanny. She has been married twice and Both names Hall. But I am sorry to say she is now a Widow with 8 children and I am the oldest being 21 years of age and I have been living in London for 6 years in a Tea Dealer Trade. Your sister Betsey is living at Broadwater and is quite well with children and all quite well. Your

---

22 Hoops was the name of the public house in Kneesworth.

Dear Mother is as well as you may expect; she is getting quite old. She has been very ill but I am happy to say she [is] quite well now. My dear Uncle, I should so like to see you, so I wish you could come home to see us all grown up. I hope we shall see you this next Spring. Dear Uncle, I hope your wife and family are all the enjoyment of good health. I hope you will write me a few lines when you can. I should so like to hear from you, I hope you will excuse me. Dear Uncle, when you think of coming to England I would meet you at the Docks; and now, Dear Uncle, you may please give my kind love to your wife and children and accept my kindest love yourself.
I remain
Your Ever Affectionate Nephew
Henry Hall
My address is Henry Hall
David Lloyd Co[23]
18 Rood Lane
London

OTHER LETTERS: 15, 145–64
Emma Muncey and Henry Hall were married some time after this letter and their first child was born about 1865. Emma wrote several of the letters that have survived.

■ 152
JOHN E. WILSON, UDORA, ONTARIO, TO OBED WILSON, EAST WHITBY TOWNSHIP, ONTARIO, 20 OCTOBER 1873
John Wilson was the oldest of Obed Wilson's sons. At the time Obed prepared his last will in 1892, he owned a hotel and land in the village of Udora.

SOURCE: Wilson Family Papers, Obed Wilson correspondence

Udora Oct 20 73
Dear Father
    I beg leave to inform you that I am at present well and getting on well hoping you and Family are all the same.
    The money you have of Richard Harrison's ($90.00) He & Mr Harrison told me you could have the use of it till the 17th of next month. I thought I could write and let you know, thinking it might be an advantage for you to have it till that time.
    Mr Sager will be down on Friday next. He can only make out $100.00 for you at that time
    Yours ever
    John E. Willson

OTHER LETTERS: 15, 145–64

---

23 The City of London Directory, 1878, records David Lloyd and Co., Tea Merchants, 18 Rood Lane, Fenchurch Street, City of London.

■ **153**

FANNY HALL, THE ROEBUCK INN, BROADWATER, HERTFORDSHIRE, TO OBED WILSON, UPPER CANADA, 8 MARCH 1875

This letter from Obed Wilson's niece Fanny Hall suggests the younger generation was quite intrigued by their Canadian cousins.

March 8 1875. The Roebuck Inn
Broadwater
N^r Stevenage
Hertfordshire
England

My dear Uncle

I have intended writing to you for some time and knowing you are always glad to hear from your English friends I determined to write to you giving you all the information respecting them I possibly could, but must first explain who I am. My name is Fanny, my age 20 years, my father was the second John Hall. I have one own brother but no doubt, dear uncle, William has told you all about us. We saw and read the nice letter my cousin Lizzie Crabtree received from your Daughter, also the Portrait of my cousin. He is a fine looking young man. I was quite in love with him. You must not tell him so or he will be shocked; should like to see you all personally very much. Mother and I often say we should like to go to America. Mother says she would have done before this if she had no children. We were very glad you were so fortunate in having a good harvest; hope you will continue to be prosperous. You deserve to be, for you must have been very very persevering when a young man.

We have had what we call a very sharp winter but I daresay you would not think so living in such a cold climate. I think I should be frozen in America for I feel the cold here very much. We often wonder how William endures it; he used to be such a cold subject.[24] Mother & We all think him very unkind & negligent not to write. Mother has not received one letter from him since his departure from home. We think it most ungrateful; I suppose it is the old saying "out of sight out of mind." My Brother John wrote to him the 22nd of last April & Mother sent him two newspapers with the account of eccentric "Hermit Lucas" & his death, but has no reply to any of them so we don't know if he got them or not

Uncle Ted [Wilson] was here the other night. He is looking remarkably well; carrys his years well, has not scarcely a grey hair in his head. It is a great misfortune his wife being to delicate he has only one son and Daughter single. The daughter is at home with her Mother as she is not fit to be alone. Aunt Crabtree[25] lives just across the road a few yards from us; she is quite well & wears well.

---

24 William, fifth child and third son of Fanny and the first John Hall, emigrated to Canada about 1874. We know nothing of the circumstances, but the fact that he evidently did not write his mother suggests estrangement. He moved on to the United States after a few years; see letter 155.

25 Obed Wilson's sister Elizabeth, who was previously married to Simeon Sell.

Mother has had very good luck with the stock, a lot of little pigs & some young lambs, but our hay crop was bad last year. We have got six or seven fields and a nice garden; we grow nearly all kinds of vegetables; it is 42 years since Mother first came here to reside; that was soon after you left England. Mother says she often thinks of your parting words on the Kneesworth Road (you said nothing would trouble you if she did not fret after you), both you and her have seen many changes since then. I am glad to tell you my Aunt Muncey[26] is a little better. My brother Henry lives with her. I think my eldest sister Ellen has written to you. She has very delicate health, never really well. We had her home eight months. I think you know she lives with her Aunt. Mother has set you the picture of our house & she will send you the portrait of her & Mr Shore as soon as she gets to Hitchin to have them taken.

I shall be very pleased to have a letter from you in answer to this. We like to hear about you all & America. I wish you would come to England and see us, but I suppose you never will now. I daresay you almost forget what old England is like after such a lapse of years and would not like to live here now. I suppose America like everywhere else has been much improved since you first went. We have lots of farmers living near us (large farmers). There are no small farms now much; I suppose you have lots of sheep? I suppose my brother William often comes to see you. Mother thanks you very much for your kindness to him. We hope you all spent a Merry Christmas. We were very quiet, had no company, only our own family. We all wish you a "Happy New Year." Hope you are all in the enjoyment of health. There has been a great deal of illness in England this winter. Mr Shore has been very ill; he has had such a bad face, large boils on it. These were very painful; he has also had the lumbago in his back. Mother is pretty well in health & looks quite young, only she has a wound in her leg which causes her a good deal of pain, but I hope it will soon heal again. I expect we shall hardly know William when he [words missing] again. I suppose he will some day. Give our love to him when you see him again and tell him he might find time to write to us once in 14 months or a little oftener if he chose. My sister Polly thinks the same, tell him. And now, dear Uncle, I think I have written you a very long letter and given you a lot of news. Give our kind[?] love to Aunt and Cousins. Accept best love

From your
Affectionate Niece
Fannie Hall

P.S. let us hear from you again soon.

OTHER LETTERS: 15, 145–64

■ **154**

MARY ANN MUNCEY, HOOPS, KNEESWORTH, CAMBRIDGESHIRE, TO OBED WILSON, UPPER CANADA, 27 MARCH 1876
This letter seems to be written in one hand and signed Mary Muncey, but obviously it is a

---

26 Mary Ann Muncey, Obed Wilson's oldest sister. Henry Hall later married his cousin Emma Muncey.

composite effort, probably by her daughter Emma and Emma's husband, Henry Hall (Obed's sister Fanny's son).

———————

SOURCE: Wilson Family Papers, Obed Wilson correspondence

Hoops Kneesworth
N^r Royston
Cambridgeshire
March 27th 1876

Dear Brother & Sister

I received your kind letter on Friday the 17th March and was very pleased to hear from you, and shall always be glad to get a letter from you at any time, and was glad to hear that you were all quite well, as I am glad to say we are quite well here now. They were all quite well at Broadwater about a fortnight ago, except Betsey, she is not very well. Dear Brother, I shall not forget you on the 11th of April being your Birthday I suppose 62 years of age.

Dear Uncle We have had a long winter here this year, a great deal of snow and very cold. Stock of all kinds are very dear here. Potatoes are about 4/- pr Bushel; Wheat from 5/- to 5/6; Barley – 4/– to 4/6 pr Bushel, now quite the top prices. We had a Merry Christmas to ourselfs and the children enjoyed a Christmas tree. We have had a great deal of sickness around us and we have like you lost a lot of our old neighbours died away this winter.

Dear Brother, I am glad to say that Henry is quite well again now and gets quite stout. He sends his kind love to you all. I hope by the time you will get this your son John will be quite well. We are sorry to hear that you had a Dull Christmas time and hope you will have a better next year.

Dear Uncle if you should see my Brother William give my kind love to him and tell him to write to me as he promised to write to me when I saw him off to America.

Dear Brother, I wish to know if you ever see John Racher that went away with you.[27] His brother Stephen died since Christmas and his sister Mary is very ill with the yellow jandess [jaundice] and has been so all winter. They do not think she will last long. John Racher her nephew lives with her, and he wants his Uncle John to write to him and he will answer the letter

And now, Dear Brother, I must conclude with our kindest love to you all.

I Remain Your affect Sister
Mary Muncey

———————

OTHER LETTERS: 15, 45–64

———————

27 John Racher settled with his family in Beverly Township, west of Toronto; Obed Wilson seems always to have lived east of Toronto.

■ 155

WILLIAM HALL, BUFFALO, NEW YORK, TO OBED WILSON, EAST WHITBY TOWNSHIP, ONTARIO, 27 NOVEMBER 1880

SOURCE: Wilson Family Papers, Obed Wilson correspondence

Buffalo
Novr 27 /80

Dear Uncle,

It is with the greatest of pleasure I now sit down to write to you after such long silence hoping this will find you & all your family well as it leaves me in the enjoyment of good health. You will no doubt be surprised to hear I am in Buffalo. I have been here since the 6th of September. I like the place better than Toronto. I have started to work at my trade but for the past 6 weeks I have been at work in the lumber yard. I do not think of staying here after the winter is over. I think of going farther west in the spring, if all is well. I may pay you a visit before I go any further in the early spring. I got tired of Canada. I think there seems to be more chance of a fellow getting along here. I was a little surprised to hear of Marry Ann's Wedding.[28] It was Mrs Muncay who told me of it. From Brooklyn[29] she called on me at Leslieville[30] this summer. I hope that all that family are well.

I must now tell you I have received a nice letter from my son & he & my brother John are thinking of coming out to me. In fact he says they have made up their minds. He tells me that he has not lived with his mother for a year, that he is in lodgings & that he is not doing well. He was apprenticed to a man but he does not say what at, only that he is a German & that he does not use him well. He says he only gives him 5 shillings per week & that is not enough to keep him, only for his Mother giving him a little & finding him a few clothes he could not get along so he wants me to send him a little money to bring him over. I am going to write to him & tell him not to come out till spring & then I will send him some money for to come. He wants me to send him directions where to land; he says he paid my sister Hannah[31] a visit last Witsuntide & stayed a week; he also saw his Grandma & he says she was going to live at Bassingbourne in October; at that time they were all well. He did not say anything about my brother Henry but he gave me James' address. I must now draw this to a close, so accept my best love to you all, from

Your Affectionate Nephew W. Hall

Remember me to all enquring friends
address: W. Hall
          120 Church St.
          Buffalo, N.Y.

---

28 Obed Wilson's daughter Mary Ann (b 1860) married Robert A.E.Vernon, and they farmed the Vernon Farm at Prospect, just north of the Wilson family farm.
29 Brooklin is in Whitby Township, a few miles south and west of the Wilson farm.
30 Leslieville is now part of Toronto.
31 Hannah Maria Hall (b c 1847) was the youngest daughter of Fanny and the first John Hall.

OTHER LETTERS: 15, 145–64

We have no further information about William Hall. Nor do we know anything further about his son or the mother of his son. The letters that survive suggest strongly that there was an estrangement between William and his mother.

■ 156

FANNY SHORE, BASSINGBOURN, CAMBRIDGESHIRE, TO OBED WILSON, EAST WHITBY TOWNSHIP, ONTARIO, 28 JUNE 1881

Fanny wrote her brother a joint letter in 1855 (149) when she had been not long married to her second husband and had just had a baby girl.

SOURCE: Wilson Family Papers, Obed Wilson correspondence

June 28/81

I have written
this with my
own hand
My dear Brother

Mrs. Shore
Bassingbourn
N^r Royston
Cambridgeshire
England

    I have at last sat down to write to you after so many years silent, altho I have not written to you & your family, and you have not been forgotten for I have so often thought & talked of our parting. I have seen many of your letters; am so glad to hear that you have done so well in that country and able to provide for your children as they grow up. I have a large family of nine, 4 sons & five daughters. They are all from home, doing pretty well, with exception of John who I am sorry to say is in a Lunatic Asylum, has been out of his mind nine months. We don't know the cause, he was in good work at the time, taken nearly £2-10s per week. He was 25 years of age last March, not married; it has been a great trouble to me but I am glad to say this week I had a letter to say he is much better.

    I must now tell you that my sister Mary had a letter from you on Monday. I saw by that you was aware of me living at Bassingbourn. I came here last October after being in Hertfordshire forty-eight years. I kept the Roe Buck Inn[32] Broadwater over 36 years and got quite tired of it. I feel much more happy in a private house and I have a good & kind Husband so all togeather I am very comfortable. I have thought it strange that my son William has never written to me since he left England. I had always been a good mother to him. I saw a letter the other day he sent to his son, a very nice one it was too; he said he was going to England shortly so I hope soon to see him and I thank you all very much for your kindness to him during his stay with you. I have often thought how much I should like to come over to see you all

---

32 The Roebuck Inn, Broadwater, near Stevenage, is still in business on the Old London Road

but then again I thought I could not leave my family. I suppose we shall never see each other in this world again but I trust we may meet in a better world than this.

I have Enclosed my likeness which was taken 3 years ago with the intention to send it to you then; I was 62 when taken; it's thought a very good likeness of me. I am 65 in August so we are all going down hill fast now. I hope your wife and family also yourself are in health. Give our love to her and all of you. My Sister Betsey also Edward brakes [is failing?] very fast, I remain your loving sister

Fanny Shore

OTHER LETTERS: 15, 145–64

▪ 157

EMMA (MUNCEY) HALL, BASSINGBOURN, CAMBRIDGESHIRE, TO OBED WILSON, RAGLAN POST OFFICE, WHITBY EAST, CANADA WEST, 28 JUNE 1881

SOURCE: Wilson Family Papers, Obed Wilson correspondence

North End, Bassingbourn
June 28th 1881

My Dear Uncle & Aunt

As my Husband's Mother[33] has just written a letter to you I thought I would write a few lines and send the same time. I hope this will find you both well, also my Dear Cousins. I saw my Mother yesterday and she had just received a letter from you. So I brought it home with me, for your brother Henry and your sister to hear the news. We were glad to hear you are likely to have good crops. My Mother will write to you soon and tell you all the news.

Dear Uncle I dair say you think it long to hear from my Husband Henry Hall. But he has not much time at home now. His business is in London. I am glad to say we are doing very well. Henry looks well after business so as to provide for us. We have 4 children, two boys at school, one little girl at home. And my eldest daughter is in a gentleman's family in Norfolk about 100 miles from here. I will write to you again soon, a longer letter. Now dear Uncle, I wish to draw to a close with kind love to you and Aunt, also my Cousins.

Believe me to remain your loveing niece, Emma Hall

OTHER LETTERS: 15, 145–64

---

33 Fanny Shore was also Emma's aunt. This letter has not survived, but Emma's mother, Mary Ann Muncey seems to refer to it in letter 158, written in August.

■ 158

MARY ANN MUNCEY, KNEESWORTH, TO OBED WILSON, EAST WHITBY
TOWNSHIP, ONTARIO, 29 AUGUST 1881

SOURCE: Wilson Family Papers, Obed Wilson correspondence

Kneesworth Augst 29th

My dear Brother & Sister

I dare say you have been expecting to hear from me before this but as my sister
[Fanny Shore] wrote I thought I would wait and tell you a little about the harvest.
They commenced Harvest about a month ago; the first ten days was very hot, the last
3 weeks it has been raining every day. Obliged to cut the corn and cart it as soon as
possible. It has caused the [price of] bread to rise twice in a fortnight, it is now [/2?]
pr loaf. The wheat is yielding very well; would have been better had it been fine. I
have not got my wheat thrashed yet, my barley and beans are not cut. The fruit there
is a fair crop of apples & plums, the potatoes are very good. Not been so good for
years. Fresh Butter is 1/7 pr pound, Beef & Mutton[10s?] pr pound, Wheat is selling well.

I think you were surprised to have a letter from your sister Fanny. I hope she will
continue her correspondence; they are all quite well. Brother Henry is very poorly
but a poor creature. I have not heard from sister Betsy & brother Edward lately. The
last I heard they were much as usual. Wool is not making very little money in England. I am glad to hear your family are all doing well My love to them. I am much as
usual. My leg is no better. Obed^{34} & wife & family are quite well. Emma & her husband and family are all well. I have enclosed the piece of paper about the storm we
had the 18th of January.^{35} I should like to hear from you by the return of post to let
me know the result of your harvest. It is raining now very fast. I must now say good
bye with love to all.

I remain your affectionate Sister
M.A. Muncey

OTHER LETTERS: 15, 145–64

■ 159

MARY ANN MUNCEY, KNEESWORTH, CAMBRIDGESHIRE, TO OBED AND
BETSY WILSON, EAST WHITBY TOWNSHIP, ONTARIO,
19 FEBRUARY 1883

Obed Wison's oldest sister, Mary Ann Muncey, appears to have been his most faithful correspondent after his mother; see letters 149, 154, 158, 161.

---

34 Her youngest son
35 This clipping has survived; it describes the storm as the most violent in many years, with train travel
  interrupted and a damaging high tide in the Thames.

SOURCE: Wilson Family Papers, Obed Wilson correspondence

Kneesworth

Feby 19th /83

My dear Brother & Sister

I received your letter with great pleasure which I had been looking for for some time. Glad to hear you are in your new house & that you like it so much. I hope you will live to enjoy it for some years to come. I should like to have been with you on Christmas day. You had quite a large party. We have had a very mild winter but very wet, raining most every day; every where is flooded with water; a great deal of the wheat has been ploughed up again. We do not get 2 fine days together. We have not had any snow or frost to speak of; the wheat is not making much with you; it is cheap here now but I am afraid it will be dearer next year.

I am much the same as usual, in very good health but my leg is very bad. My son Obed had been very ill, not done any work for 13 weeks. He has had 3 children ill, one little boy he lost, 9 years old. My daughter & husband & her family are quite well. Your sister Fanny is quite well. She thinks a great deal about her son William. She is afraid he is dead by not hearing anything about him. His son we do not know where he is but we think he is in America.

My dear Sister

I am glad to hear you have got in your new home. I dare say you have found plenty to do! But I hope you will enjoy it for many years and that you have got nearly settled now.

My dear niece

I was pleased to have a line or two from you. I do not suppose I shall ever see you as it is too long a journey. We make your age out as 15. I should like to know how many there are of you in family if you will tell me next time you write.

My dear nephew

You said you would like to correspond with one of your lady cousins. There is only one or two single now, if you would like to write to them I will send you their address next time. One is living at Broadwater the other at London

Your Uncle Henry Wilson has been very ill again this winter, did not expect he would get well again, but he is able to get out again but breaks[36] very much I think I have no more to say this time. Hope to hear from you again shortly. I must conclude now with kind love to you & all your family.

I remain your affectionate

Sister

M.A. Muncey

OTHER LETTERS: 15, 145–64

36 The *Compact Oxford Dictionary* gives one definition of break as to fail in health, decay, give way.

■ 160

[ELIZABETH CRABTREE?], LONDON, TO [CHARLES M. WILSON], EPSOM, ONTARIO, 1 SEPTEMBER [1884]

Mary Ann Muncey, in a note to a son of Obed Wilson enclosed in letter 159 of February 1883, promised to send the address of one of his female cousins. This correspondence may have been the result, although Fanny Hall refers to Lizzie Crabtree writing to one of Obed's daughters in 1875. This letter was probably sent to Obed Wilson's fifth son, Charles, who was born in March 1858 and evidently was teaching at Epsom, a village some 20 kilometres north of the family farm.

SOURCE: Wilson Family Papers, Obed Wilson correspondence

Fair Lawn
Honor Oak Road
Forest Hill
London
September 1st

My Dear Cousin

I at last sit down to write to you. I am sure you must have thought how unkind of me not to answer it before this but the reason chiefly is I lost the address and you did not put it in your letter and when they wrote from home they used to forget to put it in so I hope you will forgive me. Dear Cousin I have to thank you for the enclosed Photo. I should think it was a very good one of your Brother & I see there is a likeness of the Wilson's family. I suppose he is Married by this time. Give my love to him and tell him I don't expect we shall see him over here to choose his intended Bride; it is rather too far. How is Cousin William getting on. I saw Aunt Shore in London a few weeks ago and Emily her youngest daughter. I met them at her daughters Mrs. Fairee. They was all quite well and Aunt has gone to the seaside for three weeks with Emily. Henry Hall had taken a business in London the same as he had before; his wife [Emma] is still at Kneesworth at Present. Uncle Edward [Wilson] breakes very much he suffers very much with Rheumaise.[?] His wife has been very ill indeed this last two months, she is a little better than she was. Mother's legs has been very bad again but I am happy to say she gets about nicely although they are not quite the thing yet.

I was sorry to hear from Aunt [Mary Ann] Muncey your Father & Mother had not been well during the winter. I hope they are quite well, give my best love to them, Also Cousin William [Hall] when you see him and tell him I am still the old maid. My sister Maria has just returned from spending three weeks at home with her 2 children and am living only 5 miles from her so that is very nice for us both.

We have had a lovely Harvest here. I hope you have been favoured with the same this summer. We have had a great deal of thunder & lightening. A great many people has been killed by the lightening and a great many buildings burnt but it has been a beautifull summer and now we shall see soon the beautifull trees stripped of there green leaves and shall be looking forward to Christmas time. Mr. Bond has taken a house about 15 miles from here.

OTHER LETTERS: 15, 145–64

■ 161

MARY ANN MUNCEY, BASSINGBOURN, CAMBRIDGESHIRE, TO OBED WILSON, EAST WHITBY TOWNSHIP, ONTARIO, 8 AUGUST 1887

SOURCE: Wilson Family Papers, Obed Wilson correspondence

North End August 8th
Bassingbourn 1887

My Dear Brother

In answer to your last letter I received March 14th, we were all very pleased to hear from you. But sorry to hear such a poor account of your son John's wife.[37] Hope she has recovered her illness by this time. So you are getting your sons married one after another. I suppose you have several more yet for you have such a large family.[38] I hope your married Daughters are well and happy. How many children have they? What a large party you had at Christmas. We thought of you the 11th of April it was your real Birthday Easter Monday you was 73 years.

Dear Brother I have some sad news to tell But you may expect to hear. Your Brother Henry died the 29th of October 1886. He was taken worse and obliged to keep his bed about a fortnight. He seemed to lose his sight and speech and did not know any of us and could not take anything for days. His housekeeper stayed with him till he died. They spent all he had and the furniture was taken to pay the rent of the cottage he lived in so there was nothing left for his brothers & Sisters. We had him buried respectfully. Your Sister Betsy [Crabtree] was ill in the winter; she begins to feel old age, and your Brother Edward gets quite the old man. Your Sister Fanny [Shore] has been ill in bed some days; I am glad to say [she] is down stairs today lying upon the sofa. I feel myself pretty well in health but my limbs are so bad. William How last year fell from a plum tree [at the] time he was gathering fruit and died. Isick Racher is still living but looks quite [an] old man.

I must now tell you people are very busey in the harvest getting the corn down fast. We have had 9 weeks hot dry weather. Your wheat seems very cheap and your beef much cheaper than ours. We have to give 9 pence per pound for Beef & mutton, wheat 4 shillings pr bushel, butter 1s6d pr pound. How did you get on this Jubilee year. Fine doings here We sat down to dinner with about 9 or 10 hundred people I

---

37 John Edward Wilson (b 1848) was Obed and Betsy Wilson's oldest son; the name of his wife is not known.

38 Obed and Betsy had 13 children, 8 boys and 5 girls; see Figure 2, Obed Wilson's family.

think I must now close with Best love to yourself, wife & family. Beleave me to remain your Ever affectionate Sister

Mary Ann Muncey

Dear Uncle[39] I have just written this for mother so thought would say how we all are. Henry [Hall] is still very short of breath, not able to go to London now, the rest of us are well. William[40] will write soon he is busy just now. We have not heard from William Hall.[41]

OTHER LETTERS: 15, 145–64

■ 162

EMMA HALL, [BASSINGBOURN, CAMBRIDGESHIRE], TO OBED WILSON, EAST WHITBY TOWNSHIP, N.D. [1887?]

SOURCE: Wilson Family Papers, Obed Wilson correspondence

Dear Uncle

Mother received your letter the last day of March; hopes you will write to her very soon. She is anxious to hear from you again. I now draw to a close with kind love to you all. Beleave me to remain your loveing niece, Emma Hall

OTHER LETTERS: 15, 145–64

■ 163

WILLIAM H. HALL, BASSINGBOURN, CAMBRIDGESHIRE, TO OBED WILSON, ONTARIO, 18 JANUARY 1889

William H. Hall was the son of Emma (Muncey) and Henry Hall and therefore Obed's great-nephew.

SOURCE: Wilson Family Papers, Obed Wilson correspondence

c/o Henry Hall
North End
Bassingbourn, Cambridgeshire
January 18th /89

Dear Uncle & Aunt

I now take the pleasure of writing to you again, or perhaps you will forget about me. I have written to you once before if you remember. I am William Hall, 2nd son of Henry Hall; my age is 18. I am carpenter & joiner by trade. After having read my grandmother [Fanny] Shore's letter which she has had from you lately, it set me long-

39 Emma (Muncey) Hall is the author of this post script.
40 Emma and Henry's son, William H. Hall; see letter 163.
41 Brother of her husband. The silence of William Hall was obviously distressing to his family.

ing so much to see you all. And I intend to come out to see you soon God sparing me. About 4 or 5 years time. I have 18 months more to serve in my apprenticeship; when I am out of my time & saved a little money I mean to come & see you all. Your photos are taken excellent. Dear Uncle your photo is the very image of poor Uncle Henry,[42] I said it was as soon as I saw it. We all had a kiss off of your faces on the photos. I have sent you one of myself. I will send you a better one in the summer. I shall have some more taken then. I look so serious in this one.[43] We often talk about you, & say we should like to see you all. My brother John & my cousin talk of coming too. My brother is a tailor he is 20 years of a age & my cousin is a painter & house decorator, he is about 19. My cousin is the son of Obed Muncey, Grandmother Munceys son Obed. He Works at Royston.

We had a very cold & wet season last year. Crops were not so good as some years. A lot of the potatoes went rotten, other roots were good; the weather suited them. We have not had a very sharp winter yet, had a fortnights sharp frost, enough to give us a few days skating. We had some good skating on Lord Hardwicks Bason at Wimpole.[44]

There is a deal of stone digging going on close to us, which employs a lot of men. They are digging the field over which used to be Uncle Henry's. At Barrington & Meldreth & 2 or 3 villages round, they have found large quantities of cement which employs a lot of labour. Barrington is quite a busy place. Its about 5 miles from here. A company of London gentlemen have bought some land and are working it; They keep about 200 hands. They have 4 large kilns for burning the cement in besides mills for grinding it & all[?] The kilns are built 20 ft below ground & they run up to about 80 feet above ground. As the cement burns it falls down to the bottom & trucks run under & cart it to the mills to be ground. Then it is exported to different parts of the kingdom. This work has made it better for our trade. We have built several cottages there & a very large drying shed. We were at work there most of the summer. They also make bricks, tiles, drain pipes, lime & etc so you see its quite a busy place. We also do work at London. Some of our men are up there now. We are rather slack of work now, trade of any kinds are dull about this time of the year. How is the building trade where you are?[45] How is the tailoring trade & painting trade out there? Could any one get a living at their trades?

We have 3 stoves for heating our Church, tried them last Sunday for the first time. Mr Jarman of Kneesworth gave them to the Church. He is one of the churchwardens. We have a Cemetary for burying the dead. It has been opened now about 10 years & is getting a lot in already. There has been a lot of deaths here lately About all the old people of Bassingbourn are gone off. There is not many people got much money in Bassingbourn. Mr Jarman has all the Kneesworth farms; he has 6 farms.

42 He presumably is referring to his great-uncle, Obed Wilson's brother Henry.
43 William H. Hall and his cousin George Muncey had their photographs taken in Royston.
44 The 5th Earl of Hardwicke lived at Wimpole Hall, Caxton, Cambridge; the lake was and is a feature of the extensive grounds.
45 The question marks have been added. Hall used none in his letter.

William H. Hall and George Muncey
Courtesy W.H. Wilson

The Country is all alive again now, electing County Councillors.[46] There is to be so many Councillors to each county. Our division votes on the 22nd of this month.

My sister Annie is leaving her situation; she has not been home for nearly 2 years. She has travelled a good deal, been to Ireland once, Wales & several parts of England. She is 24 years old. My other sister goes to school yet, she is 12 years old so you see mothers family is growing up. Mother & father's silver Wedding was last year. They have been wedded 25 years. They are getting on, with their age 50 last year. My mother is going to write to you so I must soon leave off or else she will have nothing to tell you. I had a narrow escape with my life last summer. I was thrown out of a cart with 2 more. One was killed on the spot. But thank God it didn't hurt me much. It frightened me very much. I felt it for weeks afterwards. I helped to carry the poor fellow to his grave. We were going to Meldreth to work & our horse ran away. So you see you are as safe on the sea as on land. I am very fond of flower gardening. What climate is yours? Is it hot all at once & cold or is it temperate? What kind of flowers do you grow? I should very much like to have a letter from some of my cousins. I should be pleased to answer them. My cousin George Muncey has sent you his photo. Now I must draw to a close. I think I have told you about all the news with fond love to you and cousins believe me to be your affectionate nephew

William H. Hall

xxxxxxxxxx

---

46 The County Councils were a new development in local administration; they were to be elected bodies with powers (over roads, for example) overriding those previously held by the parishes.

I hope these lines will find you quite well and all in good health. Now I must wish you a happy & prosperous New Year and I hope you will see some more yet.
I have sent you a long letter & I shall expect a long one back. Write soon as we like to hear from you [written vertically across top of letter]

OTHER LETTERS: 15, 145–64

■ 164

EMMA (MUNCEY) HALL, BASSINGBOURN, CAMBRIDGESHIRE, TO OBED WILSON, WHITBY TOWNSHIP, ONTARIO, 20 JANUARY 1889

SOURCE: Wilson Family Papers, Obed Wilson correspondence

North End   January 20th
Bassingbourn   1889

My Dear Uncle, Aunt & Cousins

My son William has just written a long letter to you. So I thought I would send a few lines the same time. He has told you all the news, so I need not say much. My mother is much the same in health. But her limbs are very week; her age is great, 83 in March. She was very pleased to see your likenesses. The photos you sent to your sister Fanny are very good. We fancy we see you alive. We spend a very comfortable Christmas; had the old English dinner, roast Beef and plum pudding. Henry dined with his Mother and M[r] Shore. Your sister Mary Ann (she my mother you know) dined with me and my Children. We often talk about you, all my sons say they will come to see you some day. They have been looking at the map to night to find the best way to get to you. Now Dear Uncle I must draw to a close with kind love to you all, from your loveing niece Emma Hall

My Mother sends her love to you all. Also Henry sends his love to you all.

OTHER LETTERS: 16, 145–64

Obed Wilson is certainly one of those emigrants who worked hard and prospered. He and Betsy Martin had 13 children between 1848 and 1875; see Figure 2. The family's home farm was located on W ½ lot 16 concession 9 East Whitby Township, but Wilson acquired a number of lots in the area, including S ½ lot 29 concession 6 and S ½ lot 28 concession 7 of Scott Township, W ½ lot 9 concession 2 and SE ¼ lot 13 concession 1 Reach Township, and part of lots 14, 16, and 17 concession 9 East Whitby Township (land which he intended for his numerous sons). He also had a hotel and property in Udora Village (see letter 152). He became quite prosperous and in his will, dated 5 March 1892, left his children well provided for. Betsy's death in 1883 necessitated a codicil revoking her part of the legacy and the arrangement he had made for his youngest son to look after her and the house where she lived on the home farm. When he died on 10 February 1894, a year after Betsy, he left an estate valued at $24,000.

FIGURE 2: FAMILY OF OBEDIAH AND BETSY WILSON

Father Obed WILSON b ll Apr 1814, bap 10 Jul 1814 Bassingbourn, married 16 Feb 1847 in Canada, d 10 Feb 1894

Mother Elizabeth (Betsy) MARTIN b 1831, d 14 Jan 1894

Children:

1 John Edward WILSON b 19 June 1848, married —
  i Jack
2 William Henry WILSON b 30 June 1850, married Rebecca Margaret ENGLISH (d 31 March 1897)
  i George Matlin WILSON b 1885, d 1893 diphtheria
  ii Wilmer Edson WILSON b 1889, d 1893 diphtheria
  iii Margaret Jane WILSON b 1883, married Frank SCHELL, d 1973
  iv Murray Cecil WILSON b 1893, married Mary CHAPMAN, d 1936
  v Eva Pearl WILSON b 1895, married Clifford ENGLISH, d 1984
3 Richard A. WILSON b 3 Feb 1852, married Melissa VERNON; farmed concession 3 Reach
  i Fred or Russel WILSON
4 Obed Augustus WILSON b 22 Mar 1854, married 1897 Sarah Ann HUBBARD (b 1860, d 1843); farmed in East Whitby Township, d 1924
  i Arthur Edgar WILSON b 1888, d Feb 1941
  ii Roy Clayton WILSON b 1891, d 1913
5 Martha Maria WILSON b 29 Feb 1856, married John DAWSON
  i George DAWSON
6 Charles M. WILSON b 19 Mar 1858, school teacher at Ashburn
7 Mary Ann WILSON b 19 Jul 1860, married Robert E. VERNON; farmed Vernon farm at Prospect
  i Minnie Ida VERNON, married Ernie CHAMBERS
  ii Lou Ethel VERNON, married Charles WALES

  iii Etta May VERNON, married Milton HOLIDAY

  iv Lena Maude VERNON b 1887, married Scott GILLETTE

  v Alonzo Franklin VERNON b 1887, married Maude CROSIER

8 Coleman Elias WILSON b 29 Oct 1862, married —

  i Violet WILSON, married Frank JOHNSON

9 James Stanford WILSON B 17 Jan 1865, married Margaret Agnes GLOVER; farmed on townline of Whitby and Reach

  i Gladys WILSON, married William BLATCH

  ii Hilliard WILSON, married Ruby SMITH

  iii Charlie WILSON, married Laura CLEMENS

  iv Sadie WILSON, married (1) Art THOMPSON, (2) Roy CARNOHAN

10 Fanny Melissa WILSON b 1 Feb 1868, married William SMITH

11 Lydia Sophrona WILSON b 26 Dec 1869, married Wesley LAMB; lived at Manchester

12 Emma Jane WILSON b 19 Apr 1872, married Dan PARROT; lived at Ashburn

  i Lena PARROT, married Henry DOBLE

13 Christopher Adolphus WILSON b 19 May 1875, married Dolly McCLINTOCK; farmed in East Whitby Township

  i Fern WILSON, married Carl AVERY

  ii Frank WILSON

  iii Grant WILSON, married Ethel GLENNIE

  iv Inez WILSON, married Robert COATES

SOURCE: Family information; 1871 Census East Whitby Township; AO, RG 22/264, Ontario County Surrogate Court, file 2655

Chantler Correspondence

Nathaniel and Moses Chantler emigrated with their families from the Dorking area of Surrey to Upper Canada in 1832 (see Figures 3 and 4). Although we thought for some time that they were Petworth emigrants, they actually sailed on the *Brunswick* through London where their elder brother Joseph lived. All three brothers had grown up as members of a tight Quaker community in Horsham in Sussex, and letters from Canada were copied for Horsham relatives or carried to Horsham for them to see. The anxiety of the family grew as a long silence was broken with bad news: first that Nathaniel and his niece Ann had died of cholera, and then that Nathaniel's wife Sophia had also died at York, leaving five young orphans. Although letters to London are addressed to Joseph Chantler Sr, the correspondence is in fact carried on by the next generation of Joseph and Moses' families.

Letters written between 1830 and 1832 are part of a three-way correspondence between Joseph R. Chantler in London (165, 167, 168), William, the eldest son of Moses Chantler, who remained behind in Dorking, Surrey (also 168), and John, Moses' second son, who wrote from Upper Canada (166, 169). The 1836 letter from William's friend Arthur Gravely finds the two young men both considering emigration (170). Two letters written in Canada at a much later date show these families in Canada under happier and more normal circumstances (171 and 172). Hesther (Chantler) Dennis's reminiscences, written as a private memoir to her children in about 1896, brings us back to the searing experiences of the cholera epidemic (173).

Both Nathaniel, who was 52 in 1832, and Moses who was 13 years his junior, were having a difficult time when they left England. Because these are family letters, Joseph had no need to explain the "complicated distresses" from which his uncle Nathaniel was released by death. Nathaniel's health was obviously poor, and the 1830s were not the best time to be a weaver. His relationship to the Society of Friends was another area of "complication." In 1819, because of his second marriage to Sophia (Rowe) who was not a Quaker, Nathaniel was officially disowned by the Dorking Meeting, which nevertheless continued to register the births of their children who were all born in the Dorking area. Although we see Sophia only through the eyes of her 12-year-old daughter and her nephew, her decision to stay in York and brave the difficulties of raising a young family and the risks of cholera speaks of a strong and determined character.

In England, Moses Chantler had moved several times in search of work as a miller. Birth registrations trace the family's movements in Surrey: the first four children were registered at Abinger Mill, two at Ockley, two more at Findon not far from Worthing on the coast of Sussex, and then Emma in 1831 at Ockley, which like Abinger is near Dorking. The lives of this family were closely bound up with the Dorking Meeting of the Society of Friends. Having accepted Moses and Sarah as members in 1820, the Friends oversaw William's apprenticeship in 1828 to Robert Marsh, one of their number who was a linen draper in Dorking, and they paid John's fees at a Quaker school in Croydon in the same year. The Dorking Meeting had helped Moses out with smaller sums in the past, and in 1832 members raised a loan of £100 to send him and his family to Upper Canada.

■ 165

[JOSEPH R.] CHANTLER, LONDON, ENGLAND, TO WILLIAM NATHANIEL CHANTLER, DORKING, SURREY, 21 NOVEMBER 1830

This is the earliest of the materials in this collection, and although there is no signature we have identified it as probably written by Joseph R. Chantler, the author of 167 and 168. It is a long commentary on the events of the previous months, written to his cousin William Nathaniel Chantler, the oldest son of Moses Chantler (see figure 4). Joseph was a son of Joseph Chantler (the eldest of Moses' brothers)[1] and his letter reviews a very event-filled year, beginning with the death of George IV in April, the succession of William IV, and the summer election, which brought the issue of electoral reform to the fore. In November the Whigs and Earl Grey replaced the Tories and the Duke of Wellington as the government. In the letter, William gives an account of the unrest in London that broke out in part in response to the July Revolution in France that brought Louis Philippe to power in place of Charles X and touched off unrest in Belgium, the German states, Italy, and Poland. In Dorking, William's news would have been of rural unrest in protest against low wages and seasonal unemployment among agricultural workers and of the Swing disturbances which Joseph describes simply as acts of incendiarism.

SOURCE: Chantler Family Papers. A typescript of the letter was made by Gladys Chantler Walker, great-granddaughter of William Nathaniel Chantler, and the inserts in square brackets were done by her.

Letter Addressed to

Robert Marsh,
Clother &c,
Dorking,
For Mr. Wm. N. Chantler.   Surrey.
London, 21st of the 11th Mo., 1830.

Dear Cousin;

Thou wilt no doubt expect me to make some apology for my neglect in not writing to three before this, but as I am afraid it would be a very lame one, I will omit

1 Nathaniel Chantler and Hannah (Sayers) Chantler had eight children between 1778 and 1793: Joseph, Nathaniel, Elijah, John, Deborah, Benjamin, Thomas, and Moses. Two brothers, Joseph and John, seem to have settled in London; two brothers, Nathaniel and Moses, emigrated to Upper Canada in 1832. Deborah is mentioned in the letters, but Elijah, Benjamin, and Thomas are not and may have died. WSRO, MF 676, A Register of Births of the People Called Quakers Belonging to the Monthly Meeting of Horsham and Ifield, Sussex,.

FIGURE 3: NATHANIEL CHANTLER'S FAMILY

Father Nathaniel CHANTLER b 22 Jun 1780 Cripplegate, parish of Horsham, Sussex, son of Nathaniel CHANTLER and Hannah SAYERS; d c 15 Jul 1832 Coteau-du-Lac, Lower Canada; married (1) 7 Jul 1807 Southwark, London, Elizabeth LONG who died childless 3 Jan 1817 Wotton, Surrey, (2) 14 Sep 1819 Wotton, Surrey
Mother Sophia ROWE, d 1832 York, Upper Canada

> *Children:*
>
> 1 Hester Mary CHANTLER, known as Esther, b 28 May 1820 Broadmoor, Wotton, Surrey, d 20 Feb 1899 Whitchurch Township, Upper Canada; married 11 Mar 1841 Brooke DENNIS, b 28 July 1814 son of Cyrus and Barbara DENNIS, d 8 May 1884 in Whitchurch. Both are buried in the Newmarket Cemetery.
>> *i* Sophia DENNIS b 1843, married Hiram MALLOY 20 Dec 1865
>>> *a* Nellie MALLOY b c 1868 Canada
>>> *b* Emeline MALLOY b c1869 Canada, married William H. ORVIS.
>>> *c* Charles Henry MALLOY b c 1874 Kansas
>>> *b* Alfred MALLOY b c1885 USA
>> *ii* Charles DENNIS b 1844, d 1919, married Almeda HUGHES
>> *iii* Alfred C. DENNIS b 1846, d 22 Apr 1894 in California, married Elizabeth BUGG and/or — MOUNT
>> *iv* Emmeline DENNIS b 1848
>> *v* Barbary DENNIS b c1851, d 11 Dec 1885 Newmarket, married Benjamin BROWN
>> *vi* Daniel Milton DENNIS b c1853, d 8 Jan 1892 Newmarket
>> *vii* Walter DENNIS b c1855
>> *viii* Alfreta DENNIS b c1858, married Robert W. PHILLIPS
>> *ix* Robert Baldwin DENNIS b c1860, d 27 Apr 1924 Toronto
>> *x* Nathan DENNIS
>> *xi* Marshall Bidwell DENNIS, "practising in Norwich, Connecticut" in 1884
> 2 Joseph CHANTLER b 15 Feb 1822 Broadmoor, Wotton, Surrey, d 30 Jun 1868 Whitchurch Township, Upper Canada; married 28 Sep 1846 Ogdensburg, New York, Mary Ann MILLARD, daughter of Eleazar and Betsy MILLARD, b 24 Sep 1825, d 22 Jan 1913 Toronto

it and throw myself on thy kindness to excuse this, my first offence, at the same time assuring thee that thou hast very frequently been brought to my remembrance, and that the fraternal feeling which existed between us has suffered no diminution on my part.

Many and various have been the things which have transpired since I last addressed thee. Whether I look to the demise of the late King [George IV] – the accession of his brother [William IV] and his amiable Consort – their public visits to and thro' this part of the Metropolis – The elections – The lamentable death of our newly elected Member, J.P. Harris – The forthcoming election to fill his place – The revolutions in France and the Netherlands – The like spirit manifested in this country – the riotous conduct of some of the lower orders in the City and its Suburbs – or lastly to the recent changes in the Cabinet.

  i Jane Elizabeth CHANTLER b 15 Jul 1847 Ogdensburg, New York; married 23 Dec 1870
  John A SHARPE
   a Reverend Morton SHARPE
  ii William Henry CHANTLER b 12 Apr 1850 Canada West, d 1887 Bracebridge; married
  Mary Emily SAUNDERS 29 Sep 1874
   a Mary S. CHANTLER b 6 Aug 1875; married Edward BODEY
   b Ethel Maude CHANTLER b 28 Oct 1877; married William COX 14 Feb 1900
   c Albert Austin CHANTLER b 7 May 1879
   d Earl Millard CHANTLER b 24 Feb 1883
  iii Esther Mary CHANTLER b 6 Aug 1852 Ogdensburg, New York, d 7 Jan 1922; married 5
  Feb 1878 Andrew KINNEY, residence Brantford
   a William Reginald KINNEY; married Margaretta BRONSON
   b G.L. Milton KINNEY; married Jessie BROOKS
   c A. Albert KINNEY; married Lorraine MCMAHON
  iv Albert Nathaniel CHANTLER b 14 Aug 1855 Ogdensburg, New York, d Newmarket 22
  Aug 1889
  v George Washington CHANTLER b 2 Apr 1858 Canada West
  vi Joseph Edward CHANTLER b 12 Aug 1861 Canada West, d 23 Feb 1862
  vii Virginia Sophia CHANTLER b 8 Sep 1866 Canada West, d 4 Apr 1868
 3 Henry CHANTLER b 11 Nov 1823 Broadmoor, Wotton, Surrey; married 9 Oct 1850 Lydia
 GUERNSEY, daughter of John GUERNSEY, 9 Oct 1850 Queenston, Canada West; practised at
 Newmarket and Toronto as medical doctor
 4 Alfred CHANTLER b 2 Jul 1825 Broadmoor, Wotton, Surrey
 5 Nathaniel Rowe CHANTLER b 27 Mar 1829 Coldharbour, Dorking, Surrey

SOURCE: Project files; Brenda Dougall Merriman, "Some Descendants of Nathaniel Chantler," *Families* 34, no.2 (1995): 86–9

All these subjects, were I to enter into detail, would more than fill the whole of my paper. I shall therefore just touch upon them in as brief a manner as I can.

The death of our late king, tho' much to be deplored, (for his pacific disposition and lenity to friends) has made way for those who now hold the sceptre of these realms, and who promise to equal, if not exceed, him in doing anything that may alleviate the distresses of the poor and exalt the prosperity of the nation. May they ever cherish those sentiments with which they have commenced their reign, and long continue to enjoy the affectionate loyalty of their devoted subjects.

They several times past near our residence in their road to and from Greenwich &c; once in state accompanied by a numerous retinue. Their equipage was very stylish indeed; but what took my attention was the number of Footmen, there being no less than 4 great fat fellows behind each of the royal carriages, which had a very

FIGURE 4: MOSES CHANTLER'S FAMILY

Father Moses CHANTLER b 7 Nov 1793 Cripplegate, Horsham, Sussex, son of Nathaniel CHANTLER
   and Hannah SAYERS; d 8 Oct 1878 Meaford, Ontario; married 28 May 1812 Shipley, Sussex
Mother Sarah HOAD, bap 20 Apr 1794 Shipley, Sussex

   Children:
   1 William Nathaniel CHANTLER b 14 Oct 1813 Abinger Mill, Surrey, d 25 May 1904 Tecumseh
   Township, Ontario; married Margaret BOOKER 6 June 1839; emigrated to Canada in 1840
      i Eliza V CHANTLER b 29 Aug 1842, d July 1922; married Joseph HIPWELL 27 Sep 1860
            a Emma Jane HIPWELL b 20 July 1861
            b William R HIPWELL b 19 July 1864
            c Joseph Newton HIPWELL b 13 Sep 1866
            d Marshall Booker HIPWELL b 6 Aug 1872
            e Ernest Goodwin HIPWELL b 7 Aug 1874
      ii Joseph Robert CHANTLER b 27 June 1842; married (1) Cynthia W LAW 23 June 1864,
      (2) Elizabeth BAYCROFT 4 Jan 1893, lived at Newton Robinson
            a Rev William Newton CHANTLER b 25 Mar 1866; married Hannah M CONNELL
            b Joseph Wilford CHANTLER b 18 June 1868
            c Ida Margaret CHANTLER b 25 Oct 1870
            d Herbert Leslie CHANTLER b 25 May 1873
            e Marshall Lyman CHANTLER b 1 Nov 1880; married Ethel BUTLER
            f Ernest Baycroft CHANTLER b 10 Apr 1895
      iii James G CHANTLER b 3 Jan 1845, d 1 Jan 1920; married Elizabeth ROGERS 6 Sep 1870,
      lived at Newton Robinson
            a Milton Clark CHANTLER b 13 Aug 1871
            b daughter CHANTLER b 8 Oct 1873, d 17 Oct 1873
            c Amy CHANTLER married James COBURN
            d Eva CHANTLER married Alvin DICKINSON
            e Mina CHANTLER married Dr ____ BREWSTER
            f Orval CHANTLER married Ada McDONALD
            g Otto CHANTLER married Marguerite LEDDER
            h Winifred CHANTLER married C PELTON
      iv Sarah Jane CHANTLER b 25 Jan 1847, d 1 Mar 1847
      v Prisilla (*aka* Guilalina or Guilielmer) CHANTLER b 1 Oct 1849; married 1 Oct 1873
      William RORKE, lived in Chicago in 1904
      vi William Russell CHANTLER b 28 Mar 1851; married Emma LAW, lived at Newton
      Robinson
            a-f six children

---

ludicrous appearance. They looked well in health!!!

   The election caused a great deal of bustle and was ably contested for, and J.R.
Harris in conjunction with Robt. Wilson were returned as our representatives to
Parliament.

   I cannot leave this subject without adverting to the sorrowful event which succeeded. Scarcely was the election over and the cheering performed when the sky which
appeared before so calm and beautiful was suddenly overcast by an impending storm.

2 John CHANTLER b 3 June 1816 Abinger Mill, Surrey, d 19 March 1897 Stroud, Ontario; married Elizabeth A BELL 10 Jan 1841 at Tolendol Mills, Innisfil Township
 i Charles E CHANTLER b c1843, merchant in Stroud, Ontario
 ii John I CHANTLER b c1847, merchant in Westbourne, Manitoba, predeceased his father
 iii George CHANTLER b c1853, merchant in Stroud
 iv Sarah CHANTLER b c1857, predeceased her father
 v Jeffrey CHANTLER b c1859, railway agent in Minnedosa, Manitoba
 vi Amelia CHANTLER married Rev. Abraham NEELANDS, lived in Minnesota

3 Elizabeth CHANTLER b 22 Oct 1818 Abinger Mill, Surrey, d 1902; married Rev George Millward McDOUGALL of Flos Township 20 Jan 1842 at Tolendol Mills, went to Alberta
 i John Chantler McDOUGALL b 1842, d 1917
 ii Elizabeth Chantler McDOUGALL married Harrison YOUNG
 iii David McDOUGALL

4 Charles CHANTLER b 26 Feb 1821 Abinger Mill, Surrey; married Catherine McMILLAN 20 Feb 1844 at Whitchurch

5 Ann CHANTLER b 11 May 1823 Ockley, Surrey, d 1832 on voyage down the St Lawrence River

6 Robert CHANTLER b 19 Mar 1825 Ockley, Surrey, d 26 Nov 1825

7 George CHANTLER b 6 Oct 1826 Findon, Sussex; married (1) Augusta HUTCHINSON c1859 (2) Maria CHADWICK 15 Nov 1865 in Artemesia Township
 i Frederick CHANTLER b c1860
 ii Vincent CHANTLER b c1861
 iii William Grant CHANTLER b c1865

8 Mary Ann CHANTLER b 26 Nov 1828 Findon, Sussex; married (1) _____ McDOUGALL, (2) _____ TITMOUSE

9 Emma CHANTLER b 14 Jan 1831 Ockley, Surrey

10 Priscilla CHANTLER b Canada; married William GRIER 21 Dec 1853

11 Amina or Emina CHANTLER b c1837 in [East] Gwillimbury Township, Ontario; married James C GRANT of Owen Sound 25 Nov 1858

SOURCE: Family Information; project files.

Arrived at the summit of his ambition and in the full vigour of life, John Harris was taken seriously ill, and before 2 weeks had elapsed we heard the sad tidings that he had breathed his last. Well might the poet express himself in the following pathetic language,

Few years but yield us proof of Death's ambition,
To cull his victims from the fairest fold.
And sheathe his shafts in all the pride of life.   Young.

With respect to the late revolutions on the Continent thou hast most probably been made acquainted, yet I may inform thee that I have heard from good authority that the revolution in France is considered very favourable to the downfall of popery and the establishment of a more enlightened religion, that the Agents of the Bible Society are more at liberty to circulate the holy Scriptures than formerly and the King is also favourable to their distribution.[2]

It must be because of grief to all who have heard of those repeated instances of incendiarism in various [   ] and Sussex, which have done so much damage [   ]. It is also rather singular that no discover has yet been [made of] the aggressors; but time will tell.[3]

Accounts of the disturbances and disappointments [   ] by the good citizens of London (in not viewing the intended Procession on Lord Mayor's Day) have no [doubt reached] thee but I cannot describe the agitation which [existed] among [all] classes. Nothing was to be heard but [cries] of disappointment and disgust when it was officially announced that it was not to take place. People were busy [engaged] in taking down the lamps and devices which they [had put up]. Reports of all sorts were propagated respecting the [riots that] had and were to take place. The Bank was trebly guarded and the Tower placed in some posture of defence and garrisoned, with reinforcements of troops and Artillery from Woolwich. Orders from the Police Office were posted up, requiring all persons to desist from assembling in the streets on 3 days. Evenings the Police were drained from this part of the [town to] the West end. But I am happy to say that the [expected] shock did not take place, the Mob which had in time past created so much alarm did not do much Mischief, though several persons were wounded in the scuffle which ensued between the Mob and the police. It is reported that their intention was to extinguish all the Gas lights and attack the Guildhall while they were there assembled, but I have not heard anything further respecting their activities, though many think there is something at the [   ] with which the public are not acquainted.

I hope nothing more will occur in that way. A change in the administration has given new hope to the public mind, as Earl Grey, who is at the head, is a complete [liberal so] termed and a decided advocate for Parliamentary Reform.

I think, my dear William, thou must be almost tired from this political Epistle and ready to say "is this the best way he can interest me." As I have no wish to be tedious I will endeavour to fill up my paper with something else in the room of my former newspaper strain.

I am sorry to find thy father has been obliged to remove from his old residence, but hope he will be able to go on again comfortably at Horsham. It will, of course, be more pleasant to thee to have them so near thee.[4]

---

2 The original transcriber noted that part of the next sheet was missing so that gaps occur.

3 The disturbances, sweeping through counties in the south of England helped persuade local powers to adopt assisted emigration as one solution to problems of overpopulation and unemployment.

4 Horsham is about 13 miles south of Dorking.

Thy brother Charles met with a misfortune (very incident to Country folks) soon after his arrival here; for being inclined to take a walk with me in the morning, I took him by the hand for safety, but he had not gone far before he separated from me to look at something in the road, and was not long before he ran foul of one of the iron lamp posts, by which he received a considerable blow on the forehead and dropt a few tears with this inanimate friend.[5] Perhaps I am rather too unfeeling; but really if thee had witnessed the manner in which he stood clinging to the post, it would have taken off a little of the sorrow which it would otherwise have occasioned.

As he had got sufficiently bumped by his first excursion, it was no wonder he refused to accompany me to visit the City. He however went with me to the Coach next morning and parted in good spirits.

However fond thou mays't be of Poetry, I am determined to insert a piece for thy perusal, as I conjecture thou hast not read, or at least, not got the following, composed by Henry Kirk White. I hope thou wilt be able to Decipher it.

> *The Wandering Boy,*
> When the winter wind whistles along the wild moor,
> And the cottager shuts on the Beggar his door,
> When the chilling tear stands in my eye,
> Oh! how hard is the lot of the Wandering Boy.
>
> The winter is cold, and I have no rest,
> And my heart is cold as it beats in my breast,
> No father, no mother, no kindred have I,
> For I am a poor little parentless boy.
>
> Yet I had a name and I once had a Sire,
> A mother who granted each infant desire,
> Our cottage it stood in a wood-embow'rd vale,
> Where the ring dove would warble its sorrowful tale.
>
> But my father and mother were summoned away,
> And left me to hard-hearted strangers a prey,
> I fled from their rigour with many a sigh,
> And now I'm a poor little wandering boy.
>
> The wind it is keen, and the snow loads the gale,
> And no one will list to my pitiful tale,
> I'll go to the place where my parents both lie,
> And death shall befriend the poor Wandering Boy.

Before I close this letter I will take the liberty granted on a former occasion to express a few words of admonition, though feeling as I do mine own inability and the need I myself stand of similar advice. In the first place have a care to avoid falling

---

5 Charles was nine years old at this time.

into any wicked or immoral conversation, remembering that "Evil conversation corrupts good manners." Keep to plainness of speech as well as dress, for though they are little attended to by many among us, yet I can say from my own little experience they are as a hedge round about us. Be particular what books thou readest, knowing that "reading is to the Mind what food is to the Body" and if the food be not good, it will be hurtful.

I suppose thou art aware that the Monthly Meeting Library is open for thy perusal, so that thou needst not be without a book if thou make application for one.

On the first day of the week do not forget to read portions of the Holy Scripture, attend diligently to Meetings and when assembled with others endeavour to get into an abstracted state of mind, remembering the solemn purpose for which we profess to meet, viz. " To worship the Almighty in Spirit and in truth." I am inclined to think there was not much need for saying what I have, but a hint from those to whom we are attach'd is not always without effect. Finally, my dear Cousin, may we both so here and Happiness.

I send greetings for thee, hoping thou art quite well. I have just heard of disturbances in your town.[6] Be careful not to get into the mob, for fear of accident.

The election for the borough commenced this morning and with it a sad scuffle among some of the low classes. 4 Persons were taken to the Hospital wounded. I think C. Calvert will get in. Hoping to hear from thee soon,

I remain,

Affectionately thine, Adieu,

3rd day 23, 11th Mo. 1830.

Postscript. I closed my letter without saying anything about our health or Business. Therefore I hereby let thee know that we are all in good health but that Business is very slack at the present time, tho' I think we may not complain. Thy school mates are all well. When thou writest again direct to my father for ....

OTHER LETTERS: see 167–73

■ 166

JOHN CHANTLER, NEWMARKET, UPPER CANADA, TO JOSEPH CHANTLER AND WIFE, LONDON, 27 JULY 1832

John Chantler was Moses' second son and, at 18 years of age, was the oldest of the 8 children who emigrated.

SOURCE: Chantler Family Papers; a typescript and original is in AO, F775, MU2106, 17, Chantler letters, 1832.

---

6 On 22 November 1830, troops were called in to end a riot outside a magistrates' meeting at the Red Lion Inn in Dorking (which was not far from the Quaker Meeting House).

Typescript notes "a letter received 11th of 9th Mo. 1832 from John Chantler to his Uncle Joseph Chantler & wife."

Upper Canada,
Newmarket 27 of 7 Mo. 1832.

Dear Uncle & Aunt;

I am afraid that long before this reaches England, you will begin to think the Promised letter has been lost; (or what is really the case) been delayed; but as it was not from entire neglect, I hope this will make amends for the past.

We left Gravesend on second day the 7th of 5th Month and anchored off Deal in the evening. The wind was contrary in the morning, but changed towards evening. We passed the Isle of Wight the next morning; most of us were Sea Sick to day. On the 10th we lost sight of the Shores of Old England. The wind continued favourable until we passed the Bay of Biscaye, it then changed to North West and continued in that quarter till the 16th when a brisk wind arose from the South East. We had a sudden gust of wind from the Starboard about 12 o'clock which almost turned the vessel on her side; there were several Barrels that happened not to be lashed, which rolled from one side to the other, so that some were in danger of getting their legs broken. In the evening the ship rocked to such a degree that the boxes began to tumble about and caused some disturbance amongst Crockery, and some of the Passengers that had retired rather early getting up in much haste to see what was the matter, were thrown out of their Cribs.

17th we had very heavy rains which continued until the 20th when it cleared, but it was very cold, although the sun shone bright. We saw several ships during the Day; a transport passed us in the afternoon, she appeared to be homeward bound, but we were not near enough to speak to her.

22nd The wind changed nearly west and disappointed our hopes of being on the banks of Newfoundland by next first day. Our fresh water begins to smell very bad, but it improves a little by being exposed to the Air.

25th, The wind was favourable today and continued so during the rest of the Passage. There was a serious quarrel between a man and his Wife; they were both tipsy. He threw several of her gowns overboard and a pair of his Boys new shoes; he also threatened to murder his wife but she happened to have the key of the Box where his Razors were; the Boy slept in the Jolly Boat, for his father would not let him come near him.

27th, It was very fine today considering we were so near the banks. We saw an Iceberg about 5 miles off; it appeared to be as high as our topmast. We could plainly see Spray dash over it.

29th, On the Banks with a good opportunity for catching Cod. The sea being calm, Father caught 13 fine ones, which were divided between the two families, and others. There were 300 caught in all, which was a very reasonable supply to some of the Irish who were nearly out of Provisions.

30th, The wind was very strong so that we backed about for fear of running ashore on Newfoundland, it being very misty. We saw several Whales and Seals; some of them came within a few yards of the Ship. Towards evening we saw a vessel bottom upward with about two thirds of her keel visible. Our captain supposed her to be about 300 tons Burthen. We heard afterwards that a great number of vessels were lost this season.

6 Mo. 1st, We were within sight of the southern coast of Newfoundland, in the afternoon; the snow laid very thick on the Hills; the country here is mountainous and woody, the sea dashing against some high cliffs; which makes it look like the South Down Cliffs,[7] on account of their being covered with snow.

2nd, We entered the Gulph of St. Lawrence, with a good North East wind; we spoke with a brig from Portsmouth, the same that the emigrants from Dorking and Guildford sailed in.[8] We saw Cape Breton in the evening.

4th, We entered the River St Lawrence on the Southern Shore but could not see it on account of the mist; we took in our Pilot in the morning, from him we learnt that we should have to ride Quarantine, before we could enter Quebeck. The mist cleared off in the afternoon and we had a good view of the country round for miles, it is very woody, having villages scattered along the shore, and the Churches which were covered with Tin, glittering in the sun, so dazzle your Eyes that you can scarcely look at them.

5th, We have now a good view of Both sides of the River, on the north side there are some very high mountains, their tops are covered with snow: the land is cultivated 5 or 6 miles back all the way. We anchored in the Station at one o'clock, the Captain and Doctor went to report our Healths. There were several Ships in the Harbour that had Cholera on board and there was one Irish vessel that had 45 deaths on Board and another 16.

6th, The Doctor came on Board and examined our Healths, we all passed before him separately; we are to be here 3 days.

7th, The Clio came in this morning, she had 4 deaths of the Cholera on board, one died about an hour after she came in, she sailed from Gravesend 10 days before us, We have had the shortest passage of any vessel this Season.

8th, We weighed anchor at 11 o'clock and reached the Isle of Orleans in the evening, where we anchored for the night, for the wind was contrary, and we could only get along when the tide was favourable.

10th, We reached Quebec to day, we heard from the Custom House Officer that the Cholera was very bad in the town. John Cattermole came on board in the afternoon; he was in England in the Spring and I saw him at Guildford.[9] He advised Father to take his Passage in a steamer that was to come along side.[10]

11th, The Steamer came along side in the evening and got our goods on board,

---

7 The South Downs are chalk hills and therefore any exposed cliffs are white.

8 He seems to be referring to the Petworth emigrants on the *England*.

9 He may mean William Cattermole, who was in Guildford as part of an extensive tour promoting emigration in England.

10 The ships carrying Petworth emigrants took them through to Montreal, thus saving them this transfer to a steamboat.

with several other Passengers for Montreal. We laid by the Wharf till 12 oclock at night, so that we had an opportunity of getting what Provisions we wanted. We Heard that the sity gates are to be shut to morrow for the Cholera is increasing very fast. We slept for the first night in the open air, but the Pipes of the Steamer kept us pretty warm.

13th, Arrived at Montreal this morning: It is 180 miles from Quebeck. The town has a very dull appearance off the water; the first street being a parcel of Wooden Houses, mostly Warehouses, and in the spring and fall the roads are so bad that one may sink up to his knees in mud. Father and Uncle went to the bank for their money, and as soon as they came back they took their Passage for Prescott. We went on board the Batteaux in the afternoon, here we met with Henry Miles of Guildford, he has been here about 2 weeks, and is upon taking a mill about 3 miles from the town. As the mill laid about half a mile from the corner[?] he walked up with us. He advised Father to stop ... Montreal and look about him, but it was too late as Father had paid our passage.

We reached Luschine [Lachine] in the evening, where we entered the River again. The next morning we were towed by a steamer to Cedars where we had to pass through another Canal. Cedars is 24 miles from Luschine. After we were through the Canal we came in sight of a strong rapid, where there is a lock for the Boats to pass through. We staid here for the night and Father hired a room at an Inn. They all slept there except Father and myself.

In the morning I was sorry to hear that Uncle had been very ill during the night of the Cholera. They sent for Father directly and he sent the Innkeeper for the Doctor who lived a few miles off. The Doctor ordered him immediately to be put into Hot water which relieved him of the cramps, and pains in the chest. When the Doctor came again he was much better and he told us he was in a fair way of recovery. He advised Father to send him in a cart to Coto-du-lac [Coteau-du-lac], and there he could rest a day or two until the boat came up, which Father did and put a bed into the cart and made it as easy as he could. Aunt, Cousins and I went with him. Uncle bore the journey very well till we were within 1 mile of the place, when he began to get worse, and we could perceive he was getting insensible.

When we reached Coto I enquired for a room at all the Inns, but they all refused. I then inquired if there was any outhouse in the Place; they all said no, and one had the cruelty to give me this answer, "We are all Canadians here and could not think of such a thing." I then asked what we were to do. Let the man die and you shift for yourselves, answered the Cruel Man. We were obliged at last to go out on the Wharf and get on the underside of the storehouse. We then took the Bed and laid Uncle on it who was quite insensible. I then covered him over with a large trunk[?][11]... and what boards I could find so as to keep the wet off. Uncle continued to get worse and to complete our distress [?] ... came on to rain till ½ past 10.

---

11 In her memoir, Esther (Chantler) Dennis remembered that they had turned over a cart to shelter him.

Then sat down and went to sleep. Not slept long when Aunt awoke me and said [missing] It was not till then I had the least Idea of fe[ar?]... now remembering the danger of being near a [de[ad] ... af[fected] with the Cholera, and also being wet thro[ugh] ... spread such a chill over me that I sunk down ... Boards almost insensible, but was soon rouse[d] ... the distress of my poor Aunt and Cousins.[12] We then ... Place convinced that we do no more ... we could find some shelter, after looking abou[t] ... time we found a barge that would shelter us, ... here till the boat came up in the morning. As soon as it was known a coffin was made and his remains were interred in the ground about 3 miles from Coto Du Lac. Neither of us followed the coffin to the Grave.

We staid here till the 18th when the boat came up. It was a very wet day and all the Passengers had to walk 3 miles so that by the time they reached Coto they were all wet through. Father thought it would be very imprudent to go on board the boat in such a condition as it was just going off with a good wind. He therefore took our passage in a Steam Boat for 40 miles. When we arrived at Cornwall we could hear no tidings of our boat. The captain gave Aunt her Passage free. We took lodgings here for the night and next morning hired a waggon to take us above the Rapids 22 miles, but we could hear nothing of the Boat. We slept in a Barn here for several nights in the morning sister Ann was taken ill and showed symptoms of the Cholera. We used the same means the doctor advised for Uncle which gave her great ease, and in the evening she was much better. Next morning Father and another Passenger went down to the River in search of the Boat, through the woods. Sister was taken with the cramps again in the morning but they soon ceased by bathing her in Warm Water and applying warm flannels.

22nd, Sister continued the same during the day. There is no doctor nearer than Prescot, and her complaint was so mild that we did not think she needed a Doctor.

23rd, Sister grew considerably worse about 11 oclock her arms and legs turned Black and her breath was short. Father returned at one o'clock just in time to see ... her last she was very quiet during the last ten minutes ... departed with a sweet smile. Father buried her un[der] ... at the water side and raised a heap of stones over her ... The boat came up in the evening and we all went [aboar]d. We arrived at Prescot, after leaving Montreal 12 Days, on the 25th, a distance of ... which is generally performed in 4 days. We staid ... and then took the Steamer for York where we arrived ...

York is a very fine and improving Town. It is situated ... of the Lake Ontario but the water is very Shallow ... this defect, there are several wooden Piers about half a mile ... Warehouses at the end. Father took lodging at an Inn built on the water; and the next morning went to Newmarket (where the settlement of friends is) in search of a mill. I had a slight bowel complaint before Coto Du Lac, it continued to grow worse till we reached York, when I was so weak, and my appetite so far gone, that I could eat nothing, but a little milk thickned with Flour, for there is no sweet

---

12 Nathaniel died 15 July.

bread to be had in this Country except in Winter. I went to the Doctor on the Seventh Day, he gave me some powder which soon stopped the complaint, so that by the time Father returned I had gained my strength, my diet was principally [missing] thickened with Arrow Root.

Father returned on 7th of y Mo. He met with a kind reception from Friends and they recommended him to several Mills in the Neighbourhood but he could not find one that wanted Hands. He was recommended to a mill near Lake Sim[coe] that belonged to an Irishman, and agreed to take the Mill all but drawing up the Articles, but in the morning his Wife had persuaded him off from it, he told Father it was most likely he should let it at Michaelmas. When he returned to Newmarket he heard alarming accounts of the Cholera at York so he came down the next day to take us to Newmarket but Aunt thought it would be better for her to stay at York, as the Governor [Sir John Colborne*] would find her a house, and recommended her to several of the English Gentry in the town.

The road to Newmarket is very Pleasant, the Farmers have just begun Haying, and all is bustle and activity, if it is fine they mow in the morning and carry in the afternoon. We travelled till 11 oclock it being a fine night and then stopped [at an] Inn till day [missing] in a manger with a black Man, and the rest slept in the Cart. We arrived at the meeting house at Sun Rise, and Friends allowed us to go into the School Room until we could find a situation. Their Monthly Meeting was held here on 5th day the 12th of 7th Mo. and Friends allowed us to sit at the meeting of business.

Father heard of a situation that would be likely to suit me at a Merchants of the name of John Cawthra[13] at Newmarket, where I am now on trial. I went with Father into a new settlement of friends 15 miles distant. We had to pass over Corderoy Bridge, which is nearly a mile over, built of logs fastened together, and in the middle is a swing Bridge which rises & falls with the water. Father likes the farm very well and he is to have it for 5 years for Building a Barn and putting the fence in order, if he cannot find a mill that will suit him. It belongs to a friend of the name of Jacob Wind. When we returned we went another way thrugh the woods and were terribly annoyed by the Musquitoes which very much resemble our English Gnats. Father had an attack of the Bowel complaint on first day but Friend gave him some Bark of the Hemlock tree, which cured him in two days. Mary Ann, George and Emma have also had it, but, by drinking Bark tea, they soon recovered.

I went to my place on the 16th and like it very well, though trade is on a very different plan to what it is in England. I have three coinages to contend with, the English, Spanish, and States. A York shilling is 7½ and a states shilling is the same as the English. British Coins are worth more here than at Home, thus a Sovereign is worth 23/6, Half a crown 2/11, a shilling ½ the Sovereign varies from 22 to 25 they are regulated by the Banks of Upper and Lower Canada.

20th, We heard the news of the Reform Bill being passed by the Lords, and signed

---

13 Son of prominent Toronto merchant Joseph Cawthra and member of the House of Assembly for
   Simcoe in 1828–30.

by the King. We hear also that the Cholera is very bad at New York and Albany. Three thousand have left the Place and nearly 100 die daily. It is also at Philadelphia and Washington, and several other Towns on the sea coast.

21st, Had a letter from Aunt. They are all quite well; the Governor is building a school for her and doing all he can to assist her, Joseph and Esther[14] have situations, which if they behave well will be of great service to them.

22nd, We were all invited to dine with an English Friend from Yorkshire, he has undertaken to get Elizabeth[15] a situation as School Mistress. She is to live with him a month to try her abilities. Father has made up his mind ... and take the ... at the Half if he cannot [missing] with anything to suit him better.[16] Land sells here for 6 Dollars an acre wild, and cleared from 15 to 20 Dollars. I must now begin to draw my letter to a conclusion having disfigured my sheet of Paper. I should be obliged to Russell to write some copies of this, and send to Dorking, another to Horsham and another to my Uncle John Hoard for him to forward to my grandmother at Litchenfield. Give our love to Samuel Sturge and tell him we are very thankful for the Books and tracts he was so kind as to give us. I have distributed those papers from the Yearly Meeting amongst friends, and also the Temperance and other tracts amongst the Inhabitants of Newmarket. Spirit[s] Drinking is carried on very high here, there being no beer to be had. Whiskey and Jamaica Spirits are most drank in Canada by the lower orders.

Give our love to Brother William, to Grandmother [Hannah Chantler,] Jos. Sayers[17] and all enquiring Friends. I intend to write to Brother William in 2 months and Father will write to J Sayers when he is settled. I hope you will partake of a large share yourselves. From your affectionate Nephew.

John Chantler.

P.S. Direct to John Cawthra, Merchant, Newmarket or Joseph Pearson, Young St. Newmarket.

OTHER LETTERS: 169, 172; see also 165–8, 170–1, 173

■ 167

JOSEPH R. CHANTLER, [LONDON], TO WILLIAM NATHANIEL CHANTLER, DORKING, SURREY, [SEPTEMBER 1832]

The *Brunswick*, on which Nathaniel and Moses Chantler emigrated to Upper Canada with their families, departed Gravesend near London; therefore, one of Joseph Chantler's family would be well placed to get early word about the ship's safe arrival. When he began this letter Joseph had had no news from those in Canada.

14 Joseph was 10 and Esther 12 years of age

15 Elizabeth was not yet 14 years of age.

16 Moses was probably considering taking the farm on shares, an arrangement in which a share of the produce took the place of rent.

17 Joseph Sayers loaned the Monthly Meeting of Horsham and Ifield £100 "to defray the expence of the removal of Moses Chantler and family to Canada" (WSRO, Monthly Meeting Minutes, 12 December 1832).

Four sisters, the children of Moses Chantler. From left to right: Amina, Priscilla, Mary Ann, and Elizabeth
Courtesy Elizabeth R. Gillespie

SOURCE: Chantler Family Papers, typescript and photocopy of original.

Letter addressed to (Year 1832)

Wm. N. Chantler
Dorking.
N.B. Read this first

My dear Cousin;

I have no doubt but that thou art anxiously expecting to hear from thy dear connexions on the American Continent and perhaps surprised that I have not written to thee before this. I have been also very desirous to hear from them and have more than once enquired at the Agents respecting the *arrival of the ship at Quebec.* The last time I enquired I learnt that their passage was a very favourable one, that all arrived safe and well in the *10th of* the *7th month* and laid *5 days in quarantine.* Some vessels left here a month before the *Brunswick* which did not arrive more than a week before her. We expect to hear from them very shortly, but fearing lest anything should occur to disappoint our wishes I did not like to defer giving thee this little information I possessed with the assurance that we shall forward as early as possible any communication that may come to our hands.

In the meantime let us trust that He who has preserved them from the dangers of the deep may continue with them in the way that they go and bring them in safety to their future habitation. I have read the principal part of a second letter from David, who is, as I believe thou art aware, settled at New York. It appears to have been written in the early part of the 4th month and gives a tolerably good account of the state of things there, but not sufficiently encouraging to invite me to follow his example. It appears from his statement that work is plentiful, particularly agricultural. Provisions he says are cheaper, tho' he understands not as low as in the interior of the country. He does not mention the prices of mechanical labour but stated the agriculturalist to get from 7 to 10 dollars a month with his board & that the Farmers hire their men generally by the year. He does not tell what clothes or domestic utensils can be bought for, neither does he inform us of the rentals in that rapidly increasing City. He stated it contains about 215,000 inhabitants. The description of the Town (or rather the Island on which it stands) is short and simple: it is that it is very hilly & must be levelled before building on it. Friends are very numerous though not half the number they were before the separation. The Hickites are the largest body & possess the Meeting-House, so that the Friends have built a new one.[18] Their number is about 1 thousand.

David says that his 2 cousins who went with him are now settled at some distance from him. Johnson is at Flushing in Long Island among some kind friends and the other, Simon, is 40 miles from New York. They talk of going to the State of Ohio in the spring.

Having given thee as copious an account of America as time and space will allow, I will turn thy attention to another part of the world and present to thy imagination the residence of thy friend and the principal events that are taking place under his own observation. In the first place I may inform thee that through the blessing of God we are at the present time all quite well. Many have and still continue to be falling around us under the visitation which has been permitted to assail us.[19] Day unto day has indeed "uttered speech and night unto night shewed knowledge." Few cases (comparatively speaking) have come to my knowledge within the last week or two, tho' I know of several and one, next door but one to our house.

Such was not the case 4 or 5 weeks back; repeated instances of sudden illness and premature death came under my own observation and scarce an individual you conversed with but what added fresh instances of mortality to the long catalogue of my own recollection. In truth I was sick with every days report and would fain have been deaf for a season. I heard as it were the language "by [be?] ye also ready" proclaim'd to my understanding with each of these melancholy tales, and felt that the great work was as yet scarce begun; "that from the evil of my life nothing could be taken away" and but a short time appeared "to add anything to the good." I trust that many have been awakened to a sense of the uncertainty of Time and led to apply their hearts unto true wisdom.

We have very little business at the present time, but hope the Autumn will set us to work again soon. Great improvements are taking place on both sides of the

18 The Hicksites were a splinter group who had broken away from the Quakers in 1827.
19 Cholera was confirmed in London on 13 February 1832.

new Bridge.[20] Some handsome houses have been erected on the left hand of the approaches from the Boro' and the remaining row of Houses on that side are being pulled down, so that the whole side of the High Street from the Town Hall to the Bridge will be thrown further back and present a more handsome and a more uniform aspect than heretofore. The street, which was very narrow, will now shortly be considerably wider, which will be a great desideratum. The old rookery of St. Saviour's Cathedral known as the "Ladye Chapel" fronting the road is undergoing a thorough repair & is to be entered from the foot of the Bridge. New Houses are also in progress on the Right hand of the High Street from St. Thomas's Hospital to the river & a new Fishmonger's Hall with a number of Houses are just commenced on the City side of the Bridge. The method of building is much altered in these last few years; the bricks are laid & then covered with a wash of mortar which runs into the work without the more tedious way of spreading the Mortar. Sometimes the front bricks are cemented, which gives them the appearance of being *pointed*.

The Streets of the City are mostly paved after a new method, viz. first a good foundation is made with hard rubbish &c; then a good layer of river sand mixt with lime which makes a substantial bottom – the stones are then laid in a gentle sweep from each side of the street and after a wash of lime and sand to bind them together, which, with their Iron Gutters, form an excellent road. Thus much about paving.

The illumination in commemoration of the Reform Bills was very partial, a few simpletons in our neighborhood put up transparencies, but the thing was so stale that it passed off with very little spirit. Turning to the west end of the great metropolis I shall notice a new statue to the memory of the celebrated Geo. Canning.[21] It is a beautiful likeness of that illustrious senator standing in bold posture with a bill (I suppose Catholic Emancipation) in his hand.[22] He is wrapped in a loose mantle & the sandals on his feet combine to give him the appearance of the Roman Orators. A very substantial monument of the Duke of York is being erected on the top of a flight of steps in the St. James's Park on the site of Carlton House.

9th Month, 13th. I have just time to say that I have at length received a letter from thy <u>brother John</u>,[23] which I have copied verbatim after a tedious task. Thou wilt find it to contain some lamentable news as well as some of a pleasing nature. *Poor Uncle Nathaniel* has been removed by the cholera from his complicated distresses and tho' no one followed him to the grave we have reason to believe his soul now rests in peace like Lazarus of old, with the Just of all generations. Nor was this all; thou art no doubt aware the disease is very bad in America and I regret to inform thee that one of the beloved circle who lately owned thee as brother is now no more. I *allude to thy sister Ann* whose death is also recorded in the accompanying letter. Tho' Prov-

20 London Bridge was completed in 1831.
21 Prime minister from April to his death in August 1827.
22 The Catholic Emancipation Act was to give Roman Catholics the right to sit in Parliament. Dissenters had had this right ratified in 1828.
23 See letter 166.

idence has thus taken what he alone had Power to bestow, let us be thankful that these are the only instances in which the disease has proved fatal, several of the rest having been attacked with the complaint but mercifully spared from its effects. They are now arrived at their destination and seem likely to get comfortably settled among kind Friends.

I will not detain thee further than to request thee to send a copy of the letter to thy *Grandmother* as I do not know address &c. I will endeavour to write a copy for *Aunt Deborah* as soon as ever I can but it takes a long while to copy it. I regret my negligence which I must beg of thee to excuse for reasons which I have not time to mention at length at the present, further than to say that I waited to see the Captain of the ship as soon as he returned, having begun my letter about two weeks ago.

Farewell, my dear Cousin. Mourn not for the dead but thank the Allwise disposer of events that they are not all taken, seeing the disease rages or has done so in their path. Remember me *and my parents to Cousin Josh syers* [Sayers], thy Master and my other enquirers. I shall, in [if?] living and well, write an answer in about 6 or 8 weeks, when I shall be glad to have such information from thee as will be desirable to send them.

Wishing thee Health and every other blessing, I conclude and should be most happy to see thee whenever thy master can spare thee to come to London, which I trust thou wilt now consider as thy country Home.

> Thine with love,
> Josh R. Chantler.

N.B. The Coach is going off in ¼ of an hour.

OTHER LETTERS: 168, see also 165, 166–173.

■ 168

JOSEPH R. CHANTLER, LONDON, ENGLAND, TO JOHN CHANTLER, NEWMARKET, UPPER CANADA, 30 NOVEMBER 1832

Joseph R. Chantler wrote this letter quickly in reply to letter 166, addressed to his father, which told of the family's safe arrival and the subsequent deaths from cholera of Nathaniel and Ann Chantler. At William's request, he copied in a letter from William to his younger brother in Canada.

SOURCE: Archives of Ontario, F775, MU2106.17, Chantler Letters, 1832. Fragile original: some words are lost to holes or a tear in the paper. The letter is written on a sheet 12 inches by 16 and the handwriting is crossed on every area except that occupied by the address.

From Joseph R. Chantler, London, England to John Chantler, c/o John Cawthra, merchant, Newmarket, Upper Canada, 30[?] November 1832   *Sent via the "New York Post Line."*

My dear Cousin

Thy truly acceptable epistle of the 7th Month last, came safe to our hands (tho' partly wore out by the length of the journey) on the 13th of the 9th Month, and in compliance with thy instructions I immediately sent a copy to thy brother, and soon after, one to Horsham. I also wrote a copy for the perusal of those Friends in London who were interested in your welfare. This letter has been very deservedly commended by all who have perused or heard it, for the copious and interesting narrative of your voyage, and the subsequent account of your travel through the interior of the Country ... [with?] the hardships and misfortunes that attended it. To us ...[it ha]s been not only deeply interesting, but also affecting; yet we cannot but feel sensible of the goodness of Him "who doth all things right:" who in his mercy hath [permitted?] *so many* of you to reach in health and safety, the place of your destination. We rather feared, as soon as we heard that the Cholera was in Canada, that some of you might become the victims of its ravages, therefore it was not *quite* so surprising when we read the melancholly departure of my poor Uncle and the subsequent decease of they Sister Ann. Can we reflect on the removal of these, the late partners of your pilgrimage, and not admire the goodness of God, in thus taking from among you the weakest, instead of the strongest, and those who were least capable of service in your arduous undertakings? We trust that they were both in measure prepared to put off the shackles of mortality, and through the merits and intercession of their *Redeemer*, have entered into their everlasting rest. We could not but feel for *thee* in they trials at Coto du lac, as well as for my Aunt upon that melancolly occasion, and though we may perhaps *picture* to ourselves your deplorable condition it can be but a faint description of your feelings. I will not hide from thee that we should have felt more comfortable if you had followed the re[lics?]... [...le?] to the grave, instead of leaving it entirely to stran[gers] ... course should be the best judges of your own feelings ... been present we should have done the same.

I delivered your message to Samuel Sturge, who was much pleased with thy attention & has since seen the *letter* which he is much pleased with. I was very much interested with the style and correctness of manner in which thou hast described the different scenes which [w]ere presented to your view and hope thou will favour me in thy next with as accurate and copious an account of the face of the Country its climate soil and productions etc. It is not likely that my letter will be either so long or so interesting, as thine was to us, yet I will endeavour to send thee all the news which I think most likely to interest thee, and as I have just received a second letter from William I will give an account of him in his own words as he *first* desires me to enclose the following –

10th Mo 25th 1832

Dear Brother

I was not a little surprised and sorry to hear of the decease of dear sister Ann; but I was not so much surprised of Uncle as it was thought by a great many that he would not live through the voyage in consequence of his delicate state of health. I have felt a great deal for *thee* my dear Brother – placed in a situation so dangerous as thou wast, and it is a great pleasure to me to think thou acted thy part so well, and not a little glad that thee did not stay behind. I am very glad to hear that Ann went off so quietly and easy, and I hope their souls are gone to rest. I was glad to hear of your quick passage, and safe arrival, and that there were no *more* attacked with the Cholera exposed as you were [?]; but after all the troubles you have had to pass through, I hope you have by this time found a comfortable home and am glad as are many others that you have got situated among so many kind friends, who interest themselves on your behalf and I flatter myself with great hopes of your getting on comfortably.

I suppose by this time Father ... and ... [some]thing to suit him, either a Mill or a Farm. I am glad ... got a situation likely to suit thee; and hope that [Elizabeth is] capable of acting the part of School Mistress. I think there is no doubt but that she will. I am very glad to hear that Aunt [Sophia] is likely to get on comfortably, that the Governor has assisted her, and that cousins have situations.

I had a little holliday of about 3 days, which I spent at Gra[nd]-mother's about 2 months ago, and about 5 weeks back, I took a copy of thy letter to Horsham and shewed it to a few Friends: Margaret Deane for one, who could not help shedding a tear over it. I then took it to my Aunt Deborah [Chantler] who has got a situation as Housekeeper at a Farmer in the name of Wilson near L[o]wer Hill. She was quite well; but had a large bunch[24] in her neck which is very common with country people. I next went to Uncle Jn°. Hoard's[25] about ½ miles from Aunt's and read it to them and Uncle could not help dropping a few tears. They were all quite well and had plenty of work. I next proceeded to Grandmother's whom I found but poorly but Uncle & Aunt & Cousins were [qui]te well. I slept there that night and got back to Dorking next morn[ing] ...

...aster's Father died about 5 weeks back and his ...st daughter about 3 weeks ago and were both buried at Riegate. I went to James Chantler's this day week, who with his Wife and Children are quite well. They have left the Mill and are living at a small house on the Green. He has engaged with Mr Coleman for the winter at 13 shillings per week. Thee said nothing about Mother and Charles in thy letter but I hope thee will mention about all in thy next. I shall expect soon to have a letter from thee with a relation of thy excursions into the Country with a report of good health. Mary Greenwood (distantly related to us) wishes to be remembered to Aunt, and would be very much obliged to her if she will send her a letter, be the expense where it may. Give my dear love to Father, Mother, Brothers & Sisters with Aunt & Cousins and accept a large portion thyself.
I remain thy affectionate Brother

W.N. Chanter

22nd I now sit down to resume my letter which as I am a slow writer I fear will not be finished this evening. Thy Brother's letter of the 18th Inst informs me that [sic] has received thine (without a date[)] and expresses a little disappointment at finding it so similar to that which he has already seen and would have been glad of further information respecting your present situation etc; yet speaks in high terms of the affectionate regard which it evinces towards him. We are all sorry to hear that

---

24 a goitre
25 Or Hoad? Moses Chantler was married to Sarah Hoad.

thy Father had not met with anything to suit him but hope that that will not be the case on the receipt of this. I was pleased to find that thou likest thy place and hope that thou will endeavour to conduct thyself in all things so as [to] gain the esteem and appreciation of thy employers and be a comfort to thy friends.

Remember my dear Cousin that it is of the greatest importance to maintain a good character as our future welfare greatly depends on the good opinion of others. Endeavour therefore to guard against the least deviation from moral rectitude; as one false step is often the prelude to many others, and each new temptation increases in its weight and rises higher in its demands till we become (like the fly in the spider's webb) entangled in the net of our own corruptions, from which nothing but the mercy and grace of our Heavenly Father can ever extricate us. Let us therefore strive to walk circumspectly keeping in remembrance the high profession which we as a Society are making before the world at large; and let us not be contenting ourselves ... [ma]king a bare profession of religion and of wearing the outward garb of our sect but endeavour ... [ev]idence to the manifestations of the holy spirit of God to pursue the path of duty. So shall we be ... [fathoms?] from the many snares and allurements of the grand enemy of our souls happiness and be permit[ed] ... the doctrine of God our Saviour upon earth and finally be prepared to receive the welcome sentance ... ... [go]od and faithful servant enter thee into the joy of thy Lord." It is from an earnest desire for thy ... and under some sense of my own outgoings [sic] that I have ventured thus to express myself, earnestly desiring that thou mayst be preserved from the many temptations that surround us. The following lines which I received from Willm Chantler of Newport Pagnel are worthy of our remembrance and being applicable to my subject need no apology for their insertion.

"Think on the dangers thou may'st [...]et
Watching with care thy sliding feet.
And where thou once hast fell before,
Mark well that place and fall no more!"

As I have mentioned Wm Chantler's name I will now inform thee that he was quite well when I heard last of him (about 2 weeks ago) as was also his Father James Chantler Senr. but his Mother was but very poorly and appears to be breaking very fast. They have had another letter from David, which says that he has had an attack of the Cholera but was recovered. He intends to proceed up the Country into the State of Ohio in the ensuing Spring. Thomas Hayllar and his family are all well or as usual. Some of thy schoolfellows are still living in our neighbourhood among whom I suppose Joseph Albright Fred^k Dogget Fred^k Sims, & Robert Downs will be remembred by thee.[26] Hen^y Dymond & the other teachers were quite well when I last heard of them.

Thy brother seemed in high spirits when he wrote his last letter to me on the 18th Inst. partly occasioned by the belief that he is beginning to grow again after a long stand, he says that he has grown 2½ inches since he last measured though he does not

---

26 John Chantler had been to the Friends Boarding School in Croydon, Surrey.

say how long that was. He says that everybody tells him of it, and therefore concludes that "what everybody says *must* be true" and hails it as good news. I also unite with him and hope he may go on till he attains a man's stature. He mentions that R. Dix at my cousin King's has received a letter from thee.[sic] the particulars he had not learnt. Our yearly Meeting was pretty fully attended and we had the company of 4 Friends from your land (or rather the States) viz Stephen Griellat, a French American – Christopher Healy, John Willbur and Charles Osborne. They have been gone ever since, some to the Continent and Scotland and I think one is returned home.

SG Wm Allen is gone to the Continent with S Griellat. John Walkinson an eminent minister has lately paid a religious visit to us in conjunction with the other Monthly Meetings composing the Quarterly Meeting of London & Middlesex. The Old London Bridge has at length entirely disappeared and the new one is *quite* completed but it will be some considerable time before the approaches are entirely finished though many handsome and lofty houses have been already, and are nearly completed [sic]. On the City side is erecting a vast pile of Building intended for a new Fishmonger's Hall, on the site of the old one. It will front the river and have another facing the Bridge. The exact manner of the approaches is not (I believe) determined upon. On our side of the water the houses that stood on the left hand between the Town Hall and the Bridge have all been pull'd down and a new row will be formed further ... which will considerably widen their part of the Borough. The old church of St Saviour is undergoing a th[oro]ugh repair (or rather I should say) that part of it called the Lady Chapel, and which fronts the road) – and on the other side a new wing is being formed to the St Thomas's Hospital; so that when all is *done* we shall be very grand indeed.

I went on 1st ... to see the improvements in Westminster & St. James's Park and saw the statue of George [Canning] [w]hich has been place on the side of Parliament Street near the Abbey. It is a noble yet plain piece ...nship of representing him in a loose mantle, with the Catholic Emancipation Bill in his hand ... [coun]tenance is dignified and expressive, and his whole person presents the idea of a Roman Senator. It is ... [he]ight from the ground, and is considerably larger than life. Very different will be that of the late Duke [of York] [w]hich is being erected on the side of the late King's palace (called Carleton House.) at the top of a flight of steps which form a new communication between [the] park and Pell Mell [sic]. It is a very neat and massive edifice and in its base is a door leading to a flight of step[s by] which to ascend the summit of this lofty building which is already the height of the houses adjoining[. At] the top of the shaft will be a gallery on which will be placed the statue of his late Royal Highness. – H[igh] enough truly. A second Monument whose slight circumference seems almost incapable of supporting its towering height. I do not know for why, but it seemed to me a folly to carry it so high that the features of the Duke will be scarcely discernable to such little folk as myself. When finished it will be called the Duke of York's Column. It is in print at the head of the Stationer's Almanck.

The New Palace is in progress but the alterations do not strike me as any improvement to its appearance. Returning from John Rawling's at Islington last 6th day week was just in time to see the new Lord Mayor's Show, as it is vulgarly called; which was a very pretty sight. Sir Peter Laurie is the new Mayor & Sir John Key the late one is putting up for the representation of the City in the new Parliament. Joseph Rawlings & Alfred are quite well – we are very intimate. I think I have not told the the longest half of my story and as I do not know much more news likely to inter-est thee or there will bid thee adieu for the present as it is past bedtime and will resume the first opportunity.

30th of 11th Month. I am sorry to have again delayed the sending of this letter but have nothing further to communicate at present, therefore conclude with desires that you may all be enabled to get along comfortably in this world, trusting in the protecting care of the Great Shepherd of Israel who will never leave nor forsake those who put their trust in him – but as they are obedient to his voice will give them of the good things of this present life and finally lend them to the "green pastures" of eternal bliss.

Be so kind as to let my Aunt Sophie have either [a copy] of this or of the prin-cipal parts as she no doubt will be glad to hear of us. Tell her that we should like to hear from her perhaps thou will enclose it in thine. Do not forget to give our united Love to her & her children and inform her that a young woman whose brother had part of the opposite berth has called several times to know if we had heard of him; saying that Aunt promised to write & say how he was & where. If she know what became of him after their arrival perhaps she will say as they had not heard of him when I last saw them his name is Samuel Bidmad.

Give my love together with that of Father & Mother to thy Parents and the chil-dren; particularly to Elizabeth, also accept the same from us all to thyself, and believe me thy sincere friend and cousin.

Joseph R. Chantler

P.S. I shall send *now* with the first post   6th day evening 30/11/32
Adieu!

OTHER LETTERS: 167, see also 166–73

■ 169

JOHN CHANTLER, NEWMARKET, UPPER CANADA, TO WILLIAM
NATHANIEL CHANTLER, DORKING, SURREY, SEPTEMBER 1832
John Chantler could not be certain when he wrote his brother that the news sent in his pre-vious letter to his uncle (166) had reached William too.

SOURCE: Chantler Family Papers; modern copy in pencil in AO, F775, MU 2106, Chantler letters, 1832. There is no original on file; gaps or illegible words in the text have been marked with ellipses.

New Market near York U. Canada

Dear Brother

It is with feelings of affection that I address thee my dear Brother, and with grat-itude to the Almighty for his mercies which with a Bountiful hand, he is pleased to bestow upon us, and with a providential hand, hath preserved us thus far, both from the Perils of the Deep, and in a great degree from the raging Pestilence which is daily consuming numbers of our fellow creatures.

But I must say it is with feelings of deep regret that I have to inform thee of loss of our Sister Ann, and also of Uncle Nathanial since we arrived in this country, but I also can inform thee with great pleasure, that a provision has been made for Aunt, and cousins, which will not only ensure to Aunt a comfortable and easy living but her children will be placed out in such situations by which they may obtain a comfortable livelihood, when grown to manhood. I shall give thee more particulars in the course of this Letter.

I hope my dear Brother, thou wilt not destress thyself when thou perusest this letter, but remember that we are all of us as it were on the Brink of a Precipice not knowing when we may fall into the Gulf below. Let us therefore seek the Lord with all our hearts, so that when he cometh he may find us watching. Then we shall gain[?] the crown of Glory which is laid up for all those that fear the Lord and keep his commandments.

I shall not enter into a detail of our Voyage as thou canst obtain that from the letter I sent to Uncle Joseph, but give thee particulars of the death of my dear Sister and Uncle.

Uncle was taken ill on the morning of the 2nd day after we left Montreal at a place called Cedars. The boat was lying at the time, just below a rapid, waiting for horses to draw them up and Father had taken lodging for all, excepting himself, me and Charles; we slept in the boat to take care of our goods, the boats are open, and not so large as a common Barge. They sent for Father as soon as it was light; there was the Doctor of our ship in the boat at the time and Father requested him to go and see Uncle. The Doctor was in bed at the time but he directed Father to bathe his legs and arms in hot water and he would be at the Inn as soon as he was drest. Father then went and did as the Doctor had ordered, but his not coming in the time, Father went to the boat to see whether he was coming, but found that he had left the boat, and was run away to the next Village, and in such haste was he to get away that he did not half dress himself but we could make a little excuse for him as he was a young man about 22 years old.

Father then sent the Innkeeper for a Doctor that had lived 5 miles off and as soon as he came ordered the bath to be continued, until he was relieved from the cramps, which were very severe for the first two hours. He then gave him a strong dose of medicine and left. When he came again, Uncle was much better so that he said he was in a fair way of recovery. He then advised us to send him on a cart to the next village which we did, and I went with Aunt and Cousins, and Father staid with the boat. Uncle bore the journey very well, until we were within a mile of the place, when he grew very weak, so that he could not sit up in the cart, and by the time we reached the Village he was nearly insensible. Then I went in search of lodgings, after going to all the Inns and most of the houses in the Village, I was obliged to return, and they were even so much set against us, that they would not even let us into their out houses, they told us that the only place we could take him to was out on the wharf and, as there was no alternative but to stay in the middle of the street or on the lea side of the wharf, we chose to go out there. We made up his bed and laid him on it. I then covered him with a ... and what boards I could find but I had scarcely finished when a heavy thunderstorm came on & lasted nearly two hours. Uncle was now quite insensible, his breath grew shorter and his eyes were sunk into his head and about 1 o'clock he went off quietly without a groan, and at first we could only perceive it by not hearing him breath, which before was very strong. It was not until then, that I was in the least alarmed for my own safety but the idea of a corpse beside me, and that too of a malignant kind, chilled my ... that I was all in a shake and tremble and fell down and should have fainted away, had I not been aroused by the cries of my distressed Aunt and Cousins. I got up and after covering the body over, I persuaded Aunt to leave the place but before we could get into shelter, it came on to rain again in torrents and we were nearly all wet through to the skin.

I then remembered to have seen a barge on the side of the wharf, to which we went and found a place to shelter us at one end. We stayed there until the boat came up. In the morning as soon as it was known, the inhabitants ordered a coffin to be made and he was interred in a burying ground 3 miles from the village. After Aunt had paid the expenses of interment she had only £20 and a few shillings left. Uncle died on the 15th of 6 month, after a short illness of 18 hours and intered on the morning of the 16th. On the 18th the boat came up, the passengers had had to walk three miles on account of the rapids and it rained the whole of the way, and poor Ann was completely wet through and the rest were nearly as bad. As there was a favourable wind in the morning the boat was just going ... when they came up instead of ... towed by ...

Father then concluded to go by the steamer as there was great danger of their catching colds if they went in the boats and in the steamer they could dry their clothes. The Captain was so kind as to [let] Aunt to go free, and the Cook gave us several parcels of soup while we were in the boat. We went 40 miles in a steamer and landed in Cornwall, we expected to have found our boat here but we could neither see nor hear anything of it here, so we concluded she must have gone past. The next morning we hired a waggon to take us above the chain of rapids, the longest of which is called the Long-Scoue [Long Sault]. Here we heard that a boat had passed in the night. We then went to Williamsburgh 25 miles from Prescott and as there was no other lodging in the place we slept in a Barn on some straw. In the morning Sister Ann complained of pains in her bowels. They were also very much relaxed, in the evening she was much better but grew worse in the morning and was very much troubled with the Cramps. We then bathed her in hot water and applied bottles filled with hot water to the parts that were cramped. Father left us to go in search of the boat this morning in company with another Passenger. He was gone three days. They found the boat moored between two rocks in an obscure part of the river ... Cote-du-lac. They sailed into the middle of Lake St. Francis and then turned off to an Indian Village States side and made themselves tipsy at a Store in the Village when one of the Indians happened to hear that a man belonging to the boat had died of the Cholera he communicated it to the rest and they assembled round the Store with sticks and clubs and threatened to murder them but our Captain who was an Indian and brought up in the Village went out to them and explained to them as well as he was able the circumstances of his death[.T]hey were soon quieted and allowed them to stay 2 days.

When they sailed again the Captain quarreled with the crew and his resentment went so far that he put his right hand on his breast and cried out in broken English – me die wid boat – and let the sail loosen and the boat began to fill with water which one of the men seeing he took a cudgle and knocked him down, and stunned him. He then righted the boat and the rest baled the water but it did great damage to our goods. When Father found the boat as I have mentioned the Captain had run away into the woods and he concluded to take the Goods and hire waggons to take them to Prescott and charge the carriage to the Agents, which the Captain hearing of it he returned and told Father if he did not put the Goods into the boat again he would have to pay the carriage which Father was very glad to hear as he did not want the trouble. When he came up he found Sister just on the point of death, when he left us she continued to get worse and worse. She lost her appetite, but very eager after water and it was with difficulty we could induce her to take anything else[. F]or about an hour before she departed she was very calm and the Violence of her disorder seemed to be abated but her legs and arms were nearly Blue. Father came just in time to receive her last smile, her speech having failed her for the last ¼ hour, she closed her eyes no more to behold this transitory world and I believe, my dear Brother, that she is gone to open her eyes in the World of endless happiness where the wicked cease from troubling and the weary are at rest. Father buried her in a ... hide under an oak tree and piled a heap of stones over her grave near the Water side. She died on the 23rd of 6 month and was intered the same day. Dear Mother and Father appeared to bear their loss with great firmness, but it was a Melancholy task for him to consign his own Daughter to her lonesome grave.

I do hope, my Dear Brother, thou wilt not ... thy feelings more than thou canst possibly avoid. Perhaps thou mayst think it hard that ... thee in this way. I know the ties of affection are the strongest between Brothers ... and I know also that it is very trying to be separated from those we dearly love. But we should remember that the ways of Providence are inscrutable and past finding out. Let us therefore submit ourselves to her decrees with patience and resignation.

We arrived at Prescott on the 26th so that we were 12 days traveling ... miles which is generally done in 3 or 4 days. We took our passage in a steamer on the 28th for York and arrived there on the 30th. Father took lodgings at an Inn and the next morning went to New Market where the Settlement of Friends is. They behaved very kind to him and recommended him to several mills in the Township but he could not find one to suit him. He staid there a week but hearing that the Cholera was very bad at the time there died from eight to ten every day we left York on second day but Aunt thought it would be best for her to stay. Father went with her to the Governor [Sir John Colborne*] and he provided her an house rent free and recommended her to several English families where she might obtain work. We reach[ed] New Market on 3 day morning and Friends let us into their Meeting house where we have been ever since. Next week we heard of a situation that would suit me in the Village where I now am. I like my place quite well.

Our Half Year Meeting began yesterday; it was well atended, it last ... days. We have not yet ... certificate. Father heard of a place that would be likely to suit him from one of the Friends, Pelham between York and Niagara. He is going with the Friends to see about it.

I have not time to say much more before I shall conclude. We all enjoy good health at present except Emma who has been very poorly but is getting better. We all unite in our loves to all our kind Friends and relations and may this convey to thy heart ... of the affection which flows in pure stream in our breasts for thy welfare and happiness.

I am thy truly affectionate Brother, John Chantler.

P.S. Thou must excuse this letter but I had not time to correct mistakes. Thou must also excuse me for not mentioning the names to whom we send our loves. Thou must do that part.

My seal is a States sixpence.

Addressed to:
    Robert Marsh
        Linen Draper
        Dorking, Surrey
        Near London.
Wm. Chantler

OTHER LETTERS: 166, 172; see also 165, 167–68, 170–71, 173

Passage on the St Lawrence River was interrupted by the cholera epidemic early in the navigation season of 1832, in part because some boatmen fled the river. Although traffic was supposed to be moving again by early July, John Chantler's account suggests that some emigrants were still having difficulties.[27]

---

27 See Geoffrey Bilson, *A Darkened House: Cholera in Nineteenth-Century Canada* (Toronto: University of Toronto Press 1980).

■ **170**

ARTHUR GRAVELY,[28] CHICHESTER, WEST SUSSEX, TO WILLIAM
CHANTLER, DORKING, SURREY, 21 AUGUST 1836

SOURCE: Chantler Family Papers

Letter addressed to
Wm. Chantler,
Robt, Marsh,
Draper,
Dorking,
Surrey.

By favour   Chichester, S. August 21st, 1836.
   M. Niblen.

My dear William;

I cannot do otherwise than follow thy example in taking a foolscap sheet to answer thy last long and interesting letter, but will not promise thee that I shall be able to fill it, as Mary Niblen will leave us tomorrow morning at 9 and I have not been able to begin before. I quite concur in thy wish that it may not be so long again before we write to each other, and hope thou wilt answer this within a month. John Niblen will, I have no doubt, take charge of letters till he sends a parcel to us.

How well thou managed to get to Worthing after leaving Chichester, last summer. I was very much surprised to find it was so long since thy Relations in America had written to thee; if they should write before thou receivest this, please give me all the Particulars thou can – as everything connected with Emigration and Emigrants is particularly interesting to me.

Thou hast fallen into a trifling mistake about Stephen Hack's accompanying the Hobinsons to the States next spring. He is at present living here (near Chichester I mean) and on the 1st of next month will sail from England with his brother, John Barton Hack, and family to a new Colony not yet settled at all, called South Australia. The first settlements are to be on Kangaroo Island.

They intend being in Partnership and suppose they will be principally Sheep Farmers. The first vessel to the Colony sailed about 6 weeks back – taking the Governor, Clerk, Clergymen &c &c and all the officers of the Establishment, – and I suppose some Passengers to the Colony. A great many Persons of first rate Respectability, talent and circumstances, have bought lots of land there and will most likely shortly proceed there. The land in the Colony has been for sale nearly a year; those who bought land before some date past, bought a lot of – acres in the Country and 1 acre of land where the Town is to be made as 12/– per Acre. A believe there have been 400 lots bought. So there will be 400 lots of 1 Acre each marked

---

28 The Gravelys were a Quaker family whose name appears in the records of the Monthly Meetings of Horsham and Ifield, but we did not find any trace of Arthur.

out in the Town and 400 plots of – Acres joining the Town. The first Purchasers of the above grounds will then draw lots and No. 1 will have the liberty of choosing where he likes (or perhaps the best lot will be marked out for him – which of course will be as near the Town as possible), and so on till the whole 400 have their allotment given them. After that time no land in the Colony is to be sold at less than 21/– per Acre. The Proceeds of the above sales is to be applied entirely to the Purpose of taking out, or at any rate assisting, deserving labourers to emigrate to the Colony. The price of Land being high will be of immense good to the Colony as it will prevent the redundancy of Farmers without capital that for years crippled Swan River Settlement and makes labourers and the Price of labour so dear in Upper Canada and other British Colonies. The Plan too of appropriating the money obtained by the sale of Lands to the encouragement and assistance of Emigration is most excellent and has been followed for the last 18 months in New South Wales about Sydney.

I cannot at all enter into feeling with thee about thy emigrating prospects – and think there must be some unintentional mistake in thy letter. So I will quote from it, and wish thee to put it right in thy next if wrong. "I am at present undecided as to what I shall do when arrived there – whether to take a situation as Shopman in some part of the States or return again to England." "If things should turn out as I anticipate, I might return again to my present situation, as I think it would answer my purpose better than America."

Now carefully read over my two foregoing sentences, and if they are thy present sentiments, I advise thee most strongly *not to leave England on any account*. I consider it would be a positive waste of money to go over there with the intention of coming back. Again I advise thee to be extremely cautious in speculating. I think the safest way would be not to speculate at all, for in a Foreign Market British Produce or Manufactures that are selling 300 or sometimes 500 per cent dearer than in England are the next week or month, from a glut in the Market, selling from 20 to 50 per cent *less* than in England, – which if it should be thy case would make a strange difference in thy funds. My advice is "be extremely careful – act only on the latest intelligence." What was a good speculation 6 months back may be a Ruinous game. Now about sheep. What number and sort does thy Father wish thee to bring out and what will he give thee for them? Ascertain that *clearly* before taking them out. The risk of losing them is great. Does he wish thee to take out Rams or Ewes?

I find thou intends to go by New York. A vessel, one of the New York line of Packet Ships, sails from St. Catherine's Dock on the 10th, 20th and last day of each month during the year. Their price for Steerage Passage is £5, provisioning himself of course. The same Packets call at Portsmouth on the 10th, 20th and the last of each month. They leave London on the 7th and 17th and 27th. (I made a mistake above.)

I was sorry to hear so poor an account of Robt. Maith's health. Please remember me to him. I have not forgotten his ac/c and will settle as soon as possible. I have been poorly and have had a Doctor's Bill to pay. I can assure thee I find a great many ways for my Earnings – but Robt. may depend upon being paid. I feel

William Nathaniel Chantler, the recipient of this letter, with his wife, Margaret Booker. A son of Moses Chantler, William came to Upper Canada in 1840
Courtesy Elizabeth R. Gillespie

extremely obliged to him for his kindness in waiting so long. The amount is £4, I think. I am anxious to receive Thos. Spencer's long delayed letter. I have no doubt he thoroughly enjoyed his Kentish trip.

Canst thou send me any news of Edwin Horsnaill? I have heard that he is turned Paper Maker. Is he living near Maidstone? Has he a mill to himself or is he in Partnership? and canst thou tell me how he is getting on? I suppose he made very great sacrifice in disposing of his stock. I was a good deal surprised to hear that Mr. Smith was going away from Mrs. Deane. It is not always that high Premiums make good servants. Will Thos. Spencer leave when of age?

I was surprised to hear there was a Probability of my being readmitted a member of the Society of Friends. I applied to the Monthly Meeting about a year ago and was refused. My love to John and Hannah Trimmer. I was extremely sorry to hear of their Reverses, but they cannot be helped. It seems to be the fate of some

Persons to be constantly going down hill or Backwards; or as Franklin says come out of the little end of the Horn. Amongst whom I am sorry to say my own dear Father is one. I am glad to hear Charles has so nice a situation, and hope he will keep it. There is a young man living here who used to live with Jas. King, the Grocer. He has been here about half a year.

I have pretty much made up my mind to emigrate next spring and intend going to Sydney, which after much Reading, thinking, &c &c I prefer to Canada, as I do not wish to be an agriculturalist in which line, from all that I have heard and read, there seems more Probability of succeeding than in any other. I can tell thee more of my plan in my next which I shall write thee shortly after receiving an answer to this. I have not time to say much more as M.N. leaves at 9 tomorrow morning and I have several things to attend to in the morning, which will prevent my writing.

Jim Bevan and I arose at 3 o'clock last 3rd day morning,[29] the 16th Instant, and proceeded at 4 in F.W. Lucas Pony Gig (which he was kind enough to lend us) to Portsmouth which we reached soon after 6 – 18 miles. We walked about the Town and went to book at the shipping. Saw the Glasgow Steamer just arrived with wounded and sick Troops from Spain.[30] The Victory, Nelson's ship, was in Dock so that we did not see her as we should have liked to have done.

At 7 we stepped into a small Steam Boat and went over to Ryde in the Isle of Wight, which we reached in ½ hour. We then walked south west to the village of Brading, saw Leigh Richmond's House and Church,[31] the grave of the young Cottager &c &c. We then turned westwards and walked along the top of the Range of hills to within 2 miles of Newport. Then turned south to the village of Shide to call on a Person we knew, a Clergyman, where we had a Crust of Bread and Cheese. After which we walked to Carisbrook Castle, from which there is some most splendid scenery. After we had taken a slight survey, as we had not time to examine it thoroughly, we walked to Newport. Prowled about the Town for an hour or so, then left in boat for Cowes. Had a most delightful sail, about 5 miles for 6 pence. Cowes we found a very busy, bustling place. There are a great many Yachts there, shipping of all sorts, including King's Ships. There was a beautiful 400 Ton American Brig, which had just delivered at Cowes a cargo of Swedes Iron. Just such a vessel I should like to go to Sydney in. After waiting about Cowes an hour, we left by Powerful Steam Packet for Portsmouth, which we reached at [text missing] and had tea there. Started at 8 and reached Chichester soon after 10 in the evening, having spent a most delightful day, which cost us only 6/3 each including Gates and everything. So I think

---

29 Tuesday, the third day of the week.

30 England was supporting the Constitutionalists in Spain against Don Carlos's claims to the throne. The British government allowed the formation of a foreign legion, which may explain this reference.

31 Legh Richmond (1772–1827) was at one time rector of Brading on the Isle of Wight. His evangelical stories *Annals of the Poor* were best sellers, especially *The Dairyman's Daughter*, which had a circulation of over two million copies.

we were not extravagant and saw a great deal for our money and most thoroughly enjoyed the Trip which went off without any mishap. The Towns in the Island are good, large and have better shops than Dorking. Newport we both thought quite as large as Chichester.

Now do not let it be a year before thou answers me this time or I really shall be disappointed. The Mare Cousin Robert Swan sold my Uncle James seems to give satisfaction. My Uncle and Uncle Hack &c are again going to winter at Torquay. My love please to my Uncle, Mrs. Deane, and Willy, J. and H. Trimmer, T. Spencer &c and remembrances to enquirers whom thou mayst think I care for.

   In love, I remain,
    Thy Friend,
     Arthur Gravely.

I find since writing this letter that there are Papers for gratituous Distribution on the Colony of South Australia, giving a Plan of it &c. Perhaps thou may be able to get one.

OTHER LETTERS: see 165–69, 171-73

William Nathaniel Chantler emigrated to join his parents and brothers and sisters in Upper Canada in 1840. We do not know whether his friend Arthur Gravely carried through with his plan to go to Australia.

■ 171

HENRY CHANTLER, NEWMARKET, CANADA WEST, TO JOSEPH CHANTLER AND WIFE MARY ANN MILLARD, 12 NOVEMBER 1846

Henry Chantler was Nathaniel and Sophia Chantler's third son; in this letter he was writing to his brother Joseph who was presumably in Ogdensburg, New York, where he married Mary Ann Millard.

SOURCE: Chantler Family Papers

           Newmarket Whitechurch Nov, 12th—46
Dear Brother,

I wish you with your better half much joy in your Hymenial change. I was not a little surprised when I found in your letter of the 28th Sept that you had united in the bands of Matrimony and have transformed yourself into a Married Man. I am happy to hear also that you are united to one who is kind, affectionate, tender-hearted, and of a respectable family. I still remain unmarried and the day seems far hence when I shall be able to pronounce the assertion "I am a married Man," Though at times I feel wrought up to a sense of my own oneness and when I serve up my soul with the thoughts of being comforted with one of those creatures you talk of, my heart throbs with the greatest emotion sometimes starts off on the trot rears – pitches, bounds, and leaps to the canter rendering it difficult by times to keep from being overthrown. But when I reverse the train of thinking it settles down into a perfect calm and seems ameliorated by being unattached.

But no more of this, let me give you a detail of things less grave than that of Marriage Courting or Love, for certainly they are these things clothed with solemnity though often contemplated with mere bubbles of thought.

I have my health as usual it being by times scarcely probable but I still continue teaching school in the same place and expect to remain through the winter. My school at present numbers 45, and I have prospects of having a very large school in the winter season. Alfred still remains at his trade as firm and as staple as the Alpine hills and as steady as a town clock. Nath, I am sorry to say is not doing much for himself he has been sick all summer or nearly so and is now without a place. Esther is well and Brooks the same,[32] both and in fact all of us are anxious to see you[;] we are particularly so now when we anticipate the pleasure of seeing the person you must assuredly bring with you. We would all be glad to hear how you are situated what wages you get &C the next time you write.

Esther with all your connexions here send their best and most precious Love to you & M.A – hoping that you enjoy true happiness in every sense of the word, highly recommending too the peace you talk of, which as you say is the principal thing. Though earth with all her Laurels crowns thrones Sceptres pomp pride and gaiety be collected in one wreathe it is not to be placed on a paralel, with that peace of mind – the soul and life of man. Receive this as flowing from the heart of your affectionate brother.

H. Chantler
TO M[ary] A[nn Millard]

Dear Sister in L—

Though I have never had the privilege of beholding your face yet I form your appearance in my imagination. You will pardon my presumption in taking this liberty of addressing you. As it comes through the medium of your connexion with me influenced by the warmest affection towards you perhaps this will merit your excuse

Remember me who'll think of you
And often long to see
Though billows roll between the homes
That nurture you and me
Wilt thou permit a wandering thought
To cast its flight on me
Whose heart is filled with deep desire
And friendly love to thee
Remember too a married life
Is always filled with care,
But at the theme of Love have vent
And give to J— his share.

---

32 Esther Chantler married Brooke Dennis in 1841 in Whitchurch Township; see her memoir 173

If through the day thy anger rise
Or something go Amiss
Be reconciled before you sleep
An seal it with a Kiss

Your H— Chantler

OTHER LETTERS: see 165–70, 172–73
Joseph and Mary Ann Chantler were to have seven children; their birthplaces indicate that the family moved between Ogdensburg, New York, and Canada West several times before settling in the latter (see figure 3).

■ **172**

JOHN CHANTLER, INNISFIL TOWNSHIP, CANADA WEST, TO HIS NIECE ELIZA, 15 MARCH 1863
John Chantler was apparently writing to his niece Elizabeth McDougall, daughter of his younger sister Elizabeth, who had married the Reverend George Millward McDougall in 1842.

SOURCE: Chantler Family Papers

Innisfil
15th Mar 1863

Our Dear Niece Eliza
I have just been writing to your papa & mama and have sent your love to them all. I expect you have had a letter from them lately as we have; they are all well they tell of two stranger relative to the family babies as you once were. I have told them that you have grown much lately; we had your letter and ought to have written long ago. You must come and see us again this Summer.

I suppose you have heard that David[33] leaves Canada by the spring boats for your Parents home in the North West; he received a letter from his Father and came down here to be ready for a start from Collingwood with the first steamer; he is now gone on a visit to his friends at Orillia and Rama.

Your Aunt Elizabeth is not so healthy this winter she and Charles are now on a visit to Penetanguishene, they had a [Ten?] Meeting there last week. Miss Jeffry was down here lately they are all well.

With our love I remain
Your affectionate Uncle
John Chantler

P.S. If you want to write to him you can do so enclosed to us anytime before the middle of April.

33 Eliza's brother

OTHER LETTERS: 169; see also 165–68, 170–73.

Eliza's father, George, was a Methodist missionary, ordained in 1854, who served first at Garden River and at Rama, near Orillia. In 1860 he was appointed to a mission in the west near Norway House in Hudson's Bay Company territory. In 1863 David was probably hoping to join the family for the trip they took that year up the Saskatchewan River to become residents of the Saskatchewan Valley, perhaps the first white family to do so.

■ 173

MEMOIR BY ESTHER (CHANTLER) DENNIS FOR HER CHILDREN, WRITTEN ABOUT 1896

We hesitated over Esther's express wish that she wrote only for her children, "it is not for the public," and hoped that the passage of so many years have legitimized sharing her memories outside her family. She seems to have feared that the small tricks she knew time had played with her memory would weaken her account, but the immediacy with which she relived the experience makes this a remarkable document. She was 12 at the time of the events she describes in 1832.

SOURCE: Chantler Family Papers. A handwritten copy of this memoir and typescript copies are in private hands; Surray Record Office (Guildford Muniments Room) holds a typescript in an uncatalogued folder labelled "emigration."[34] Part of the left margin of the final page of the earliest version is missing; we have compared the typescript to the handwritten copy. It is entirely unpunctuated and unparagraphed.

To My Dear Children from there Mother
My Children I know you have often wondered why I have had so little to say of my Childhood & early part of my life not that my People or Myself have comited any crime that I have been ashamed of[. M]y Parents were poor & I can remember my Father having very poor health & I also remember seeing My Mother shed tears when they talked of coming to America but did not realize it as I did after what it ment, but my history was so sad so filled with sad events on every hand that I avoided refering to it in every way that I could had I have been old enough to have given dates but my Parents died & was buried & I could not tell the day of the month or where there remains was laid as not a friend was present to drop a tear, & my dear ones you can imagine how I have been reminded when attending funerals ever since of the difference. I was to[o] young to describe the situation of the country & when my father was taken with that dreadful desease cholera of which he died[.]

I remember after leaving the ship at Quebec we traveled in boats drawn by horses up what was called the rapids & at night we all had to stop & the night my father was taken we was stoping at a house near the river – it might have been a house for travellers but I do not know where – but in the morning we had to leave the

34 The story of how the editors of this volume found Esther Chantler Dennis's memoir is told in *Families* 34, no.2 (1995): 85-9.

boats, had to go on. My uncle & family went on with the boats, but my mother, John Chantler[35] & us little ones was left behind to take our sick father in a waggon; I think we was not allowed to stay there but the boats had gone on and our luggage, so we came to a place called Coto [Coteau] du lac, but it was known we had Cholera among us[and] we was not alowed even a shed. Everyone was afraid of us, would not open there doors when we went to buy milk. I often think of it & what must have been the feelings of that dear Mother – a dying hustand and five little children in a strange place where every one was afraid of us – & as a last resort our dying father was laid on the wharf on a bed with no shelter but a cart turned over it & night coming on. There was a boat tied at the wharf that us little ones got into. John Chantler our cousin and our own dear Mother with a lantern watched at the side of the dying bed. A storm came up I well remember & we were so frightened as the boat rocked about on the water; the wind blew & the rain fell. Is it any wonder my dear ones that I have not wanted to refer to those scenes of misery & sadness but that heart rending seen [scene] seems stamped on my memory for life & other sceens to[o] sad to pen can never be erased while life & consiousness remains. My uncle lost a daughter [Ann] with that desease & had to dig her grave himself but I do not remember weather it was before or after my fathers death.

After we were left little friendless orphans my pillow was often wet with tears when none but god was near. I often prayed that he would take my dear Little brother Nat that was so dear to me as my own life, but I seemed to have so much trouble on his account, he being only three years old when our parents died, & when he was blamed or corrected for any thing it seemed to hurt me more than him & being separated as I was from my other brothers. But through all I never lost track of any of my brothers. I do not know about my brother Joseph but that dear lady[36] knew where my Mother had let him go & to whom as there was no one else to tell my uncle when he came to look after us in Toronto from a dream he had. He came said he could not rest.

I have here got ahead of my sad story – the death on the wharf in the storm and darkness. In the morning my fathers remains were laid in a coffin & just as he died taken to his last resting place by strangers, I know not where. If I remember right the boats came on by that time that we came on, but the journey from there to Toronto is all gone from me. My dear ones, I am about to take a journey to Kansas with Sophia and have not time to copy any more of my sad history & if not spared you will see that I had put it off to long.

My dear children after an absence of nearly four months I was permited to return to my home but it was under very sad circumstances similar to what have occured in our family several times. To stand at the death bed of another of our loved ones taken in the prime of life with every thing seemingly to live for, as also was the case of his

---

35 Her cousin and author of letters 166 and 169, which gives his version of his uncle's last hours.
36 Elizabeth Colborne, wife of the lieutenant governor, Sir John Colborne*, remained at York with him during the epidemic and took a special interest in the family.

dear sisters, & me that have almost lived out my usefulness left. But such is life & we must submit to him that doeth all things well. But the loved ones all left a full assurance of that peaceful happy rest in that home not made not made hands eternal in the heavens where if faithful we can all meet them. & I will again commence my sad life. Our uncle and his family left us come up Young Street; we was then left alone among strangers in a strange land but my Mother understood the straw Millinery and found she could do well at that or at least would try it. I well remember her saying to me if I am spared & have my health I think I can do well here, but that dreadful desease was rageing then in Toronto & my Mother was asked to take charge of some rooms that was aranged for taking care of the homeless & friendless orphans & she had decided to do so. The Govener of Canadas man, Sir John Colbourn, his lady, & a sister of hers, a Miss Young, seemed to take great interest in that class and they both came to see my Mother. I well remember them, they was so nice, but dear ones how they found my Mother out & wanted her I cannot tell. It seemed to please my Mother to be able to get the situation but before any thing was done only the rooms ready & us in them my Mother was taken with the dreaded desease. I remember it was sabath day she had got up in the morning to dress & was taken with Cramps in her limbs. I went for a neighbour woman & a Doctor was sent for. Mother plead with him not to have her sent to the hospital. we lived not far from it & so few ever came out alive that went there, so she dreaded it, But I well remember her sufferings was terrible. I was not allowed in the room but it was a sad day for me & I watched every move with anxious fears that our all was to be taken & in the evening she was taken to the hospital on a bed. The Dr was so nice, seemed to do every thing to save her. My dear ones, young as I was I realized that our doom was sealed. I went to see how she was in the morning; she had changed for the better but did not let me see her. I can never forget the kindness of that Dr; he seemed to feel so sorry for me & after that morning one of my brothers and I was alowed to see her & she seemed quite better, could talk to us. I do not remember how the goveners lady knew my Mother was in the hospital but she sent Jelies & Wine & lots of nice things to nourish her, & I well remember, when we went to the hospital to see her each morning, we went to the Govenment house to tell her how she was & we was taken to her room by one of the girls & she would ask all about her. There are few such ladies as her & to wards the last of that week we was told to bring her Cloths in as she was going to get up. We took the cloths in, but she had a relaps instead & gradually grew worse & our hopes were blighted. We went on Saturday morning & she did not seem to know us, was verry ill & the next morning we was not alowed to see her. The Dr said she would not know us and in the afternoon I was laying on the bed crying & I heard the Dr ask where is Mrs Chantlers little girl her Mother is gone. He was a dear man, so full of sympathy for her little ones, not many Drs like him. I asked him if we could [see] her but he said that we could not. She was burried, I do not know where,[37] none to shed a tear over her remains, all strangers & one of my brothers and I went to let that dear lady know

---

37 No record remains of a Chantler buried in Potters Field or St James Cemetery in Toronto.

that she was gone & her & her sister talked so nicely to us little orphans. How often I have thought of those dear ladies & there kind & loving words & often wish I could remember more about them but god [h]as long ago taken them to himself.

They asked if we had any friends & where they had gone, gave me to understand that we would be cared for. We was then under the care of a woman that took my Mother place, & the lady herself & sister came to see about our things as we did not know where our uncle & family had gone. So she said our things had better be sold & she would see that the money was put in the saving bank of us, but told me and the woman to keep our cloths out & to keep any little things that I wished out. She seemed to want to get good places for us. Our brother Joseph was not with us in that trying time; our Mother had got a place for him with one known to us as Captain Davis, near Lake Simcoe in the township of Oro.[38] That Lady must have known where, as she was the only one to tell our uncle when he came to look after us from a dream that he had. He could not rest; if it had not been for that dream we might have been separated as many families at that time was, one here and another there, among strangers. But through a kind & all wise providence & that dear lady I was able to keep track of my brothers. She did not seem in a hurry to get places & seemed sorry that we did not know where our uncle had gone. But the dear old man came, but not before our things had been sold & places had been got for Henery & Alfred.

One man pretended to take them both, said that he would keep them together, & he seemed to be so kind made so much of the boys that Lady Colbourn thought she had got a good place for them and they was taken away. My dear one I then began to realize our sad lot; young as we was we all felt the parting & there last look seemed stamped on my memory, particularly Alfreds. He was the youngest & seemed to feel it most but he told them nice stories about there new home. But it was me that felt it but I had so much confidence in that dear lady that she would see to them as she talked so kind to me about them. My little brother of three years old was then left to the mercies of a woman who did not care for us only to get every thing she could of our things before they was taken away. Every little relic that my Mother had left in her bedroom was taken, even my dolls & lots of little presents that was given me by school mates in England was taken to[o]. That lady told my uncle that she found that she drank & was not fit to have charge of the friendless orphans & after my Mother was taken to the hospital no money could be found. So she had taken all there was. She had taken advantage of our helpless condition. My Mother was taken so bad that she could not do any thing. I remember so well that she could not finish dressing herself for cramps in her limbs & I remember going to visit some friends with my Mother in London, I think they were Cousins, & they gave her & I some very nice things, but they all went that she wanted. But I think she lost her

---

38 A Captain E. Davis was granted about 1000 acres of crown land in Oro Township in December 1831 (AO, Ontario Land Records Index), but directories do not show a Davis in Oro or surrounding locations in 1837.

situation from what my uncle said lady Colbourn went to see her but she denied having been drunk or of robing us of any thing.

Now he was not satisfied without finding where the boys had been taken to. He went to see for himself. This man had let Alfred go to another man; it was in a new place in the woods, I think in the township of [Scarbor..?]. He said they was so pleased to see him and he brought them away with him & then he brought us all up Young Street. Henry & we was placed among the friends. Henry at Isaac Lundy[39] on Second Street had a good home, used him as there own I think, and Alfred went to live in Pickering with an old couple by the name of Wright. They was friends. I cannot remember how long but I think he was a large boy almost grown when he left them; he then went to live with James Coldwell of Newmarket to learn chair making & painting.[40] He liked him so much he was very kind to him. Henry got sufficient education to teach school & earned money to put himself through as a Doctor but he & my other two Brothers Joseph & Alfred died in the prime of life. Myself & my little brother of three years was adopted by an English family by the name of Simpson.[41] I then young as I was had to work for my living. I was the only help, my brother was to[o] young, but as soon as possible he had to work. We was both sent to school some but was kept home so much that it did not do us the good it otherwise would; had I not have been able to read & write I never would have with the chance they gave me. It was at the old Mcleod school house[42] that we went to. They were farmers & built a brewery & several other buildings kept imported horses & cattle, had lots of men. The old gentleman[43] was very kind to us but as my brother got older he had to run here & run there so many to please that could seldom do enough he being the only boy. I had many heart aches on his account & often wish it had been the Lords will to have taken him when our dear Mother died. It did not cost much to dress us & was exposed to all kinds of weather from early morning until late at night. My dear Children if you knew what I went through with in my early days you would not wonder that I have suffered so much from Rheumatism that my fingers are crooked & the joints enlarged. All there floors was white from the garret to the cellar; all had to be scrubbed on my hands & knees, not a mop used in the house, no carpets or painted floors, no cooking stove, all the cooking done in an open fire place & in summer did it in an open shed quite a little dis-

---

39 Lundys were among the original Quaker settlers of the Newmarket area. Isaac Lundy was located at lot 25 concession 2 Whitchurch in 1837 (*The City of Toronto and the Home District Commercial Directory ... for 1837* [repr. Toronto, Toronto Branch of the Ontario Genealogical Society 1987]).

40 We have not been able to establish the Wrights referred to, but chairmaker and painter James B. Caldwell was located at lot 95 concession 1 Whitchurch Township, the location of Newmarket, in 1837 (*City of Toronto ... Directory ... 1837*)

41 George Simpson was on lot 83 concession 1 Whitchurch in 1837 (*City of Toronto ... Directory ... 1837*); Simpson was a brewer and a Quaker.

42 Located on Yonge Street.

43 George Simpson took over the property from his father, Joseph, perhaps the "old gentleman" mentioned by Esther.

tance from the house for fear of fire, posts planted & a pole fixed across to hang the pots & kettles on. If a baked pudding or pie was wanted, it was baked in what was called a bake kettle with a lid and hot coals laid on the top & the same for the bottom – the bread was baked in a brick oven – you can imagine how easy that cooking would be done for a lot of men. No one had the conveniences of to day. Others had the same way of cooking.

My adopted Mother was an old woman so the most of the hard work fell to my lot. I had no flanel under cloths, no rubers or over shoes in those days, no over coats for little boys. My Brother never had such a thing while he lived there. They had what was quite common in those days, an old fashioned thrashing machine. I had to cut the bands day after day, & when they would stop for dinner I had to run & help in the house until they would start again. Helped plant potatoes & pick them, top the turnips & carrots & often helped in the hay field and at any thing that it was possible for me to do in doors or out. The washing was done for all the hired help. Many days I had to wash & help with the work it would often be dark before I was done. They had no soft water only what was caught in a rain trough – a large log dug out, no cisterns in those days. They had quite a large hop garden. Having a brewery they needed hops. Every moment I had to spare I had to help pick them. We had to do the milking rain or shine. The men never thought of such a thing. No one to see that we had proper clothing for such work; many times we have both cried with the cold. From a child I have been afflicted with sick head aches & several years before leaving there my health began to fail. Had head ache much oftener felt weak & tired when at my work felt the nead of a Mothers care. My adopted Mother thought more of the stimulant that was being made there than of my ill health, had a supply constantly on hand. My health kept getting worse; I was not able to do there work so I went to live with the Father & Mother of Samuel & Elias Rogers. Her Mother, an old lady, kindly took an interest in me & made a strength[en]ing syrup. I did not have to work so hard or to expose myself & my health improved. I shall always & have remembered there kindness. The old Lady died while I was with them & they left the farm on Yonge St went to live in Marriposa and I went to live with Seth and Ann Armitage, Parents of Jane Taylor.[44] She was married & had left home. Her Mother a dear woman treated me as her own daughter.

It was there that your Father and I became acquainted & married. I came into the family with his Father & Mother and three single sisters the Eldest made her home with Aunt Betsy Pearson. His Grand Mother Dennis lived with them then but she soon went to be with her son Nathan Dennis & died there. She lived with us until after Charles was born her & I was great friends always. The two sisters married shortly after we were married & left home. My Mother in law was a dear woman. I think I can say of a truth that we never had a word, she was like an own

---

44 Seth Armitge married Ann Phillips in 1816 and their daughter Jane was born in 1818 (*Genealogical Index to the Records of the Canada Yearly Meeting of the Religious Society of Friends (Quakers), vol. One: Yonge Street Monthly Meeting* [Canadian Friends Association 1988]).

Mother to me. She lived until after Barbara was born; do not remember how old she was taken she died. She was named after her Grandmother.

The Grand Father lived until Marshall was two years old, our youngest child. After he had a stroke & became unconcious he would notice him he was a great man for children they never seemed to anough [annoy] him as they do the most of old men. He was a great help to me in raising my large family. When even sitting down to read it was no trouble for him to rock the cradle if needed & the younger ones he would sit & rock & sing to them by the hour when not reading, & he had given up working hard so that he spent a good deal of time in the house. He & I got along nicely, never had any trouble that amounted to anything. He was not so easy to get along with as my Mother in law. But my dear ones, when I look back at my younger day I cannot but feel that the good sheperd watched over me & kept me from harm, exposed as I was on every hand. Our adopted parents had two daughters, both married, one to the father of James Pearson now in the Register Office in this town, the other married a Joseph Baldwin[45] of King near Alaska now called, had a new farm nearly all woods. They had a saw mill. He was the Father of the Baldwin now living in Aurora. I was sent there to keep house for 4 or 5 weeks at a time & she would go to her home to visit & do quilting as there house was to[o] small for that purpose. It consisted of two rooms one below & what would be now called a loft with ladder for steps a bed in the lower room & open fireplace, a cave for celler quite a distance from the house. There nearest neighbours Smelsons a family well known then,[46] I often went there, took the child left to my care with me. They had a daughter that came often to stay with me. She was the wife of Joseph Wood, a farmer, was township Clerk many years. He is still living but his wife died several years ago. We both had large families; your Father & I visited them & they was all nice people. King township was nearly all woods at that time now.

My dear children, when you read this sad history, & I do hope you will, I think you will not blame your Mother. Your Father knew it all & did not blame me for keeping it to myself as I did. I was to[o] young to remember dates the day of the month or even the month that my Parents died or where there remains are laid. This [h]as been a source of much sorrow to me when at funerals & having ones paying the last tribute of respect, taking the last sad look, how keenly have my thoughts wandered back to these days when none but strangers was near & they anxious to have them laid away as quick as possible. In my Mothers case more particularly as no doubt there were others dieing or needing care & I do suppose they were laid in there coffins as they died. No one to shed a tear & a Mother left with five of us

---

45 In 1857 Joseph Baldwin was a general merchant in the village of Laskay (concession 5 King Township) and propietor of Laskay flouring and saw mills (*Directory of the Province of Ontario, 1857* [Lambertville, NJ: Hunterdon House 1987]).

46 Perhaps this should be Smelzer; a John Smelzer was at lot 1 concession 5 of King and Henry Smelzer was an auctioneer and appraiser at Laskay village in 1857 (*City of Toronto ... Directory ... 1837*; *Directory of the Province of Ontario, 1857*).

little ones among strangers in a strange land not knowing what moment she would be taken down with that dreadful desease. But how thankful I have been that God in his infinite mercy and all saving power so ordered it that we never lost track of each other, & had it not have been for Lady Colborns kindness keeping trace of where she had let Henery & Alfred go & to whom, when dear old uncle would not have known where to go to look for them, as I have told you before of his dream that caused him to look after us.

My dear ones, I have told you the truth as near as I can remember & I can also truthfully say that I have tried from youth to old age to live a respectable life, have not done any thing that will bring disgrace on my children or there ofsprings. I was poor, had to work hard for a living. My brothers you have known what there lives have been. They have long since gone to reap the rewards of there labor. They was all dear to me as my own life the one left I never expect to meet on this side of the grave but hope to meet all the loved ones when parting will be no more; & when I am gone dear ones do not forget him if living he will be pleased to hear from any of you. I have neglected to finish this until to day, my 76th birthday. You see many mistakes & some repetition but I feel that you will excuse me as you know how my memory has failed. In writing this poor epistle have had to copy it two or three times & in writing short letters I often have to copy them over in turning from sheet to another but I have resorted to the pencil & can rub out mistakes. If I am spared I fear I will lose my memory altogether. It may be from having suffered so with neuralgia in my head for the last 8 or 9 years, have to keep a Diary as I cannot remember from one day to another things that I have done or who I have met. Had I have written this in my younger day while my memory was better, it was never very good, had to depend on your Father many times as he had an extra memory, or if I could have told you but that was my weakness. But my dear children I trust that you can forgive my wrong & miss guided steps towards you. As a mother I have looked back & seen where I could & ought to have done differently. You know that I have been a great sufferer from Rheumatism had the inflamatory rheumatism when Sophia was but a year old, was 9 weeks almost entirely helpless, my joints swolen & inflamed. Had the Doctors have known how to treat it as they do now I might have got over it, but for years after I had attacks of joints be swolen & inflamed & have suffered from the relicks ever since, as the Drs have the neuralgia is a form of rheumatism & I can truthfully say for 25 years of my [missing] more that I was very seldom clear of it; had it so much in my hands, had so much, several severe attacks of it when exposed more than usual; suffered so at night. Had your dear Father not have been such a good hand [to do] [ev]ery thing to releive my suffering & for the children, as you will all [re]member his untiring faithfulness in sickness, from the youngest to the oldest. He was always ready. He took a cold ... [journal ?] & he always used it in fevers of any kind, in Measels, in croup. As you can remember, how often he got up at night for croup, Baldwin being quite subject to that desease in his young days.

I hope my dear children you will read [missing] poorly composed account of your Mothers life. It is not for the public [missing] feel that you can excuse all mistakes

& I trust you & yours may [ne]ver see many of the dark shades of life & may you live long and [u]seful lives doing by others as you would that others should do to [y]ou. And lastly may we all meet in the house not made with hands eternal in the heavens is the most sincere prayer of your
Mother Esther Dennis

OTHER LETTERS: Letters 166–67, 169 report the news of the voyage and the deaths from cholera to family in England and how that news was received in England.

Moses was at Whitchurch on 11 October 1832 when he settled his brother's estate, took responsibility for his children, and placed them in families as described by Esther. In the same month, the Yonge Street Meeting of the Society of Friends sent word of the safe arrival of Moses and his own family to the Dorking and Horsham Meeting. Moses and Sarah had two more daughters and stayed in the Newmarket area until 1844 when Moses purchased a grist mill and about 15 acres of land on the future site of Meaford in St Vincent Township. John Chantler left John Cawthra to work as a miller, at first under his father and then on his own at Tolendol Mills in Innisfil Township. He married in 1842 and moved to Barrie where he opened a general store and joined the Methodist church "there being no society of friends in that part of the country." William Chantler, Moses' other son of this correspondence, also settled in Simcoe County where he lived out his life as a storekeeper and postmaster at Newton Robinson.

Moses decision to buy his mill was a good choice in that the Meaford area was settling rapidly and there was good demand for a mill. A series of petitions to the Department of Crown Lands, however, revealed a case study of the problems that could plague such an enterprise on the frontier. Moses built himself a house and outbuildings and put a bridge across the river only to find that a corrected survey put most of his improvements on land reserved for the town plot. As he petitioned to buy the land he needed from government, David Miller, the original owner (in jail for debts occasioned by construction of the mill) sold it again as part of a package of all his land in the township to a second miller. Arrangements to compensate the Chantlers seem never to have been settled to their satisfaction in a relationship that was now acrimonious and litigious.

Despite these problems, business must have been brisk, for John Chantler invested in a new mill and bought the ten acres of government land on which it was sited from his father. Although John does not appear to have lived in Meaford or to have run this mill at any time, he seems to have considered doing so, and he took a leading role in petitioning as a new generation of difficulties emerged over the next four years. The Chantlers became embroiled in disputes related to water control with the new owner of the first mill and experienced more trouble with boundaries. When John applied for a patent, the lot was found to include more of the river bank than was allowed, but the adjustments reduced the value of the Chantler mill. The correspondence about the mill ends in 1851 with an able statement of the Chantlers' case in a letter written to the commissioner of crown lands by William Lyon Mackenzie*, and the Chantler mill was not rebuilt when it burnt about 1866.

Moses Chantler lived on in Meaford where he died on 8 October 1878, reportedly 80 but actually older as he was baptized in 1793. John Chantler left Barrie after losing his business there (according to his obituary, he was "unfairly treated by some whom he had trusted"). A broken leg at a mill in Newmarket ended his milling career. He returned to Simcoe County and his wife's village of Stroud in Innisfil Township where, after a year teaching school, he opened a store and kept the post office for some 20 years.

John Chantler was probably still alive when his cousin Esther started work on her auto-biographical memoir, but the two families had apparently lost touch with each other. Thus Esther, who otherwise tells her own story, was left with questions about the deaths of her parents and her early life that her uncle and cousin might have answered.

FREDERICK HASTED LETTERS

In England, Frederick Hasted had made a large acquaintance by travelling as a hawker. His statement that he had at one time had the vote suggests a loss of property, but he was able to pay his passage from Arundel, West Sussex, and that of his daughter, Mary Ann. They arrived at Quebec on 22 August 1833 and travelled to Hamilton and from there to Adelaide. A series of petitions and other document pertaining to his land in the Adelaide settlement help to flesh out the picture of himself he chose to give in his two published letters of 1834 and 1839 (174 and 175). Hasted wrote at length to the Department of Crown Lands, though apparently in vain, always wanting to negotiate special terms for himself.

On first coming to Adelaide, Hasted tried to buy land belonging to an absentee loyalist because it was close to some new friends he had met. After this plan fell through, he discovered he could buy the rights to lots assigned by Roswell Mount* to indigent settlers. Between December 1833 and April 1834, Hasted acquired the rights to the E ½ lots 13, 14, and 15 concession 2 SER. He settled on E½ lot 14, concession 2 SER, which he named Dairy Farm. Mary Ann was with him when he wrote the first of these two letters, but she left about the fall of 1834 "not liking the bush." Despite the work he had invested in this lot, by 1836 he petitioned to exchange it for another – preferably the one abandoned early on by Petworth emigrant Charles Mann, one of the sons of Ann Mann (127) who had emigrated in 1832.

Hasted wanted to move because his land proved swampy even after clearing, because the people from England whom he had hoped would come and take up his extra lots had disappointed him, and because his only neighbours for half a mile or more, the family of James Knight, were terrorizing him: killing chickens, breaking his fences to let cattle in the crops, and, he claimed, engaging in petty theft. He purchased Mann's interest in W½ lot 19 concession 4 for two pounds fifteen shillings,[1] believing Mann's lot (which was in the cluster of lots settled by Petworth emigrants) to be in "a more honest and respectable neighbourhood."[2] The transaction was complicated for Hasted, and for the next two purchasers after him, by the fact that goveernment would not issue a deed until the settlement duties on the lot were performed and the instalments paid. Until that time, all Hasted could do was to buy

---

1 George Crossfield in 1845 said the price had been $4 and an old musket valued at $6.

2 AO, RG1, C-IV, Township Papers, Adelaide.

An idealized view of the bustle of clearing land …

Sarah Ann (Johnson) Carter, "The Woodcutters," Dunn Township near Port Maitland, Upper Canada, c. 1840, Toronto Reference Library, T14800

Mann's interest and to take a bond from Mann to insure that the deed would be handed over.

■ 174

FREDERICK HASTED, DAIRY FARM, ADELAIDE TOWNSHIP, UPPER CANADA, 7 FEBRUARY 1834

SOURCE: *Brighton Herald*, 17 May 1834

Frederick Hasted
Dairy Farm, 7th Feb., 1834.

I now come to say I cannot add much to the good accounts you have already received of this country, but confirm their correctness, especially the description of climate and soil given out with the map. I must say, I find the country hitherto answers my expectations, except as respects game and wild animals, neither of which are as numerous as I expected. Many people in England are terrified at the sound of bears, wolves and rattlesnakes, but I have not seen either of them, although I have hunted for some. There are such things, but they are neither numerous nor daring.

About the latter end of November we had snow, knee deep, but not very cold weather – not enough to freeze the puddles. On the 17th of December, we had 24 or 25 inches fall of snow, but this washed down to about 12 or 14 inches; when on

and the lonely reality that drove Mary Ann Hasted from the bush
Philip John Bainbrigge, "A Clearing in the Woods," Upper Canada, 1839, NA C3119

the 2nd of January, we had nine or ten inches more, and the next day very sharp frost. The cold is not so sensibly felt as in England, it being dry, and but little wind.

Some people at home were ignorant enough to say that those sent out by the Earl of Egremont,* other gentlemen, and their respective parishes, were going out like convicts; but let those people say which is most like a convict, – a man chained, as it were, to his parish because he cannot get work out of it, is obliged to take what they will give him, and if no work, go on the parish, be looked upon as a useless being, an evil, yea, a pest to society, and scoffed at like a dog, half starved, in debt, in rags, his children brought up in idleness (which is the first step to ruin), having nothing to do; or a man that has all Canada before him, can obtain what land he please to employ his family or himself, go where he like, work for whom he will, live well, get good wages, pay his way, and be respected as a useful member of society; this is a true picture; and I hope they will send more; but send industrious, sober men – it is the best thing you can do for them. The two Whites, told me they had their expences paid by the kind interposition of Squire Hawkins of Bognor Park,[3] and for which they seemed grateful. Thus you see some, at least, do not forget their benefactors. But the greatest evil is, people in general are not persevering enough. You know I am not accustomed to chopping, or out of doors labour; yet I have, since the new year began, shovelled away the snow from the roots of trees so as to cut them close to the ground, and chopped about an acre – cut up part, and brought it home and burnt it; while others, settled last summer twelve months, did nothing.

3 Bignor, West Sussex

For the good of the poor, and for the satisfaction of my friends, and all who it may concern, I shall be glad if the Rev. Mr. Tripp, Mr. Sockett, or someone else, would have this letter printed, either in bills, books or newspapers: bills I think would be best, as they could be sold at 1d. each, or given away. Shew this letter to Mr. Tripp and Miss. Hawkins.

OTHER LETTERS: 175
This letter as published omits to mention that Hasted hired for some of the work on his lot and also leaves out the intriguing detail that he kept a tally of the trees he had cut, a tally which by November 1836 had reached 372, besides underbrushing and grubbing small trees. At that date, he claimed ten acres cleared. A separate, detailed account of his improvements made over "three of the roughest years, I ever encountered in my life"[4] give some idea of what a ten-acre clearing might look like: about 1700 square rods "more or less chopped," with a little better than half cleared, "some laid down in grass, and some fit for crop, nearly fenced, and will be quite soon," in addition to statutory work on the road allowance and some beginnings on the side lines. He had made improvements to the log house built by government in 1832 and he had put up outbuildings such as cowsheds and pigsties.

■ 175

FREDERICK HASTED, LONDON, UPPER CANADA, TO HENRY AYLING, TREYFORD, NEAR MIDHURST, SUSSEX, 15 DECEMBER 1839
Although he seems to have lived mainly in London in these years, Hasted occupied his lot on concession 4 long enough to build a log house and start clearing.

Hasted added a note to a letter of 25 January 1841 to the commissioner of crown lands as follows: "Inclosed I send you a copy of a letter I sent to a friend in England, which the Revd T. Socket [sic] Rector of Petworth got printed, and sent me two copies back last spring, that you might [see] wether I am a welwisher to the country or not."[5]

SOURCE: Printed by John Phillips at Petworth, n.d. A copy is found at Toronto Library, bound with a copy of *Emigration: Letters* (1833); another copy is in Archives of Ontario, Pamphlet 1839, 1910.

The writer of the following letter emigrated to Upper Canada at his own expence in 1833, and settled in the Township of Adelaide, where many Sussex emigrants reside.

He was well known throughout Sussex, Hampshire, and parts of the adjoining counties, where he had been in the habit of travelling for several years as a hawker, with a small carriage drawn by dogs, and provided with a good assortment of various articles.

London, Upper Canada, December 15th. 1839.

Dear Friend,

It is now a long time ago since I wrote to you, but I have wrote since to some of my acquaintance, and requested them to communicate the same to you, but I have never

4 NA, RG1, L3, UCLP H20/86, Hasted, 20 November and 29 October 1836. Colonel Thomas Radcliff attested to the truth of his description.
5 AO, RG1, C-IV, Township Papers, Adelaide, 396, Frederick Hasted to R.B. Sullivan, 25 January 1841.

London, Dundas Street in 1840
James Hamilton, "London, Canada West, Dundas Street, 1840," Toronto Reference Library, T15406

heard from you, or any of them, except Mr. Faulks of Portsea; I received a letter from him about three years ago, wherein he requested me to write to him, and give him my opinion of the country again, stating all particulars, and whether I thought it would answer his purpose to commence the shoemaking business in this country, and in what part: I accordingly gave him my ideas on the subject, and recommended him to buy a town lot, and settle in London, it being a central town, and likely to become a place of considerable importance, although it was but a small place at that time. It is now the principal Town, and the most flourishing place in Upper Canada, west of Hamilton, and pleasantly situated, and property in it has advanced and is still advancing rapidly. Had he come at the time I wrote to him I have no doubt but he would have been worth full a thousand pounds more now, than when he came. Whether he sailed for this country or not, I do not know, as I have not heard from him since, and I know there were several vessels lost about the time I expected him to come. I wrote a letter to him last spring, and sent it by the drum major of the 32nd. regiment, who was discharged from length of service, having served more than 25 years in the army.

I have been rather unsettled for these last two years, owing to the disturbances in the country, arising from the intrigues of designing men, who endeavoured to plunge the country into civil war, in order to separate it, if possible, from England; but all those who were attached to the crown and constitution of Great Britain, and who wished still to be governed by the laws of our ancestors, came forward and opposed those who wished to establish republican laws and institutions, and they soon drove the rebels into the United States for shelter. What ground they had for complaint against the government I am not exactly aware, as the excellence of the British constitution is admitted by all, but they say it is not administered in its purity. In this, I confess, there may be some truth; and as man is not perfect, I fear we may always have that to complain of, let us be under what government we may, because those in office will generally favour their friends most; and although the constitution provides equal justice to all, yet it is sometimes perverted in the administration thereof, and I have no doubt but there is room for reform in that respect, not only here, but all over the world.

I have no doubt but many have been deceived and led away by the arguments of designing men, because some of the old settlers have complained to me, of the duty on salt, tea, &c., while they do not complain of the direct taxes on land, houses, cattle, &c., or what is called the assessed taxes, except that they want to know what is done with it, and that is right. People must be very ignorant to suppose that any government can be supported without duties or taxes of some kind, and it displays greater ignorance for farmers to complain of trifling duties on salt, tea, &c., at a time when they get cash for wheat, pork, beef, hay, rye, indian corn, and some other kinds of produce, now selling at high prices: whereas some few years ago, they had to trade it away, at about half or one third the price, for articles they were then charged double what they are now, and could not get cash.

Many of the heads of the rebel party have accumulated considerable fortunes, under the government of which they complain; I suppose the fact is, they want to govern the country themselves now, but we do not want to be under such governors, and I hope we never shall. It is very evident that this country could never exist as an Independent State, it must either remain under Great Britain or the United States of America. Many people say, were we under the States Government, the country would be improved more rapidly; but I say, the States cannot pay for the improvements they have already made in their own country; and it is admitted on all hands, that our taxes would be higher, and I fully expect that the country would be inundated with people from the States. What good then would British subjects gain by a union with the States? Their laws do not afford protection to persons and property as ours do; the weakest generally go to the wall, as some say.

I say then, let us remain as we are, except making some necessary alterations in the government, and let England lend her assistance to improve our country, and all will I think be well; although the task to improve the country generally, is greater now than three years ago, because the rebels, instead of improving it, have retarded the improvement in a public light, except the bringing troops into the country, building of barracks, &c. &c. New and handsome barracks are built at London, for the accommodation of I think two regiments of foot, they are not quite finished yet. There are stationed here at the present time, the 73rd. regiment, and 4 companies of the 85th. regiment, about 30 artillery men, and two troops of volunteer cavalry, in the town, this makes London brisk. The regular soldiers cannot be trusted on the frontiers so well as the militia, because they desert over to the States, therefore I expect London will be always full, as they can be then sent when and where they may be needed.

I am at present assisting Mr. Perin, the contractor, having the management of his baking business, supplying the troops with bread: we make them good bread, from fine white flour, but not superfine. I give good satisfaction both to him and the troops. I have engaged for six months, ending the 31st. of March next, and am to receive 156 dollars, besides what bread I may want.[6] And my daughter lives next door to me, with English people; she is well, sends her best respects to you, Mrs. Ayling, and all the family, and hopes you are all alive and well; but I fear you are not all alive, having dreamed two or three years ago, that I was at Treyford, the shutters of your windows were closed, I thought you were gone to church, or to a funeral, and just as I attempted to lift the latch of the door, something shook me, and I awoke, and I thought some of you were dead. I should like to be informed how this is, I intended to put down the exact time, but neglected it, until I forgot it.

I have wrote letters to England for several of my neighbours, stating several particulars respecting the rebellion[7], &c. &c., but as these may not come within your reach, I will state a few to you. I am not aware whether you know it or not, but many of my acquaintance know, that I always advocated whig principles when in England, and voted (when I had a vote) for opposition members to parliament; but this being only a Colony of the British Empire, opposition to the government cannot be carried to such a high pitch here, I consider, as at home, without risking the overthrow of the country altogether, instead of reforming it; on which account the government ought to be more particular not to give room for complaint, and more particularly after the late display of loyalty and attachment to the crown and constitution of Great Britain by the people of this Province; for I am fully aware that thousands of reformers came forward and made common cause with the tories, to prevent this country being separated from England, many of whom had nothing to fight for, but the ties that bind them to their native country, and the enjoyment of those laws with which they are satisfied.

When Sir Francis Bond Head* dissolved the house of assembly, William Lion M'cKenzie*, or some of his party, sent printed circular letters to, I believe, every Township in the Province, directed to the Township clerk, calling upon the people to come forward, and support the old members against the Governor, and return them again.[8] One of these was sent to Adelaide; a meeting of the inhabitants was called, and the letter laid before them, accompanied with a copy of the Lieutenant Governor's speech at the dissolution of parliament, and from the insolence of the members towards his Majesty's representative, and the drift of their arguments, it was easy to discover their intentions; and in order to prevent as much as in us lay the overthrow of the country, we drew up and signed an address to his Excellency, to strengthen his hands against

6 In January 1841, Hasted's terms with Perin were 204 dollars per year and board, but he appeared to be growing tired of the job (AO, RG1, C-IV, Township Papers, Adelaide, Hasted, 25 January 1841).

7 Cooper's letter (133) with the postscript summarizing events of the "war," and Rapley's letter (135) which concludes with a prominent mention of Hasted's land he wanted to sell, were sent by Adelaide emigrants known to Hasted and could have been written by him.

8 He is probably referring to a series of reform meetings in the London district in the early autumn of 1837. Some established Political Unions and endorsed resolutions passed at an earlier meeting in Toronto (Read and Stagg, *Rebellions of 1837*, xxxi-iii).

evil doers, and I proposed, as a resolution of the meeting, that the Township clerk be requested to write the following answer to Mr. Mc'Kenzie.

"Sir,

I have to inform you, that I laid your letter before the people of the Township of Adelaide, at a public meeting, and they had his Excellency's the Lieut. Governor's speech before them at the same time, and I beg to state, on their behalf, that they highly approve of his Excellency's speech, and manly conduct, and they believe him to be the defender of the constitution, and the redresser of all real grievances, and have placed their confidence in him as such.

Whereas, you appear to them to be throwing a false colour over your intentions and designs, and under pretence of defending the constitution, and benefitting the people of Upper Canada, are endeavouring to sap the foundation, destroy the great principles of the constitution; overturn the government; and cause a separation between this, and the mother country. Such a reform the people of Adelaide neither need nor wish."

This was unanimously adopted, and ordered to be printed. The result of the elections was, that Bidwell,[9] the speaker of the house, Mc'Kenzie, and [Peter] Perry,[10] the three principal agitators, lost the election, and got out altogether. Having now no power to overturn the country in a constitutional way, the next thing was, to have recourse to arms, when an opportunity offered. The French Canadians in Lower Canada having revolted, the commander of the forces (as I understand) sent to our governor, to know what troops he could spare him. Sir F.B. Head supposing that no outbreak would take place in Upper Canada, said he could spare all, and accordingly sent them, leaving the military stores, &c., in charge of the civil power.

M'cKenzie and his party, supposing this a favourable opportunity, took advantage of it, and about the 6th. of December, 1837, was about to enter the city of Toronto with an armed force, to kill, burn, and destroy whom and what they pleased, but was foiled in their enterprise, by the loyal inhabitants, rising spontaneously, and rushing to assist the Governor and Government, who were enabled soon to put them to flight. Soon after this, a strong party rose in the London District, under Dr. Duncomb,[11] near to a place called Scotland, and on the 13th. of December the Adelaide people were called out as militia men, under Colonel Radcliff*, to march against Duncombe's men. It was cold weather for campaigning, with six or eight inches of snow on the ground. But when they got to London, news arrived that the loyalists having almost surrounded him, his men had dispersed, except about 18, who were

---

9 Marshall Spring Bidwell, an American by birth, was a member of the House of Assembly from 1825 to 1836 and a prominent reformer.

10 Peter Perry, a leading reformer and a member of the House of Assembly from 1834. Like, Bidwell, he was defeated in the election of 1836.

11 Dr Charles Duncombe, the leader as Hasted reported of an abortive rising based on the village of Scotland, near Brantford, in the London District. He escaped to the United States where he supported the Patriot cause in 1838.

taken prisoners; and the Adelaide men were detained to protect London, which was threatened to be burnt; they assisted the magistrates in searching houses for arms, &c., ammunition, and taking people up, and putting them to prison, &c. &c.

After this it was reported that the rebels that had escaped, had mustered a strong party at Detroit, and was about to cross into Canada, and the Adelaide militia was sent to stop them, accompanied by Indians and others: they went first to Sandwich,[12] and then to Amherstburgh, but a day or two before they got there, the Kent militia and others, took a schooner[13] with three cannon, 4 or 500 stand of arms, ammunition, &c. &c., manned by 21 men, without any loss on our side: this was a death blow to the rebels.

About the 19th. of January I joined our regiment at my own expence, travelling through a terrible wet country, beyond Chatham, the water overflowing the road at different places for I believe more than ten miles, I was often up to, and over my knees; the weather having broke up for part of the time; in some places the ice would bear. I stood sentinel three nights with a loaded musket, at Amherstburgh, on the cliff wharf, &c., at a time when we expected them across every night. Three companies of regular troops arrived about the end of January 1837, and then some of us were sent home, except those who volunteered for six months. Had it not been for the loyal militia, Upper Canada must have been lost to Great Britain. Last winter we were threatened with an invasion again from the States, and we were then about to be ballotted, as many as were wanted to make up a regiment, over and above what had volunteered their services, and as I do not like soldiering or fighting, I engaged with Mr. Perin, to bake for the troops, for six months, and as he wanted me this winter, he sent for me again. All is quiet here at present; the Governor General has arrived at Toronto, and opened parliament in person;[14] the dissatisfied party seem pretty well pleased with Mr. Thompson's words and professions, and look forward to a more liberal line of policy to be pursued by the government, and I hope they will do the best they can to satisfy all parties.

I hold at present, in Adelaide, four hundred and fifty acres of land, out of which I have 300 for sale, on easy terms, to any acquaintance. If the Great Western Railroad should go on, and I expect it will when things are settled, it will go through or near my land. Government have reduced the price of land to 8s. currency per acre, sold by auction, and to be paid for in one month. But if you will come here, and want a farm, you know where to get one without money. If I am spared, and nothing unforeseen happens, I expect to return to my farm next April, I have improvements making on it now, and another person is taking care of my cattle on shares. I have at present, ten heifers and steers.

About two years ago I sent home to Messrs. Horne and Whittington, bakers, of Portsea, Hants, a statement of the weather for twelve months, and requested them

---

12 Windsor, Ontario
13 The *Anne*, which was captured 8 January 1838.
14 Charles Edward Poulett Thomson was commissioned governor-in-chief on 6 September 1839, arrived at Quebec on 19 October and was in Toronto in November. He became 1st Baron Sydenham in August 1840.

to forward it to the Rev. T. Sockett*, Petworth, for the use of the Petworth Committee, and the information of the public. I also request you to send this by the Petworth postman, to Mr. Sockett, and I should feel obliged, if he would have the kindness to get it printed, and send a copy of it to each of the undermentioned persons; John Carpenter, Cocking; Mr. John Mitchell, Wheeler, &c. Ditchling; Mr. S. Hasted, Angmering; Mr. John Parlett, Hairdresser, &c. Worthing; Mr. C. Newman, Broyle, Chichester; Mr. George Dalton, Carpenter, Arundel; Mr. William Marshall, Baker, &c. Felpham; Mr. George Hawkins, Fittleworth; and Mr. F. Gilbert, Innkeeper, Steyning; all in Sussex; and Mr. Wm. Faulks, Boot and Shoe maker, Portsea, Hants.

Write now via Halifax, to Frederick Hasted, London, or Adelaide. Tell G. Dalton, and Geo. Cortness, that carpenters and harness makers do well here. I remain with best respects to al enquiring friends,

Yours sincerely,
FREDERICK HASTED.

MR. HENRY AYLING,
    Treyford, near Midhurst, Sussex.

OTHER LETTERS: 174

When Hasted wrote his second letter in 1839, he described how the events of the rebellion had taken him to London to work for the baker, Perin, and said that Mary Ann was living there next door to him. He was in London in 1841 when he sold Mann's lot to James Parker (88) for 500 dollars to be paid over five years.[15] In October 1842, he signed a petition from settlers in the New Survey in London asking for more time to make their cash down payments. At this point, Hasted's actions depend on hearsay from George Crossfield who bought the lot and Parker's improvements in 1843. Crossfield wrote that Hasted, while employed as foreman in a storehouse in London in 1842, was convicted of embezzling his employer's money and fined heavily. Hasted sold what he could and absconded to the United States, living for several months as a wandering artist. After brief contact with Parker, who still held back half the purchase money, he had again disappeared.

The matter of Hasted's sale then rested unresolved until August 1849 when Hasted himself, "just returned from a tour through the United States" and using James Parker's address, wrote hoping that he might have the missing deed without further payment. Neither Parker nor Crossfield trusted Hasted, and it took them another year to sort the matter out.

At the time of his death in Sarnia in 1868, an obituary in the *Sarnia Observer* described Hasted as formerly of Buffalo, New York, and said that he had for many years followed the "avocation" of "colporteur."[16] His daughter, Mary Ann, was living in Sarnia with her husband, William Holden, and Hasted willed her an estate of about $700 with the provision that after their deaths it should go to the Buffalo Protestant Orphan Home.

---

15 Parker, who signed these documents with a mark, seems sometimes to have take his literate son along when transacted business.

16 A hawker of books, newspapers and other printed matter, perhaps employed by a society to distribute Bibles and religious tracts.

WELLS' LETTER

■ 176

GEORGE AND EMILY WELLS, YORK, UPPER CANADA, TO MISS WELLS,
WALBERTON, WEST SUSSEX, 7 FEBRUARY 1832

George and Emily Wells were not Petworth emigrants; they emigrated from the parish of
Walburton in 1831. They were in a party of Walburton emigrants who appear to have paid
their own way to Canada. George Jordan, who emigrated at the same time as the Wells, wrote
that George and his wife left Quebec for Little York (Toronto) as soon as they arrived.

As part of his promotion for the 1832 emigration, Thomas Sockett* published letters from
Jordan and another single Walburton emigrant, Mark Ruel.[1] Jordan and Ruel found work
near Quebec City. On 3 August 1831, they said goodbye to Mark's brother James at Quebec
and set out at the invitation of Jordan's uncle to join him and his family at Pittsford in Monroe County, New York. These young men are mentioned by the Wells.

SOURCE: *Letters from Sussex Emigrants*, 5-6

Young Street, York, Upper Canada,
February 7, 1832.

MY DEAR SISTER,

I now take the pleasure of writing you and stating our welfare. We are in perfect
health, and most sincerely hope this will find you in the same condition. We like
the country much better than we did at first, *because in this province an honest and industrious mechanic will always earn more than in England, and by a prudent course of conduct
may soon become independent. George gets 7s. 6d. Canada* [Halifax] *Currency per day* in
the summer season, but during the winter little work in his line of business (bricklaying) is to be had. We have no intention of an immediate return to England, *because
in this beautiful colony of the British Empire industry and honesty will at all times procure
a comfortable living. The taxes are very trifling,* and lands may be purchased at a moderate rate. We like most old country people, are, and ever will continue to be, affectionately attached to our friends and our native land. We may perhaps return to
England, or should it prove otherwise, we shall be very glad to see our friends here,
but desire to be distinctly understood to invite none, because they might after arrival
feel dissatisfied with the manners and habits of the country, and thereby censure us

---

1 WSRO, MP 320 and MP 1070.

for our good intentions. In a letter to you, dear Sister, we are to be understood as stating the language of truth.

If any of our friends should come to this country, we are of opinion *they would shew but little or no inclination to return to England, because here we have peace and plenty, and (which we sincerely lament to observe by the public prints) is not the case with you.*

If you shall receive this letter, my dear Sister, write to your Father and Mother, also to my Father and Mother, transmitting this letter, and desiring all our Friends (and we love them affectionately) to pay the inland postage of their letters to us, or to get them franked.

Such letters as your friends and mine wish to direct to us, you will have the goodness to send to Miss Emma Trew at Mr. G. Halsted's Walberton, as that young lady is expected to arrive at Quebec in the Spring, likewise respectfully desiring all letters for us to be addressed to the care of Thomas E. Trew, Esq., Commissary, Quebec. At your desire combined with my own inclination and affection for you, I wrote to you on our arrival at Quebec, but to my surprise and disappointment have not received a single line from you. The reason is, I think, you had forgotten to pay the inland postage of your letters, without which they will not find their way to a distant colony.

We are extremely anxious to hear how you all do, and whether Fanny is gone to Gibraltar or not. We have written three letters and others but received no answers. We sincerely desire you and all friends will write us without fail. From yourself we look for a letter in the spring, and surely it will contain as much news as the bounds of a single sheet will contain. We have not for the last 5 months seen either James or Mark Ruel or Jorden. We left them at Quebec and have reason to think they have gone to the United States.

Desiring you to remember us very kindly and affectionately to all enquiring friends, We remain, dear Eliza, your affectionate brother and sister,

GEORGE and EMILY WELLS.

To Miss Wells, Walberton.

The Wells may have written this letter from Thornhill, which was on "Young Street." They were certainly settled in Thornhill by 1835. In that year, three Walberton letter-writers all mentioned George Wells: see letter 102 written by Frank Mellish, 107 from Mary and Edmund Birch (Burch), and 110 from John Ayling.

KNIGHT CORRESPONDENCE

■ **177**

JAMES KNIGHT, NELSONVILLE, OHIO, TO UNKNOWN RECIPIENT, WEST SUSSEX, 29 AUGUST 1832

Before he and his wife Sarah Redman emigrated from Wisborough Green in 1821, Knight had been an innkeeper and maltester and well known locally. In Nelsonville he was both promoting the sale of his own lands and acting as an agent for members of the Courtauld family who had returned to England after a sojourn in Ohio. Knight conducted a letter campaign to England trying to attract settlers, and several of his letters are published in Sussex papers of this period. The emigrants who sailed from Wisborough Green on the *England* in 1832 went at his urging. J.C. Hale, the superintendent of the *England*, was engaged to take them to his land in Nelsonville.

SOURCE: *Portsmouth, Portsea & Gosport Herald*, 13 October 1833; Thomas Sockett* also published this letter in the Petworth Emigration Committee's "Statement" in defence of Hale in 1833; in that publication he made some changes to the punctuation and two words – indicated in square brackets below – were omitted there.

Extract of a letter from Mr. James Knight, of Nelsonville, (United Sates) formerly of Wisborough Green, Sussex, dated August 29th, 1832.

Charles Wheeler came on the 19th July; he had not seen any one he knew since he left England until he met me at my door. He informed us that a party had sailed before him, and he expected they might have been arrived; this strengthened our opinion that the cholera had set in with considerable violence at Montreal and Quebec, [and we] were fearful that there might be such obstacles in the way as altogether to prevent their ever reaching us, not knowing, at that time, that the party were under the care of a superintendent, who was to deliver them here. Happily for the party that such was the case; and, but for the extreme vigilance of Capt. Hale, and his determined efforts to fulfil to the letter every promise of his engagement made at Wisborough Green, they could not have got here ever at this time, for they all say, if they had to manage for themselves, that they would not have enough to carry them through; and it is generally believed by the party that, although Capt. Hale has fulfilled to them all that he promised to do, that he expended more than the amount that he was to receive, trusting to the honor of those who engaged him to make the amount good, which I hope, if that is the case, will be done, as I really believe he has done full justice to his engagement.

The Church of St Peter ad Vincula, Wisborough Green, West Sussex
Photograph: Patrick Burrows

■ 178
JAMES KNIGHT, NELSONVILLE, OHIO TO GEORGE COURTAULD (II), 15
DECEMBER 1832

SOURCE: BL, Courtauld Family Letters, VI 2039–41

JAMES KNIGHT TO GEORGE COURTAULD (II). The part of the letter relating to Petworth emigrants is given below.

NELSONVILLE O.
Dec. 15 – 1832.

Dᴿ SIR–

    After the receipt of your very long two sheet Letter of the date of Febʸ last, I
had intended to have set down and given you a very long answer, but having just
then so many occupations which continually took up my time so as to prevent me
– I had then also a series of letters in hand which seemed to claim my immediate
attention on the subject of advice to Emigrants – those letters have many of them
been published – and the result has been what you may have perhaps heard – a host
of English people surrounding us — we are now quite an English settlement – Judge
what must have been my situation in having to act as the adviser to the heads of 8
or 10 families – who look to me for almost everything they want – Judge what must
have been the pleasure in first having a Brother of Mrs. Knight (Mr Edward Redman his wife and Daughter) to join us in the spring – totally unknown to us of their
coming but a few Days before – I had a House which they soon went into and Mr
Redman was a happy aid to me in my business I then hoped to have some more
leisure – but his health has not been good – something of a pulmonary affection[1]
– which has latterly totally unfitted him for business from some time past and I am
now comparitively single handed – – shortly after they were settled came a young
man a Carpenter from Wisboro Green – who informed me that a great many more
were on the way on another Ship – but whether they would reach here he did not
know – I recommended him to stay – he has bought a lot (the same that Mr
Billinghurst formerly owned) and intends building him a House in the Spring – he
had not been here more than 10 Days when a person drove up to my Door and
asked me if I did not expect to see some familys from Wisboro Green – I informed
him that I had not any decided information to that effect – he then informed me
that in less then 2 hours there would be about 40 at my Door! – this was no time
to talk what was to be done – but to set about and prepare for their reception – We
were happily well provided with everything that they would require – I first ordered
all the Pots and Kettles to be in immediate requisition – and soon had a Ham or
two and some Apple Dumplings under way and then set about the arrangement of
tables for their Dinner – I had just completed a large frame warehouse 40 feet by
20 – with a carriage House adjoining – in this I placed long tables – and in 3 hours

1 Sarah Knight states that Edward came in May 1832 and that he died in February 1833.

I had the satisfaction of seeing 40 of my countrymen women and Children with their superintendent set down at once at my table – hale, hearty and stout hearted English men – all come to this country to fly from starvation – it was really a happy sight to see so many happy faces – tho worn down with fatigue – being just at the time the cholera was raging at its most violent height in Montreal (where they were chartered to by ship) I cannot here particularize to you what they had to endure on that account – but you can in some measure imagine – the next care, what is to be done with them – I happen[d] to own the Biggerstaff House which you recollect (dont be surprized at this – for I have been favour so much in my exertions here as to own now 4 good houses besides about 20 town Lots and several other build-ings such as Warehouses, Stables &c in the town) – this House I had vacant for the purpose of repairs which was only partly done – and in this emergency I converted into a complete Barrack for Six families – until further arrangements could be made – a few Days after came on another family from Cranly (Sussex) of 10 in number – these I gave up a part of my Warehouse to – for their present convenience – they are now living in town – I ought to have said before that the first number of 40 all came out from the neighbourhood of Wisborough Green – most of them I knew as little boys and Girls – come out now as Men and Women with *their* children –

■ 179

SARAH (REDMAN) KNIGHT, NELSONVILLE, OHIO, EXTRACT FROM HER JOURNAL FOR 1832

In April 1861, in her seventieth year, Sarah Redman decided to write down some of the events of her life. Life and death on the frontier, the hardships of settling, natural disasters, and much moving about in search of a living gave her dramatic subject matter. The later part of her "Epit-ome" covering 1861-7 is in the form of a journal with dated entries, and she seems to have used some sort of written record for her early years. One of the events she described was the arrival of the 1832 party from Wisborough Green. The pertinent passages are quoted below.

SOURCE: WSRO, MP1790, Sarah Redman, "Epitome of the Life of Sarah Redman" (typescript copy)

In August 1832 there came out to us a party from our own village, Wisbo Green, six families (sent by the parish) consisting of:

Mr. Burberry & wife & 8 children	10
Mr. Older & wife & 7 Do	9
Mr. Thair & wife & 2 Do	4
Mr. Saunder & wife & 3 Do	5
Mr Smart & wife & 2 Do	4
Mr. Tribe & wife & 2 Do	4
George Hook }	
Thomas Older } Single men	3
Ch Wuler [Wheeler] }	—
	39

We put them all into our Bickerstaff house for a few days. Provided a good dinner and supper for them and gave them suficient for breakfast. Captain Hale came with them. He staid with us two weeks and was very pleased. During that time Mr. T. Evershed came (an old friend of ours). Ought to have said that a man of the name of Charles Wheeler came two weeks before. The Collory [cholera] was ragin when they arrived at Monteral so that they were greatly exposed, and were not suffered to land at Cleveland, but had to hire wagons and go to Pittsburg; And thence down the Ohio river to Marietta. But they all enjoyed good health. The second week after they were here Mrs Launder [Saunder?] and I took sick. She had one babe die. But after a few weeks we recovered.

Then Mr. Thair took sick and Mrs. Burberry, who both died. Mr. And Mrs. Grapham came on soon after – with seven children, one died. They all continued here a few months & were doing well. We let them have every thing we could. But they soon became dissastified and went off to Lancaster.

———————

Some of the emigrants who went to Knight's settlement at Nelsonville must have reported unfavourably. The *Hampshire Telegraph* of 3 March 1834 printed part of a letter from Knight explaining that the first part, which was omitted, contained Knight's refutation of "malignant charges" made by people who had emigrated from Wisborough Green and Pulborough.

James Knight died on 26 August 1836 of a "nervous fever." Sarah remarried and out lived her second husband. She spent her last years in Athens County, recording in 1863 that she was the last surviving member of the party of 1821 immigrants from England still living there. She continued to write in her journal until July 1867, one month before she died.

Charles Adsett
Autobiography

■ 180

CHARLES ADSETT, AUTOBIOGRAPHY, WRITTEN AFTER 1874, PROBABLY
AT GUELPH, ONTARIO

Charles Adsett travelled to Upper Canada in 1832 when his father, Thomas Adsett (22, 49,
61, 71) emigrated, taking his family with him. Charles begins his own story at the age of six.
Apart from a brief mention of their adoption, he says nothing more of his two sisters, and
we have been unable to trace them in their adoptive families. According to the family, this
account of his life was taken down by one of his granddaughters.

SOURCE: Brighton Reference library, Sussex Pamphlets, Box 38 (typescript)

AUTOBIOGRAPHY OF CHARLES ADSETT (1826–1908)

Was born in Parish of North Chaple, county of Sussex, England, on 24th of May
1826 and immigrated with my parents Thomas and Sarah Adsett, and three sisters
in the spring of 1832 to Canada, leaving Portsmouth harbour on the 5th day of April
and after a very rough voyage in the ship called the "Eveline" (65 days) we arrived
at Montreal on the 9th of June.

Our next move was from Montreal to (then) Little York, (now Toronto), part of
the way by canal boats drawn by oxen traveling at the rate of about 14 miles in 15
hours. ... From Little York to Hamilton thence by way of Dundas and Beverly swamp
(a rough road it was then) to Preston, our destination, sometime in the latter part
of June. I think there were 3 houses then in Preston and one of them was a tavern
with what was then considered a large stable and driving shed – where we – with
many other immigrants were glad to take shelter for the time being, until we could
find or build something better than a stable but unfortunately some never left that
old stable alive of which my poor dear mother was one and my little sister another.

But what a sad fix for my poor dear father to be left alone in a strange country, with
3 helpless children, the oldest 7 years a girl and myself about 6 years and the youngest
then living a girl between 4–5 years without friends and very little money left.

But thank God we were not long without friends; my two sisters were soon
adopted by a kind friend in Galt and I soon found a place in Preston with a weaver
where I was to learn to weave and in one of those places, where we were first adopted
there was no family of their own. But the weaver started tavern keeping soon after

I went to live with him and as I and my father were tea-totalers I could not stop with him so I went to help a farmer (Uncle Sam Cornell) get in his harvest and while I was there we heard of a place where there was an apprentice wanted to learn the tanning and currying business (Mr. John Betchel) and we at once decided that I should try that trade but Mr. Betchel was not prepared to take on a green horn, so I had to lie off and take a rest for a shorttime.

However in November 1832 Mr. Betchel thought he could find enough work for another hand so I was taken on trial for 2 months and in January 1833 (the trial having proved satisfactory) the indentures were drawn up by Wm. Scollick Esquire, in his office in a part of old Mr. Isaac master's house about a mile from Preston on the way to Galt between John Betchel tanner *master* and Charles Adsett apprentice to serve from date until 24th of May 1847. Only 14½ years from the time I went on trial in November 1832 and I should attain to full 21 years. The last 2 years of my apprenticeship I was promoted to be foreman of the whole shop and while serving the 14 years I was rented twice to parties who rented the tannery like any of the chattels so rented. The first time to Messrs Toul and Till – and the second time to Baldwin and Jackson. However I went with them each time, but came back and finished with the same old master on May 24th, 1847 that I started with in November 1832.

From being called by my old master – the laziest boy he had ever had about the place – the last few years of my apprenticeship he told several parties that I was the best boy he ever raised and several times when we were doing business in the country together he introduced me to strangers as his oldest son.

After finishing my apprenticeship on advice of my father I took up 100 acres of land in the township of Woolwich to make a home for my father while he lived and while taking a few holidays in Guelph my good old master followed me and persuaded me to hire with him by the year and take full charge of the business in his tannery which I consented to do and stopped with him until his death in August 1849, then I managed his business for his executors until December 1849. My old master appeared to be well satisfied with my management of his business while he was living, but his executors for some reason unknown to me or his family wished to have some other person run the show for them so I packed my kit and left the old home and friends to return no more.

My next invitation was from an old friend in Saginau, Michigan, Mr. Wm. Baldwin and old apprentice in the tannery with Mr. John Betchel. I left Canada in January 1850 and worked for him until the following September. I returned home riding an Indian Pony all the way back from Saginau City via Flint, Port Huron, London, Woodstock to my home in Woolwich. I was always fond of riding horseback, but I got enough of it this time to do me awhile and as the pony was small I was obliged to take it easy as there were no railroads or express carriers at the time I was obliged to carry my traps on one of the old fashioned saddle-bags across the pony's back and with my weight it was too much for my little pony for such a long distance. That was the way the good old-fashiond methodist ministers used to travel in those days and I was sometimes taken for one of that worthy clan. I have seen the women at the door of their housed and have heard them say "There goes the methodist minister, but whether it was the trappings or the appearance of things in general I did not stop to enquire.

Soon after I returned I was take sick with genuine Michigan ague[1] and had it all fall and again next spring and although I had it very hard I worked every day while I would be shaking while the fever lasted after shaking.

I worked sometimes at currying for Mr. John Wissler in the township of Waterloo. From there I went to Hespeler and worked for Mr. Robert Forbes. He was about the best boss I ever had after leaving the old home. Mr. Adam Shaw managed the business for him and Mr. James Jackson (an old shop mate) as foreman. I kept on there until sometime in 1852, then moved to Guelph and worked for Mr. Jackson for sometime and next for Mr. Gorie where I worked until his tannery burned down with all that was in it. All my clothers and all else that I had (some precious keepsakes of my mothers and several others) except for the duds on my back (my working harness) were burned. This happened on Christmas day 1853. Then I went home and worked for my father on the farm all summer and in October 1854 came back to Guelph and went into business with Mr. F.W. Galbraith and Wm. Heather forming a co-partnership of Galbraith, Heather and Adsett. Mr. Heather carried on his business in his old stand and Mr. Galbraith carried on his, facing the market square (both of them saddlers) and I managed the tannery that we leased from Mr. Jackson on Huskinson Street and although we each had our own department or shop to look after it was all one business. Our term of co-partnership was for 5 years and we stuck together until the end of the term, then dissolved partnership and I think that was where we all made a mistake. We were doing well and should have stuck together.

I was married to my dear wife Sarah Jane Kirkland on the 21st day of January 1859 and a happy day it was for me. In January 1860 we moved to our farm in Woolwich Township and bought a smaller farm (40 acres) for my father near by but we only stopped about 11 months on the farm then sold the farm and moved back to Guelph again and settled down for several years doing very little.

I was in the leather and binding business for a time with Mr. Heather in his old shop but it did not turn out very satisfactory and we gave it up for a bad job. In the early part of the year 1867 I was offered and induced to take a ⅓ share in what was represented to be a good paying business in a woolen mill near New Dundee on the town line between the Township of Wilmot and Blenheim with Graham Watson and John Tilt. Started business April 1st, 1867 under the name of Watson, Tilt, and Adsett and lost nearly all that I had made and saved in former years, farm and all and came back to Guelph in the fall 1872 leaving my family in Wilmot, where my dear wife died in the month of March, 1873. I then moved my children back to

---

1 Presumably malaria, which was quite prevalent in some areas at the time.

Guelph and Miss Rogers kept house for me for a while. When I came back to Guelph last fall it was to go into the foundry business with Messrs. Harley and Heather, but after looking over the business and books for a shorttime I thought they were losing instead of making anything and I declined going in with them, and in a short time they made an assignment to Mr. John Smith and he engaged me to look after the business for him until he could dispose of the business and property and as he did not wish to be bothered with it he rented it to me until he could dispose of the whole affair.

Engaged with James Hough Deputy clerk of the court in 1874. Married Elizabeth Hough April 1874, who died of heart failure very suddenly, while alone near her bed. Continued with James Hough till his death, when I resigned. I then retired and made my home with my son John the rest of my life.

OTHER LETTERS: See letters 22, 61, 62, 71 from Thomas Adsett.

Noted on the typescript is the following: Some family records from Grandpa Adsett's family Bible. Charles Adsett born May 24, 1826 in the County of Sussex England. Married January 21st, 1858 to Sarah Jane Kirkland, born September 20th 1833 of the country of Nottingham, England. Sarah Jane Adsett (Kirkland) died March 23rd 1873. Charles died March 7th, 1908 in Guelph, Ontario aged 81 years, 9 months, 12 days.

There is no Bible record of Charles Adsett's second wife or Bible record of marriages of any of the family.

Although Charles bought a farm at his father's urging, his one brief attempt at farming after his marriage to Sarah Jane Kirkland in 1858 seems to have convinced him that this was not the life for him. Some of the more entrepreneurial of Petworth letter-writers mention the advantages of arriving with a small amount of capital. Although they provide stories, and some examples, of people who arrived poor and amassed considerable wealth in one generation, Charles – who managed always to make a living without ever founding a lasting business – was perhaps more typical. After their first two children died as infants, he and Sarah had four sons. His son John lived in Guelph where Charles died on 7 March 1908. His obituary in the *Guelph Weekly Mercury and Advertizer* described Charles as a tanner by trade, but one who had "followed many different occupations during his life." This source described him as a devout Methodist and stated that he had been clerk of the District Court for a number of years before his retirement.

Mark Mann and his wife, Sophia Rapley Mann, on their fiftieth wedding anniversary, 1891, surrounded by family
Courtesy Margaret Parsons

Appendices

APPENDIX A
TRANSCRIBED ORIGINAL MANUSCRIPT LETTERS

These three letters sent from England by the mothers of Richard Pullen and Obediah Wilson give the flavour of a correspondence without punctuation and with erratic spelling and capitalization. A photograph of letter 145 is at page 304.

■ 132

Petworth April 22 1838

My Dear Children

I Now Write these few lines to you hopeing it Will find you All in Good Health As it leaves Me At Presen I thank the lord I Am A graet Deal Better then I Was in the Winter for We Had A very Severe Winter More So then Ever Was known since the Memory of Mn for it kild All the furs bushes on the Commons And in the farmers feilds Except on the South Side of the Hills Witch I Never Remember Seeing the furs All Dead I Hope that you Have Not Had it Colder in Canada We Was in Hopes of Haveing A letter from you Before this time But As We Have An opportunity of sending it By James Lanaway that was Lord Egremonts Cotchman He is Coming to Blandford His Lordship is Dead And Colonel George Has Got the Estate And your Sister Martha is Come Down to the lodge in the Tilington Road to live Were the Poultry is kept She Has Got a Good House But Sarahs Husband Have Nothing to Do they Have Been in vew of A Place several times But it is All A Blank And she Have Been very Poorly And the Children Have All Had the Hoping Coff And Poor little Charels Died With it And the youngest Has Been very ill But she is A little Better And your Brother William is very ill And Has Been for this 18 Weeks With His old Complaint And I Am very Much Afraid He Will Never Be No Better But We Hope He will if it is the lords Will. But He is A little Better Again Now And so He Have been several times And then He Gets Worse He just Crals out to the Gate Now But we Must . . . the Lords will Be Done . . . I hope And Pray And Believe that He is very serious I bless the Lord He Have A Good Hope Beyond the grave His Wife And Children Are very Will And I Bless the Lord they Dos Pretty Well for A living they Have ther Club Muney And they Have 5 loves of Bread And A Half Ccrown from the youn.. A Week your Brothers Petters Wife Have Got A Nother little one And She is Pretty Well And All of them Elizabeth will soon Have Another And they Are All Well But Thomases Wife is Not like to Have Aney family At Present they Was Along Here the 17 from Bilingshurst the Have got A peice of Ground Now At Midhurst had plenty of work they Are Both Well But Poor James Has lost His Master And Mistress Have Died Both in one week With the Titus fever But I Bless the lord He Has Ecapt As yet And I Hope He Will They Have Been Busy ... these weeks But He Have Been in A Great Deal of troble There Was No one Belonging to them Anear that Every thing layes on Him I had 5 letters from Sunday to the Next Munday Morning I Have Been up to Him once And Am A going Again He is upon taking the Bisiness for He Says He is quit Master of the Bisiness And Have Done it for A Great Wile

And so People says About Gildford I Bless the lord He Have An Excellent Caracter And I Hope And Pray He will Do Well it Will Be A Good thing for Him if He Keeps Himself stedy And Be paruent in Bysiness Serving God I Hope He Will Not forget His Duty to King and Be thankfull He Has Got A littel Muney of His own And I Have found Him A freind to lend Him A little Master Hooker is very Well He Send His Well Wishes to you And Mrs Winter And her Husband And James Hooker And His famyly I See old Jane Baker About A Week Since Poor old Creatuer she Was A Planting of Pertatoes Hoping Abut As usel All Colehook Peopel Are All Well Except William I forgot to tell you yong Sister Sarah Was Got out in Collhook to live to that House Were Master May died. I hope My Dear Children you Received our letter As We sent to you And I Hope it found you Well And I Hope We Will Soon Hear from you Again And I Hope My Dear Granchildren Goes to School or learns to Read And Not only learns to Read But to Searve their Creator in the days of there youth I long to know wether you Have the Gospel Preachd thier or Not But Blessed Be God you Have the Bible So My Dear Children there is troble And vexashon of Spirit for us All No Doubt But you finds it in Canada for that is Not our Rest Because it is Perluted But we Must look Beyond the Grave unto that Happy Shore Were I Hope to Meet to Part No More All your Brothers And Sisters join And All freinds in love to you We often talks of you When We Meet So Now My Dear Children And Grand Children I Commend you to God And to the [. . .]rde of His Grece So No More from your loveing Mother Elizabeth Hooker

My dear sister and brother this comes with with our kind love to you all in hopes it will find you all well and thank God it leaves us all at present all that is spared my dear sister i am sorry to inform you of the death of my dear baby who departed this life the 6 of March after six weeks ilness the poor little dear died with the hopping coff she had sevrell fits with it poor little dear but you now my dearsister and brother that the lords will must be done poor little dear we hope she is at rest but we have had a Great Deal of troubel but i hope you all that is now Liveing will try your Best and Get Back to Old England again for we do hear every week in the News Papper from Canaday that there is Bad Going on with some and i your Brother John Summersell hope and wish that them that wish for you to go from Old England will be force to pay your passage Back again for it have Gave me a Great Deal of troubel to see your Sister in so much troubbel about you all and i am sorry my self and it hurt us to hear our Daughters Hariott and Ann talk about you all so much and i wish you all well so no more from your brother John Summersell

My dear sister i now take my pen to rite about all our dear ralions and my dear children harriott and ann both sends their aunt and uncle and all their cousins their kind love and the hopes and we all hopes we shall all meet in this world again our aunt meriah and all her famaly sends their kind love to you all and the are all very well our cuosens [missing][1] wife is near her confindment if she is [missing] with the second child my dear sister [missing] not heard from guildford since i rote [missing] last i rote to them but i have not rese[missing] answer from them my husbands friend [missing] their kind respects to you all i saw [missing] danger tow or three days ago master di[missing] been very ill all the winter but he is [missing] now the both sends their respecks to [missing] I saw misses [holden] yesterday and she s[missing] all the people was all very well in the family except your poor brother William old Jane baker is about the same she goes to [missing] d as she use to do wen you lived their Lord egremont is dead and your brother John have dran him to church we had a very grand funiral there was hundreds of people your brother

---

1 A piece of the letter measuring 1 inch by 3 ½ inches, which probably contained a stamp, is missing.

had a sut of close my dear sister i have not been down in the commonds since i rote to you before we have had a great deal of trouble all the winter my dear children have had the hopping coff all the winter but thank God my dear little ann is a great deal better it pleased God to take my dear baby to himself i hope and trust to a better world were i hope we shall all meet to part no more i hope God will be with you all so now to conclude we remain your loving sister and brother Ann and John Summersell.

> ADDRESS Mr Robinson, Ekfrid
> Delaware, London District
> Upper Canada
> for Richard Pullen at Mr. Seabrook
> Delaware U C

■ 145

Bassingbourn August 1838

My Dear Son
This is the second time I have taken up my pen to right to you And have not reseived hanay Answar if this Should reach your hands I hope you will right As soon As possabel or I shall think you are know more whe hope you still live And wonce Again will come to old England to see your Affectionate mother Has your Are in my thoughts Day And night this leaves me well And All your brothers & sisters As thay Are more numerous then when you Left as Edward was maried 20th November 1837 to Charlotte Corse And faney on the 30 of January 1838 to Marie Jhon Hall near Broadwater Elizabeth on 23th Juley 1838 to Simen Sell of Bassingbourn your uncal Henery is Living with me And your brother Henery your cousons Willsons Are well & send thar kind love to you know my Dear Boy I must conclude with my kind Love and Hall your Brothers and Sisters Join with me I hope the Lord is with you from your ever Loving Mother Maria Wilson

> Bassingbourn
> Cambridge Shire
> North of England

PS If this is not Answard some wone of the Familey will come over

■ 147[2]

June 21 1841 Bassingbourn

My Dear and Ever Blessed son I received your kind letter june 11 1841 and was so glad to hear from you I cannot Express my fealings to Wards you my Dear Child as have now husband my Childern are al my Comforts I ham glad to hear you are well as Bless the lord at this time it leves us all well your grand mother and grand father Stamford are living She is 80 fore this june your sister faney as bin to se me and her Littel gail name Ellien the son Henery 2 the priteys Children your Ever did see and such a kind husband she as married in to such A respectable famley and she wishes so much to see you I post the letter to her and sent word she flud in to tears for joy to hear from her dear Brother home she thort was dead my dear son pray write ofin your sister Betcey as ad 3 stil Born your sister mary muncey as got 4 children 2 boys 2 gals the oldes g... Named frances lives witch me as I now due witch out

---

2 This letter, also from Maria Wilson, is written by a different hand.

a sirvand she is very andey fore me I have ad the reumatims in my leg so bad But it is better now I have a nise poney and I drive my self out Edward as got a littel gal and a son he and is wife sends thare kind love to you he lives near to faney thay all say pray mother tel my brother obed to sel is farm and Com home to England and live happey to gather witch us all as we are all Comfortable one witch another my dear son Thare is a living hear for you as wel as the reast thay all dind with me on witsunday last but the thorts of your absence was a grafe to us all o my son if I cood Com over the warter i cood soon be with you Old Mrs Muncey is alive and sends her kind Love to you and ses how she shod Likki to see you and meney more as wel your Hunkel Henry is at home witch us 3 years and Better my dear son I thort you was married acording to your Letter my dear if you have got A yong woman Bring her to England and we shal Love her and youse her well your sister fanney wil write to you soon we eare apor acont of the yeunite steats for the Banks are Borok and thare bad during thare thare is several gorne from hear But glad to Come Back again for thay cannot find a better plase Bassingbourn is Wonderful inroved hower Crops are in som places very good Isack Racher sends is Love to you and ses you must Com home as he wil spend a happey hoer witch you he as got 4 Childern William Hose is so glad to hear of you he is a fin young man he is A miller Henry Cullep cosin Judey as bin very bad thort she wod of dide but she is better Rechard and Betcy are wel and thay feail very much Consirnd about your seprashon from the rest of the famerly Mr and Mrs Chambling and famley sends thare kind Love to you and meney mor I Cannot menchen al that wich me to send to you Asher Racher & his wife send there kind love to you and hope you will find there son John Racher as he at Dundas Upper Canada they are a canvasing here and we expect to have a reform please to give my kind love to the Gentleman that wrote to me Pray write to me as soon as possible & we all shall [be] glad to here from you I remain your loving and affectionate Mother Maria Wilson

Appendix B
IDENTIFICATION OF PERSONS, PLACES, TERMS

This appendix is intended to familiarize readers with some of the people and terms that are referred to or used many times in the letters. An asterisk following a name in the text indicates that the person is identified in this appendix. Persons who are mentioned only a few times are identified when possible in notes. Brief explanations of some of the places and terms that may be unfamiliar on one side of the Atlantic or the other are also provided below.

BARCLAY, CHARLES, of Bury Hill, Dorking, Surrey, was a sponsor of the Dorking emigration. He edited the collection of letters from Dorking emigrants published in 1833.

BATTEAU, light, shallow-draft, flat-bottomed boat with pointed bow and stern (*Canadian Oxford Dictionary*); if they were not being towed, the crew might use a sail, oars, or poles.

BLANDFORD, townplot of Blandford Township, Upper Canada, renamed Woodstock

BRYDONE, JAMES MARR (1779-1866), born in Scotland, army surgeon and veteran of Trafalgar, surgeon and superintendent of Petworth Emigration Committee ships from 1834 to 1837. After 1837, he became private secretary to George Wyndham, Egremont's eldest son and the heir to Petworth. He rose to a responsible position as Wyndham's land steward.

BUCHANAN, JOHN S., the son of the British consul in New York and the nephew of Alexander Carlisle Buchanan, the emigration agent at Quebec, owner of a large grant in Adelaide Township. He opened a sawmill in 1833 and a grist mill in 1836 at a site which became Strathroy.

BUSHBY, LEVI, of Field Place, Goring, made a loan for emigration to the parish of Goring in 1836.

CANADA COMPANY, land and colonization company in Upper Canada chartered in 1825; its publications on emigration circulated widely in England. Approximately half the roughly 2.5 million acres purchased by the company from government in 1826 were in the Huron Tract, which lay to the north of the townships of Adelaide and Plympton (see map 6 at page xlviii). The remainder of the company's land consisted mainly of crown reserves in townships surveyed before the sale was made.

CHICHESTER, HENRY THOMAS PELHAM, 3RD EARL (1804-1886), large landowner and the principal magistrate of East Sussex. He was the patron of the Lewes and Brighton emigration committees, which were formed in 1834 using Sockett's scheme as their model. Over 50 emigrants from parishes in and around Brighton and Lewes travelled under his protection on the *British Tar*.

CHRIPPES, THOMAS, a cabinetmaker and upholster, he also worked as a surveyor and auctioneer. He served on Thomas Sockett's Petworth Emigration Committee with his brother-in-law James Knight.

COBBETT, WILLIAM (1763-1835), a maverick English political writer and politician, publisher of *Cobbett's Weekly Political Register*. Born in Surrey and working class in origin, he made himself a spokesman for the rural labourer. His *Rural Rides* describe a journey which took him through Petworth in 1823.

COLBORNE, JOHN, 1ST BARON SEATON (1778-1863), soldier, colonel of the 52nd Regiment at Waterloo, and colonial adminstrator. He was lieutenant governor of Upper Canada, 1828 to early 1836, commander in chief of the forces in Upper and Lower Canada, 1836 to 1839, and hence during the Rebellions, governor general 1838-9. Anxious to increase British settlement, he took a personal interest in the Petworth emigrants. He and his wife, Elizabeth, stayed in Toronto during the cholera epidemic of 1832 and Esther Chantler records their concern for widows and orphans.

CROWN LANDS DEPARTMENT, UPPER CANADA, headed by a commissioner who was responsible for the sale or granting of land in all new townships surveyed after 1826. Arrangments for Petworth emigrants assisted in travelling or settling by the Upper Canadian government were made by agents of this department.

DISTRICT, a unit of local government in Upper Canada. The four original districts were subdivided from time to time as settlement increased. Authority rested with justices of the peace, appointed by the lieutenant governor, who met in district Quarter Sessions four times a year to try legal cases, supervise administration, and appoint officials. The districts to which Petworth emigrants went are (from east to west) Newcastle, Home, Gore, Niagara, London, and Western (see map 3, at page xlvi). Elections for district councils were not introduced until the 1840s.

DORKING EMIGRATION SOCIETY, based in Dorking, just over the border from Sussex in Surrey. This society sent over 70 emigrants on a Petworth ship in 1832, supplying their provisions and sending its own superintendent. Although Sockett grouped a total of 102 Petworth emigrants of 1832 as from "Dorking and neighbourhood," a number were sent from nearby parishes rather than from Dorking and they were not included in the society's report.

DREWITT, JOHN, a tenant of the Duke of Norfolk at Little Peppering and Great Peppering Farm, Burpham, West Sussex, he apparently helped fund a number of emigrants from Arundel.

DURHAM BOAT, a larger type of barge than the batteaux, also flat bottomed but with a keel.

EGREMONT, GEORGE O'BRIEN WYNDHAM, 3rd Earl (1751-1837), patron and principal sponsor of the Petworth emigrations. Lord Lieutenant of Sussex from 1819 to 1835, Egremont is identified with the "Golden Age" of Petworth House and is remembered especially for his patronage of British artists (J.M.W. Turner is the most famous of those he helped). He was widely noted for his benevolence towards the poor and sponsored emigration for humanitarian reasons as much as to benefit his property.

GREETHAM, JOHN KNIGHT, vicar of Kirdford, 1831-9, a living belonging to the Earl of Egremont. Greetham was a strong supporter of Sockett's scheme and in 1832 he personally conducted the emigrant party from Kirdford down to the ship at Portsmouth.

GURNETT, GEORGE (c.1792-1861), an Upper Canadian journalist. Originally from Horsham, Sussex, he settled first in Virginia and then in Ancaster, Upper Canada, before moving to York (Toronto) where he published the *Courier of Upper Canada*. He was mayor of Toronto in 1837 at the time of the Rebellion. As a nephew of Egremont's steward, he felt a connection with the Petworth emigrations and took a particular interest in the emigrants.

HAMILTON, Upper Canada, often written Hambledon by immigrants who confused it with Hamledon in Surrey.

HATCH, JOHN (1789-1853), a farmer on land now partly within the town, Hatch was one of two magistrates in Woodstock, Upper Canada. He made local arrangements for the reception of Petworth immigrants.

HAWKE, ANTHONY BEWDEN (d. 1867), immigration agent 1832-64, at Lachine in 1832. In 1833, Colborne brought him to Toronto where he became in fact, and later in name, chief emigration officer for the province. His responsibilities included supervising .emigration agents, providing information, and taking charge of assistance given to indigent immigrants. Hawke claimed credit for devising the five-acre lot plan pioneered by Petworth immigrants in Woodstock.

HEAD, SIR FRANCIS BOND (1793-1875), author, adventurer, and administrator. He succeeded Colborne as lieutenant governor of Upper Canada, arriving in January 1836 after serving as assistant poor law commissioner in Kent in 1834-5. Head took an active political role and swept the election of 1836 on the issue of loyalty, but his autocratic style and erratic policies alienated moderate opinion and contributed to the grievances leading to rebellion at the end of 1837. True to the tenets of the new poor law, he reduced aid to able-bodied immigrants.

HILL, NOAH, landlord of the public house the Noah's Ark, site of parish meetings where emigration was discussed and the decision made to sponsor emigrants.

KNIGHT, WILLIAM (d. 1846), corn chandler, insurance agent, and one of the three members of the Petworth Emigration Committee. He served as auditor of the Sutton Gilbert Union and the Petworth Poor Law Union.

MACKENZIE, WILLIAM LYON (1795-1861), journalist and politician. A prominent agitator and Reformer before the Rebellion, he led the rebel forces in the Toronto area in 1837. He escaped to the United States and lived there until 1849 when he was pardoned, returned to Canada, and resumed his political career.

MOUNT, ROSWELL (1797-1834), surveyor and politician; appointed crown lands agent and superintendent of the government settlement in Adelaide and Warwick townships in 1832. He successfully located some 2000 immigrants under difficult circumstances and found work for many more, but his cost overruns caused his superiors serious problems. As postmaster of Delaware, he was in a good position to encourage immigrant correspondence from his settlement.

PARISH, a unit of local goverment in England as the civil parish. In this era, the parish vestry made decisions affecting the parish and appointed the officials who would carry them out. Vestries were variously constituted but in Petworth the vestry was controlled by Sockett and, through him, by Egremont. Under the new poor law legislated in 1834 parishes lost much of their importance.

PHILLIPS, JOHN, printer, Church St, Petworth, West Sussex. He printed all the advertisements, notices, and collections of letters published by Sockett's Petworth Emigration Committee. He also gave out information and took reservations for the Petworth ships.

POOR LAWS, laws making parishes responsible for their poor were first passed in the sixteenth century to fill the gaps in social services (and in social control of the poor) left by the suppression of the monasteries. An act passed under Elizabeth I in 1601 is often taken as the starting point of the poor laws in force in the early nineteenth century. Local administration took many forms, but, speaking generally, Petworth emigrants often came from parishes where there was a strong sponsor willing to incur some extra costs in exchange for the added benefits of sending emigrants under the Petworth committee rather than on their own.

POOR LAW AMENDMENT ACT, passed in 1834, gave centralized authority over poor relief to three poor law commissioners who had the assistance of a secretary and a team of inspectors in the field. They endeavoured to bring all parishes into poor law unions, although some older forms of union continued to exist. The poor law commissioners had the power to authorize government backing for loans raised by parishes to send emigrants abroad. They were replaced in 1847 by a Poor Law Board.

POOR RATES, a rate (or tax) levied on property owners in a parish for the relief of the poor

PRIME, RICHARD (1784-1866), a magistrate and landowner in the parish of Walberton, which sent some 50 emigrants on Petworth ships. Sockett used Prime as an example of a sponsor who was well satisfied to pay the full price of a passage with the Petworth committee in order to be "relieved from all personal trouble in the matter."

RADCLIFF, THOMAS (1794-1841), army officer, settler, and magistrate. He settled in Adelaide Township in 1832, was appointed a colonel in the Upper Canadian militia in 1837, and took command on the Niagara frontier in January 1838. He became lieutenant-colonel of the 11th Provisional Battalion of Militia on 9 November 1838.

SCOVILLE, PETER, innkeeper at the King's Arms, Haslemere, Surrey, he handled the official correspondence concerning prospective emigrants from his area.

SOCKETT, GEORGE, eldest son of the Reverend Thomas Sockett of Petworth. After selling out of the army, he emigrated to Upper Canada on the *Ottawa* on 29 October 1833 and settled in Eramosa Township. Although he had no formal connection with the Petworth emigrations, Brydone visited him on his trips to Upper Canada and he is mentioned in immigrant letters.

SOCKETT, THOMAS (1777-1859), went to Petworth House as tutor to Egremont's sons in 1797, was supported through livings in Egremont's gift from 1808, rector of Petworth 1816, and personal chaplain to Egremont. The originator and organizer of the Petworth emigrations, Sockett collected and edited many of the letters in this volume.

TITHE, one-tenth of the annual produce of agriculture formerly claimed as a tax, originally in kind but later in money, for the support of the Church of England and its clergy

TOWNSHIP, subdivision of a district and the basic unit of local government. Rural settlers described their property in terms of township surveys that laid out concession lines and numbered the lots. Some minor officials were elected at the township level and settlers might meet on local issues or to prepare a petition (see 175 Frederick Hasted), but the powers vested in a township were local in nature and quite restricted.

WOODSTOCK, the town plot of the Township of Blandford and the site in 1834 of a first experiment in giving Petworth families temporary occupancy of five-acre lots and a log house in a community where there was a demand for labour. The project was expanded to other parish emigrants, and to Brantford and the Township of Paris, but it was not continued after 1837.

WYNDHAM, COLONEL GEORGE, LATER 1ST BARON LECONFIELD (1787-1869), the eldest son of the Earl of Egremont. He inherited Petworth and the largest share of Egremont's lands but, being of illigitimate birth, could not inherit the entailed title, which went to Egremont's nephew. Wyndham's involvement with emigration was mainly from his estates in Ireland in counties Clare and Limerick – in all he sent roughly the same number of Irish emigrants as his father had sent from Sussex. Wyndham himself sponsored relatively few emigrants from Sussex.

YALDWYN, WILLIAM HENRY, of Blackdown, a magistrate and landowner in Lurgashall, West Sussex. He worked with Sockett to organize the 1832 emigration in his area and accompanied the Lurgashall emigrants to Portsmouth. Yaldwyn emigrated to Australia and died in Sydney in 1866.

YORK, UPPER CANADA, renamed Toronto in 1834

A NOTE ON CURRENCY[1]

The most important rate to remember in reading these letters is that one US dollar was widely accepted as equivalent to 5s sterling and 4s 6d Halifax currency. Halifax currency was a currency of account which A.B. McCullough describes as equivalent to bookkeeping credits and debits as opposed to "cash" or physical money. As government and merchants kept their accounts in Halifax currency, it is often mentioned in the letters. The nominal par value was £111.11 currency to £100 sterling (although commercial exchange rates varied over time and from year to year and, by the 1830s, tended to put a somewhat higher value on sterling). The Province of Canada did not adopt decimal accounting for government departments or a coinage of its own until the 1850s.

Petworth emigrants explained the currency in various ways in their letters. Some gave the difference in value between sterling and (Halifax) currency. Others who specified "English" money probably intended to distinguish between sterling coins and [American] dollars – coins from both currencies were in daily use.

1 Based on A.B. McCullough, *Money and Exchange in Canada to 1900* (Toronto: Dundurn 1984)

Notes to Preface and Introduction

PREFACE

1 Charlotte Erickson, *Invisible Immigrants: The Adaptation of English and Scottish Immigrants in Nineteenth-Century America* (London: Weidenfeld and Nicholson 1972), and *Leaving England: Essays on British Emigration in the Nineteenth Century* (Ithaca and London: Cornell University Press 1994); Robin F Haines, *Emigration and the Labouring Poor: Australian Recruitment in Britain and Ireland, 1831-60* (Basingstoke, Hampshire: Macmillan 1997).

INTRODUCTION

1 Bruce Elliott, "Regional Patterns of English Immigration and Settlement in Upper Canada," "Migration Conference," University of Edinburgh, 1998, conference paper.

2 Webb, Sydney and Beatrice Webb, *English Poor Law Policy* (London: Longmans Green 1910); Michael E Rose, *The English Poor Law 1780-1930* (Newton Abbot, England: David and Charles 1971). In this era only English and Welsh parishes assisted emigration. The poor law in Scotland did not permit this kind of aid to able-bodied people and Ireland had no poor law until 1838.

3 Helen I. Cowan, *British Emigration to British North America: The First Hundred Years* (rev. ed., Toronto: University of Toronto Press 1961), Table 1.

4 A full list of publications relating to the Petworth emigrations is given in the Sources, p 419.

5 This list evolved each time it appeared at the back of one of Phillip's publications. The books included: Joseph Bouchette, *Topographical and Statistical Description ... of Lower and Upper Canada ...*, 2 vols. (London 1832); William Cattermole, *The Advantages of Emigration to Canada* (London 1831); Martin Doyle [William Hickey], *Hints on Emigration to Upper Canada* (2nd ed., London 1832; 3rd ed. London 1834); Robert Mudie, *The Emigrant's Pocket Companion* (London 1833); Andrew Picken, *The Canadas* (London 1832; 2nd ed., 1836); Joseph Pickering, *Inquiries of an Emigrant* (3rd ed., London 1832); *Information* published by His Majesty's Commissioners for Emigration (London 1832 and subsequent years); J.C. Hale, *Instructions to Persons Intending to Emigrate* (Petworth 1833 and subsequent years); Thomas Radcliff, ed., *Authentic Letters from Upper Canada* (1833; repr., Toronto: Macmillan 1953).

6 PRO, MH 12/13061, Petworth Union, Phillips to the Poor Law Commissioners, 20 March 1837.

7 Wendy Cameron, "'Till they get tidings from those who are gone ..': Thomas Sockett and Letters from Petworth Emigrants, 1832-1837," *Ontario History* 85, no. 1 (1993): 1-16. A number of the authors of books written in the early 1830s had connections to the Canada Company or wrote in the hope of some recognition from the company.

8 Josephine Wtulich, ed and trans., *Writing Home: Immigrants in Brazil and the United States, 1890-1891* (New York: Columbia University Press for East European Monographs 1986).

9 See, for example, Charlotte Erickson, *Invisible Immigrants: The Adaptation of English and Scottish Immigrants in Nineteenth-Century America* (London: Weidenfeld and Nicholson 1972); Patrick O'Farrell, *Letters from Irish Australia, 1825-1929* (Sydney: New South Wales University Press, and Belfast: Ulster Historical Foundation 1984); Kerby A Miller, *Emigrants and Exiles, Ireland and the Irish Exodus to North America* (New York: Oxford University Press 1985); Patricia Clark and Dale Spender, *Lifelines: Australian Women's Letters and Diaries, 1788-1840* (North Sydney: Allen and Unwin 1992); Stephen Fender, *Sea Changes: British Emigration and American Literature* (Cambridge and New York: Cambridge University Press 1992); David Fitzpatrick, *Oceans of Consolation: Personal Accounts of Irish Migration to Australia* (Ithaca and London: Cornell University Press 1994).

10 For example, H. William Thomas and Florian Znanieki, *The Polish Peasant in Europe and America*, 4 vols. (1st ed. 1918; New York 1927), vol. 1; Arnold Barton, *Letters from the Promised Land: Swedes in America, 1840-1914* (Minneapolis: University of Minnesota Press for the Swedish Pioneer History Society 1975); Niels Peter Stilling and Anne Lisbeth Olsen, *A New Life: Danish Emigration to North America as Described by the Emigrants Themselves in Letters, 1842-1946*, Studies in Emigration History No. 6 (Aalborg, Denmark: Danes Worldwide Archives 1994); Walter D. Kamphoefner et al., eds., *News from the Land of Freedom: German Immigrants Write Home* (Ithaca: Cornell University Press 1991); Herbert J. Brinks, ed., *Dutch American Voices: Letters from the United States, 1850-1930* (Ithaca and London: Cornell University Press 1995).

11 Marianne McLean, *The People of Glengarry: Highlanders in Transition, 1745-1820* (Montreal and Kingston: McGill-Queen's University Press 1991), 202-4.

12 Peter Way, *Common Labour: Workers and the Digging of North American Canals, 1780-1860* (Cambridge: Cambridge University Press 1993).

13 Fitzpatrick, *Oceans of Consolation*, 26-7.

14 Erickson, *Invisible Immigrants*, 4.

15 Wendy Cameron and Mary McDougall Maude, *Assisting Emigration to Upper Canada*, 21; Cowan *British Emigration*, Table 11.

16 Colin Read and Ronald J Stagg, eds., *The Rebellion of 1837 in Upper Canada* (Ottawa: Carleton University Press 1988); Alan Greer, "1837-38: Rebellion Reconsidered," *Canadian Historical Review* 76, 1 (1995): 1-18.

17 WSRO, PHA 1069, Account of Emigrants sent by Colonel Wyndham to Canada and Australia from Ireland.

18 Bruce S. Elliott, "English," in *An Encyclopedia of Canada's Peoples*, ed. Paul Robert Magosi (Toronto: University of Toronto Press 1999); Robin F. Haines, *Emigration and the Labouring Poor: Australian Recruitment in Britain and Ireland, 1831-60* (Basingstoke, Hampshire: Macmillan 1997), 24-6, 48-52. The work of some Australian historians who have investigated the lives and letters of immigrant labourers is summarized in the continuing series *Visible Immigrants*: Eric Richards, Richard Reid, and David Fitzpatrick, eds., *Visible Immigrants: Neglected Sources for the History of Australian Immigration* (Canberra: Australian National University 1989), and the sequels: *Visible Immigrants, Two: Poor Australian Immigrants in the Nineteenth Century*, ed. Eric Richards (1991); *Visible Immigrants, Three: Home or Away? Immigrants in Colonial Australia*, ed. David Fitzpatrick (1992); *Visible Immigrants, Four: Visible Women: Female Immigrants to Colonial Australia*, ed. Eric Richards (1995); and *Visible Immi-*

grants, Five: The Australian Immigrant in the 20th Century: Searching Neglected Sources, ed. Eric Richards and Jacqueline Templeton (1998).

19 Alan Armstrong, *Farmworkers: A Social and Economic History 1770-1980* (London: BT. Batesford 1988; *The Agrarian History of England and Wales: 1750-1850*, vol. 6, ed. G.E. Mingay (Cambridge: Cambridge University Press 1989).

20 Cameron and Maude, *Assisting Emigration to Upper Canada*, chap 3.

21 WSRO, Goodwood MS 1460, f.112.

22 Elizabeth Jane Errington, *Wives and Mothers, Schoolmistresses and Scullery Maids: Working Women in Upper Canada, 1790-1840* (Montreal and Kingston: McGill-Queen's University Press 1995), chap. 5.

23 As part of our search for first-generation Petworth emigrants and their letters, we have corresponded with a number of their descendants living in the United States. No letters with an American mark came to light, but they will perhaps be found in sources south of the border.

24 PRO, CO 384/41, 352, and MH 12/13060, Petworth Union: both are copies of a chart prepared by Sockett listing sending parishes and numbers of "Emigrants sent out to Canada by the Petworth Emigration Committee." The five parishes were Petworth, Tillington, Northchapel (all well represented), and the two small parishes of Duncton and Egdean. Of the thirteen, our collection includes letter-writers sent by Billinghurst, Felpham and Merston (combined on the list), Kirdford, Lurgashall, Pulborough, Sullington, Sutton, West Grinstead, and Wisborough Green. The other parishes were Coates, Fittleworth, Barlavington, and Storrington.

25 Erickson, *Invisible Immigrants*, 6-7; Fender, *Sea Changes*, 18-20; Dudley Baines, "European Emigration, 1815-1930: Looking at the Emigration Decision Again," *Economic History Review* 47, no. 3 (1994): 525.

26 WSRO, PHA 1068, Sockett to Wyndham, 23 August 1838.

27 Barton, *Letters from the Promised Land*, 4-5, describes a modern editor's considerations in balancing the "typical" with letters selected "with an eye to variety, interest, and appeal to the reader."

28 O'Farrell, *Letters from Irish Australia*, 5.

29 Erickson, *Invisible Immigrants*, 6.

30 Terry Crowley, "Rural Labour," in *Labouring Lives: Work and Workers in Nineteenth-Century Ontario*, ed. Paul Craven (Toronto: University of Toronto Press 1995), 15. J.K. Johnson, "Gerald Craig's *Upper Canada: The Formative Years* and the Writing of Upper Canadian History," and E. Jane Errington. "'And What About the Women?' Changing Ontario's History," *Ontario History* 90, no 2 (1998): 121-2 and 144 are other Canadian authors calling for research in sources which will retrieve the lives of ordinary people in Upper Canada.

31 E.J. Hobsbawm and George Rudé, *Captain Swing* (London: Lawrence and Wishart 1969), 12.

32 Thomas Sokoll, "Old Age in Poverty: The Record of Essex Pauper Letters, 1780-1834," in *Chronicling Poverty: The Voices and Strategies of the English Poor, 1640-1840*, ed. Tim Hitchcock, Peter King, and Pamela Sharp (Houndsmill, Basingstoke: Macmillan 1997).

33 Gary Howells, "'For I was tired of England Sir': English Pauper Emigrant Strategies, 1834-60," *Social History* 23, no 2 (May 1998): 181-94.

34 R.S. Schofield, "Dimensions of Illiteracy in England, 1750-1850," *Explorations in Economic History* 10 (1973), reprinted in *Literacy and Social Development in the West: A Reader*, ed.

Harvey J. Graff (Cambridge: Cambridge University Press 1981); Haines, *Emigration and the Labouring Poor*, 68-76, discusses records of literacy and emigrants to Australia in the 1840s and 1850s.

35 Schofield, "Dimensions," 204 and note 11. To be valid under Lord Hardwick's Marriage Act of 1754, a marriage in England had to be registered in the Anglican registers and signed by the parties and two witnesses. Jews, Quakers, and members of the royal family were exempt. This law was not relaxed for the benefit of Nonconformists until 1839.

36 If available, such evidence is given in a note to the letters. We omitted William Green (97) from this count because of uncertainty whether we had the right William Green.

37 David Vincent, *Literacy and Popular Culture: England, 1750-1914* (Cambridge: Cambridge University Press 1981), 50-1.

38 Flora Thompson, *Larkrise to Candleford* (1st pub in 3 pts, 1839-43; Harmondsworth, Middlesex: Penguin Books 1973), adds nervousness and modesty to the reasons for people who might sign using a mark when they could have written their name.

39 British Parliamentary Papers 1837-38 (658), xx, Pt 2, Second Report of the Select Committee on Postage, Thomas Sockett, 23 May 1838.

40 J.M.R. Cameron *Ambirion's Fire: The Agricultural Colonization of Pre-Convict Western Australia* (Nedland, W. Australia: University of Western Australia Press 1981).

41 G. Poulett Scrope, *Extracts of Letters from Poor Persons who Emigrated Last Year to Canada and the United States* (London 1831).

42 British Parliamentary Papers 1837-38 (658), xx, Pt 2, Second Report on Postage, Sockett, 23 May 1838.

43 Brydone, *Narrative*, 26

44 William Smith, *The History of the Post Office in British North America, 1639-1870* (Cambridge 1920); CR. McGuire, "Mail Transportation in Nineteenth-Century Ontario," *BNA Topics* 39, nos 1-6 (1982); Jane Harrison, *Until Next Year: Letter Writing and the Mails in Canada, 1640-1830* (Waterloo, Ont.: Wilfrid Laurier University Press for the Canadian Postal Museum and the Canadian Museum of Civilization 1997).

45 WSRO, Goodwood MS 1470, f.104, Sockett to Richmond, 5 November 1833. Sockett grumbled at paying 3 shillings and eight pence for a letter that the emigrant agent at Toronto has put in a cover (and perhaps sent through Halifax) for the sake of "official regularity."

46 Upper Canada, House of Assembly, Journal, 1835, Appendix, Bill for the Management and Regulation of the Post Office in Upper Canada. This bill was preceded by an Act of the Imperial Parliament, 24 March 1834, providing for postal revenues to be used in the colonies rather than being sent to Britain, a change that was made 1 January 1836.

47 Smith, *Post Office*, 131-2.

48 Jameson, *Winter Studies*, 2, 220.

49 WSRO, Goodwood MS 1461, f.151, Sockett to Richmond, 6 November 1832; MS 1470, f.104, Sockett to Richmond, 5 November 1833.

50 Fender, *Sea Changes*, 42-3.

51 Terry McDonald, "'Come to Canada While You Have a Chance': A Cautionary Tale of English Emigrant Letters in Upper Canada," *Ontario History*, 91, no 2 (1999): 111-30.

52 PRO, CO384/30, 545, "Copies and Extracts of Letters from the United States of America."

53 PRO, CO 384/30, 545; *Emigration: Letters .. 1833*, vii-viii.

54 WSRO, Goodwood MS 1463, f434, Sockett to Richmond, 12 February 1833.

55 WSRO, Goodwood MS 1406, f98, Sockett to Richmond, 15 October 1832.

56 Petworth Emigration Committee, "Statement," 1833.

57 Frances Hoffman and Ryan Taylor, *Across the Waters: Ontario Immigrants' Experiences, 1820-50* (Milton, Ont.: Global Heritage Press 1999), gathers extracts from many settlers and travellers' accounts.

58 British Parliamentary Papers 1831-32 (724), XXXII, Report of the Emigration Commissioners, 15 March 1832.

59 Eric Richards, *Voices of English and Irish Migrants in Nineteenth-Century Australia, in Migrants, Emigrants, and Immigrants: A Social History of Migration*, ed. Colin Pooley and Ian D. Whyte (London and New York: Routledge 1991).

60 WSRO, Goodwood MS 1474 f.104, Sockett to Richmond, 5 November 1833.

61 British Parliamentary Papers 1837-38 (658), XX, Pt 2, Second Report on Postage, Sockett, 23 May 1838.

62 K.D.M. Snell, *Annals of the Labouring Poor: Social Change and Agrarian England, 1600-1900*, Cambridge Studies in Population, Economy, and Society in Past Time 2 (Cambridge: Cambridge University Press 1985), 9-14; Peter Russell, *Attitudes to Social Structure and Mobility in Upper Canada, 1815-1840: "Here we are Lairds to Ourselves,"* Canadian Studies 6 (Lewistown: Edwin Mellen Press 1990), 88-97.

Sources

LETTERS IN THIS COLLECTION

Private holders of letters in this volume are given in the source line in the text. Archival repositories holding letters printed here are given first in the list below, followed by contemporary published sources, arranged by year of publication, and newspapers. We have not listed single sheets or small pamphlets with one or two printed letters. These are also identified in the source lines if they are the only copies we found.

LETTERS IN ARCHIVES

Archives of Ontario (AO)
F 775 Miscellaneous Collections
MU 2106, 17, Chantler letters, 1832

British Library (BL), *London*
Courtauld Family Letters

West Sussex Record Office (WSRO)
Goodwood Estate Archives
MP 1790, Sarah (Redman) Knight, Diary
Ann Mann's letter

PUBLISHED LETTERS
(listed in order of publication)

Hale, J.C. *Instructions to Persons Intending to Emigrate.* [1832; Petworth: John Phillips 1833? and thereafter].

Emigration: Letters from Sussex Emigrants, Who Sailed from Portsmouth, in April 1832, on Board the Ships, Lord Melville and Eveline, for Upper Canada: Extracts from Various Writers on Emigration to Canada, and from Canadian Newpapers, with References to the Letters: Capt. Hale's Instructions to Emigrants: and a Gazetteer of the Places Named in the Letters. Petworth: John Phillips, and London: Longman 1833; 2nd (shortened) ed. 1833.

[No. 1 to 6] *Continuation of Letters from Sussex Emigrants in Upper Canada for 1833.* Petworth: John Phillips 1833. Published as six eight-page pamphlets plus covers and unnumbered pages, the letters are paginated consecutively from 1 to 48. The New York Public Library has a copy of a publication that brings all six together as *Canada: Letters from Persons Who Have Emigrated to Upper Canada, under the Management of the Petworth Emigration Committee, Written in the Year 1833.* Petworth: John Phillips, and London: Longman 1834.

Petworth Emigration Committee, "Statement," [October 1833]

Letters from the Dorking Emigrants Who Went to Upper Canada, in the Spring of 1832. Ed. Charles
  Barclay. London: J. and A. Arch, Cornhill, and Dorking: Robert Best Ede 1833.

*Emigration: A Letter to a Member of Parliament, Containing a Statement of the Method Pursued by
  the Petworth Committee, in Sending out Emigrants to Upper Canada, in the Years 1832 and 1833.
  And a Plan upon Which the Sums Required for Defraying the Expence of Emigration May Be
  Raised.* [Wolryche Whitmore] Petworth: John Phillips, and London: Longman 1833; 2nd.
  ed. 1834. This publication contains no letters but describes the emigrations of 1832 and
  1833.

*Emigration: Extracts from Various Writers on Emigration, with Authentic Copies of Letters from Emi-
  grants from Norfolk, Suffolk, and Sussex.* Norwich: Bacon and Kinnbrook [1834].

Brydone, James Marr. *Narrative of a Voyage with a Party of Emigrants, Sent out from Sussex, in
  1834, by the Petworth Emigration Committee to Montreal, Thence up the River Ottawa and through
  the Rideau Canal, to Toronto, Upper Canada, and Afterwards to Hamilton; Also of the Journey
  from Hamilton to the Township of Blandford, Where the Families Were Settled; and of a Journey
  through a Large Portion of the London and Gore Districts, with a Map, Shewing the Route, a
  Description of the State of the Country Generally, and the Nature of the Soil; to Which Is Added
  a Comparison of the Route to Upper Canada by Quebec, with That by New York; and Observa-
  tions on the Proper Mode of Fitting out Emigrant Ships.* Petworth: John Phillips, and London:
  Effingham Wilson 1834. Reprinted 1987 as *Voyage of Emigration to Toronto, Canada.*

Continuation of Letters from Sussex Emigrants in Upper Canada, Written in 1836. Petworth: John
  Phillips [1837].

Continuation of Letters from Sussex Emigrants in Upper Canada. Petworth: John Phillips 1837.

Letters from Sussex Emigrants Gone out from the South Side of the Hills to Upper Canada. Chichester: William Hayley Mason 1837.

Letters from Emigrants sent out to Upper Canada by the Petworth Committee in 1832, 1833, and 1837.
  Petworth: John Phillips 1839.

NEWSPAPERS

All likely newspapers were searched for letters, and letters were found in those noted here.

Brighton Gazette and Lewes Observer

Brighton Guardian, Lewes Free Press and Sussex, Surrey, Kent and Hampshire Journal

Brighton Herald or Sussex, Surrey, Hampshire and Kent Advertiser

Brighton Patriot and Lewes Free Press, 1835–6; *Brighton Patriot and South of England Free Press,*
  1836–9

*Portsmouth, Portsea and Gosport Herald, Chichester Reporter, United Service Chronicle and Hants
  and Sussex Advertiser,* 1831–5 [incorporated with the *Hampshire Advertiser*]

Sussex Advertiser, or Lewes and Brighthelmston Journal, 1830–9

A NOTE ON SOURCES

We found letters from Petworth immigrants in a great variety of sources. They exist as manuscripts, in manuscript copies, and in printed form. At the beginning of the project, we published a preliminary list of the names of Petworth emigrants and circulated questionnaires
and requests for information through genealogical and historical societies in England and in

Canada. Our collection of family letters grew from this beginning. Manuscript letters from family collections were often tracked down with the help of several members of the family interested in genealogy. In some cases, letters copied by descendants of an earlier generation now exist only as copies. There are also manuscript letters deposited in public repositories.

Contemporary manuscripts of immigrant letters are not necessarily original. We know that letters were frequently copied privately for circulation – as it is written on one side of the paper only, Ann Mann's (127) may be one such manuscript. The Goodwood Estate Archives holds the largest single collection of copied manuscript letters included here, copies possibly made by Sockett's daughters. Sockett annotated these letters as to the method of transcription and included most of them in his published collections. Sussex newspapers printed immigrant letters quite regularly – some from Petworth immigrants are found only in this source. On occasion, an editor noted that the original or an attested copy might be seen at his office. If newspapers printed a different version of a letter also used by Sockett (and perhaps obtained from him), their version was usually the same or shorter than his. We owe to newspaper editors the probing that led to the publication of letters critical of the administration of the Petworth emigrations.

The largest single source for this book is letters printed, and published in collections, by the Petworth printer, John Phillips. Phillips did all the printing for Sockett's project, including printing letters. The popularity of immigrant letters in England in the 1830s is attested by two collections of Petworth immigrant letters published in addition to those Phillips issued at Petworth: a collection from Dorking, Surrey, in 1833 and another from Chichester, West Sussex, in 1837.

There is no one repository for all of Sockett's publications, but the Canadian Institute for Historical Microreproductions (CIHM) has compiled a good collection on microfiche. The best place to see the actual original publications is, as might be expected, in the West Sussex Record Office (WSRO) at Chichester, where most of the books and pamphlets listed in our sources can be found in the Petworth House Archives (PHA), the Goodwood Estate Archives, or the parish records. Publications sent by Sockett are also at the Public Records Office (PRO) at Kew Gardens in the files of the Colonial Office (CO) and of the Ministry of Health (MH). Copies of one or more of his publications can be found in a number of archives or libraries with a nineteenth-century collection in both Britain and North America.

Where Sockett and Phillips issued the same letter in more than one form, we have tried to cite the one that is easiest to locate. This decision was most difficult with the letters written in 1833 where we have made an exception to our rule of using the source that seems most substantial. In this case, we favoured six pamphlets (*No. 1-6 Continuation*) over a single collection (*Canada: Letters from Persons*). We made reference to the pamphlets because they contain interesting supporting material, such as William Robinson's letter (122), and because five of them are more widely available than a volume which we found in a single source after an extensive search. The exception is *No. 5 Continuation*, which we have not found in a completed version, although we do have the title page and references to it. Sockett's "Statement" on Hale's conduct was issued at much the same time as this pamphlet, but it is not part of the numbered sequence for 1833. In cases where we found letters only in a four-page pamphlet or on a folio sheet printed by Phillips, we have given that as our source and indicated where a copy or copies may be found. We have given more than one source for letters when we found them in a different form or when they were printed in more than one version.

Although Sockett's name appears within his first volume of immigrant letters and in his *Letter to a Member of Parliament*, which are thus often attributed to him, his title pages did not name an author. When his first edition of the letters of 1832 emigrants sold out in December 1833, he had Phillips run off a second edition that had been shortened to include only the introduction and the section containing the letters. He did this to reduce the price in half – to one shilling – in order to make the letters "more generally accessible." When he collected the letters written in 1833 into a single volume stripped of most of the supporting material originally in the pamphlets, he also labelled this volume a second edition. His small pamphlets of four or eight pages and the letters on single sheets are identified as his through the presence of Phillips's name as printer.

Sockett, whose father had been a printer and stationer in London until his business failed, and Phillips developed a distinctive style for presenting immigrant letters. Examples of early productions exist in the files of R.W. Hay, the undersecretary at the Colonial Office who had responsibility for the Canadas (PRO, CO 384/30, 543-66v, with a covering letter from Sockett to [Hay], 22 February 1832, 541-2). In promoting his first emigrations, Sockett had had to rely on the Canada Company for letters from Canada, for example "Letters from Settlers in Upper Canada to their Friends here, containing important practical Information relating to that Country, for the guidance of Emigrants." One example printed by Phillips copied the plain presentation and crowded page of the Canada Company letters: "Copies and Extracts of Letters from the United States of America" (letters of Petworth area emigrants including two from young men who had travelled to Quebec with George and Emily Wells). Phillips' second small pamphlet, "Letters and Extracts of Letters from Swan River," letters from three Petworth area immigrants who went to Australia, looked forward to later publications in its presentation. In it, Phillips used a variety of fonts and spacing to differentiate the text from other elements and to make a more attractive page. The advertisement for material on Upper Canada at the end of this pamphlet was expanded in later publications into a list including a number of recent books approved by Sockett and available from Phillips. Sockett updated this list from one publication to the next.

Authors of Sockett's day were eclectic in their borrowings. In addition to reprinting notices from emigration agents and passages from Canadian newspapers, Sockett included extracts from a number of recent books on Upper Canada to accompany the letters written in 1832 and 1833. Sockett's material was borrowed by Charles Barclay, who obtained four letters from Sussex emigrants in the version sent to the Duke of Richmond and printed them with his *Letters from the Dorking Emigrants* (9, 10, 17, 18), and by the editor of *Emigration: Extracts . . . with Authentic Copies of Letters from Emigrants from Norfolk, Suffolk, and Sussex* (8, 10, 17, 27, 30). The latter book promoted an emigration proposed by Edward Harbord, third Baron Suffield, a friend and correspondent of Richmond, and also included a few of Sockett's extracts from books on Upper Canada, complete with cross-references to immigrant letters that are in Sockett's book but not included here.

BIOGRAPHICAL NOTE

Biographical notes are based on the project files on both sides of the Atlantic. The International Genealogical Index was consulted and genealogical research pursued in the record offices of West Sussex, East Sussex, and, to a more limited extent, Surrey, Cambridgeshire, and Hampshire. London sources include the Public Record Office at Kew, the newspaper library at Colindale, and the Family Records Centre.

North American sources were consulted mainly in the Archives of Ontario, although we had occasionally to go farther afield. They include Upper Canada Land Petitions, Upper Canada Sundries, Crown Land Papers, census returns 1842-71, property registration records, wills and estate files, district census and assessment rolls, district and country marriage collections, civil registrations (mainly deaths), church registers, maps, early newspapers, and cemetry transcriptions of the Ontario Genealogical Society and other groups.

ACKNOWLEDGMENTS

From the time we began investigating the history of the Petworth emigrations and collecting material on the families and individuals involved, we have had an enthusiastic and generous response from individuals and institutions in Canada and England. We owe a great debt to all those who have helped us, from the people working in archives and record offices who have generously shared their knowledge and collections, to the descendants of emigrants who have sent us family histories, letters, photographs, and anecdotes.

The project has been underwritten by the Jackman Foundation and has been part of the Northrop Frye Centre at Victoria University in the University of Toronto. We wish to acknowledge the very generous financial assistance of the Foundation. Eva Kushner at Victoria oversaw the beginnings of the project in her dual role as president of the university and director of the Frye Centre. We are grateful to her and her successors, Roseann Runte at Victoria and Brian Merrilees at the Centre, for a friendly and stimulating academic home for our project. We also thank the staff of the Robarts Library of the University of Toronto and in particular those on whom we made great demands for interlibrary loans and microtexts.

There are some institutions and individuals to whom we appealed time and again, and we should like to acknowledge their help. We cannot name all the individuals who assisted us within public repositories but we are grateful for their knowledge and attention. In England, all the record offices in our research area were helpful – Cambridge County Record Office, East Sussex Record Office, Hampshire County Record Office, Norfolk County Record Office, Surrey County Record Office, Guildford Muniment Room, Isle of Wight Record Office, Wiltshire County Records Office, but we relied most heavily on the West Sussex Record Office and we thank archivist Richard Childs and his predecessor Patricia Gill. Special thanks are due to Alison McCann, the archivist for the Petworth House Archives, and Tim McCann, in charge of the Goodwood Estate Archives, for sharing knowledge beyond their impressive familiarity with these wonderful collections.

Lord Egremont kindly gave us permission to consult and quote from the Petworth House Archives, and Diana Owen has been an able liaison with the National Trust. Quotations from the Goodwood manuscripts are made by courtesy of the Trustees of the Goodwood Collections and with acknowledgments to the West Sussex Record Office and the County Archives. We wish also to acknowledge the assistance of the Brighton Reference Library, the British Library Newspaper Library, Courtauld Institute of Art, Dorking and District Museum, Public Record Office,

Religious Society of Friends (Quakers) Dorking Preparative Meeting, Archives and Special Collections of the Durham University Library, Sussex Archaeological Society, Sussex University Library, Tate Gallery, United Reformed Church, West St, Dorking, and the University College Library of the University of London. Barbara Brydone shared family papers left by her ancestor, James Marr Brydone.

In the United States we thank the Rare Book and Manuscript Library in the Butler Library of Columbia University. In Canada, we relied on help from both local and national institutions, and we would like to acknowledge the assistance of the National Archives of Canada, the Archives of Ontario, the D.B. Weldon Library Regional Collection of the University of Western Ontario, the United Church Archives, the Baldwin Room at the Toronto Reference Library, Queen's University Archives, Kitchener Public Library, Hamilton Public Library, Strathroy Middlesex Museum, Stratford-Perth Archives, Special Collections at the University of Waterloo, and the Wellington County Museum and Archives. Staff and members of the Ontario Genealogical Society, both at the provincial and the branch levels, were of great assistance; in particular, we would like to mention Mary Evans of the Oxford County Branch and Claudia McArthur of the Simcoe County Branch. Sylvia Wray of East Flamborough Archives and Helen Maddock of Lambton County Library went to extra efforts to locate material for us, as did Eleanor Nielsen, Margaret Parsons, and Jane E. Thompson. Dan Walker and Gerry Tordiff helped us with research in the Huron Diocese Archives. We would also like to thank the staff of the Dictionary of Canadian Biography for help with many and sundry questions. Ellen Megannety deserves a special thanks for uncovering some valuable nuggets of information about some of the emigrants.

A number of our colleagues read all or part of our work, shared their own work in progress, or assisted with particular aspects of either history or genealogy. Any errors that remain are our responsibility, but we should like to acknowledge their help in making this a better book. We were most fortunate in having the advice of Professor G.S. French who read and commented on drafts; we owe him a particular debt. We thank the readers for McGill-Queen's University Press for thoughtful comments, as well as Alison McCann and Tim McCann, who read text in addition to the help they gave us as archivists. In addition, we thank Peter Brandon, Clifford Collier, Bruce Elliott, Barry Fletcher, Brian Gilchrist, Gary Howells, Alexandra Johnston, Terry McDonald, Henri Pilon, Guy St Denis, Brian Short, Ryan Taylor, Morley Thomas, and Joan Winearls.

Many other individuals from different walks of life contributed in a variety of ways to our search for Petworth emigrants and their stories – historians, librarians, archivists, genealogists, and interested people researching their families. These contacts were made at various times and places, and we apologize to those who are not mentioned by name. Our correspondence stretched from Great Britain to Australia with stops across Canada and the United States. We wish to acknowledge the assistance of Frances Acres, Rosemary Ambrose, Roy Adsett, Phyllis Alcorn, Shelley Banks, Constance Bayley, Edna Bell, Elizabeth Bloomfield, Robert T. Bell, Mary L. Black,

Shirley Blakely, Eunice M. Brake, William K. Cairns, Arthur J. Capling, Harvey Carver, Kenneth M. Cates, Roger A. Chalwin, Roy Coleman, Ken Cook, Beatrice and Harold Cosens, Ralph D. Courtnage, Ronald E. Cox, Virginia Curulla, John Dennis, Marjorie Dow, Pat Duguid, Yvette H. Dwyer, Edna Featherston, Rachel and Barry Fletcher, Helen Fortney, Elizabeth R. Gillespie, Nancy W. Graden, R.A. Golds, Doris Gray, A.J. Haines, Alfred Haslett, John H., Beth, and Stuart Harwood, Gerald W. Hilman, Elizabeth Hodges, Jean Hodges, Richard Holt, Richard H. Howick, Mavis and Tony Howlett, Patricia Pay Keefe, Helen M. Kerr, Agnes M. Kelcher, Diane Khoury, E. Jack Langstaff, Donna Longhurst, Lyle Longhurst, Sandra and David Longhurst, O.G. Luton, James M. MacDonald, Jeanette Mahler, Margaret Major, Doreen Mann, Grace and Isobel Mann, Sharon Martin, Roy Marvel, H. Roger Miller, June Moffatt, Barbara Monasch, Richard Moon, Nanette Neville, Peter A. Noice, Arnold Orchard, Lesley Parker, Betty Patterson, Janet Pennington, Glenn Racher, John W. Racher, Blake Rapley, Charlotte Rapley, David Rapson, Marjorie Robbins, Dennis Ruhl, Thomas A. Ryerson, Guy St Denis, Virginia Streeter Sande, John Sayers, Mary and Ian Short, R.J. Simmonds, John J. Skilton, Berenice A. Smith, John Ward Smith, Nancy Smith, Claire Stemp, Margaret Stockton, Clifford L. Stott, Helen Stover, S.R. Suter, Sally Swenson, C. William Terry, Wilbert and Doreen Thompson, Maurice and Vera Titmuss, Donald W. Tomlinson, Pat Tripp, Eleanor C. Tuckey, H.E. Turner, H.M. Upton, Lesley and Tony Voice, Heather Wallis, John Ward-Smith, Eileen Whitehead, Jai Williams, W.H. Wilson, and Jane Zavitz.

We would also like to thank the people at McGill-Queen's University Press. Don Akenson and Philip Cercone gave advice and encouragement at various points during the project's history. Joan McGilvray added her deft editorial touch and was always a pleasure to deal with, as were her colleagues at the press. We should like to thank Miriam Bloom who devised an apt and attractive design.

Finally, we should like to thank our families for their support, especially the late Joe Haines for research help and cheerful encouragement to both sides of the Atlantic.

LETTER–WRITERS BY LETTER NUMBER

1 Mrs Sarah Eliza (Cooper) Jones, Quebec, Lower Canada, to her brother, 2 June 1832 / 8

2 James Rapson, Montreal, to his father, Philip Rapson, Lodsworth, Sussex, 4 June 1832 / 8

3 Mrs J. Burchell, Adelaide Township, Upper Canada, [circa June 1832] / 11

4 Stephen Goatcher, en route to Kettle Creek, Upper Canada, to his wife, Elizabeth Burchill, Pulborough, West Sussex, 6 July 1832 / 13

5 Richard Neal, Dundas, Upper Canada, to friends and relations, [Sutton, West Sussex], 20 July 1832 / 16

6 [Jane Payne?, July 1832] / 18

7 Edward and Catharine Boxall, Adelaide Township, Upper Canada, to mother, 28 July 1832 / 20

8 William Cooper, Adelaide Township, Upper Canada, to his father and mother, brothers and sisters, 28 July 1832 / 21

9 William Phillips, Adelaide, Upper Canada, to his father and mother, William and Ellen Phillips, Merston, West Sussex, 28 July 1832 / 22

10 John Luff, Nelson Township, Upper Canada, to the Overseer of Bury, West Sussex, 29 July 1832 / 24

11 John Luff, Nelson Township, Upper Canada, to Aunt Foster, Fittleworth, West Sussex, 29 July 1832 / 25

12 James Rapson, Galt, Upper Canada, to his father, Philip Rapson, Lodsworth, Sussex, August 1832 / 26

13 William Phillips, Ancaster, Upper Canada, to Mrs Newell, 5 August 1832 / 29

14 William Wright, Nelson Township, Upper Canada, to James Wright, his father, near Dorking, Surrey, [circa August 1832] / 30

15 Obed Wilson, Ernest Town, Upper Canada, to his parents, John and Maria Wilson, [Bassingbourn, Cambridgeshire], 5 August 1832 / 31

16 George Hills, Ancaster, Upper Canada, 5 August 1832 / 32

17 George Hills, Ancaster, Upper Canada, to his brother and sister Elizabeth, 6 August 1832 / 33

18 John Stedman, Malahide Township, Upper Canada, to James G. Stedman, Hascomb, Surrey, 7 August 1832 / 34

19 Charlotte (Tribe) Evans, Waterloo Township, Upper Canada, to her brother, Robert Tribe, Dean, near Petworth, Sussex. 18 August 1832 / 36

20 Charlotte and William Willard, Dundas, Upper Canada, to Mrs Maria Wolgar, Charlotte's sister, Milton Street, Dorking, Surrey, 26 August 1832 / 38

21 John Capling, South Easthope Township, Upper Canada, to his brother, Lurgashall, West Sussex, 28 August 1832 / 43

22 Thomas Adsett, Galt, Upper Canada, to his father-in-law, Thomas Scutt, Bignor, near Petworth, West Sussex, 9 September 1832 / 45

23 Simeon Titmouse, Dundas, Upper Canada, to — Jackson, 11 September 1832 / 46

24 William Spencer, Nelson Township, Upper Canada, to his father-in-law, Francis Cooper, Petworth, West Sussex, 16 September 1832 / 48

25 George and Mary Boxall and William Tilley, Nelson Township, Upper Canada, to James Tilley, Petworth, West Sussex, [16 September 1832] / 50

26 William Taylor Upton, Andross [Ardross] Mills, Nelles Settlement, Upper Canada, to George Warren, Petworth, West Sussex, 16 September 1832 / 51

27 William Taylor Upton, Andross [Ardross] Mills, Nelles Settlement, to his mother, Frances Taylor Upton, Petworth, West Sussex, 16 September 1832 / 52

28 Elias Elliot, near Fort George, Upper Canada, to his brother Richard Elliott, Sutton, West Sussex, 24 September 1832 / 54

29 Martin Martin, Guelph, Upper Canada, to Mr Sparks, Felpham, West Sussex, 24 September 1832 / 55

30 Edward Francis Heming, Nyton Farm, near Guelph, Upper Canada, to his mother, Anna Maria (Payne) Hemming, [Bognor, West Sussex], 25 September 1832 / 59

31 Rebecca Longhurst, Little York, Upper Canada, to Mrs Weller, her mother, Cold Harbour, Dorking, Surrey, 4 October 1832 / 60

32 Rebecca Longhurst, Township of Little York, Upper Canada, to Robert Swan, [4 October 1832] / 61

33 George Scott, Trafalgar Township, Upper Canada, to James and Mary Scott, his father and mother, [Dorking, Surrey], 6 October 1832 / 62

34 Cornelius Cosens, Waterloo Township, Upper Canada, to John Bartlett, Dorking, Surrey, 7 October 1832 / 63

35 William Pannell, London District, Upper Canada, to his father and mother, William and Jane Pannell, Kirdford, West Sussex, 14 October 1832 / 64

36 John Allen Tribe, Southwold Township, Upper Canada, to George Fielder, Hambleton House, Godalming, Surrey, 14 October 1832 / 66

37 Ann Thomas, Waterloo Township, Upper Canada, to her father, Thomas Puttock, Stroud Green, Kirdford, West Sussex, 15 October 1832 / 68

38 James Rapson, Galt, Upper Canada, to Philip Rapson, Lodsworth, Sussex, 16 October 1832 / 69

39 Humphrey and Charlotte Cooper, York, Upper Canada, to Mr J. Turner, Fittleworth, West Sussex, 25 October 1832 / 71

40 Henry Smart, Ancaster, Upper Canada, to John and Sarah Baker, his father- and mother-in-law, Kirdford, West Sussex, 5 November 1832 / 73

41 William Baker, [Ancaster, Upper Canada], to his mother, Sarah Baker, Kirdford, West Sussex, [5 November 1832] / 75

42 Frank Nash, Ancaster, Upper Canada, to his mother and father, [Kirdford, West Sussex], [5 November 1832] / 76

43 Henry Smart, Ancaster, Upper Canada, to James and Charles Rapley, Gownfield, West Sussex, [5 November 1832] / 77

44 Henry Smart, Ancaster, Upper Canada, to James Napper, Kirdford, West Sussex, [5 November 1832] / 77

45 Henry Smart, Ancaster, Upper Canada, to the Reverend J.K. Greetham, Kirdford, West Sussex, [5 November 1832] / 78

46 Richard Neal, Dundas, Upper Canada, to his father and mother, William and Abigail Neal, [Sutton, West Sussex], 18 November 1832 / 79

47 Mary Holden, Adelaide Township, Upper Canada, to Sergeant Holden, 2nd Regiment, Tower Hamlets Militia, Light Infantry, London, England, [postmark 21 November 1832] / 80

48 John Worsfold, Hamilton, Upper Canada, to his father and mother, Dorking, Surrey, 15 December 1832 / 83

49 Thomas Adsett, Waterloo Township, Galt Post Office, Upper Canada, to the Reverend Robert Ridsdale, Rector, Northchapel, West Sussex, 21 December 1832 / 87

50 Jesse Penfold, Galt, Upper Canada, to Mr and Mrs Noah Hill, Noah's Ark, Lurgashall, Sussex, 1 January 1833 / 93

51 Stephen Goatcher, Adelaide Township, Upper Canada, to his wife, Elizabeth Burchill, Nash, Pulborough, West Sussex, 17 January 1833 / 95

52 William Cooper, Adelaide Township, Upper Canada, to his brother, Christopher Cooper, Graffham, near Petworth, West Sussex, 5 February 1833 / 97

53 Edward and Catharine Boxall, Adelaide, Upper Canada, to his mother, Widow Boxall, Graffham, near Petworth, West Sussex, 9 February 1833 / 100

54 Henry and Charlotte Tribe, Galt, Upper Canada, to Noah Hill, Noah's Ark, Lurgashall, Sussex, 12 February 1833 / 101

55 Henry Smart, Ancaster, Upper Canada, to James Napper, Kirdford, West Sussex, 1 March 1833 / 103

56 Henry Smart, Ancaster, Upper Canada, to Sarah Baker, [Kirdford, West Sussex], 1 March 1833 / 104

57 Henry Smart, Ancaster, Upper Canada, to Charles Rapley, [Kirdford, West Sussex,] 1 March 1833 / 105

58 Henry Smart, Ancaster, Upper Canada, to his brothers and sisters, [Kirdford, West Sussex], 1 March 1833 / 105

59 Henry Smart, Ancaster, Upper Canada, to the Reverend J.K. Greetham*, Kirdford, West Sussex, 1 March 1833 / 106

60 Henry Smart, Ancaster, Upper Canada, to Charles Street, [Kirdford, West Sussex], 1 March 1833 / 106

61 Thomas Adsett, Waterloo Township, Upper Canada, to friends, 4 March 1833 / 107

62 Thomas Adsett, Waterloo Township, Upper Canada, to father and mother, 4 March 1833 / 107

63 George and Ann Hills, Ancaster, Upper Canada, to Father, Mother, brothers and sisters, [Sullington, West Sussex], 8 March 1833 / 108

64 Charles Haines, [Ancaster, Upper Canada], 8 March 1833 / 110

65 William Baker, Adelaide, Upper Canada, to his father and mother, John and Sarah Baker, and to his brothers and sisters, [Kirdford, West Sussex], 13 March 1833 / 110

66 Ann and Charles Cosens, Waterloo Township, Upper Canada, to her father, mother, and sister, [Dorking, Surrey], 31 March 1833 / 112

67 James S. and William Goldring, York, Upper Canada, to their uncle, Thomas Goldring, South Bersted, West Sussex, 9 April 1833 / 114

68 William Spencer, Nelson Township, Upper Canada, to friends (addressed to his father-in-law Francis Cooper), Montpellier, near Petworth, West Sussex, 6 May 1833 / 117

69 Charles Moore, Blenheim, Waterloo Township, Upper Canada, to his father, William Moore, [Petworth, West Sussex], [circa June 1833] / 119

70 Extract from a letter by Rhoda Thair, Montreal, 22 June [1833] / 120

71 Thomas Adsett, Galt, Dumfries Township, Upper Canada, to his father, Thomas Adsett, Northchapel, West Sussex, 25 June 1833 / 121

72 Elizabeth (Nash) Wackford, Waterloo Township, Upper Canada, to Mrs Sarah Green, Petworth, West Sussex, 25 June 1833 / 124

73 Elizabeth (Nash) Wackford, Waterloo Township, Upper Canada, to her father and mother, Richard and Massey Nash, and friends, [Petworth, West Sussex, 25 June 1833] / 125

74 Extract from a letter of William Phillips Sr, Adelaide Township, Upper Canada, [summer] 1833 / 126

75 Extract of a letter from Mary Barnes, York, Upper Canada, July 1833 / 128

76 James Rapson, Galt, Upper Canada, to his father Philip Rapson, Lodsworth, Sussex, 9 July 1833 / 129

77 Extract of a letter from John Saunders, York, Upper Canada, 11 July 1833 / 131

78 Rhoda and George Thair to Philip Rapson, Lodsworth, Sussex, 13 July 1833 / 132

79 William and Elizabeth Daniels, Wilmot Township, Upper Canada, to brothers and sisters, addressed to Mr George Sharp, Petworth, West Sussex, 14 July 1833 / 135

80 Henry Habbin, York, Upper Canada, 17 July 1833 / 137

81 Henry Habbin, York, Upper Canada, to his mother, Petworth, West Sussex, 17 July 1833 / 137

82 Edward and Hannah Bristow, Woolwich Township, Upper Canada, to his brother, Shipley, West Sussex, 20 July 1833 / 138

83 James and Hannah Tilley, Nelson Township, Upper Canada, to friends and neighbours, [addressed to Thomas Lucas, Red Lion Yard,] Petworth, West Sussex, 29 July 1833 / 140

84 [James and Hannah Tilley to friends and neighbours] Continued. / 143

85 John and Caroline Dearling, Galt, Upper Canada, to her father, John Francis, Lickfold, Lodsworth, West Sussex, 30 July 1833 / 144

86 Edmund Sharp, Sandwich, Upper Canada, 11 August 1833 / 145

87 George Carver, London, Upper Canada, to his father and mother, James and Sarah Carver, Bignor, West Sussex, 18 August 1833 / 148

88 James Parker, Adelaide Township, Upper Canada, to [Harvey Whitington, Pulborough, West Sussex,] 1 September 1833 / 149

89 William Moore and James Moore, Thorold Township, Upper Canada, to William Moore, Petworth, West Sussex, 5 September 1833 / 151

90 James Helyer, Toronto Township, Upper Canada, to Peter Scovell, Haslemere, Surrey, 29 September 1833 / 152

91 John and Elizabeth White, Guelph, Upper Canada, to his father, Edward White, and mother, Lurgashall, West Sussex, 27 October 1833 / 153

92 William Baker, Delaware Township, Upper Canada, to his mother and father, John and Sarah Baker, Kirdford, West Sussex, 3 November 1833 / 155

93 John Holden, Delaware Township, Upper Canada, to Thomas and Sophia Holden, his father and mother, 6 November 1833 / 157

94 Extract of a letter from Henry Harwood, Blandford (Woodstock), Upper Canada, [1834] / 163

95 George Carver, Delaware Township, Upper Canada, to his father and mother, James and Sarah Carver, Bignor, West Sussex, 30 June 1834 / 165

96 Henry Heasman, Blandford (Woodstock), Upper Canada, to his father, Henry Heasman Sr, sisters, and brothers, West Grinstead, West Sussex, 19 October 1834 / 166

97 Extract of a letter from William Green, Blandford (Woodstock), Upper Canada, recipient unknown, 20 October 1834 / 168

98 William Voice, Blandford (Woodstock), Upper Canada, to his sister, Mary Elliot, Ashington, West Sussex, 27 October 1834 / 169

99 Joseph and Ann Webb, St Catharines, Upper Canada, to his father, William Webb, brothers, and sisters, Felpham, West Sussex, 11 January 1835 / 178

100 John and Ann Gamblen, Blandford (Woodstock), Upper Canada, to Daniel King, Brighton, East Sussex, 18 February 1835 / 180

101 Cornelius and Elizabeth Voice, Blandford (Woodstock), Upper Canada, to brother and sister, 20 September 1835 / 183

102 Frank Mellish, Thornhill, Upper Canada, to his father, William Mellish, and his mother, Walberton, West Sussex, 8 November 1835 / 187

103 George Coleman, Woodstock, Upper Canada, to Mr J. Marten, Rodmell, East Sussex, 17 December 1835 / 188

104 John and Ruth Waldon, St Catharines, Upper Canada, to friends, [James Cooper], Tillington, West Sussex, 9 January 1836 / 194

105 Timothy Trussler, Plympton Township, Upper Canada, to William Luff, Farnhurst Cross, Sussex, 8 February 1836 / 198

106 Edward Longley, Guelph, Upper Canada, to William Mitchell, Heene, West Sussex, 28 September 1835 and 20 March 1836 / 200

107 Mary and Edmund (Edward) Birch (Burch), George St, Thornhill, Upper Canada, to his uncle, George Burch, and his aunt, 13 April 1836 / 204

108 William Hewitt, Woodstock, Upper Canada, to his father and mother, William and Elizabeth Hewitt, Cocking, West Sussex, 6 July 1836 / 205

109 George Older, Hamilton, Upper Canada, to John Drewitt, Little Peppering, Burpham, West Sussex, 7 July 1836 / 207

110 John Ayling, Yonge Street, Thornhill, Upper Canada, to William and Mary Ayling, his father and mother, Walberton, West Sussex, 24 July 1836 / 207

111 John and Caroline (Francis) Dearling, Waterloo Township, Upper Canada, to Thomas Francis, Lodsworth, Sussex, 24 July 1836 / 209

112 James and Ann Woods, Woodstock, Upper Canada, to mother and father, 10 August 1836 / 212

113 David Clowser Sharp, Sandwich (Windsor), Upper Canada, to his sister, Mary Ward, 21 August 1836 / 213

114 John and James Moore, Sandwich (Windsor), Upper Canada, to friends and relations, [21 August 1836] / 215

115 Extract of a letter from James Rapson, Waterloo Township, Upper Canada, 30 August 1836 / 215

116 John Barnes, Toronto, Upper Canada, to his father, brothers, and sisters (addressed to Robert Haslett), Petworth, West Sussex, 4 September 1836 / 217

117 John Denman, East Flamborough Township, Upper Canada, to William Booker, Billingshurst, West Sussex, 4 September 1836 / 221

118 Luke Joyes (Joice), Nelson Township, Upper Canada, to his father and mother, [Billingshurst, West Sussex], 4 September 1836 / 222

119 George and Lydia Hilton, Toronto, Upper Canada, to brother, Henry Hilton, and
    mother and sisters, Bignor, West Sussex, 10 September 1836 / 223

120 George and Mary Hills, West Flamborough Township, Upper Canada, to John Drewitt,
    Peppering, West Sussex, 18 September 1836 / 227

121 Mary and George Boxall, Nelson Township, Upper Canada, to his father, William Box-
    all, mother, brothers and sisters, Farnhurst near Haslemere, West Sussex, 25 September
    1836 / 229

122 William Robinson, Delaware Township, Upper Canada, to the Reverend Thomas
    Sockett, Petworth, West Sussex, 14 October 1836 / 230

123 Alexander Hilton, Delaware Township, Upper Canada, to his uncle, Henry Hilton, and
    his aunt, Bignor, West Sussex, 16 October 1836 / 233

124 William and Sarah Jackman, Brantford, Upper Canada, to their son, Stephen, [Goring,
    West Sussex,] 29 October 1836 / 235

125 William Spencer, Bronte, Upper Canada, to his father and mother, 10 November
    1836 / 238

126 John Barnes, Toronto, Upper Canada, to his father, brother and sisters, [Petworth, West
    Sussex,] 1 January 1837 / 246

127 Ann Mann, Adelaide Township, Upper Canada, to her sons, Henry and George Mann,
    and friends, [Wisborough Green, West Sussex,] 2 January 1837 / 251

128 William Courtnage, Niagara District, Upper Canada, to his brother and sisters,
    10 January 1837 / 255

129 Ann Courtnage, Niagara District, Upper Canada, to John Randall, Farnhurst, West
    Sussex, [10 January 1837] / 257

130 Author unknown, Toronto, Upper Canada, 25 October 1837 / 258

131 Richard and Frances Pullen to sister and brother [Ann and John Summersell,
    Petworth, West Sussex], 9 September 1837 / 260

132 Elizabeth (Pullen) Hooker and Ann and John Summersell, Petworth, Sussex, to
    Richard and Frances Pullen, Delaware, Upper Canada, 22 April 1838 / 267

133 James Cooper, Adelaide Township, Upper Canada, to family and friends, c/o James
    Cooper, Graffham, West Sussex, 26 May 1838 / 270

134 John and Caroline Dearling, Waterloo Township, Upper Canada, to brothers and sisters
    (addressed to John Francis), Lodsworth, West Sussex, 15 July 1838 / 276

135 Charles Rapley, Adelaide Township, Upper Canada, to his family, [Kirdford, West
    Sussex,] 14 October 1838 / 278

136 Richard and Frances Pullen, Delaware Township, Upper Canada, to Ann and John
    Summersell, and Elizabeth Hooker, Petworth, West Sussex, 31 December 1838 / 281

137 [Richard and Frances Pullen, to Elizabeth Hooker] To her mother. / 283

138 Author unknown, West Flamborough Township, Upper Canada, to her uncle and aunt,
    17 January 1839 / 284

139 Elizabeth (Pullen) Hooker and Ann and John Summersell, Petworth, West Sussex, to
    Richard and Frances Pullen, Delaware, Upper Canada, 4 April 1839 / 288

140 William Phillips, Galt, Upper Canada, to his brother, Thomas Phillips Jr, of Singleton,
    West Sussex, 14 July 1839 / 293

141 Charles and Ann Cosens, Blenheim Township, Upper Canada, to her father and
    mother, [Dorking, Surrey], 28 September 1839 / 295

142 James and Sarah Lannaway (Lanaway), Woodstock, Upper Canada, to William Thorp,
    Petworth, West Sussex, 24 September 1840 / 297

143 Thomas Trussler, Bexleyhill, West Sussex, to George Trussler, Waterloo Township, Upper Canada, 10 August 1863 / 299

144 Thomas Trussler, Bexleyhill, West Sussex, to George Trussler, Waterloo Township, Ontario, 22 November 1879 / 300

145 Maria Wilson, Bassingbourn, Cambridgeshire, to Obed Wilson, Mariposa Township, Upper Canada, 9 August 1838 / 307

146 Maria Wilson, Bassingbourn, Cambridgeshire, to Obed Wilson, Mariposa Township, Upper Canada, 22 August 1839 / 309

147 Maria Wilson, Bassingbourn, Cambridgeshire, to Obed Wilson, Upper Canada, 21 June 1841 / 311

148 Maria Wilson, Bassingbourn, Cambridgeshire, to Obed Wilson, East Whitby Township, Canada West, 21 September 1848 / 312

149 Frances Ann Hall, Broadwater, Elizabeth Crabtree, Mary Ann Muncey, Kneesworth, and Maria Wilson, North End, Bassingbourn, Cambridgeshire, to Obed Wilson and his wife Betsy Maria, East Whitby Township, Upper Canada, written between 19 and 26 March 1855 / 313

150 Maria Wilson, Bassingbourn, Cambridgeshire, to Obed Wilson, East Whitby Township, Canada West, 4 May 1859 / 316

151 Maria Wilson, Bassingbourn, Cambridgeshire, Emma Muncey, Hoops, Kneesworth, and Henry Hall, London, to Obed Wilson, East Whitby Township, Canada West, 7 November 1859 and 12 January 1860 / 317

152 John E. Wilson, Udora, Ontario, to Obed Wilson, East Whitby Township, Ontario, 20 October 1873 / 319

153 Fanny Hall, The Roebuck Inn, Broadwater, Hertfordshire, to Obed Wilson, Upper Canada, 8 March 1875 / 320

154 Mary Ann Muncey, Hoops, Kneesworth, Cambridgeshire, to Obed Wilson, Upper Canada, 27 March 1876 / 321

155 William Hall, Buffalo, New York, to Obed Wilson, East Whitby Township, Ontario, 27 November 1880 / 323

156 Fanny Shore, Bassingbourn, Cambridgeshire, to Obed Wilson, East Whitby Township, Ontario, 28 June 1881 / 324

157 Emma (Muncey) Hall, Bassingbourn, Cambridgeshire, to Obed Wilson, Raglan Post Office, Whitby East, Canada West, 28 June 1881 / 325

158 Mary Ann Muncey, Kneesworth, to Obed Wilson, East Whitby Township, Ontario, 29 August 1881 / 326

159 Mary Ann Muncey, Kneesworth, Cambridgeshire, to Obed and Betsy Wilson, East Whitby Township, Ontario, 19 February 1883 / 326

160 [Elizabeth Crabtree?], London, to [Charles M. Wilson], Epsom, Ontario, 1 September [1884] / 328

161 Mary Ann Muncey, Bassingbourn, Cambridgeshire, to Obed Wilson, East Whitby Township, Ontario, 8 August 1887 / 329

162 Emma Hall, [Bassingbourn, Cambridgeshire], to Obed Wilson, East Whitby Township, n.d. [1887?] / 330

163 William H. Hall, Bassingbourn, Cambridgeshire, to Obed Wilson, Ontario, 18 January 1889 / 330

164 Emma (Muncey) Hall, Bassingbourn, Cambridgeshire, to Obed Wilson, Whitby Township, Ontario, 20 January 1889 / 333

165 [Joseph R.] Chantler, London, England, to William Nathaniel Chantler, Dorking, Surrey, 21 November 1830 / 337

166 John Chantler, Newmarket, Upper Canada, to Joseph Chantler and wife, London, 27 July 1832 / 344

167 Joseph R. Chantler, [London], to William Nathaniel Chantler, Dorking, Surrey, [September 1832] / 350

168 Joseph R. Chantler, London, England, to John Chantler, Newmarket, Upper Canada, 30 November 1832 / 354

169 John Chantler, Newmarket, Upper Canada, to William Nathaniel Chantler, Dorking, Surrey, September 1832 / 359

170 Arthur Gravely, Chichester, West Sussex, to William Chantler, Dorking, Surrey, 21 August 1836 / 364

171 Henry Chantler, Newmarket, Canada West, to Joseph Chantler and wife Mary Ann Millard, 12 November 1846 / 368

172 John Chantler, Innisfil Township, Canada West, to his niece Eliza, 15 March 1863 / 370

173 Memoir by Esther (Chantler) Dennis for her children, written about 1896 / 371

174 Frederick Hasted, Dairy Farm, Adelaide Township, Upper Canada, 7 February 1834 / 382

175 Frederick Hasted, London, Upper Canada, to Henry Ayling, Treyford, near Midhurst, Sussex, 15 December 1839 / 384

176 George and Emily Wells, York, Upper Canada, to Miss Wells, Walberton, West Sussex, 7 February 1832 / 391

177 James Knight, Nelsonville, Ohio, to unknown recipient, West Sussex, 29 August 1832 / 393

178 James Knight, Nelsonville, Ohio to George Courtauld (II), 15 December 1832 / 395

179 Sarah (Redman) Knight, Nelsonville, Ohio, extract from her journal for 1832 / 396

180 Charles Adsett, Autobiography, written after 1874, probably at Guelph, Ontario / 398

LETTER-WRITERS BY PLACE OF ORIGIN

Letter-writers and letter numbers are listed below according to the writer's place of origin. The list is divided into two. The first covers the letters in sections 1832 to 1837, and 1838 and After and is organized by emigrant's parish of settlement. The second covers the section Additional Correspondence and Memoirs and is organized by address or location. Letters or memoirs not included in this listing can be found in an explanatory note at its end.

I 1832 TO 1837, 1838 AND AFTER

Most of these emigrants were assisted by the parish in which they had a legal settlement. Some, such as Edward and Catherine Boxall, may have been living away from their parish of settlement when they emigrated.

CAMBRIDGESHIRE
Bassingbourn
Wilson, Obediah 15
Titmouse, Simeon 23

SURREY
Chapel
Longhurst, Rebecca 31, 32

Chiddingfold
Tribe, John Allen 36

Dorking
Wright, William 14
Willard, Charlotte and
  William 20
Scott, George 33
Cosens, Cornelius 34
Worsfold, John 48
Cosens, Ann and
  Charles 66, 141

Hascomb
Stedman, John 18

Haslemere
Helyer, James 90

SUSSEX
Arundel
Burchell, Mrs J. 3
Hilton, George and
  Lydia 119

Ashington
Haines, Charles 64

Billingshurst
Voice, William (son of
  Cornelius) 98
Voice, Cornelius 101
Denman, John 117
Joyes, Luke 118

Brighton
Gamblen, John and Ann 100

Burpham
Hills, George and Mary 120

Burton
Cooper, William 8, 52

Bury
Luff, John 10, 11

Climping
Walden, John and Ruth 104

Cocking
Hewitt, William 108

Felpham
Martin, Martin 29
Webb, Joseph and Ann 99

Fernhurst
Boxall, George and
  Mary 25, 121
Trussler, Timothy
  (son of John) 105, 105
Courtnage, William 128, 129

Goring
Jackman, William and
  Sarah 124

Heene
Longley, Edward 106

Kirdford
Pannell, William 35
Thomas, Ann 37

Smart, Henry 40–45, 55–60
Baker, William 41, 65, 92
Nash, Frank 42
Holden, Mary 47

Lewes (and Kingston by Lewes)
Harwood, Henry 94
Coleman, George 103

Lodsworth
Rapson, James 2, 12, 38, 76,
    115
Thair, Rhoda 70, 78
Dearling, John and
    Caroline 85, 111, 134

Lurgashall
Evans, Charlotte (Tribe) 19
Capling, John 21
Penfold, Jesse 50
Tribe, Henry and
    Charlotte 54
Saunders, John 77
White, John and Elizabeth 91

Merston
Phillips, William Jr 9
Phillips, William Sr 74

Northchapel
Adsett, Thomas 22, 49, 61,
    62, 71
Pullen, Richard and
    Frances 131, 136, 137

Petworth
Boxall, Edward and
    Catherine 7, 53
Spencer, William 24, 68, 125
Upton, William Taylor 26, 27
Moore, Charles 69
Wackford, Elizabeth
    (Nash) 72, 73
Habbin, Henry 80, 81
Tilley, James and
    Hannah 83, 84
Sharp, Edmund 86
Moore, William and James 89
Sharp, David 113
Moore, John and James 114
Barnes, John 116, 126
Lannaway, James and
    Sarah 142

Pulborough
Goatcher, Stephen 4, 51
Green, William 97
Parker, James 88

Shipley
Bristow, Edward and
    Hannah 82

Singleton
Phillips, William 13, 140

South Bersted
Goldring, James S. and
    William 67

Sullington
Hills, George 16, 17, 63

Sutton
Neal, Richard 5, 46
Elliott, Elias 28
Carver, George 87, 95
Hilton, Alexander 123

Tillington
Cooper, Humphrey and
    Charlotte 39
Barnes, Mary 75
Daniels, William and
    Elizabeth 79
Woods, James and Ann 112
Cooper, James 133

Walberton
Mellish, Frank 102
Birch, Mary and Edward 107
Ayling, John 110

Washington
Holden, John 93

West Grinstead
Heasman, Henry 96

Wisborough Green
Older, George 109
Mann, Ann (wife of
    Samuel) 127
Rapley, Charles 135

II ADDITIONAL CORRESPONDENCE AND MEMOIRS

Letters are arranged by address of the letter-writer.

ENGLAND
CAMBRIDGESHIRE
Bassingbourn
Hall, Emma (Muncey) 157,
    162, 164
Hall, William H. 163
Muncey, Mary Ann 161
Shore, Fanny 156
Wilson, Maria 145–8; 150, 151

Broadwater
Hall, Frances Ann et al 149
    (Fanny) 153

Kneesworth
Muncey, Mary Ann 154,
    158, 159

LONDON, ENGLAND
Chantler, Joseph R 165,
    167, 168
[Crabtree, Elisabeth] 160

SUSSEX
Bexley Hill, West Sussex
Trussler, Thomas 143, 144

Chichester
Gravely, Arthur 170

UPPER CANADA /
CANADA WEST /
ONTARIO
Adelaide Township
Hasted, Frederick 174

Innisfil Township
Chantler, John 172

Guelph
Adsett, Charles 180

Newmarket
Chantler, John 166, 169
Chantler, Henry 171

London, Upper Canada
Hasted, Frederick 175

Udora
Wilson, John E. 152

York (Toronto)
Wells, George and Emily
    176

UNITED STATES
Buffalo, New York
Hall, William 155

Nelsonville, Ohio
Knight, James 177, 178
Knight, Sarah 179

LETTERS NOT INCLUDED

Sarah Elizabeth (Cooper) Jones, 1, was a cabin passenger whose place of origin is unknown.
Jane Payne, Edward Heming's aunt and the probable author of 6, wrote from England.
Edward Francis Heming, 30, was a cabin passenger from Bognor, Sussex.
William Robinson, 122, wrote from Delaware Township, Upper Canada, as a prospective
    employer.
Unknown writers sent 130 and 138.
Hooker, Elizabeth (Pullen), 132 and 139, wrote from Petworth, Sussex.
Esther (Chantler) Dennis 173 did not give a date or place for her memoir. She spent most
    of her life in rural areas north of Toronto.

INDEX

This index reflects the language of the letters and should be consulted with that in mind: for example, most instances of childbirth will be found listed under the term confinement. A □ indicates that the number following refers to a letter number.

Abel, Christopher, 63n140
Abinger Mill, 336
able-bodied immigrants: aid to reduced, 194, 411
accident, 76, 238
Adams, Frances, *see* Rapley
Adelaide, 66, 73n161, 82, 92, 96n10, 104n28, 120n59, 133, 223, 225, 234, 235, 267, 271, 274n27, 279; emigrants, 387n7; militia, 169, 267, 388, 389
Adelaide settlement, xxiii, 68, 69, 100, 103n25, 126, 166, 169, 178, 227, 251, 254, 266, 381
Adelaide Township, xlii, 4, 7, 64, 66, 97, 98, 101, 156, 177, 194n3, 198n11, 233, 244, 252, 255, 394, 387, 388, 389, 409, 411, 412; letter from, 11, 20, 21–2, 80, 95, 97, 100, 110, 126, 149, 251, 270, 278
adoption, 122n61, 398
Adsett, Charles, xxv, xliii, 45, 46, 87, 107, 121, 122, 126, □ 180 (398–402)
Adsett, Elizabeth (Hough), 401
Adsett, Emma, 45, 46, 87n189, 121, 122
Adsett, Harriet, 45, 46
Adsett, John, 402
Adsett, Matilda (Penfold), 93, 123, 216
Adsett, Sarah, 45, 87n189, 121, 122
Adsett, Sarah (Scutt), 45, 46, 70, 398
Adsett, Sarah Jane (Kirkland), 400, 402
Adsett, Thomas (father), 121
Adsett, Thomas, xxix, xxx, 45,

□ 22 (45–6), □ 49 (87–8), □ 60 (107), □ 62 (107–8), □ 71 (121–4), 126, 216, 278, 398
Adsett family, 4
agricultural labourer, 167, 204, 205, 207, 221, 222, 251; definition of, xxiv
agriculturalist: wages reported in New York, 352
ague, 47, 54, 65n143, 67, 77n170, 83, 112, 240
aid: to immigrants, 92
Albany, 350
Albright, Joseph, 357
Albury, sending parish, 38
Allen, William, 358
American settlers, 7
American-born population, 266
Amherstburg, 214, 267, 280, 280n36, 389; action at, 272
Ancaster, 7, 48, 111, 118, 164, 294, 410; letter from, 29, 32, 73, 75, 76, 77, 78, 103, 104, 105, 106, 108, 110
Andrews, Mrs, 143
Andross (Ardross) Mills, 51, 52, 53
Anglican minister, 66n152
Angmering, 157, 207n24, 225n76, 234
animals, domestic, 28, 33, 39, 59, 172, 183, 185, 189, 198, 199, 202, 225, 228, 234, 252, 255, 271, 277, 283; sent to George Sockett, 201; *see also* calves, cows, cattle, dogs, fowl, hogs, horses, oxen, sheep
animals, wild, 18, 20, 41, 66, 70, 78, 85, 90, 94, 98, 101, 118, 156, 173, 203; *see also* hunting,

bears, deer, game, ground hogs, hares, porcupines, rabbits, racoons, squirrels
anker (cask), 214n44
Anne (schooner), 280n36
Anticosti, 10
apples, 48, 70, 98, 118, 199, 217
apprentice, 206, 323, 399; to blacksmith, 31, 138, 164, 274; to butcher, 129, 273; to cabinet maker, 274; to carpenter, 223, 247; conditions, 167; to tailor, 274; to tanner, 107, 121; at Toronto, 160; to weaver, 87n188
apprentice fee, 52
apprenticeship, xxv, 53, 117, 331, 337; terms, 399; in Upper Canada, 25, 25n48
Armitage, Ann (Phillips), 376
Armitage, Jane, *see* Taylor
Armitage, Seth, 376
army pension, 213; army pensioner, 146, 272n19
artisans, work for, 178
artist, 390
Arundel, West Sussex, 226, 381, 410; party from, 11; sending parish, 223
ashery, 140
Ashington, West Sussex, 110, 186n17; letter to, 169
assistance: to emigrate, 110, 183, 227, 235, 350n17; from parish, 260; for travelling, 92; through winter, 27; *see also* emigration, parish-assisted emigration
assistant poor law commissioner, 193, 245, 411

assisted emigration, 258, 265; solution to overpopulation, 342n3

asthma, 300

Athens County, Ohio, 397

attitudes: class, 165, 167; to emigration, 183; social, 33, 35, 40–1, 87, 165, 172, 195, 205; to work, xxiv; see also Upper Canada

Aurora, 377

Austin, Reverend John, 16

Australia, 217, 259n18, 412; and government-assisted passage, xxiv

author unknown, □ 130 (258–60), □ 138 (284–8)

autobiography, 398

axes, 65, 237; see also tools

Ayling, Henry, 208, 384

Ayling, J. (in England), 188

Ayling, John, 188, □ 110 (207–9)

Ayling, Mary, 207

Ayling, Mr, 136

Ayling, William, 192, 207

Bachelor, Benjamin, 65, 155, see also Batchelor

bachelors, 203

bacon, 51, 74, 111, 116; for sea-sickness, 196

badger's hair softener, 85

bailiff, working as, 128

bake kettle, 376

Baker, Amanda, 156

Baker, Charles, 156

Baker, Dame, 283, 282, 289

Baker, Frederick, 111

Baker, Henry, 37

Baker, Jane, see Smart

Baker, Jane, 269, 270

Baker, John (father of William), 73, 110, 155

Baker, John, 65

Baker, Martha, 75

Baker, Sarah, 73, 75, 104, 110, 155

Baker, Thomas, 65, 76, 77, 110

Baker, William, 65, 73, □ 41 (75–6), 104, □ 65 (110–12), □ 92 (155–6)

baker and confectioner, 195n4

bakery, 157

Baldwin, Joseph, 377

Baldwin, William, 399

Baldwin and Jackson, 399

ball room, 115

Balls Cemetery, 131, 217

Balsam Lake, 176

Banks of Upper and Lower Canada, 349

Baptist, 48, 68, 131, 217

Barclay, Charles, 30, 34, 42, 62n136, 409

barges, 222, as shelter, 361, 348

Barlavington, near Sutton, 226n80

barley, 44, 109, 111, 125, 148, 150, see also crops

Barlow (chief mate Lord Melville), 8

Barlton, 226

barn, 57, 98, 199; emigrants housed in, 162, 171, 348, 361; raising, 165

Barnes, Charlotte (Woodford), 217, 246

Barnes, Ellen, 217, 219, 249

Barnes, Emma, 217, 219, 247, 249

Barnes, Henry (son of John), 217, 218, 219, 220, 247

Barnes, Henry, 219, 248

Barnes, John, xxxiv, 192, 194, 226, □ 116 (217–20), □ 126 (246–50)

Barnes, John Jr, 217, 219, 248

Barnes, Mary (from Tillington), 11

Barnes, Mary, 95n8, □ 75 (128–9), 154, 273

Barnes, William, 95, 101, 128

Barnes family, 246

Barnet's Mills, 218

Barns, Benjamin, 65

barracks, built at London, Upper Canada, 386; for emigrants, 396

Barrie, 379

Barrington, 331

barter, 29

Bartlett, John, 63

Base Line Church, 131, 217

Bassam, J., 163n2

Bassingbourn, Cambridgeshire, 46, 305, 306, 310n5, 311, 331; emigrants from, 32; letter from, 307, 309, 312, 316, 317, 324, 329, 325, 330, 333, 405–7; letter to, 31; vicar of, 47

Batchelor, see also Bachelor

Batchelor, Matthew, 156

batteaux, 13, 131, 347, 409; see also travel inland

Battle of the Windmill, 266

Bay of Biscay, 9, 345

Bays, James, 118

beans, 70, 125

Bear Creek, 20, 98, 225

bears, 70, 85, 98, 104, 101, 118, 134, 156; see also animals, wild

Beasley, Richard, 209, 210

Beasley's Lower Block, 278

Beasley's new survey, 95; old survey, 209

Beasley's Tract, Waterloo Township, 123

beds and bedding, 98, 100, 150, 248

beef, 44, 47, 51, 57, 61, 73, 85, 86, 94, 99, 111, 123, 124, 135, 148, 154, 236

beer, 85, 111, 123, 134, 147, 148; and cider, 94; lack of, 34, 46, 172, 350

beet, variety of, 100n18

beggars: lack of, 34, 88

Belchamber, Aunt: literate, 253

Belchamber, James, 252n7

Belchamber, Jane (Downer), 252n7

Beldam, Charles: sponsor, 32, 32n66

Belfast, Ireland, 316, 318

Belgium: unrest, 337

Bell, Mary, see Thomas

benevolence, 178, 410

bent seed, 65, 111

Berry, Edward, 255, 256, 257

Berry, Emma (Curtis), 133n74, 217n56

Berry, George, 133

Berry, Isaac, 133, 133n74, 216

berths: collapse of on Lord Melville, 4, 11, 61, 82

Betchel, John, 87n188, 107, 121, 399

Bettridge, William Craddock, 185n16

Bevan, Jim, 367

Beverly Township, 48, 86, 322n27; swamp, 4, 398

Bexleyhill, West Sussex: letter from, 299, 300

Bible, 290, 296

Bible record, 402

Bible Society, 342

Bickerstaff (Biggerstaff) House, 396, 397

Biddulph, Ann, *see* Rapley

Bidmad, Samuel, 359

Bidwell, Marshall Spring, 388

Biggs, T., 214

Bignor, West Sussex, 46n102; letter to, 45, 148, 165, 223, 233

bilious fever, 65n144, 79, 106

bill (billhook), 65n145

Billingshurst, West Sussex, 187, 268; emigrants, 221n63; letter to, 221, 222; parish church, 170n10; sending parish, 184, 221

Birch, Charles, 204

Birch (Burch), Edmund (Edward), □ 107 (204–5), 208

Birch, Edmund Jr, 188n19, 204, 205

Birch, Emma, 204

Birch, Frances (Viney), 188, 188n21, 205

Birch, George, 204, 205

Birch, James, 188, 188n19, 204, 205

Birch, Mary (Caiger), □ 107 (204–5), 208

Birch, Mary Ann, 204

Birch, Mr, 164

Birch, William, 204

Bird, Sally, 315

birds: game, 17, 20, 46, 65, 70, 85, 94, 98, 101, 110, 115, 134, 156, 180; *see also* hunting

Birmingham reap hooks, 199

births, 11, 160, 170; on shipboard, 8, 42, 250; still birth, 289

biscuit, 58, 61

Bishop, Mr, assisted Luff, 25

black man, 156

Blackdown, 412

Blackman, George, 205

blacksmith, 63, 67, 95, 167, 206

blacksmithing, 63, 256

Blandford (Woodstock), 171, 185, 201, 206, 409; letter from, 163, 166, 168, 169, 180, 183

Blandford Township, 180, 207, 293n54, 409, 412; description of, 163

blankets, 78, 98; *see also* bedding

Blenheim Township, 38, 45, 123, 296, 297, 400; letter from, xxiv, 119, 295

Bloes, Elizabeth, 48n106

Bloes, Isaac, 48n106

Bloes, William, 47, 48, 48n106

boatmen, 127; flee river, 363

Bognor, 58, 60

Bognor, West Sussex: letter to, 59

Bognor Lodge, 19

Bognor Park, 383

bonnet makers, 287; *see also* milliners

Booker, George, 208

Booker, Jane, *see* Capling

Booker, Lydia, *see* Hilton

Booker, William, 221

books, 344; and tracts, 350

boot and shoe maker, 154

boots and shoes, 155, 172, 181; Wellingtons, 72, 155; *see also* shoes

border raids, 266

Boswell, Charlotte, *see* Cooper

Botting, William, 173

bowel complaint, 145, 251, 349

Bowley, William, 158

box: for goods, 53, 66, 85, 120, 137, 145

Boxall, Alfred, 50

Boxall, Catharine, □ 7 (20), □ 53 (100–1)

Boxall, Charles, drowned at Montreal, 11, 100, 136

Boxall, Edward, xxx, 4, □ 7 (20), 21, 23, □ 53 (100–1), 128

Boxall, George, □ 25 (50–1), 141, 142, □ 121 (229–30)

Boxall, Granny, 143

Boxall, Harriet (Hall), 273n26

Boxall, Mary (Tilley), □ 25 (50–1), 141, □ 121 (229–30)

Boxall, Sarah, *see* Tickner

Boxall, Widow (mother of Edward), 100

Boxall, William, 273, 273n26, 274

Boxall, William (brother of George), 50, 229

Boxall, William (father of George), 229

Boxall, William (of Whites Green), 11

Boxall family, 241n100

Boxgrove, 154

boy: for farm work, 231; from Isle of Wight, 146n106

Brading, 367

brandy, 67, 73, 111, 116, 118, 123, 141n88, 148, 156, 220, 286; and shipboard births, 154n120

Brantford, 176, 178, 186, 194, 201n17, 223; letter from, 235–7, 251, 253, 388n11, 412; uncollected letters at, xxxv

bread, 28, 87, 100, 114, 147, 298; baking, 286

breeches, 197

brewery, 286, 375, 375n41, 376

bricklayer, 16, 63, 80, 101, 118, 131, 157, 217, 391; wages of, 18, 218

brickmaker, 120, 208n25, 279

brickmaking, 11

Bridger, Barbara, *see* Hilton

Bridger, Mrs, 143

Bridger, Thomas, 249

Bridgwater, John, 221, 222

Brighton, East Sussex, 55, 181, 182, 244; letter to, 180

Brighton emigration committee, 161, 409

Brighton Gazette, 90, 207n24

Brighton Guardian, xix, 293n56

Brighton Herald, 213, 227

Brighton Patriot, xxxix, 246, 258, 259, 260

Bristow, Edward, 69, □ 82 (138–40)

Bristow, Hannah (Streeter), □ 82 (138–40)

Bristow, John (brother of Edward), 139n84, 140

Bristow, John (son of Edward), 138

Bristow, John, 140

Bristow, Sarah (Streeter), 140

Bristow, Susan (Eisenhauer), 138n83

Bristow post office (West Woolwich), 140

Britannia (steamboat), 176

British American Land Company, 176

British Tar, 58n128, 53, 161, 162, 164, 169, 170n11, 177, 180, 190, 409

Brixham, Devon, 144n100

broadcloth, super fine, 31

Broadmore, Surrey, 42
Broadwater, Hertfordshire, 306, 309, 310, 312, 313, 318, 322, 327
Broadwood, Thomas, 60
Brockburn, Charles, 77
Brockville, 142
Bronte, 119; description of, 238, letter from, 238
Brooklyn, 323
Brooks, Eliza, 109
brother, search for, 224
Broughton, George, 31n65
Broughton, Richard, 31n65
Brunswick, 336, 350, 351
Brydone, James Marr, xix, 24, 53, 108n35, 126, 161, 163n2, 167, 169, 171, 173, 176, 178, 180, 183, 184, 185, 192, 193, 194, 201, 204, 215, 216, 223, 228, 229, 232, 244, 245, 246, 258, 259, 259n18, 293, 412; allegations against contradicted, 260; carried letters, xxxv; charges against, xxxix; as superintendent, 162; see also Narrative of a Voyage
Buchanan, Alexander Carlisle, 409
Buchanan, James, 150
Buchanan, John S., 15n15, 409
buck wheat, 109; see also crops
Budd, Barbara Ann, 206n23
Budd, Charlotte (Denman), 221, 222n67
Budd, George, 206, 206n23, 274
Budd, Henry, 206n23, 274
Budd, James, 100, 206, 206n23, 273, 294, 294n60
Budd, James Jr, 206n23, 274
Budd, John, 206, 206n23, 221n67, 274
Budd, Joseph, 206, 206n23
Budd, Maria, see Pullen
Budd, Mary, 206n23
Budd, Mary (Carter), 100, 206n23, 273n26, 274, 294n60
Buffalo, New York, letter from, 323
Buffalo Protestant Orphan Home, 390
builder, 234
building churches, 235
building trades, 144; in England, 16
bull frogs, 156

bunch (goitre), 356
Bunker's Hill, 142
Burberry, Mr, emigrates to Ohio, 396
Burch, see also Birch
Burch, George, 204
Burch, Thomas, 205
Burchell, John, 16
Burchell, Mrs J., □ 3 (11–13)
Burchill, Elizabeth, see Goatcher
Burgess, Mrs, 141
Burgess, Mrs Clement, 143
burial, 11, 75, 122, 213, 221, 355; en route, xxxvii, 44, 44n97, 348, 362; expenses, 361; of rebels, 282; at sea, 10; service, 122
Burley, Plumer, 222n68
Burley's Inn, 222
Burlington Bay, route via, 7
Burns, Ann, see Racher
Burpham, West Sussex, 227, 410
Burrell, Sir Charles, 138, 176
Burrell, 109n36, 140, 176, 177, 194, 200, 236n96
Burrett's Rapids, 160
Burton, parish of settlement, 21
Bury, West Sussex, overseer of, 24–5
Bury Common, 249
Bury Hill, Dorking, 409
Bury Mill, 249
burying ground, 361
bush: dislike of, 381; land, 196; road, 273
Bushby, Levi, 235, 237, 237n97, 409
Bushby, Mr, 114
Butchell, T., 97
butchering, 156
butcher's boy, 208
butler, 44, 51, 57, 109, 111, 124, 135, 148, 150, 153, 186, 189, 202, 211
butter print, 222
Buttery, Charlotte, see Rapley
Bytown (Ottawa), xxxviii

cabbage, 70, 125
cabin passengers, 8, 142, 259; provisions for, 14, 40
cabinet maker, 121, 296; wages, 52
Caiger, Mary, see Birch

cakes, 146n106
Caldwell, James B., 375n40
calf, 59, 150, 153
calico, 67
Calvert, C., 344
Camlachie, Plympton Township, 301
Canada boats, 35
Canada Company, 4, 43, 45, 86, 94n5, 129, 152, 160, 163, 178, 237, 409; agents of, 53; carried mail, xxxv; lands bought from, 20; money sent via, 5; road, 37; stage waggon route, 28n59
Canada Villas, 60
Canadian Courant, 56n126
Canadian Emigrant, 90, 146n105
canal, 127; digging, 285; travel inland by, 398; see also Rideau; travel inland
candles, 51, 100, 124, 148, 150, 181, 185, 189, 190n24, 255
Canning, George: statue to, 353, 358
cannons, 276
Cape Breton, 10, 17, 145, 346
Cape Ray, Newfoundland, 163
Capel, 60
Capelain (Caplin), see also Capling
capital, advantage of, 402
Caplen, Charles, 206
Capling, George, 45
Capling, Jane (Booker), 43, 70
Capling, John, xxxvii, 37; □ 21 (43–5)
Capling, Mary (Morley), 45
Capling (Capelain), William, 44
Captain Swing, xxviii
Caradoc plains, 274
Caradoc Township, 83, 225, 292
Caradoc-Adelaide-Warwick road, 111n41
Carillon Canal, 160
Carisbrook Castle, 367
Carleton House, 358
Caroline, burning of, 266
Carpenter, John, Cocking: copy of letter requested, 390
carpenter, 38, 53, 59, 61, 67, 95, 178, 184, 208, 190n52, 395; apprenticed to, 236; and joiner, 330; wages in Upper Canada, 233; work of, 64

carriages, 147; lack of, 34
Carrick (Carricks), deaths on, 8–9
Carter, Harriet, *see* Cooper
Carter, Mary, *see* Budd
Carter, Mr, 183
Carter, Richard, 274; seen at York, 21
Carter and Bonus, xxxviii, 5: ships, 266, 298
Carver, George, xl, □ 87 (148–9), □ 95 (165–6), 226
Carver, Isabell (Marrell), 166
Carver, James, 148, 165
Carver, James Jr, 166
Carver, Sarah, 148, 165
Cascades, 90, 127
casks, 58, 150, 212, 215
casualties (1837–8) 276
Catholic Emancipation, 353, 353n22, 358
Cattermole, John, 346
Cattermole, William, 29, 346n9
cattle, 59, 69; price for 240; *see also* animals, domestic
caul, 132, 132n71
Cawthra, John, 349, 354, 379
Cawthra, Joseph, 349n13
Cedars, 347, 360; Island of, 13; rapids and village, 12
cellars, 233
cement, 331
cemetery: in Delaware, 293; opened, 331
census: 1840, 95; 1851, 100, 116, 124, 126, 156, 136, 207, 299, 292; 1861, 200; 1871, 131, 299
chain migration, *see* emigration
chair making, 375
Chalcraft, Charlotte, 273n26
Chalcraft, Matthew, 273, 273n26
Challen, Harriet, *see* Cooper
Challen, Mr, 14, 97, 206
Challen, Mr, of Pulborough: assisted emigrants, 149
Chalwin, B., 70
Chalwin, Caroline, 43
Chalwin, Charlotte, 43
Chalwin, Edmund, 43
Chalwin, George, 43
Chalwin, James, 43
Chalwin, Jane, 43
Chalwin, John, 43
Chalwin, Mary, 43
Chalwin, Ralph, 95

Chalwin, Robert: dead, 37, 43, 44
Chalwin, Stephen, 43
Chalwin, Thomas, 43
Chalwin, William, 43
Chambling, Mr and Mrs, 312, 315
Champion and Weekly Herald, 295, 295n63
Champlain, Lake, 176
Chancellor, Captain, 5, 8, 40
Chantler, Alfred, 374, 375, 369, 378
Chantler, Ann, 336, 353, 354, 355, 360, 361, 372; death of, 362
Chantler, Baldwin, 378
Chantler, Benjamin, 337n1
Chantler, Charles, 343, 356, 370
Chantler, David, 352, 357
Chantler, Deborah, 337n1, 356, 354
Chantler, Elijah, 337n1
Chantler, Elizabeth, *see* McDougall
Chantler, Emma, 336, 350, 363
Chantler, Esther, *see* Dennis
Chantler, Hannah (Sayers), 337n1, 350
Chantler, Henry, 374, 375, 378, □ 171 (368–70)
Chantler, Hesther, *see* Dennis, Esther
Chantler, James, 356
Chantler, James Sr, 357
Chantler, John, 337n1
Chantler, John (son of Moses), xxviii, xxx, 337, □ 166 (344–50), 353, 354, □ 169 (359–63), 372, □ 172 (370–1), 379, 380
Chantler, Joseph R., xxviii, □ 165 (337–44), □ 168 (354–9), □ 167 (350–4)
Chantler, Joseph (son of Nathaniel), 350, 360, 368, 372, 374
Chantler, Joseph Sr, 336, 337, 337n1, 344
Chantler, Mary Ann (Millard), 368
Chantler, Moses, 336, 337, 337n1, 344, 350, 350n17, 379; family chart, 340–1; mill bought, 379
Chantler, Nathaniel (father of Moses and Nathaniel), 337n1

Chantler, Nathaniel, 60n132, 336, 337n1, 350, 353, 354, 368; death of described, 360–1; death described by Esther, 372; family chart, 338–9
Chantler, Nathaniel Jr, 369, 372
Chantler, Sarah, 337, 379
Chantler, Sophia (Rowe), 60, 60n132, 61, 336, 356, 368; death described by Esther, 373
Chantler, Sophie, 359
Chantler, Thomas, 337n1
Chantler, William, xxx, 336, 337, 350, 354; letter from enclosed in, □ 168 (355–6), 354, 379
Chantler, William: of Newport Pagnel, 357
Chantler, William Nathaniel, 337, 350, 359, 368
Chantler families: leave Montreal, 4; and cholera, 6
Chantler mill, 379
chapel, 39
chapel warden, 200n14
Chapman, Mr, 46
character (reference), 232
Charles X, 337
Charman, Ann, *see* Hills
Charman, Edward, 109
Charman, Hannah, 54
Charman, James, 109
Charman, Mr, 54
Charman, Sefton, 151n115
Charman, William, 109
Chase, Charles, 60
Chase, Edwin, 180
Chase, Lucy (Gregory), 59n130, 180
Chase, Mr, 153
Chase, Walter, 60
Chase, William, 59, 59n130, 179, 180
Chatfield's Farm, 223
Chatham, Upper Canada, 389
Chatham and Kent people, 280
cheese, 51, 104, 109, 114, 116, 124
cheese ware cloths, 150
Chelsea pensioner, 272n18
Chesman, Hannah, *see* Tilley
Chesman, Henry, 143
Chesman, Sarah, 143n94
Chichester, Henry Thomas Pelham, 3rd Earl, 161, 163, 183, 409

Chichester, West Sussex, 56, 90, 132, 150, 284, 368; letter from 364

Chiddingfold, Surrey, 66, 67; sending parish, 34

Child, Elizabeth, see Kinshott

child allowance, 43, 246, 251

childbirth, see confinement, deaths

children, 64, 161; barefoot, 195; fatherless, 140; health of, 299; separated, 372; work for, 39, 195, 279

Childs, Jane, see Trusler

Chiltington, 82

Chippewa, Upper Canada, 23, 65

chisels, 98; see also tools

Chisholm, George, 143, 230

Chisolm, George, 230n85

Chitty, Charles, 222

cholera, 4, 6, 29, 37, 44, 58, 61, 64, 65, 69, 70, 75, 78, 79, 92, 111, 142, 168, 170, 172, 346–8, 352n19, 355–7, 371, 396, 397; on Carrick, 8–9; death from, 353, 354, 336; effects of in 1832, 6; epidemic, 162, 336, 363; fear of, 14, 362, 372; at Montreal and Quebec, 393; threat of, 13; in Toronto, 373; treatment of, 347–8; in United States, 350; at York, 349

chopping, 133, 277, 383

Chrippes, Thomas, 71, 147, 130, 409

Christmas, 321, 322, 327, 329, 333

church, 67, 79, 172, 185, 188, 201, 205, 206, 224, 282, 283, 346; at Delaware, 265

Church of England, 412; clergyman, 280; preacher, 185

Church of St Saviour, 358

churchwarden, 221n63, 227

cider, 71, 118, 146n106, 123, 156, 199

cisterns, 376

Clarke, James, 18

Clarksland, Billingshurst, West Sussex, 221n63

Clear, Edward, 32

clearing land, 56, 98, 119, 133, 237, 279; and fencing, cost, 203; method, 98; see also land

Clements, Mr, 14, 97

clergyman, Church of England, 280

Cleveland, Ohio, 397

climate, 57, 61, 87, 119, 153, 168, 203, 257

Climping, Sussex, 188, 205; sending parish, 194

clock, recommended to bring, 37, 111, 150, 221

clothes, 66, 67, 78, 135, 137, 154, 188, 195, 197, 248, 286; on board ship, 257; received from parish, 217

clothing, 18, 47, 61, 66, 96, 100, 118, 148, 150, 172, 179, 181, 213; available and cheap, 36, 42; recommended, 226; very little dearer, 124

club money, 268

coaches, 127

coachmaker, 298

coachman, 268, 297

Cobbett, William, 214, 258

Cobbett's Weekly Political Register, 409

Cobourg, Upper Canada, 35, 66, 68, 160, 164

Cocking, West Sussex, 273n26, 293n54; letter to, 205; sending parish, 206

cod, 345

coffin, 348

coinages, 349

Colborne, Elizabeth, 374, 372n36, 378, 410

Colborne, Sir John (later 1st Baron Seaton), 92, 101, 115n53, 171, 176, 178, 180, 184, 192, 193, 349, 356, 363, 372n36, 373, 410, 411; Goatcher met, 14; response to cholera epidemic, 6; settlement initiative, 7

Cold Harbour, Dorking, 61; letter to, 60

Coldwell, James, 375

Cole, George, 208

Cole, William, 188, 188n19, 205, 208, 209

Colebrook, Mr, 147

Coleman, Elizabeth (Voice), 172, 185n15, 187, 190

Coleman, George, xxxiv, xlii, 164, □ 103 (188–90)

Coleman, George Jr, 187, 190

Coleman, Lucy Susannah, see Harwood

Coleman, Mr, 356

Coleman, Sarah, see Lannaway

Coleman, Sarah (Pollard), 188

Coleman family, 173

Colhook Common, Northchapel, West Sussex, 260, 269, 269n10

Collection of Letters from Sussex Emigrants, 1832, 141n89

Collingwood, Ontario, 370

Collins, Mary, see Rapley

Colonial Office, 92, 101, 178

colporteur (hawker of books), 390

commissary (army), 283

Comper, Henry, 97, 14n14

Condor, William, 310n9

Conestogo, 139n84

confinement, 48, 68, 74, 138, 145, 154, 270, 277, 283, 290

Congregational Church, 209

Congregationalists, 26

constable, special, 13

Constitutionalists: England supporting, 367n30

consumption, 300

contractor, 234

convicts, 259, 383

Cook, Cornelius, 208

cooking utensils, 98

Cooper, Albert, 4

Cooper, Amelia, see Ford

Cooper, Caroline, 271, 275

Cooper, Charlotte (Boswell), □ 39 (71–3)

Cooper, Charlotte, 276

Cooper, Christopher, 97

Cooper, Emma, 271

Cooper, Francis, 48, 48n107, 117

Cooper, George, 271

Cooper, Harriet, 271

Cooper, Harriet (Carter), 100, 270, 275, 276

Cooper, Harriet (Challen), 100

Cooper, Henry, 271

Cooper, Humphrey, □ 39 (71–3), 226

Cooper, James, xxx, 99, 194, 198n11, 207, 267, □ 133 (270–6)

Cooper, James (father), 270

Cooper, James (brother of William), 21
Cooper, James King, 271, 276
Cooper, John, 100
Cooper, John, 282n39
Cooper, Mary, 270, 274, 275n29
Cooper, Richard, 208
Cooper, Sarah, *see* Spencer
Cooper, Sarah, 271, 275
Cooper, William, xxx, xxxviii, 20, □ 8 (21–2), 23, □ 52 (97–100), 178, 194n3, 207, 214, 244, 266–7, 271, 272, 274
Cooper, William (son of Humphrey), 73
Cooper, William (son of James), 271
Cooper's Black Horse Tavern, Church Street, York, 128
Corbett, William, 409
Corderoy Bridge, 349
corn, 47, 111, 148; *see also* crops
corn mills, 94
Cornell, Sam, 399
Cornwall, Upper Canada, 90, 127, 134, 348, 361
Corse, Charlotte, *see* Wilson
Corsley, Wiltshire, emigration letters reported as faked, xxxi
Cortness, George, 390
Cosens, Ann, 63n138
Cosens, Ann (Goodchild), 63
Cosens, Ann (Miller), xxiv, xxxiv, 63, □ 66 (112–14), □ 141 (295–7)
Cosens, Caroline, *see* Tilt
Cosens, Charles Sr, 296, 297
Cosens, Charles Jr, 63, □ 66 (112–14), □ 141 (295–7)
Cosens, Charles (son of Charles Jr), 296
Cosens, Cornelius, xxxii, □ 34 (63–4), 112, 114, 296, 297
Cosens, Elizabeth (Betsy), 63n138, 296, 297
Cosens, Emily, 296
Cosens, Esther, 296
Cosens, Francis, 296, 296n66
Cosens, Francis William, 63n138
Cosens, George, 296
Cosens, Henry, 296
Cosens, Hester, 63n138
Cosens, Jane, *see* Tilt
Cosens, Jesse, 63n138, 297

Cosens, John, 63n138, 297
Cosens, Mary, 63n138, 64n141, 296
Cosens, Mary Ann, 113
Cosens, Nathaniel, 63n138, 296
Cosens, Thomas, 63n138, 296
Coteau-du-Lac, 347, 348, 355, 361, 372
cottages, 177; rent, 269n10
cotton, 67, 150
cotton stockings, 150
County Clare, Ireland, 265
County Councils, 332n46
County Limerick, Ireland, 265
Courier of Upper Canada, 33n73, 410
Course, Charlotte, *see* Wilson
Court, Henry, 153
Court, Mary, 77
Courtauld (II), George, 395
Courtauld family, 7, 393
Courtnage, Ann (Madgwick), 255, □ 129 (257–8)
Courtnage, Hannah, 255, 255
Courtnage, James, 255, 257
Courtnage, John, 257, 258
Courtnage, Maria, 258
Courtnage, Mary Ann, 257, 258
Courtnage, Susan, 258
Courtnage, Thomas, 258
Courtnage, William, xxxii, □ 128 (255–7)
Courtnage family, 246
Covey, Hannah, 111n42
Covey, William, 111
Cowes, 367
Cowper, Amelia, *see* Peacock
cows, 48, 57, 59, 71, 82, 94, 95, 111, 115, 119, 124, 138, 135, 148, 150, 153, 156, 255, 256
Crabtree, Elizabeth (daughter), 305, 315, 320, □ 160 (328–9)
Crabtree, Elizabeth (Wilson) (formerly Sell), 305, 309, 311, 312, □ 149 (313–16), 322, 325, 326, 329
Crabtree, Henry, 315
Crabtree, James, 315
Crabtree, Maria Frances, 315, 328
cradle, 41
Cranly (Sussex), 396
Crawford, Robert, 161, 166
credit notes, 129
cricket, 114, 186, 296, 297
crookhorn peas, 150
Crooks, Matthew, 78

crop seed, 97, 100
crops, 15, 36, 87, 172, 185, 199, 216, 225, 240, 274, 277; grown, 271; yield, 189; *see also* wheat
Cross, Dr, 198
Crossfield, George, 390
Crossing, Charles, 163n2
Crouch Common (near Bignor, West Sussex), 46n102
croup, 378
crown lands, 176; commissioner of, 384; offer to purchase, 192
Crown Lands Department, 20, 92, 379, 381, 410
crown reserves, 409
Croydon, Surrey, 337
crude oil, 116
Cullep, Henry, 311
currency, 67n153, 413
Curtis, Emma, *see* Berry
Cushing's warehouse, 160
Customs House Officer, 346

dairy, 96, 97, 186
Dairy Farm, Adelaide Township, 381; letter from, 382
Dalton, George, of Arundel (carpenter), 390
Daniels, Elizabeth (Horton), □ 79 (135–7), 141, 141n92
Daniels, William, □ 79 (135–7), 141n92
David Lloyd and Co., 319, 319n23
Davis, Captain E., 274, 374n38
Davis, William, 122
Deadman, Mr, 257
Deal: anchored off, 345
Dean, near Petworth, letter to, 36
Deane, Margaret, 356
Dearling, Caroline (Francis), 90, 91, 126, □ 85 (144–5), □ 111 (209–12), 209, □ 134 (276–8), 300, 300n73
Dearling, Caroline (daughter), 144, 210
Dearling, Hannah, 209, 210n31, 277
Dearling, James, 277
Dearling, Jane, 144, 210, 277
Dearling, John, 90, 92, 129, 134, □ 85 (144–5), □ 111 (209–12), 216, 267, □ 134 (276–8), 300n73
Dearling, John Jr, 209, 277

Dearling, Phoebe, 144, 210, 211, 277

Dearling family, 120; farm sold, 278

deaths, 11, 43, 44, 49, 60, 69, 74, 77, 79, 87, 95, 100, 101, 107, 113, 121, 126, 128, 137, 142, 181, 182n7, 183, 190, 192, 198, 213, 221, 224, 237, 240, 251, 253, 278, 290, 296n66, 300, 397; in childbirth, 297n67; from cholera, 37, 346; of rebels, 276; on voyage, 10, 42, 129; from whooping cough, 8, 268, 269; see also cholera

deed to land, 210; requirements before issue, 381

deer, 46, 65, 67, 70, 85, 98, 101, 102, 134, 180, 274; deer's fat, 100; see also hunting

Delaware, 22, 156, 225, 235, 270, 282, 283; letter to, 267, 288

Delaware Post Office, xxxiv, 97, 270n14, 283, 292; postmaster, 411

Delaware Township, 207, 227, 255; letter from, 155, 157, 165, 230, 233, 281

Delaware Village, 223, 234

Denison, George Taylor, 224n72, 226

Denman, Charlotte, see Budd

Denman, David, 222

Denman, George, 221

Denman, Hannah (Ede), 221

Denman, Harriette, 221

Denman, Henry, 221

Denman, James, 221

Denman, Job, 221

Denman, John, xxxiv, □ 117 (221–2)

Denman, Mary, 222

Denman, Sampson, 221, 221n66, 222

Denman, Samuel, 222

Denman, Sarah, 221, 222n67

Denman, Susan, 221

Denman, William, 221

Dennett, Hannah, see Joyes

Dennis, Barbara, 377

Dennis, Brooke, 369

Dennis, Charles, 376

Dennis, Esther (Chantler), 336, 369, □ 173 (371–80), 410

Dennis, Grandfather, 377

Dennis, Marshall, 377

Dennis, Nathan, 376

Dennis, Sophia, 378

Denyson, George, see Denison

destitute poor, housing of, 177

Detroit, 389

Detroit River, 92

Dial Green, Lurgashall, 101; emigrated from, 36

Diana, 215, 227, 230, 234n89, 244, 245, 258, 260, 284; difficulty filling, 245

Dighton, William: fell overboard, 160

Dilloway, Charles, alias Bridger, 268n5

Dilloway, Sarah, 268

directories, 116

discharge, military, 20

district, 410

District Court clerk, 402

disturbances, Dorking, 344; see also Swing disturbances

ditching, 142

Ditton, Ann, 170n8

Ditton, Tabitha, 160, 170n8

Ditton, Thomas, 170n8

Ditton family, 173

Dix, R., 358

doctor, 74, 75, 85, 115, 121, 133, 145, 170, 289, 310, 346, 347, 348, 349, 360, 373, 375, 378; care, 77n170; home doctors, 134; at Kingston, 28; Yankee, 23

dog cart, 274n27; van, 288

dogs, 59; for cattle or hunting, 271; requested for hunting, 21, 98

Dogget, Frederick, 357

Dorking, Surrey, 42, 85, 240, 337, 350, 356, 368; letter to, 62, 63, 83, 112, 295, 337, 350, 359, 364; sent from, 30

Dorking and Horsham Meeting, 379

Dorking area, 336; emigrants from, 34, 409, 410; letters from, xxvii

Dorking Emigration Society, 38, 62, 63n140, 410

Dorking fair day, 40

Dorking Meeting, 336, 337

Dorking post, 85

Dornorman, William, 31

Downer, Ann, see Mann

Downer, Avis (Avice), see Napper

Downer, Jane, see Belchamber

Downer, John, 252n6, 278

Downer, John (of Marshall's farm), 111

Downer, Lucy (Rapley), 278, 280

Downs, Robert, 357

Doyle, Martin, 29

Doyle's Hints to Emigrants, 52, 78n174

dressmakers: scarce, 286

Drewitt, Frances Ann, 227, 228

Drewitt, John, 192, 207, 232, 227, 410

drink, 136n81, 248, 350; effects of, 11; given up, 148; price of, 214; see also beer, drunkenness, spirits

driving, 182

Drove, 293

drownings, 10, 11, 17, 152, 136, 250; see also death

drum major, 32nd regiment: letter sent by, 385

Drummond, Jessie, 239

drunkenness, 17, 100, 144, 146, 146n105, 259; see also drink, spirits

dry goods: requested, 37

Dublin, Ireland, 8

Duchess Street, Toronto, 208n25

Dumfries Township, 46, 93n3, 95, 102, 124

Duncombe, Charles, xxiii, 388, 388n11

Dundas, 7, 18, 48, 55n124, 70, 79, 80, 84, 90, 120, 135, 141, 192, 207n24, 286, 311, 398; letter from, 16, 38, 46, 79

Dundas Post Office, 43

Dundas St, Ontario, 238

Dunsfold, Surrey, 217n57, 250

Durham boats, 6, 26, 46, 52, 74, 82, 90, 126, 192, 193, 201, 410

Durrant (Deront), Elizabeth, see Thomas

Dutch, 87, 107, 121, 125; midwife, 277

duties, 190n24; complained of, 386; none on goods brought, 37

Eade, Robert, 299
eagles, 98, 101
earthenware, 96
Easebourne, 152, 275n29; poor-house, 119n57; workhouse, 155, 253
East Flamborough Township, 84, 86; letter from, 221
East Sussex, 161; emigrants, 163
East Whitby Township, 326, 333; letter to, 312, 313, 317, 319, 323, 324, 329, 330
East Zorra Township, 164, 222
economic difficulties, 193
Ede, Hannah, see Denman
Edward, John, 61
Edwards, Charles (of Tillington?), 212
Edwards, Charles (of Petworth?), 52
Edwards, Mr (coachmaker), 298
Edwards, Sarah, see Randall
Edwards, William, 142
economic migrants: described, xxiv
Egdean, 148; fair, 213
eggs, 146n106
Egremont, George O'Brien Wyndham, 3rd Earl of, xxxviii, 4, 9, 45, 71, 91, 92, 107, 108n44, 124, 128, 130, 138, 146, 147, 156, 176, 177, 178, 213, 215, 227, 244, 245, 246, 265, 268, 270, 294, 297–8, 383, 410, 411, 412; assumption of risk, 5; bust of, 244; death of, xxiii, 298; passages paid, xxvi–xxvii; patronage of, xvi, xvii; pleasure ground, 147
Egremont Road, 92, 275, 279
Eisenhauer, Michael, 138n83
Eisenhauer, Susan, see Bristow
Ekfrid Park, near Delaware, 230
Ekfrid Post Office, 270n14
Ekfrid Township, 230, 233
elder wine, 274
election, 194, 337, 338, 340, 388
Elgin County, 68
Eliza, 259n18
Elliot, Daniel, 54
Elliot, Elias, 17, □ 28 (54–5), 79, 148, 152, 165
Elliot, James, 186n17
Elliot, Mary (Voice), 169, 186
Elliot, Mr, 67

Elliott, Richard, 54
Elliot, T., 90
Elliott, William, 157
Elmira, 140
Elora, 58
embden grits, 40
emigrants: advice for, 20; connec-tions, xv; indigent, 151; from Ireland, 294n57; from Isle of Wight, 245; list of Petworth, xv; office, 35; preparation for leaving, 5; returned to England, 97, 136, 146n108, 157, 218n60, 272n19; undesirable, 200
emigration, 265, 365; agent, 178, 409, 411; chain migration, xxxix–xxxlx, 99, 241; consid-ered, 336; encouragement of, 294; enthusiasm for, 5; finan-cial support hoped for, 91; promoted, 295, 346n9, 391; prospects, 365; recommended, 203; to Sydney, considered, 367; warned against, 258
Emigration Commission, xix
employers: choice of, 246; not masters, 41; see also attitudes, social
employment: abundant, 37, 164; conditions, 47, 231
England: attitude to, 189, 195; compared to Upper Canada, 165; return to, 30, 210n30, 235, 293; state of, 198
England, xxxviii, xxxix, 4, 5, 90, 160, 133n72, 137, 177, 276, 346n8, 393
English farmers, 104; manners, 231
Enniskillen, 169
Enticknap, Charles, 102
Enticknap, George, 212
Enticknap, Hannah, 212
Enticknap, James, 256
Enticknap, Thomas, 212
Enticknap, William, 257
Epsom, Ontario, letter to, 328
Epsom salts, 287, 288n46
Eramosa road, 19
Eramosa Township, 90, 201n18, 210, 216, 412
Erickson, Charlotte, xx, xxi
Erie, 247
Erie, Lake, 67, 92, 276n31

Erie Canal, xxxviii, 160; travel via, 21
Ernestown, Upper Canada: letter from, 31
estate, 116, 177, 333, 390; bought, 19; value, 38, 151, 165, 180, 278
estrangement: from family, 320n24, 324
Etherington, James, 123
Etobicoke, 115n51, 116
Evans, Ann (Hilton), 225, 233, 234
Evans, Charlotte (Tribe), □ 19 (36–8), 101, 102, 123, 133, 216
Evans, David, 225, 225n76, 234
Evans, Elizabeth (wife of Joseph Jr), 38
Evans, Joseph Neuroke, 36, 37, 102
Evans, Joseph (son of Char-lotte?), 38
Evans, Mrs (in England), 37
Evans family, 235
Eveline, 4, 5, 9, 24, 30, 35, 52, 60, 224n73, 225n76, 271n16, 398
Evershed, T., 397
Ewens, John, 208
Ewens, Mary Ann, see Hills
exciseman, 190
expenses, 56; to New York, 286, 288; of transporting goods, 252

Fair, Ann, 222
Fairee, Mrs, 328
fair-keeping, 274
Falkner, Thomas, 205
families, 37, 161, 162, 184, 185, 178, 203; with children, 245; correspondence with, xxxix–xxxi; opportunities for, 165
fanning, 57
Farhall, Charles, 221n63
farm, 84, 155, 179, 196, 206, 219, 349; cleared, 47, 119; by halves, 202; on shares, 117, 152, 350n16; for sale, 203; size, 321
farm labourer, 5, 68, 178, 227, 201n16, 260, 279
farmer, 87, 234, 321; emigrated, 13; partnership with, 226; sheep. 364
farmer's men, 86, 111, 236n96; wages of, 22, 233

farming, 205, 306; implements, 57; method, 15; work, 119, 209, 248

Farnhurst, West Sussex: letter to, 229, 257

Farnhurst Cross: West Sussex, letter to, 198

farthings: recommended to bring, 42, 99, 111

Faulks, William, Portsea, Hants, (boot and shoe maker), 385, 390

Fawkes, Guy, 74n163

fellmonger, 61

Felpham, West Sussex, 58, 179n3, 194n2, 115n54; letter to, 55, 178

Fernhurst, West Sussex, 50, 133n72, 212n36, 217n56; sending parish, 198, 255

fever, 74, 112, 117, 127, 240, 258; and ague, 60, 64; see also ague

field peas, 150n113

Field Place, Goring, West Sussex, 235, 237n97, 409

field work: described, 376

Fielder, George, 66

Fielder, William, 67, 252

Fielding, Mr, 153

Findon, 336

Findon Place, West Flamborough, 229

fire: arson, England, 317; camp (Canada), 127; house (Canada), 240

fire irons, 98

firewood, 229, 257, 261; firing, 115, 189

fish, 20, 65, 115, 134

fish lot, 116

fisherman's licence, 116

Fishmonger's Hall, 353, 358

fistula, 181

Fittleworth, West Sussex, 51, 117; letter to, 25, 71

FitzGibbon, James, 27, 57

Flamborough Township, 48

Flanders, John, 48, 310

flannel, 73, 78, 153

Flemish bond, 80

flies: grass flies, 26; troublesome, 13; see also mosquitos

flintstone, 197

Flood, Reverend Richard, 282n38

florist and seed business, 289n49

flour, 44, 51, 58, 82, 83, 86, 94, 111, 123, 124, 125, 135, 213; mill, 238; price of, 203

flower seeds, 211

Flushing, Long Island, 352

Foard, Michael, 216

food, 194; allowance, 225; cheap, 179; cost of, 41; plenty of, xl, 156; price of, 172, 181220, 249, 256; see also beef, flour, meat, provisions

Ford, Amelia (Cooper), 155

Ford, Ann, 236n96

Ford, Charles, 155, 156

Ford, John, 236n96, 237

foreign legion, 367n30

forest, 118

forks: recommended to bring, 98

Fort George, Niagara District, 17; letter from, 54

Fortier, Dr, 170n12

Foster, Mrs (Luff's aunt), 25

foundry business, 401

fowl, domestic, 59, 109, 118, 185, 283; domestic birds, 181; guinea, 111

Fowler, Elizabeth, see Sturt

Fox and Hound, North End, Bassingbourn, 306, 313

Fox at Felpham, 58

Fozer, Mr, 36

France, 337

Francis, Caroline, see Dearling

Francis, James, 54

Francis, John, 144, 276, 300

Francis, Phoebe, 209n27

Francis, Thomas, 209, 209n27

franking for free postage, 108n34, 140; requested, 392

Frederick Street, Toronto, 116

free country, 67

French Canadians, 17, 127, 276

French Land, Ashington, 110

Friends, 354, 356; in London, 355; in New York, 352; reception from, 349; settlement of, 362; from United States, 358; see also Society of Friends

Friends Boarding School, Croydon, Surrey, 357n26

Frightfold (Frithfold), West Sussex, 155, 155n125; farm, 282, 282n39

frock, 211

frogs, 66

frost-bite, 274

fruit, 18, 61, 51, 98, 118, 211; cuttings requested, 23; wild, 180

Fryfogel Inn: deaths at, 7

Fuller, John, 85

funeral, 278; of Lord Egremont, 270, 270n13

furnishings, 51

furniture: advice on, 285, 286

furze (gorse), 268n2

Galbraith, F.W., 400

Galbraith, Heather and Adsett, 400

Galt, 90, 122, 277, 294, 398, 399; letter from, 26, 45, 69, 93, 101, 121, 129, 144, 293

Galt Post Office, 87

Gamble, John, 114

Gamblen, Ann, xxiv, □ 100 (180–3)

Gamblen, John, xxiv, □ 100 (180–3)

Gamblen family, 173

game, 17, 41, 46, 65, 70, 85, 94, 98, 110, 115, 134, 156; laws, 22; see also birds, deer, hunting

gamekeeper, 110, 240, 268n5

garden, 115, 116, 228; seeds, 98, 111, 150; vegetable, 29, 100n17, 185, 211, 225

Garden River, 371

gardener, 20, 236n96

gardening, 332

Garrafraxa Township, 56

Gates, James, 235, 237, 237n99

Gates, Mr (shoemaker at Ancaster), 163

Gates, William, 236, 236n92

geese, 70, 109, 111, 118

general merchant, 377n45

general store, 140

gentlefolks, 130

Gentleman's Magazine, 270n13

gentlemen, 130, 181, 187; farmers, 102

George St, Thornhill, 204

George IV, 337, 338; death of, 339

George, Mr, 153

George, William, and family, 90

German Company Tract, 69, 95, 139n84, 200

German immigrants, 136
German states: unrest, 337
Gibbs, Mr, 126
Gibraltar, 392
Gibson, George John (sponsor), 108, 109n36
Gilbert, Elizabeth, *see* Trussler
Gilbert, F., Steyning (innkeeper), 390
Gilbert, Sarah, *see* Older
Gilbert, William, 299
Gillisby, Thos, 293
gimblets: requested, 98
gin, 67
gingerbread: blocks and moulds, 196; makers, 270; nuts, 197n8; prints, 196n8
Glasgow steamer, 367
gleaning, 43, 195n4; *see also* lease
Glengarry Scots, xx
Goatcher, Elizabeth (Burchill), 11n11, 13, 95
Goatcher, Mrs, 195
Goatcher, Robert, 195
Goatcher, Stephen (superintendent), 4, 5; □ 4 (13–16), 27, □ 51 (95–7), 150, 151, 157, 255
Goble, Charlotte, *see* Helyer
Goble, George, 272
Goddard, Mr, 59n130
Goderich, 19, 94, 136, 176, 192, 194, 44
Goderich Township, 131, 217
Gogger, Henry, 37, 70
Goldring, Caroline, 114
Goldring, Edward, 114
Goldring, Eleanor, 114
Goldring, Emma, 114
Goldring, Frances, 114
Goldring, George, 114
Goldring, Henry, 114, 115, 116
Goldring, James S., □ 67 (114–18)
Goldring, James Sr, 114, 116
Goldring, Mary Ann (Rayner), 114
Goldring, Michael, 114
Goldring, Richard, 116
Goldring, Samuel, 114
Goldring, Sarah (Pratt), 114, 116
Goldring, Thomas, 114
Goldring, William, xliii, □ 67 (114–16)
Goldring fleet, 116

Goldsmith, Mr: at York, 27
good character: importance of, 357
Goodchild, Ann, *see* Cosens
Gooderham and Worts, 238
goods: cheap, 132; prices of, 249, 256; recommended to bring, 39–40, 226, 230, 234, 248, 252, 286; requested, 256, 287; sent from England, 210
Goodwood House, 154
gooseberry trees or slips: requested, 44, 214; *see also* fruit
Gore District, 92; emigrants, 7
Gorie, Mr, 400
Goring, West Sussex, 82, 237n97; letter to, 235
Goring, Mrs, 157
Goulds, Jane, 237
government, 104, 114, 142, 172; agents, 7; assistance, 101; complaints of, 386; reserve, 299; work, 111, 146; *see also* roads
government house, 373
Gownfield, letter to, 77
Graffham, West Sussex, 21, 23, 98, 271; letter to, 97, 100, 270
Graffham/Woolavington, 100
grafting tools, 150; *see also* tools
grain, 65, 84, 240; plentiful, 271; price of, 172, 234
graining and flatting, 84
Grand River, 51n115, 52, 53, 71, 94n4, 162, 209n26
Grand River Navigation, 285n42
Grantham Township, 180, 256
Gravely, Arthur, 336, □ 170 (364–8)
Gravesend, 90, 345, 346
Great Britain, 40, 90, 152, 386
great house, 247
Great Lakes, 238
Great Peppering Farm, 227, 410
Great Western Railroad, 389
Greavatt, Ann (Trussler), 299n71, 300
Greavatt, James, 300
Greavatt, John, 299, 299n71, 300
Green, Ann (sister of James), 249
Green, Ann (daughter of Sarah?), 125, 126
Green, James, 249
Green, Mary, 125, 126
Green, Mary (Hawkins), 168n7

Green, Sarah, 124
Green, Thomas, 124n63
Green, William, □ 97 (168–9), 180, 267
Greenfield, Arthur, 168
Greenfield, C., 96
Greenfield, Daniel, 214
Greenfield, James, 236n95
Greenfield, Mary, *see* Jackman
Greenfield, Mrs, 214
Greenfield, Sarah, 236n95
Greenwood, Mary, 356
Greetham, John Knight, xxvii, 69, 78, 106, 410
Gregory, Lucy, *see* Chase
Grey, Earl, xix, 337, 342
Griellat, Stephen, 358
Griggey family, 257
Grimwood, Mary, *see* Poland
Grinstead, Charles, 86
Grinyer (Gringyer), Thomas, 235, 237, 237n99
grist mill, 17, 19, 71, 122, 157, 379
grocer, 124n63 157, 238
grog, 115, 121, 146; *see also* spirits
Grosse Île, 6, 90, 120, 137, 145, 160, 163, 170, 176, 177, 200, 224
groundhogs, 98, 101
Guelph, Upper Canada, 28, 53, 56, 58n128, 64, 70, 73n161, 154, 179, 192, 201, 202, 216, 296, 297, 399, 400, 401, 402; letter from, 19, 55, 153, 200, 398
Guelph Township, 8, 60
Guernsey, Island of, 218n60
Guildford, Surrey, 268, 289, 290, 346, 347
Guildford Goal, 62n136
Guildhall, 342
Gulf of St Lawrence, 10, 40, 346
guns, 98, 115, 180, 221; *see also* rifle
Gunshot, 77
Gurnett, Gabriel, of Horsham, 33
Gurnett, George, 33n73, 78, 184, 410
Gurr, Samuel, 249

Habbin, Henry, xxxix, □ 80 (137), □ 81 (137), 147
Hack, John Barton, 364
Hack, Stephen, 364
Haines, Charles, xxix, □ 64 (110)

Hale, Captain J.C., 4, 5, 90, 91, 120, 128, 131, 132, 133n72, 134, 141, 144n101, 146, 147, 154n120, 200, 393, 397; conduct of, xxxviii–xxxix, 130; "Instructions," 91; journal, 134; takes party to Ohio, 7
Half Moon Inn, 192
half-pennies: recommended to bring, 42, 99, 111
Halliday's shop, 248
Halifax, Nova Scotia, 390
Halifax currency, 98n13, 181n5, 412
Hall, Annie, 332
Hall, Edward, 315, 326
Hall, Ellen, 311, 313, 321
Hall, Emma (Muncey), 305, 315, □ 151 (317–18), 322, 326, 328, □ 162 (330); □ 164 (333), □ 157 (325)
Hall, Fanny, 314, □ 153 (320–1)
Hall (Hale), Frances, 135
Hall, Frances Ann (Fanny) (Wilson), see Shore
Hall, Hannah Maria, 313, 323, 323n31
Hall, Henry, 305, 307, 311, 313, □ 151 (317–19), 321, 322, 325, 326, 328, 330, 330, 333,
Hall, James, 210, 293
Hall, James (son of Frances Ann), 313
Hall, John (1st), 309, 314, 320n24, 323n31
Hall, John (2nd), 314, 320
Hall, John Jr, 320, 323, 324, 331
Hall, Mary Ann, 313
Hall, William, 305, 306, 313, 320, 321, 322, □ 155 (323–4), 327, 328, 330, 333
Hall, William H., 305, 330, 331n43, 332; □ 163 (330–3)
ham, 286; see also bacon
Hambleton, 143
Hambleton, Upper Canada, see Hamilton
Hambleton House, Godalming, Surrey, letter to, 66, 67n154
Hamilton, 4, 27–8, 40, 42, 45, 46, 52, 53, 54, 56, 57, 70, 75, 84, 86, 90, 90, 92, 105, 106, 109, 111, 122, 126, 133, 134, 154, 162, 171, 172, 176, 185, 201, 207,

210, 223, 228, 238, 293, 294, 381, 385, 398, 410; to Adelaide Township, cost of transportation, 274; to Blandford Township, travel by wagon, 160; letter from, 27, 83; route via, 7
Hamilton Post Office, 53, 86
Hamman, Jane, 211
Hampshire Telegraph, 397
Hampton, John (sponsor), 108, 110, 124n63
hand bills, 65
harbourmaster, 54
hardware, 157
Hardwicke, Earl of, 331n44
hares, 17, 94
harness makers, 390
Harper, James, 40n88, 42, 43, 84, 85, 86
Harper, Sarah, 40n88, 85, 86
Harper's Corners, 86
Harris, John R., 338, 340, 341
Harrison, Richard, 319
hartshorn, 229
harvest, 59, 117, 145, 147, 153, 211, 216, 261; in England, 326; method used, 41
Harwood, Alfred, 163, 164
Harwood, Edmund, 79
Harwood, George, 190
Harwood, Henry, xxix, □ 94 (163–5), 190, 222
Harwood, Henry Jr, 163, 164, 165, 190
Harwood, John, 173
Harwood, Lucy Susannah (Coleman), 164–5, 190
Harwood, Mary, 173
Harwood, Mrs, 173
Harwood, Richard, 163, 164
Harwood, Sarah (Holden), 164
Harwood, Sarah (Wise), 164n3
Hascomb, Surrey, 36; sending parish, 34
Haslemere, Surrey, 153, 256; letter to, 152
Haslett, Robert, 217, 219
Haslett, William, 65, 79
Hasted, Frederick, xxix, 151, 255, 266, 272n17, 274, 279n35, 281, 381, □ 174 (382–4), □ 175 (384–8)
Hasted, Mary Ann, see Holden
Hasted, S., Angmering, 390

Hastlett, William, 106
Hatch, John, 160, 171n14, 410
hats, 250; making, 124
Hawke, Anthony Bewden, 411
hawker, 381, 384
Hawkins, Charles, 150
Hawkins, G., 53
Hawkins, George, Fittleworth, 390
Hawkins, Mary, see Green
Hawkins, Squire, 383
Haws, William, 310, 311
hay and harvest time, 103
hay: cutting knife, 111, 150; fork, 199n13
Hayes Independent Chapel, Slinfold, West Sussex, 170n10, 185n16
Hayllar, Thomas, 357
Haylor, Mrs, 203
Head, Sir Francis Bond, 192, 193, 233, 276n30, 387, 388, 411
Head of the Lake, 92, 118; see also Hamilton
health, xl, 117, 138, 141, 164, 180, 214, 234, 238, 281, 284
healthy situation, 182
Healy, Christopher, 358
heart, ailment, 229
Heasman, Anne, 167
Heasman, George, 167
Heasman, Harriet, 167
Heasman, Henry, xl, xlii, □ 96 (166–8)
Heasman, Henry Sr., 166
Heasman, Mary, 167
Heasman, Sarah, 167
Heath, Counsellor, 42
Heath family, 42
Heather, John, 216
Heather, George, 141, 156n127
Heather, Thomas, 156
Heather, William, 212, 400
Heber, 100, 192, 193, 207, 212, 213, 235, 238, 249, 251, 252, 271, 275n29
hedges, ditches or posts, 104
Heene, West Sussex: letter to, 200; sending parish, 200
Hellyer, Henry, 65
Hellyer, James, 65
Helyer, Charlotte (Goble), 152
Helyer, Edward, 153
Helyer, Eliza, 152
Helyer, Henry, 153

Helyer, James, □ 90 (152–3)

Helyer, James Jr, 152, 153

Helyer, Jane, 153

Helyer, John, 10, 152

Heming (Hemming), Anna
    Maria (Payne), 18, 19, 59

Heming (Hemming), Edward
    Francis, 8, 18, 19, 57, 90, □ 30
    (59–60), 202

Heming, Canon George, of
    Chichester, 18

Heming, Sarah Eliza (Jones), 8

hemlock, 117, 349

Henley, Chas., 214

Henley, Mrs (aunt of John Luff),
    117

Henly, West Sussex, 50

Henry Street, Woodstock, 299

Herington, Reverend, 292

herrings, 116, 146n106

Hespeler, 400

Hetherington's Twopenny Dispatch,
    295, 295n63

Hetzel, Wm., 153

Hewitt, Elizabeth, 205

Hewitt, Sarah, 207

Hewitt, William (father), 205

Hewitt, William, □ 108 (205–7),
    273, 273n26, 293, 293n54

Heyshott, 152

Hibernia, 298

Hicks, Mr, 134

Hicksites, 352, 352n18

Hide, George, 236

Hill, Mr and Mrs
    (of Lurgashall?), 37

Hill, Mrs Noah, 102

Hill, Noah, 93, 94, 95, 101, 411

Hill, Thomas (overseer), 200n14

Hills, Amy (Emma), 228, 228n82

Hills, Ann, 32, 108

Hills, Ann (Charman), 32, □ 63
    (108–10)

Hills, Caroline, 32

Hills, Charles, 109, 227

Hills, Eleanor (Ellen), 227, 228,
    228n82

Hills[?], Elizabeth, xxix, 33

Hills, Emma, 227

Hills, George (emigrated 1836),
    □ 120 (227–9)

Hills, George (emigrated 1832),
    xxix, xlii, □ 16 (32–3), □ 17
    (33–4), □ 63 (108–10)

Hills, George Jr, 32, 33, 108, 110

Hills, Henry, 32, 108

Hills, Hester (Esther), 227, 228,
    228n82

Hills, Hugh, 109, 109n37

Hills, Jane, 32, 33, 108

Hills, John, 32, 108

Hills, Lucy, 227, 228, 228n82

Hills, Lydia, 194

Hills, Mary, 192

Hills, Mary Ann (Ewens), □ 120
    (227–9)

Hills, Mary Ann (daughter), 227

Hills, William, 110

Hilton, Alexander, 17n25, 223,
    225, 227; □ 123 (233–5)

Hilton, Ann, see Evans

Hilton, Barbara (Bridger), 223

Hilton, Charles, 17n25, 79, 148,
    165, 223, 224n73, 225, 225n76,
    226, 227, 233, 280

Hilton, Charles Jr, 225, 225n75,
    233

Hilton, Charles (son of Alexan-
    der), 234

Hilton, Charlotte, 223, 224n71,
    234

Hilton, Emily, 223, 224n71

Hilton, Friend, 223, 224, 227

Hilton, George, □ 119 (223–7),
    225, 233

Hilton, George Jr, 233, 224

Hilton, Harriet, 225, 225n75, 234

Hilton, Harriet, see Rapley, Jane

Hilton, Henry (brother of
    Charles and George), 223, 225,
    226, 227, 233

Hilton, Henry (son of George),
    223

Hilton, James, 223, 224, 225, 227,
    133

Hilton, James (son of George),
    233

Hilton, Jane, see Rapley

Hilton, Lydia (Booker), xxxii, 73,
    223, □ 119 (223–7)

Hilton, Maria, 234

Hilton, Martha, 223, 224, 227,
    234

Hilton, Martha (Humphries),
    234

Hilton, Mary Ann (Webb),
    17n25, 23, 225, 225n75, 233,
    234n89

Hilton, Rachel, 234

Hilton, Sarah (Overington), 225,
    227, 234

Hilton, Sarah Ann, 225, 233

Hilton, William, 225, 233

hire: by year, 35; 115, 207; with
    large farmer, 112

Hoad, Sarah, 356n25

Hoard, John, 350, 356

hobbing (hand-raising) a calf, 211

hogs, 70, 73, 111, 115, 153, 205

Holden, Ann, see Summersell

Holden, Ann, 80, 82

Holden, Frances, see Pullen

Holden, Harriet, 80, 82, 292

Holden, Henry Edward, 158

Holden, James, 80, 255

Holden, John, □ 93 (157–8), 294,
    294n60

Holden, Joseph, 157

Holden, Mary, □ 47 (80–3); see
    also Pannell

Holden, Mary Ann (Hasted),
    381, 390

Holden, Moses, 80, 255

Holden, Ruth, see Mann

Holden, Sarah, see Harwood

Holden, Sarah, 158

Holden, Sarah, of Slinfold, 82

Holden, Sergeant, 80

Holden, Sophia, 157

Holden, Thomas, xlii, 80,
    82n180, 83, 252, 253, 254, 280

Holden, Thomas Jr, 80

Holden, Thomas (father of
    John), 157

Holden, William (brother of
    John), 157

Holden, William (married Mary
    Anne Hasted), 390

Hollis, Fanny, see Martin

Hollis, Jane, 55, 179n4

Hollis, Jane (daughter), 55

Hollis, John, 115, 179, 179n4

Hollis, John (son), 55

Hollis, Mary, 55

Hollis, Sarah, 55

Hollist, Catharine, 214

Hollist, John, 214

Holmwood, Mr, 207n24

Honor Oak Road, Forest Hill,
    London, 328

Hook, George: emigrates to
    Ohio, 396

Hooker, Caroline, 280
Hooker, Elizabeth (Pullen), □ 132 (267–9), □ 139 (288–93), 405–7
Hoops, Kneesworth, Cambridgeshire, 306, 317; letter from, 321
hops, 96; garden, 376
Horezen, Mr, 42
Horne and Whittington, 389
Horning, John, 154
horse racing, 274
horses, 56, 57,111, 125, 132, 155, 182, 201, 209, 218, 224; boats drawn by, 13, 27, 250
Horsham, West Sussex, 172, 173, 183, 184, 336, 342, 350, 355, 356, 410
Horsnaill, Edwin, 366
Horton, Elizabeth, see Daniels
Horton, Thomas, 136
Hosmer or Osmer, Sarah, see Longhurst
hospital, 170, 373
Hough, Elizabeth, see Adsett
Hough, James, 401
Hough, R.: Obed Wilson working for, 32
house, 44, 47, 57, 61, 72, 83, 112, 115, 133, 145, 157, 201, 225, 228, 229; built, 86, 171; burned down, 280; described, 172, 185; let, 224; raising, 165, 280; rented, 33; two-storey built, 28
House of Assembly, 194, 387, 388n9
House of Industry, 146n106, 244, 260n29
housebreaking, 147
housekeeper, 53, 157
housework: described, 375–6
How, William, 329
Hudson's Bay Company, 371
humming birds, 101
Humphries, Martha, see Hilton
hunger, 113
Hunt, Edward, 85
Hunt, Henry, 250
hunting, 94, 99, 115; dog for deer, 22; free, 20, 173
Huntly, Mr, 58
Hurley, Henry, 164
Huron, Lake, 59, 94n5, 105, 146, 176
Huron County, 131, 217

Huron Tract, xxxv, 7, 28, 44n97, 56, 58, 70, 94n5, 96n10, 135, 136, 178, 237, 296, 297, 409
hurricane, 9
hurts (bilberries), 134
Huskinson Street, 400
hymns, 210
Hyson tea, 86

icebergs, 170, 200, 208
Ile d'Orléans, 346
Illinois, 187n18
illness, 52, 115, 124, 127, 189, 214, 289, 361; during voyage, 8; see also cholera
immigrant quarters, 6
incendiarism, 337, 342
indenture: in Upper Canada, 25n48
indentured, 107
Independence, 160
independence, feeling of, xli–xlii, 198, 195, 212, 231, 285, 391
Independent and Congregational Chapel, 120
Independent (Congregational) West Street Chapel, 86
Indian corn, 46, 70, 83, 98, 109, 149
Indian lands, 178; reserve, 90, 92; village, 362
Indians, xl, 85, 99, 100, 156, 362, 389; selling venison, 22; woman, 122
inflammation: on the brain, 261
Ingersoll, 164
inheritance, 317–18
inland postage, payment of requested, 392
Innisfil Township, 379, 380; letter from, 370
innkeeper and maltester, 393
inns, 73, 224, 349; refused travellers, 347
intermarriage, 281
invasion: threatened from United States, 389
Ireland, 306, 332
Irish, 170, 349
Iroquois, 56n126
Isle of Wight, xxvii, 91, 146n105, 161, 260n29, 345; emigrants sent from, 246; visit described, 367–8

Islington, 358
Italy, unrest, 337
Itchingfield, 222n69

Jackman, Ann, 235, 236
Jackman, Ann (mother of William), 236
Jackman, Barbara (Smith), 237
Jackman, Ellen, 235, 236
Jackman, Francis (Frank), 235, 236, 238, 239
Jackman, Henry William (Harry), 235, 236, 238, 239
Jackman, Mary, 235, 236
Jackman, Mary (Greenfield), 236, 237
Jackman, Sarah (Lillywhite), xix, 235; □ 124 (235–6)
Jackman, Stephen, 235, 237
Jackman, William, xix, □ 124 (235–8)
Jackman family, 194
Jackson, James, 400
Jackson, Sarah, see Titmouse
Jameson, Anna, xxxv
Janes, Sarah, see Mann
jaundice, 322
Jay, Henry, 205
John, Randall, 256
John Bull, 10, 17, 34
Johnson, James, 123
Johnston, William M., 69
Joice, see also Joyes
Joice, Rachel, 115n52
Joice, Thomas, 115
Joiner, Hannah, see Covey
Joiner, James, 111
Jones, Eliza, 290
Jones, Eliza Sarah, 59
Jones, Harriet, 67
Jones, Henry John, 146, 146n107, 200
Jones, Mr, blacksmith, 167
Jones, Sarah Eliza, see Heming
Jones, Sarah Eliza (Cooper), □ 1 (8)
Jones, Thomas, 8
Jordan, George, 391, 392
journal, 396
journal entries, 126
journeyman, 72, 85, 155
Joyes, Albert Emanuel, 223
Joyes, Anna, 223
Joyes, Cyrus, 223

Joyes, Daniel, 222

Joyes, Edward, 223

Joyes, Frederick, 222

Joyes, Hannah (Dennett), 222

Joyes (Joice), Luke, □ 118 (222–3)

Joyes, Richard, 223

Joyes, Robert, 223

Joyes, Solomon, 223

Joyes, William Henry, 223

Jubilee celebrations, 329

July Revolution, 337

Jupp, Jane, 168

Jupp's Farm, Goring, 237n99

Kangaroo Island, new colony, 364

Kansas, 187n18, 372

Katesville Post Office, xxxiv, 275

Kemp, Ann, 299

Kemp, M., 163

Keen, master, 283

Keen, Meriah, 290

Keen, Mrs, 289

Keen, William, 290

Kent, 411

Kent militia, 389

Kettle Creek (Port Stanley), 4, 7, 21, 22, 23, 35, 53, 66, 68, 82; letter from, 13

Key, Sir John, 359

King, Charles (overseer of Bury), 25n46

King, Daniel, 180, 183

King Street, 182

King Township, 377, 377n45

King's Arms, Haslemere, 153, 412

Kingett, Eliza, 280

Kingshott, see also Kinshott

Kingshott, Robert (in England), 37

Kingston, East Sussex, 27, 132, 164, 184, 187n18 201; sending parish, 188

Kingston Mills, 160

Kinshott, Eleanor, 45

Kinshott, Elizabeth (Child), 38, 45

Kinshott, George, 102

Kinshott, James, 102

Kinshott, John, 45

Kinshott, Joseph, 37, 44, 70, 123

Kinshott, Robert, 102

Kinshott, Sarah, see Morley

Kinshott's, 118

Kirdford, West Sussex, 66, 79, 80, 102n24; 111, 156, 282n39; 289, 410; letter to, 64, 73, 75, 76, 77, 78, 103, 104, 105, 106, 110, 155, 278; people, xxvii, 65; sending parish, 252n6

Kirkland, Sarah Jane, see Adsett

Kneesworth, 306, 315, 328, 331; letter from, 326

Knight, George, 214, 214n43

Knight, J., 84, 86

Knight, James, xxxiii, 4, □ 177 (393), □ 178 (395–6), 409; as agent for the Courtauld family, 7

Knight, James (Guelph area), 381

Knight, Mrs, of White Hart Inn, Petworth, 215

Knight, Sarah (Redman), 393, 395n1; □ 179 (396–7)

Knight, William (member of the Petworth Emigration Committee), 147, 265, 411

knives, 98; see also tools

labour, 73, 136, 140, 144, 199, 213, 238; to clear, 153; demand for, 103; , payment in kind, 228; price of, 172

labourers, 57, 59n130, 62, 73, 78n175, 103, 116, 123, 124, 135, 138, 151, 168, 183, 188, 189, 200, 215, 223, 231, 258; wages, 181, 240, 290; wanted, 178, 232

lace, 150

Lachine, 90, 126, 160, 347, 411

Lachine Canal, 6, 26, 126

Ladd family, 240

Lady Chapel, 358

Lake Road, 114

Lambkin, Silvester, 32

Lanaway, see Lannaway

Lancaster, 397

land, xli, 56, 59, 64, 94, 96, 148, 167, 172; 50 acres of, 145; 100 acres of, 44, 61, 94, 110, 150, 135, 146, 148; 200 acres of, 133; at Adelaide, 23, 225; agents, 27; available, 27, 98; bought, 28; cleared, 153, 216; clearing of, 15, 185; description of, 237; five-acre lots, xlii, 160, 162, 178, 180, 184, 194, 298, 299, 411; importance of, 36;

improvements, 384; land, payment, 210; payment by instalments, 180; at Plympton, 199; price in South Australia, 364; price of, 19, 20, 31, 36, 94, 163, 172, 203; proposed purchase, 162–3, 177, 265, 293; rental, 255; rights to lots acquired, 381; sale, 8, 24; speculator, 209; uncleared, 47; in Upper Canada, 176

land grant, 169; military, 95, 115

land jobber, 294n59

Land's End, 163, 164

Lander, George, 37, 44, 70

Lander, Henry, 37, 44, 70

Landers, see Lander

landing money, xvii, 5, 146n106

Lane, Edward, 245, 260

Langleys, 272

Lannaway (Lanaway), James, 246, 266, □ 142 (297–9)

Lannaway, Joseph, 298, 299

Lannaway, Leah, 298

Lannaway, Lucy, 298

Lannaway, Rachel, 298

Lannaway, Sarah, 298

Lannaway, Sarah (Coleman), □ 142 (297–9)

Lascelles, Dr, 40

Laskay village, 377n45

laudanum, 141n88

laundry, 115, 206

Laurie, Sir Peter, 359

Lavant Hill, 126

lease or glean, 41, 41n90

leather, 67, 98, 124

leaven, 100

Leggatt, see Leggett

Leggett, Charles, 188, 188n19, 205, 209

Leggett, George, 208

Leggett, Joseph, 17, 54, 55, 79, 148, 165

Leggett, Ruth, 208

legislation, 91

Leslieville, 323

letters, 43, 58, 64, 69, 80, 83, 85, 92, 94n6, 102, 103, 107, 109, 114, 115, 118, 119, 121, 124, 126, 130, 134, 137, 138, 140, 141, 149, 156, 157, 162, 173; advice to emigrants, 395; against emigration, 258; alteration of, 9; carried to England, 297; collected and edited, 412; collections, arrive in Upper Canada, xxxii, 141; composite, 322; copied, 20, 78, 336, 350, 354, 390; cost of, 249; crossed, 354; editing of, liv–lv, 141, 267n1; for emigrants, 393; expensive, 101; extracts of, 293n56, 295; and fears of tampering, xxxi; forms of surviving, xix–xx; importance to emigration, xxxix–xl; joint, xxvi, xxix, 305, 313, 324; in manuscript, xxi, 267; method of verifying, xxix–xxxii, 16; not answered, 298; omission, xxxviii, 18, 180, 206, 384; opened, 82, 195; original, 235; paper, taken out, 256n13; place of, xviii; of Polish immigrants, xx; post in Onslow Arms, 252; published, xix–xx, 241, 305, 384, 391; on rebellions, 266; received, 277, 293; sent with, 268, 313; shared, 325; show to others, xxx, 186, 241, 248, 250; sources of xxvi–xxvii; as sources, xxvii–xliii; unanswered, 290; see also Sockett, Thomas

letter-writers: background of, xx–xxii; clusters of, xvii, xx; description of, xxiv–xxv; and first stage of settlement, xxi; literacy of, xxviii–xxix; profile of, xxiv–xxv

Lewes, East Sussex, 163, 164

Lewes emigration committee, 161, 409

Lewis, Captain John, 5, 91, 142

libel, 147, 213

Lickfold, Thomas, 95

Lickfold, Lodsworth, West Sussex, 144, 218

Light, Colonel Alexander Whalley, 182

Lillywhite, Daniel, 235

Lillywhite, Elizabeth, 236

Lillywhite, George, 235

Lillywhite, Reuben, 235

Lillywhite, Sarah, see Jackman

lime burning, 70

Linchmere, Surrey, 48

linen drapery, 157

Lintot, Benjamin, 209

Lintot, George, 208, 209

liquor, 63, 118

Litchenfield, 350

literacy, xxviii–xxix, 223, 305; see also marriage registers, signing of

Litlington, 310

Little Park, 102

Little Peppering, Burpham, West Sussex: letter to, 207, 410

Little Walberton, 208

Little York, 55, 146, 179, 398; see also York

Littlehampton, 79, 118

Liverpool, 176

living: comfortable, 209, 229; compared to England, 282; on ship, 107

Lizard, 90

Lloyds of London, 5

loan, 206; approval for, 193; for emigration, 337; guarantee, 177, 206n22

Lobo Township, 77n170, 278

locks, 127

locktender, 180

lodgings, 127, 348; refused, 360; at York, 348, 362

Lodsworth, West Sussex, 70, 120, 135, 143, 275, 300n73; immigrants from, 7; letter to, 8, 26, 69, 129, 132, 144, 209, 276

Lodsworth Common, 217, 218

Lodsworth-Tillington area, 272n21

log house, 7, 19, 57, 59, 67, 94, 98, 99, 100, 126, 152, 160, 162, 171, 173, 185, 189, 194, 384; logging bee, 57

London, England, 42, 50, 266, 307, 325, 353, 359; disturbances, 342; letter from, 328, 337, 354; letter to, 80, 344; improvements, 1832, 352–3; post, 85; sailed from, 298, 336; visit to City, 343

London, Upper Canada, 166, 224, 252, 272, 280, 282, 283, 389, 390; flourishing, 385; letter from, 148, 384; military stationed at, 386; town lot recommended, 385

London bridge, 353

London District, 7, 65, 152, 232, 388, 387n8; letter from, 64

London/North Dorchester, 68

London Standard, 245

London Township, 148

Long, Henry, 249

Long, Wm., 212

Long Island, 160

Long Sault rapids, 56n126 134, 361

Longhurst, Charlotte, see Willard

Longhurst, Christiana, 60, 61

Longhurst, George, 60

Longhurst, Hester, 10n5, 42n92, 61

Longhurst, Joseph, 60

Longhurst, Rebecca (Weller), □ 31 (60–1), □ 32 (61–2)

Longhurst, Sarah (Hosmer or Osmer), 60

Longley, Edward, xxxiv, 60, 176, 178, 192, □ 106 (200–4)

Longley, Lucy, 200

Longley, William, 204

loom, 255

Lord Mayor's Show, 359

Lord Melville, 4, 6, 5, 8, 9, 17, 38, 46, 52, 68, 75, 82n179, 97n12, 138, 139, 155n149

Lotton, Louise, see White

Louth Township, 55, 258

Lower Canada, xv, journey through described, 10, 13, 17; rebellion in, 388; see also Lachine, Montreal, Quebec, rebellions

Loxwood, 252, 252n8

Loyalist, 51n115

Lucas, Ann (Mitchell), 141n91

Lucas, F.W., 367

Lucas, Hermit, 320

Lucas, J., 52

Lucas, Maria, see Smith

Lucas, Ned, 52

Lucas, Thomas, 140, 141

lucern seed, 65, 111, 111n42

Luff, Edward (Ned), 37, 43, 45, 70

Luff, John, □ 10 (24–5), □ 11 (25–6), 117

Luff, Mrs, 298

Luff, William, 198

luggage, 35, 58, 64, 126, 185;

expensive to transport, 226;
and passengers, 56
lumber yard, work at, 323
lunatic asylum, 324
Lundy, Isaac, 375
Lurgashall, 66, 124, 102n23, 131,
278, 290, 412; deaths among
party from, 37; Lurgashall,
West Sussex, immigrants from,
7; letter to, 43, 93, 101, 153;
sending parish, 8
luxuries, 181
Lyons, Joseph, 223

McCrea, John, 202, 203
McDougall, David, 370, 371
McDougall, Elizabeth
(Chantler), 350, 359, 370
McDougall, Elizabeth (daughter), 370
McDougall, George, 371
McDougall, George Millward, 370
McKean, Richard, 296
Mc'Kensey, Mr, 53
Mc'Kensey's saw mills, 52
Mackenzie, James Hector, 51n114
Mackenzie, William Lyon, xxiii,
244, 266, 379, 387 388, 411
Mackenzie Creek, 51n114
Mcleod school house, 375
MacNab, Allan Napier, xxiii
McPherson's warehouse, 90
Madgwick, Ann, see Courtnage
Madgwick, Aunt, 133
Madgwick, James, 257n15
Maguire, John, 153
Maidstone, 366
Maith, Robert, 365
Malahide Township, 35, 68; letter
from, 34
malaria, see Michigan ague
malt, 148
malt mill, 71, 96, 150; requested,
21
mandrakes, 211; may-apple (wild
mandrake), 211n35
mangel wurzel seed (variety of
beet), 100, 100n18
Mann, Ambrose, 251n5
Mann, Ann (Downer), xxviii,
xxix, xxx, 83, □ 127 (251–5),
280, 281, 381
Mann, Charles, 251, 252, 254,
255, 381, 382, 390

Mann, Edwin, 251
Mann, Eli, 251, 252, 254
Mann, Elizabeth (Sherwin), 251
Mann, Ellen, 251n5, 253
Mann, George, xxx, 251, 253, 255
Mann, Hannah, 251n5
Mann, Henry, xxx, 251, 253, 255
Mann, John, 123, 251, 252, 254
Mann, Lucy, 253n9
Mann, Mark, 251, 252, 254, 281,
401
Mann, Meshec, 251n5
Mann, Moses, 251, 252
Mann, Noah, 251, 252, 253
Mann, Noah (son), 251
Mann, Ruth (Holden), 80, 82,
83, 253. 254
Mann, Samuel, 83, 251, 252
Mann, Samuel (son), 251
Mann, Sarah (Janes), 255
Mann, Shadrac, 251n5
Mann, Sophia (Rapley), 254, 281,
401
Mann, Thomas, 83, 251, 254, 255
Mann family, 246
Manning, Reverend Henry, 101
manufacturing, 78
manure, 104
maple sap: uses for, 272
maple sugar, 39, 65, 173, making,
185; see also sugar
marbles, 317
Marietta, 397
Mariposa Township, 307, 376; letter to, 309
market, 84, 201, 249
Marlborough, 9
Marrell, Isabell, see Carver
marriage, 37, 109, 167, 187
marriage register, xxviii–xxix, 79;
mark in, 43n95, 45n100,
48n105, 48n108, 68n155,
73n162, 140n87, 145n104,
204n20; signed, 32n68, 43n95,
45m100, 46n103, 48n108,
48n105, 48n108, 68n155,
73n162, 93n2, 112n45, 119n56,
138n82, 140n87, 144n99,
149n110, 152n116, 153n119,
163n1, 168n7, 178n1, 183,
194n1, 204n20, 213n27, 221n62,
222n69, 221n62, 223, 227n81,
251n4, 255n12, 260n21, 270n15,
278n34, 297n68; see also literacy

Marsh, Robert, 64, 337
Marshall, Mary, see Pannell
Marshall, William (Felpham
baker): copy of letter
requested, 390
Marten, J., 188, 189
Martin, Betsy Maria, see Wilson
Martin, Esther, 55
Martin, Fanny (Hollis), 55, 59,
179n3
Martin, Frances, 55
Martin, Jane, 181n6, 183
Martin, Louisa, 55
Martin, Marion, 55
Martin, Martha, 237
Martin, Martin, xl–xli, 19, 20,
□ 29 (55–9), 179
Martin, Richard, 55
Martin, William, 180, 181, 181n6
Martin, William (son of Martin),
55, 59
Martin family, 173
Mason, Wm., 114
masters, 26, 79, 85, 102, 114, 121,
189
Matilda (Iroquois) Rapid, 27
matrimony, 368
Matthews, Charles Stephens,
218n60, 246, 250
Matthews, Solomon, 118
May, James, 269, 269n10
Meaford, 379
measles, 160, 170, 378; see also
sickness
meat, 73, 104, 134, 189, 259; price
of, 22, 41, 181, 195, 203, 213
mechanic, 57; wages, 240
medicine, 228, 360
Medonte Township: land grant
in, 37
meetings, 278, 344; meeting
house, 224, 352, 363
Melbourne, Lord (prime minister), 312n15
Meldreth, 331, 332
Mellish, Frank, 178, □ 102
(187–8), 205, 208, 209
Mellish, William, 187
melons, 70, 98, 125; see also fruit
memoir, 378
mending, 111, 115; see also washing
merchandise, 56
Merston, West Sussex, 126; sending parish, 22

mess, 142

Messenger, Mark, 208

Messenger, Thomas, 188

Messrs Harley and Heather, 401

metal plates, 98

Metcalf, Captain J., 177, 201

Methodist church, 379; ministers, 399; missionary, 371; preacher, 280

Methodists, 107, 278, 402

Michigan, 48, 83, 178, 234, 255

Michigan ague, 400; see also ague

Middlesex Light Infantry, 244, 272

Midhurst, West Sussex, 152, 206, 268, 289

Midhurst Poor Law Union, 206n22

Miles, Ann, 236n94

Miles, George, 236n94

Miles, Henry, 347

military land grant, 20, 37, 69, 102

military service, 169

militia, 276, 279; 11th Provisional Battalion of, 412; general muster day, 279; service, 266, 272

mill, 199, 347, 348, 349, 366

Millard, Mary Ann, see Chantler

Miller, Ann, see Cosens

Miller, David, 379

Miller, Jane, 112

miller, 336, 379

millinery, 373

Mills, Mr, 123

Millyard, James, 208

Milton Street, Dorking, 38

ministers, 87

misbehaviour, 260

Mitchell, Ann, see Lucas

Mitchell, John (Ditchling, wheeler), 390

Mitchell, Thomas, 103

Mitchell, Tom, 78

Mitchell, William, 200

Mitchenor, James, 65

molasses, 210

money, 78, 94, 196, 226; foreign, 58; payment in, 228; received at York, 201, 261; recommended to bring, □ 42; sent from England, 210, 292; see also landing money

Montgomery, Thomas, 61

Monthly Meeting, 349, 358, 366; of Horsham and Ifield, 350n17; library, 344

Montpelier, near Petworth: letter to, 117

Montreal, 17, 46, 48, 52, 56, 65, 70, 74, 76, 82, 82, 85, 90, 105, 109, 111, 121, 130, 131, 132, 142, 145, 146, 164, 167, 172, 181, 192, 193, 201, 235, 244, 250, 251, 286, 346n10, 347, 397; arrived at, 40; disembarked at 1832, 6; emigrants arrive, 4, 10; emigrants left at, 163n2; letter from, 8; paid way from, 30; Wesleyan ministers at, 26; work available, 25

Montreal Gazette, 90

Moore, Charles, □ 69 (119–20)

Moore, Edward (brother of James and William), 54n123, 152, 215

Moore, Frances, 119

Moore, Frank, 120

Moore, George, 120

Moore, Hannah, 151

Moore, Hannah (mother of James), 215

Moore, James (in England), 119

Moore, James, □ 89 (151–2), 214, □ 114 (215)

Moore, John, 151, 214; □ 114 (215)

Moore, Luke, 215

Moore, Mary Ann, 151n115

Moore, Rhoda (Willett), 119

Moore, Sarah, 215

Moore, William, 54, □ 89 (151–2), 215

Moore, William Sr, 151, 152, 215

Moore, William (father of Charles), 119

morels, 17

Morgan, George, 167

Morley, Jesse, 257

Morley, Mary, see Capling

Morley, Nathan, 44

Morley, Sarah, 37, 70

Morley, Sarah (Kinshott), 44

mosquitoes: compared to English gnats, 349; troublesome, 14

Moulton, Mr, 65

Mount, Roswell, xxxii, xxxv, 7,

22, 23, 69, 83, 97, 99, 112, 156, 278, 381, 411

Mount Pleasant, Michigan, 280

Mountpillier, near Petworth, 48n107

Mount Zion 4th line cemetery, 66n152, 83, 111, 151

Mulmur Township, 61

Muncey, Emma, see Hall

Muncey, Frances, 311

Muncey, George, 306, 331n43, 332

Muncey, Henry, 315

Muncey, John, 314, 315

Muncey, Mary, 310, 310n7, 311

Muncey, Mary Ann (Wilson), 305, 306, 310, 311, 313, 314, □ 149 (315), 316, 318, □ 154 (321–2), 324, 325n33, □ 158 (326), □ 159 (326–7), 328, □ 161 (329–30), 333

Muncey, Obed, 315, 318, 326, 327, 331

Murnick, James, 62

Murray, Mr, 198

musket, 255

Musselman, David, 139n84

Musselman's mills, 139, 139n84

mutton, 44, 47, 51, 57, 86, 94, 123, 124, 148, 156; see also beef; meat

Napoleonic Wars, 168

Napper, Amy (Parker), 149, 150, 151

Napper, Avis (Downer), 13n12, 151, 252n6

Napper, Charles, 151, 252n6

Napper, George, 252n6

Napper, James, 13, 105, 151, 252

Napper, James, of Kirdford, 73, 77, 103

Napper, James Jr, 151

Napper, William, 252n6

Narrative of a Voyage, xix, 162, 170n9; advertised, 166, 169–70

Nash, Elizabeth, see Wackford

Nash, Frank, 73, □ 42 (76), 126

Nash, Massey, 125

Nash, Richard, 125

Nash, William, 76

Nash, Pulborough, West Sussex: letter to, 95

Natal, South Africa, 238

natives, 118; *see also* Indians
Navy Island, 266
Neal, Abigail, 18, 79
Neal, Richard, xli, □ 5 (16–18), 48, 55, □ 46 (79–80), 148, 165
Neal, William, 18, 79, 80
nectarines, 98
needles, 98
needlewoman, 298
needlework, 112; earnings, 299
Negroes, 286
Nelles, Henry, 51n115
Nelles, Robert, 51n115
Nelles, Warren, 51n115
Nelles Settlement: letter from, 51, 52
Nelson Post Office, 31, 119
Nelson Township, 143, 144, 230, 238; letter from, 24, 25, 30, 48, 50, 117, 140, 222, 229
Nelsonville, Athens County, Ohio, 4, 7; letter from, 393, 395, 396
nervous fever, 397
neuralgia, 378; James Rapson suffers from, 26, 27, 28
Nevett, John, 143, 143n97, 284, 284n41
Nevett, Mrs, 143
Nevett, Rebecca, 143n98
Nevett, Thomas, 143, 143n97
New Dundee, 400
new poor law, 178, 246, 411; relief, 193
New South Wales, 365
New Survey, London, 390
New York, 118, 141, 156, 176, 182n7, 350, 365; conditions in, 352; mail via, 18; packet ships schedule to, 365; prison, 62; travel via, 33, 157, 204, 280
New York State, 51n115, 152, 153, 255
Newcastle district, 294n57
Newell, Mrs, letter to, 29
Newfoundland, 13, 160; banks of, 55, 74, 170, 200, 345; description of, 346
Newfoundland dog: picture of 22; requested, 21
Newman, C., Broyle, Chichester, 390
Newman, Charles, 75n166, 106
Newman, James, 140

Newmarket, 348, 362, 363, 375, 379, 380; letter from, 344, 354, 359, 368; Quaker settlers in, 375n39; road to (Yonge St.), 349
Newport, 367, 368
Newport Pagnel, 357
newspaper, 295; accusations, 128; advertisement for son, 153; attention, 92; letters, 8, 188; radical, 295n63; received in England, 317; reports of rebellions, 269
Newton Robinson, 379
Niagara, 73n161
Niagara District: letter from, 255, 257
Niagara Falls, 4, 13, 65, 182; staircase under, 23; view, 24
Niagara frontier, 412
Niagara-on-the-Lake, 54n122
Niagara River: travel via, 23
Niblen, John, 364
Niblen, Mary, 364
Nicholl Township, 56
Nicolet, 176
Nile, 237
Noah's Ark, 93, 101, 411
non-conformist, 120
Norfolk, Duke of, 227, 410
Norfolk, 238, 325
Norris, Charlotte, 188n20, 209
Norris, Henry, 188n20, 209
Norris, John, 208
Norris, Thomas, 208
North Easthope, 45
North End, Bassingbourn, Cambridgeshire, 333; letter from, 313
North Street, 252; in Peworth, 284
Northchapel, West Sussex, 278, 290n50, 292, 398; letter to, 87, 121; parish of, 45
Northlands, 52n119
Northhamptonshire, 79
North-West Territories, 370
Northwood, John, 234
Norway House, 371
Nye, Charlotte, 215
Nyton Farm, near Guelph: letter from, 59

Oakshott, W., 214

oats, 46, 125, 148, 153; onesided; 44; *see also* crops, grain
Ockley, 336
Ogdensburg, New York, 368
Ohio, 276n31, 352, 357, 393
Ohio River, 397
Old London Bridge, 358
Old St Pauls, 158
Older, George, □ 109 (207), 227, 232
Older, Mr: emigrates to Ohio, 396
Older, Sarah (Gilbert), 207
Older, Thomas: emigrates to Ohio, 396
onions, 125, 286; seed, 100
Onslow Arms, xxx, 252n8
Ontario, Lake, 114, 118, 127, 238, 240, 348
open boat, 132, 134, 235
opportunities, 178
opposition to the government, 387
orchards, 29, 228
Oregon Boundary Dispute, 312n16
Orillia, 370
Oro Township, 374, 374n38
orphans, 101, 372–4; *see also* children
Osborne, Charles, 358
Ostand, George, 205
Ottawa, 90
Ottawa, 412
Ottawa River, 160
outbuildings, 94, 384; outhouses, 57, 132
outfit, 5, 213; cost of, 38, 217
oven cakes, 226
Overington, Sarah, *see* Hilton
overseers, 96, 189, 189n23, 200n14
Owen Sound, 60
oxen, 57, 69, 95, 98, 111, 125, 127, 132, 135, 138, 156; boats drawn by, 13, 23, 27, 250; cost of, 256
Oxford, 45
Oxford Township, 237, 252
Oxfordshire, 57

packet-boat, 76, 164
Page, Charles, 163
Pagham, 59n130
painter, 86, 183; and decorator, 83, 331

painting, 181, 375
Pall Mall, 358
Pallant, Chichester, 286
Palmer, Hannah, 54
pamphlet, 128
panekins, 98
Pannell, Mary (Holden), xxxii, 4, 66, □ 47 (80–3)
Pannell, Mary (second wife), 66
Pannell, Mrs, xxxii, 256
Pannell, William (father), 64
Pannell, William, □ 35 (64–6), 83, 156
parcel, received, 271
Paris Township, 412
parish, 91, 176, 178, 245, 383; aid, 73; assistance, 201n16; as local government unit, xvii, 411; reasons for assisting emigration, xxii; register, 79n176; relief, 251, 260; sale of parish poorhouses, 177
parish-assisted emigration, xxii–xxiii, 91, 177, 193, 245; from Norfolk and Suffolk, xxviii; outfit emigrants, 5
Parker, Amy (Steer), 13n12, 97, 149, 149n110
Parker, Amy, see Napper
Parker, George, 149
Parker, James, 13, 13n12, 14, 96, 97, □ 88 (149–51), 255, 390
Parker, James (son), 149
Parker family, 235
Parkins, Charles, 67
Parlett, John, Worthing (hairdresser), 390
parliamentary reform, 342
parliamentary select committee, 245
Parry, Mr, 14, 97
passage, 47, 60, 62, 64, 213, 235; cost of 32, 38; defined, xviii; in 1832, 16; passage inland paid, 172; paid by Egremont, 298; rough, 43
Passengers' Acts, 5
paupers, 55, 178, 189, 245, 246, 251, 271
Payne, Anna Maria, see Hemming
Payne, Jane, □ 6 (18–20)
pea soup, 170n11
Peacock, Amelia (Cowper), 282, 282n39

Peacock, Charles, 282n39, 290
Peacock, Jane, 215
Peacock, Mrs, 141
Peacock, T., 214
Pearson, Betsy, 376
Pearson, James, 377
peas, 70, 125, 153; see also crops
Peel, Sir Robert, 312n15
Peel Township, 126
Pelee Island: rebels attack, 266, 276
Pelham, 363
Penfold (Samuel or William), 53, 109
Penfold, Caroline, 93, 95
Penfold, Esther, 93
Penfold, Harriet, 93
Penfold, James, 70, 95
Penfold, Jane (Tribe), 9, 10, 26, 27, 37, 69, 94n7, 102
Penfold, Jesse Sr, 94, 123
Penfold, Jesse, xxx, 9, 28, 37, 38, 45, 69, 70, 87n190, □ 50 (93–5), 102, 123, 154, 216, 278
Penfold, Jesse (son), 93
Penfold, Matilda, see Adsett
Penfold, Sarah, 8n1
Penfold, William (superintendent), 5, 8, 19n34, 52, 122, 155
Penfolds, 52
Pennell, Jane, 64
Peppering: letter to, 227
Percival, David: 43
Percival, David, at York, 43
Perin, Mr, 386, 289
Perry, Peter, 388
persuasion: to emigrate, 229; reluctance to use, 18, 33, 50, 67, 80, 103, 113, 140, 150, 157, 173, 179, 285
Petworth, West Sussex, 52, 94, 120, 128, 273n26, 143, 145, 137, 186, 192, 195n4, 201n18, 217, 230n18, 120n84, 238, 240, 258, 265, 266, 284n41, 289, 409; letter from, xxiv, 267, 288, 405; letter to, 48, 50, 51, 52, 119, 124, 125, 135, 137, 140, 151, 217, 230, 246, 260, 281, 297; market, 242; parish, 152; parish contribution to cost, 298; sending parish, 20, 213, 217; suspicion of letters, xxxi
Petworth emigrants, 205, 278,

281, 245, 381, 410, 266–7, 346n8; Adelaide cluster, 7; immigrants, 179, 195, 241
Petworth Emigration Committee, 4, 30, 31–2, 43, 59n130, 60n132, 76, 77n171, 91, 92, 128, 132, 130, 134, 147, 152, 161, 162, 166, 176, 178, 193, 200, 204, 218n58, 230, 232, 244, 245, 246, 247n27, 251, 258, 260, 265, 271, 272n19, 276, 284, 298, 305, 390, 409, 409, 411, 412; assistance in 1838, 246; exertions of, 9; management 1832, 5; organization of, xv; provisioning by, 38; sends Dorking emigrants, 34; "Statement," xxxviii–xxxix, 134, 137, 141, 144n101
Petworth House, 244, 265, 297, 410, 412; staff assisted to emigrate, 298
Petworth Poor Law Union, 245, 411
Petworth Union Workhouse, 221n63
pheasants, see birds, game
Philadelphia, 350
Phillips, Ann, see Armitage
Phillips, Ellen, 22, 126, 127
Philips, James, 294
Phillips, John, xix, 55, 90, 115, 411; and attested copies of letters, xxix
Phillips, Mary (Pullen), 24
Phillips, Thomas Jr, 293
Phillips, William Jr, of Merston, 21, □ 9 (22–4), 127
Phillips, William (from Singleton), □ 13 (29–30), 158, 210n30, □ 140 (293–5)
Phillips, William Sr, of Merston, 22, □ 74 (126–7)
photographs, exchanged, 328, 331, 331n43, 332
piano-manufacturing, 60
Pickering, 375
pigeons, see birds, game
pigs, see animals, domestic
Pilkington, Robert, estate of, 265
Pilkington Township, 59, 265
pitsaw, 42, 70
Pittsburgh, 217, 397
Pittsford, Monroe County, New York, 391

place, *see* work, children
plain muslin, 150
Plympton party, 135
Plympton Township, 90, 92, 133n72, 133n75, 146, 146n107, 152n117, 200; letter from, 198
poaching, 200
Poland, George, 201
Poland, Mary (Grimwood), 201n16
political discontent, 194
Political Unions, 387n8
Pollard, James, 150
Pollard, Sarah, *see* Coleman
Poor Law Amendment Act, xxiii, 176, 177, 411; passed, 160
Poor Law Board, 412
poor law commissioners, 177, 206n22, 245, 251, 411, 412
Poor Law Unions, 177
poor laws, xvii
poor rates, 57, 96, 153, 412
poor relief, 135
poorhouse, 253; *see also* workhouse
Poor-house-hill, 226
Pope, Thomas, 79
porcupines, 98, 101
pork, 47, 51, 86, 99, 111, 123, 124, 135, 146, 148, 156; *see also* meat
porpoises, 17, 200
Port Hope, 129
Port Stanley, 162; *see also* Kettle Creek
Port Stanley Post Office, 67
port wine, 73, 127, 259
porter, 258, 259
Portland Bay, 144
Portland Roads, 90
portrait: sent to Canada, 320, 321, 325
Portsea, Hants, 385, 389
Portsmouth, 51, 52, 56, 46, 65, 73, 90, 133, 147, 150, 168, 201, 235, 244, 246, 294, 305, 346, 365, 367, 410, Cambridgeshire emigrants travel from, 32n66; transportation to, 5
Portsmouth Herald, 4, 9
post office, 137, 141, 293; complaints of, 313; opened in Adelaide, xxxiv
post master, 295
postage, xxxiii–xxxiv, 183, 204;

impediment to emigration, xxxv; pay through England, 114, 123; to the water, 280
postal order, 300
postal service, xxxiii–xxxiv
postmaster, 101, 140, 295, 379
potatoes, 46, 47, 58, 70, 83, 125, 148, 149, 153, 228; failure of, 314; sent to Upper Canada, 277
Potter, Richard, 220
potter's clay, 114
pottery, 114, 156, 225, 228
Pound Street, Petworth, 299
poverty, 193
powder, 98, 133
Pratt, John, 218, 273, 273n26, 274
Pratt, Sarah, *see* Goldring
preachers, wanted, 252
pregnancy, 9; *see also* confinement
Presbyterian: charge, 28; Church 235; minister, 71
Prescott, 6, 34, 56n126, 74, 75, 82, 85, 86, 90, 111, 122, 127, 127, 131, 132, 192, 193, 201, 206, 235, 348, 361, 362; incursions at, 266; passage to 347
preserved meats, 259
Preston, 4, 46n101, 192, 277, 398, 399
Preston Post Office, Waterloo Township, xxxiv, 297
prices, 51, 109; of land, 56, 135; of provisions, 123, 135; of spirits, 181; *see also* produce, spirits, meat, grain, clothing, shoes
Prime, Richard, of Walburton, 32n66, 187
Prime, Thomas (Bassingbourn overseer), 32n66
Primitive Methodist, 296n65
prince's feather (flower), 211
printing: business, 184
prison, 31, 62n136, 129
prisoners, 272, 276, 280n36, 282
produce: prices of, 31, 234, 274
Promenade Hotel, Hamilton, 222n68
prong (hay fork), 199
prospects: better in Upper Canada, 44, 47, 61, 148, 150, 167; improved in England, 292
Providence: faith in, 39, 42

Provident and District Society, 183, 183n8
provisions, 57, 61, 104, 111, 121, 124, 134, 148, 172, 199, 271; cost of, 284, 298, 261; Irish nearly out of, 345; shared, 240; on ship, 196, 221; for voyage, 40, 225, 256
public houses, 94, 316; keeping, 306
public works, 232
Puget, John Hey, 183n8
Pulborough, West Sussex, 77n171, 151, 252n6; letter to, 13, 149; sending parish, 168
Pulborough Poor House, 71
Pullen, Ann, 260, 261
Pullen, Eliza, 268n8, 289n49
Pullen, Elizabeth, *see* Hooker
Pullen, Elizabeth, 268, 289
Pullen, Elizabeth (daughter of Richard), 260
Pullen, Emily, 292
Pullen, Frances (Holden), □ 131 (260–1), 265, 267, 279n35, □ 136 (281–3), □ 137 (283–4), 288, 292, 298
Pullen, Frances (daughter), 292
Pullen, Frederick, 289n49
Pullen, George, 283, 290n51, 292
Pullen, Hannah, 260
Pullen, Harriet, 268n7
Pullen, Henry, 260
Pullen, James, 268, 289
Pullen, James (son of Richard), 292
Pullen, John, 289n49
Pullen, John (son of Richard), 292
Pullen, Mara Ann, 292
Pullen, Maria (Budd), 268n7
Pullen, Martha, 268, 288
Pullen, Mary, *see* Phillips
Pullen, Peter, 268, 289
Pullen, Richard (father of Mary), 24
Pullen, Richard, 24, □ 131 (260–1), 267, □ 136 (281–3), □ 137 (283–4), 288
Pullen, Richard Jr, 260
Pullen, Sarah, 289
Pullen, Sarah (daughter of Richard), 260, 292
Pullen, Thomas, 268, 268n8, 289

Pullen, William (brother of Richard), 268, 269, 270, 283, 289
Pullen, William (son of Richard), 260, 290
pumpkins, 70, 98, 125
Puslinch Township, 204
Puttick, Mary, 166
Puttick, Mary (Smart), 78n175
Puttick, Matthew, 78
Puttock, Ann, see Thomas
Puttock, Elizabeth, 105
Puttock, Sarah, 68, 69
Puttock, Thomas, 68, 69, 140
Puttock, William, 69

Quaker community, 336; school, 337
Quaker Meeting House, 344n6
Quakers, 352n18; see also Society of Friends
quarantine, 6, 8, 10, 120, 145, 160, 224, 346, 351
Quarantine Island, see Grosse Île
quarrelling: on ship, 40, 345
Quarterly Meeting of London & Middlesex, 358
Quebec, Lower Canada, 8, 46, 47, 54, 65, 70, 74, 82, 85, 90, 121, 123, 137, 152, 160, 163, 166, 170, 171, 176, 184, 189, 192, 193, 201, 208, 225, 230, 235, 244, 259, 346, 351, 371, 381, 391, 392; arrival at, 17, 34; city gates to shut, 347; description of 1832, 10, emigrants arrive 1832, 4
Queenston, 160
Quelch, John, 220, 250

rabbits, see animals, wild
Racher, Ann (Burns), 48
Racher, Asher, 311
Racher, Edith (Titmouse), 47, 48, 312n14
Racher, Isaac, 310, 311, 315, 317, 329
Racher, John, 47, 48, 312n14, 322, 322n27
Racher, Mary, 322
Racher, Stephen, 322
Rackett, William, 163n2
racoons, 98, 101
Radcliff, Colonel Thomas, 101, 169, 267, 388, 412

raft, 71
Raglan Post Office, Whitby East, letter to, 325
rail fences, 104
Rama, near Orillia, 370, 371
Randall, Abraham, 192, 250, 250n2
Randall, Abraham (son), 250n2
Randall, Isaac, 250n2
Randall, Jacob, 90, 250n2
Randall, John, 257
Randall, Mesheck, 250n2
Randall, Sarah (Edwards), 250n2
Randall, Sarah, 250n2
Randall, Shadrack, 250n2
Rapley, William, 278
Rapley, Ann (Biddulph), 278, 280
Rapley, Charles, 97, 267, □ 135 (278–81); as drummer, 279
Rapley, Charles (brother of William), 77
Rapley, Charlotte (Buttery), 278, 280
Rapley, David (son of Charles), 278, 280
Rapley, David (son of James), 278
Rapley, Elizabeth, 278, 279
Rapley, Frances (Adams), 278n34
Rapley, Harriet (Hilton), 278
Rapley, James (son), 77
Rapley, James, 65, 77n170, 101, 105n30, 110n40, 278
Rapley, Jane (Hilton), 225, 233, 234, 278
Rapley, Jesse, 278, 280
Rapley, Lucy, see Downer, Lucy
Rapley, Mary (Collins), 77
Rapley, Sophia, see Mann
Rapley, Sophia (Sophy), 278, 279, 280
Rapley, Thomas, 278, 280
Rapley, Thomas (brother of Charles), 279
Rapley, William, 77, 110, 280
Rapley family, 112, 235
Rapson, Charlotte (Tribe) [daughter of Sarah, wife of Thomas], 8, 27, 71
Rapson, Fanny, 216
Rapson, Hannah, 8, 28, 130, 133, 216
Rapson, Isaac, 8, 9, 11, 130, 216
Rapson, James (son), 9, 10, 11

Rapson, James, xxix, xxxiv, xxxvii, □ 2 (8–11), □ 12 (26–9), 37, 38, □ 38 (69–71), 45, 87n190, 92, 102, 120, 123, 125, 126, □ 76 (129–31), 133, 134, 145, 155, 209, 210, 212, □ 115 (215–17), 277, 293n55
Rapson, Jane, 130
Rapson, Jesse, 102
Rapson, John, 133, 216
Rapson, Maria, 154n120
Rapson, Maria (Thair), 120, 121n60, 129, 216, 217
Rapson, Mary, 28
Rapson, Mary (daughter of James), 8, 130
Rapson, Philip (father of James), 8, 9, 26, 69, 129, 132
Rapson, Philip (son of James), 8, 11, 28, 130, 216
Rapson, Rhoda, see Thair
Rapson, Rhoda, 9, 11, 28, 130, 216
Rapson, Sarah (daughter of James), 216
Rapson, Sarah (Tribe), 8, 9, 26, 28, 37, 69, 71, 102, 130, 131, 133, 216
Rapson, William (brother of James), 90, 92, 120, 121n60, 129, 133, 134, 209, 212, 215, 216, 217, 278
rates and taxes, 316; see also poor rates
rations: on shipboard, 5, 91, 258
rattlesnakes, 86
Rawling, John, 358
Rawlings, Joseph, 359
Rayner, Mary Ann, see Goldring
Raynor, C., 115
Reach Township, 333
Rebellions of 1837–8, xxiii, 169, 246, 261, 266, 272, 279, 282, 294, 309n3, 410, 411; and aftermath, 267; described, 385–6; in Lower Canada, 244, 276; news of reaches England, 298; in Upper and Lower Canada, 265, 269n11
Red Lion Inn, Dorking, 344n6
Red Lion Yard, 140
Redhill, Surrey, 217
Redland Farm, 63
Redman, Edward, 395, 395n1

Redman, Sarah, *see* Knight
Reeves, William, 118
Reform Bill, 14, 53, 349, 353
reformers, 387, 411; reform meetings, 387n8
regiment of foot, 68; of militia, 279
Regiment of Foot, 24th, 276; 32nd, 276; 36th, 20, 168; 57th, 95
regular troops, 276, 389
Reigate, 356
religion (in Upper Canada), 87, 278
religious beliefs, 210, 268, 269, 295, 344, 357; expressions, 107; gospel preached, 54, 142; sacrament, received, 283; services, lack of, 28
revolution: on the European Continent, 338, 342
Rewell or Rule, Ruth, *see* Waldon
rheumatism, 375, 378
Rice, Frances, 142n93
Rice, Mary, 142
Richards, Ann, *see* Webb
Richards, Charles, 208
Richards, Eric, xxxix
Richards, Robert, 102
Richardson, Joseph, 298
Richmond, Charles Lennox, 5th Duke of, xix, xxxi, xxxv, 11, 21, 26, 34, 95, 128, 131, 137, 147, 154
Richmond, Legh (author): house and church, 367
Riddle, Mr, 108n35
Rideau Canal, xxxviii, 4, 126, 131, 132, 176, 177, 193, 235, 244, 250, 171n13; travel via, 160
Rideau Lake, 160
Ridsdale, Robert, xxx, 87
rifle, 41, 94, 102
roads, 127; allowance, statutory work on, 384; bush, 7; government, 98; London District, 15; new, 285; work on, 25, 31
robbery, 128
Robert Marsh Clother &c, 337
Roberts, Captain, 39, 42
Robinson, Charles, 233
Robinson, George, 157
Robinson, Mr, 270

Robinson, William, 207, □ 122 (230–3)
Robson, George, 149
Rodmell, East Sussex: letter to, 188
Roebuck Inn, Broadwater, Hertfordshire, 306, 307, 316n29, 324; letter from, 320
Rogers, Elias, 376
Rogers, Miss, 401
Rogers, Mr, 164
Rogers, Samuel, 376
Rolph, Thomas, 294, 294n59, 295, 295n64
Rood Lane, London, 318
Rose, James, 62
Rosebank Cemetery, Waterloo Township, 301
Rossshire, Scotland, 51n114
round-frock, 197, 197n10; not worn in Canada, 234, 250; white smock-frock, 270n13
Roundstreet Common, West Sussex, 253
routes: Canadian, xxviii; via New York recommended, 21, 234; *see also* voyage, travel inland
Rowe, Sophia, *see* Chantler
Rowland, James, 296
Royal, Captain, 5, 14
Royal Navy, 53, 294
Royston, 306, 318
Royston Union, 310n5
rubbers, 66, 150
Rubidge, Charles, 294, 294n57
Rudgwick, 251
Rue, Captain, 193
Ruel, James, 391, 392
Ruel, Mark, 392
rum, 67, 111, 147, 148, 156; and brandy, 94; for neuralgia, 28; *see also* beer, drink, spirits, whisky
Rural Rides, 409
rural unrest (England), 337
rush-lights, 190n24
Ryde, 367
rye, 70, 109, 148; *see also* crops, grain

Sabbath School, 289, 290
sacks, 199
saddle: requested, 19
saddler, 400; working for, 33

Sadler, James, 67
Sageman, Bertha, 214
Sageman, Charles, 272, 272n22
Sageman, James Boxall, 214n46
Sageman, Mary, 214n41, 272n22
Sageman, William, 119, 214, 272n22
Saginau, Michigan, 399
sailors, 91, 106, 116, 132, 145, 183; and captain, 134; death of, 11; drowned, 17
St Catharines (England), dock, 365
St Catharines (Upper Canada), 59n130, 178, 256; letter from, 178, 194
St Clair, Lake, 92, 147n109
St Clair River, 90, 92, 147n109
St Francis, Lake, 13, 361
St George, 163
St James Anglican Church (Toronto), 182
St James's Park (London, England), 353, 358
St John's, York Mills, 218n60
St Lawrence River, 54, 60, 131, 170n11, 183, 192, 200, 250, 346; effects of cholera, 4, 363; description of, 10, 17, 27; rapids, 6, 13, 33, 56, 127, 131, 193, 235, 347, 348, 361; route, 126; hardships of travel on, xxxvii, 26–7, 126–7
Saint-Louis, Lake: towed across, 26
St Mary the Virgin Church, Petworth, 291, 292
St Paul's church (Warwick), 127
St Paul's Island, 10
St Saviour's Cathedral (London, England), 353
St Thomas, 235
St Thomas's Hospital (London, England), 353, 358
St Vincent Township, 379
salt: for cattle, 202
salt rising: used upcountry, 286
salvage, 116
Sandgate Lodge, Sullington, 109n36
Sandwich (Windsor), 90, 92, 137, 147n109, 152, 169, 192, 389; editor, 146; letter from, 145, 213, 215

Saratoga, 182n7

Sarnia, 92, 198, 390

Saskatchewan River, 371

Saunder, Mr: emigrates to Ohio, 396

Saunders, John, □ 77 (131–2), 153

Saunders, Wm., 102

Savage, Eliza, 188

savings, 173, 228

saw mills, 15, 50, 53, 115, 150, 238; near Guelph, 19

sawyers, 8, 50, 51, 76, 198, 199; work for, 11

Sayers, Hannah, *see* Chantler

Sayers, Joseph, 350, 350n17

Sayers, Josh, 354

scarlet fever, 46, 108, 113

school, 45, 67, 121, 123, 179, 195, 210, 247, 269, 332, 350, 369, 375; Blenheim Township, 38; national, xxix

school mistress, 356

schooner, 23, 82, 133, 280, 389

Scollic, Wm., Esquire, 399

Scotch, 179, 206, 216, 277, 294

Scotland, 388n11

Scott, George, □ 33 (62–3)

Scott, John (son), 62

Scott, John, 62

Scott, Mary, 62

Scott Township, 333

Scovell, Peter, 152, 153, 412

Scutt, Thomas, 45

scythes: sharpen, 150

Seabrook, Mr, 270, 282

Seagull, 238, 239

sealing wax, 61

seals, 345

seasickness, 9, 17, 20, 30 , 31, 32, 74, 91, 111, 116, 124, 133, 134, 141, 141n88, 150, 170, 181, 196, 206, 208, 212, 219, 225, 236, 256, 261, 286, 345

seaside, 328

seed cakes, 196n8

seed warehouse, 268n8

seeds: requested, 19, 20, 23; sent 271, 207n24

Select Committee on Postage, 43n96

Selham parish, 144n99

Sell, Edith Fossey, 317, 317n21

Sell, Elizabeth (Wilson), *see* Crabtree

Sell, Hemp, 317

Sell, Simeon Leat (grandfather), 316, 317, 318

Sell, Simeon Leat (Leete), 312, 315, 316, 317, 318

servants, 247; attitude to, 148; live-in, 146

service: in, 33, 68, 105, 125, 153, 172, 217, 221, 225, 228, 231, 236, 247, 252, 325

setting and hauling, 116

settlement: duties, 69, 381; parish of, 6, 7, 38, 79, 154

Shambrink, *see* Shambrook

Shambrook, Hannah, 47n104

Shambrook, John, 47, 47n104

Shambrook, Lydia, 47n104

Shambrook, Mary (Titmouse), 47, 47n104, 312n14

Shambrook, Sophia, 47n104

Shannon: ship sent from, 265

shanty, 21, 99, 136, 167, 173, 184; boards provided for, 23

Sharp, Clara (Ware), 213

Sharp, David Clowser (Clouds-ley), xxvii, 137, 146n108, 148, 192, □ 113 (213–15), 272, 272n19

Sharp, Edmund, 92; □ 86 (145–8), 213, 214

Sharp, Edmund (son), 213

Sharp, Elizabeth, *see* Turner

Sharp, George, 135

Sharp, Mary, *see* Ward

Sharp, Sarah (Clowser, née West), 145, 213

Sharp, Thomas, 146, 147, 151, 213, 214, 215, 272, 272n19

Shaw, Capt., 222

shed, 170

sheep, 111, 124; Leicester, 60

Sheer: sending parish, 38

Shepherd, James, 249

Sherwin, Elizabeth, *see* Mann

Shide, 367

Shingay Mill, 310

shingle, 57; shingled roof, 173; shingle-making, 210n30, 217

shipboard life, 161–2

Shipley: letter to, 138

ship's lists, xv

shoemaker, 29, 39, 67, 116, 153, 163, 227; wages, 155

shoemaking, 72, 116, 385

shoes, 96, 124, 133, 154, 181, 197, 250; high, 37, 72, 96, 98; low, 72; men's fine, 155

Shop Farm, 290

shops, 56, 94, 185, 198

Shore, Emily, 328

Shore, Frances Ann (Fanny) (Wilson) (formerly Hall), 305, 309, 311, 312, 316, □ 149 (313–15), 323n31, 327, □ 156 (324–5), 326, 328, 329, 330

Shore, Mr, 321

Short Hills: incursions at, 266

shot guns, 94, 134; *see also* rifle

sickness, 34, 122, 135, 144, 145; of fever, 151; during voyage, 13, 137; *see also* seasickness

signatures, *see* marriage register

silk, 150

Simcoe, Lake, 58, 71

Simcoe County, 379, 380

Simpson, George, 375n41, 375n43

Simpson, Joseph, 375n43

Sims, Frederick, 357

single men, xxvi, 53, 161, 165, 168, 187, 204, 207, 215, 246

single women, xxvi, 53, 173, 203, 214n46, 246

Singleton, near Midhurst, West Sussex, 29, 30; letter to, 293

Sir James Kempt (steamer), 27

situations, 53, 350, 356; with a gentleman, 141; as house-keeper, 356; with merchant, 349; as school mistress, 350

Skildon, Thomas, 114

Slaughter, Luke, 279

sleighing, 24

sleighs, 276

Slinfold, 82

smallpox, 272

Smallwood, Elizabeth, *see* Voice

Smart, David, 78

Smart, Francis, 98

Smart, Frederick, 73, 74, 75

Smart, Henry, xxix, 65n146, 69, □ 40 (73–5), 76, □ 43 (77), □ 44 (77–8), □ 45 (78–9), □ 55 (103–4), □ 56 (104), □ 57 (105), □ 58 (105–6), □ 59 (106), □ 60 (106), 110, 111

Smart, Jane (Baker), 65, 73, 75, 76, 111

Smart, Mary, *see* Puttick

Smart, Mr: emigrates to Ohio, 396

Smart, Rhoda, *see* Whitington

Smelzer, Henry, 377n46

Smelzer, John, 377n46

Smith, Barbara, *see* Jackman

Smith, Daniel, 272, 272n21, 278

Smith, Daniel (son), 272n21

Smith, Emma, 272n21

Smith, George, 249

Smith, Jemima, 272n21

Smith, John, 401

Smith, John (from Woolbeding), 294, 294n62

Smith, John (son of Daniel), 272n21

Smith, Lucy, 272n21

Smith, Maria (Lucas), 272n21

Smith, Mary, 272n21

Smith, Rebecca (Turrell), 294n62

Smith, Thomas, 249

Smither, Avis, 289

smock-frock, 197n10, *see also* round-frock

smuggling, 114

Snider, Breugremen (Bürgersmann), 114

Snider, C.H.J., 116

snow, 13, 73n161, 80, 98, 112, 117, 120, 123, 138, 145, 192, 203, 208, 382

snowball fight: on deck, 192, 250, 208

soap, 51, 100, 148, 150, 185, 189, 255, 299; salt water, 98

social aspirations, 266

Society for the Propagation of the Gospel, 185n16

Society for the Relief of Strangers in Distress, 27n57

Society of Friends, 336, 337, 357; readmission to, 366; Yonge Street Meeting, 379; *see also* Quakers, Friends

Sockett, Caroline, 143n95

Sockett, Frances, 143n95

Sockett, George, 90, 108n35, 201, 202, 204, 210, 216, 412

Sockett, Henry, 143n95

Sockett, Sarah, 143, 143n95, 147

Sockett, Thomas, xv, xviii, xxi, xl, 43n96, 52n119, 71, 80, 82n178, 90, 94n6, 95, 120, 122n61, 128, 129, 130, 131, 43n96, 122n61

132n70, 134, 141, 143, 143n95, 144n101, 147, 152, 154, 169, 169, 173, 177, 186 188, 192, 193, 201n18, 207, 217, 223, 230, 232n87, 245, 258, 259, 260 265, 266, 292, 295, 384, 384, 390, 391, 410, 411, 412; collecting of letters, xxvi–xxviii, xxx; decides against land purchase, 246; editing of letters, xxvii, xxxv–xxxix, 165, 170, 305; land belonging to, 45; sermon on the Pullen's letter, 292; *see also* letters, Petworth Emigration Committee

soil: types of, 117, 189

soldier, 94, 146n108, 156

South Australia, 165, 364; colony of, papers on, 368

South Bersted, 178, 225n75; letter to, 114

South Down Cliffs, 346

South Easthope Township, letter from, 43, 45

Southdown sheep, 60

Southwold Township, letter from, 66

Spain, 367n30

spasms, 127

speculation: advice on, 365

Speed River, 78

Spencer, James, 118

Spencer, Samuel, 118

Spencer, Sarah (Cooper), 48

Spencer, Thomas, 366

Spencer, William, xxx, 25, □ 24 (48–50), □ 68 (117–19), □ 125 (238–41), 144

Spencer Creek, 78

spirits, 111, 123, 172, 189, 350; and ale, 87; cheap, 22; Jamaica, 350; prices of, 10; and wines, 73

Spithead, 90, 144, 160, 163, 176, 180, 192

sponsors, xxii, 5, 91, 108, 124n63, 177, 187, 192, 412; mistrust of motives, xxi; in Petworth area, 161

Spooner, Aunt, 126

Spooner, Elizabeth, 212

Spooner, John, 212

spring crop, 98, 110

spring work, 277

Springs Farm, 279

squirrels, 65, 98, 101, 156

stable, 133; immigrants sheltered in, 398

Stamford, grandparents, 311

Stamford, Louisa, 314

Stamford, Maria, *see* Wilson

Stamford, Uncle, 314

Stamford, William, 310, 316

stamp, 270n12; mark, 220; removed from cover, 310n10

Standen, Caroline, 280

Standen, Harriet, 237

Standen: seen at Hamilton, 109

Standing, William, 135, 141

Statement, *see* Petworth Emigration Committee

statues, 353

stays, 150, 287; stay-maker, 287

Steadman, Mr, 62

steam packets, 82, 240

steamboats, 6, 35, 52, 56, 93, 177, 201, 222, 286, 348; steam packets, 82, 240; wood-fired, 50n111

steamer, 127, 127, 132, 132, 134, 135, 347, 361; transfer to, 346

Stedman, John, □ 18 (34–6), 68

Stedman, James G., 34

Steer, Amy, *see* Parker

Steer, George, 120

Steer, William, 120, 215

steerage passage: price of, 365

Stemp, Arthur, 141n90

Stemp, Mary (Tanner), 141n90

Stenning, Mr, 154

Stephens, Henry, 275

Stevens, Henry Jr, 275n29

stiff cambrick, 150

stock, 98

stockings, 133, 257

stone: shaped, for sharpening tools, 66n151; *see also* tools

stone digging, 331

stone turnip seed, 100

storehouse, 132, 146; waited in, 34, 40

storekeeper, 379

stores, 157, 261

Stovelds, Messrs., 143

Strathroy, 15, 234, 235, 409; site of, 99n16

Street, Ann, 75

Street, Charles, 75, 105, 106

Street, Mr, 237

Streeter, George, 138
Streeter, Hannah, *see* Bristow
Streeter, Sarah, *see* Bristow
Streets, Josh., 214
Stroud Green, Kirdford, 139, 140;
  letter to, 68
Stroud Post Office, 380
Sturge, Samuel, 350, 355
Sturt, Elizabeth (Fowler), 194n2
Sturt, John, 62
Sturt, Tom, 58
Sturt, William, 194, 194n2, 198
sugar, 47, 51, 57, 100, 111, 124,
  135, 150, 189, 213, 255, 272,
  274, 298; goods, 196; making,
  210; *see also* maple sugar
Sullington, 109, 124n63; letter to,
  108; sending parish, 32
Sullington Farmhouse, 108n35
Summersell, Ann (Holden), 260,
  ☐ 132 (267–70), 281, ☐ 139
  (288–93), 405–7
Summersell, Ann, 269, 270, 283,
  292
Summersell, Harriett, 269, 283,
  292
Summersell, Henry, 290, 292
Summersell, John, 260, ☐ 132
  (267–70), 281, ☐ 139 (288–93),
  405–7
superintendent, 91, 258; care of,
  393
surgeons, 247; chest, 288n46;
  examine ship, 8; inspections of
  immigrants, 14
Surrey, 91, 297, 336
survey, 178; party, 176; into townships, 118
Sussex, 92, 152, 266; emigrants,
  384; labourers, as barrier to
  American habits, 295n64;
  parishes, disturbances feared,
  178; people, 183, 293, 294
Sussex Advertiser, 178, 293n56
Suter, George, 188, 188n22
Suter, George (son), 188n22
Suter, R., 188
Sutton Gilbert Union, 266, 411
Sutton, West Sussex, 142, 148,
  151n115, 227; letter to, 54, 79;
  sending parish, 16, 165, 233, 280
Sussex: rural occupations,
  xxiv–xxv
Swan, Robert, 61

Swan Inn, Fittleworth, 117
Swan River Settlement, Western
  Australia, xxxi, 365
swede turnip, 100; seed, 111
Swing disturbances, xxii, 13, 337
Sydenham, Lord, *see* Thomson
Sydenham River, *see* Bear Creek
Sydney, 367

tailor, 55, 57, 143, 206, 331; wages,
  47
Talbot, Thomas, 35
Talbot settlement, 35, 67, 68
Tanner, Eliza, 141n90
Tanner, Mary, *see* Stemp
Tanner, Mrs, 141
Tanner, Richard, 153
tanner, 87; and currier, 107
tannery, 400; and currying, 296,
  399
tares, 65, 109, 111
tavern, 58, 73, 102, 201, 224, 226,
  230, 398; keeping, 398; keepers, letter for, 35
taxes, 57, 87, 153, 271, 391; direct,
  386
Taylor, Jane (Armitage), 376
Taylor, Jos., 114
Taylor, Mr, preacher, 252
tea, 47, 51, 57, 83, 109, 111, 127,
  135, 212, 229, 252; dealer, 318;
  merchant, 307
teacher, 68, 375; teaching, 369
teasels, 211n33
teetotallers, 399
temperance tracts, 350
Terry, James, 109
Thair, Fanny, 120, 133
Thair, George, 71, 90, 92, 120,
  129n66, ☐ 78 (132–5), 293n55,
  209, 210, 217, 278, 293n55
Thair, John, 120, 133, 134
Thair, Maria, *see* Rapson
Thair, Mr: emigrates to Ohio,
  396, 397
Thair, Rhoda (Rapson), xxxix,
  71, ☐ 70 (120–1), 126, 129,
  129n66, ☐ 78 (132–5), 198
Thair, Sarah, 130
Thair, Thomas, 120, 129, 133, 134
Thames River, Upper Canada, 280
thatch, 173, 205
Thomas, Ann (Puttock), ☐ 37
  (68–9), 75, 102n24, 129n85

Thomas, David, 68
Thomas, Edmund, 68, 69, 102,
  104n29, 139
Thomas, Elizabeth (Durrant or
  Deront), 68
Thomas, Henry, 68
Thomas, James, 65, 68, 69,
  104n29, 280
Thomas, Mary (Bell), 68
Thomas, Rhoda, 68
Thomas, Thomas, 65, 68, 104,
  280
Thomas, William, 68
Thomson, Charles Edward
  Poulett, 1st Baron Sydenham,
  389
Thorah Township, 188n22
Thornhill, Upper Canada, 55,
  187, 392; letter from, 187, 204,
  207
Thorold Township: letter from,
  151
Thorp, Mrs, 298
Thorp, William, 297
thrashing, 199, 274; machine, 57,
  376
thread, 98, 150
tic douloureux, *see* neuralgia
Tickner, Edmund, 44
Tickner, Jane, 136n81
Tickner, Mary, 44
Tickner, Sarah (Boxall), 136n81
Tickner, William, 44, 45, 136n81
Till, Dame, 210
Tilley, Frederick, 140, 142
Tilley, Hannah (Chesman), xxxii,
  xxxix, 50, 51, ☐ 83 (140–2),
  ☐ 84 (143–4)
Tilley, Henry, 140, 142
Tilley, James, xxxii, 50, 51, ☐ 83
  (140–2), ☐ 84 (143–4), 212,
  230n84, 241, 241n100
Tilley, John, 143n94
Tilley, Maria, 140, 142
Tilley, Mary, *see* Boxall
Tilley, William, ☐ 25 (50–1),
  241n100
Tillington, West Sussex, 71, 73,
  119, 128, 135n78, 136n81,
  141n92, 198n11, 270, 273n26;
  letter to, 194; parish of settle-
  ment, 271; sending parish, 212,
  135
Tillington Road, 268

Tilt, Caroline (Cosens), 63n138, 297, 297n67

Tilt, Ellen, 297

Tilt, Jane (Cosens), 63, 113, 113n47, 297n67

Tilt, John, 400

Tilt, William, 63, 113n47, 278, 296, 297, 297n67

timber, 44, 63, 65, 65, 71, 117, 146, 147, 172, 199; compared to England's, 15; kinds of, 19, 117; number of trees cut, 383; rafts, 27, 261; size of, 23

tithe, 412; system, 153

Titmouse, Ann, 46

Titmouse, Benjamin, 48

Titmouse, Catherine, 48

Titmouse, Charles, 46

Titmouse, Edith, see Racher

Titmouse, Elizabeth, 48

Titmouse, George, 46, 48

Titmouse, Joseph (brother of Simeon), 48

Titmouse, Joseph (son of Simeon), 48

Titmouse, Mary, see Shambrook

Titmouse, Richard, 48

Titmouse, Sarah (Jackson), 46, 46n101

Titmouse, Simeon, □ 23 (46–8), 312n14

Titmouse, William, 48

tobacco, 51, 111, 156, 181, 203, 213, 220; see also exotics

Tocker, Mrs, of Albury, 40

Tolendol Mills, 379

tools, 20, 44, 111, 156; cheaper in Upper Canada, 287

Torbay, Brixham, Devon, 144, 146n106

Tories, 337, 387

Toronto, 69, 92, 154, 160, 160, 167, 176, 180, 181, 182, 184, 192, 193, 194, 208, 217–19, 225, 233, 233, 237, 238, 247, 261, 266, 272, 273; 387n8; city guards, 294; letter from, 217, 223, 246, 258; money received at, 235; to Niagara, cost by steamer, 197; Toronto Hospital, 226

Toronto Township, 54; letter from, 152

Torquay, 368

Tottles, Mr (Dumfries), 46

Toul and Till, Messrs, 399

town lot: five acres, 232, 274

town plot, 180; see also Blandford, Woodstock

Townsend, Charles, 163

Townsend, George, 163n2

township clerk, 387, 388

trade, 94, 157, 186, 247; of emigrants, xxiv; in Upper Canada compared to England, 349

tradesmen, 93, 123; wages, 181; wanted, 232

Trafalgar, 90

Trafalgar Township, 230n85, 241; letter from, 62

transportation, see travel

transported, 317

travel inland, xxxii–xxxiii, 7, 171; conditions, 9; to Blandford paid for, 184; charge for shelter, 127; convoy of emigrants, 54; description of 1832, 26–8; drawn by horses or oxen, 127, 201, 249; expensive, 253; by foot, 35, 237, 348; of goods, xviii; from Hamilton, 28; by land, 56; from Montreal, 171, 184, 347; St Lawrence and Rideau routes compared, 162; in winter, 203

Trew, Emma, 392

Trew, Thomas E., Esq., Commissary, Quebec, 392

Treyford, near Midhurst, West Sussex, 387; letter to, 384

Tribe, Ann, 101, 216

Tribe, Benjamin, 26, 28, 37, 38, 45, 87n190, 101, 102, 123, 154, 216

Tribe, Charlotte. see Evans

Tribe, Charlotte (Tickener), 36, 38, 69, 95, □ 54 (101–3), 123, 133, 154, 154n121, 216

Tribe, Charlotte (mother of Sarah), 9, 28

Tribe, Charlotte (daughter of Sarah), 8, 71

Tribe, Henry (father of Sarah), 9

Tribe, Henry, 36, 38, 69, 71, 95, □ 54 (101–3), 154n121, 216

Tribe, Henry Jr, 101, 102

Tribe, James, 66, 68

Tribe, Jane, see Penfold

Tribe, John Allen, 34, □ 36 (66–8)

Tribe, Jonathan, 101, 216

Tribe, Mary, 101, 216

Tribe, Mr, 210, 277

Tribe, Mr: emigrates to Ohio, 396

Tribe, Richard, 101, 133, 216

Tribe, Robert (brother of Charlotte), 36

Tribe, Robert, 11, 71, 94, 95, 101, 102, 133

Tribe, Sarah, see Rapson

Tribe, Thomas, 66, 67

Trigg, John, 102

Triller, Jacob, 49, 51, 117, 119; farm, 25, 25n47

Trimmer, Hannah, 366

Trimmer, John, 366

Tripp, Mr, 384

troops: from Spain, 367; sent to Lower Canada, 388

Trowbridge, 297

Troy hotel, 140

Truller, see Triller

Trusler, see also Trussler

Trusler, Absolom, 199

Trusler, Eleanor, 199

Trusler, Eliza, 199

Trusler, Elizabeth, 121n60

Trusler, George, 121n60

Trusler, Harriet, 121n60

Trusler (Trussler), Jane (Childs), 133n75, 198

Trusler (Trussler), John, 90, 133n75, 198, 200, 299

Trusler, Timothy, □ 105 (198–200), 299

Trussler, see also Trusler

Trussler, Ann, see Greavatt

Trussler, Eli, 300

Trussler, Elizabeth (Gilbert), 133n72, 198

Trussler, George, 90, 92, 92, 129, 132, 133, 133n72, 198, 200, 278, 299, 300

Trussler, Harriet, 133n72

Trussler, James, 299

Trussler, James (son of George), 132, 135, 198

Trussler, Reuben, 199

Trussler, Thomas, □ 143 (299–300), □ 144 (300–1)

Trussler, William, 300

Tuckersmith Township, 296, 297
turkeys, 65, 94, 98, 101, 109; *see also* fowl, domestic
Turner, Elizabeth (Sharp), 145, 213
Turner, George, xxxviii, 90, 92, 137, 147, 146, 90, 145, 213n40, 214
Turner, J., 71
Turner, J.M.W., 410
Turner Cemetery, 113n47, 297
Turrell, Rebecca, *see* Smith
Twelve Mile Creek, 238
Tyler, William (Egremont's steward), 147, 213, effigy, of, 148, 213
typhoid fever, 268, 299
typhus fever, 49

Udora, Ontario, 333; letter from, 319
unemployment (in England), 317
United Brethren Church, 38
United Kingdom, 90, 132
United States, 57, 136, 147, 157, 231, 247, 266, 282, 386, 390, 392, 388n11; advice to travel through, xxxviii; as destination, xviii; emigrants to, 187n18; hundreds gone to, 294; neighbours from, 34; rebels driven into, xxiii, 276
unrest, 1830, 337
up country, 186
Uphold, Mr, 296
Upper Canada, 368; account of, 138, 382; bad account in first letter on, 284; books on, xix; compared to England, 18, 25, 240; cost of living, 202; description of, xl–xlii, 15, 29, 35–6, 103; districts emigrated to, xvii; exodus of emigrants, 178; good land, 65, 104; good living, 87, 212, 252; not for old people, 119; plans for Egremont to purchase land, 177; reaction to, 54, 80, 94, 172; recession in begins, 178; settlement in 1830s, xvi; tract chosen, 178, weather, 123; a wooden world, 46
Upper Canada College, 115n53, 218n59, 250n3

Upper Canadian government, 244, 251; response to cholera epidemic, 6
Upper Nash House, Pulborough, 97
Upton, Albert, 54
Upton, Clifford, 51, 52, 53
Upton, Egbert, 53
Upton, Frances Taylor, 51, 52, 54
Upton, Frances Jr, 51
Upton, Frederick, 53, 161, 241, 241n101
Upton, Percival, 53
Upton, William, 51
Upton, William Taylor, xxiv, □ 26 (51–2), □ 27 (52–3), 112

Vansittart, Admiral Henry, 182, 185n16
Varndell, George, 273, 273n26
Vaughan Township, 188, 205, 209
vegetables, 61, 70, 98, 100, 125, 189, 271, 298; *see also* gardens
venison, 94, 99, 111; *see also* game
Verdley Wood, 300
Vernon, Mary Ann (Wilson), 323
Vernon, Robert A.E., 323n28
Vernon Farm, Prospect, 323n38
veterinary surgeon, 309n4
Victoria, Queen of England, 244
Victory, 367
victuals, 146; price of, 214; *see also* provisions
Vincent, David, xxix
vinegar, 286; from molasses, 211
Viney, Emily, 188n21
Viney, Frances, *see* Birch
violin, 280
Virginia, 410
Voice, Cornelius, 162, 169, 173, 176, 184, □ 101 (183–7)
Voice, Elizabeth, *see* Coleman
Voice, Elizabeth (Smallwood), xxiv, 169, □ 101 (183–7)
Voice, George, 170
Voice, Ham, 187
Voice, Ham Jr, 221
Voice, John, 169, 171, 172, 176
Voice, Joseph, 170
Voice, Martha, 172, 185n15
Voice, Mary, *see* Elliot
Voice, William, xxx, 162, □ 98 (169–73), 176, 184, 185, 186, 187

voyage, 68, 82, 204, 208; account of, 345–6; advice for, 286, 225; danced on deck, 170n11; description of, 9–11, 17, 30, 31, 40, 55, 169, 166–7, 163–4, 170, 235, 163–4, 371–2; goods stolen during, 42; memories of, 371; short and pleasant, 206; tedious, 200; troublesome, 283

Wackford, Abraham, 124, 125
Wackford, Elizabeth (Nash), xxx, □ 72 (124–5), □ 73 (125–6)
Wackford, Emma, 124, 125
Wackford, James, 28, 124, 125, 126
Wackford, James (son), 124, 126
Wackford, Sarah, 124, 125
Wackford, Thomas, 124, 125, 126
Wackford, William, 124, 125
wages, 31, 32, 202, 256; and conditions, 17; expectations of, 168; labourer, 298; Montreal, 17; by shop goods, 48; Upper Canada compared to England, 179
wagons (waggons), 82, 122, 133, 176, 182, 185, 198, 249, 255, 274, 348, 362, 397; Canada Company transport, 28n59; harness, 155; hired, 361; in Upper Canada, 201
Walberton, 178, 412; emigrants, 187, 188; letter to, 187, 207, 391; sending parish, 187, 204, 208
Waldon, Ann, 194
Waldon, Charles, 194
Waldon, Elizabeth, 194
Walden, George, 163n2
Waldon, Jane, 194
Waldon, John, 178, □ 104 (194–8)
Waldon, Mary, 194
Waldon, Ruth (Rewell or Rule), □ 104 (194–8)
Wales, 233, 332
Walker, Gladys Chantler, 337
Walkinson, John, 358
Wallace Township, 140, 297
"The Wandering Boy," 343
Ward, James, 214
Ward, John, 213n38
Ward, Mary (Sharp), 213

Ward, Unis, 68
Ware, Clara, *see* Sharp
Warminghurst, Heath Common, 227
Warren, George, 51, 53
Warwick Township, 7, 24, 103n25, 127, 150, 411
washing, 86, 93, 111, 121, 138, 145, 148
Washington, West Sussex, 157, 158, 294n60, 350
water: control, disputes over, 379; in Upper Canada, 46;
water keepers, 240
Waterloo, 28, 46, 102, 107, 265, 120n59, 294n57
Waterloo Post Office, 139
Waterloo Township, 63, 95, 131, 200, 209n26, 217, 278, 296, 297, 300n73, 400; letter from, 36, 63, 68, 87, 107, 112, 124, 125, 209, 215, 276; 300; letter to, 299
Watson, Graham, 400
Watson, Tilt, and Adsett, 400
Watt Township, Muskoka District, 61
Wawanosh Township, 237
weather, 73, 125, 130; comparison to England, 16, 383; heat, 117
weaver, 46, 255, 258, 336, 398; weaving flannel, 255
Webb, Ann (daughter), 178, 179
Webb, Ann (Richards), □ 99 (178–80)
Webb, James, 178
Webb, Joseph, 59n130, □ 99 (178–80)
Webb, Joseph Jr, 178, 179
Webb, Sarah, 178
Webb, William (grandfather), 178
Webb, William, 178
well, 124, 224; digging, 233
Welland Canal, 90, 92, 180, 198; description, 23; route via, 7
Weller, Mrs (mother), 60, 61
Weller, Rebecca, *see* Longhurst
Wellington, Duke of, 14, 337
Wellington Square, 119; Post Office, 241
Wells, Emily, 187, 205, □ 176 (391–2)
Wells, George, 187, 188, 205, 208, 209, □ 176 (391–2)

Wells, George (of Goring), 237
Wells, Mary, 208
Wells, Miss (sister of George), 391–2
Wenger, Martin, 139n84
Wesleyan chapel, 11, 122; minister, 26
Wesleyan Methodists, 66n152, 124; minister, 221n67
West (Clowser), Sarah, *see* Sharp
West, Elizabeth, *see* White
West, Mary, 160
West, Thomas, 199
West Flamborough Township 78; letter from, 227, 284
West Grinstead, West Sussex: letter to, 166
West St Independent [Congregational] Chapel, 39n86
West Sussex, 91, 230
West Sussex parishes, 177, 193
West Woolwich Post Office, 140
Western District, English settlers, 7
western frontier, 272
Western Rangers, 169
Westminster, 358
Westminster Township, 143, 148, 223, 284n41
Wey and Arun canal, 252n8
whales, 17, 145, 200, 345
wharf, 198; shelter by, 361
wheat, 46, 70, 82, 83, 84, 85, 98, 104, 108, 109, 117, 125, 135, 148, 149, 150, 152, 153, 155, 156, 165, 179, 195, 199, 277; price of, 22; sowing, 13, 23; for two hats, 125
Wheeler, Charles, 393, 397
wheelers, 95
wheelwright, 64, 156
Whigs, 337; principles, 387
whip poor will, 101
whisky, 46, 57, 71, 73, 94, 102, 109, 111, 118, 123, 147, 148, 156, 171, 285, 350; plenty of, 67, price of, xl, 13, 34, 142
Whitby Township: letter to, 333
Whitchurch Township, 369n32, 375n39, 375n40, 375n41, 379
White, Captain (Lobo Township), 4
White, Edward (father), 153, 155
White, Edward, 155, 155n124, 217, 383

White, Elizabeth (West), □ 91 (153–5), 216
White, England, 154
White, Harriet, 133
White, Henry Kirk, 343
White, John, 90, 92, 129, □ 91 (153–5), 216, 383
White, John (son), 154
White, Louisa (Lotton), 155n124, 218n58
White, Mary, 54
White, Mary Ann, 67
White, William, 153
White Hart Inn, Petworth, 214, 214n43, 215n47
Whitechapel in London, 182
White's Green, near Lurgashall, West Sussex, 11
whitesmith, 169
Whitington, Harvey, 149, 149n111
Whitington, Rhoda (Smart), 77, 77n173, 78, 105n31
Whitington, Thomas, 77n173, 105
Whitley, Surrey, 79
Whittington, George, 236, 236n93
Whittington, Henry, 149n111
Whittington, James, 214
Whittington, Mary, 149n111
Whittington, William, 149n111, 150
wholesale produce merchant, 238
whooping cough, 138, 268, 270
whortleberry or bilberry, 134n76
widows and orphans: concern for, 410
Willard, Charles, 38
Willard, Charlotte (daughter), 38, 39
Willard, Charlotte (Longhurst), xlii, □ 20 (38–43), 85n185
Willard, David, 38
Willard, George, 38
Willard, Henry, 38
Willard, Henry (brother of William Sr), 38, 39
Willard, James, 38, 39
Willard, James (England), 42
Willard, John, 38, 39
Willard, Maria, 38, 42
Willard, William, □ 20 (38–43), 85n185

Willard, William Jr, 38, 39
Willbur, John, 358
Willet, Mary, 120
Willett, Eliza, 119
Willett, Rhoda, *see* Moore
Willet, Thomas, 120
Willey, William, 141
William IV, 337, 338
Williamsburgh, 361
Wilmot Township, 56, 136,
141n92, 400; letter from, 135
Wilson, Betsy Maria (Martin),
313, 333
Wilson, Betsey, 310, 311, 313, 315,
317
Wilson, Charles, 148
Wilson, Charles M., 328
Wilson, Charlotte (Course), 309,
310
Wilson, Edward, 32, 306, 309,
310, 311, 314, 315, 317, 318, 320,
325, 326, 328, 329
Wilson, Elizabeth (Betsy), *see*
Sell; Crabtree
Wilson, Frances Ann (Fanny), *see*
Hall, Shore
Wilson, Henry (uncle), 309, 310,
311, 317
Wilson, Henry (brother of
Obed), 309, 316, 322, 325, 326,
327, 329, 331
Wilson, John (father of Obed), 31
Wilson, John Edward, □ 152
(319), 322, 329
Wilson, Judy, 310, 311, 313, 315,
317
Wilson, Maria (Stamford), 31,
305, 306, □ 145 (307–9), □ 146
(309–10), □ 147 (311–12),
□ 148 (312–13), □ 149
(315–16), □ 150 (316–17),
□ 151 (317–19), 407–8
Wilson, Maria, 266
Wilson, Mary Ann, *see* Vernon
Wilson, Mary Ann, *see* Muncey
Wilson, Obed (son of Edward),
314
Wilson, Obediah (Obed), xliii, 6,
□ 15 (31–2), 47, 266, 305, 306,
307, 309, 311, 312, 313, 316, 317,
319, 320, 321, 323, 324, 325,
326, 328, 329, 330, 333; letters
sent to, xxvii
Wilson, Richard, 310, 311

Wilson, Robt., 340
Wilson family charts, 306–7,
334–5
Wilson letters, xxi, xxix
Wiltshire, 91
Wimpole Hall, Caxton, 331n44
Wind, Jacob, 349
Windsor, incursions at, 266
wine, 118; spirits, prices of, 17
Wingham, Mrs, 206
winter, 73, 80, 82, 98, 105, 112,
113, 115, 128, 156, 189, 203,
210, 383; barley, 46, 70; damage, 131; of 1837–38, 274;
severe in England, 268
Wisborough Green, West Sussex,
4, 65n143, 73, 77n170, 77n172,
97n12, 110n40, 217, 219, 220,
249, 252, 278, 393; dinner for
emigrants from, 395; letter to,
251; party from, 11, 395, 396–7;
sending parish, 207, 251; settlers to Nelsonville, 7
Wise, Sarah, *see* Harwood
Wissler, John, 400
Wolgar, John, 40, 41
Wolgar, Maria (Longhurst?): letter to, 38
Wolgar, Mary, 40
wolves, 70, 85, 98, 101, 104, 156;
see also animals, wild
women, 166; and children, 132,
134, 259; work for, xxix, 195,
280
Wonham, R., 115
Wonish, Surrey, 289
wood, 98, 113, 228; *see also* tim-
ber, firewood
Wood, Joseph, 173
Wood, Joseph, farmer, 377
Woodcut Farm, 271
Woodford, Charlotte, *see* Barnes
Woodhull, Benjamin, 166
Woodhull's Mills, 4; staging
point, 166
woodpeckers, 101
Woods, Ann, □ 112 (212–13)
Woods, Ann (wife of Thomas),
273n26
Woods, George, 212
Woods, James, □ 112 (212–13)
Woods, Thomas, 273, 273n26
woods: free for all cattle, 202
Woodstock, Upper Canada, xx,

xlii, 54, 100, 158, 160, 162, 164,
169, 176, 178, 188n22, 205,
222, 244, 246, 266, 273, 294,
299, 410, 411, 412; letter from,
188, 205, 212, 297
Woodstock Post Office, 207
Woodward, Mrs, 168
Woodward, W.P., 168
wool, 326
Woolbeding, West Sussex, 294n62
woollen, 98; mill, 400
Woolwich congregation, 124
Woolwich Township, 56, 69, 95,
124, 126, 139, 280, 399, 400;
letter from, 138
work, 46, 102, 118, 185, 188, 202,
206, 208, 212, 228, 229, 240;
for boys and girls, 185; on
canals, 160, 162; carpenters,
184n9; for children, xxv, 224,
236, 251; conditions of, xli, 29,
33, 179, 164, 165, 194; for girls,
42, 256; hard in Upper
Canada, xl, 258; at Montreal,
164; mowing and harvesting,
35; plenty of, 21, 29, 61, 80,
148, 240, 258, 290; on roads,
49, 111n41; in Upper Canada
compared to England, 181,
258; for women, 181, 187
workhouse, 193, 310n5
working, 149; for board, 163,
228; conditions, 18; by the
month, 165; tools, 100
Worsfold, John, xxxv, xl, 40, 43,
□ 48 (83–6)
worsted, 150; stockings, 98
Worthing, 157, 336, 364
Wright, David, 30
Wright, George, 30
Wright, James, Jr, 30
Wright, James, Sr, letter to, 30
Wright, Rebecca, 31
Wright, William, □ 14 (30–1)
Wtulich, Josephine, xx
Wuler [Wheeler], Ch, emigrates
to Ohio, 396
Wyndham, Colonel George, 1st
Baron Leconfield, 265, 268,
292, 293, 294, 409. 412; decides
against buying land, 295; pays
half passage, 298; and Petworth
Emigration Committee,
xxiii–xxiv

Yaldwin, William Henry, 50, 71, 95, 130, 198, 217, 412

Yankeefied, 231

Yankees, 185, 282

Yapton Bridge, 205

Yearly Meeting, 350, 358

yeast, 83, 298

yeoman farmer, 221n63

Yonge Street, 187, 244, 373, 375, 375n42, 376, 391

York, Duke of, statue of, 353, 358

York, Seneca Township, 51n114

York (Toronto), 14, 32, 46, 49, 50, 55n115, 52, 53, 56, 56, 61, 65, 68, 69, 70, 79, 82, 84, 85, 95, 101, 105, 115, 121, 127–9, 132–4, 135, 141, 147, 150, 152, 153, 154, 164, 172, 187, 198, 201, 204, 205n21, 336, 348, 362, 410; arrival at, 4, 17, 25, 27; conditions at, 19, 40, departure from, 23; letter from, 60, 61, 71, 114, 128, 131, 137, 391; money received at, 30; numbers of immigrants, 6; unhealthy situation, 19; work near, 31; *see also* Toronto

Yorkshire, 350

Zorra Township, 108n35, 169